THE NEEDLECRAFT
BOOK

THE NEEDLECRAFT BOOK

MAGGI GORDON, SALLY HARDING, ELLIE VANCE

DK

LONDON, NEW YORK, MUNICH, MELBOURNE, DELHI

Project Editor Danielle Di Michiel

Project Art Editor Katie Eke

Editors Katie Hardwicke, Sarah Hoggett,
and Sally Harding

Designers Mandy Earey, Anne Fisher,
and Helen McTeer

Photography Peter Anderson

Managing Editors Dawn Henderson
and Angela Wilkes

Managing Art Editors Christine Keilty
and Marianne Markham

Senior Jacket Creative Nicola Powling

Senior Presentations Creative
Caroline de Souza

Production Editor Maria Elia

Senior Production Controller Alice Sykes

Creative Technical Support
Adam Brackenbury and Sonia Charbonnier

DK INDIA

Head of Publishing Operations
Aparna Sharma

Managing Art Editor Malavika Talukder

Managing Editors Glenda Fernandes
and Julie Oughton

Designers Neha Ahuja, Arijit Ganguly,
and Rajnish Kashyap

Editors Alicia Ingty, Suchismita Banerjee,
Steffenie Jyrwa, and Garima Sharma

Photography Deepak Aggarwal

Technical Consultants Anu Jain
and Arijit Ganguly

First published in Great Britain in 2010
by Dorling Kindersley Limited
80 Strand, London WC2R 0RL

A Penguin Company

2 4 6 8 10 9 7 5 3 1

Copyright © 2010 Dorling Kindersley Limited

A CIP catalogue record for this book is available
from the British Library.

ISBN 978-1-4053-51720-0

Colour reproduction by Colourscan, Singapore

Printed and bound in China by L-Rex

Discover more at
www.dk.com

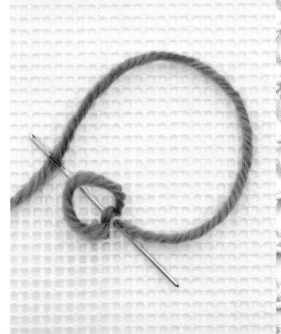

CONTENTS

INTRODUCTION

The Needlecraft Book is a comprehensive guide to the needle arts.

The book is divided into key needlecrafts: knitting; crochet; embroidery; needlepoint; patchwork, appliqué, and quilting; and finishing techniques. The chapters include an outline of the essential materials and tools required, the basic skills for learning the craft, and techniques or stitches that experienced practitioners will want to master. Every technique, from the easiest to the more complex, is illustrated with easy-to-follow step-by-step photographs and illustrations that can be referred to time and again.

The Knitting and Crochet chapters guide you through the basic techniques and stitches and onto more complicated textures and skills, covering all the relevant abbreviations and symbols on the way. The Patchwork, Appliqué, and Quilting chapter outlines the fundamental skills of quiltmaking; from general techniques for starting out, to the specifics of each skill. The Embroidery chapter takes you through the tips for beginners and onto surface embroidery, openwork, smocking, and beadwork. The Needlepoint chapter covers the starting and finishing techniques and the relevant stitches, from diagonal stitches to Florentine work. A final chapter covers the relevant finishing techniques, including bindings, zips, and buttonholes.

We hope the book will provide a valuable reference tool for anyone who wants to master an existing skill, or to learn a new kind of needlecraft.

Happy stitching!

Maggi Jordon

ABOUT THIS BOOK

This book is suitable for readers with no previous experience of needlecraft, for needlecrafters hoping to improve their technique, and will serve as an excellent reference for anyone with more advanced skills. If you are new to a craft, start by familiarizing yourself with the relevant tools and materials for that discipline, found at the beginning of the chapter. The pages that follow serve

to ease you into the essential skills for that discipline. For example, in the Basic Techniques section of the Knitting chapter, you will learn how to hold the yarn and needles and how to knit a simple knit and purl stitch. Once you've mastered these "basics", you are free to move through the chapter, refining your skills, and practising the techniques you enjoy the most. Then perhaps try another of the crafts in this book – you have plenty to choose from!

KNITTING

All you need to know to gain the basic hand-knitting techniques for making individual items, such as scarves, throws, sweaters, socks, accessories, and toys.

TOOLS AND MATERIALS

If you have never knit before, take your time to read this simple explanation of the yarns and equipment required for the craft. A little understanding of yarn and knitting needles will help you make decisions about the minimal purchases needed to get you started.

YARNS

Here are some examples of the vast array of yarns available to tempt you to get knitting. Smooth yarns are perfect for colourwork and lace stitch patterns. Textured yarns are useful for adding interest to plain knits, and multicoloured yarns introduce a variety of colour with a single strand.

SMOOTH YARNS

≪ WOOL
Traditional pure wool is still the ideal knitting yarn, and lightweight wool yarn, like double knitting, is perfect for novices, as the needles glide smoothly in and out of the elastic loops. Wool takes dye beautifully, is durable, and comes in machine washable versions.

COTTON AND BAMBOO ≫
With a smooth finish and easy care, natural cotton and bamboo yarns are popular for knitted garments. Cotton produces crisp textured and lace stitch patterns. Bamboo is similar to mercerized cotton and is strong and flexible, yet soft and comfortable.

⌄ LUXURY YARNS
Silk (below) and cashmere yarns can be an expensive option but have a luxurious feel and finish. Check the care label for special after-care instructions.

SYNTHETIC YARNS
Synthetic fibre yarns, like acrylic, or synthetic and natural fibre mixes are economical choices and produce yarns that are easy to knit and easy to care for.

TEXTURED AND NOVELTY YARNS

≪ NOVELTY YARN
Unique novelty yarns change with fashion. This shaggy yarn creates a knitted fabric that looks like fur.

TEXTURED YARNS
With minimal effort, simply by knitting them in plain, easy stocking stitch, you can turn balls of textured yarn into interesting and appealing knits. These are a small selection of the types of yarn textures available.

Mohair: This yarn produces a fluffy effect and creates a very warm knitting fabric.

metallic yarn: These yarns add sparkle to a project.

Tape yarn: A variety of different types of tape (or ribbon) yarns are available. They form distinctive, bold knit stitches.

Slubbed and bouclé yarns: These highly textured yarns look very seductive in the ball. The lumps (or knots) in the strands of slubbed yarn produce a bobbled effect. Bouclé yarn is made with a loose strand that forms a loop around an "anchor" strand and produces a curled texture.

MULTICOLOURED YARNS

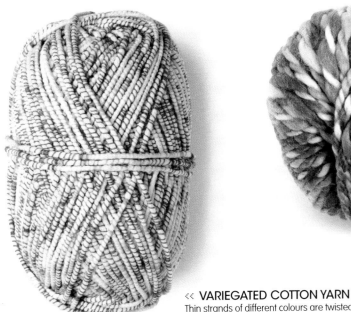

‹‹ VARIEGATED WOOL YARN

Two strands of different colours are twisted around each other in this super-bulky-weight yarn (see below for a close-up). Each strand changes from dark to light and back again along its length.

‹‹ VARIEGATED COTTON YARN

Thin strands of different colours are twisted around a core yarn to create this fairly smooth multicoloured yarn.

"SOCK" YARN

There are "sock" yarns available that have been carefully space-dyed so that a colourwork type pattern appears on the socks (or other item) as they are knitted from a single ball.

UNUSUAL YARNS

FABRIC STRIPS ››

Recycled rag strips produce strong knitted items, and are suitable for accessories or household items, such as bags or cushions (see page 90).

STRING

Ideal for knitting practical items, such as containers, string is available in a range of natural colours and different sizes (see page 91).

STRIPS CUT FROM PLASTIC BAGS ››

Bags, tablemats, and other household items can be knitted from recycled strips of plastic bags (see page 90).

YARN UNRAVELLED FROM OLD SWEATERS

Recycling unravelled yarn is easier than you think; even thin sweater yarns can be used by knitting with several strands held together (see page 89).

YARN
PUT-UPS

A yarn "put-up" is a specific quantity of yarn packaged for sale. The most common put-ups for knitting yarn are balls, hanks, and skeins. You can also buy bigger put-ups in cones, although these are more commonly sold for machine knitting than for hand knitting.

◁◁ BALLS
One of the most common put-ups, balls of yarn are also practical as they are ready to use; just pull the yarn from the centre to start knitting.

SKEINS ⌃
Similar to balls but an oblong shape, skeins of yarn are also ready to use. Keep the label in place to ensure that the skein doesn't unravel as you work.

⌄ HANKS
A hank is a twisted ring of yarn that needs to be wound into a ball see page 33) before it can be used.

CONES
Cones of yarn are often too heavy to carry around in your knitting bag and are best wound into a ball before you start knitting (see page 33).

YARN
LABELS

Yarn put-ups are most commonly packaged with a label that provides you with all the information you need to knit successfully. Before you buy, always read the label carefully to establish the type of yarn, suggested needle size, care instructions, and ball length.

READING A YARN LABEL ⟫
Decide whether you require an easy-care yarn and check the care instructions. Fibre content will indicate whether the yarn is synthetic or a synthetic mix, or 100 per cent natural, each giving a different effect as it ages. The ball length will enable you to calculate how many balls are required when you are substituting yarn (see opposite page). Check the dye-lot number if you are purchasing several balls, as variations in colour can occur across different dye-lots.

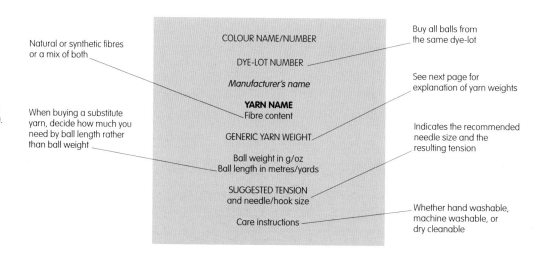

Natural or synthetic fibres or a mix of both

When buying a substitute yarn, decide how much you need by ball length rather than ball weight

COLOUR NAME/NUMBER

DYE-LOT NUMBER

Manufacturer's name

YARN NAME
Fibre content

GENERIC YARN WEIGHT

Ball weight in g/oz
Ball length in metres/yards

SUGGESTED TENSION
and needle/hook size

Care instructions

Buy all balls from the same dye-lot

See next page for explanation of yarn weights

Indicates the recommended needle size and the resulting tension

Whether hand washable, machine washable, or dry cleanable

YARN WEIGHTS

• **The yarn "weight"** refers to the thickness of a yarn. Some yarns are spun by manufacturers to fall into what are considered as "standard" yarn weights, such as US sport or worsted and UK double-knitting and aran. These standard weights have long histories and will probably be around for some time to come. However, even within these "standard" weights there is slight variation in thickness, and textured novelty yarns are not easy to categorize by thickness alone.

• **Visual yarn thickness** is only one indicator of a yarn-weight category. A yarn can look thicker than another yarn purely because of its loft, the air between the fibres, and the springiness of the strands. By pulling a strand between your two hands you can see how much it has by how much the thickness diminishes when the yarn is stretched. The ply of a yarn is also not an indication of yarn thickness. Plies are the strands spun together around each other to form the yarn. A yarn with four plies can be very thick or very thin depending on the thickness of each individual ply.

• **In order to help knitters** attempting to match like for like when looking for a substitute yarn for their knitting pattern, the Craft Yarn Council of America has devised a table of yarn weights. This table (below) demonstrates how to find the perfect yarn substitute if you are unable to purchase the yarn specified in a knitting pattern. The very best indication of a yarn weight is the manufacturer's recommended tension and needle size for the yarn. (These recommendation will produce a knitted fabric that is loose enough to be soft and flexible but not so loose that it loses its shape.) Two yarns with the same fibre content and the same recommended tension and needle size will be perfect substitutes for each other.

STANDARD YARN-WEIGHT SYSTEM

YARN WEIGHT SYMBOL & CATEGORY NAMES	0 LACE	1 SUPER FINE	2 FINE	3 LIGHT	4 MEDIUM	5 BULKY	6 SUPER BULKY
Types of yarns** in category	Fingering, 10-count crochet thread	Sock, baby, fingering, UK "4-ply"	Sport, baby	Double knitting, light worsted	Worsted, afghan, aran	Chunky, craft, rug	Bulky, roving
Knit tension ranges* in stocking stitch to 10cm/4in	33–40*** sts	27–32 sts	23–26 sts	21–24 sts	16–20 sts	12–15 sts	6–11 sts
Recommended needle in metric size range	1.5–2.25 mm	2.25–3.25 mm	3.25–3.75 mm	3.75–4.5 mm	4.5–5.5 mm	5.5–8 mm	8 mm and larger
Recommended needle in US size range	000 to 1	1 to 3	3 to 5	5 to 7	7 to 9	9 to 11	11 and larger
Crochet tension ranges* in dc to 10cm/4in	32–42*** trebles	21–32 sts	16–20 sts	12–17 sts	11–14 sts	8–11 sts	5–9 sts
Recommended hook in metric size range	1.6–2.25 mm	2.25–3.5 mm	3.5–4.5 mm	4.5–5.5 mm	5.5–6.5 mm	6.5–9 mm	9 mm and larger
Recommended hook in US size range	6 steel, 7 steel, 8 steel, B-1	B-1 to E-4	E-4 to 7	7 to I-9	I-9 to K-10½	K-10½ to M-13	M-13 and larger

GUIDELINES ONLY The above reflect the most commonly used tensions and needle sizes for specific yarn categories. The categories of yarn, tension ranges, and recommended needle and hook sizes have been devised by the Craft Yarn Council of America (YarnStandards.com).

** The generic yarn-weight names in the yarn categories include those commonly used in the UK and US.
*** Ultra-fine lace-weight yarns are difficult to put into tension ranges; always follow the tension given in your pattern for these yarns.

KNITTING
NEEDLES

Finding the right knitting needles is mostly down to personal preference. If you are a beginner, purchase a pair of quality 4mm (US size 6) needles and a ball of double-knitting wool yarn (see page 12) to learn and practise techniques with.

◄◄ STRAIGHT KNITTING NEEDLES

Ordinary knitting needles with rigid shanks and a stopper at one end are called straight needles or pins. They come in a range of sizes (see opposite) and lengths. The most common material for straight needles is metal like these. Metal needles have very good points and are extremely long-lasting.

⯆ BAMBOO KNITTING NEEDLES

Some knitters swear by bamboo needles and say that the loops slide beautifully along them.

PLASTIC KNITTING NEEDLES ⯈⯈

Plastic needles come in a range of attractive colours. As they are inexpensive, special short ones are produced specially for children to learn to knit with.

JUMBO NEEDLES ⯅

Knitting needle sizes from 12mm (US size 17) up are sometimes called jumbo needles. These needles are used for super-chunky yarns to make super-fast sweaters or scarves and for rag knitting (see page 90).

CIRCULAR NEEDLES »

These have long or short plastic wire between the straight, stiff ends. Long circular needles are used for knitting very wide items (like blankets) back and forth in rows, because very many stitches can be packed onto the wire. Knitting can also be worked round and round in a tube on circular needles, for example, sweaters are sometimes knit in the round up to the armholes. Short circular needles are designed for tubular hats, neckbands, armhole bands, and sleeves, eliminating the need for seams. Some very short circular needles are produced specially for knitting socks.

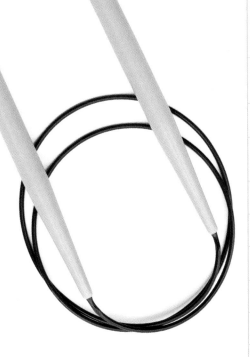

CONVERSION CHART

This chart gives the closest conversions between the various needle-size systems. The sizes don't match exactly in many cases but are the closest equivalents.

EU METRIC	US SIZES	OLD UK
1.5mm	000 00	
2mm	0	14
2.25mm 2.5mm	1	13
2.75mm	2	12
3mm		11
3.25mm	3	10
3.5mm	4	
3.75mm	5	9
4mm	6	8
4.5mm	7	7
5mm	8	6
5.5mm	9	5
6mm	10	4
6.5mm	10½	3
7mm		2
7.5mm		1
8mm	11	0
9mm	13	00
10mm	15	000
12mm	17	
15mm	19	
20mm	35	
25mm	50	

« DOUBLE-POINTED NEEDLES

Designed so that stitches can be slipped on and off both ends, double-pointed needles are used for circular knitting (see page 78), for certain fancy colour stitch patterns, and for knitting cords (see stems on leaves on page 47).

OTHER EQUIPMENT

Aside from knitting needles, there are a few other tools that are necessary for knitting and some that are not essential but are very handy. The only item not shown here that you should have is a dedicated large soft bag to carry your knitting around in wherever you go.

THE ESSENTIALS

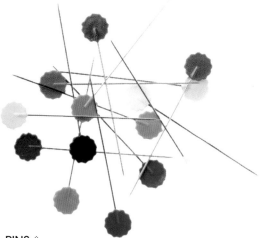

PINS ⌃
Use pins with large heads for aiding seaming and blocking (see pages 69–71).

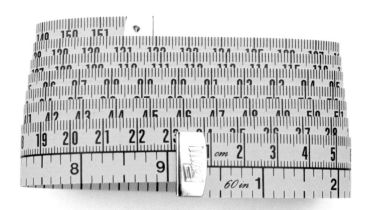

TAPE MEASURE ⌃
Always have a tape measure to hand for checking your tension (see page 67) and measuring your knitting. Use either metric or imperial measures, never a mixture of both.

BLUNT-ENDED YARN NEEDLES ⌃
These are useful for darning in ends and sewing seams. They can also be used for embellishing your knitting with embroidered decorations.

SCISSORS »
Keep a pair of good-quality scissors to hand for cutting off yarn and trimming off yarn ends.

CABLE NEEDLES «
These are essential if knitting cables (see page 48).

HANDY EXTRAS

STITCH HOLDERS ⋏

These are used to hold stitches you will return to later. You can make your own stitch holder (or stitch marker, see below), from a length of lightweight cotton yarn, or a safety pin or paper clip.

POINT PROTECTORS ⋏

Useful for protecting you and your knitting bag from knitting needle punctures and for keeping stitches from slipping off.

STITCH MARKERS ⋏

These are sometimes placed on the needle to mark the beginning and end of a panel of stitches, for example when working panels of different cables. They can also be used to mark the right-side of the knitting or to mark a particular row or individual stitch.

ROW COUNTER ⋏

This can be slipped onto the end of a knitting needle and used to keep track of which row you are working on.

⋘ YARN BOBBINS

Use these for holding short lengths of yarn in colourwork knitting (see page 58).

KNITTING NEEDLE GAUGE ⋙

Use this to test double-pointed needles, circular needles, and other unmarked needles for size.

U.S.	mm
0	2.00
1	2.25
-	2.50
2	2.75
3	3.00
3	3.25
4	3.50
5	3.75
6	4.00
7	4.50
8	5.00
9	5.50
10	6.00
10½	6.50
.	7.00
.	7.50
11	8.00
13	9.00
15	10.00

BASIC TECHNIQUES

Learning to knit is a very quick process. There are only a few basic techniques to pick up before you are ready to make simple shapes like scarves, baby blankets, cushion covers, and throws. The basics include casting stitches onto the needle, the knit and purl stitches, and casting the stitches off the needles.

HOLDING YARN
AND NEEDLES

Before starting to make loops on the needle, familiarize yourself with how to hold the yarn and needles. Although all knitting is formed in exactly the same way, you can hold the yarn in either the right or left hand. These two yarn-holding techniques are called the "English" and "continental" methods. Knitting is ambidextrous, so right-handed and left-handed knitters should try both knitting styles to see which one is easier for them.

KNITTING "ENGLISH" STYLE

1 The yarn is laced around the fingers of the right hand. Try lacing the yarn through your fingers like this to see if it feels comfortable. The aim is to control the yarn firmly but with a relaxed hand, releasing it to flow through the fingers as the stitches are formed.

2 Try this alternative yarn-lacing technique as well or make up one of your own. You need to be able to tension the yarn just enough with your fingers to create even loops that are neither too loose nor too tight.

3 Hold the needles with the stitches about to be worked in the left hand and the other needle in the right hand. Use the right forefinger to wrap the yarn around the needle.

Right forefinger controls yarn-wrapping action

KNITTING "CONTINENTAL" STYLE

1 Lace the yarn through the fingers of the left hand in any way that feels comfortable. Try this lacing technique to see if you can both release and tension the yarn easily to create uniform loops.

2 This alternative yarn-lacing technique may suit you better. Here the yarn is wrapped twice around the forefinger.

3 Hold the needle with the unworked stitches in the left hand and the other needle in the right hand. Position the yarn with the left forefinger and pull it through the loops with the tip of the right needle.

Left forefinger controls yarn-wrapping action

KNITTING

MAKING A
SLIP KNOT

After reading about the two knitting styles on the previous page you are ready to place the first loop on the needle to start a piece of knitting. This loop is called the slip knot and it is the first stitch formed when casting on stitches.

1 Begin by crossing the yarn coming from the ball over the yarn end (called the yarn tail) to form a circle of yarn.

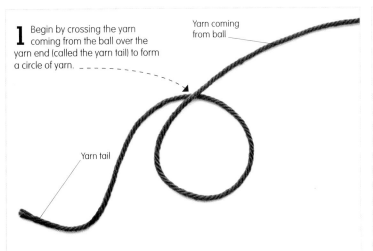

Yarn coming from ball

Yarn tail

2 Insert the tip of a knitting needle through the circle of yarn, then wrap the needle tip around the ball end of the yarn and pull the yarn through the circle.

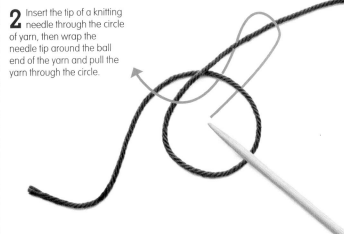

3 This forms a loop on the needle and a loose, open knot below the loop.

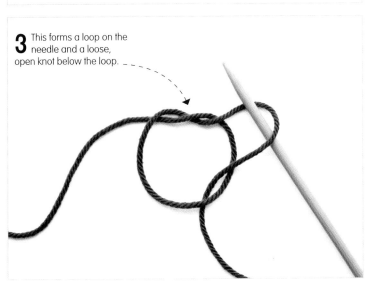

4 Pull both ends of the yarn firmly to tighten the knot and the loop on the needle.

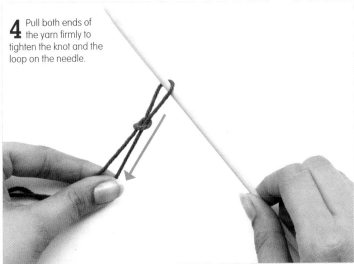

5 Make sure the completed slip knot is tight enough on the needle that it won't fall off but not so tight that you can barely slide it along the needle.

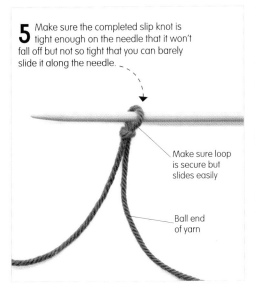

Make sure loop is secure but slides easily

Ball end of yarn

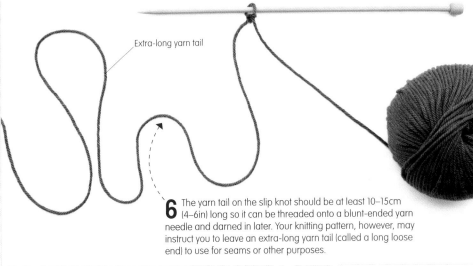

Extra-long yarn tail

6 The yarn tail on the slip knot should be at least 10–15cm (4–6in) long so it can be threaded onto a blunt-ended yarn needle and darned in later. Your knitting pattern, however, may instruct you to leave an extra-long yarn tail (called a long loose end) to use for seams or other purposes.

WINDING UP A
LONG YARN TAIL

A long loose end on your slip knot can start to get tangled around your needles and yarn ball when it is packed away and unpacked for knitting. To keep it tidy, after you have worked a few rows wind it into a yarn "butterfly" close to your knitting.

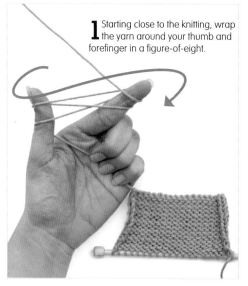

1 Starting close to the knitting, wrap the yarn around your thumb and forefinger in a figure-of-eight.

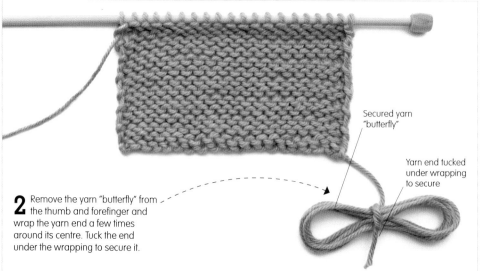

2 Remove the yarn "butterfly" from the thumb and forefinger and wrap the yarn end a few times around its centre. Tuck the end under the wrapping to secure it.

Secured yarn "butterfly"

Yarn end tucked under wrapping to secure

CASTING ON
TECHNIQUES

Once the slip knot is on the needle, it is time to form the rest of the knitting loops next to it. This is called casting on. Your knitting pattern will tell you how many loops (called stitches) to cast on. When you are learning to cast on, practise until the movement becomes automatic. There are numerous cast-on methods and only the easiest and most popular are shown here. Try each method to see which one you like the best.

SINGLE CAST-ON (also called *thumb cast-on*)

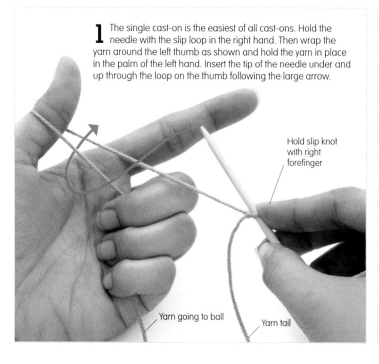

1 The single cast-on is the easiest of all cast-ons. Hold the needle with the slip loop in the right hand. Then wrap the yarn around the left thumb as shown and hold the yarn in place in the palm of the left hand. Insert the tip of the needle under and up through the loop on the thumb following the large arrow.

Hold slip knot with right forefinger

Yarn going to ball

Yarn tail

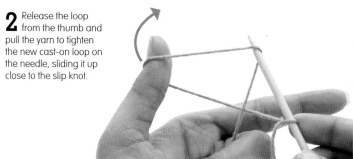

2 Release the loop from the thumb and pull the yarn to tighten the new cast-on loop on the needle, sliding it up close to the slip knot.

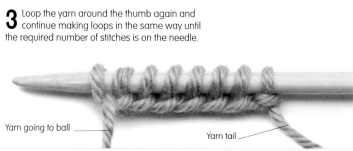

3 Loop the yarn around the thumb again and continue making loops in the same way until the required number of stitches is on the needle.

Yarn going to ball

Yarn tail

DOUBLE CAST-ON (also called *long-tail cast-on*)

1 Make a slip knot on the needle, leaving a very long yarn tail – allow about 3.5cm (1⅜in) for each stitch being cast on. Hold the needle in your right hand. Then loop the yarn tail over the left thumb and the ball yarn end over the left forefinger as shown. Hold both strands in the palm of the left hand.

Long yarn tail

Yarn going to ball

2 Insert the tip of the needle under and up through the loop on the thumb.

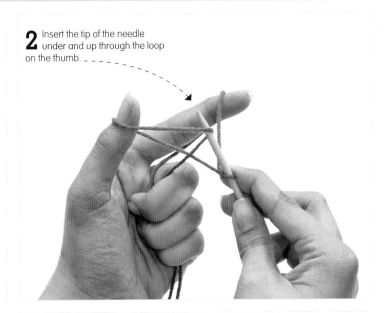

3 Wrap the tip of the needle around the loop on the forefinger from right to left and use it to pull the yarn through the loop on the thumb as shown by the large arrow.

4 Release the loop from the thumb.

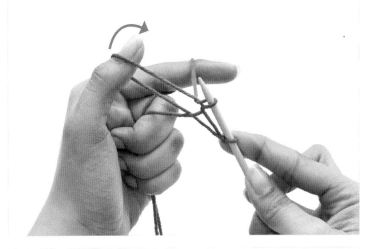

5 Pull both yarn ends to tighten the new cast-on loop on the needle, sliding it up close to the slip knot.

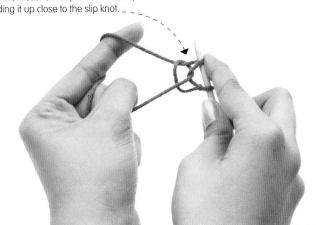

6 Loop the yarn around the thumb again and cast-on another stitch in the same way. Make as many stitches as you need.

Yarn going to ball

Yarn tail

KNITTING

KNIT-ON CAST-ON (also called *knit-stitch cast-on*)

1 Holding the yarn in the left or right hand as explained on page 20, place the needle with the slip knot on it in the left hand. Then insert the tip of the right needle from left to right through the centre of the loop on the left needle. (Although the loops are opened out in these steps to show the technique clearly, they should be snugly hugging the needles in the usual way.)

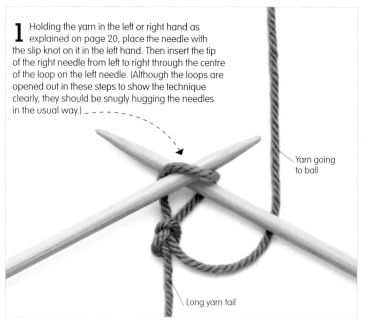

Yarn going to ball

Long yarn tail

2 With the yarn behind the needles, wrap it under and around the tip of the right needle. (While casting on, use the left forefinger or middle finger to hold the loops on the left needle in position.)

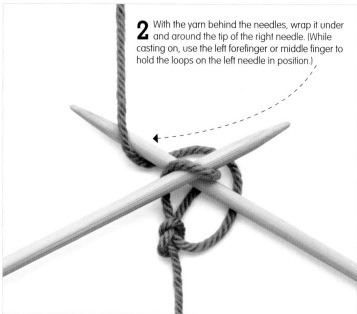

3 With the tip of the right needle, carefully draw the yarn through the loop on the left needle. (This is the same way a knit stitch is formed, hence the name of the cast-on.)

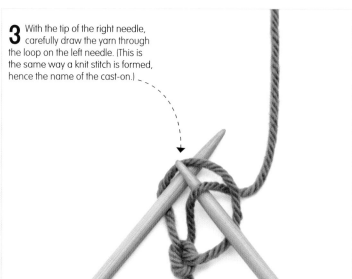

4 Transfer the loop on the right needle to the left needle by inserting the tip of the left needle from right to left through the front of the loop.

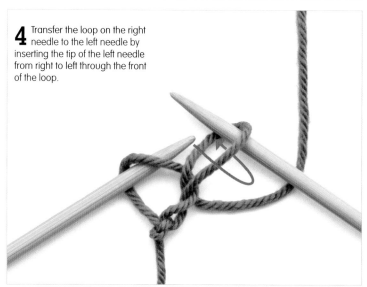

5 Pull both yarn ends to tighten the new cast-on loop on the needle, sliding it up close to the slip knot.

6 Continue casting on stitches in the same way until you have the required number of stitches.

Yarn tail   Yarn going to ball

CABLE CAST-ON

The cable cast-on gets its name from the distinctive double-threaded "cabled" edge that you can see forming in Step 3. Although it is not as elastic as the single, double, and knit-on cast-ons (which can be used for all types of knitting), it is more hard-wearing and more decorative. The cable cast-on is suitable for most items and stitch patterns that call for a firm, durable edge, except for lace knitting, which requires a more elastic cast-on.

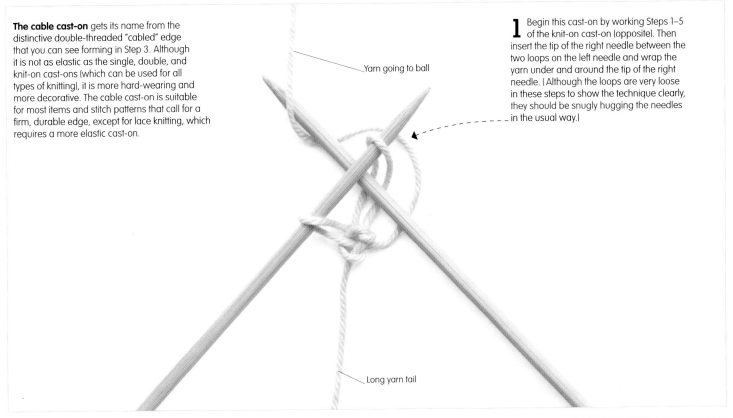

Yarn going to ball

Long yarn tail

1 Begin this cast-on by working Steps 1–5 of the knit-on cast-on (opposite). Then insert the tip of the right needle between the two loops on the left needle and wrap the yarn under and around the tip of the right needle. (Although the loops are very loose in these steps to show the technique clearly, they should be snugly hugging the needles in the usual way.)

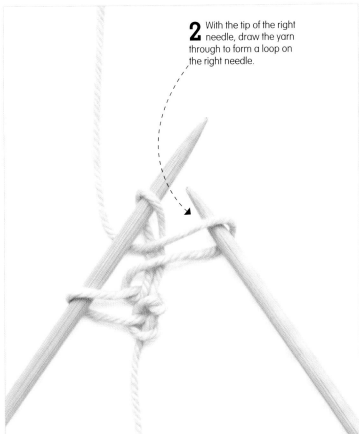

2 With the tip of the right needle, draw the yarn through to form a loop on the right needle.

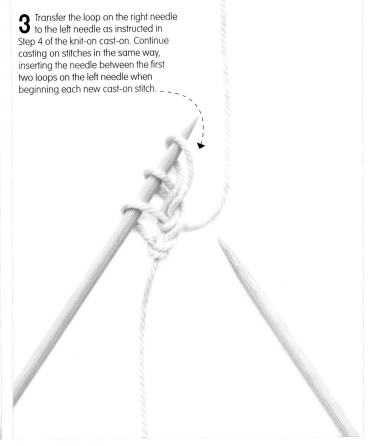

3 Transfer the loop on the right needle to the left needle as instructed in Step 4 of the knit-on cast-on. Continue casting on stitches in the same way, inserting the needle between the first two loops on the left needle when beginning each new cast-on stitch.

KNIT STITCH

Abbreviation = K (or k)

All knitting is made up of only two basic stitches – the knit stitch and the purl stitch. If you are an absolute beginner, do not attempt to learn the knit stitch on cast-on loops. Ask an experienced knitter to knit four or five rows for you and work to the middle of the row so you can practise the steps below. Once you have mastered it, cast on your own stitches (see pages 22–25) and try the knit stitch on these.

1 Hold the needle with the unworked stitches in your left hand and the other needle in your right hand as explained on page 20. With the yarn at the back of the knitting, insert the tip of the right needle from left to right through the centre of the next stitch to be worked on the left needle.

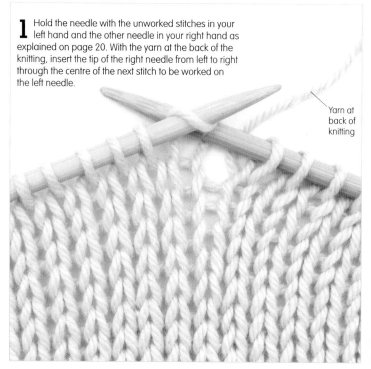

2 Wrap the yarn under and around the tip of the right needle, keeping an even tension on the yarn as it slips through your fingers.

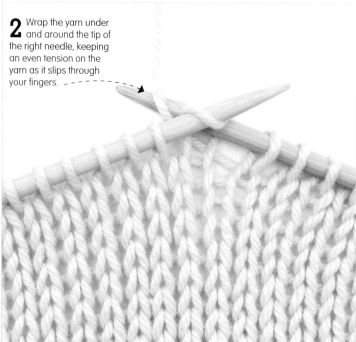

Yarn at back of knitting

3 With the tip of the right needle, carefully draw the yarn through the stitch on the left needle. Try to hold the yarn firmly but not too tightly.

4 Let the old loop drop off the left needle to complete the knit stitch on the right needle. Work all the stitches on the left needle onto the right needle in the same way to complete the knit row. To start a new row, turn the work and transfer the right needle to the left hand.

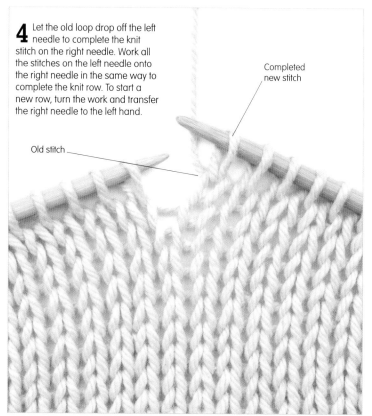

Completed new stitch

Old stitch

PURL
STITCH
Abbreviation = P (or p)

The purl stitch is a little more difficult to make than the knit stitch, but like the knit stitch it becomes effortless after a little practice. Once you are a seasoned knitter, you will feel as if your hands would know how to work these simple basic stitches in your sleep. It is very difficult to learn the purl stitch on cast-on loops, so get an experienced knitter to work a few rows for you first, stopping in the middle of a row so that you can continue.

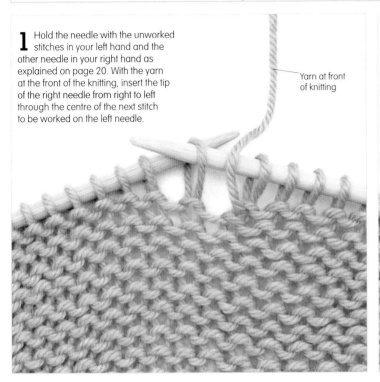

1 Hold the needle with the unworked stitches in your left hand and the other needle in your right hand as explained on page 20. With the yarn at the front of the knitting, insert the tip of the right needle from right to left through the centre of the next stitch to be worked on the left needle.

Yarn at front of knitting

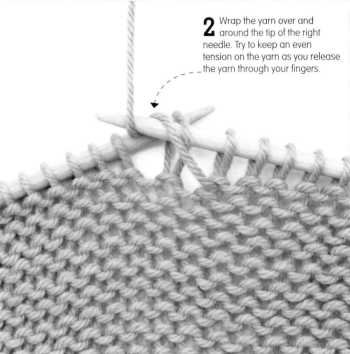

2 Wrap the yarn over and around the tip of the right needle. Try to keep an even tension on the yarn as you release the yarn through your fingers.

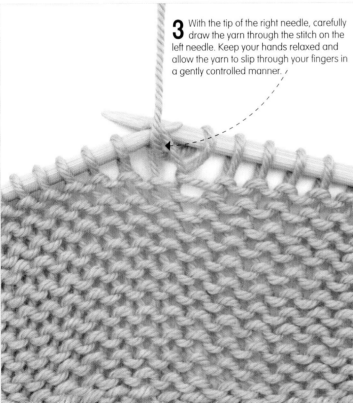

3 With the tip of the right needle, carefully draw the yarn through the stitch on the left needle. Keep your hands relaxed and allow the yarn to slip through your fingers in a gently controlled manner.

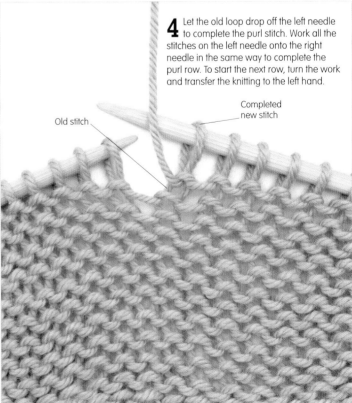

4 Let the old loop drop off the left needle to complete the purl stitch. Work all the stitches on the left needle onto the right needle in the same way to complete the purl row. To start the next row, turn the work and transfer the knitting to the left hand.

Old stitch

Completed new stitch

KNITTING

BASIC KNIT AND PURL STITCHES

Once you know how to work the knit and purl stitch with ease, you will be able to work the most frequently used stitch patterns – garter stitch, stocking stitch, reverse stocking stitch, and single ribbing. Stocking stitch and reverse stocking stitch are commonly used for plain knitted garments, and garter stitch and single ribbing for garment edgings.

GARTER STITCH (Abbreviation = g st)

Knit right-side (RS) rows: Garter stitch is the easiest of all knitted fabrics as all rows are worked in knit stitches. When the right side of the fabric is facing you, knit all the stitches in the row.

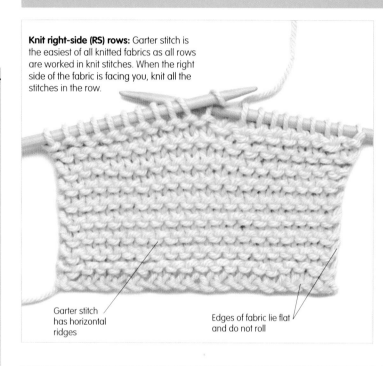

Garter stitch has horizontal ridges

Edges of fabric lie flat and do not roll

Knit wrong-side (WS) rows: When the wrong side of the fabric is facing you, knit all the stitches in the row. The resulting fabric is soft, textured, and slightly stretchy.

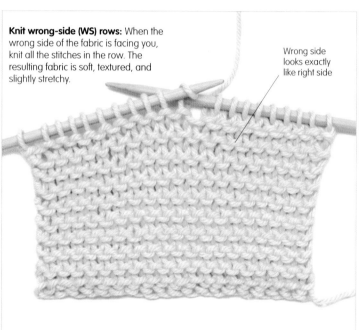

Wrong side looks exactly like right side

STOCKING STITCH (Abbreviation = st st)

Knit right-side (RS) rows: Stocking stitch is formed by working a row of knit stitches and a row of purl stitches alternately. When the right side of the fabric is facing you, knit all the stitches in the row.

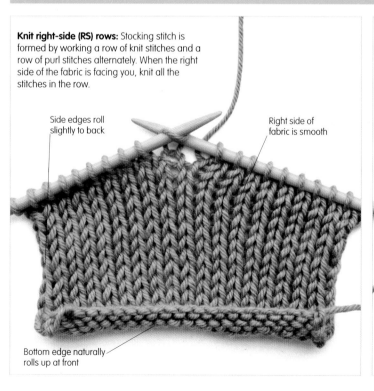

Side edges roll slightly to back

Right side of fabric is smooth

Bottom edge naturally rolls up at front

Purl wrong-side (WS) rows: When the wrong side of the fabric is facing you, purl all the stitches in the row. The wrong side is often referred to as the "purl side" of the knitting.

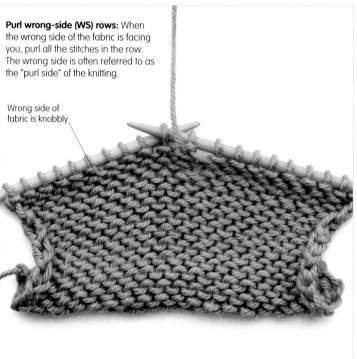

Wrong side of fabric is knobbly

REVERSE STOCKING STITCH (Abbreviation = *rev st st*)

Purl right-side (RS) rows: Reverse stocking stitch is formed exactly like stocking stitch but the sides are reversed. When the right side of the fabric is facing you, purl all the stitches in the row.

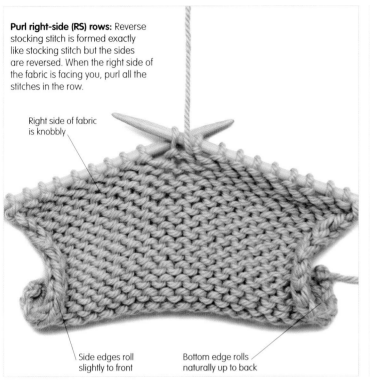

Right side of fabric is knobbly

Side edges roll slightly to front

Bottom edge rolls naturally up to back

Knit wrong-side (WS) rows: When the wrong side of the fabric is facing you, knit all the stitches in the row.

Wrong side of fabric is smooth

SINGLE RIBBING (Abbreviation = *K1, P1 rib*)

Right-side (RS) rows: Single ribbing is formed by working a knit stitch and a purl stitch alternately. After a knit stitch, take the yarn to the front of the knitting between the two needles to purl the next stitch. After a purl stitch, take the yarn to the back between the two needles to knit the next stitch.

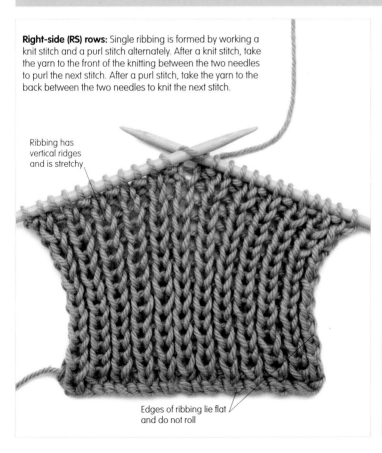

Ribbing has vertical ridges and is stretchy

Edges of ribbing lie flat and do not roll

Wrong-side (WS) rows: On the wrong-side rows, knit all the knit stitches that are facing you and purl all the purl stitches. Work the following rows in the same way to form thin columns of alternating single knit and purl stitches.

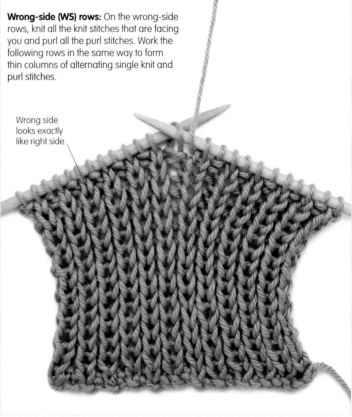

Wrong side looks exactly like right side

SIMPLE KNIT AND PURL STITCH PATTERNS

Here are a few of the vast array of stitch patterns created by combining knit and purl stitches. They all create a flat, reversible knitted fabric and are easy to work. Those that have no specific right side (RS) look exactly the same on both the front and the back, and the few with a marked right side have an attractive texture on the wrong side as well. Because the edges of these stitches do not curl, they are ideal for making simple scarves, baby blankets, and throws. The instructions are given in words and symbols; use whichever you find easier to follow.

MOSS STITCH (RICE STITCH)

KNITTING CHART

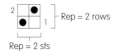

KNITTING INSTRUCTIONS
Cast on an even number of sts.
Row 1 *K1, P1; rep from *.
Row 2 *P1, K1; rep from *.
Rep rows 1 and 2 to form patt.

DOUBLE RIB

KNITTING CHART

KNITTING INSTRUCTIONS
Cast on a multiple of 4 sts.
Row 1 *K2, P2; rep from *.
Rep row 1 to form patt.

LITTLE CHECK STITCH

KNITTING CHART

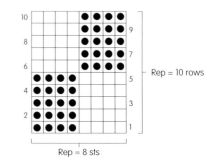

KNITTING INSTRUCTIONS
Cast on a multiple of 8 sts.
Rows 1–5 *K4, P4; rep from *.
Rows 6–10 *P4, K4; rep from *.
Rep rows 1–10 to form patt.

SPECIAL NOTES AND SYMBOL KEY

• See page 37 for a list of knitting abbreviations and for how to work from a stitch symbol chart. Explanations for how to follow a simple stitch pattern are given on page 35.

• Avoid using black or the very darkest yarns if you are using one of these stitches for the main section of your knitting. The shadows around the stitch textures on knit and purl combinations create the patterning effects, and these will not show up very well on such deep shades.

KEY

☐ = K on odd-numbered rows
   = P on even-numbered rows

⬤ = P on odd-numbered rows
   = K on even-numbered rows

TEXTURED CHECK STITCH

KNITTING CHART

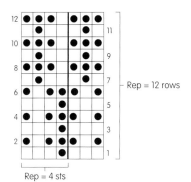

Rep = 12 rows

Rep = 4 sts

KNITTING INSTRUCTIONS
Cast on a multiple of 4 sts, plus 3 extra.
Row 1 K3, *P1, K3; rep from *.
Row 2 K1, *P1, K3; rep from * to last 2 sts, P1, K1.
Rows 3–6 [Rep rows 1 and 2] twice.
Row 7 K1, *P1, K3; rep from * to last 2 sts, P1, K1.
Row 8 K3, *P1, K3; rep from *.
Rows 9–12 [Rep rows 7 and 8] twice.
Rep rows 1–12 to form patt.

STRIPED CHECK STITCH

KNITTING CHART

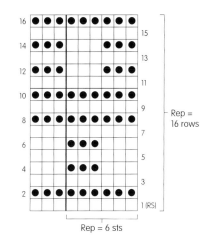

Rep = 16 rows

Rep = 6 sts

KNITTING INSTRUCTIONS
Cast on a multiple of 6 sts, plus 3 extra.
Row 1 all odd-numbered rows (RS) K.
Row 2 K.
Rows 4 and 6 P3, *K3, P3; rep from *.
Rows 8 and 10 K.
Rows 12 and 14 K3, *P3, K3; rep from *.
Row 16 K.
Rep rows 1–16 to form patt.

DIAMOND STITCH

KNITTING CHART

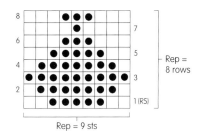

Rep = 8 rows

Rep = 9 sts

KNITTING INSTRUCTIONS
Cast on a multiple of 9 sts.
Row 1 (RS) K2, *P5, K4; rep from * to last 7 sts, P5, K2.
Row 2 P1, *K7, P2; rep from * to last 8 sts, K7, P1.
Row 3 P.
Row 4 Rep row 2.
Row 5 Rep row 1.
Row 6 P3, *K3, P6; rep from * to last 6 sts, K3, P3.
Row 7 K4, *P1, K8; rep from * to last 5 sts, P1, K4.
Row 8 Rep row 6.
Rep rows 1–8 to form patt.

CASTING OFF

When your piece of knitted fabric is complete you will need to close off the loops so that they can't unravel. This is called casting off the stitches. Although casting-off is shown worked across knit stitches, the principle is the same for purl stitches. Sometimes a knitting pattern instructs the knitter to stop knitting but retain the stitches for future use. In this case, you will have to slip your stitches onto a spare needle or a stitch holder.

CASTING OFF KNITWISE

1 Begin by knitting the first two stitches. Then insert the tip of the left needle from left to right through the first stitch and lift this stitch up and over the second stitch and off the right needle.

2 To cast off the next stitch, knit one more stitch and repeat Step 1. Continue in this way until only one stitch remains on the right needle. (If your pattern says "cast off in pattern", work the stitches in the specified stitch pattern as you cast off.)

3 To stop the last stitch from unravelling, cut the yarn, leaving a yarn tail 20cm (8in) long, which is long enough to darn into the knitting later. (Alternatively, leave a much longer yarn end to use for a future seam.) Pass the yarn end through the remaining loop and pull tight to close the loop. This is called fastening off.

SLIPPING STITCHES OFF NEEDLE

Using a stitch holder: If you are setting stitches aside to work on later, your instructions will tell you whether to cut the yarn or keep it attached to the ball. Carefully slip your stitches onto a stitch holder large enough to hold all the stitches.

Stitch holder

Using a length of yarn: If you don't have a stitch holder or don't have one large enough, you can use a length of cotton yarn instead. Using a blunt-ended yarn needle, pass the yarn through the stitches as you slip them off the knitting needle. Knot the ends of the cotton yarn together. If you are only slipping a few stitches onto a holder, use a safety pin.

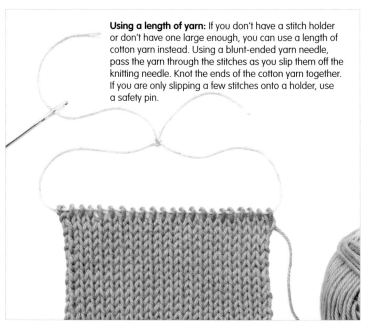

BEGINNER'S TIPS

Here are some useful tips for absolute beginners. Knowing how to wind a hank of yarn into a ball is a handy skill as lots of luxury yarns still come put-up as hanks (see page 14). Beginners also need to learn how (and where) to join on a new ball of yarn when the first ball runs out (see below) and what to do with yarn ends when the knitting is complete (see next page).

WINDING A HANK INTO A BALL

1 Untwist the hank and carefully undo the knot joining the two ends of the yarn. Have someone hold the hank for you, or place it over a chair back. Pull out one of the yarn ends from the hank and wind it into a little yarn "butterfly" (see page 22). Then pinch the butterfly together at the centre and slip it off the left hand.

Yarn tail

2 Start wrapping the yarn around the butterfly and the thumb to create a hole in the centre of the ball. Keep winding until the whole hank is used up. Be sure to change the positioning of the wraps frequently to keep the ball round. Secure the yarn end under a few of the outer wraps. When you start knitting, pull the butterfly out of the centre and use this end. Pulling the yarn from inside the ball stops it from rolling around.

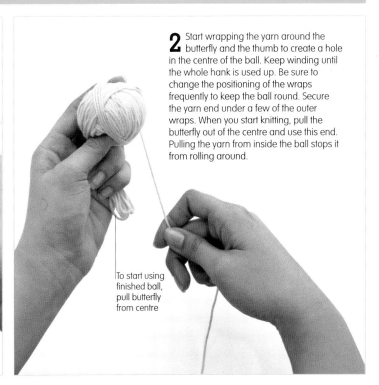

To start using finished ball, pull butterfly from centre

JOINING ON A NEW BALL

1 Always join on a new ball of yarn at the beginning of a row. Knot the new end of yarn onto the old yarn.

End of old ball

New ball

2 Slide the knot up very close to the knitting. The knot can be hidden in the seam later. If you are knitting a scarf or blanket, tie the knot loosely so you can undo it later and darn in the ends.

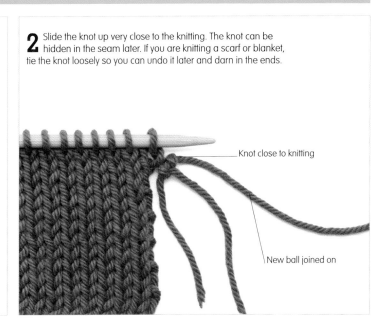

Knot close to knitting

New ball joined on

KNITTING

DARNING IN A YARN END

Freshly completed knitting will have at least two yarn ends dangling from the piece – one at the cast-on edge and one at the cast-off edge. For every extra ball used, there will be two more ends. Thread each end separately onto a blunt-ended yarn needle and weave it through stitches on the wrong side of the work as shown.

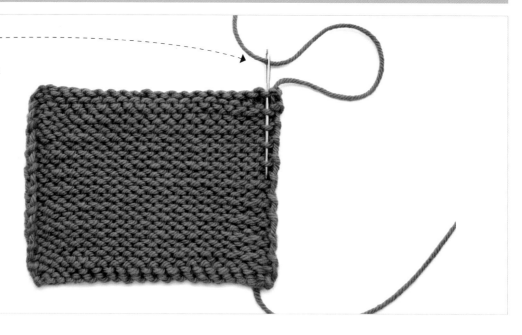

CORRECTING MISTAKES

The best thing to do if you make a mistake in your knitting is to unravel it back to the mistake by unpicking the stitches one by one. If you drop a stitch, be sure to pick it up quickly before it comes undone right back to the cast-on edge.

UNPICKING A KNIT ROW

Hold the needle with the stitches in your right hand. To unpick each stitch individually, insert the tip of the left needle from front to back through the stitch below the first knit stitch on the right needle, then drop the old knit stitch off the needle and pull out the loop.

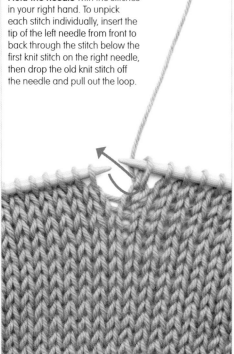

UNPICKING A PURL ROW

Hold the needle with the stitches in your right hand. Unpick each purl stitch individually with the tip of the left needle in the same way as for the knit stitch.

PICKING UP A DROPPED STITCH

If you drop a stitch on stocking stitch, you can easily reclaim it with a crochet hook. With the right side of the knitting facing you, insert the hook through the dropped loop. Grab the strand between the stitches and pull a loop through the loop on the hook. Continue up the rows in this way until you reach the top. Then slip the stitch back onto your needle.

FOLLOWING A SIMPLE STITCH PATTERN

Stitch pattern instructions are written or charted directions for making all sorts of textures – knit and purl combinations, lace and cables. Knitting stitch pattern swatches is the best possible introduction to row instructions. Beginners should try some out before attempting to follow a proper knitting pattern (see pages 66 and 67). Once you understand row instructions, a first knitting pattern won't look so daunting.

UNDERSTANDING WRITTEN INSTRUCTIONS

Anyone who can cast on, knit and purl, and cast off will be able to work from simple knit-and-purl-combination stitch pattern instructions with little difficulty. It is just a question of following the instructions one step at a time and getting used to the abbreviations. A full list of knitting abbreviations is given on page 37, but for simple knit and purl textures all you need to grasp is that "K1" means "knit one stitch", "K2" means "knit two stitches", and so on. And the same applies for the purl stitches – "P1" means "purl one stitch", "P2" means "purl two stitches", and so on.

To begin a stitch pattern, cast on the number of stitches that it tells you to, using your chosen yarn and the yarn manufacturer's recommended needle size. Work the stitch row by row, then repeat the rows as instructed and the stitch pattern will grow beneath the needles. When your knitting is the desired size, cast off in pattern (see page 32).

The best tips for first-timers are to follow the rows slowly; mark the right side of the fabric by knotting a coloured thread onto it; use a row counter to keep track of where you are (see page 19); and pull out your stitches and start again if you get in a muddle. If you love the stitch pattern you are trying out, you can make a scarf, blanket, or cushion cover with it – no need to buy a knitting pattern.

The principles for following stitch patterns are the same for cables and lace (see pages 50–51 and 54–57), which you will be able to work once you learn cable techniques and how to increase and decrease.

Some stitch patterns will call for "slipping" stitches and knitting "through the back of the loop". These useful techniques are given next as a handy reference when you are consulting the abbreviations and terminology list.

SLIPPING STITCHES PURLWISE

1 Always slip stitches purlwise unless instructed otherwise. For example, when slipping stitches onto a stitch holder, slip them purlwise. To slip a stitch purlwise, insert the tip of the right needle from right to left through the front of the loop on the left needle.

2 Slide the stitch onto the right needle and off the left needle without working it. The slipped stitch now sits on the right needle with the right side of the loop at the front of the needle just like the worked stitches next to it.

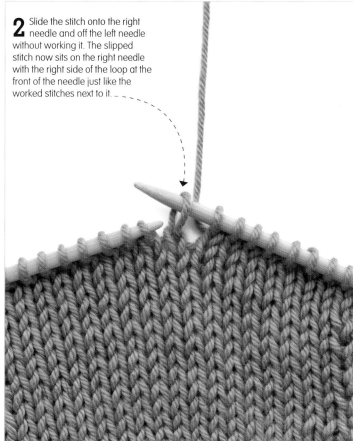

SLIPPING STITCHES KNITWISE

1 Slip stitches knitwise only if instructed to do so or if working decreases (see pages 43 and 44). To slip a stitch knitwise, first insert the tip of the right needle from left to right through the front of the loop on the left needle.

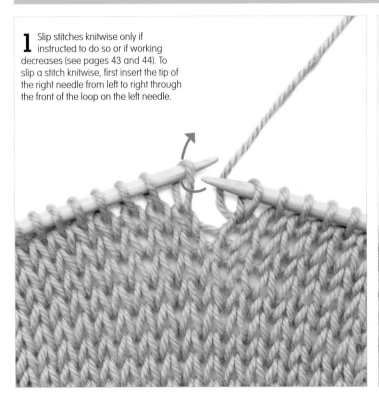

2 Slide the stitch onto the right needle and off the left needle without working it. The slipped stitch now sits on the right needle with the left side of the loop at the front of the needle unlike the worked stitches next to it. ----

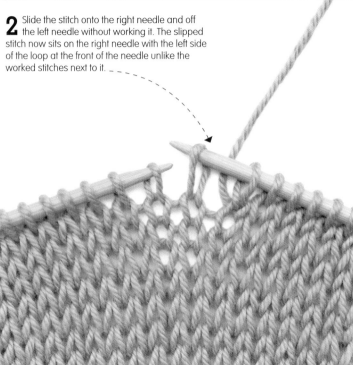

KNITTING THROUGH BACK OF LOOP

1 When row instructions say "K1 tbl" (knit one through the back of the loop), insert the right needle from right to left through the side of the stitch behind the left needle (called the back of the loop). ----

2 Wrap the yarn around the tip of the right needle and complete the knit stitch in the usual way. This twists the stitch in the row below so that the legs of the stitch cross at the base. (The same principle applies for working P1 tbl, K2tog tbl and P2tog tbl.) ----

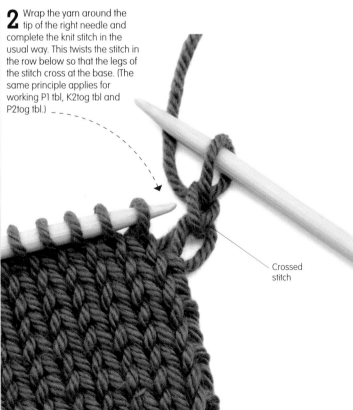

Crossed stitch

UNDERSTANDING STITCH SYMBOL CHARTS

Knitting instructions for stitch patterns can also be given in chart form. Some knitters prefer working stitch-symbol charts because they are easy to read, and they build up a visual image of the stitch repeat that is quick to memorize.

Even with charted instructions, there are usually written out directions for how many stitches to cast on. But if there aren't, you can figure out how many stitches to cast on by looking at the chart. The number of stitches in the pattern "repeat" is marked clearly on the chart, so cast on a multiple of this number, plus extra for any edge stitches outside the stitch repeat.

Each square on the chart represents a stitch and each horizontal line of squares represents a row of knitting. After casting on, start at the bottom of the chart and follow it upwards. Read odd-numbered rows (usually right-side rows) from right to left and even-numbered rows (usually wrong-side rows) from left to right. Work the edges stitches, then repeat the stitches inside the repeat as many times as required. Note that some symbols mean one thing on a right-side row and another on a wrong-side row (see stitch symbol key below).

Once you have worked all the charted rows, start again at the bottom of the chart to begin the "row repeat" once more.

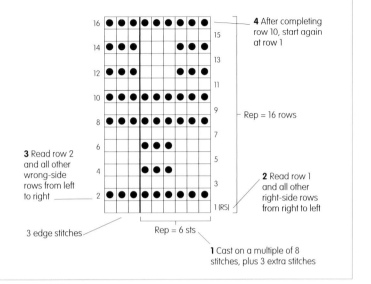

4 After completing row 10, start again at row 1

Rep = 16 rows

3 Read row 2 and all other wrong-side rows from left to right

2 Read row 1 and all other right-side rows from right to left

3 edge stitches

Rep = 6 sts

1 Cast on a multiple of 8 stitches, plus 3 extra stitches

KNITTING ABBREVIATIONS

These are the most frequently used knitting abbreviations. Any special abbreviations used in knitting instructions are always explained within the pattern.

alt	alternate	**rev st st**	reverse stocking stitch
beg	begin(ning)	**RH**	right hand
cm	centimetre(s)	**RS**	right side (of work)
cont	continu(e)(ing)	**skp**	sl 1-K1-psso (see page 44)
dec	decreas(e)(ing)		
foll	follow(s)(ing)	**sk2p**	sl 1, K2tog, psso (see page 45)
g	gram(s)		
g st	garter stitch	**ssk**	slip, slip, knit (see page 45)
in	inch(es)		
inc	increase(e)(ing)	**sl**	slip
K	knit	**sl 2-K1-p2sso**	slip 2, knit one, pass slipped stitches over (see page 45)
K1 tbl	knit st through back of loop		
K2tog	knit next 2 sts together (see page 43)	**st(s)**	stitch(es)
		st st	stocking stitch
Kfb	knit into front and back of next st (see page 38)	**tbl**	through back of loop(s)
		tog	together
LH	left hand	**WS**	wrong side (of work)
m	metre(s)	**yd**	yard(s)
M1	make one stitch (see pages 39 and 40)	**yfwd**	yarn forward (US yo; see page 41)
mm	millimetre(s)	**yfrn**	yarn forward round needle (US yo; see page 42)
oz	ounce(s)		
P	purl		
P2tog	purl next 2 sts together (see page 44)	**yon**	yarn over needle (US yo; see page 42)
patt	pattern; or work in pattern	**yrn**	yarn round needle (US yo; see page 41)
Ptb	purl into front and back of next st (see page 38)	**[ ] ***	Repeat instructions between brackets, or after or between asterisks, as many times as instructed
psso	pass slipped stitch over		
rem	remain(s)(ing)		
rep	repeat(ing)		

KNITTING TERMINOLOGY AND SYMBOLS

The following terms are commonly used in knitting patterns. Most knitting terminology is the same in the UK and the US, but where they differ, the US equivalent is given in parentheses.

cast on Create a series of loops on a knitting needle which form the foundation for the piece of knitting.

cast off Close off stitches and drop them from the knitting needle (US: bind off).

cast off knitwise/purlwise Cast off while working the stitches in the knit/purl stitch.

cast off in pattern Cast off while working the stitches in the pattern used in the previous row.

cast off in ribbing Cast off while working the stitches in the ribbing used in the previous row.

decrease Decrease the number of stitches in a row (see pages 43–45).

garter stitch Knit every row. In circular knitting (see page 78), knit one round and purl one round alternately.

tension The size of the stitches in a piece of knitting (US: gauge), measured by the number of stitches and rows to 10cm (4in), or to 2.5cm (1in) on fine knitting (see page 67).

increase Increase the number of stitches in a row (see pages 38–43).

knitwise Insert the right needle into the stitch on the left needle as if starting a knit stitch.

pick up and knit Draw loops through the edge of the knitting and place them on the needle (see page 68).

purlwise Insert the right needle into the stitch on the left needle as if starting a purl stitch.

stocking stitch Knit all RS rows and purl all WS rows (US: stockinette stitch).

reverse stocking stitch Purl all WS rows and purl all RS rows (US: reverse stockinette stitch).

work straight Work in the specified pattern without increasing or decreasing stitches (US: work even).

yarn-over increase Wrap yarn around right needle to make a new stitch; abbreviated yfwd, yfrn, yon or yrn (US yo; see pages 41–43).

STITCH SYMBOLS
These are the stitch symbols used in this book. Knitting symbols vary, so be sure to follow the explanations for symbols given in your pattern.

☐ = K on RS rows, P on WS rows

⊡ = P on RS rows, K on WS rows

Ⓞ = yarn over (see page 43)

╱ = K2tog (see page 43)

╲ = ssk (see page 45)

⋀ = sk2p (see page 45)

Ⱶ = sl 2-K1-p2sso (see page 45)

⧄⧄ = T2R (see page 51)

⧅⧅ = T2L (see page 51)

⧓ = C4F (see page 50)

⧓ = C4B (see page 50)

⧓ = C6F (see page 50)

⧓ = C6B (see page 50)

KNITTING

INCREASES AND DECREASES

Increasing the number of stitches on the needle and decreasing the number of stitches is the way knitting is shaped, changing the edges from straight vertical sides to curves and slants. But increases and decreases are also used in combinations with plain knit and purl stitches to form interesting textures in the knitted fabric, from lace to sculptured relief.

SIMPLE INCREASES

The techniques that follow are the simple increases knitters need to know how to work when shaping is called for in a knitting pattern. They create one extra stitch without creating a visible hole in the knitting and are called invisible increases. Multiple increases, which add more than one extra stitch, are used less frequently and are always explained fully in the knitting pattern – only one is given here as an example.

KNIT INTO FRONT AND BACK OF STITCH (Abbreviation = *Kfb* or *inc 1*)

This is the most popular invisible increase for a knit row and is sometimes called a bar increase because it creates a little bar between the stitches.

1 To begin, knit the next stitch, but leave the stitch being worked into on the left needle. Then insert the right needle through the back of the loop from right to left.

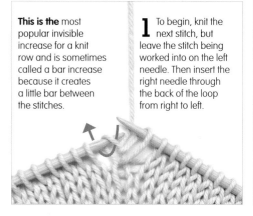

2 Wrap the yarn around the tip of the right needle, draw the yarn through the loop to form the second stitch and drop the old stitch off the left needle.

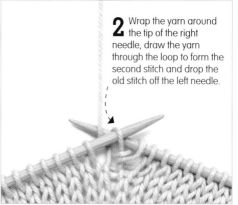

3 Knitting into the front and the back of the stitch like this creates two stitches out of one and increases one stitch in the row.

New stitch

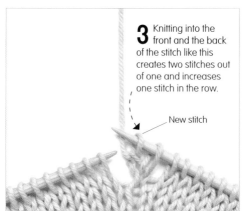

PURL INTO FRONT AND BACK (Abbreviation = *Pfb* or *inc 1*)

1 Purl the next stitch, but leave the stitch being worked into on the left needle. Then insert the right needle through the back of the loop from left to right.

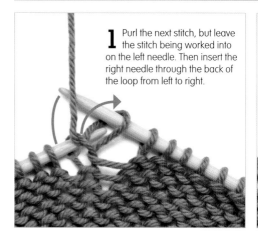

2 Wrap the yarn around the tip of the right needle, draw the yarn through the loop to form the second stitch and drop the old stitch off the left needle.

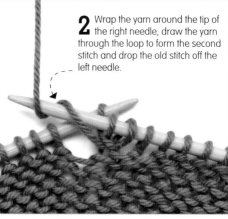

3 Purling into the front and the back of the stitch like this creates two stitches out of one and increases one stitch in the row.

New stitch

LIFTED INCREASE ON KNIT ROW (Abbreviation = *inc 1*)

1 Insert the tip of the right needle from front to back through the stitch below the next stitch on the left needle and knit this lifted loop.

2 Knit the next stitch (the stitch above the lifted stitch on the left needle) in the usual way.

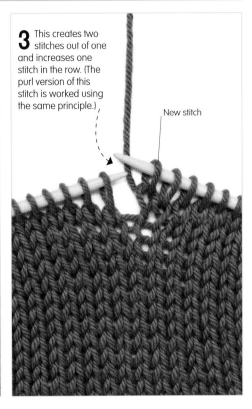

3 This creates two stitches out of one and increases one stitch in the row. (The purl version of this stitch is worked using the same principle.)

New stitch

"MAKE-ONE" INCREASE ON A KNIT ROW (Abbreviation = *M1* or *M1k*)

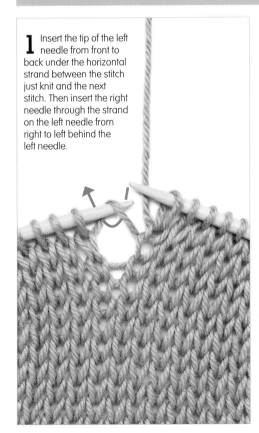

1 Insert the tip of the left needle from front to back under the horizontal strand between the stitch just knit and the next stitch. Then insert the right needle through the strand on the left needle from right to left behind the left needle.

2 Wrap the yarn around the tip of the right needle and draw the yarn through the lifted loop. (This action is called knitting through the back of the loop.)

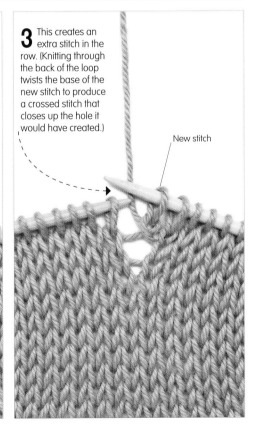

3 This creates an extra stitch in the row. (Knitting through the back of the loop twists the base of the new stitch to produce a crossed stitch that closes up the hole it would have created.)

New stitch

KNITTING

MAKE-ONE INCREASE ON PURL ROW (Abbreviation = *M1* or *M1p*)

1 Insert the tip of the left needle from front to back under the horizontal strand between the stitch just knit and the next stitch. Then insert the right needle through the strand on the left needle from left to right behind the left needle.

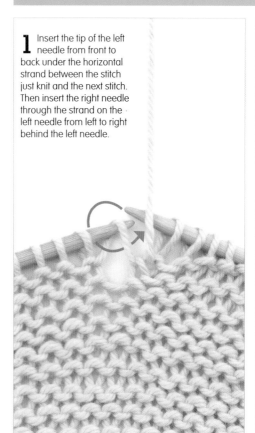

2 Wrap the yarn around the tip of the right needle and draw the yarn through the lifted loop. (This action is called purling through the back of the loop.)

3 This creates an extra stitch in the row. (Purling through the back of the loop twists the base of the new stitch to produce a crossed stitch that closes up the hole it would have created.)

New stitch

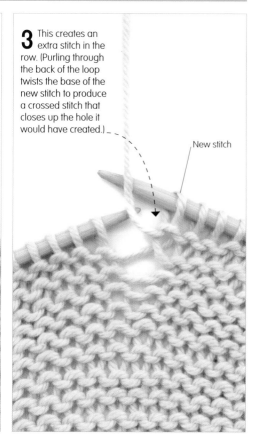

MULTIPLE INCREASES (Abbreviation = *[K1, P1, K1] into next st*)

1 This is a very easy increase to use if you need to add more than one stitch to an existing stitch, but it does create a small hole under the new stitches. To begin the increase, knit the next stitch but leave the old stitch on the left needle.

2 Then purl and knit into the same loop on the left needle. This action is called knit one, purl one, knit one all into the next stitch. It creates two extra stitches in the row. You can keep alternating K and P stitches in the same loop to create even more stitches if desired.

K1　P1　K1

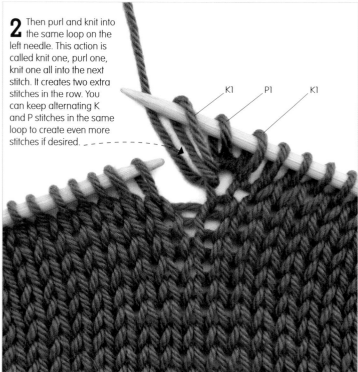

YARN-OVER
INCREASES

Yarn-over increases add stitches to a row and create holes at the same time, so are often called visible increases. They are used to produce decorative laces (see pages 54–57). A yarn-over is made by looping the yarn around the right needle to form an extra stitch. It is important to wrap the loop around the needle in the correct way or it will become crossed when it is worked in the next row, which closes the hole.

YARN-OVER BETWEEN KNIT STITCHES (Abbreviation = UK *yfwd*; US *yo*)

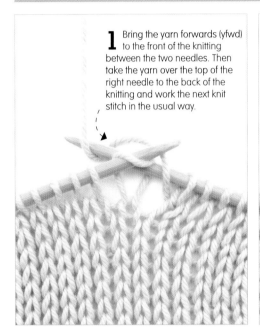

1 Bring the yarn forwards (yfwd) to the front of the knitting between the two needles. Then take the yarn over the top of the right needle to the back of the knitting and work the next knit stitch in the usual way.

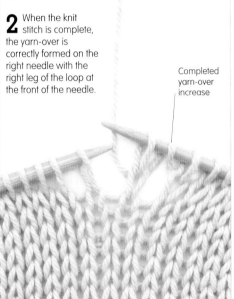

2 When the knit stitch is complete, the yarn-over is correctly formed on the right needle with the right leg of the loop at the front of the needle.

Completed yarn-over increase

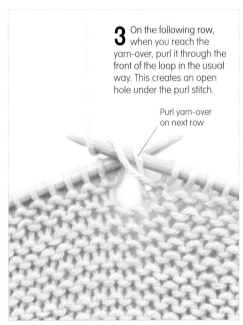

3 On the following row, when you reach the yarn-over, purl it through the front of the loop in the usual way. This creates an open hole under the purl stitch.

Purl yarn-over on next row

YARN-OVER BETWEEN PURL STITCHES (Abbreviation = UK *yrn*; US *yo*)

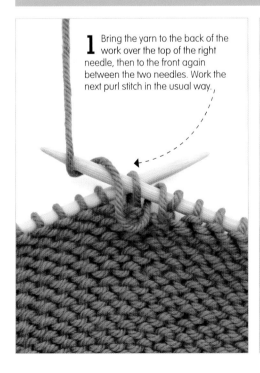

1 Bring the yarn to the back of the work over the top of the right needle, then to the front again between the two needles. Work the next purl stitch in the usual way.

2 When the purl stitch is complete, the yarn-over is correctly formed on the right needle with the right leg of the loop at the front of the needle.

Completed yarn-over increase

3 On the following row, when you reach the yarn-over, knit it through the front of the loop in the usual way. This creates an open hole under the knit stitch.

Knit yarn-over on next row

YARN-OVER BETWEEN KNIT AND PURL STITCHES (Abbreviations = UK *yfrn* and *yon*; US *yo*)

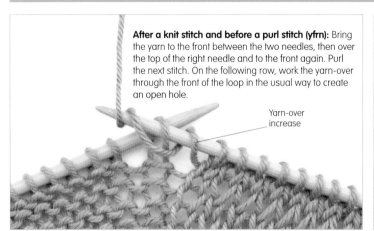

After a knit stitch and before a purl stitch (yfrn): Bring the yarn to the front between the two needles, then over the top of the right needle and to the front again. Purl the next stitch. On the following row, work the yarn-over through the front of the loop in the usual way to create an open hole.

Yarn-over increase

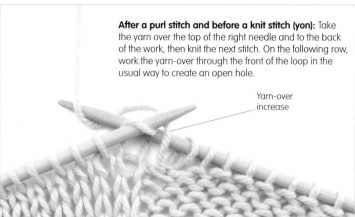

After a purl stitch and before a knit stitch (yon): Take the yarn over the top of the right needle and to the back of the work, then knit the next stitch. On the following row, work the yarn-over through the front of the loop in the usual way to create an open hole.

Yarn-over increase

YARN-OVER AT THE BEGINNING OF A ROW (Abbreviations = UK *yfwd* and *yrn*; US *yo*)

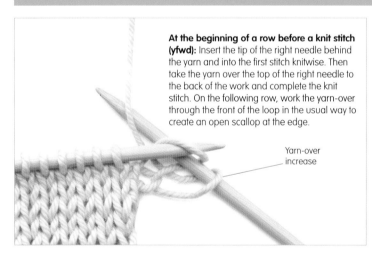

At the beginning of a row before a knit stitch (yfwd): Insert the tip of the right needle behind the yarn and into the first stitch knitwise. Then take the yarn over the top of the right needle to the back of the work and complete the knit stitch. On the following row, work the yarn-over through the front of the loop in the usual way to create an open scallop at the edge.

Yarn-over increase

At the beginning of a row before a purl stitch (yrn): Wrap the yarn from front to back over the top of the right needle and to the front again between the two needles. Then purl the first stitch. On the following row, work the yarn-over through the front of the loop in the usual way to create an open scallop at the edge.

Yarn-over increase

DOUBLE YARN-OVER (Abbreviation = UK *yfwd twice*; US *yo2*)

1 For a double yarn-over between two knit stitches, take the yarn over the top of the right needle to the back of the work, between the two needles to the front again and over the top of the right needle to the back again, ready to knit the next stitch.

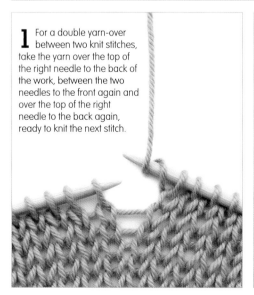

2 Knit the next stitch in the usual way. This creates two new loops on the right needle.

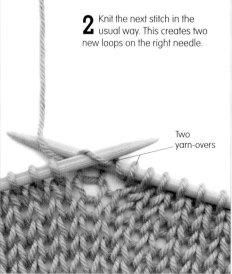

Two yarn-overs

3 On the following row (a purl row), purl the first yarn-over and knit the second yarn-over. The double yarn-over creates a bigger hole than the single yarn-over. It is frequently used in lace knitting and for buttonholes.

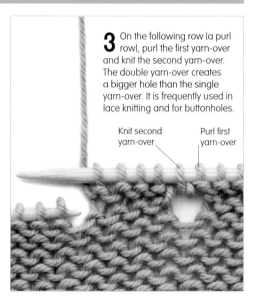

Knit second yarn-over

Purl first yarn-over

CLOSED YARN-OVER ON GARTER STITCH

1 The closed yarn-over is used as an "invisible" increase and is an especially good increase for garter stitch. Take the yarn from back to front over the top of the right needle, then around the needle to the back of the work between the two needles. Knit the next stitch in the usual way.

Yarn-over increase

2 On the next row, knit the yarn-over through the front loop (the strand at the front of the left needle).

Knit yarn-over though front on next row

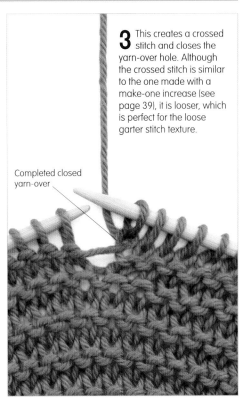

3 This creates a crossed stitch and closes the yarn-over hole. Although the crossed stitch is similar to the one made with a make-one increase (see page 39), it is looser, which is perfect for the loose garter stitch texture.

Completed closed yarn-over

SIMPLE DECREASES

The decreases explained here are the simple ones that are most frequently used for shaping knitting and, paired with increases, for textured and lace stitches. More complicated decreases than these are always explained in detail in knitting instructions. Most of the decreases that follow are single decreases that subtract only one stitch from the knitting, but a few double decreases are included.

KNIT TWO TOGETHER (Abbreviation = *K2tog* or *dec 1*)

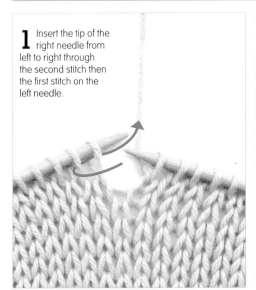

1 Insert the tip of the right needle from left to right through the second stitch then the first stitch on the left needle.

2 Wrap the yarn around the tip of the right needle, draw the yarn through both loops and drop the old stitches off the left needle.

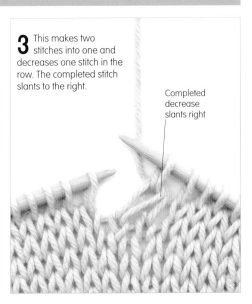

3 This makes two stitches into one and decreases one stitch in the row. The completed stitch slants to the right.

Completed decrease slants right

PURL TWO TOGETHER (Abbreviation = *P2tog or dec 1*)

1 Where a knitting pattern instructs the knitter to "decrease 1" on a purl row, the P2tog decrease should be used. Insert the tip of the right needle from right to left through the first stitch then the second stitch on the left needle.

2 Wrap the yarn around the tip of the right needle, draw the yarn through both loops and drop the old stitches off the left needle.

3 This makes two stitches into one and decreases one stitch in the row.

Completed decrease slants right on right side of work

SLIP ONE, KNIT ONE, PASS SLIPPED STITCH OVER (Abbreviation = *skp or sl 1-K1-psso*)

1 Slip the first stitch on the left needle knitwise (see page 36) onto the right needle without working it. Then knit the next stitch.

Slipped knitwise onto right needle

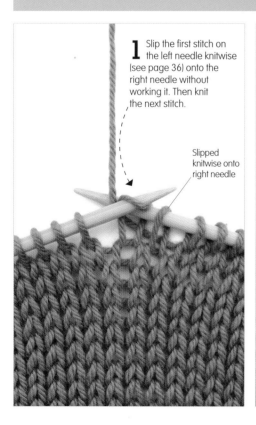

2 Pick up the slipped stitch with the tip of the left needle and pass it over the knit stitch and off the right needle.

3 This makes two stitches into one and decreases one stitch in the row.

Completed decrease slants left

SLIP, SLIP, KNIT (Abbreviation = *ssk*)

1 Slip the next two stitches on the left needle knitwise (see page 36), one at a time, onto the right needle without working them.

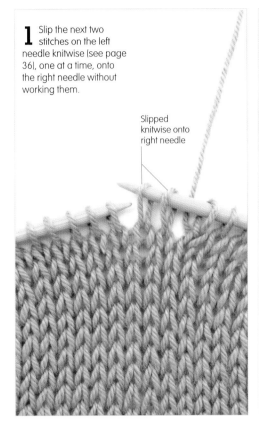

Slipped knitwise onto right needle

2 Insert the tip of the left needle from left to right through the fronts of the two slipped stitches (so that the right needle is now behind the left needle). Knit these two stitches together.

3 This makes two stitches into one and decreases one stitch in the row.

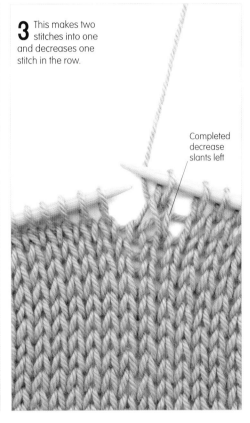

Completed decrease slants left

DOUBLE DECREASES

K3tog: Insert the tip of the right needle from left to right through the third stitch on the left needle, then the second, then the first. Knit these three together. This decreases two stitches at once.

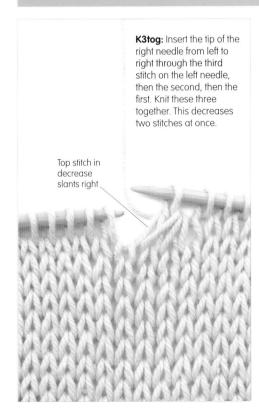

Top stitch in decrease slants right

sk2p (sl 1-K2tog-psso): Slip one stitch knitwise onto the right needle, knit the next two stitches together, then pass the slipped stitch over the K2tog and off the right needle. This decreases two stitches at once.

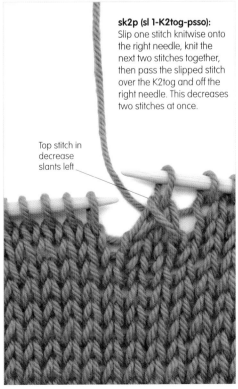

Top stitch in decrease slants left

sl 2-K1-p2sso: Slip two stitches knitwise TOGETHER onto the right needle, knit the next stitch, then pass the two slipped stitches together over the knit stitch and off the right needle. This decreases two stitches at once.

Top stitch in decrease is upright

SIMPLE FLOWER PATTERNS

These flowers have all been designed to be easy to make using simple increasing and decreasing techniques. Knitting them is a fun way to practise the shaping techniques explained on the previous pages in this section. Each flower is worked as one piece, starting at the petals and working inwards towards the centre. As a bonus, there are no yarn ends to darn in on the flowers because the yarn tails are used to plait a simple stem. The shapes are perfect for use as appliqué on blankets, cushion covers, bags, scarves, and sweaters, or to decorate greeting cards.

TWELVE-PETAL FLOWER

KNITTING INSTRUCTIONS
Worked in yarns A (petals) and B (flower centre).
Using knit-on cast-on method (see page 24) and A, cast on 12 sts, leaving a yarn tail at least 25cm (10in) long.
Row 1 (RS) Cast off 10 sts knitwise and slip st on RH needle back onto LH needle. 2 sts.
Note: Do not turn work when working petals, but keep RS always facing.
Row 2 (RS) Cast on 12 sts onto LH needle using knit-on cast-on method, then cast off 10 sts knitwise and slip st on RH needle back onto LH needle. 4 sts.
Rows 3–12 [Rep row 2] 10 times more to make a total of 12 petals. 24 sts (2 sts at base of each petal).
Cut off A.
Using B and working across all 24 sts, cont in usual rows for flower centre as foll:
Row 13 (RS) [K2tog] 12 times. 12 sts.
Row 14 (WS) K.
Row 15 (RS) K.
Slip all sts back onto LH needle. Then cut off yarn, leaving a yarn tail at least 25cm (10in) long. Thread yarn tail onto a blunt-ended yarn needle. With RS facing, thread yarn through rem sts, slipping them off knitting needle as you proceed. Pull yarn tight to gather sts firmly. With WS facing and still using threaded yarn needle, sew row ends of flower centre together using overcast stitches, working from centre to beginning of petal yarn. Knot ends of matching yarn together, close to work on WS, then knot all yarn ends together close to WS. To form stem, plait together yarn ends, holding two ends of A together and using B strands singly for three strands of plait. Knot end of stem and trim yarn ends.
Do not press.

SPINNING-PETAL FLOWER

KNITTING INSTRUCTIONS
Worked in yarns A (petals) and B (flower centre).
Using knit-on cast-on method (see page 24) and A, cast on 10 sts, leaving a yarn tail at least 25cm (10in) long.
Row 1 (RS) K8 and turn, leaving rem sts unworked.
Row 2 (WS) K to end.
Rows 3 and 4 Rep rows 1 and 2.
Row 5 (RS) Cast off 8 sts loosely knitwise, slip st on RH needle back onto LH needle. 2 sts.
Note: Do not turn work after last row of each petal (cast-off row), but keep RS facing for next row.
Row 6 (RS) Cast on 10 sts onto LH needle using knit-on cast-on method, K 8 and turn.
Rows 7, 8, 9, and 10 Rep rows 2–5 of first petal. 4 sts.
[Rep rows 6–10] 5 times more to make a total of 7 petals. 14 sts (2 sts at base of each petal).
Cut off A.
Using B and working across all 14 sts, cont in usual rows for flower centre as foll:
K 3 rows.
P 1 row.
K 1 row, so ending with a RS row.
Finish as for twelve-petal flower from ** to **.
Do not press.
Decorate centre with small button if desired.

LOOP-PETAL FLOWER WITH SMALL CENTRE

KNITTING INSTRUCTIONS
Worked in yarns A (outer petal), B (inner petal), and C (flower centre).
Using double cast-on method (see page 23) and A, cast on 90 sts, leaving a yarn tail at least 25cm (10in) long.
Row 1 (WS) K6, sk2p, *K12, sk2p; rep from * to last 6 sts, K6.
Cut off A and change to B.
Row 2 (RS) *K1, cast off next 11 sts knitwise; rep from *. 12 sts.
Cut off B and change to C.
Row 3 P.
Row 4 *K2tog, K1; rep from *. 8 sts.
Finish as for twelve-petal flower from ** to **, but also using A to sew beginning and end of cast-on sts together and making plait with two strands each of A, B, and C. Do not press.

SPECIAL NOTES

• To produce firm flowers and leaves, use a knitting needle size one size smaller than the yarn's recommended size and knit tightly. See page 37 for a list of knitting abbreviations.

• Be sure to leave a yarn tail at least 25cm (10in) long when casting on the stitches for the flowers and when fastening off. These long ends will be needed for gathering stitches, working short seams, and making plaited stems.

• Do not press or block the leaves or flowers because pressing or blocking will flatten the knitted texture and alter the natural shapes.

LOOP-PETAL FLOWER WITH LARGE CENTRE

KNITTING INSTRUCTIONS

Worked in yarns A (outer petal), B (inner petal), and C (flower centre).
Using double cast-on method (see page 23) and A, cast on 72 sts, leaving a yarn tail at least 25cm (10in) long.
Cut off A and change to B.
Row 1 (RS) K.
Row 2 *Kfb, cast off next 10 sts knitwise; rep from *. 18 sts. Cut off B and change to C.
Row 3 K.
Row 4 *K4, K2tog; rep from *. 15 sts.
Row 5 K.
Row 6 P.
Row 7 *K1, K2tog; rep from * to end. 10 sts.
Finish as for twelve-petal flower from ** to **, but also using A to sew beginning and end of cast-on sts together and making plait with two strands each of A, B, and C.
Do not press.
Decorate centre with small button if desired.

ANEMONE

KNITTING INSTRUCTIONS

Note: Slip all slip stitches purlwise with yarn at WS of work.
Worked in yarns A (petals) and B and C (flower centre).
Using double cast-on method (see page 23) and A, cast on 41 sts, leaving a yarn tail at least 25cm (10in) long.
Row 1 (RS) *Sl 1, K7; rep from * to last st, P1.
Row 2 *Sl 1, K to end.
Row 3 Rep row 1.
Row 4 *Sl 1, P7, *sl 1, take yarn to back of work between two needles then around knitting over cast-on edge, over top of knitting between two needles and around cast-on edge again, so ending at front of work, pull yarn to gather knitting tightly, P7; rep from * to last st, K1. Cut off A and change to B.
Row 5 *K2tog; rep from * to last 3 sts, sk2p. 20 sts.
Row 6 K.
Cut off B and change to C.
Row 7 [K2tog] 10 times. 10 sts.
Finish as for twelve-petal flower from ** to **, but also using A to sew short petal seam (leaving part of seam unworked to create indent between petals as between other petals) and making plait with two strands each of A, B, and C.
Do not press.

LARGE LEAF

KNITTING INSTRUCTIONS

Note: Although the stem is worked on two double-pointed needles, you can change to ordinary needles after row 1.
Using any cast-on method, cast on 3 sts onto a double-pointed needle and K 1 row (this is RS).
Cord row (RS) With RS still facing, slide sts to opposite end of needle, then take yarn across WS of work, pull yarn tightly and K to end.
Rep cord row until stem is desired length.
Row 1 (RS) With RS of work still facing, slide sts to opposite end of needle, then take yarn across WS of work, pull yarn tightly and work K1, [yfwd, K1] twice. 5 sts.
Cont in rows, turning work in usual way.
Row 2 (WS) K2, P1, K2.
Row 3 K2, yfwd, K1, yfwd, K2. 7 sts.
Row 4 (WS) Cast on 1 st onto LH needle (using knit-on cast-on method), cast off 1 st (knitwise), K to centre st, P centre st, K to end. 7 sts.
Row 5 Cast on 1 st onto LH needle, cast off 1 st, K to centre st, yfwd, K centre st, yfwd, K to end. 9 sts.
Rows 6–9 [Rep rows 4 and 5] twice. 13 sts.
Row 10 Rep row 4. 13 sts.
Row 11 Cast on 1 st onto LH needle, cast off 1 st, K to end. 13 sts.
Row 12 Rep row 4. 13 sts.
Row 13 Cast on 1 st onto LH needle, cast off 1 st, K to 2 sts before centre st, K2tog, K centre st, ssk, K to end. 11 sts.
Rows 14–19 [Rep rows 4 and 13] 3 times. 5 sts.
Row 20 K2, P1, K2.
Row 21 K2tog, K1, ssk. 3 sts.
Row 22 K1, P1, K1.
Row 23 Sk2p and fasten off.
Darn in yarn ends. Do not press.

CABLES AND TWISTS

Many interesting textures can be created by combining knit and purl stitches in various sequences (see pages 30–31), but if you are looking for textures with higher relief and more sculptural qualities, cables and twists are the techniques to learn. Both are made by crossing stitches over each other in different ways to form an array of intricate patterns.

SIMPLE TWISTS	Unlike a cable, a simple twist is made over only two stitches and without a cable needle. Although twists do not create such high relief as cables, their ease of execution and more subtle beauty makes them very popular. Twists are shown here worked in stocking stitch on a stocking stitch ground, but they can also be worked with one knit stitch and one purl stitch – the principle of the technique is always the same.

RIGHT TWIST (Abbreviation = T2R)

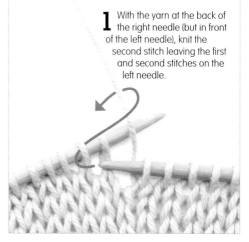

1 With the yarn at the back of the right needle (but in front of the left needle), knit the second stitch leaving the first and second stitches on the left needle.

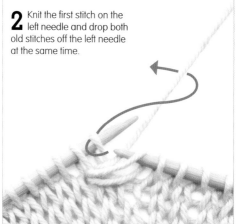

2 Knit the first stitch on the left needle and drop both old stitches off the left needle at the same time.

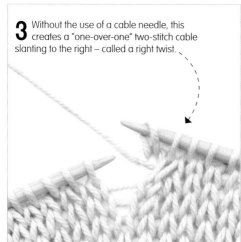

3 Without the use of a cable needle, this creates a "one-over-one" two-stitch cable slanting to the right – called a right twist.

LEFT TWIST (Abbreviation = T2L)

1 Insert the tip of the right needle behind the first stitch on the left needle and through the next second stitch knitwise. Wrap the yarn around the right needle.

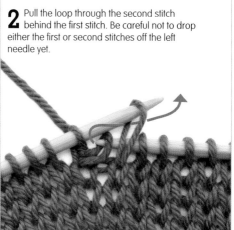

2 Pull the loop through the second stitch behind the first stitch. Be careful not to drop either the first or second stitches off the left needle yet.

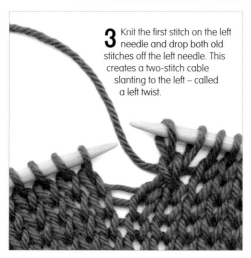

3 Knit the first stitch on the left needle and drop both old stitches off the left needle. This creates a two-stitch cable slanting to the left – called a left twist.

CABLES

Cables are usually worked in stocking stitch on a reverse stocking stitch (or garter stitch) ground. They are made by crossing two, three, four or more stitches over other stitches in the row. This technique is illustrated here with the cable 4 front and cable 4 back cables below, which are crossed on every sixth row. These are very simple cables, but once you master them you will be able to work cables of all different widths and styles.

CABLE 4 FRONT (Abbreviation = C4F)

1 Work to the position of the 4 stocking stitches that form the cable and slip the first 2 stitches onto a cable needle. With the cable needle at the front, knit the next 2 stitches on the left needle.

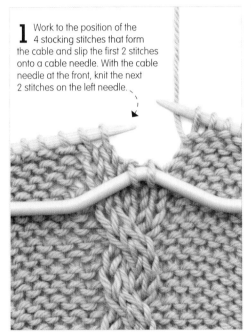

2 Knit the 2 stitches from the cable needle.

3 This creates a cable crossing that slants to the left. For this reason, a "front" cable is also called a "left" cable.

CABLE 4 BACK (Abbreviation = C4B)

1 Work as for Step 1 of cable 4 front, but knit the first 2 stitches from the left needle with the cable needle at the back of the knitting.

2 Knit the 2 stitches from the cable needle.

3 This creates a cable crossing that slants to the right. For this reason, a "back" cable is also called a "right" cable.

SIMPLE CABLE AND TWIST STITCH PATTERNS

These cable and twist stitch patterns are all easy to work and are a good introduction to these textures for beginners. Work the patterns from the written instructions for the first repeat; then follow the chart for the next repeat to see how much easier it is to use a chart for cables and twists. Any of these simple stitches would make a good cushion cover. The twist pattern has a garter stitch background so it does not curl up at the edges and would make a perfect throw – and with no cable needle involved it is quick to work, too.

FOUR-STITCH CABLE PATTERN

KNITTING CHART

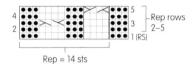

Rep = 14 sts

KNITTING INSTRUCTIONS

C4F (cable 4 front) = slip next 2 sts onto cable needle and hold at front of work, K2 from LH needle, then K2 from cable needle.
C4B (cable 4 back) = slip next 2 sts onto cable needle and hold at back of work, K2 from LH needle, then K2 from cable needle.

Cast on a multiple of 14 sts, plus 3 extra.
Row 1 (RS) P3, *K4, P3; rep from *.
Row 2 K3, *P4, K3; rep from *.
Row 3 P3, *K4, P3, C4F, P3; rep from *.
Row 4 Rep row 2.
Row 5 P3, *C4B, P3, K4, P3; rep from *.
Rep rows 2–5 to form patt.

SIX-STITCH CABLE PATTERN

KNITTING CHART

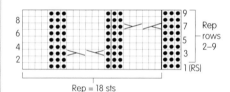

Rep = 18 sts

KNITTING INSTRUCTIONS

C6F (cable 6 front) = slip next 3 sts onto cable needle and hold at front of work, K3 from LH needle, then K3 from cable needle.
C6B (cable 6 back) = slip next 3 sts onto cable needle and hold at back of work, K3 from LH needle, then K3 from cable needle.

Cast on a multiple of 18 sts, plus 3 extra.
Row 1 (RS) P3, *K6, P3; rep from *.
Row 2 and all even-numbered (WS) rows K3, *P6, K3; rep from *.
Row 3 P3, *K6, P3, C6F, P3; rep from *.
Row 5 Rep row 1.
Row 7 P3, *C6B, P3, K6, P3; rep from *.
Row 9 Rep row 1.
Rep rows 2–9 to form patt.

CHAIN CABLE STITCH

KNITTING CHART

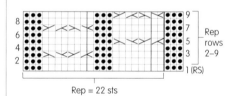

Rep = 22 sts

KNITTING INSTRUCTIONS

C4F and C4B: See four-stitch cable pattern left.

Cast on a multiple of 22 sts, plus 3 extra.
Row 1 (RS) P3, *K8, P3; rep from *.
Row 2 and all even-numbered (WS) rows K3, *P8, K3; rep from *.
Row 3 P3, *K8, P3, C4B, C4F, P3; rep from *.
Row 5 P3, *C4B, C4F, P3, K8, P3; rep from *.
Row 7 P3, *K8, P3, C4F, C4B, P3; rep from *.
Row 9 P3, *C4F, C4B, P3, K8, P3; rep from *.
Rep rows 2–9 to form patt.

SPECIAL ABBREVIATIONS AND SYMBOL KEY

- **T2R (twist 2 right)** = skip first st on LH needle and K 2nd st through front of loop (do not drop st off LH needle), then K first st on LH needle and drop both sts off LH needle at same time.

- **T2L (twist 2 left)** = skip first st on LH needle and K 2nd st by taking RH needle behind first st to do so (do not drop st off LH needle), then K first st on LH needle and drop both sts off LH needle at same time.

- See individual patterns and page 37 for other abbreviations, and page 35 for how to follow a stitch pattern.

KEY

☐ = K on RS rows, P on WS rows
⬤ = P on RS rows, K on WS rows
⟋ = T2R
⟍ = T2L
⟋⟍ = C4F   ⟋⟍ = C6F
⟍⟋ = C4B   ⟍⟋ = C6B

CABLE-EFFECT STITCH

KNITTING CHART NOTE
There is no chart provided for this stitch pattern as it is easier to follow written instructions for it.

KNITTING INSTRUCTIONS
Cast on a multiple of 5 sts, plus 2 extra.
Note: The stitch count varies from row to row.
Row 1 (RS) P2, *yarn to back of work between 2 needles, sl 1 purlwise, K2, pass slipped st over last 2 K sts and off RH needle, P2; rep from *.
Row 2 K2, *P1, yrn, P1, K2; rep from *.
Row 3 P2, *K3, P2; rep from *.
Row 4 K2, *P3, K2; rep from *.
Rep rows 1–4 to form patt.

HORSESHOE CABLE STITCH

KNITTING CHART

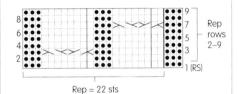

Rep = 22 sts

KNITTING INSTRUCTIONS
C4F and C4B: See four-stitch cable pattern on previous page.

Cast on a multiple of 22 sts, plus 3 extra.
Row 1 (RS) P3, *K8, P3; rep from *.
Row 2 and all even-numbered (WS) rows K3, *P8, K3; rep from *.
Row 3 P3, *K8, P3, C4B, C4F, P3; rep from *.
Row 5 Rep row 1.
Row 7 P3, *C4B, C4F, P3, K8, P3; rep from *.
Row 9 Rep row 1.
Rep rows 2–9 to form patt.

GARTER STITCH ZIZAG TWIST PATTERN

KNITTING CHART

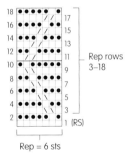

Rep = 6 sts

KNITTING INSTRUCTIONS
T2L and T2R: See Special Abbreviations above.

Row 1 (RS) K.
Row 2 *K5, P1; rep from * to last st, K1.
Row 3 K1, *T2L, K4; rep from *.
Row 4 K4, P1, *K5, P1; rep from * to last 2 sts, K2.
Row 5 K2, T2L, *K4, T2L; rep from * to last 3 sts, K3.
Row 6 K3, P1, *K5, P1; rep from * to last 3 sts, K3.
Row 7 K3, T2L, *K4, T2L; rep from * to last 2 sts, K2.
Row 8 K2, P1, *K5, P1; rep from * to last 4 sts, K4.
Row 9 *K4, T2L; rep from * to last st, K1.
Row 10 K1, *P1, K5; rep from *.
Row 11 *K4, T2R; rep from * to last st, K1.
Row 12 Rep row 8.
Row 13 K3, T2R, *K4, T2R; rep from * to last 2 sts, K2.
Row 14 Rep row 6.
Row 15 K2, T2R, *K4, T2R; rep from * to last 3 sts, K3.
Row 16 Rep row 4.
Row 17 K1, *T2R, K4; rep from *.
Row 18 Rep row 2.
Rep rows 3–18 to form patt.

LACE KNITTING

The light, airy openwork texture of knitted lace is formed by combining yarn-overs and decreases to create holes (also called eyelets) all over the fabric. Although lace knitting looks complicated to make, the techniques employed are relatively easy. If you pick a lace stitch that has a short row repeat, you can work the openwork fabric quickly and still produce impressive delicate textures.

TIPS FOR LACE KNITTING

Eyelets arranged in various ways around each other are the basis of all lace stitches. Eyelets are made up of yarn-overs (see pages 41 and 42), which produce the holes in the fabric, and decreases, which frame the eyelets and compensate for these increases in the row to keep the knitting the same width. The techniques for two simple eyelets are given here, but there are other ways of producing eyelets and these methods are always explained in full in the stitch instructions. For example, bigger eyelet holes can be made by working double yarn-overs paired with double decreases (see grand eyelet mesh stitch on page 54). Here are some tips to keep in mind when you are first trying out the simple lace stitches on pages 54–57.

● **Cast on loosely** for lace patterns. This is best achieved not by trying to make loose loops but by spacing the cast-on stitches farther apart on the knitting needle, with at least 3mm (⅛in) between the loops. If you find this difficult to do evenly, then use a needle one or two sizes larger than the size you are using for the lace and switch to the correct needle size on the first row.

● **Lace stitch patterns** sometimes have yarn-overs and decreases in the very first row. These are not easy to work on cast-on loops, so you can start with a plain knit or purl row then begin the lace pattern on the following row. This will usually not effect the delicacy of the lace at all.

● **Lace stitch patterns** worked on a larger knitting needle size than the one recommended by the manufacturer for the yarn will produce an airy texture but this softens the definition of the design, so it is best to stick to the recommended needle size and let the eyelets create the airiness.

● **Use a row counter** when working lace stitches to keep track of which pattern row you are on. This is especially important for intricate lace worked over a long row-repeat. If you do get lost in your pattern, stop and start over.

● **It is a good idea** to count your stitches frequently when knitting lace to make sure you still have the right number of stitches. If you are missing a stitch (or two) you may have left out a yarn-over (or two) – an easy thing to do in lace knitting. There is no need to undo stitches all the way back to the missing yarn-over if it was left out on the row before. Simply work to the position of the missing yarn-over on the following row, then insert the left needle from front to back under the strand between the stitch just worked and the next stitch on the left needle (see below). Work this stitch through the front of the loop in the usual way.

Picking up and working a missing yarn-over

CHAIN EYELET

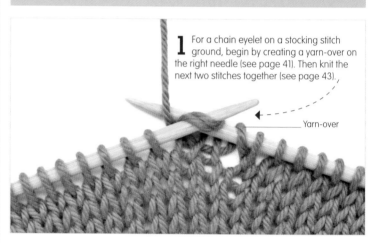

1 For a chain eyelet on a stocking stitch ground, begin by creating a yarn-over on the right needle (see page 41). Then knit the next two stitches together (see page 43).

Yarn-over

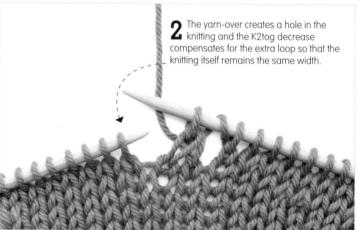

2 The yarn-over creates a hole in the knitting and the K2tog decrease compensates for the extra loop so that the knitting itself remains the same width.

3 On the following row, purl the yarn-over in the usual way. A single chain eyelet is shown here so that its structure is clear, but eyelets can be arranged separated by several rows and several stitches or sitting side by side.

Completed chain eyelet

OPEN EYELET

1 For an open eyelet on a stocking stitch ground, begin by creating a yarn-over on the right needle (see page 41). Then work a "sl 1, K1, psso" decrease (see page 44) right after the yarn-over.

Yarn-over

2 The yarn-over creates a hole in the knitting and the decrease compensates for the extra loop so that the knitting itself remains the same width.

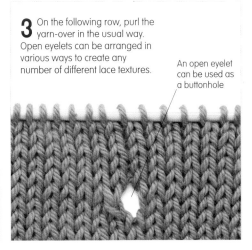

3 On the following row, purl the yarn-over in the usual way. Open eyelets can be arranged in various ways to create any number of different lace textures.

An open eyelet can be used as a buttonhole

YARNS
FOR LACE

Knitted lace was first designed to look similar to traditional needle lace, so it was worked on fine needles in white cotton thread. Fine yarn does enhance the delicacy, but openwork knitting can look interesting in other yarns as well. Here are a few examples.

PSEUDO LACE

The quickest way to produce knitting with an airy, delicate appearance is to knit garter stitch using fine yarn and very large needles. You can make an attractive lacy scarf this way in a flash, and any type of yarn, including this metallic one, is suitable for the pseudo lace technique.

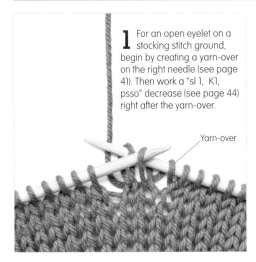

MULTICOLOURED OPENWORK

For added interest, use a double-knitting-weight yarn with variegated colours for your openwork textures. The stitch pattern here is grand eyelet mesh stitch (see page 54), which looks the same on both sides and is extremely easy to work.

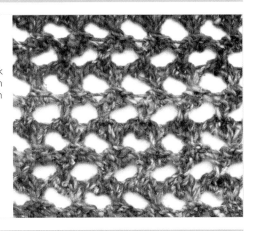

MOHAIR LACE

Fine mohair yarn highlights the delicacy of the lacy stitches. Stick to easy lace patterns like this mini-leaf stitch (see page 55) when using mohair, as it is more difficult to knit with than smooth yarn, and complicated lace doesn't show up clearly in textured yarns.

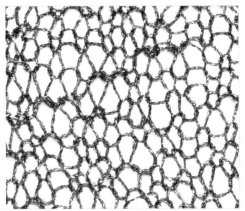

TRADITIONAL-STYLE KNITTED LACE

Traditional-style knitted lace is worked in fine cotton thread on very fine needles. You can see how much more delicate this domino eyelet pattern looks when knitted with super-fine yarn instead of a lightweight cotton yarn as on page 57.

SIMPLE LACE
STITCH PATTERNS

Many of these lace patterns are suitable for baby blankets or shawls. If the ground of the lace is stocking stitch and you are making one of these, be sure to include a garter stitch border around the piece. Either pick up stitches and work the border after the piece is complete (see page 68); or work four rows of garter stitch at the beginning and end of the knitted piece and four stitches of garter stitch at the sides of the knitting. Alternatively, sew a knitted edging all around the finished piece (see pages 76 and 77).

EYELET MESH STITCH

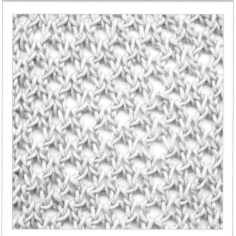

KNITTING CHART

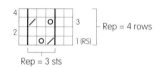

Rep = 4 rows
Rep = 3 sts

KNITTING INSTRUCTIONS
Cast on a multiple of 3 sts.
Row 1 (RS) K2, *K2tog, yfwd, K1; rep from * to last st, K1.
Row 2 P.
Row 3 K2, *yfwd, K1, K2tog; rep from * to last st, K1.
Row 4 P.
Rep rows 1–4 to form patt.

LEAF EYELET PATTERN

KNITTING CHART

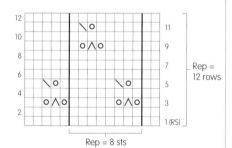

Rep = 12 rows
Rep = 8 sts

KNITTING INSTRUCTIONS
Cast on a multiple of 8 sts, plus 7 extra.
Row 1 (RS) K.
Row 2 and all even-numbered (WS) rows P.
Row 3 K2, yfwd, sk2p, yfwd, *K5, yfwd, sk2p, yfwd; rep from * to last 2 sts, K2.
Row 5 K3, yfwd, ssk, *K6, yfwd, ssk; rep from * to last 2 sts, K2.
Row 7 K.
Row 9 K1, *K5, yfwd, sk2p, yfwd; rep from * to last 6 sts, K6.
Row 11 K7, *yfwd, ssk, K6; rep from *.
Row 12 P.
Rep rows 1–12 to form patt.

GRAND EYELET MESH STITCH

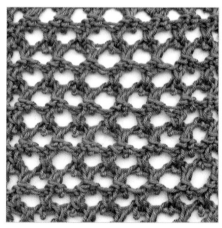

KNITTING CHART NOTE
There is no chart provided for this stitch pattern as it is easier to follow written instructions for it.

KNITTING INSTRUCTIONS
Note: This fabric looks the same on both sides. When blocking, stretch vertically to open eyelets.
Cast on a multiple of 3 sts, plus 4 extra.
Row 1 K2, *sk2p, yfwd twice; rep from * to last 2 sts, K2.
Row 2 K2, *[P1, K1] into double yfwd, P1; rep from * to last 2 sts, K2.
Row 3 K.
Rep rows 1–3 to form patt.

SPECIAL ABBREVIATION AND SYMBOL KEY

- **sl 2-K1-p2sso** = insert RH needle through 2nd and first sts on LH needle (as if beginning K2tog) and slip both sts onto RH needle, knit next st, then pass 2 slipped tog over knit st and off RH needle.

- See page 37 for a full list of other abbreviations and for how to work from a stitch symbol chart. Explanations for how to follow a simple stitch pattern are given on page 35.

KEY

☐ = K on RS rows, P on WS rows   ◺ = ssk

● = P on RS rows, K on WS rows   ◬ = sk2p

○ = sl 2-KL-p2sso   ◭ = sl 2-K1-p2sso

◿ = K2tog

VERTICAL MESH STITCH

KNITTING CHART NOTE
There is no chart provided for this stitch pattern as it is easier to follow written instructions for it.

KNITTING INSTRUCTIONS
Cast on an odd number of sts.
Row 1 K1, *yfwd, K2tog; rep from *.
Row 2 P.
Row 3 *Ssk, yfwd; rep from * to last st, K1.
Row 4 P.
Rep rows 1–4 to form patt.

MINI-LEAF STITCH

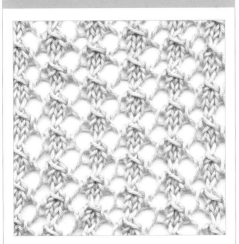

KNITTING CHART

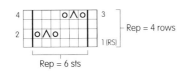

Rep = 4 rows

Rep = 6 sts

KNITTING INSTRUCTIONS
Cast on a multiple of 6 sts, plus 2 extra.
Row 1 (RS) K1, *K3, yfwd, sk2p, yfwd; rep from * to last st, K1.
Row 2 P.
Row 3 K1, *yfwd, sk2p, yfwd, K3; rep from * to last st, K1.
Row 4 P.
Rep rows 1–4 to form patt.

ARROWHEAD LACE PATTERN

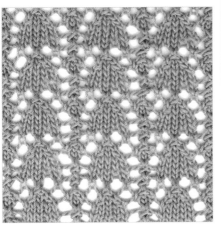

KNITTING CHART

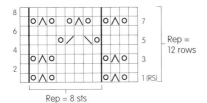

Rep = 12 rows

Rep = 8 sts

KNITTING INSTRUCTIONS
Cast on a multiple of 8 sts, plus 5 extra.
Row 1 (RS) K1, *yfwd, sk2p, yfwd, K5; rep from * to last 4 sts, yfwd, sk2p, yfwd, K1.
Row 2 and all even-numbered (WS) rows P.
Row 3 Rep row 1.
Row 5 K4, *yfwd, ssk, K1, K2tog, yfwd, K3; rep from * to last st, K1.
Row 7 K1, *yfwd, sk2p, yfwd, K1; rep from *.
Row 8 P.
Rep rows 1–8 to form patt.

KNITTING

ZIGZAG MESH STITCH

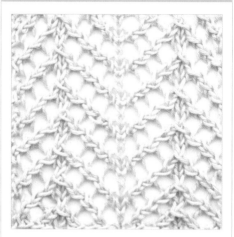

KNITTING CHART

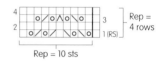

Rep = 10 sts

Rep = 4 rows

KNITTING INSTRUCTIONS
Cast on a multiple of 10 sts, plus 1 extra.
Row 1 (RS) K1, *[yfwd, ssk] twice, K1, [K2tog, yfwd] twice, K1; rep from *.
Row 2 P.
Row 3 K2, *yfwd, ssk, yfwd, sk2p, yfwd, K2tog, yfwd, K3; rep from *, ending last rep K2 (instead of K3).
Row 4 P.
Rep rows 1–4 to form patt.

BIG LEAF LACE

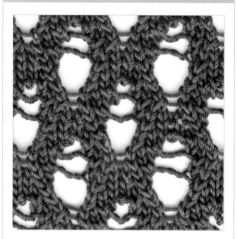

KNITTING CHART

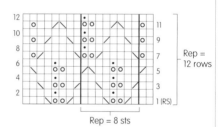

Rep = 8 sts

Rep = 12 rows

KNITTING INSTRUCTIONS
Cast on a multiple of 8 sts, plus 2 extra.
Row 1 (RS) K3, *K2tog, yfwd twice, ssk, K4; rep from * to last 7 sts, K2tog, yfwd twice, ssk, K3.
Row 2 and all even-numbered (WS) rows P, working [K1, P1] into every double yfwd and P1 into single yfwd at beg and end of row.
Row 3 K2, *K2tog, K1, yfwd twice, K1, ssk, K2; rep from *.
Row 5 K1, *K2tog, K2, yfwd twice, K2, ssk; rep from * to last st, K1.
Row 7 K1, yfwd, *ssk, K4, K2tog, yfwd twice; rep from * to last 9 sts, ssk, K4, K2tog, yfwd, K1.
Row 9 K1, yfwd, *K1, ssk, K2, K2tog, K1, yfwd twice; rep from * to last 9 sts, K1, ssk, K2, K2tog, K1, yfwd, K1.
Row 11 K1, yfwd, *K2, ssk, K2tog, K2, yfwd twice; rep from * to last 9 sts, K2, ssk, K2tog, K2, yfwd, K1.
Row 12 Rep row 2.
Rep rows 1–12 to form patt.

STAR EYELET STITCH

KNITTING CHART

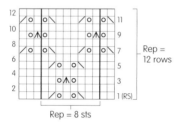

Rep = 8 sts

Rep = 12 rows

KNITTING INSTRUCTIONS
Cast on a multiple of 8 sts, plus 5 extra.
Row 1 (RS) K4, *ssk, yfwd, K1, yfwd, K2tog, K3; rep from * to last st, K1.
Row 2 and all even-numbered (WS) rows P.
Row 3 K5, *yfwd, sl 2-K1-p2sso, yfwd, K5; rep from *.
Row 5 Rep row 1.
Row 7 Ssk, yfwd, K1, yfwd, K2tog, *K3, ssk, yfwd, K1, yfwd, K2tog; rep from *.
Row 9 K1, *yfwd, sl 2-K1-p2sso, yfwd, K5; rep from *, ending last rep K1 (instead of K5).
Row 11 Rep row 7.
Row 12 P.
Rep rows 1–12 to form patt.

DOMINO EYELET PATTERN

KNITTING CHART

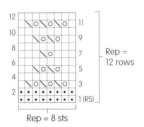

Rep = 12 rows

Rep = 8 sts

KNITTING INSTRUCTIONS
Cast on a multiple of 8 sts.
Row 1 (RS) P.
Row 2 K.
Row 3 *K1, [yfwd, ssk] 3 times, K1; rep from *.
Row 4 and all foll even-numbered (WS) rows P.
Row 5 *K2, [yfwd, ssk] twice, K2; rep from *.
Row 7 *K3, yfwd, ssk, K3; rep from *.
Row 9 Rep row 5.
Row 11 Rep row 3.
Row 12 P.
Rep rows 1–12 to form patt.

LEAVES LACE

KNITTING CHART

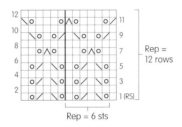

Rep = 12 rows

Rep = 6 sts

KNITTING INSTRUCTIONS
Cast on a multiple of 6 sts, plus 1 extra.
Row 1 (RS) K1, *yfwd, ssk, K1, K2tog, yfwd, K1; rep from *.
Row 2 P.
Rows 3–6 [Rep rows 1 and 2] twice.
Row 7 K2, *yfwd, sk2p, yfwd, K3; rep from *, ending last rep K2 (instead of K3).
Row 8 and all foll even-numbered (WS) rows P.
Row 9 K1, *K2tog, yfwd, K1, yfwd, ssk, K1; rep from *.
Row 11 K2tog, *yfwd, K3, yfwd, sk2p; rep from * to last 5 sts, yfwd, K3, yfwd, ssk.
Row 12 P.
Rep rows 1–12 to form patt.

DIAMOND LACE STITCH

KNITTING CHART

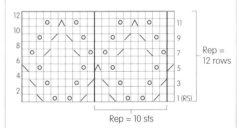

Rep = 12 rows

Rep = 10 sts

KNITTING INSTRUCTIONS
Cast on a multiple of 10 sts, plus 1 extra.
Row 1 (RS) K2, *K2tog, [K1, yfwd] twice, K1, ssk, K3; rep from *, ending last rep K2 (instead of K3).
Row 2 and all even-numbered (WS) rows P.
Row 3 K1, *K2tog, K1, yfwd, K3, yfwd, K1, ssk, K1; rep from *.
Rows 5 K2tog, *K1, yfwd, K5, yfwd, K1, sk2p; rep from *, ending last rep ssk (instead of sk2p).
Row 7 K1, *yfwd, K1, ssk, K3, K2tog, K1, yfwd, K1; rep from *.
Row 9 K2, *yfwd, K1, ssk, K1, K2tog, K1, yfwd, K3; rep from *, ending last rep K2 (instead of K3).
Row 11 K3, *yfwd, K1, sk2p, K1, yfwd, K5; rep from *, ending last rep K3 (instead of K5).
Row 12 P.
Rep rows 1–12 to form patt.

KNITTING

COLOURWORK

You have many technique choices if you like adding lots of colours to your knitting. The easiest method of all is to knit plain stocking stitch using a multicoloured yarn with many colours twisted into it or a variegated yarn, which changes colour along the strand (see page 13). But if you want to work the colours into the knitting yourself to give more colour options, you can work simple stripes, easy colourwork stitch patterns, or charted Fair Isle or intarsia motifs.

SIMPLE STRIPES

Horizontal stripes are the perfect vehicle for colour for knitters who want to have fun playing with colour without having to learn more advanced techniques. Here are a few examples of the variety of stripe widths, colours, and textures that are available to experiment with. You can follow any plainly coloured knitting pattern and introduce stripes without interfering with the tension or shape of the knitting.

TWO-COLOUR GARTER STITCH STRIPE

This stripe pattern is worked in garter stitch in two colours (A and B). To work the stripe, knit 2 rows in each colour alternately, dropping the colour not in use at the side of the work and picking it up when it is needed again.

TWO-COLOUR KNIT AND PURL PINSTRIPE

Knit this stripe in two colours (A and B). Work 6 rows in stocking stitch in A. Then drop A at the side of the work and knit 2 rows in B – the second of these rows creates a purl ridge on the right side of the knitting. Repeat this stripe sequence for the pinstripe effect. To avoid long loose strands of B at the edge, wrap A around B at the beginning of every right-side row.

FIVE-COLOUR STOCKING STITCH STRIPE

To work stripes of any number of rows like this one and still carry the colours up the side edges, use a circular needle. Work the stripes back and forth in rows on this needle, and if a yarn you need to pick up is at the opposite end of the needle, push all the stitches back to the other end of the circular needle and work the next row with the same side of the knitting facing as the last row.

TEXTURED STOCKING STITCH STRIPE

This stripe is worked in a mohair yarn in two colours (A and B) and a smooth cotton yarn (C). The cotton yarn provides a good contrast in texture and sheen and highlights the fuzziness of the mohair.

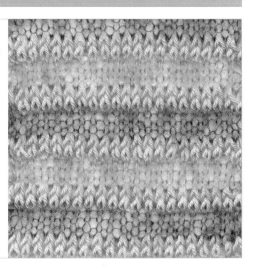

COLOURWORK
STITCH PATTERNS

Another easy way to introduce colourwork into knitting is with slip-stitch patterns. These are designed specially to use more than one colour in the overall pattern but only ever one colour in a row of knitting. With this technique, geometric patterns are created by working some stitches in a row and slipping others. The pattern here is shown in two different colourways and is one of the easiest of all slip-stitch colourwork patterns.

CHECK SLIP-STITCH PATTERN

Follow this pattern to work the stitch and use the steps below as a guide.

Use three colours for the pattern that contrast in tone: A (a medium-toned colour), B (a light-toned colour), and C (a dark-toned colour).

Note: Slip all slip stitches purlwise with the yarn on the WS of the work.

Using A, cast on a multiple of 4 stitches, plus 2 extra.

Row 1 (WS) Using A, P to end.
Row 2 (RS) Using B, K1, sl 1, *K2, sl 2; rep from * to last 3 sts, K2, sl 1, K1.
Row 3 Using B, P1, sl 1, *P2, sl 2; rep from * to last 3 sts, P2, sl 1, P1.
Row 4 Using A, K to end.
Row 5 Using C, P2, *sl 2, P2; rep from *.
Row 6 Using C, K2, *sl 2, K2; rep from *.
Rep rows 1–6 to form patt.

WORKING A COLOURWORK SLIP-STITCH PATTERN

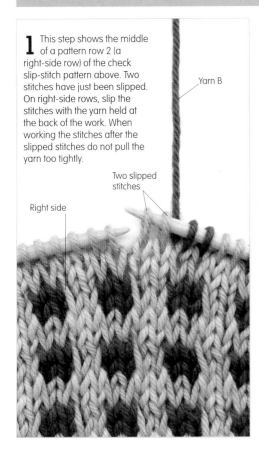

1 This step shows the middle of a pattern row 2 (a right-side row) of the check slip-stitch pattern above. Two stitches have just been slipped. On right-side rows, slip the stitches with the yarn held at the back of the work. When working the stitches after the slipped stitches do not pull the yarn too tightly.

Yarn B

Two slipped stitches

Right side

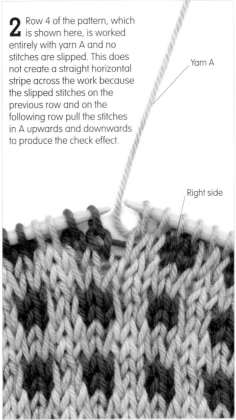

2 Row 4 of the pattern, which is shown here, is worked entirely with yarn A and no stitches are slipped. This does not create a straight horizontal stripe across the work because the slipped stitches on the previous row and on the following row pull the stitches in A upwards and downwards to produce the check effect.

Yarn A

Right side

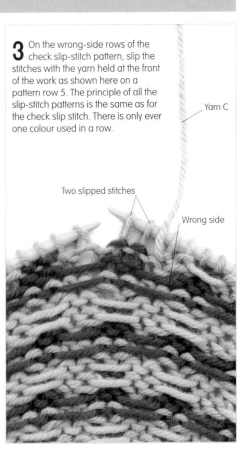

3 On the wrong-side rows of the check slip-stitch pattern, slip the stitches with the yarn held at the front of the work as shown here on a pattern row 5. The principle of all the slip-stitch patterns is the same as for the check slip stitch. There is only ever one colour used in a row.

Yarn C

Two slipped stitches

Wrong side

CHARTED COLOURWORK

The techniques for charted stocking stitch colourwork – Fair Isle and intarsia – are worth mastering as they open up a world of richly coloured designs. With the Fair Isle technique, a yarn colour is carried across the wrong side of the work until it is required again. In intarsia knitting a separate length of yarn is used for each area of colour and the yarns are twisted around each other at the colour change junctures.

FOLLOWING A COLOURWORK CHART

The first step in understanding charted colourwork is to grasp how easy the charts are to follow. Rather than writing out how many stitches in which colours to work across a row, your knitting pattern provides a chart with the colours marked on it in symbols or in blocks of colour.

If a pattern covers the whole sweater back, front, and sleeve and cannot be repeated, a large chart is provided for each of these with all the stitches on it for the entire piece. Where a pattern is a simple repeat, the repeat alone is charted. Each square on a stocking-stitch colourwork chart represents a

stitch and each horizontal row of squares represents a knitted row. You follow the chart from the bottom to the top, just as your knitting forms on the needles.

The key provided with the chart tells you which colour to use for each stitch. All odd-numbered rows on a colourwork chart are usually right-side (knit) rows and are read from right to left. All even-numbered rows on a colourwork chart are usually wrong-side (purl) rows and are read from left to right. Always read your knitting pattern instructions carefully to make sure that the chart follows these general rules.

FAIR ISLE CHART

This example of a Fair Isle chart illustrates very clearly how easy it is to knit simple Fair Isle patterns. No more than two colours are used in a row, which makes it ideal for colourwork beginners. The colour not in use is stranded across the back of the knitting until it is needed again.

To identify if a colourwork chart should be worked in the Fair Isle technique, check that both colours in a row are used across the entire row. If each colour is used after every 3 or 4 stitches (as in this chart), use the stranding technique. If the colours are not used over a span of more stitches, use the weaving-in technique so that the loose strands (called floats) don't become too long.

KEY

☐ = background colour
● = motif colour

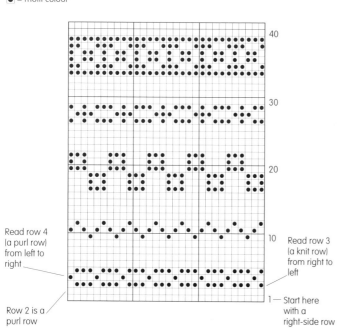

Read row 4 (a purl row) from left to right

Row 2 is a purl row

Read row 3 (a knit row) from right to left

Start here with a right-side row

INTARSIA CHART

This heart is an example of a simple intarsia colourwork chart. Each colour on the chart is represented by a different symbol. The blank square (the background) also represents a colour.

You can tell that a charted design should be worked in the intarsia technique if a colour appears only in a section of a row and is not needed across the entire row. Use a separate long length of yarn, or yarn on a bobbin, for each area of colour in intarsia knitting (including separated background areas). Twist the colours where they meet as explained on the opposite page.

KEY

☐ = background colour
● = motif colour 1
● = motif colour 2
✕ = mtoif colour 3

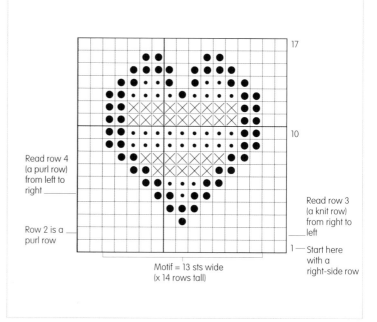

Read row 4 (a purl row) from left to right

Row 2 is a purl row

Read row 3 (a knit row) from right to left

Start here with a right-side row

Motif = 13 sts wide (x 14 rows tall)

FAIR ISLE STRANDING TECHNIQUE

1 On the knit rows, knit the stitches in the first colour, then drop it at the back and knit the stitches in the second colour. Strand the colour not in use loosely across the back of the work until it is needed again.

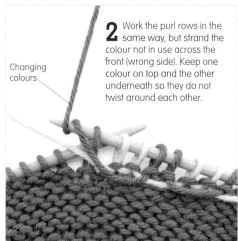

Changing colours

2 Work the purl rows in the same way, but strand the colour not in use across the front (wrong side). Keep one colour on top and the other underneath so they do not twist around each other.

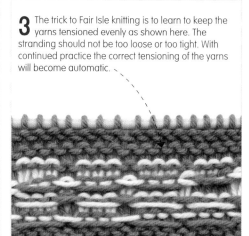

3 The trick to Fair Isle knitting is to learn to keep the yarns tensioned evenly as shown here. The stranding should not be too loose or too tight. With continued practice the correct tensioning of the yarns will become automatic.

FAIR ISLE WEAVING-IN ON A KNIT ROW

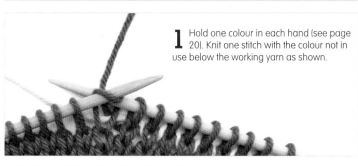

1 Hold one colour in each hand (see page 20). Knit one stitch with the colour not in use below the working yarn as shown.

2 Knit the next stitch with the colour not in use above the working yarn as shown. Continue moving the colour not in use up and down so it is woven around the working yarn.

FAIR ISLE WEAVING-IN ON A PURL ROW

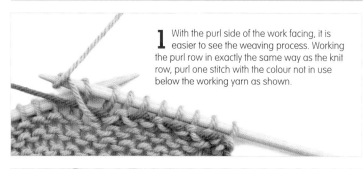

1 With the purl side of the work facing, it is easier to see the weaving process. Working the purl row in exactly the same way as the knit row, purl one stitch with the colour not in use below the working yarn as shown.

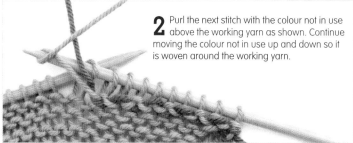

2 Purl the next stitch with the colour not in use above the working yarn as shown. Continue moving the colour not in use up and down so it is woven around the working yarn.

INTARSIA TECHNIQUE

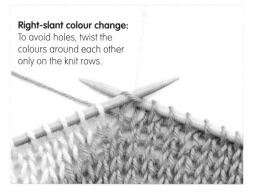

Right-slant colour change: To avoid holes, twist the colours around each other only on the knit rows.

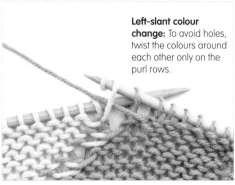

Left-slant colour change: To avoid holes, twist the colours around each other only on the purl rows.

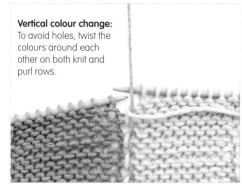

Vertical colour change: To avoid holes, twist the colours around each other on both knit and purl rows.

KNITTING

SIMPLE COLOURWORK PATTERNS

Here are some easy-to-work stocking-stitch colourwork patterns. A few of the patterns are suitable for the Fair Isle technique, and the remainder for the intarsia technique or a combination of the intarsia technique and the Fair Isle technique. The borders can be worked individually for simple bands of colour, or repeated to make up an item in stripes. If you have never knit colourwork, start with the Fair Isle patterns as they use only two colours in every row. Refer to pages 60 and 61 for how to read the charts and master the techniques.

SIMPLE BORDERS

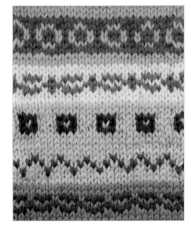

KNITTING CHART

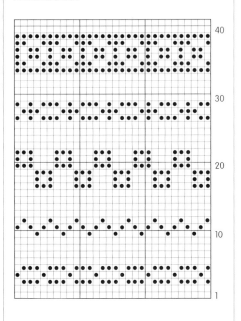

KNITTING INSTRUCTIONS
Use the Fair Isle technique to work these border patterns. Change background and motif colours as desired for each band of pattern.

REPEATING CIRCLES

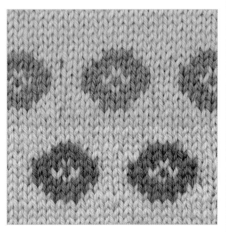

KNITTING CHART

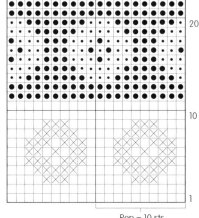

Rep = 10 sts
(x 22 rows)

KNITTING INSTRUCTIONS
Use the Fair Isle technique to work this repeating pattern. Choose four colours: two motif colours and two background colours.

HEART MOTIF

KNITTING CHART

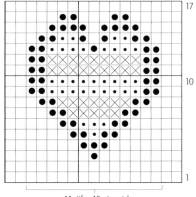

Motif = 13 sts wide
(x 14 rows tall)

KNITTING INSTRUCTIONS
Use the intarsia technique to work this heart. Choose four colours: three motif colours and one background colour. Work a single motif on the knitting or arrange motifs across the knitting at random intervals or in regular repeating positions.

SPECIAL NOTES

• The charts here are designed with symbols so that they are easy to read and so that you can use the colours of your choice with them.

• To try out a small amount of colourwork, why not knit a small sample following one of the motif charts? Cast on eight stitches more than the width of the chart using the background colour. Work four stitches and four rows of garter stitch around the outer edge and the chart in the centre of this. Stitch the completed swatch to the front of a small bag or cushion cover.

BIRD MOTIF

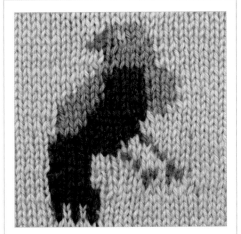

KNITTING CHART

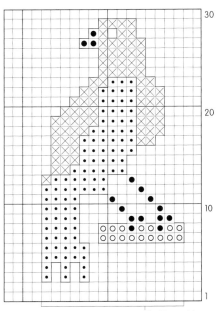

Motif = 15 sts wide
(x 27 rows tall)

KNITTING INSTRUCTIONS

Use the intarsia technique to work this bird. Choose five colours: four motif colours and one background colour. Work a single motif on the knitting or arrange motifs across the knitting at random intervals or in regular repeating positions.

FAIR ISLE BLOSSOMS

KNITTING CHART

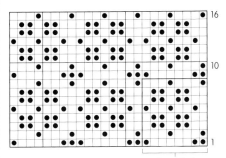

Rep = 8 sts
(x 8 rows)

KNITTING INSTRUCTIONS

Use the Fair Isle technique to work this repeating pattern. Choose two colours: one motif colour and one background colour.

INTARSIA FLOWERS

KNITTING CHART

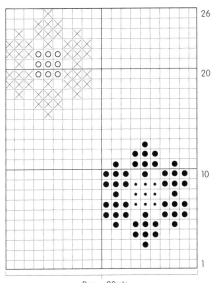

Rep = 20 sts
(x 26 rows)

KNITTING INSTRUCTIONS

Use the intarsia technique to work the flowers in this repeating pattern and the Fair Isle technique to work only the background colour. Choose four colours, two motif colours for each flower and one background colour.

KNITTING

FLOWER MOTIF

KNITTING CHART

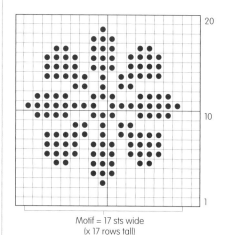

Motif = 17 sts wide
(x 17 rows tall)

KNITTING INSTRUCTIONS

Use the intarsia technique to work the flower motif in this pattern and the Fair Isle technique to work only the background colour. Choose two colours, one motif colour and one background colour. Work a single motif on the knitting or arrange motifs across the knitting at random intervals or in regular repeating positions.

TULIP MOTIF

KNITTING CHART

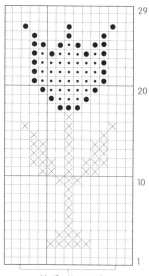

Motif = 11 sts wide
(x 25 rows tall)

KNITTING INSTRUCTIONS

Use the intarsia technique to work the tulip motif and the background around the tulip head in this pattern. When working the stem, use the Fair Isle technique to work only the background colour. Choose four colours: three motif colours and one background colour. Work a single motif on the knitting or arrange motifs across the knitting at random intervals or in regular repeating positions.

LITTLE LADY MOTIF

KNITTING CHART

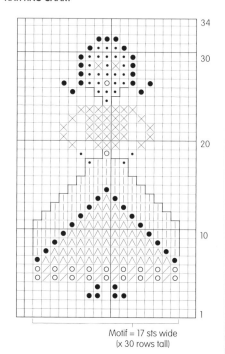

Motif = 17 sts wide
(x 30 rows tall)

KNITTING INSTRUCTIONS

Use the intarsia technique to work this motif. Choose eight colours: seven motif colours and one background colour. Work a single motif on the knitting or arrange motifs across the knitting at random intervals or in regular repeating positions.

PUSSY CAT MOTIF

KNITTING CHART

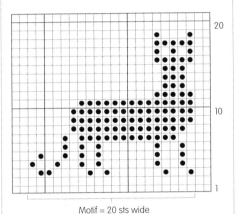

Motif = 20 sts wide
(x 17 rows tall)

KNITTING INSTRUCTIONS
Use the intarsia technique to work this cat motif. Choose two colours: one motif colour and one background colour. Work a single motif on the knitting or arrange motifs across the knitting at random intervals or in regular repeating positions.

NUMBERS AND LETTERS

KNITTING CHART

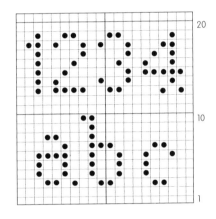

KNITTING INSTRUCTIONS
Use the intarsia technique to work these motifs and the Fair Isle technique to work only the background colour. Choose eight colours: seven motif colours and one background colour. Work as a block of numbers and letters like this or arrange to form dates and names, charting further numbers and letters as required.

DUCK MOTIF

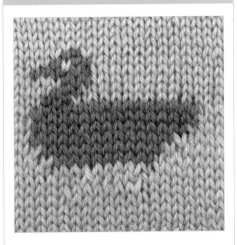

KNITTING CHART

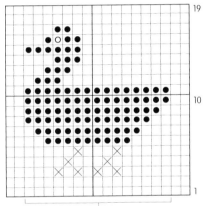

Motif = 15 sts wide
(x 15 rows tall)

KNITTING INSTRUCTIONS
Use the intarsia technique to work this duck motif. Choose four colours: three motif colours and one background colour. Work a single motif on the knitting or arrange motifs across the knitting at random intervals or in regular repeating positions.

FOLLOWING A KNITTING PATTERN

Knitting patterns can look daunting to a beginner knitter, but if approached step by step they are easy to understand. This section provides an explanation of how to follow simple knitting patterns. It also gives tips for finishing details and seams, which are often more difficult to execute than knitting the pieces.

SIMPLE ACCESSORY PATTERNS

The best advice for a beginner wanting to knit a first project from a knitting pattern is to start with a simple accessory. Cushion covers are especially good practice as the instructions are straightforward and usually the only finishing details are seams. Here is an example of a pattern for a simple striped stocking stitch cushion cover with a step-by-step guide to the directions.

1 At the beginning of most patterns you will find the skill level required for the knitting. Make sure you are confident that the skill level is right for you.

2 Check the size of the finished item. If it is a simple square like this cushion, you can easily adjust the size by adding or subtracting stitches and rows.

3 Try to use the yarn specified. But if you are unable to obtain this yarn, choose a substitute yarn as explained on page 15 for how to substitute yarn.

8 Make a tension swatch before starting to knit and change the needle size if necessary (see opposite page).

9 Instructions for working a piece of knitted fabric always start with how many stitches to cast on and what yarn or needle size to use. If there is only one needle size and one yarn, these may be absent here.

10 Consult the abbreviations list with your pattern (or in your book) for the meanings of abbreviations (see page 37).

14 The back of a cushion cover is sometimes exactly the same as the front or it has a fabric back. In this case, the stripes are reversed on the back for a more versatile cover.

15 After all the knitted pieces are complete, follow the Finishing (or Making Up) section of the pattern.

STRIPED CUSHION COVER

Skill level
Easy

Size of finished cushion
40.5 x 40.5cm (16 x 16in)

Materials
3 x 50g (1³/₄oz)/125m (137yd) balls in each of branded Pure Wool DK in Lavender 039 (**A**) and Avocado 019 (**B**)
Pair of 4mm (US size 6) knitting needles
Cushion pad to fit finished cover

Tension
22 sts and 30 rows to 10cm (4in) over stocking stitch using 4mm (US size 6) needles or size necessary to achieve correct tension. To save time, take time to check tension.

Front
Using 4mm (US size 6) needles and A, cast on 88 sts.
Beg with a K row, work in st st until work measures 14cm (5¹/₂in) from cast-on edge, ending with RS facing for next row.
Cut off A and change to B.
Cont in st st until work measures 26.5cm (10¹/₂in) from cast-on edge, ending with RS facing for next row.
Cut off B and change to A.
Cont in st st until work measures 40.5cm (16in) from cast-on edge, ending with RS facing for next row.
Cast off.

Back
Work as for Front, but use B for A, and A for B.

Finishing
Darn in loose ends.
Block and press lightly on wrong side, following instructions on yarn label.
With wrong sides facing, sew three sides of back and front together. Turn right-side out, insert cushion pad, and sew remaining seam.

4 Always purchase the same total amount in metres/yards of a substitute yarn; NOT the same amount in weight.

5 If desired, select different colours to suit your décor; the colours specified are just suggestions.

6 Alter the needle size if you cannot achieve the correct tension with the specified size (see 8 left).

7 Extra items needed for your project will usually be listed under Materials or Extras.

11 Work in the specified stitch pattern, for the specified number of rows or cm/in.

12 Colours are usually changed on a right-side row, so end with the right-side facing for the changeover row.

13 If no stitch is specified for the cast-off, always cast off knitwise.

16 See page 34 for how to darn in loose ends.

17 Make sure you look at the yarn label instructions before attempting to press any piece of knitting. The label may say that the yarn cannot be pressed or to press it only with a cool iron. (See page 69 for blocking tips.)

18 See pages 70 and 71 for seaming options. Take time with seams on knitting, and when working your very first seams get an experienced knitter to help you.

GARMENT PATTERNS

Most garment instructions start with the Skill Level, followed by the Sizes, Materials, and finally the instructions. Choosing the right size and knitting a tension swatch are the two most important things to get right if you want to create a successful garment.

TIPS

• **Choose a knitting skill level** that suits your knitting experience. You will quickly advance to the next level with a little practice.

• **If you choose** white yarn for a first sweater, wash your hands every time you start knitting, and put away the yarn and sweater in a bag in between knitting to keep them from becoming soiled.

• **Avoid black** or other very dark yarns for a first knitted sweater, as the stitches are difficult to see clearly.

• **Make sure** the dye-lot number on all the yarn balls you are purchasing all match (see page 14).

• **It is handy** to have a set of knitting needles in different sizes if you are starting to knit sweaters. When checking tension (see below), you will need to have other sizes at hand if you need to change your needle size.

• **Always knit the pieces** in the order given in the pattern instructions; this is true for all types of patterns, including those for accessories and toys. On a garment, the back is usually knit first, followed by the front (or fronts if it is a cardigan), and lastly the sleeves. Pockets that are integrated into the fronts are knit before the fronts and those applied as patches are knit last.

• **Don't attempt** to alter sweater patterns. Garment patterns are specially designed for the back, front/s and sleeves to fit precisely together. For example, if you alter the armhole length the sleeve head will not fit into it the right way. The sweater length or the sleeve length are sometimes adjustable, however, at the points specified in the pattern – usually right before the armhole shaping on the body and the sleeve head shaping on the sleeve.

CHOOSING A GARMENT SIZE

Try to avoid looking at specific "sizes", whether they are bust sizes or dress sizes, when choosing which size to knit in a knitting pattern. The size you choose should relate more on how you want the garment to fit. The best way to select your size to make, for example, a sweater, is to find one in your wardrobe that has a similar knitted fabric weight and a similar shape, and that fits you in a comfortable and flattering manner. Lay this sweater flat and measure its width. Then choose the sweater width on the sweater diagram that is the closest to this width – this will be the size for you.

Once you have chosen the size you are going to knit, make a photocopy of your pattern and circle or highlight the figures for your size throughout the pattern. This will start with the number of balls of yarn to purchase, then the number of stitches to cast on for the back, the length to knit to the armhole, and so on. The figure for the smallest size is given first and all the figures for the larger sizes follow in parentheses. Where there is only one figure given in the instructions – be it a measurement, the number of rows, or the number of stitches – this figure applies to all sizes. Before starting your knitting, always check your tension.

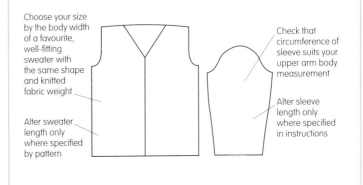

Choose your size by the body width of a favourite, well-fitting sweater with the same shape and knitted fabric weight

Alter sweater length only where specified by pattern

Check that circumference of sleeve suits your upper arm body measurement

Alter sleeve length only where specified in instructions

MEASURING TENSION

Alway knit a swatch before starting your knitting in order to make sure that you can achieve the stitch size (tension) recommended in your pattern. Only if you achieve the correct tension will your finished knitted pieces have the correct measurements.

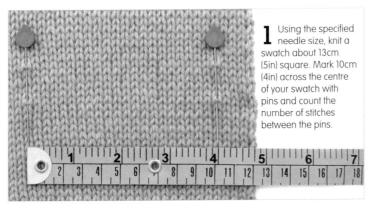

1 Using the specified needle size, knit a swatch about 13cm (5in) square. Mark 10cm (4in) across the centre of your swatch with pins and count the number of stitches between the pins.

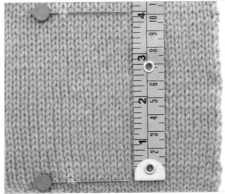

2 Count the number of rows to 10cm (4in) in the same way. If you have fewer stitches and rows than you should, try again with a larger needle size; if you have more, change to a smaller needle size. Use the needle size for your knitting that best matches the correct tension. (Matching the stitch width is much more important than matching the row height.)

FINISHING DETAILS

The last section in a knitting pattern covers the finishings. These can be simply darning in yarn ends (see page 34) and blocking, such as on throws and baby blankets. Other finishing details include adding borders, sewing seams, sewing on pockets and buttons, and making button loops. Picking up stitches along the knitting when adding borders is one of the trickiest finishings to master, so it is explained here in detail.

PICKING UP STITCHES ALONG A CAST-ON OR CAST-OFF EDGE

With the right side facing, insert the tip of the needle through the first stitch. Leaving a long loose end, wrap the yarn around the needle and pull it through the stitch – as if knitting a stitch. Continue along the edge in this way, picking up and knitting one stitch through every cast-on or cast-off stitch.

PICKING UP STITCHES ALONG ROW-ENDS

1 On lightweight or medium-weight yarn, pick up about three stitches for every four row-ends. To begin, mark out the row-ends on the right side of the knitting, placing a pin on the first of every four row-ends as shown here.

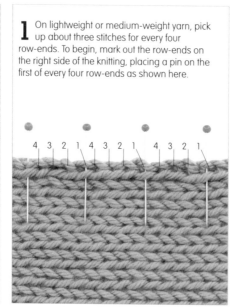

2 Pick up and knit the stitches as for picking up stitches along a cast-on edge, inserting the tip of the needle through the centre of the edge stitches. Skip every fourth row-end.

Remove pin before picking up stitch

Skipped row-ends

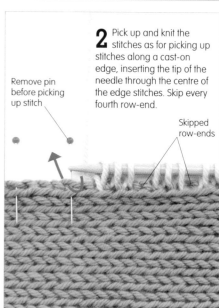

PICKING UP STITCHES WITH A CROCHET HOOK

1 Choose a hook size that fits easily through the stitches. With the right side facing, insert the hook through the first stitch. Then wrap the hook behind and around the yarn from left to right and pull the yarn through the stitch as shown.

Yarn going to ball

Yarn tail

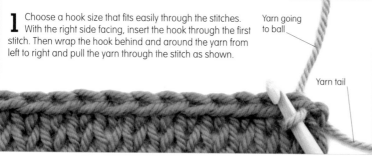

2 Transfer the loop on the hook onto the knitting needle and pull the yarn to tighten it on the needle. Continue in this way, pulling loops through the knitting and transferring them onto the knitting needle.

TIPS FOR PICKING UP STITCHES

• **A yarn in a contrasting colour** is being used in the step-by-step instructions for picking up stitches to clearly illustrate the process. You can hide picking-up imperfections, however, if you use a matching yarn to pick up stitches. For a contrasting border, switch to the new colour on the first row of the border.

• **Always pick** up and knit stitches with the right side of the knitting facing you, as picking up stitches creates a ridge on the wrong side.

• **Your knitting pattern** will specify which needle size to use for picking up stitches for a border – usually one size smaller than the size used for the main knitting.

• **After you have picked up** the required number of stitches, work the border following the directions in your pattern, whether it is ribbing, moss stitch, garter stitch, or a fold-over hem.

• **Even experienced knitters** find it difficult to pick up stitches "evenly" along an edge, so don't be disheartened if your border doesn't look just right when it is complete. First, try casting it off again, either looser or tighter. If this doesn't work, pull out the border and try again, adjusting the number of stitches or spreading them out in a different way if necessary. Alternatively, try a smaller needle size if the border looks too stretched out, or a larger needle size if it looks too tight.

PICKING UP STITCHES ALONG A CURVED EDGE

1 When working picked-up armhole borders or neckbands, you will be required to pick up stitches along a curved edge. As a general rule, you can follow this diagram when picking up stitches along a curved edge. Pick up one stitch in each cast-off stitch and three stitches for every four row-ends. Along the actual curve, ignore the corner stitches along the stepped decreases to smooth out the curve.

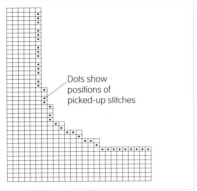

Dots show positions of picked-up stitches

2 Once all the stitches have been picked up, work the border as instructed in your knitting pattern.

A picked-up border with 5 rows of single ribbing

MAKING BUTTON LOOPS

1 Leaving a short loose end, pass the needle from back to front through the knitting at one end of the loop position and through the knitting again at the other end of the loop.

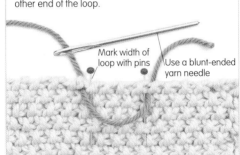

Mark width of loop with pins   Use a blunt-ended yarn needle

2 Pass the needle again through the knitting from back to front at the first pin. This creates a doubled strand for the base of the loop.

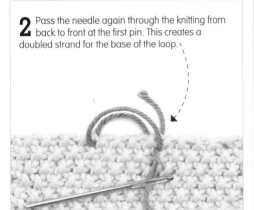

3 Work buttonhole stitches tightly over the doubled strand and the short yarn end. Secure the yarn to the knitting at the other end, then pass the yarn through a few of the buttonhole stitches and trim.

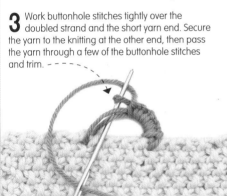

BLOCKING

Always refer to your yarn label before blocking. Textured stitch patterns, such as garter stitch, ribbing, and cables, are best wet blocked or steamed extremely gently so that their texture is not altered – but they should not be pressed or stretched.

WET BLOCKING

If your yarn allows it, wet blocking is the best way to even out your knitting. Using lukewarm water, either wash the knitting or simply wet it. Squeeze out the water and lay the knitting flat on a towel. Roll the towel to squeeze out more moisture. Pat, then pin the piece into shape on layers of dry towels covered with a sheet. Leave the piece to dry completely.

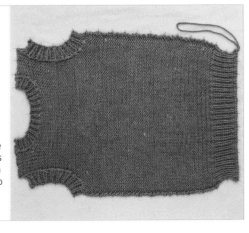

STEAM BLOCKING

Only steam block if it is suitable for your yarn. Pin out the piece to the correct shape. Then place a clean damp cloth on top. Use a warm iron to create steam, barely touching the cloth with the iron. Do not let the weight of the iron rest on the knitting, and avoid any garter stitch or ribbed areas. Move the cloth around, dampening again if necessary. Before removing the pins, let the piece dry completely.

SEAMS

The most popular seam techniques for knitting are mattress stitch, edge-to-edge stitch, backstitch, and overcast stitch. Two other seams that are sometimes called for in knitting patterns are cast-off and grafted seams. Armed with all these seaming methods, you will be able to sew most of the types of seams that you will come across in knitting patterns. Any more unusual techniques will be covered in detail within the directions.

TIPS FOR SEAMS

• **Remember to block** knitted pieces before sewing them together. After seams are completed, open them out and steam very lightly if the yarn allows this.

• **Always use** a blunt-ended yarn needle for all seams on knitting. A pointed needle will puncture the yarn strands and you won't be able to pull the yarn through the knitting successfully.

• **Although the seams** are shown here worked in a contrasting yarn for clarity, use a matching yarn for all seams.

• **Before starting a seam**, pin the knitting together at wide intervals. At the starting end of the seam, secure the yarn to the edge of one piece of knitting with two or three overcast stitches.

• **Make seams firm** but not too tight. They should have a little elasticity, to match the elasticity of the knitted fabric.

MATTRESS STITCH SEAM

1 Mattress stitch is practically invisible and is the best seam technique for ribbing and stocking stitch. Start by aligning the edges of the pieces to be seamed with both the right sides facing you.

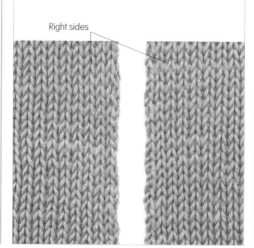

Right sides

2 Insert the needle from the front through the centre of the first knit stitch one piece of knitting and up through the centre of the stitch two rows above. Then make the same type of stitch through the other piece of knitting. Continue in this way up the seam, pulling the edges together after each stitch.

EDGE-TO-EDGE SEAM

This seam is suitable for most stitch patterns. To start, align the pieces of knitting with the wrong sides facing you. Work each stitch of the seam through the little pips formed along the edges of knitting as shown.

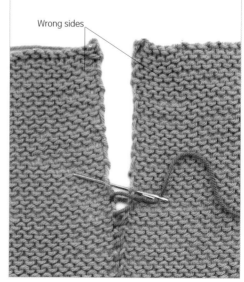

Wrong sides

BACKSTITCH SEAM

Backstitch can be used for almost any seam on knitting, but is not suitable for super-bulky yarns. Align the pieces of knitting with the right sides together. Make one stitch forward, and one stitch back into the starting point of the previous stitch as shown. Work the stitches as close to the edge of the knitting as possible.

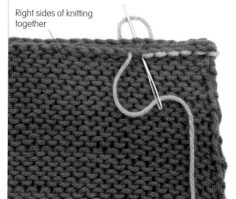

Right sides of knitting together

OVERCAST SEAM

This seam is also called a whipped stitch seam. With the right sides together, insert the needle from back to front through both layers, working through the centres of the edge stitches on the knitting (not through the pips). Make each stitch in the same way.

Right sides of knitting together

CAST-OFF SEAM

1 This seam can be worked on the right side of the knitting (as here) to form a decorative seam, or on the wrong side. Hold the needles with the stitches to be joined together with the wrong sides facing each other. Insert a third needle through the centre of the first stitch on each needle and knit these two stitches together.

2 Continue to knit together one stitch from each needle as you cast off the stitches in the usual way. (A contrasting yarn is used here to show the seam clearly.)

3 When the pieces of knitting are opened out, you will see that this technique forms a raised chain along the seam.

GRAFTED SEAM

1 This seam can be worked along two pieces of knitting that have not been cast off or along two cast-off edges as shown here; the principle for both is the same. With the right sides facing you, follow the path of a row of knitting along the seam as shown.

2 When worked in a matching yarn as here, the seam blends in completely with the knitting and makes it look like a continuous piece of knitting.

SEWING ON AN EDGING

1 Pin the edging to the knitting with the right sides facing each other.

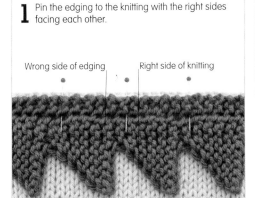

Wrong side of edging   Right side of knitting

2 Sew the edges together with even, closely worked overcast stitches.

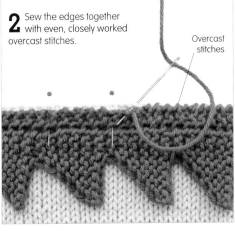

Overcast stitches

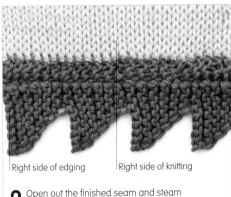

Right side of edging   Right side of knitting

3 Open out the finished seam and steam very lightly if the yarn allows it (see page 69 about how to steam block).

EMBELLISHMENTS FOR KNITTING

Plain knitting sometimes calls out for a little embellishment. The simplest flourish of embroidery, a few well-placed beads or a decorative edging are good candidates for the perfect finishing touch. An embroidered motif or two on a pocket or collar, a beaded band above the ribbing, or a narrow edging sewn to cuffs or collars can add enough to totally transform an otherwise plain garment.

EMBROIDERY ON KNITTING

Swiss darning, bullion stitch, lazy daisies, and chain stitch are the embroidery stitches most commonly used on knitting. Always use a yarn for your embroidery that is the same weight as the yarn used for the knitting or a slightly thicker one, and thread it onto a blunt-ended yarn needle. A needle with a sharp point will split the knitting yarn and prevent you from pulling the embroidery yarn through the fabric.

SWISS DARNING CHART

As Swiss darning embroidery imitates and covers the knit stitches on the right side of the stocking stitch, you can work any charted colourwork motif (see pages 62–65) using the technique. (Cross stitch books are also good sources of motifs for Swiss darning.) The completed embroidered motif will look as if it has been knitted into the fabric.

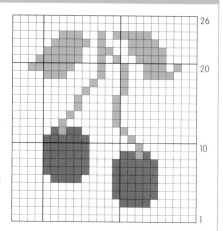

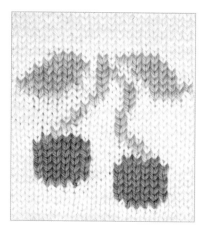

SWISS DARNING WORKED HORIZONTALLY

1 Secure the embroidery yarn to the wrong side of the stocking stitch, then pass the needle from back to front through the centre of a knit stitch, and pull the yarn through. Next, insert the needle from right to left behind the knit stitch above as shown and pull the yarn through.

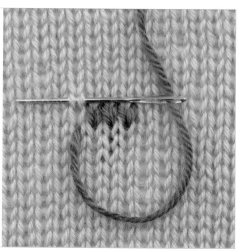

2 Insert the needle from right to left into the knit stitch below and out at the centre of the next knit stitch to the left to complete the stitch as shown. Continue in this way, tracing the path of the knitting horizontally.

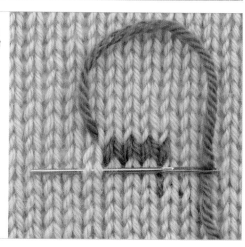

SWISS DARNING WORKED VERTICALLY

1 Secure the embroidery yarn to the wrong side of the stocking stitch, then pass the needle from back to front through the centre of a knit stitch and pull the yarn through. Next, insert the needle from right to left behind the knit stitch above as shown and pull the yarn through.

2 Insert the needle from front to back and to front again under the top of the stitch below so it comes out in the centre of the stitch just covered, as shown. Continue in this way, tracing the path of the knitting vertically.

BULLION STITCH

To begin the stitch, secure the yarn on the wrong side of the knitting and bring the needle through to the right side at one end of the position for the stitch. Then insert the needle through to the back a short distance from the starting point and out to the front again at the starting point. Wrap the yarn at least six times around the needle close to the knitting, and holding the wraps with your fingers, pull the needle carefully through the wraps. To complete the stitch, reinsert the needle through the knitting at the same place (as shown by the big arrow). Arrange the bullion stitches in spirals to form rose shapes, or as here to form simple star or flower-petal shapes.

LAZY DAISY STITCH

Lazy daisy stitches are individual chain stitches held down at the loop end by a short stitch. They are traditionally used to form flower shapes. To begin the stitch, secure the yarn on the wrong side of the knitting and bring the needle through at the centre of the flower. Reinsert the needle through to the back at the starting point and bring it out to the front a short distance away as shown. Secure the loop with a short stitch. Work all the "petals" in the same way, starting each one at the flower centre.

CHAIN STITCH ON STRIPES

Knitted stripes can be turned into a plaid or check pattern with simple vertical lines of chain stitch. To begin, bring the needle out in position for the first stitch. Reinsert the needle where it emerged and bring the tip out a short distance below with the yarn looped under it. Then pull the yarn through. For the following stitches, insert the needle back into the hole from which it has just emerged and bring it out a short distance below as shown.

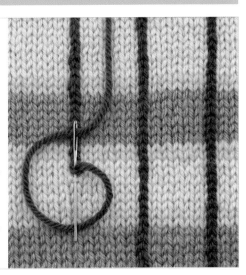

BEAD KNITTING

There are several techniques for working bead knitting, and the two most popular and easiest are provided here – slip-stitch beading and garter-stitch beading. Choose your beads carefully – glass beads look the most attractive on knitting, but there are a wide selection of plastic and wood beads available as well. Check your chosen bead to make sure that the bead hole is large enough for the yarn.

THREADING BEADS ONTO YARN

Make sure you have the right beads before starting to thread them onto the yarn. Consider their size and weight. If your knitting is to be entirely covered with scattered beads, large heavy beads will not be suitable as they would weigh the knitting down too much. Adding a little weight to the knitting can, however, produce the extra drape needed for a graceful shawl, scarf, or evening knit.

Thread the beads onto the knitting yarn before you begin knitting. Your knitting pattern instructions will tell you how many beads to thread onto each ball. If the beads are of different colours and form a specific colour pattern, the instructions will also specify what order to thread the colours on – the last bead to be used is threaded on first and the first bead to be used is threaded on last.

Fold a short length of sewing thread in half, thread both cut ends together through the eye of an ordinary thin sewing needle needle, and pass the end of the knitting yarn through the sewing-thread loop. Thread the beads onto the sewing needle, over the sewing thread and onto the yarn.

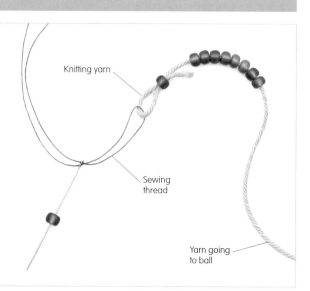

Knitting yarn

Sewing thread

Yarn going to ball

SLIP-STITCH BEADING

1 There is usually a chart provided for positioning the beads on slip-stitch beading, unless only a few beads are to be added, in which case the bead placements will be within the written instructions. The sample chart here illustrates how slip-stitch beads are staggered. This is because the slipped stitches at the bead positions pull in the knitting and alternating the bead placements evens out the fabric.

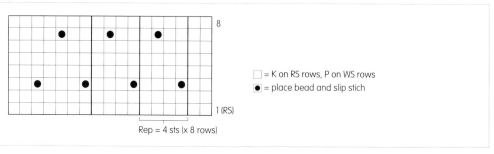

8

1 (RS)

Rep = 4 sts (x 8 rows)

☐ = K on RS rows, P on WS rows
● = place bead and slip stich

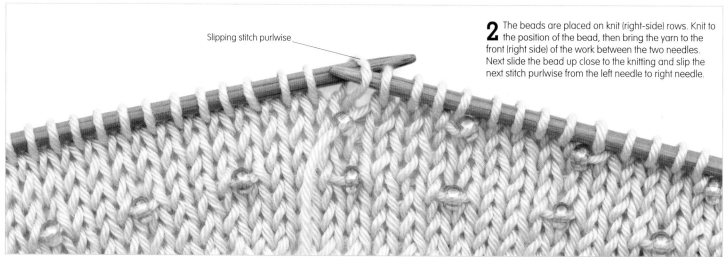

Slipping stitch purlwise

2 The beads are placed on knit (right-side) rows. Knit to the position of the bead, then bring the yarn to the front (right side) of the work between the two needles. Next slide the bead up close to the knitting and slip the next stitch purlwise from the left needle to right needle.

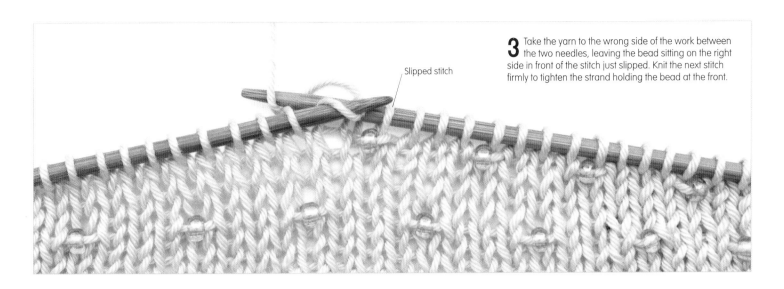

3 Take the yarn to the wrong side of the work between the two needles, leaving the bead sitting on the right side in front of the stitch just slipped. Knit the next stitch firmly to tighten the strand holding the bead at the front.

Slipped stitch

SIMPLE GARTER-STITCH BEADING

1 This method can be used to create bands of beads along borders or at intervals for beaded stripes. Start with a right-side row and work at least three rows of plain garter stitch before adding any beads. On the next row (a wrong-side row), knit two edge stitches before adding a bead. Then push a bead up close to the knitting before working each stitch. At the end of the row, add the last bead when two stitches remain on the left needle, then knit the last two stitches.

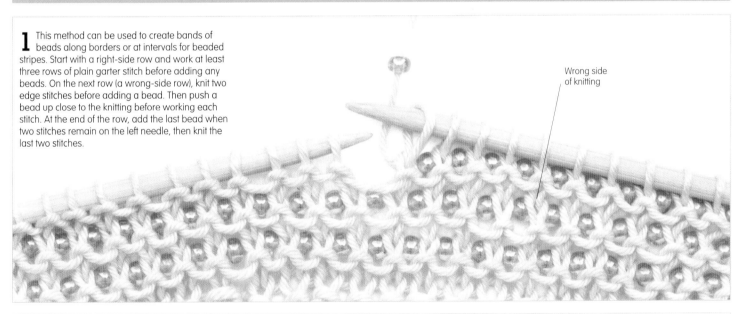

Wrong side of knitting

2 Knit the next row with no beads. Alternate a bead row and a plain row to form a band of beads of the desired depth. This technique could be used to create a piece entirely covered with beads for a small bag, but would create a fabric too heavy for a large garment.

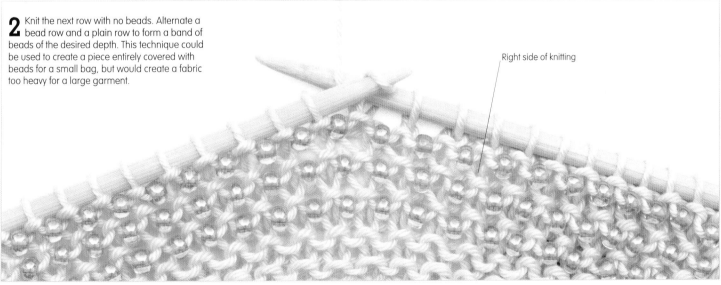

Right side of knitting

SIMPLE EDGING PATTERNS

Here are a few easy-to-work edgings that knit up quickly. Most of them are worked lengthways. Lengthways edgings are handy because you can simply work them until they are long enough. If adding the edging to a baby blanket or throw, knit a little extra to gather at each corner. Do not cast off when the edging is the desired length; instead, slip the stitches onto a stitch holder and sew the edging on around the blanket. Before casting off, you can then work more rows if you need them. With most lengthways edgings the number of stitches changes from row to row, so use the stitch count at the end of the rows to make sure it matches the number of stitches on your needle. See page 37 for abbreviations.

PETAL EDGING

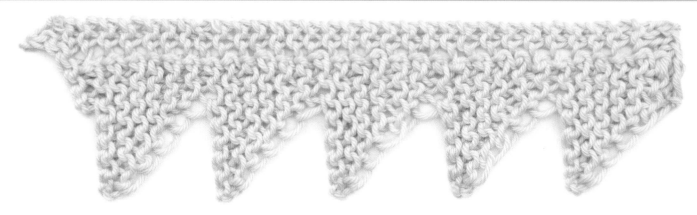

KNITTING INSTRUCTIONS
Cast on 6 sts.
Row 1 (RS) K.
Row 2 Yfwd, K2, K2tog, yfwd, K2. 7 sts.
Row 3 K.
Row 4 Yfwd, K to last 4 sts, K2tog, yfwd, K2. 8 sts.
Rows 5–10 [Rep rows 3 and 4] 3 times. 11 sts.
Row 11 K.

Row 12 Cast off 5 sts loosely knitwise, K1, K2tog, yfwd, K2.
6 sts.
Rep rows 1–12 until edging is desired length, ending with a
row 12.
Cast off knitwise.

PEAKS EDGING

KNITTING INSTRUCTIONS
Cast on 6 sts.
Row 1 and all odd-numbered (RS) rows K.
Row 2 Yfwd, K2, K2tog, yfwd, K2. 7 sts.
Row 4 Yfwd, K3, K2tog, yfwd, K2. 8 sts.
Row 6 Yfwd, K4, K2tog, yfwd, K2. 9 sts.
Row 8 Yfwd, K5, K2tog, yfwd, K2. 10 sts.
Row 10 Yfwd, K6, K2tog, yfwd, K2. 11 sts.
Row 12 Yfwd, sk2p, K4, K2tog, yfwd, K2. 10 sts.

Row 14 Yfwd, sk2p, K3, K2tog, yfwd, K2. 9 sts.
Row 16 Yfwd, sk2p, K2, K2tog, yfwd, K2. 8 sts.
Row 18 Yfwd, sk2p, K1, K2tog, yfwd, K2. 7 sts.
Row 20 Yfwd, sk2p, K2tog, yfwd, K2. 6 sts.
Rep rows 1–20 until edging is desired length, ending with a
row 20.
Cast off knitwise.

GODMOTHER'S EDGING

KNITTING INSTRUCTIONS

Note: Slip first st of even-numbered rows purlwise, then take yarn to back of work between 2 needles ready to K next st.
Cast on 15 sts.
Row 1 (RS) K.
Row 2 Sl 1, K2, [yfwd, K2tog] 5 times, yfwd, K2. 16 sts.
Row 3 and all odd-numbered (RS) rows K.
Row 4 Sl 1, K5, [yfwd, K2tog] 4 times, yfwd, K2. 17 sts.
Row 6 Sl 1, K8, [yfwd, K2tog] 3 times, yfwd, K2. 18 sts.
Row 8 Sl 1, K11, [yfwd, K2tog] twice, yfwd, K2. 19 sts.
Row 10 Sl 1, K18.
Rows 11 Cast off 4 sts knitwise, K to end. 15 sts.
Rep rows 2–11 until edging is desired length, ending with a row 11.
Cast off knitwise.

FRINGE EDGING

KNITTING INSTRUCTIONS

Note: When making this edging, hold 2 strands of yarn together throughout and knit tightly. You can alter length of fringe by adding to or subtracting from number of knit stitches at end of row 1 and adjusting purl stitches at beg of row 2 by same number.
Cast on 12 sts.
Row 1 (RS) K2, yfwd, K2tog, K8.
Row 2 P7, K2, yfwd, K2tog, K1.
Rep rows 1 and 2 until edging is desired length, ending with a row 2.

Cast off (RS) Cast off first 5 sts knitwise, cut yarn and draw through loop on RH needle to fasten off, then drop rem 6 sts off LH needle and unravel them to form fringe. Smooth out unravelled strands, and, if necessary, lightly steam to straighten the strands. Then cut through loops at end of fringe. Knot strands together in groups of four strands, positioning knots close to edge of knitting. Trim fringe ends slightly if necessary to make them even.

PICOT RUFFLE EDGING

KNITTING INSTRUCTIONS

Note: This edging is worked widthways.
Cast on odd number of sts.
Row 1 (RS) K.
Row 2 K.
Row 3 *K2tog, yfwd; rep from * to last st, K1.
Rows 4, 5 and 6 K.
Row 7 K1, *[K1, P1, K1] into next st, [K1, P1] into next st; rep from *. (This row increases the number of stitches on the needle by about two and one half times.)
Row 8 P.

Row 9 K.
Rows 10, 11, 12 and 13 [Rep rows 8 and 9] twice.
Row 14 (WS) P.
Rows 15 and 16 K.
Work picots along cast-off as follows:
Picot cast-off *Cast on 2 sts onto LH needle using knit-on cast-on method, cast off 5 sts knitwise, transfer st on RH needle back to LH needle; rep from *, ending last cast-off as required by sts remaining.

CHRISTENING EDGING

KNITTING INSTRUCTIONS

Cast on 7 sts.
Row 1 (RS) K2, yfwd, K2tog, yfwd twice, K2tog, K1. 8 sts.
Row 2 K3, P1, K2, yfwd, K2tog.
Row 3 K2, yfwd, K2tog, K1, yfwd twice, K2tog, K1. 9 sts.
Row 4 K3, P1, K3, yfwd, K2tog.
Row 5 K2, yfwd, K2tog, K2, yfwd twice, K2tog, K1. 10 sts.
Row 6 K3, P1, K4, yfwd, K2tog.
Row 7 K2, yfwd, K2tog, K6.
Row 8 Cast off 3 sts knitwise, K4, yfwd, K2tog. 7 sts.
Rep rows 1–8 until edging is desired length, ending with a row 8.
Cast off knitwise.

CIRCULAR KNITTING

Circular knitting, also called knitting in the round, is worked on a circular needle or with a set of four or five double-pointed needles. With the right side of the knitting always facing, the knitting is worked round and round to form a tube, or round and round to form a flat shape (a medallion), started from the centre. The technique for using a circular needle can be easily acquired by beginners, but working with sets of double-pointed needles is best left for knitters to try once they have achieved intermediate skills.

KNITTING
TUBES

For those who don't enjoy stitching seams, knitting seamless tubes is a real plus. Large tubes can be worked on long circular needles, for example for the body of a pullover up to the armholes, a cushion cover, or a bag. Short circular needles are used for seamless neckbands and armhole bands, and hats. Because circular needles are too long for items like mittens and socks, double-pointed needles are used instead.

WORKING WITH A CIRCULAR KNITTING NEEDLE

1 Cast-on the required number of stitches (the stitches should fit around the needle from one end to the other without stretching). Ensure that the stitches are untwisted and they all face inwards, then slip a stitch marker onto the end of the right needle to mark the beginning of the round.

Stitch marker

2 Hold the needle ends in your hands and bring the right needle up to the left needle to work the first stitch. Knit round and round on the stitches. When the stitch marker is reached, slip it from the left needle to the right needle.

Knit first stitch of first round tightly

3 If you are working a stocking stitch tube on a circular needle, the right side of the work will always be facing you and every round will be a knit round.

WORKING WITH A SET OF FOUR DOUBLE-POINTED NEEDLES

1 Your knitting instructions will specify how many double-pointed needles to use for the project you are making – either a set of four or a set of five. When working with a set of four double-pointed needles, first cast on all the stitches required onto a single needle.

2 Slip some of the stitches off onto two other needles – your knitting pattern will tell you precisely how many to place on each needle. Ensure that the bottoms of the cast-on loops are all facing inwards.

Make sure stitches are not twisted

3 Place a stitch marker between the first and second stitches on the first needle to mark the beginning of the round. Then pull the first and third needles close together and start to knit with the fourth needle. Knit round and round in this way as for knitting with a circular needle.

Knit first stitch on each needle tightly to avoid holes

Stitch marker

WORKING WITH A SET OF FIVE DOUBLE-POINTED NEEDLES

1 Cast on, distribute the stitches and position a stitch marker as for working with four needles, but distribute the stitches over four needles.

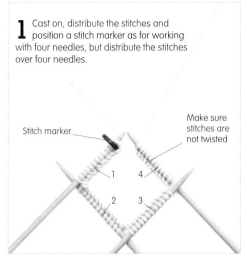

Stitch marker

Make sure stitches are not twisted

1 4

2 3

2 Use the fifth needle to knit with. Knit the first stitch tightly to close the gap between the first cast-on stitch and the last.

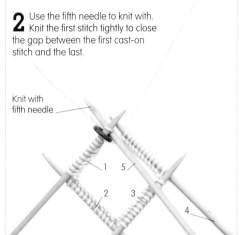

Knit with fifth needle

1 5

2 3

4

3 When all stitches on the first needle have been knit off onto the spare needle, use this empty needle to work the stitches on the second needle. Continue round and round like this, slipping the stitch marker from the left needle to the right needle when it is reached.

KNITTING
MEDALLIONS

Knitted medallions are flat shapes knitted from the centre outwards. They are worked on a set of four or five double-pointed needles. Although the steps below show a square being worked, the technique is the same for knitting circles, hexagons, octagons, and so on (see pages 80 and 81).

WORKING A SIMPLE SQUARE

1 Cast on 8 stitches onto a single needle and distribute 2 stitches onto each of four needles. Using a fifth needle to knit with, knit through the back loop (see page 36) of each stitch on all four needles.

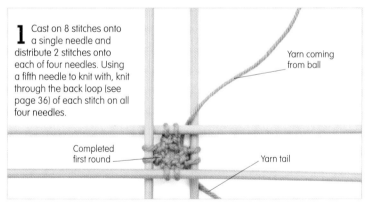

Yarn coming from ball

Completed first round

Yarn tail

2 On round 2, knit into the front and back of each stitch (see page 38). There are now a total of 16 stitches on the needles – 4 on each of the needles.

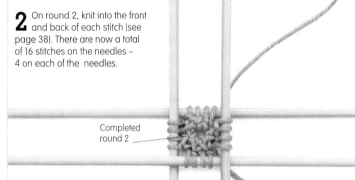

Completed round 2

3 Knit each stitch in round 3. On round 4, knit into the front and back of the first and last stitches on each needle. For rounds 5–8, repeat rounds 3 and 4 twice.

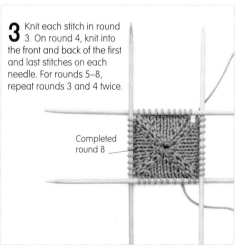

Completed round 8

4 Continue in this way, increasing 8 stitches in every alternate round, until the square is the desired size.

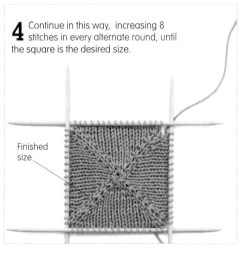

Finished size

5 Cast off in the usual way, leaving a long yarn tail. Using a blunt-ended yarn needle, pass the yarn tail under the top of the first cast-off stitch and back though the centre of the fastened off stitch. Darn in the yarn ends on the wrong side of the work, using the yarn end at the centre to pull the hole together if necessary.

KNITTING

SIMPLE MEDALLIONS

These simple medallions can be used in the same way as crocheted afghan motifs (see page 154), stitched together to form larger pieces of fabric for throws, bags, and cushion covers. They can also be worked singly into pieces big enough for a cushion cover or table mat. Alternatively, the square and circle can form the base of a container worked in the round (see page 91). For ideas on how to join the shapes into interesting patterns for throws, see the patchwork section (pages 282–373). For example, by working the medallions in different colours and tones and then arranging them in different formats you can form simple stripes.

SIMPLE CIRCLE

KNITTING INSTRUCTIONS
Cast on 8 sts onto one needle. Then distribute 2 sts onto each of 4 double-pointed needles and knit with a 5th double-pointed needle as foll:
Round 1 [K1 tbl] twice on each of 4 needles.
Round 2 [Kfb in each st] on each of 4 needles. 16 sts.
Rounds 3, 4, and 5 K.
Round 6 [Kfb in each st] on each of 4 needles. 32 sts.
Rounds 7, 8, 9, 10, and 11 K.
Round 12 Rep round 6. 64 sts.
Rounds 13, 14, 15, 16, 17, 18, and 19 K.
Round 20 [Kfb into every 2nd st] on each of 4 needles. 96 sts.
Rounds 21, 22, 23, 24, and 25 K.
Round 26 [Kfb into every 3rd st] on each of 4 needles. 128 sts.
Rounds 27, 28, 29, 30, and 31 K.
Round 32 [Kfb into every 4th st] on each of 4 needles. 160 sts.
Cont in this way, increasing 32 stitches in every 6th round and working the next increase round with Kfb into every 5th stitch, the following into every 6th stitch, and so on, until the circle is the desired size.
Cast off knitwise.

SIMPLE SQUARE

KNITTING INSTRUCTIONS
Cast on 8 sts onto one needle. Then distribute 2 sts onto each of 4 double-pointed needles and knit with a 5th double-pointed needle as foll:
Round 1 [K1 tbl] twice on each of 4 needles.
Round 2 [Kfb in each st] on each of 4 needles. 16 sts.
Round 3 K.
Round 4 [K, working Kfb in first and last st] on each of 4 needles. 24 sts.
Rep rounds 3 and 4 (increasing 8 sts in every alt round) until square is desired size.
Cast off knitwise.

SQUARE WITH SWIRLING INCREASES

KNITTING INSTRUCTIONS
Cast on 8 sts onto one needle. Then distribute 2 sts onto each of 4 double-pointed needles, and knit with a 5th double-pointed needle as foll:
Row 1 [K1 tbl] twice on each of 4 needles.
Row 2 [K, working yfwd before first st] on each of 4 needles. 12 sts.
Rep round 2 (increasing 4 sts in every round) until square is desired size.
Cast off knitwise.

SPECIAL NOTES

• All of these medallions are worked with a set of either four or five double-pointed needles (see pages 16–17). A list of knitting abbreviations are given on page 37.

• You can work the simple circle, square and octagon in stripes, using two or more colours. Work thin or thick stripes randomly or in a regular repeat as desired.

• Be sure to use a row counter when working medallions to keep track of where you are in the pattern. Alternatively, write down each row number on a piece of paper after it is complete and try not to stop in the middle of a round.

SQUARE WITH OPENWORK INCREASES

KNITTING INSTRUCTIONS
Cast on 8 sts onto one needle. Then distribute 2 sts onto each of 4 double-pointed needles and knit with a 5th double-pointed needle as foll:
Round 1 [K1 tbl] twice on each of 4 needles.
Round 2 [Yfwd, K1, yfwd, K1] on each of 4 needles. 16 sts.
Round 3 K.
Round 4 [Yfwd, K2, yfwd, K1] on each of 4 needles. 24 sts.
Round 5 K.
Round 6 [Yfwd, K to last st, yfwd, K1] on each of 4 needles. 32 sts.
Rep rounds 5 and 6 (increasing 8 sts in every alt round) until square is desired size.
Cast off knitwise.

HEXAGON

KNITTING INSTRUCTIONS
Cast on 12 sts onto one needle. Then distribute 4 sts onto each of 3 double-pointed needles and knit with a 4th double-pointed needle as foll:
Round 1 [K1 tbl] 4 times on each of 3 needles.
Round 2 [Yfwd, K2, yfwd, K2] on each of 3 needles. 18 sts.
Round 3 K.
Round 4 [Yfwd, K3, yfwd, K3] on each of 3 needles. 24 sts.
Round 5 K.
Round 6 [Yfwd, K half of rem sts on needle, yfwd, K to end of needle] on each of 3 needles. 30 sts.
Rep rounds 5 and 6 (increasing 6 sts in every alt round) until hexagon is desired size.
Cast off knitwise.

SIMPLE OCTAGON

KNITTING INSTRUCTIONS
Cast on 8 sts onto one needle. Then distribute 2 sts onto each of 4 double-pointed needles and knit with a 5th double-pointed needle as foll:
Round 1 [K1 tbl] twice on each of 4 needles.
Round 2 [Kfb in each st] on each of 4 needles. 16 sts.
Round 3 and all odd-numbered rounds K.
Round 4 [K1, Kfb, K1, Kfb] on each of 4 needles. 24 sts.
Round 6 [K2, Kfb, K2, Kfb] on each of 4 needles. 32 sts.
Round 8 [K3, Kfb, K3, Kfb] on each of 4 needles. 40 sts.
Round 10 [K4, Kfb, K4, Kfb] on each of 4 needles. 48 sts.
Round 12 [K5, Kfb, K5, Kfb] on each of 4 needles. 56 sts.
Cont in this way (increasing 8 sts in every alt round) until octagon is desired size.
Cast off knitwise.

KNITTED TOYS

Toys are a delight to knit. If you have never knit a toy before, try this very easy striped monkey. These step-by-step instructions for making a toy include lots of tips for knitting toy pieces, for stuffing, for assembling parts, and for stitching facial features. (Directions for the toy pieces are given on page 388.)

MAKING THE TOY

Knit on a pair of needles instead of in the round, the monkey toy is easy, even for a beginner. The toy pattern has been specially devised to be easy to understand as well. Follow the steps as you knit the pieces and learn practical toy-making tips.

CHOOSING MATERIALS

YARN
You will need scraps of a lightweight or medium-weight yarn (see page 15) in six colours (A, B, C, D, E, and F) as shown below

KNITTING NEEDLES
Pair of knitting needles that are one to two sizes smaller than size recommended on yarn label

EXTRAS
Black six-stranded cotton embroidery thread for eyebrows, nose and mouth
Two small black buttons (10mm in diameter) for eyes and strong button thread (or black toy saftey eyes)
Toy filling

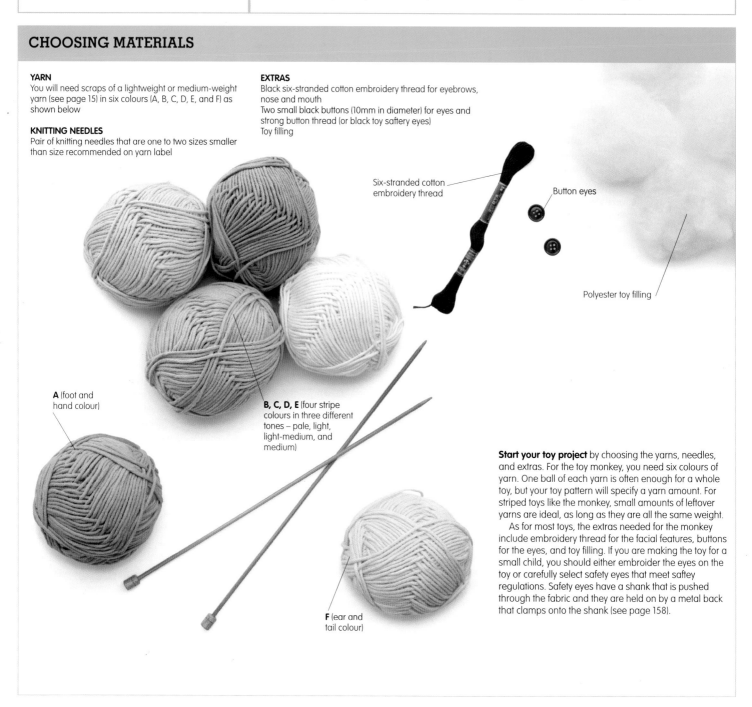

Six-stranded cotton embroidery thread

Button eyes

Polyester toy filling

A (foot and hand colour)

B, C, D, E (four stripe colours in three different tones – pale, light, light-medium, and medium)

F (ear and tail colour)

Start your toy project by choosing the yarns, needles, and extras. For the toy monkey, you need six colours of yarn. One ball of each yarn is often enough for a whole toy, but your toy pattern will specify a yarn amount. For striped toys like the monkey, small amounts of leftover yarns are ideal, as long as they are all the same weight.

As for most toys, the extras needed for the monkey include embroidery thread for the facial features, buttons for the eyes, and toy filling. If you are making the toy for a small child, you should either embroider the eyes on the toy or carefully select safety eyes that meet saftey regulations. Safety eyes have a shank that is pushed through the fabric and they are held on by a metal back that clamps onto the shank (see page 158).

KNITTING THE BODY AND HEAD

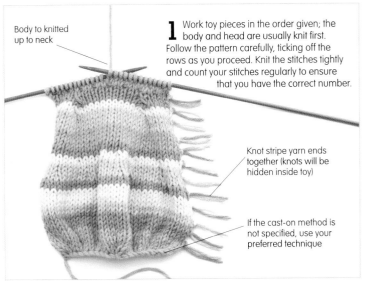

Body to knitted up to neck

1 Work toy pieces in the order given; the body and head are usually knit first. Follow the pattern carefully, ticking off the rows as you proceed. Knit the stitches tightly and count your stitches regularly to ensure that you have the correct number.

Knot stripe yarn ends together (knots will be hidden inside toy)

If the cast-on method is not specified, use your preferred technique

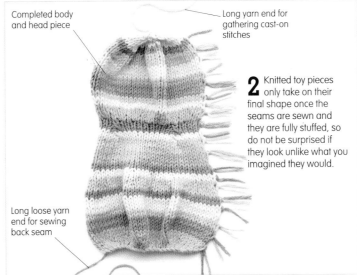

Completed body and head piece

Long yarn end for gathering cast-on stitches

2 Knitted toy pieces only take on their final shape once the seams are sewn and they are fully stuffed, so do not be surprised if they look unlike what you imagined they would.

Long loose yarn end for sewing back seam

KNITTING THE LEGS AND ARMS

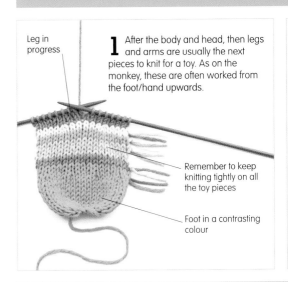

Leg in progress

1 After the body and head, then legs and arms are usually the next pieces to knit for a toy. As on the monkey, these are often worked from the foot/hand upwards.

Remember to keep knitting tightly on all the toy pieces

Foot in a contrasting colour

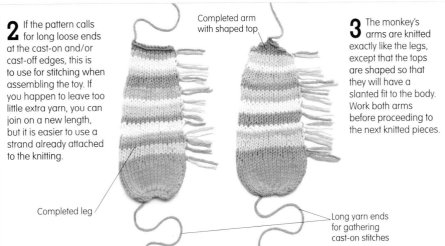

2 If the pattern calls for long loose ends at the cast-on and/or cast-off edges, this is to use for stitching when assembling the toy. If you happen to leave too little extra yarn, you can join on a new length, but it is easier to use a strand already attached to the knitting.

Completed arm with shaped top

Completed leg

3 The monkey's arms are knitted exactly like the legs, except that the tops are shaped so that they will have a slanted fit to the body. Work both arms before proceeding to the next knitted pieces.

Long yarn ends for gathering cast-on stitches

KNITTING OTHER BODY PARTS

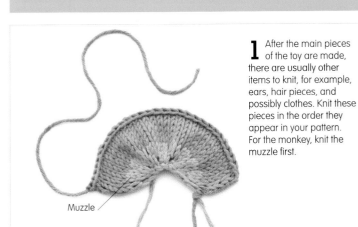

1 After the main pieces of the toy are made, there are usually other items to knit, for example, ears, hair pieces, and possibly clothes. Knit these pieces in the order they appear in your pattern. For the monkey, knit the muzzle first.

Muzzle

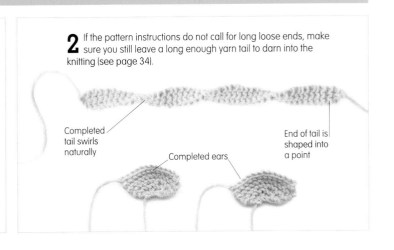

2 If the pattern instructions do not call for long loose ends, make sure you still leave a long enough yarn tail to darn into the knitting (see page 34).

Completed tail swirls naturally

End of tail is shaped into a point

Completed ears

FINISHING THE TOY

Finishing the toy successfully is the most difficult part of the toy-knitting process. Take your time and stitch slowly. Do not be afraid to unpick and redo any sewing that you are unhappy with. The finishing tips with the monkey are useful for all knitted toys.

STUFFING AND ASSEMLING THE MAIN TOY PIECES

1 Follow finishing steps in the order given. For the monkey, prepare the legs first. Using the long yarn end, weave in and out of the cast-on stitches, then pull to gather these stitches. Next, sew the leg seam, stuffing as you proceed.

Stuff firmly and evenly

Push knots to inside of leg

Sew toy seams using mattress stitch

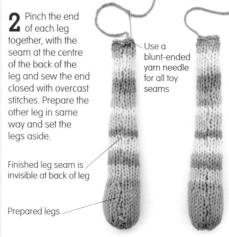

2 Pinch the end of each leg together, with the seam at the centre of the back of the leg and sew the end closed with overcast stitches. Prepare the other leg in same way and set the legs aside.

Use a blunt-ended yarn needle for all toy seams

Finished leg seam is invisible at back of leg

Prepared legs

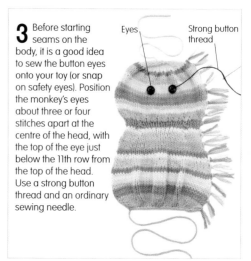

3 Before starting seams on the body, it is a good idea to sew the button eyes onto your toy (or snap on safety eyes). Position the monkey's eyes about three or four stitches apart at the centre of the head, with the top of the eye just below the 11th row from the top of the head. Use a strong button thread and an ordinary sewing needle.

Eyes

Strong button thread

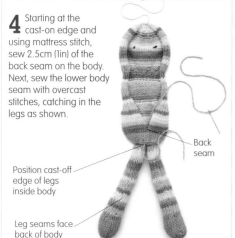

4 Starting at the cast-on edge and using mattress stitch, sew 2.5cm (1in) of the back seam on the body. Next, sew the lower body seam with overcast stitches, catching in the legs as shown.

Position cast-off edge of legs inside body

Leg seams face back of body

Back seam

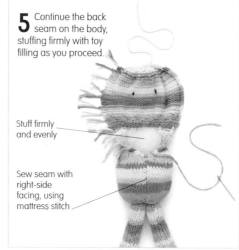

5 Continue the back seam on the body, stuffing firmly with toy filling as you proceed.

Stuff firmly and evenly

Sew seam with right-side facing, using mattress stitch

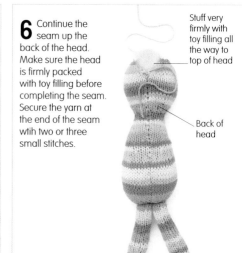

6 Continue the seam up the back of the head. Make sure the head is firmly packed with toy filling before completing the seam. Secure the yarn at the end of the seam with two or three small stitches.

Stuff very firmly with toy filling all the way to top of head

Back of head

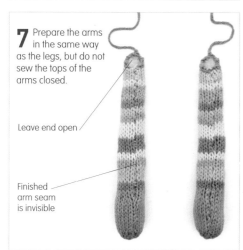

7 Prepare the arms in the same way as the legs, but do not sew the tops of the arms closed.

Leave end open

Finished arm seam is invisible

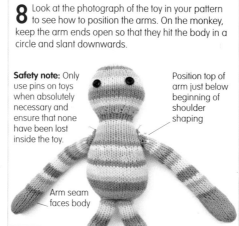

8 Look at the photograph of the toy in your pattern to see how to position the arms. On the monkey, keep the arm ends open so that they hit the body in a circle and slant downwards.

Safety note: Only use pins on toys when absolutely necessary and ensure that none have been lost inside the toy.

Position top of arm just below beginning of shoulder shaping

Arm seam faces body

9 Sew the arms in place, turning the edge of the arm inside the arm as you stitch. Remove the pins carefully as you stitch.

ADDING SMALL BODY PIECES AND FACIAL FEATURES

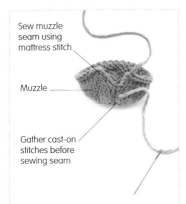

Sew muzzle seam using mattress stitch

Muzzle

Gather cast-on stitches before sewing seam

1 Using the yarn end, stitch in and out of cast-on stitches and pull to gather these stitches together. Sew the muzzle seam, starting at the cast-on end of the seam.

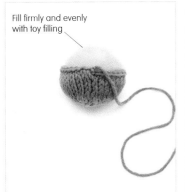

Fill firmly and evenly with toy filling

2 Clip off the seam yarn to about 5cm (2in) long and place inside the muzzle. Then fill the muzzle with toy filling.

3 Pin the muzzle to the head just below the eyes, forming an oval shape covering about 10 stitches across the face and about 12 rows. Sew the muzzle in place with short overcast stitches.

Muzzle seam at centre of bottom of muzzle

Darn in yarn end

Ear

Gather straight edge

4 Make widely spaced overcast stitches along the straight edge of each ear, and use these stitches to gather the ear into a cup shape.

5 Still using the gathering yarn, sew the ears to the sides of the head. Position toy ears following the photograph with your pattern.

Pull stitches tight so they disappear

6 Sew the tail to the centre of the back of the monkey. Darn in the other yarn end at the cast-off edge of the tail.

Use long yarn ends to sew on small toy pieces

Slanting eyebrows upwards towards centre gives monkey an innocent, relaxed expression

7 Use a blunt-ended yarn needle and all six strands of the embroidery thread for all the monkey's facial features. Embroider the mouth in backstitch along the centre of the muzzle. Work toy features carefully and redo them if necessary.

Use thick enough thread on toy features to make the stitches stand out boldly

8 For each nostril, work two stitches in the same place, the second on top of the first. Position the nostrils close together as shown.

9 For each eyebrow, work two stitches in the same place, the second on top of the first. The slant of the eyebrows will give your toy its expression. To personalize your toy, alter the position and size of the eyes, and the shape of the mouth and eyebrows. Even changing the ear positions can give your toy its unique look.

FELTED KNITTING

When felted, knitting shrinks, and it is not possible to control the exact amount of shrinkage. Luckily, there are many things you can make from felted knitting that do not require precise sizes, from cushion covers to simple bags. Motifs cut from felt also make great brooches or decoration on other knitting.

FELTING BASICS

If you are a beginner, avoid attempting a felted garment pattern until you have gained some experience with felting smaller items. Before taking the plunge into a specific project, read all about the felting basics below and discover some helpful tips.

CHOOSING THE YARN

Super-fine and lightweight 100 per cent wool tweed yarn will create a knitted felt of average thickness

Medium-weight wool-blend yarn containing mohair will felt very readily because of the mohair content

Medium-weight and bulky-weight 100 per cent wool tweed yarn will create a thick knitted felt

The best yarns for felted knitting are 100 per cent wool yarns, and other animal fibre yarns, that have not been too tightly spun. As a rule, the longer the fibres of a yarn, the more easily they felt. Avoid wool yarns marked "machine washable".

PREPARING A SWATCH FOR TEST-FELTING

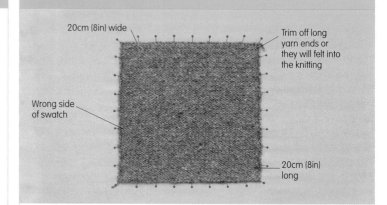

20cm (8in) wide

Trim off long yarn ends or they will felt into the knitting

Wrong side of swatch

20cm (8in) long

By testing a swatch of your yarn you can determine how much it will shrink when felted. But keep in mind that felting is not an exact science because of all these variables – washing machine agitation, water temperature, detergent type, and yarn fibre content, spin, and colour.

Knit a swatch of stocking stitch at least 20cm (8in) square; accurate shrinkage measurements cannot be obtained with smaller swatches as they shrink more than is usual. Block the swatch carefully. If unblocked, the side edges will felt too thickly due to the curling of the knitting.

HAND FELTING

Hand felting is useful for pre-testing the yarn before running a whole washing machine cycle. First, hand test the yarn to see if it is likely to felt at all. Roll a 90cm (36in) long strand of yarn into a ball. Squirt a drop of liquid dish detergent on it. Then, keeping the yarn in the palm of your hand, run hot water over it and rub it together with both hands for about 2 minutes, rinsing repeatedly in the hot running water. If the yarn clumps and is difficult to pull apart, it is a good candidate for test-felting. (If it has not stuck together at all it is unlikely to felt.)

Next, knit a 10cm (4in) swatch and block it. Submerge the swatch in a sink full of soapy hand-hot water. Squeezing and kneading it gently, keep agitating the piece and adding more hot water when needed for up to 30 minutes. Rinse and squeeze out the water (do not wring). Then roll the swatch in a towel to remove more moisture. Pat the felt, right-side up, into a rectangular shape and leave to dry overnight. If the yarn has felted successfully, you can test it again using a bigger swatch and a washing machine.

MACHINE FELTING

Prepare a swatch as explained above. Then put the swatch in your washing machine and add in a large hand towel. (The towel increases the agitation in the water to enable the felting process and should be put in for all felting.) Add half the amount of laundry detergent normally used for a full load. Use a water temperature of about 40°C (104°F) for yarn that contains any mohair, and a temperature of about 60°C (140°F) for 100 per cent wool yarns. Wash the sample using the full washing cycle and the full spin for that cycle. (If you have a top-loading machine, you can check the felting process at intervals during the cycle.)

Tug the washed swatch gently in both directions, then lay it right-side up on your ironing board and pat it into a rectangular shape. Leave it to dry completely – the shrinkage is only complete when the felt is totally dry. If necessary, do more tests with new swatches, altering the temperature or the length of the wash cycle. Keep detailed records of your testing, listing tension, needle size, sizes of the pre-felted and felted swatch, machine setting, and the type and amount of detergent.

TIPS FOR FELTING

- **If you are trying** out felting for the first time, make several test swatches in different weights of yarn and felt them together in the same washing-machine load. This way you can get a feel for the different thicknesses of knitted felt.

- **When using** highly contrasting colours in the same piece of knitting or putting highly contrasting colours in the same felting load, put a colour catcher in the washing machine. This absorbs loose dye and will prevent colours from running.

- **Wool will fade** slightly when felted, due to the high temperatures and the detergent, but this adds an attractive quality to the felt.

- **Clean your washing machine** after a felting load by wiping it out with a damp cloth to remove any stray fibres.

BEFORE FELTING
AND AFTER FELTING

Knitting changes character when it is felted, softening and shrinking usually more lengthways than widthways. Integrated decorative effects can be achieved with knitted stripes or embroidery worked onto the knitting prior to felting.

100 per cent wool yarn: The wool yarn used for these two samples is a lightweight, loosely spun tweed. A 60°C (140°F) wash was used to felt the knitting.

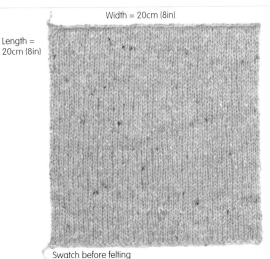

Width = 20cm (8in)

Length = 20cm (8in)

Swatch before felting

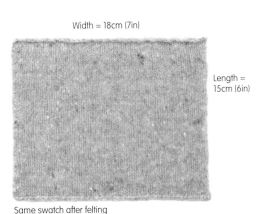

Width = 18cm (7in)

Length = 15cm (6in)

Same swatch after felting

Mohair-mix yarn in stripes: The yarn used for these two striped samples is a medium-weight mohair mix containing 70 per cent lambswool, 26 per cent kid mohair, and 4 per cent nylon. A 40°C (104°F) wash was used to felt the knitting. Felted stripes merge together gently in the felting process. When making striped knitting for felting, cut off the old colour each time a new colour is started. Then knot the yarn ends together at the edge of the knitting. Clip off the yarn ends close to the knot so that these ends do not become felted into the knitting.

Width = 20cm (8in)

Length = 20cm (8in)

Swatch before felting

Width = 16.5cm (6¼in)

Length = 15cm (6in)

Same swatch after felting

Felted knitting with embroidered lines: The yarn used for these two samples is the same medium-weight mohair mix used for the striped swatches above; and the same felting wash was used. Prior to felting, contrasting horizontal lines were embroidered in backstitch using the same yarn as the base knitting. This embroidery merges attractively into the felt. (Notice how the backstitch shrinks and narrows the swatch more than usual during the felting.) This technique can be used to integrate a variety of embroidered motifs into your felt. Why not try backstitch hearts, running-stitch swirls, or chain-stitch circles?

Width = 20cm (8in)

Length = 20cm (8in)

Swatch before felting

Width = 14.5cm (5¾in)

Length = 15cm (6in)

Same swatch after felting twice

FELTED DECORATIONS

Felted knitting is a great base for freehand embroidery because it is firm and stable. The perfect first felting project would be a plain felted cushion cover that you could embroider with shiny cotton stitches or, alternatively, appliqué with simple motifs cut from contrasting knitted felt. Cut-out motifs also make ideal decorations for knitted hats, or they can be made into stand-alone brooches.

EMBROIDERING FELTED KNITTING

Simple star stitches are easy and stand out beautifully on knitted felt. Try out this stitch (or other embroidery stitches) on a 20cm (8in) stocking-stitch square worked in lightweight 100 per cent wool yarn and felted as explained on page 86.

1 To work star stitches, first mark the desired positions for the stars with pins. Then thread a sharp-pointed crewel (embroidery) needle with a contrasting doubled six-strand cotton embroidery thread.

2 Work the two arms of the base crosses on each star 2cm (³/₄in) long and the arms of the small crosses on top 1.5cm (⁵/₈in) long.

3 Your finished sample provides a good starting point for designing your own cushion cover.

MAKING FELTED CUT-OUT DECORATIONS

For a simple flower, knit two 20cm (8in) stocking-stitch squares – one striped and one plain – and felt as explained on page 86. Use a medium-weight wool yarn with some mohair content for a good firm appliqué felt.

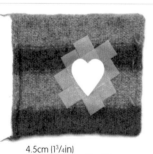

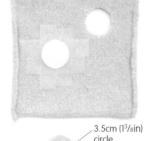

4.5cm (1³/₄in) tall heart

3.5cm (1³/₈in) circle

1 Make a paper template for the petal shape and the circle centre. Tape the petal to the wrong side of the striped piece and the circle to the solid piece.

2 Using very sharp small scissors, cut out the shapes, cutting through the tape as you proceed. Cut a total of five petals and two circles in this way.

4 With the wrong side of the petals still facing upwards, place the second felt circle right-side up on top of the petals and aligned with the circle underneath. Sew the circle in place with neat overcast stitches.

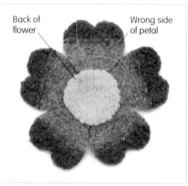

Back of flower

Wrong side of petal

3 Lay one of the circles wrong-side up, then pin the petals wrong-side up on top of it. Using a thread that matches the circle and a sharp sewing needle, sew the petals to the circle underneath with running stitches, catching the circle with each stitch but not sewing all the way through it.

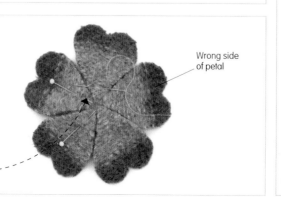

Wrong side of petal

5 Turn the flower over so it is right-side up and decorate it with beads as here or with contrasting embroidery.

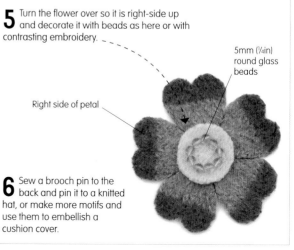

5mm (¹/₄in) round glass beads

Right side of petal

6 Sew a brooch pin to the back and pin it to a knitted hat, or make more motifs and use them to embellish a cushion cover.

UNUSUAL YARNS

Knitting is even more fun if you know you are helping the environment. Undoing old sweaters and reusing the yarn is the most obvious type of recycling for knitters. But you can also head for more "unusual" yarns – rag strips, plastic strips, and string – for your eco knitting.

RECYCLING YARN

Sweaters you no longer wear are perfect candidates for recycling, whether they are hand-knit or machine-made. The thickness of the yarn is irrelevant, as you can use thin strands doubled or tripled to create yarns thick enough to hand knit with.

PREPARING RECYCLED YARN

1 Carefully undo all the seams on the sweater. This is very easy on some manufactured sweaters because the seams pull out in a chain. Cut other seams carefully stitch by stitch with sharp scissors.

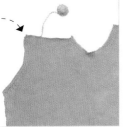

2 Unravel the knitting, starting at the top of the piece and winding the yarn into a ball as you proceed. If the yarn breaks, simply knot the ends together to form a continuous strand.

KNITTING WITH VARIEGATED RECYCLED YARN

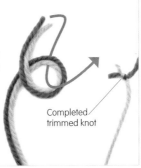

1 To enliven your rescued yarns, cut them in 30–61cm (12–24in) lengths and knot them together to form a unique yarn with variegated colours. Use yarns of similar thicknesses, doubling thin yarns if necessary.

Completed trimmed knot

2 Roll the newly formed yarn into a ball as you knot the ends together.

3 Use the yarn for your chosen project. A garter stitch scarf is perfect for showing off your unique variegated yarn. The knots are a decorative feature, so make sure some fall on each side of the scarf.

RAG KNITTING

Old shirts, cotton blouses, and patchwork remnants provide the best fabrics to recycle for rag knitting. Knitting thicker fabric strips is strenuous on the hands, and very thin fabrics are more liable to tear during the knitting process.

1 To make your rag "yarn", start by trimming the fabric pieces into even straight-edged shapes. Press remnants and cut off any ragged edges. On clothing, trim off all the seams, then press the fabric.

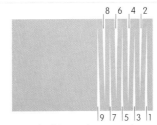

8 6 4 2

9 7 5 3 1

2 Cut or tear the fabric to form a continuous strip, making the cuts/tears 2.5cm (1in) apart in the order shown. Stop each tear/cut about 1.5cm (⅝in) from the fabric edge.

3 As you cut the continuous strip, wind it into a ball. At the end of a strip, knot on the next strip of the same colour. Keep the fabric colours separate so that you can use the different shades to create patterns in your knitting.

KNITTING WITH RAG STRIPS

1 The easiest stitch to work with rag strips is garter stitch. For 2.5cm (1in) wide patchwork-fabric-weight cotton strips, use 10mm (US size 15) needles.

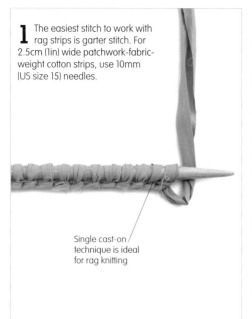

Single cast-on technique is ideal for rag knitting

2 Add interest to rag knitting, by working it in stripes. To change colours, knot on the new colour using the knot technique on page 89. Position the knot as close as possible to the edge of the knitting.

Trim ends to 3cm (1¼in) from knot

3 When you finish your piece of rag knitting, cast off the stitches knitwise (see page 32).

4 You can use your rag knitting to make a rag rug or a simple bag. For a bag, make one long rectangle, fold it in half (with the knots inside the bag) and sew the seams using a sewing thread. Then add a plaited bag handle.

PLARN KNITTING

Most of us have a collection of plastic shopping bags in the house. Cutting them into strips for knitting is a great way to put these bags to use. Because plastic strips (called plarn) are so flexible, they are even easier to knit with than rag strips.

1 Select lightweight plastic bags, as these are easier to knit with than thicker ones and they produce a springier knitted fabric. To cut strips from a bag, begin by smoothing it out flat. Then fold it in half lengthways.

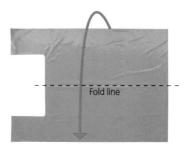

Fold line

2 Smooth the bag out flat again and fold again at the second, third, and fourth fold lines as shown, smoothing the bag out flat after each fold.

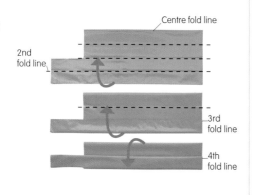

Centre fold line

2nd fold line

3rd fold line

4th fold line

3 Trim off the handles and the seam at the bottom of the folded bag. Then cut segments 3cm (1¼in) wide; each of these form a ring of plastic. Keep these rings folded until you need them.

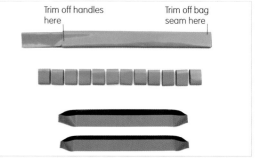

Trim off handles here

Trim off bag seam here

4 To link the rings together, lay one ring out horizontally on the table. Lay a second ring out vertically next to it. Then pass the first ring through the top of the second ring and pass the tail of the second ring through the centre of the first ring. Pull the tail of the second ring to knot it tightly to one end of the first.

Knots linking rings

5 Continue looping the rings together in the same way, rolling the continuous plarn strip into a ball. When the ball gets too big to handle, start a new one.

KNITTING WITH PLARN STRIPS

1 Plarn is very easy to knit into a tube that can be used to make a bag of any size. Prepare the plarn as explained opposite and cast your stitches onto a 9mm (US size 13) circular knitting needle. Knit every round to form stocking stitch (see page 78).

2 At the top of the tube work several rounds in knit and purl alternately to form a garter stitch border. (For handles, cast off and cast on stitches in the first two rounds to form a slot on each side of the bag.) Sew the bottom seam with overcast stitches and a blunt-ended yarn needle threaded with plarn.

KNITTING WITH STRING

If you have balls of old string languishing on a shelf or in a drawer, why not put them to use by knitting them into a useful household item? Because of its relative stiffness, string is perfect for making attractive knitted boxes.

DESIGNING A STRING BOX

Choose a twine of medium thickness. Brightly coloured strings are useful for adding contrasting seams or a border. Using a needle size that will produce a very stiff fabric, knit a tension swatch and calculate how many stitches to cast on for the sides of your box.

KNITTING A STRING BOX

1 So that the top edge of the box won't curl, begin each of the four sides of the box with two rows of garter stitch. Then complete each side in stocking stitch and cast off knitwise on the right side.

2 Once the four sides of the box are complete, work the base of the box in stocking stitch only, making sure the sides will fit it exactly.

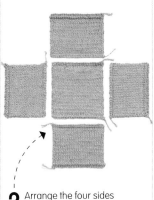

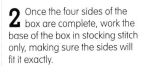

3 Arrange the four sides around the base as shown.

4 Use a length of string in a contrasting colour and a blunt-ended yarn needle to sew the seams. Sew one side to the base with wrong sides together using spaced overcast stitches (see page 70).

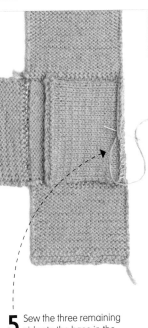

5 Sew the three remaining sides to the base in the same way.

6 Sew the seams joining the sides together in the same way.

CROCHET

All the basic crochet stitches and techniques needed to make the full range of popular crocheted items – including blankets, sweaters, scarves, shawls, accessories, and toys.

TOOLS AND MATERIALS

To get started with crochet, have a look first at the wonderful variety of yarns available. Crochet can be used to create an astounding range of textiles, from sturdy textures suitable for coats to graceful, alluring lace. It requires very little equipment, so is probably the most economical needlework craft.

YARNS

All the yarns available for knitting can also be used for crochet (see pages 12–13). Any yarn can usually be crocheted into an attractive textile using a small range of hook sizes, each of which produces a slightly looser or slightly tighter fabric that holds its shape well.

SMOOTH WOOL YARNS

≪ WOOL YARN WEIGHTS
Super-fine, fine, and lightweight wool yarns work best for crochet garments; the thicker yarns are only suitable for blankets. (A full explanation of yarn weights is given on page 15.)

SYNTHETIC YARNS
Many synthetic fibre yarns or synthetic and natural fibre mixes are very good imitations of pure wool. So if you are looking for a less expensive alternative to wool, try some of these out. They do not age as well as wool, but they are easy to care for.

SMOOTH COTTON YARNS

FINE-WEIGHT COTTON YARNS ≫
This thicker yarn is a good weight for garments and accessories and will show the texture of stitch patterns clearly.

COTTON CROCHET THREADS ≫
Traditionally, crochet was worked in cotton threads that were suitable for lace. Today cotton threads are still used for lace edgings and filet crochet (see pages 144–147 and pages 120–123).

MULTICOLOURED YARNS

"SOCK" YARN
"Sock" yarn is a spaced-dyed yarn originally designed for knitting socks – as the sock is knitted the yarn changes colour along its length and forms patterns. The fine-weight versions of this type of multicoloured yarn can be used for crochet as well, to produce interesting effects.

‹‹ VARIEGATED YARN
Yarns flecked with different colours or dyed different colours along the length of one strand are useful for achieving multi-coloured effects without needing to change yarn or colours.

TEXTURED AND NOVELTY YARNS

‹‹ METALLIC THREAD
A fine, metallic thread is ideally suited to fine openwork crochet for evening shawls and scarves.

FINE MOHAIR YARN ››
This textured yarn will produce a tactile crocheted piece, partially obscuring the stitches.

TEXTURED NOVELTY YARNS
Highly textured yarns, such as bouclés and shaggy "fur" yarns are difficult to crochet with, so stick to simple double crochet when using them. They obscure the crochet stitches and produce an allover textured-effect fabric.

UNUSUAL YARNS

‹‹ COLOURED WIRE
Thin 0.3mm (28 gauge) wire is flexible enough to work in crochet for jewellery (see page 163).

STRING ››
Ideal for crocheting bags and containers (see page 162), string is available in many colours and thicknesses.

FABRIC STRIPS ⌃
Fabric strips can be crocheted to produce household items and accessories.

‹‹ STRIPS CUT FROM PLASTIC BAGS
Crochet works well with unusual materials, such as strips of plastic, for making items with simple double crochet stitches (see page 165).

CROCHET

CROCHET
HOOKS

If you are a beginner, start learning to crochet with a good-quality standard metal crochet hook. Once you know how to work the basic stitches with a lightweight wool yarn and a 4.5mm (US size 7) hook, branch out and try some other types of hooks in order to find the one that suits you best.

STANDARD METAL HOOK

Hook tip

Throat

Hook lip

Shank

Thumb rest

Handle

PARTS OF A CROCHET HOOK ⌵
The hook lip grabs the yarn to form the loops and the shank determines the size of the loop. The crochet handle gives weight to the tool and enhances a good grip.

ALTERNATIVE HOOK HANDLES

COMFORT HANDLE »
Hook handles come in different shapes. If you find the standard crochet hook uncomfortable to hold because it is too narrow, investigate hooks with alternative handles. This is a high-quality Japanese hook designed and refined especially for comfort and good grip.

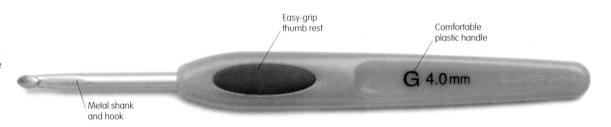

Easy-grip thumb rest

Comfortable plastic handle

Metal shank and hook

G 4.0mm

HOOK TYPES

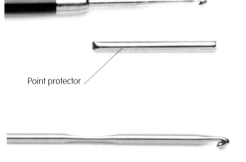

Point protector

‹‹ LACE HOOK
Because lace crochet hooks are so fine, ranging from 0.6mm (US size 14 steel) to 1.75mm (US size 5 steel), they are always manufactured in metal. Keep them with their metal point protectors in place to avoid accidents.

JUMBO HOOKS ⌃
The largest crochet hook sizes – from a 10mm (US size N-15) to a 20mm (US size S) are made in plastic. They are used for making thick crochet fabric very quickly.

‹‹ METAL HOOKS
Some ranges of aluminim hooks are available in bright colours – a different colour for each size, which is handy for picking up the right size at a glance.

HOOK SIZES

Crochet hooks are manufactured in the various sizes (diameters) listed in the hook conversion chart on the opposite page. The millimetre sizes are the diameters of the hook shank, which determines the size of the crochet stitches.

‹‹ WOODEN HOOKS
Hardwood and bamboo hooks are very attractive and lighter in weight than metal hooks. They also provide a good grip to prevent your fingers slipping when crocheting.

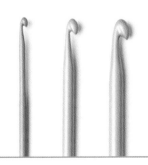

Although the middle range of hook sizes – from 2mm (US size B-1) to 9mm (US size M-13) – are the most commonly used, the finer and thicker hooks are also very popular for lace crochet and jumbo crochet. See page 15 for which hook size to use with the different yarn weights.

‹‹ PLASTIC HOOKS
Plastic hooks are not as precisely made as metal and wooden hooks, but they come in great colours, so are enjoyable to work with.

CONVERSION CHART

This chart gives the conversions between the various hook-size systems. Where there are no exact conversions possible the nearest equivalent is given.

EU METRIC	US SIZES	OLD UK
0.6mm	14 steel	
0.75mm	12 steel	
1mm	11 steel	
1.25mm	7 steel	
1.5mm	6 steel	
1.75mm	5 steel	
2mm		14
2.25mm	B-1	
2.5mm		12
2.75mm	C-2	
3mm		10
3.25mm	D-3	
3.5mm	E-4	9
3.75mm	F-5	
4mm	G-6	8
4.5mm	7	7
5mm	H-8	6
5.5mm	I-9	5
6mm	J-10	4
6.5mm	K-10½	3
7mm		2
8mm	L-11	
9mm	M-13	
10mm	N-15	
12mm	P	
15mm	Q (16mm)	
20mm	S (19mm)	

OTHER EQUIPMENT

To get started you only need a crochet hook and a blunt-ended yarn needle. You may have some of the other essentials in your sewing kit already.

THE ESSENTIALS

TAPE MEASURE ⌃
Keep a tape measure to hand for checking your tension and measuring your crochet.

PINS ⌃
Use pins with glass heads or large heads (such as knitting pins), for seams and blocking (see page 140).

SCISSORS ⌃
Keep a sharp pair of scissors on hand for cutting off yarn and trimming off yarn ends.

BLUNT-ENDED YARN NEEDLES ⌃
Use these for sewing seams and darning in yarn ends (make sure the needle has a big enough eye for your chosen yarn).

HANDY EXTRAS

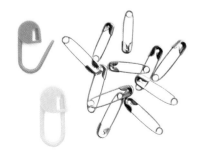

ROW COUNTER ⌄
These are useful for keeping track of where you are in your crochet. String on a length of cotton yarn and hang it around your neck – change it each time you complete a row.

STITCH MARKERS ⌃
These can be hooked onto the crochet to mark a specific row or a specific stitch in the row, or to mark the right-side of your crochet.

YARN BOBBINS ⌃
Useful for holding short lengths of yarn for jacquard crochet (see page 128).

BASIC STITCHES

Learning to crochet takes a little longer than learning to knit because there are several basic stitches to master. But there is no need to learn all the stitches at once. With only chain stitches and double crochet at your disposal, you can make attractive striped blankets and cushion covers in luscious yarns.

GETTING STARTED

Before making your first loop, the slip knot (see opposite page), get to know your hook and how to hold it. First, review the detailed explanation of the parts of the hook on page 96. Then try out the various hook- and yarn-holding techniques below when learning how to make chain stitches. If you ever learned crochet as a child, you will automatically hold the hook the way you originally learned to, and you should stick to this whether it is the pencil or knife position.

HOLDING THE HOOK

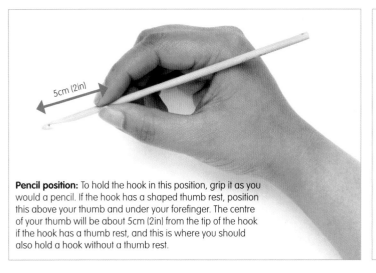

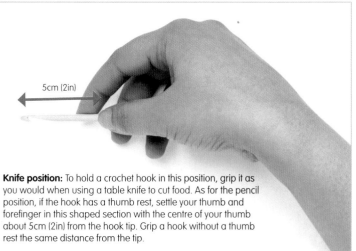

Pencil position: To hold the hook in this position, grip it as you would a pencil. If the hook has a shaped thumb rest, position this above your thumb and under your forefinger. The centre of your thumb will be about 5cm (2in) from the tip of the hook if the hook has a thumb rest, and this is where you should also hold a hook without a thumb rest.

Knife position: To hold a crochet hook in this position, grip it as you would when using a table knife to cut food. As for the pencil position, if the hook has a thumb rest, settle your thumb and forefinger in this shaped section with the centre of your thumb about 5cm (2in) from the hook tip. Grip a hook without a thumb rest the same distance from the tip.

HOLDING THE YARN

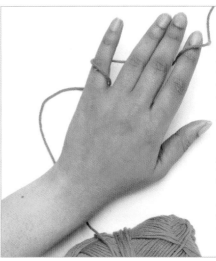

In order to control the flow of the yarn to your hook, you need to lace it around the fingers of your free hand. Both of the techniques shown here are only suggestions, so feel free to develop your own.

Method one: Start by winding the yarn around your little finger, then pass it under your two middle fingers and over your forefinger. With this method the forefinger is used to position the yarn.

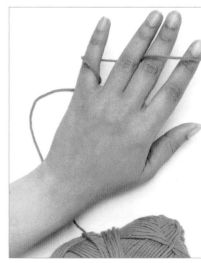

Method two: Wrap the yarn around your little finger, then pass it behind the next finger and over the top of the middle finger and forefinger. This method allows you to position the yarn with either the forefinger or middle finger, whichever is more comfortable and gives you more control (see Tensioning Your Yarn on the opposite page).

MAKING A SLIP KNOT

1 To make the first loop (called the slip knot) on your needle, begin by crossing the yarn coming from the ball over the yarn end (called the yarn tail) to form a circle of yarn.

Yarn coming from ball

Yarn tail

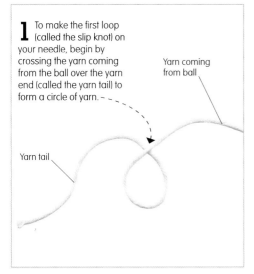

2 Insert the tip of the hook through the circle of yarn.

3 Then use the hook to grab the ball end of the yarn and pull the yarn through the circle.

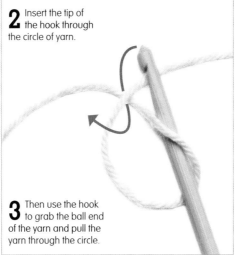

4 This forms a loop on the hook and a loose, open knot below the loop.

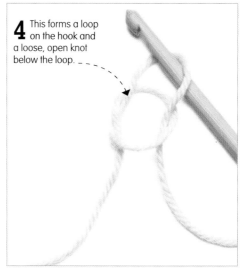

5 Pull both ends of the yarn firmly to tighten the knot and the loop around the shank of the hook.

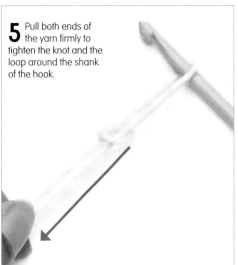

6 Make sure the completed slip knot is tight enough on the hook that it won't fall off but not so tight that you can barely slide it along the hook's shank.

Make sure loop is secure but slides easily

Ball end of yarn

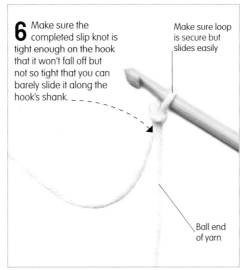

7 The yarn tail on the slip knot should be at least 15cm (6in) long so it can be threaded onto a blunt-ended yarn needle and darned in later. However, a crochet pattern may instruct you to leave an extra-long yarn tail (called a long loose end) to use for seams or other purposes.

Extra-long yarn tail

TENSIONING YOUR YARN

1 With your slip knot on your hook, try out some yarn holding techniques. Wrap the yarn around your little finger and then lace it through your other fingers as desired, but so that it ends up over the tip of your forefinger (or your forefinger and middle finger).

Yarn going to ball

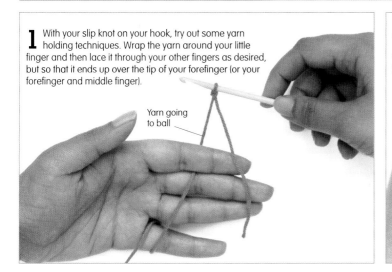

2 As you crochet, grip the yarn tightly with your little finger and ring finger and release it gently as you form the loops. Use either your forefinger or your middle finger to position the yarn, and hold the base of the crochet close to the hook to keep it in place as the hook is drawn through the loops.

Yarn going to ball

Hold your crochet firmly close to the hook

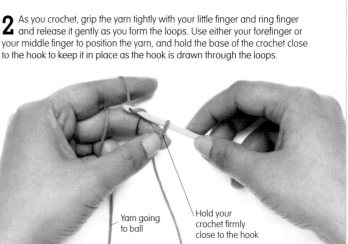

# CHAIN STITCHES
Abbreviation = *ch*

Chain stitches are the first crochet stitches you need to learn because they form the base for all other stitches – called a foundation chain – and for turning chains (see page 108). They are used in combination with other basic stitches to create a vast array of crochet stitch patterns, both dense textured stitches and lacy ones. Practise chain stitches until you are comfortable holding a hook and releasing and tensioning yarn.

MAKING A FOUNDATION CHAIN

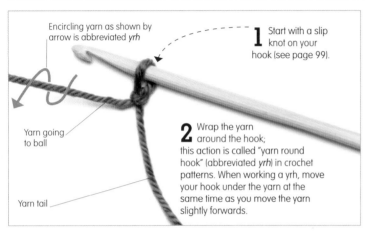

Encircling yarn as shown by arrow is abbreviated *yrh*

Yarn going to ball

Yarn tail

1 Start with a slip knot on your hook (see page 99).

2 Wrap the yarn around the hook; this action is called "yarn round hook" (abbreviated *yrh*) in crochet patterns. When working a yrh, move your hook under the yarn at the same time as you move the yarn slightly forwards.

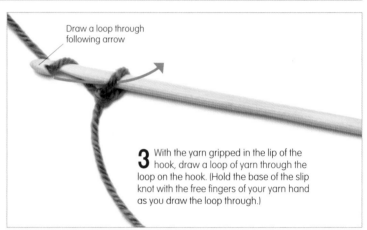

Draw a loop through following arrow

3 With the yarn gripped in the lip of the hook, draw a loop of yarn through the loop on the hook. (Hold the base of the slip knot with the free fingers of your yarn hand as you draw the loop through.)

4 This completes the first chain.

1 chain made

5 Yrh and draw a loop through the loop on the hook for each new stitch.

Front of chain

6 Continue making chains in the same way until you have the number specified in your crochet pattern.

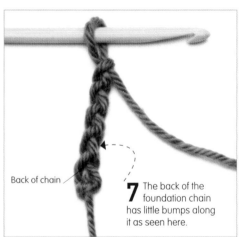

Back of chain

7 The back of the foundation chain has little bumps along it as seen here.

COUNTING CHAIN STITCHES

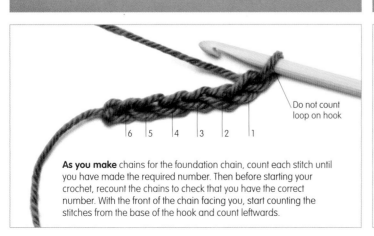

6 5 4 3 2 1

Do not count loop on hook

As you make chains for the foundation chain, count each stitch until you have made the required number. Then before starting your crochet, recount the chains to check that you have the correct number. With the front of the chain facing you, start counting the stitches from the base of the hook and count leftwards.

SIMPLE CHAIN STITCH NECKLACE

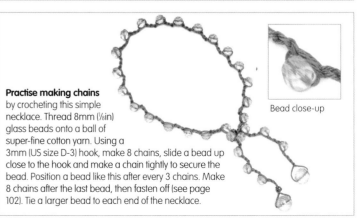

Bead close-up

Practise making chains by crocheting this simple necklace. Thread 8mm (⅛in) glass beads onto a ball of super-fine cotton yarn. Using a 3mm (US size D-3) hook, make 8 chains, slide a bead up close to the hook and make a chain tightly to secure the bead. Position a bead like this after every 3 chains. Make 8 chains after the last bead, then fasten off (see page 102). Tie a larger bead to each end of the necklace.

# SLIP STITCH
Abbreviation = ss

Slip stitches are the shortest of all the crochet stitches. Although they can be worked in rows, the resulting fabric is so dense that it is only really suitable for bag handles. However, slip stitches appear very frequently in crochet instructions – to join in new yarn (see page 107), to work invisibly along the top of a row to move to a new position (see page 137), and to join rounds in circular crochet.

WORKING SLIP STITCH AS A FABRIC

1 Make a foundation chain of the required length. To begin the first stitch, insert the hook through the second chain from the hook, passing the hook under only one strand of the chain. Then wrap the yarn around the hook (yrh).

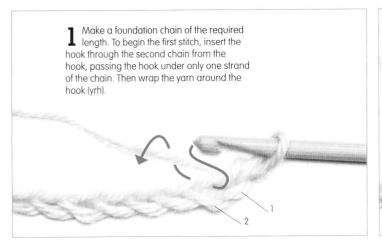

2 Holding the base of the chain firmly with the fingers of your left hand and tensioning the yarn (see page 99), draw a loop back through the chain and through the loop on the hook as shown by the large arrow.

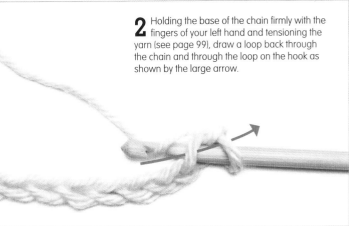

3 Continue across the foundation chain, working a slip stitch into each chain in the same way. Always work slip stitches fairly loosely for whatever purpose you are using them.

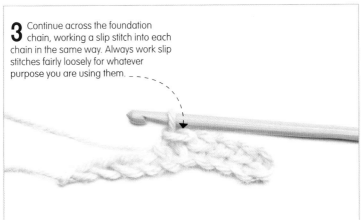

4 After the last stitch of the row has been completed, and if you want to work another row, turn your crochet to position the yarn at the right edge of the piece of crochet ready to begin the second row.

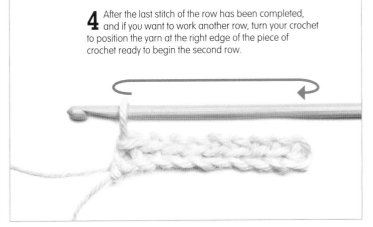

5 To begin a second row of slip stitches, make one chain stitch. This chain is called the turning chain.

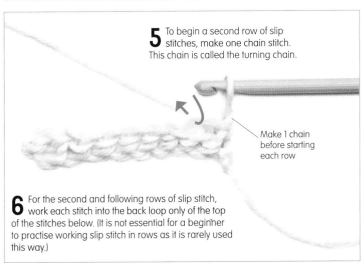

Make 1 chain before starting each row

6 For the second and following rows of slip stitch, work each stitch into the back loop only of the top of the stitches below. (It is not essential for a beginner to practise working slip stitch in rows as it is rarely used this way.)

USING SLIP STITCHES TO FORM A FOUNDATION RING

Slip stitches are also used to form the foundation rings for circular crochet (see page 150). Make the required number of chains for the ring, then insert the hook through the first chain made, wrap the yarn around the hook and draw a loop through the chain and the loop on the hook to close the ring.

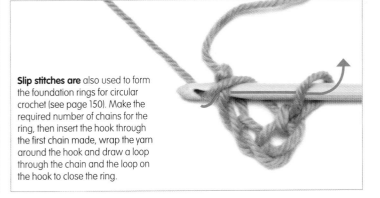

FASTENING OFF
CHAINS AND SLIP STITCHES

Stopping your crochet when it is complete is called fastening off. As there is only one loop on your hook, the process is extremely simple, much quicker and easier than casting off stitches in knitting! Here is a visual aid for how to fasten off a length of chains or a row of slip stitches. The principle is the same for all stitches.

FASTENING OFF A LENGTH OF CHAINS

1 Remove the loop from the hook.

2 Pull out the loop to enlarge it so that it does not start to unravel.

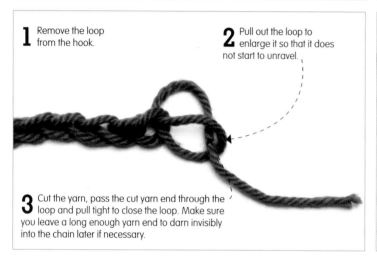

3 Cut the yarn, pass the cut yarn end through the loop and pull tight to close the loop. Make sure you leave a long enough yarn end to darn invisibly into the chain later if necessary.

FASTENING OFF SLIP STITCHES

Fasten off in the same way as for the chain stitches. Alternatively, you can use the hook to draw the cut end through the remaining loop as shown here by the large arrow.

DOUBLE
CROCHET
Abbreviation = *dc*

Double crochet is the easiest crochet stitch to learn and the one crocheters use most frequently, either on its own or in combination with other stitches. Take your time learning and practising the stitch, because once you become proficient in double crochet the taller stitches will be much easier to master. It forms a dense fabric that is suitable for many types of garments and accessories. It is also the stitch used for toys and containers because it can be worked tightly to form a stiff, firm textile.

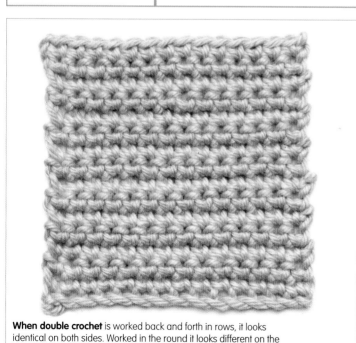

When double crochet is worked back and forth in rows, it looks identical on both sides. Worked in the round it looks different on the right and wrong sides, which you can see page on 150.

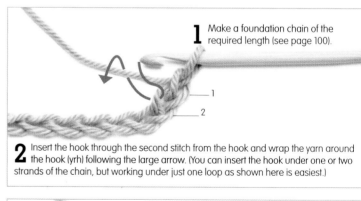

1 Make a foundation chain of the required length (see page 100).

2 Insert the hook through the second stitch from the hook and wrap the yarn around the hook (yrh) following the large arrow. (You can insert the hook under one or two strands of the chain, but working under just one loop as shown here is easiest.)

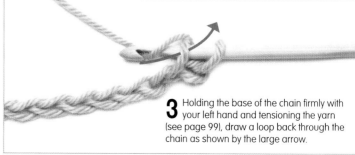

3 Holding the base of the chain firmly with your left hand and tensioning the yarn (see page 99), draw a loop back through the chain as shown by the large arrow.

4 There are now 2 loops on the hook. Next, yrh as shown by the large arrow.

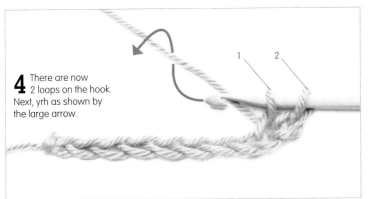

5 Draw a loop through both loops on the hook in one smooth action. As you use the yarn, allow it to flow through the fingers of your left hand while still tensioning it firmly.

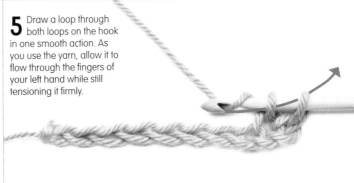

6 This completes the first double crochet. The missed chain at the beginning of this first row does NOT count as a stitch on its own (in other words it is not counted when you count how many stitches are in the row and it is not worked into in the next row).

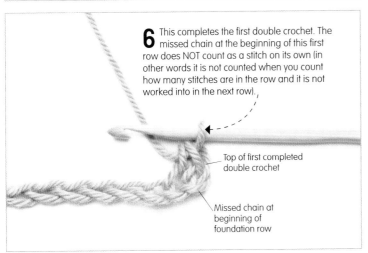

Top of first completed double crochet

Missed chain at beginning of foundation row

7 Continue across the foundation chain, working one double crochet into each chain in the same way.

8 At the end of the row, turn your crochet to position the yarn at the right edge of the piece of crochet, ready to begin the second row.

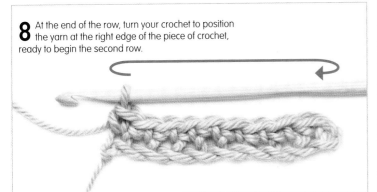

9 To begin the second row, make one chain stitch. This chain is called the turning chain, and it brings the work up to the height of the double crochet stitches that will follow.

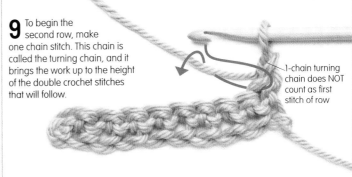

1-chain turning chain does NOT count as first stitch of row

10 Work the first double crochet into the top of the first stitch in the row below. Work a double crochet into the top of each of the remaining double crochets in the row below.

Insert hook under both strands of top of stitch

11 At the end of the row, work the last stitch into the top of the last double crochet of the row below. Work following rows as for the second row.

12 When you have completed your crochet, cut the yarn leaving a long loose end – at least 15cm (6in) long.

13 Remove the hook from the remaining loop, pass the yarn end through the loop and pull tight to close it. Fastening off like this is done the same way for all crochet stitches.

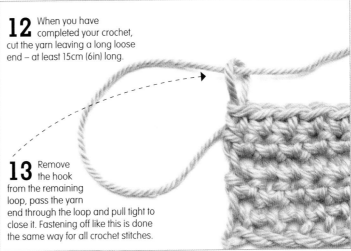

HALF TREBLE
CROCHET
Abbreviation = *htr*

After slip stitches and double crochet, half treble crochet comes next in order of stitch heights (see page 108). It is firm like double crochet and fairly dense, but produces a slightly softer texture, which makes it ideal for warm baby garments. Don't attempt to learn how to work half trebles until you make double crochet stitches with confidence.

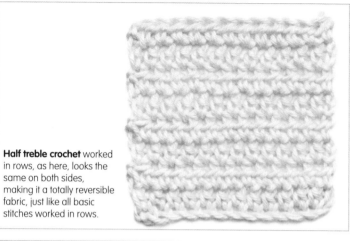

Half treble crochet worked in rows, as here, looks the same on both sides, making it a totally reversible fabric, just like all basic stitches worked in rows.

1 Make a foundation chain of the required length (see page 100). To begin the first stitch, wrap the yarn around the hook (yrh).

2 Insert the hook through the third chain from the hook, yrh again (as shown by the large arrow) and draw a loop back through the chain.

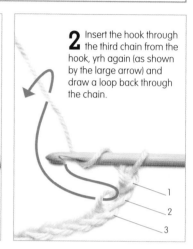

1
2
3

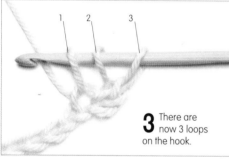

1 2 3

3 There are now 3 loops on the hook.

4 Yrh and draw a loop through all 3 loops on the hook as shown by the large arrow. (This motion becomes more fluid with practice.)

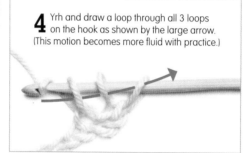

5 This completes the first half treble. (The 2 missed chain stitches at the beginning of the chain do NOT count as the first stitch of the row.)

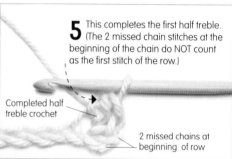

Completed half treble crochet

2 missed chains at beginning of row

6 Work one half treble crochet into each chain in the same way. Remember to start each half treble by wrapping the yarn around the hook before inserting it through the chain.

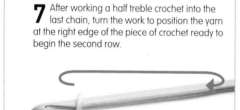

7 After working a half treble crochet into the last chain, turn the work to position the yarn at the right edge of the piece of crochet ready to begin the second row.

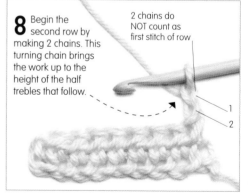

8 Begin the second row by making 2 chains. This turning chain brings the work up to the height of the half trebles that follow.

2 chains do NOT count as first stitch of row

1
2

9 Yrh and work the first half treble into the top of the first stitch in the row below.

Insert hook under both strands of top of stitch

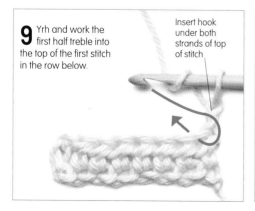

10 Work a half treble into each of the remaining half treble crochets in the row below. Work the following rows as for the second row.

Top of last half treble crochet of previous row

Leave an end at least 15cm (6in) long, so it can be darned in later

11 When the crochet is complete, cut the yarn. Remove the hook from the remaining loop, pass the yarn end through the loop and pull tight to close the loop and fasten off securely.

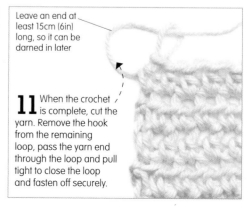

TREBLE CROCHET
Abbreviation = *tr*

Treble crochet produces a more open and softer crochet fabric than the denser double and half treble crochet. Because treble crochet is a tall stitch, the fabric grows quickly as you proceed, which makes it the most popular of all crochet stitches.

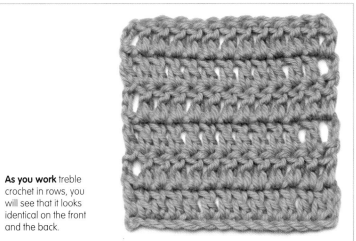

As you work treble crochet in rows, you will see that it looks identical on the front and the back.

1 Make as many chains as required (see page 100). To begin the first stitch, wrap the yarn around the hook (yrh).

Make foundation chain of any length to practise trebles

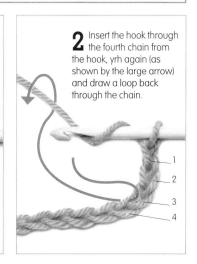

2 Insert the hook through the fourth chain from the hook, yrh again (as shown by the large arrow) and draw a loop back through the chain.

1
2
3
4

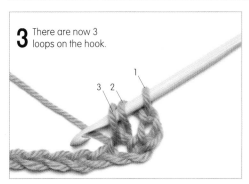

3 There are now 3 loops on the hook.

3 2 1

4 Yrh and draw a loop through the first 2 loops on the hook.

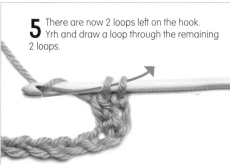

5 There are now 2 loops left on the hook. Yrh and draw a loop through the remaining 2 loops.

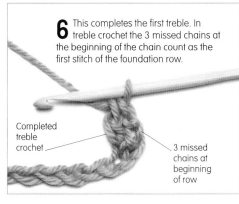

6 This completes the first treble. In treble crochet the 3 missed chains at the beginning of the chain count as the first stitch of the foundation row.

Completed treble crochet

3 missed chains at beginning of row

7 Work one treble crochet into each chain in the same way. Remember to start each stitch with a yrh before inserting the hook through the chain.

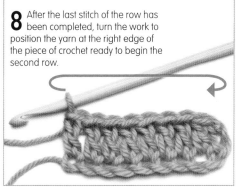

8 After the last stitch of the row has been completed, turn the work to position the yarn at the right edge of the piece of crochet ready to begin the second row.

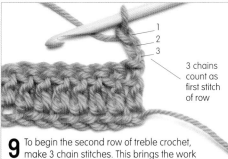

1
2
3

3 chains count as first stitch of row

9 To begin the second row of treble crochet, make 3 chain stitches. This brings the work up to the height of these tall stitches.

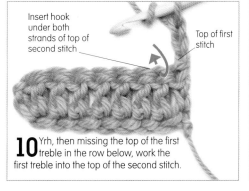

Insert hook under both strands of top of second stitch

Top of first stitch

10 Yrh, then missing the top of the first treble in the row below, work the first treble into the top of the second stitch.

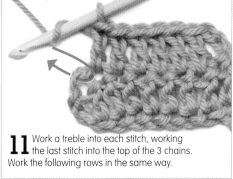

11 Work a treble into each stitch, working the last stitch into the top of the 3 chains. Work the following rows in the same way.

CROCHET

DOUBLE TREBLE CROCHET
Abbreviation = dtr

Worked in a very similar way to treble crochet, double treble crochet stitches are approximately one chain length taller because the stitch is begun with two wraps instead of only one (see page 108). Double trebles are often used in lace crochet (see pages 124–126) and in crochet medallions (see pages 153 and 155).

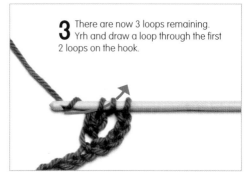

Identical on the front and the back, double treble crochet worked in rows is even softer than treble crochet. It also grows more quickly because the stitches are taller but not that much slower to work.

1 Make a foundation chain, then wrap the yarn twice around the hook (yrh) and insert the hook through the fifth chain from the hook.

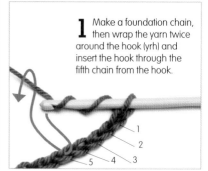

2 Yrh and draw a loop through the chain. There are now 4 loops on the hook. Yrh and draw a loop through the first 2 loops on the hook.

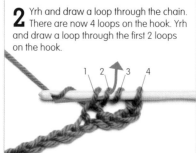

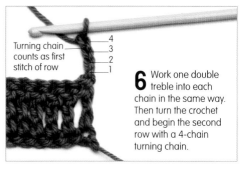

3 There are now 3 loops remaining. Yrh and draw a loop through the first 2 loops on the hook.

4 There are 2 loops remaining. Yrh and draw a loop through these 2 loops.

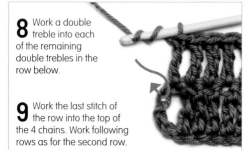

Completed double treble crochet

4 missed chains at beginning count as first stitch of row

5 This completes the first double treble. As for all tall crochet stitches, the missed chain stitches at the beginning of the foundation chain count as the first stitch of the foundation row.

Turning chain counts as first stitch of row

6 Work one double treble into each chain in the same way. Then turn the crochet and begin the second row with a 4-chain turning chain.

Top of first stitch

7 Miss the top of the first double treble in the row below and work the first double treble into the top of the second stitch.

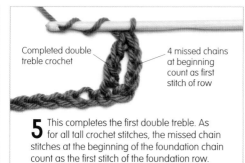

8 Work a double treble into each of the remaining double trebles in the row below.

9 Work the last stitch of the row into the top of the 4 chains. Work following rows as for the second row.

TRIPLE TREBLE CROCHET
Abbreviation = trtr

Stitches taller than double trebles are all worked in the same way as double trebles, except that more wraps are wound around the hook before the stitch is begun and they require taller turning chains. Once you can work triple trebles easily, you will be able to work quadruple and quintuple trebles without much effort.

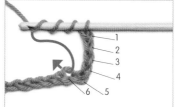

Triple treble crochet worked in rows looks the same on both sides of the fabric. Notice how airy the crochet texture becomes as the basic stitches get taller.

1 Wrap the yarn 3 times around the hook and insert the hook through the sixth stitch from the hook.

5 missed chains count as first stitch of row

2 Work the loops off the hook two at a time as for double trebles. Remember to wrap the yarn three times around the hook before starting each stitch. Start following rows with 5 chains.

BEGINNER'S
TIPS

It is important to learn how to count stitches so you can make sure you retain the same number as your crochet grows. Two other essential techniques are how to join in a new ball of yarn and how to darn in yarn ends when your piece of crochet is complete.

COUNTING CROCHET STITCHES

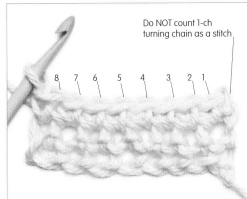

Do NOT count 1-ch turning chain as a stitch

8 7 6 5 4 3 2 1

Counting double crochet stitches: With the front of the last row facing, count the top of each stitch. If you are losing stitches as your crochet grows, then you are probably failing to work into the last stitch in the row below; if you are gaining stitches, you may have worked twice into the same stitch.

Count 3-ch turning chain as first stitch

8 7 6 5 4 3 2 1

Counting trebles: With the front of the last row facing, count the turning chain as the first stitch, then count the top of each treble. If you are losing stitches as your crochet grows, you are probably failing to work into the top of the turning chain; if you are gaining stitches, you may be working into the first treble of the row, instead of missing it.

JOINING IN NEW YARN

New yarn

Old yarn

Method one: Always join on a new yarn at the beginning of a row if possible. Simply drop the old yarn and pull the new yarn through the loop on the hook, then begin the row in the usual way. Darn in the yarn ends later.

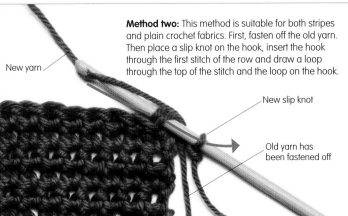

New yarn

New slip knot

Old yarn has been fastened off

Method two: This method is suitable for both stripes and plain crochet fabrics. First, fasten off the old yarn. Then place a slip knot on the hook, insert the hook through the first stitch of the row and draw a loop through the top of the stitch and the loop on the hook.

DARNING IN YARN

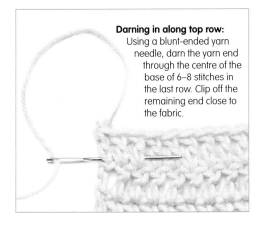

Darning in along top row: Using a blunt-ended yarn needle, darn the yarn end through the centre of the base of 6–8 stitches in the last row. Clip off the remaining end close to the fabric.

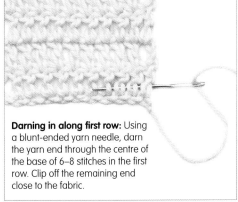

Darning in along first row: Using a blunt-ended yarn needle, darn the yarn end through the centre of the base of 6–8 stitches in the first row. Clip off the remaining end close to the fabric.

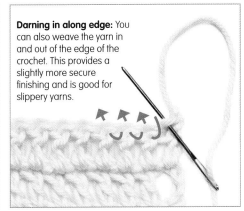

Darning in along edge: You can also weave the yarn in and out of the edge of the crochet. This provides a slightly more secure finishing and is good for slippery yarns.

BASIC STITCHES IN SYMBOLS AND ABBREVIATIONS

Crochet row instructions can be written out with abbreviations or using symbols for the stitches. There is a more detailed explanation for reading stitch pattern instructions on page 114, but directions for the basic stitches are given here in both symbols and abbreviations. This provides an introduction to crochet instructions and a quick reference for how to work crochet fabrics with basic stitches.

STITCH HEIGHTS

The diagram below shows all the basic stitches in symbols and illustrates approximately how tall the stitches are when standing side by side. A double crochet is roughly one chain tall, a half treble crochet two chains tall, a treble crochet three chains tall, and so on. These heights determine the number of turning chains you need to work at the beginning of each row for each of the basic stitches. Also provided here is a reference for which chain to work into when working the first stitch into the foundation chain.

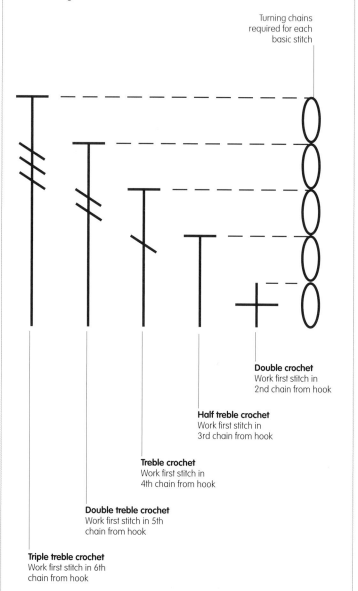

Turning chains required for each basic stitch

Double crochet
Work first stitch in 2nd chain from hook

Half treble crochet
Work first stitch in 3rd chain from hook

Treble crochet
Work first stitch in 4th chain from hook

Double treble crochet
Work first stitch in 5th chain from hook

Triple treble crochet
Work first stitch in 6th chain from hook

DOUBLE CROCHET INSTRUCTIONS

Crochet symbol instructions, especially for the basic stitches, are super-easy to understand. Roughly imitating the size and shape of the stitch, the symbols are read from the bottom of the diagram upwards. To get used to very simple crochet instructions, try working double crochet following the written directions and the symbol diagram at the same time (see page 115 for abbreviations list), then try this with the other basic stitches as well.

DOUBLE CROCHET IN ABBREVIATIONS
Make any number of ch.
Row 1 1 dc in 2nd ch from hook, 1 dc in each of rem ch to end, turn.
Row 2 1 ch (does NOT count as a st), 1 dc in each dc to end, turn.
Rep row 2 to form dc fabric.

3 Follow the diagram from left to right as per arrow

4 Continue working rows back and forth as many times as desired

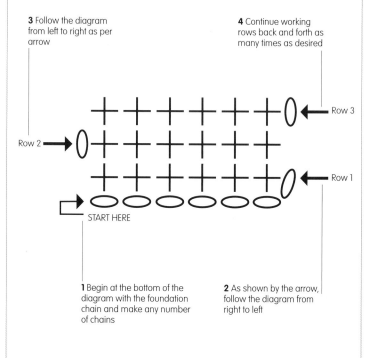

Row 2 →

Row 3

Row 1

START HERE

1 Begin at the bottom of the diagram with the foundation chain and make any number of chains

2 As shown by the arrow, follow the diagram from right to left

HALF TREBLE CROCHET INSTRUCTIONS

The symbol for half treble is a vertical line with a horizontal bar at the top, and it is about twice as tall as the double crochet symbol, just like the stitch is in real life. Read the written instructions for this basic stitch (below) and look at the chart at the same time. The direction of each arrow indicates whether to read the chart from left to right or right to left.

HALF TREBLE CROCHET IN ABBREVIATIONS
Make any number of ch.
Row 1 1 htr in 3rd ch from hook, 1 htr in each of rem ch to end, turn.
Row 2 2 ch (does NOT count as a st), 1 htr in each htr to end, turn.
Rep row 2 to form htr fabric.

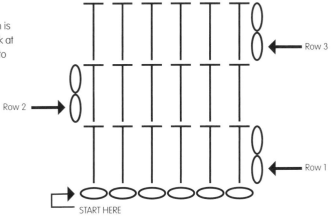

Row 3

Row 2

Row 1

START HERE

TREBLE CROCHET INSTRUCTIONS

The treble symbol has a short diagonal line across its "waist". The diagram shows clearly how the 3-chain turning chain counts as the first stitch of each row.

TREBLE CROCHET IN ABBREVIATIONS
Make any number of ch.
Row 1 1 tr in 4th ch from hook, 1 tr in each or rem ch to end, turn.
Row 2 3 ch (counts as first tr), miss first tr in row below, *1 tr in next tr; rep from * to end, then work 1 tr in top of 3-ch at end, turn.
Rep row 2 to form tr fabric.

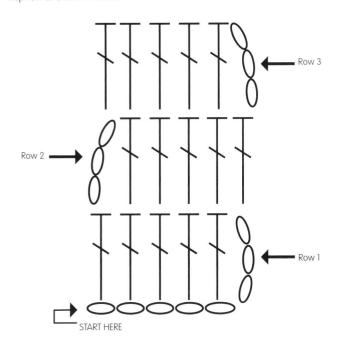

Row 3

Row 2

Row 1

START HERE

DOUBLE TREBLE CROCHET INSTRUCTIONS

Two short diagonal lines cross the "waist" of the double treble symbol, echoing the two diagonal yarn strands on the stitch itself.

DOUBLE TREBLE CROCHET IN ABBREVIATIONS
Make any number of ch.
Row 1 1 dtr in 5th ch from hook, 1 dtr in each of rem ch to end, turn.
Row 2 4 ch (counts as first dtr), miss first dtr in row below, *1 dtr in next dtr; rep from * to end, then work 1 dtr in top of 4-ch at end, turn.
Rep row 2 to form dtr fabric.

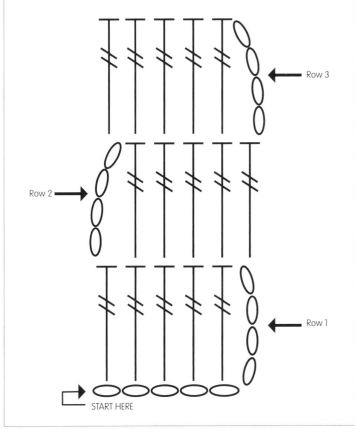

Row 3

Row 2

Row 1

START HERE

STITCH TECHNIQUES

The basic crochet stitches can be combined together in various ways to create endless textures and sculptured effects. Not all the vast range of crochet stitch techniques can be included, but the most commonly used are explained here in detail. When attempting the stitch patterns on pages 116–118, refer back to these step-by-step instructions to see more clearly how to achieve the textures.

SIMPLE TEXTURES

The simplest and most subtle crochet textures are created by working into various parts of the stitches or between the stitches in the row below. Before trying out any of these techniques, learn about the parts of the stitches so you can identify them easily.

PARTS OF STITCHES

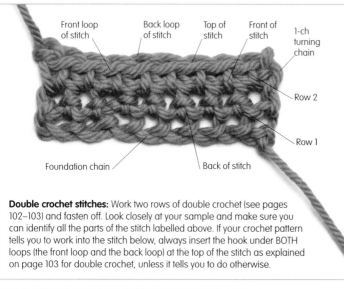

Double crochet stitches: Work two rows of double crochet (see pages 102–103) and fasten off. Look closely at your sample and make sure you can identify all the parts of the stitch labelled above. If your crochet pattern tells you to work into the stitch below, always insert the hook under BOTH loops (the front loop and the back loop) at the top of the stitch as explained on page 103 for double crochet, unless it tells you to do otherwise.

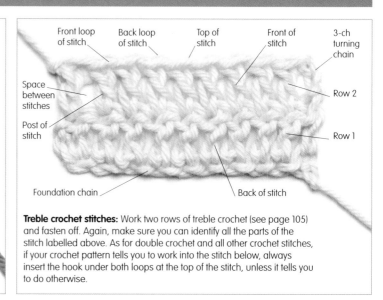

Treble crochet stitches: Work two rows of treble crochet (see page 105) and fasten off. Again, make sure you can identify all the parts of the stitch labelled above. As for double crochet and all other crochet stitches, if your crochet pattern tells you to work into the stitch below, always insert the hook under both loops at the top of the stitch, unless it tells you to do otherwise.

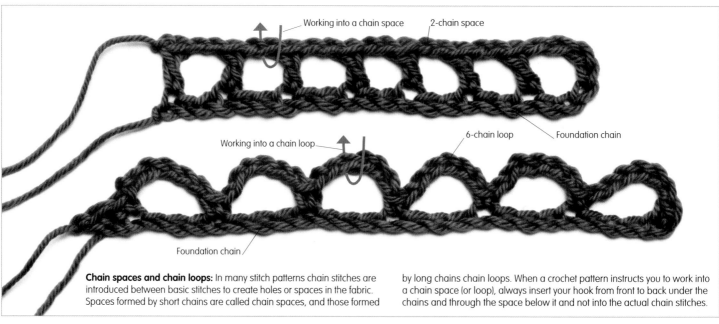

Chain spaces and chain loops: In many stitch patterns chain stitches are introduced between basic stitches to create holes or spaces in the fabric. Spaces formed by short chains are called chain spaces, and those formed by long chains chain loops. When a crochet pattern instructs you to work into a chain space (or loop), always insert your hook from front to back under the chains and through the space below it and not into the actual chain stitches.

WORKING INTO THE BACK OF A DOUBLE CROCHET

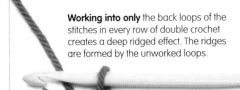

Working into only the back loops of the stitches in every row of double crochet creates a deep ridged effect. The ridges are formed by the unworked loops.

WORKING INTO THE FRONT OF A DOUBLE CROCHET

Working into only the front loop of each double crochet in the row below, on every row, creates a less pronounced texture than working into only the back loop.

WORKING INTO THE BACK OF A TREBLE CROCHET

The same techniques shown for working into the back or front of a double crochet can be used on all crochet stitches to create ridges. The fabric looks the same on both sides.

WORKING INTO SPACES BETWEEN STITCHES

Another way to achieve a subtly different texture with basic stitches is to work the stitches into the spaces between the stitches in the row below, instead of into the tops of the stitches.

WORKING INTO A CHAIN SPACE

Tweed stitch illustrates the simplest of all textures created by working into a chain space. Here double crochet stitches are worked in the 1-chain spaces between the stitches in the row below instead of into the tops of the stitches.

Tweed stitch pattern
Because it is such a popular stitch and a perfect alternative for basic double crochet, the pattern for it is given here. (See page 115 for abbreviations.) Start with an even number of chains.
Row 1 1 dc in 2nd ch from hook, *1 ch, miss next ch, 1 dc in next ch; rep from * to end, turn.
Row 2 1 ch (does NOT count as a stitch), 1 dc in first dc, 1 dc in next 1-ch sp, *1 ch, 1 dc in next 1-ch sp; rep from * to last dc, 1 dc in last dc, turn.
Row 3 1 ch (does NOT count as a stitch), 1 dc in first dc, *1 ch, 1 dc in next 1-ch sp; rep from * to last 2 dc, 1 ch, miss next dc, 1 dc in last dc, turn.
Rep rows 2 and 3 to form patt.

SCULPTURAL TEXTURES

These easy raised and grouped crochet stitch techniques produce attractive sculptural textures. Although they can be used to create fairly dense stitch patterns (see pages 116–118), they are also found in lace stitches (see pages 124–126).

WORKING A TREBLE CROCHET AROUND POST FROM FRONT

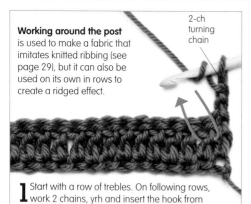

Working around the post is used to make a fabric that imitates knitted ribbing (see page 29), but it can also be used on its own in rows to create a ridged effect.

2-ch turning chain

1 Start with a row of trebles. On following rows, work 2 chains, yrh and insert the hook from the front around the post of the second treble.

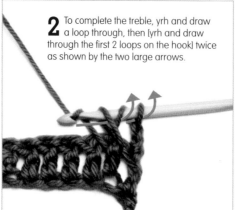

2 To complete the treble, yrh and draw a loop through, then [yrh and draw through the first 2 loops on the hook] twice as shown by the two large arrows.

3 Work a treble around each of the following trebles in the row below in the same way.

4 At the end of the row, work a treble into the top of the turning chain. Repeat the second row to form a ridged texture.

WORKING A TREBLE CROCHET AROUND POST FROM BACK

1 Start by working a base row of treble crochet. To start the second row, work 2 chains, yrh and insert the hook from the back around the post of the second treble.

2-ch turning chain

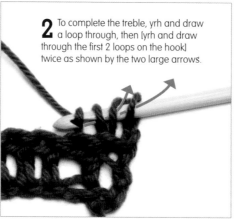

2 To complete the treble, yrh and draw a loop through, then [yrh and draw through the first 2 loops on the hook] twice as shown by the two large arrows.

3 Work a treble around each of the trebles in the row below in the same way. Continue as for Step 4 of the technique above.

SHELLS

4-tr shell: Shells are the most frequently used of all crochet stitch techniques. Usually made with trebles, they are formed by working several stitches into the same stitch or space. Here 4 trebles have been worked into the same chain to form a 4-tr shell.

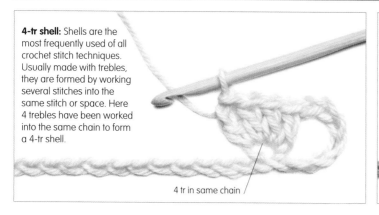

4 tr in same chain

5-tr shell: Here 5 trebles have been worked into the same chain to form a 5-tr shell. Any number of trebles can be used to form a shell, but the most commonly used crochet shells have 2, 3, 4, 5, or 6 stitches. Shells can also be made with half trebles and taller basic stitches.

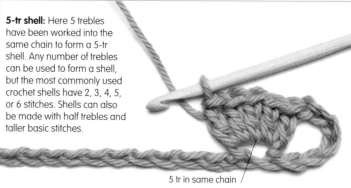

5 tr in same chain

CLUSTERS

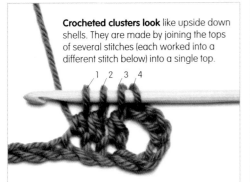

Crocheted clusters look like upside down shells. They are made by joining the tops of several stitches (each worked into a different stitch below) into a single top.

1 To make a 3-tr cluster, work a treble up to the last yrh that completes the treble. Then work an incomplete treble into each of the next 2 stitches in the same way. There are now 4 loops on the hook.

2 Wrap the yarn around the hook and draw a loop through all 4 loops on the hook.

3 This completes all of the trebles at the same time and joins them at the top. Clusters can be made with 2, 3, 4, 5, 6 or more trebles, and with half trebles or taller basic stitches as well.

BOBBLES

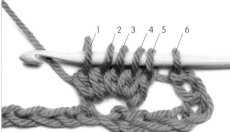

Bobbles are formed using the shell technique and the cluster technique so that the stitches are joined together at the top and the bottom.

1 To work a 5-tr bobble, work 5 incomplete trebles (as for a cluster) into the same stitch (as for a shell). There are now 6 loops on the hook.

2 Wrap the yarn around the hook and draw a loop through all 6 loops on the hook.

3 This completes all of the trebles at the same time and joins them at the top. Some bobbles are completed with an extra chain as shown by the large arrow. Bobbles are usually made with 3, 4, or 5 trebles. Bobbles made with half trebles are called puff stitches.

POPCORNS

1 Popcorns are started like shells. To make a 5-tr popcorn, begin by working 5 trebles in the same stitch.

2 Remove the hook from the loop and insert it from back to front through the top of the first treble of the group. Draw the working loop through the top of the first treble as shown by the large arrow.

3 This pulls the tops of the shells together to form a bobble-type shape. Unlike the top of a bobble, the top of a popcorn protrudes forwards because of the method of construction. Popcorns are usually made with 3, 4, or 5 trebles.

FOLLOWING SIMPLE STITCH PATTERNS

Working a project from a crochet pattern for the first time can seem difficult for a beginner, especially if an experienced crocheter is not at hand as a guide. The best way to prepare for a crochet pattern is first to practise crocheting rectangles of various stitch patterns using simple stitch techniques. This is a good introduction to following abbreviated written row instructions and symbol diagrams.

UNDERSTANDING WRITTEN INSTRUCTIONS

As long as you know how to work all the basic stitches and can work them from the simple patterns on pages 108 and 109 and have reviewed pages 110–113 where special stitch techniques are explained, there is nothing stopping you trying to work the simple textures stitch patterns on pages 116–118. Simply consult the list on the opposite page for the meanings of the various abbreviations and follow the written row instructions one step at a time.

Begin by making the required number of chains for the foundation chain, using your chosen yarn and one of the hook sizes recommended for this yarn weight on page 15. Crochet a swatch that repeats the pattern only a few times

to test it out. (If you decide to make a blanket or cushion cover with the stitch later, you can adjust the hook size before starting it to obtain the exact flexibility of fabric you desire.)

Work each row of the stitch pattern slowly and mark the right side of the fabric (if there is one) as soon as you start, by tying a contrasting coloured thread to it. Another good tip is to tick off the rows as you complete them or put a sticky note under them so you don't lose your place in the pattern. If you do get lost in all the stitches, pull out all the rows and start from the foundation-chain again.

UNDERSTANDING STITCH SYMBOL DIAGRAMS

Crochet stitch patterns can also be given in symbols (see opposite page). These diagrams are usually even easier to follow than directions with abbreviations because they create a visual reference of approximately how the finished stitch will look. Each basic stitch on the chart is represented by a symbol that resembles it in some way. The position of the base of each stitch symbol indicates which stitch or chain space it is worked into in the row below. If the symbols are joined at the base, this means that they are worked into the same stitch in the row below.

The beginning of the foundation chain will be marked as your starting point on the diagram. Read each row on the diagram either from right to left or left to right following the direction of the arrow. Although you can consult the

written instructions for how many chains to make for a foundation chain and how to repeat the stitch repeat across a row (or a row repeat up the fabric), it is easy to work these out yourself from the diagram once you become proficient in reading diagrams. But to begin with, work from the written instructions and use the diagram as a visual aid. Once you have completed the first few rows of the pattern, you can dispense with the written instructions all together and continue with the diagram as your sole guide. If the stitch is an easy one, you will very quickly be able to work it without looking at any instructions at all.

This symbol diagram for the open shell stitch (see page 124) is a good introduction to working from a symbol diagram. Start at the bottom of the diagram and follow it row by row with the aid of the numbered tips.

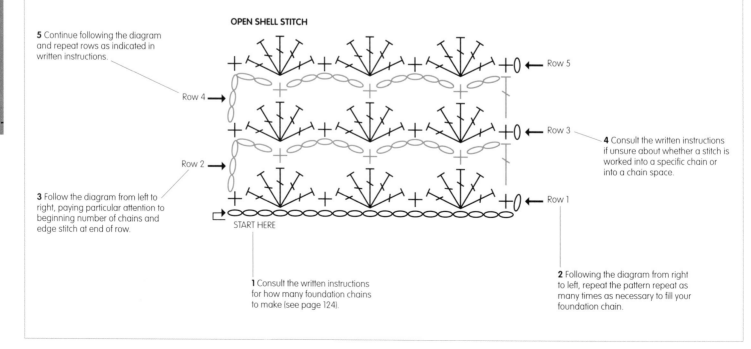

OPEN SHELL STITCH

5 Continue following the diagram and repeat rows as indicated in written instructions.

Row 4 ➡

3 Follow the diagram from left to right, paying particular attention to beginning number of chains and edge stitch at end of row.

Row 2 ➡

← Row 5

← Row 3

4 Consult the written instructions if unsure about whether a stitch is worked into a specific chain or into a chain space.

← Row 1

START HERE

1 Consult the written instructions for how many foundation chains to make (see page 124).

2 Following the diagram from right to left, repeat the pattern repeat as many times as necessary to fill your foundation chain.

CROCHET

CROCHET ABBREVIATIONS

These are the abbreviations most commonly used in crochet patterns. The abbreviations for the basic stitches are listed first and the other abbreviations found in crochet patterns follow. Any special abbreviations in a crochet pattern will always be explained in the pattern.

Abbreviations for basic stitches
Note: The names for the basic crochet stitches differ in the UK and the US. This book uses UK crochet terminology, so if you have learned to crochet in the US, be sure to take note of the difference in terminology.

ch	chain
ss	slip stitch
dc	double crochet (US single crochet – sc)
htr	half treble (US half double crochet – hdc)
tr	treble (US double crochet – dc)
dtr	double treble (US treble crochet – tr)
trtr	triple treble (US double treble crochet – dtr)
qtr	quadruple treble (US triple treble crochet – trtr)
quintr	quintuple treble (US quadruple treble – quadtr)

Other abbreviations
alt	alternate
beg	begin(ning)
cm	centimetre(s)
cont	continu(e)(ing)
dc2tog	see Crochet Terminology
dc3tog	see Crochet Terminology
dec	decreas(e)(ing)
foll	follow(s)(ing)
g	gram(s)
htr2tog	see Crochet Terminology
htr3tog	see Crochet Terminology
in	inch(es)
inc	increase(e)(ing)
m	metre(s)
mm	millimetre(s)
oz	ounce(s)
patt(s)	pattern(s)
rem	remain(s)(ing)
rep	repeat(s)(ing)
RS	right side
sp	space(s)
st(s)	stitch(es)
tog	together
tr2tog	see Crochet Terminology
tr3tog	see Crochet Terminology
WS	wrong side
yd	yard(s)
yrh	yarn round hook (US yarn over hook – yo)

* Repeat instructions after asterisk or between asterisks as many times as instructed.
[ ] Repeat instructions inside square brackets as many times as instructed.

CROCHET TERMINOLOGY

The following terms are commonly used in crochet patterns. Many crochet terms are the same in the UK and the US, but where they differ, the US equivalent is given in parentheses. Turn to the pages indicated for how to work the various increases, decreases, or stitch techniques listed.

bobble: Several stitches worked into the same stitch in the row below and joined together at the top (see page 113).
cluster: Several stitches worked into different stitches in the row below, but joined together at the top (see page 113).
dc2tog (work 2 dc together): See page 136. (US sc2tog)
dc3tog (work 3 dc together): [Insert hook in next st, yrh and draw a loop through] 3 times, yrh and draw through all 4 loops on hook – 2 sts decreased. (US sc3tog)
fasten off: Cut the yarn and draw the yarn tail through the remaining loop on the hook (see page 102).
foundation chain: The base of chain stitches that the first row of crochet is worked onto.
foundation row: The first row of a piece of crochet (the row worked onto the foundation chain) is sometimes called the foundation row.
htr2tog (work 2 htr together): [Yrh and insert hook in next st, yrh and draw a loop through] twice, yrh and draw through all 5 loops on hook – 1 st decreased. (US hdc2tog)
htr3tog (work 3 htr together): [Yrh and insert hook in next st, yrh and draw a loop through] 3 times, yrh and draw

through all 7 loops on hook – 2 sts decreased. (US hdc3tog)
miss a stitch: Do not work into the stitch, but go on to the next stitch. (US "skip" a stitch).
shell: Several stitches worked into the same stitch in the previous row or into the same chain space (see page 112).
pineapple: A bobble made with half trebles; also called a puff stitch.
popcorn: A type of bobble (see page 113).
puff stitch: See pineapple.
tr2tog (work 2 tr together): See page 137. (US dc2tog.)
tr3tog (work 3 tr together): [Yrh and insert hook in next st, yrh and draw a loop through, yrh and draw through first 2 loops on hook] 3 times, yrh and draw through all 4 loops on hook – 2 sts decreased. (US dc3tog)
turning chain: The chain/s worked at the beginning of the row (or round) to bring the hook up to the correct height for working the following stitches in the row (see page 108).

CROCHET STITCH SYMBOLS

These are the symbols used in this book, but crochet symbols are not universal so always consult the key with your crochet instructions for the symbols used in your pattern.

Basic stitches

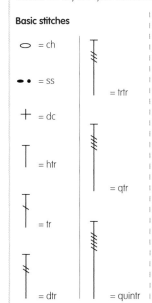

Special stitches and stitch combinations

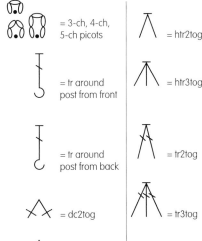

 = 3-ch, 4-ch, 5-ch picots

 = htr2tog

 = htr3tog

= 3 dc in same st

= 2 htr in same st

= 3 htr in same st

Shells, cluster, bobbles, popcorns

 = 2-, 3-, 4-, 5-, 6-tr shells (see page 112)

 = 2-, 3-, 4-, 5-, 6-tr clusters (see page 113)

 = 3-, 4-, 5-tr bobbles (see page 113)

 = 3-, 4-, 5-tr popcorns (see page 113)

CROCHET

SIMPLE TEXTURES STITCH PATTERNS

Selected for how easy they are to work, these stitch patterns cover an array of crochet textures, including those made using the techniques explained on pages 110–113. Although crochet is often identified with lacy openwork fabrics, there are also lots of solid textures like these to choose from. Quick to work and easy to memorize after the first few rows, the following stitches would make lovely cushion covers, baby blankets, or throws. They all look good on both sides of the fabrics and two are completely reversible (see Special Notes).

CROCHET RIB STITCH

CROCHET DIAGRAM

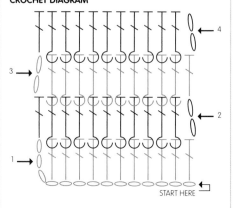

CROCHET INSTRUCTIONS
Make a multiple of 2 ch.
Row 1 1 tr in 4th ch from hook, 1 tr in each of rem ch, turn.
Row 2 2 ch (counts as first st), miss first tr, *1 tr around post of next tr from front, 1 tr around post of next tr from back; rep from * to end, 1 tr in top of turning ch at end, turn.
Rep row 2 to form patt.

SIMPLE CROSSED STITCH

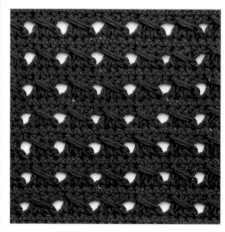

CROCHET DIAGRAM

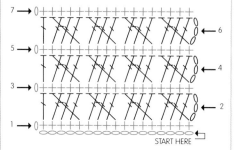

CROCHET INSTRUCTIONS
Make a multiple of 4 ch, plus 2 extra.
Row 1 1 dc in 2nd ch from hook, 1 dc in each of rem ch, turn.
Row 2 (RS) 3 ch (counts as first tr), miss first dc, 1 tr in each of next 3 dc, yrh and insert hook from front to back in first dc (the missed dc), yrh and draw a long loop through (extending the loop that so it reaches back to position of work and does not squash 3-tr group just made), (yrh and draw through first 2 loops on hook) twice – called long tr–, *miss next dc, 1 tr in each of next 3 dc, 1 long tr in last missed dc; rep from * to last dc, 1 tr in last dc, turn.
Row 3 1 ch (does NOT count as a st), 1 dc in each tr to end (do NOT work a dc in 3-ch turning chain), turn.
Rep rows 2 and 3 to form patt.

CLOSE SHELLS STITCH

CROCHET DIAGRAM

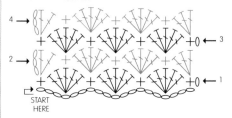

CROCHET INSTRUCTIONS
Make a multiple of 6 ch, plus 2 extra.
Row 1 1 dc in 2nd ch from hook, *miss next 2 ch, 5 tr in next ch, miss next 2 ch, 1 dc in next ch; rep from * to end, turn.
Row 2 3 ch (counts as first tr), 2 tr in first dc, *miss next 2 tr, 1 dc in next tr, 5 tr in next dc (between shells); rep from *, ending last rep with 3 tr in last dc (instead of 5 tr), turn.
Row 3 1 ch (does NOT count as a st), 1 dc in first tr, 5 tr in next dc (between shells), miss next 2 tr, 1 dc in next tr; rep from *, working last dc in top of 3-ch at end, turn.
Rep rows 2 and 3 to form patt.

SPECIAL NOTES

• Both written and symbol instructions are given for all the Simple Textures Stitch Patterns. To get started, beginners should follow the written instructions for the first few rows, referring to the symbols for clarification. See page 115 for a list of crochet abbreviations and basic stitch symbols. If a special symbol is used in a diagram, this symbol is explained in the accompanying key. A complete explanation of how to read a crochet symbol diagram is included on page 114.

• Where there is no right side or wrong side marked in the instructions of a stitch, it looks exactly the same on both sides of the fabric. The crochet rib stitch and the close shells stitch (opposite) are examples of this – they are completely reversible.

SIMPLE BOBBLE STITCH

CROCHET DIAGRAM

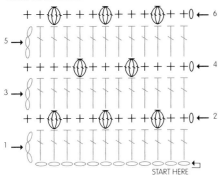

CROCHET INSTRUCTIONS
Note: bobble = (yrh and insert hook in specified st, yrh and draw a loop through, yrh and draw through first 2 loops on hook) 4 times all in same st (5 loops now on hook), yrh and draw through all 5 loops on hook (see page 113).
Make a multiple of 4 ch, plus 3 extra.
Row 1 (WS) 1 tr in 4th ch from hook, 1 tr in each of rem ch, turn.
Row 2 (RS) 1 ch (does NOT count as a st), 1 dc in each of first 2 tr, *1 bobble in next tr, 1 dc in each of next 3 tr; rep from * to last 2 tr, 1 bobble in next tr, 1 dc in next tr, 1 dc in top of 3-ch at end, turn.
Row 3 3 ch (counts as first tr), miss first dc and work 1 tr in each st to end, turn.
Row 4 1 ch (does NOT count as a st), 1 dc in each of first 4 tr, *1 bobble in next tr, 1 dc in each of next 3 tr; rep from *, ending with 1 dc in top of 3-ch at end, turn.
Row 5 Rep row 3.
Rep rows 2–5 to form patt, ending with a patt row 5.

CLUSTER AND SHELL STITCH

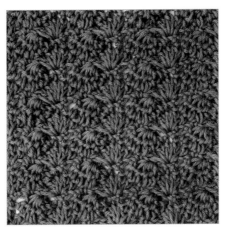

CROCHET DIAGRAM

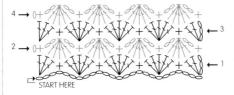

CROCHET INSTRUCTIONS
Note: cluster (also called dc5tog) = over next 5 sts (which include 2 tr, 1 dc, 2 tr) work (yrh and insert hook in next st, yrh and draw a loop through, yrh and draw through first 2 loops on hook) 5 times (6 loops now on hook), yrh and draw through all 6 loops on hook (see page 113).
Make a multiple of 6 ch, plus 4 extra.
Row 1 (RS) 2 tr in 4th ch from hook, miss next 2 ch, 1 dc in next ch, *miss next 2 ch, 5 tr in next ch, miss next 2 ch, 1 dc in next ch: rep from * to last 3 ch, miss next 2 ch, 3 tr in last ch, turn.
Row 2 1 ch (does NOT count as a st), 1 dc in first tr, *2 ch, 1 cluster over next 5 sts, 2 ch, 1 dc in next tr (centre tr of 5-tr group); rep from *, working last dc of last rep in top of 3-ch at end, turn.
Row 3 3 ch (counts as first tr), 2 tr in first dc, miss next 2 ch, 1 dc in next st (top of first cluster), *5 tr in next dc, miss next 2 ch, 1 dc in next st (top of next cluster); rep from *, ending with 3 tr in last dc, turn.
Rep rows 2 and 3 to form patt.

SHELLS AND CHAINS

CROCHET DIAGRAM

CROCHET INSTRUCTIONS
Make a multiple of 6 ch, plus 2 extra.
Row 1 (RS) 1 dc in 2nd ch from hook, *miss next 2 ch, work (1 tr, 1 ch, 1 tr, 1 ch, 1 tr) all in next ch, miss next 2 ch, 1 dc in next ch; rep from * to end, turn.
Row 2 4 ch (counts as 1 tr and a 1-ch sp), 1 tr in first dc, miss next tr, 1 dc in next tr (centre tr of shell), *work (1 tr, 1 ch, 1 tr, 1 ch, 1 tr) all in next dc (between shells), miss next tr, 1 dc in next tr (centre tr of shell); rep from *, ending with (1 tr, 1 ch, 1 tr) in last dc, turn.
Row 3 1 ch (does NOT count as a st), 1 dc in first tr, *work (1 tr, 1 ch, 1 tr, 1 ch, 1 tr) all in next dc, miss next tr, 1 dc in next tr (centre tr of shell); rep from *, working last dc of last rep in 3rd of 4-ch made at beg of previous row, turn.
Rep rows 2 and 3 to form patt.

CROCHET

• Refer to page 115 for a complete list of crochet abbreviations and an explanation of all the most commonly used crochet symbols. The written instructions explain how many chains to start with and which rows to repeat to form the pattern. So if working from the diagram, be sure to read the written instructions first for guidance.

• Make a test swatch of your chosen stitch pattern before starting to make a cushion cover, baby blanket, or throw from any of these textured stitches. Try out various yarns to see which suits your purpose. Tightly spun yarns are the best for showing off the sculptural aspects of textured stitches. Keep in mind that dense crochet textures need not be stiff and unyielding. If your sample swatch is not soft and pliable enough, try working another swatch with a larger hook size to loosen up the fabric a little. For baby blankets, super-fine cotton, or washable wool yarns are the most baby friendly.

POPCORN PATTERN STITCH

CROCHET DIAGRAM

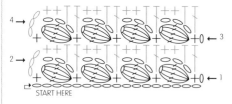

CROCHET INSTRUCTIONS
Note: popcorn = 5 tr all in same st, carefully remove loop from hook and insert it through top of first tr of this 5-tr group, pull loop (the one removed from hook) through first tr (see page 113).
Make a multiple of 4 ch, plus 2 extra.
Row 1 (RS) 1 dc in 2nd ch from hook, *3 ch, 1 popcorn in same place as last dc, miss next 3 ch, 1 dc in next ch; rep from * to end, turn.
Row 2 3 ch (counts as first tr), *work [2 dc, 1 htr] all in next 3-ch sp, 1 tr in next dc; rep from * to end, turn.
Row 3 1 ch (does NOT count as a st), 1 dc in first tr, *3 ch, 1 popcorn in same place as last dc, miss next 3 sts, 1 dc in next tr; rep from *, working last dc of last rep in top of 3-ch at end, turn.
Rep rows 2 and 3 to form patt.

SIMPLE PUFF STITCH

CROCHET DIAGRAM

KEY

4-htr puff stitch

CROCHET INSTRUCTIONS
Note: puff stitch = [yrh and insert hook in st] 4 times all in same st (9 loops now on hook), yrh and draw through all 9 loops on hook to complete 4-htr puff stitch.
Make a multiple of 2 ch.
Row 1 (RS) 1 dc in 2nd ch from hook, *1 ch, miss next ch, 1 dc in next ch; rep from * to end, turn.
Row 2 2 ch (counts as first htr), 1 puff st in first 1-ch sp, *1 ch, 1 puff st in next 1-ch sp; rep from *, ending with 1 htr in last dc, turn.
Row 3 1 ch (does NOT count as a st), 1 dc in first htr, *1 ch, 1 dc in next 1-ch sp; rep from *, working last dc of last rep in top of 2-ch at end, turn.

SIMPLE TEXTURE STITCH

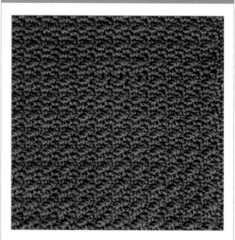

CROCHET DIAGRAM

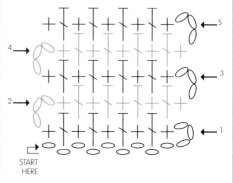

CROCHET INSTRUCTIONS
Make a multiple of 2 ch.
Row 1 (RS) 1 dc in 4th ch from hook, *1 tr in next ch, 1 dc in next ch; rep from * to end, turn.
Row 2 3 ch (counts as first tr), miss first dc, *1 dc in next tr, 1 tr in next dc; rep from *, ending with 1 dc in top of 3-ch at end, turn.
Rep row 2 to form patt.

OPENWORK

Whether worked with fine threads for lace collars, pillow edgings, and tablecloths or with soft wools for shawls, throws, and scarves, openwork crochet has an enduring appeal. As illustrated by the easy techniques on this page and the next, these airy lace textures are produced by working chain spaces and chain loops between the basic stitches.

SIMPLE LACE TECHNIQUES

A few of the openwork stitch patterns on pages 124–126 are explained here to provide an introduction to some popular openwork crochet techniques – chain loops, shells, and picots. Refer to the instructions for the stitches when following the steps.

CHAIN LOOP MESH

1 After working the first row of chain loops into the foundation chain as explained (see page 124), work the 5-chain loops of the following rows into the loops below, joining them on with a dc as shown here.

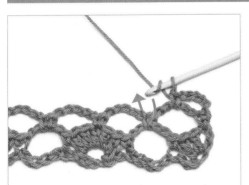

2 Remember to work the last dc of each row into the space inside the turning chain made at the beginning of the previous row. If you forget this, your lace will become narrower.

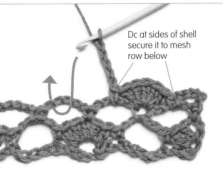

SHELL MESH STITCH

1 On the shell row of this stitch (see page 125) start each shell with a dc in a chain loop. Then work all the tr of the shell into a single dc as shown.

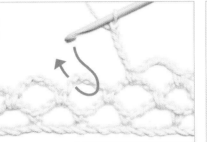

Dc at sides of shell secure it to mesh row below

2 Complete the shell with a dc worked into the following chain loop. Then work a chain loop and join it to the next chain loop with a dc as shown.

3 Continue alternating shells and chain loops to complete the shell row.

Partial shell

Full shell

4 Work mesh and shell rows alternately, working partial shells at ends on alternate shell rows.

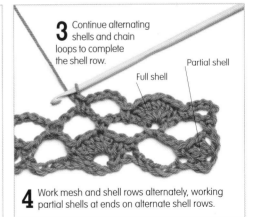

PICOT NET STITCH

1 In this stitch pattern (see page 124), work 4 chains for each picot. Close the picot-ring by working a slip stitch in the fourth chain from the hook as shown.

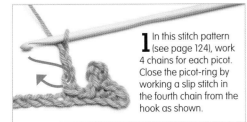

2 Work 3 dc between each of the picots in each picot row as shown.

3 After each picot row, work a 2-chain space above each picot and a tr between the picots as shown.

FILET CROCHET

Filet crochet is the easiest of all the openwork techniques. Once you learn how to work the simple structure of the open filet mesh and the solid filet blocks, all you need to do is follow is a simple chart to form the motifs and repeating patterns.

MAKING BASIC FILET MESH

When working the foundation chain for the basic filet mesh, there is no need to start with an exact number of chains, just make an extra long chain and unravel the unused excess later when finishing your crochet.

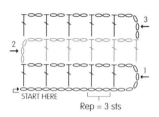

START HERE

Rep = 3 sts

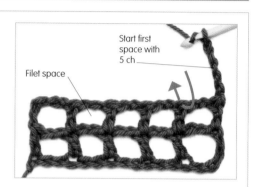

Start first space with 5 ch

Filet space

Filet mesh in symbols and words: The diagram provides the best explanation of how filet mesh is worked. If in doubt, work a mesh from the written pattern as follows:

Make a multiple of 3 ch (3 ch for each mesh square needed), plus 5 extra (to form the right side edge and top of the first mesh square of the first row).
Row 1 1 tr in 8th ch from hook, *2 ch, miss next 2 ch, 1 tr in next ch; rep from * to end.
Row 1 5 ch, miss first tr, 1 tr in next tr, *2 ch, 1 tr in next tr; rep from * working last tr in 3rd ch from last tr in row below.

MAKING FILET BLOCKS

The pattern motifs on filet crochet are created by filling in some of the mesh squares and leaving others empty. In other words, the designs are built up with solid squares and square holes. Having learned how to work the filet mesh, understanding how to fill them in to form blocks is easy.

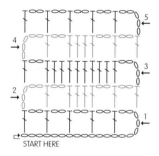

START HERE

Filet blocks in symbols: The diagram illustrates how the blocks are made – instead of working 2 chains to form an empty square, work 2 trebles fill in the square. An individual block consists of a treble on each side and 2 trebles in the centre. To work a block above a filet space, work the 2 centre trebles into the 2-chain space. To work a block above another block, work a treble into each of the trebles below.

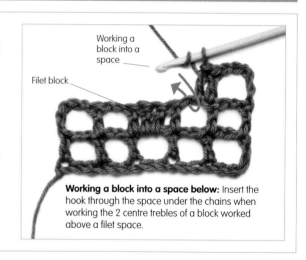

Working a block into a space

Filet block

Working a block into a space below: Insert the hook through the space under the chains when working the 2 centre trebles of a block worked above a filet space.

READING FILET CHARTS

This chart on the right shows the simple motif in the block symbol diagram above. Although actual filet charts are bigger and have elaborate patterns (see pages 121–124), the principle is the same as for this tiny chart. Each square on the chart represents either a filet space or a filet block.

To start working from a chart, make 3 chains for each of the squares along the bottom row of the chart, plus 5 chains extra. (You can work the chart stitch-repeat as many times as desired.) Working the chart from the bottom upwards, make the blocks and spaces on the chart, while reading the first row and all following odd-numbered rows from right to left, and the even-numbered rows from left to right.

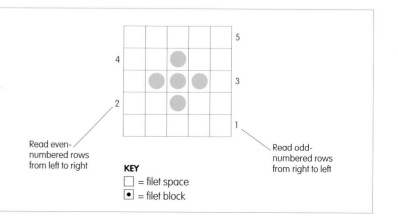

Read even-numbered rows from left to right

Read odd-numbered rows from right to left

KEY

☐ = filet space
◉ = filet block

FILET STITCH
PATTERNS

Follow the instructions on the opposite page to work filet crochet from these charts. The best yarn to use for filet lace is a super-fine cotton yarn and a suitably small size crochet hook (see recommended hook sizes on page 15). Because filet crochet is reversible, it makes great curtains. It can also be used for edgings or insertions along the ends of pillowcases and hand towels.

SPECIAL NOTE AND SYMBOL KEY

• Repeat the charted motifs as many times as desired widthwise, and work across the stitches in rows until the chart is complete. To continue the pattern upwards, start at row 1 again.

KEY
☐ = filet space
⊡ = filet block

FLOWERS AND CIRCLES

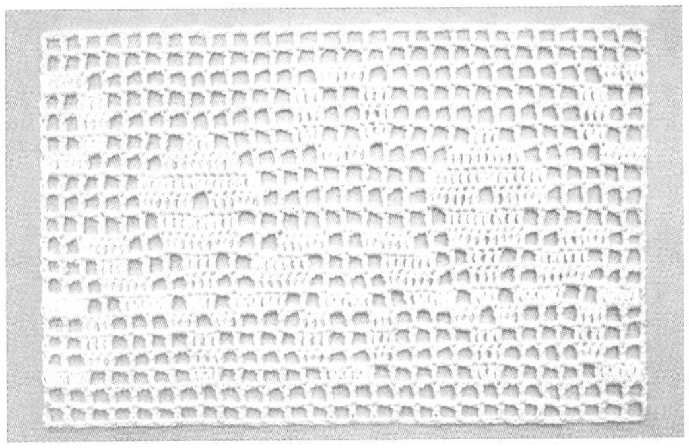

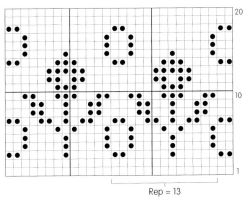

CROCHET CHART

Rep = 13

DIAMONDS BORDER

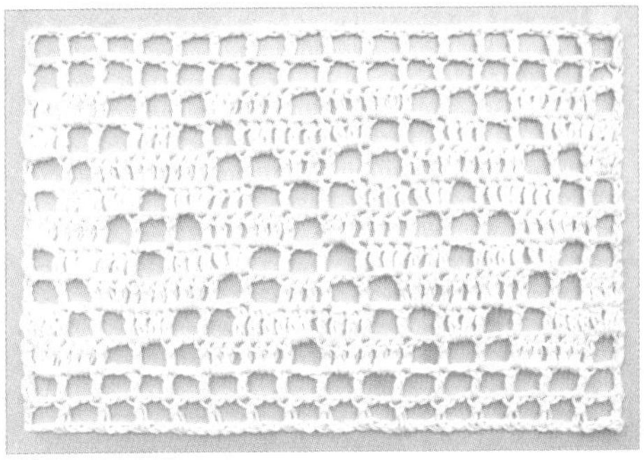

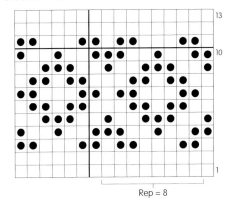

CROCHET CHART

Rep = 8

ZIGZAG BORDER

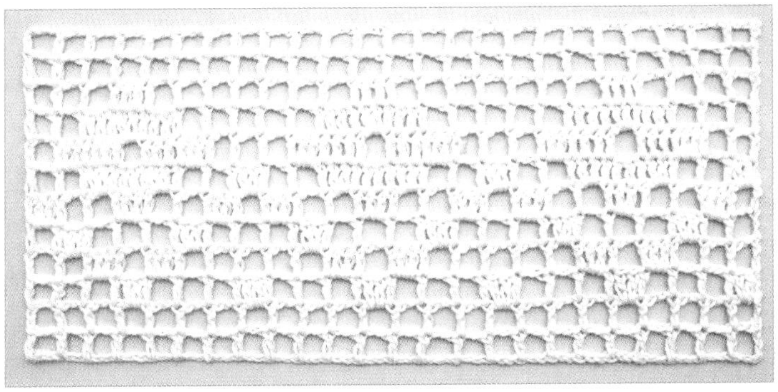

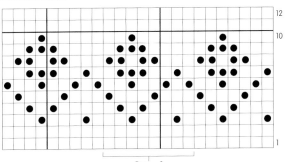

CROCHET CHART

Rep = 8

BLOOM

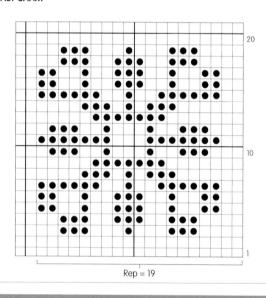

CROCHET CHART

20

10

1

Rep = 19

APPLE

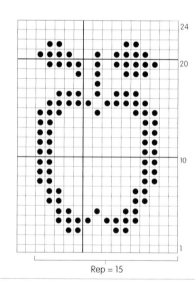

CROCHET CHART

24

20

10

1

Rep = 15

CROSSES BORDER

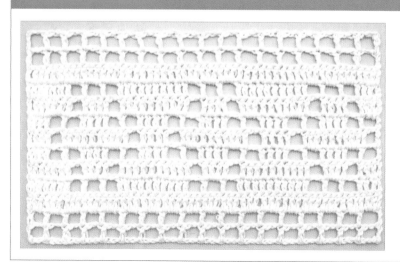

CROCHET CHART

13

10

1

Rep = 6

HEART

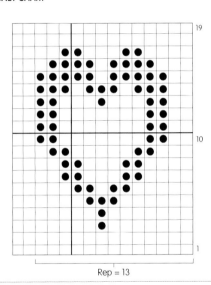

CROCHET CHART

19

10

1

Rep = 13

DOG

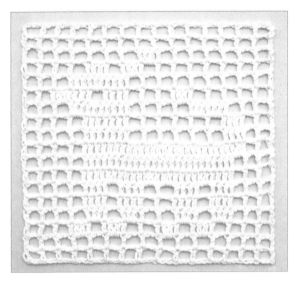

CROCHET CHART

18

10

1

BIRD

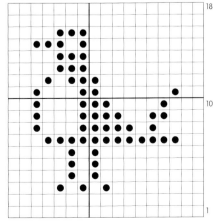

CROCHET CHART

18

10

1

SIMPLE OPENWORK STITCH PATTERNS

Openwork crochet stitches are always popular because of their lacy appearance and because they are quicker to work than solid crochet textures. They also drape gracefully due to their airy construction. Any of these easy stitch patterns would make an attractive shawl or scarf. Why not make small samples of the stitches to try them out? Then work your favourite in a range of yarns to see which texture you prefer (see Special Notes on page 126). A glance at the symbol diagram will reveal which basic stitches and simple stitch techniques are involved.

CHAIN LOOP MESH

CROCHET DIAGRAM

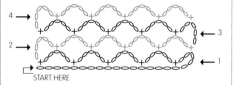

CROCHET INSTRUCTIONS
Make a multiple of 4 ch, plus 2 extra.
Row 1 1 dc in 6th ch from hook, *5 ch, miss next 3 ch, 1 dc in next ch; rep from * to end, turn.
Row 2 *5 ch, 1 dc in next 5-ch loop; rep from * to end, turn.
Rep row 2 to form patt.

PICOT NET STITCH

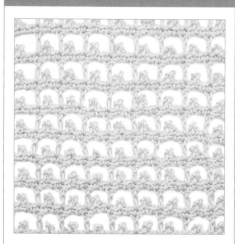

CROCHET DIAGRAM

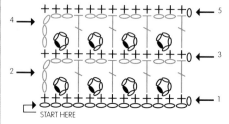

CROCHET INSTRUCTIONS
Make a multiple of 3 ch, plus 2 extra.
Row 1 (RS) 1 dc in 2nd ch from hook, 1 dc in next ch, *4 ch, 1 ss in 4th ch from hook – called 1 picot –, 1 dc in each of next 3 ch; rep from * omitting 1 dc at end of last rep, turn.
Row 2 5 ch (counts as 1 tr and a 2-ch sp), miss first 3 dc (which includes 2 dc before picot and 1 dc after picot), 1 tr in next dc, *2 ch, miss next 2 dc (which includes 1 dc on each side of picot), 1 tr in next dc; rep from * to end, turn.
Row 3 1 ch (does NOT count as a st), 1 dc in first tr, *work (1 dc, 1 picot, 1 dc) all in next 2-ch sp, 1 dc in next tr; rep from * working last dc of last rep in 3rd ch from last tr, turn.
Rep rows 2 and 3 to form patt.

OPEN SHELL STITCH

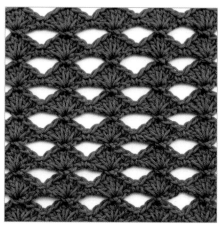

CROCHET DIAGRAM

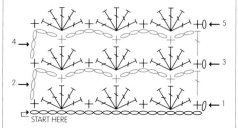

CROCHET INSTRUCTIONS
Make a multiple of 6 ch, plus 2 extra.
Row 1 (RS) 1 dc in 2nd ch from hook, *miss next 2 ch, 5 tr in next ch, miss next 2 ch, 1 dc in next ch; rep from * to end, turn.
Row 2 5 ch (counts as first tr and a 2-ch sp), 1 dc in centre tr in of first shell, *5 ch, 1 dc in centre tr of next shell; rep from *, ending with 2 ch, 1 tr in last dc, turn.
Row 3 1 ch (does NOT count as a st), 1 dc in first tr, *5 tr in next dc, 1 dc in next 5-ch loop; rep from * working last dc of last rep in 3rd ch from last dc, turn.
Rep rows 2 and 3 to form patt.

SPECIAL NOTES

• Both written and symbol instructions are given for all the Simple Openwork Stitch Patterns. To get started, beginners should follow the written instructions for the first few rows, referring to the symbols for clarification. See page 115 for a list of crochet abbreviations and basic stitch symbols. A complete explanation of how to read a crochet symbol diagram is included on page 114.

• The written instructions explain how many chains to start with. So if working from the diagram, consult the written instructions to make the foundation chain. When working a very wide piece, such as a blanket, it is difficult to count and keep track of the number of foundation chains being made. In this case, you can make a chain a few centimetres longer than the correct approximate length and then unravel the excess later.

ARCHED MESH STITCH

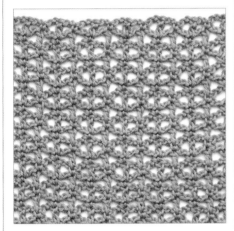

CROCHET DIAGRAM

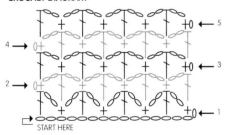

START HERE

CROCHET INSTRUCTIONS
Make a multiple of 4 ch.
Row 1 1 dc in 2nd ch from hook, 2 ch, miss next ch, 1 tr in next ch, *2 ch, miss next ch, 1 dc in next ch, 2 ch, miss next ch, 1 tr in next ch; rep from * to end, turn.
Row 2 1 ch (does NOT count as a st), 1 dc in first tr, 2 ch, 1 tr in next dc, *2 ch, 1 dc in next tr, 2 ch, 1 tr in next dc; rep from * to end, turn.
Rep row 2 to form patt.

BANDED NET STITCH

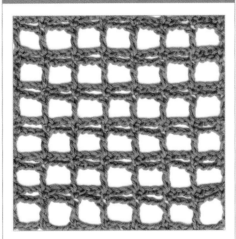

CROCHET DIAGRAM

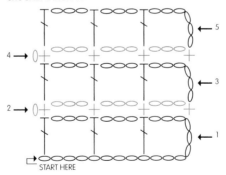

START HERE

CROCHET INSTRUCTIONS
Make a multiple of 4 ch, plus 2 extra.
Row 1 (RS) 1 tr in 10th ch from hook, 3 ch, miss next 3 ch, 1 tr in next ch; rep from * to end, turn.
Row 2 1 ch (does NOT count as a st), 1 dc in first tr, *3 ch, 1 dc in next tr; rep from *, ending with 3 ch, miss next 3 ch, 1 dc in next ch, turn.
Row 3 6 ch (counts as 1 tr and a 3-ch sp), miss first dc and first 3-ch sp, 1 tr in next dc, *3 ch, 1 tr in next dc; rep from * to end, turn.
Rep rows 2 and 3 to form patt.

SHELL MESH STITCH

CROCHET DIAGRAM

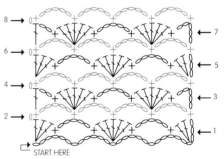

START HERE

CROCHET INSTRUCTIONS
Make a multiple of 12 ch, plus 4 extra.
Row 1 (RS) 2 tr in 4th ch from hook, *miss next 2 ch, 1 dc in next ch, 5 ch, miss next 5 ch, 1 dc in next ch, miss next 2 ch, 5 tr in next ch; rep from *, ending last rep with 3 tr (instead of 5 tr) in last ch, turn.
Row 2 1 ch (does NOT count as a st), 1 dc in first tr, *5 ch, 1 dc in next 5-ch loop, 5 ch, 1 dc in 3rd tr of next 5-tr shell; rep from * working last dc of last rep in top of 3-ch at end, turn.
Row 3 *5 ch, 1 dc in next 5-ch loop, 5 tr in next dc, 1 dc in next 5-ch loop; rep from *, ending with 2 ch, 1 tr in last dc, turn.
Row 4 1 ch (does NOT count as a st), 1 dc in first tr, *5 ch, 1 dc in 3rd tr of next 5-tr shell, 5 ch, 1 dc in next 5-ch loop; rep from * to end, turn.
Row 5 3 ch (counts as first tr), 2 tr in first dc, *1 dc in next 5-ch loop, 5 ch, 1 dc in next 5-ch loop, 5 tr in next dc; rep from * ending last rep with 3 tr (instead of 5 tr) in last dc, turn.
Rep rows 2–5 to form patt.

SPECIAL NOTES

• Lacy shawls and scarves look best worked in super-fine to lightweight yarns of various textures. Always make a swatch with your chosen yarn before beginning to make a project with one of these openwork stitch patterns. Gossamer mohair-mix yarns will work with the very simplest stitches, but to show off intricate laces, use a smooth, tightly twisted wool or cotton yarn.

• Notice how the symbol diagrams for a stitch pattern usually show more rows than appear in the accompanying written instructions. This is done on purpose so that the build-up of the rows is completely clear to the crocheter. With simple openwork patterns like these, once you have completed all the rows of the diagram you will probably have committed the pattern to memory and will not have to refer to the instructions again.

BLOCKS LACE

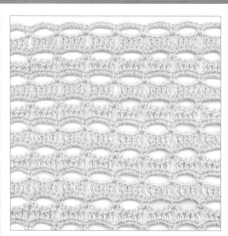

CROCHET DIAGRAM

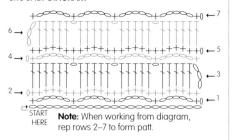

Note: When working from diagram, rep rows 2–7 to form patt.

CROCHET INSTRUCTIONS
Make a multiple of 5 ch, plus 2 extra.
Row 1 (RS) 1 dc in 2nd ch from hook, *5 ch, miss next 4 ch, 1 dc in next ch; rep from * to end, turn.
Row 2 1 ch (does NOT count as a st), 1 dc in first dc, *5 dc in next 5-ch loop, 1 dc in next dc; rep from * to end, turn.
Row 3 3 ch (counts as first tr), miss first dc, 1 tr in each of next 5 dc, *1 ch, miss next dc, 1 tr in each of next 5 dc; rep from * to last dc, 1 tr in last dc, turn.
Row 4 1 ch (does NOT count as a st), 1 dc in first tr, *5 ch, 1 dc in next 1-ch sp; rep from * working last sc of last rep in top of 3-ch at end, turn.
Rep rows 2–4 to form patt.

FANS STITCH

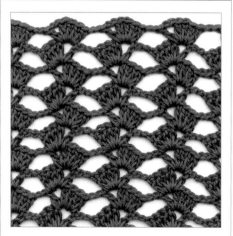

CROCHET DIAGRAM

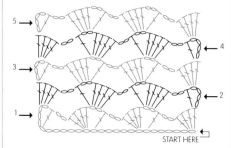

CROCHET INSTRUCTIONS
Make a multiple of 7 ch, plus 4 extra.
Row 1 1 tr in 5th ch from hook, 2 ch, miss next 5 ch, 4 tr in next ch, *2 ch, 1 tr in next ch, 2 ch, miss next 5 ch, 4 tr in next ch; rep from * to end, turn.
Row 2 4 ch, 1 tr in first tr, *2 ch, miss next 2-ch sp and work [4 tr, 2 ch, 1 tr] all in following 2-ch sp; rep from * to last 2-ch sp, miss last 2-ch sp and work 4 tr in 4-ch loop at end, turn.

TIARA LACE

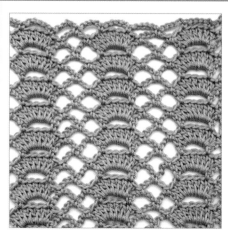

CROCHET DIAGRAM

CROCHET INSTRUCTIONS
Make a multiple of 12 ch.
Row 1 (WS) 1 dc in 2nd ch from hook, *5 ch, miss next 3 ch, 1 dc in next ch; rep from *to last 2 ch, 2 ch, miss next ch, 1 tr in last ch, turn.
Row 2 (RS) 1 ch (does NOT count as a st), 1 dc in first st, miss next 2-ch sp, 7 tr in next 5-ch loop, 1 dc in next 5-ch loop, *5 ch, 1 dc in next 5-ch loop, 7 tr in next 5-ch loop, 1 dc in next 5-ch loop; rep from *, ending with 2 ch, 1 dtr in last dc, turn.
Row 3 1 ch (does NOT count as a st), 1 dc in first dtr, 5 ch, 1 dc in 2nd of next 7-tr shell, 5 ch, 1 dc in 6th tr of same shell, *5 ch, 1 dc in next 5-ch loop, 5 ch, 1 dc in 2nd of next 7-tr shell, 5 ch, 1 dc in 6th tr of same shell; rep from *, ending with 2 ch, 1 dtr in last dc, turn.
Rep rows 2 and 3 to form patt.

COLOURWORK

One-colour crochet has its charms, but using your creative imagination to combine colours is both more challenging and more rewarding. All of the crochet colourwork techniques are easy to master and worth experimenting with. They include colourwork stitch patterns (see pages 129–131), stripes, jacquard, and intarsia (see page 128).

SIMPLE STRIPES

Stripes worked in basic stitches have more potential for creativity than most crocheters realize. The only techniques you need to learn is how and when to change colours to start a new stripe, and how to carry the yarns up the side edge of the crochet.

CHANGING COLOURS

Work the last yrh of row with next stripe colour

Drop old colour at side edge

1 When working stripes in any stitch, always change to the next colour on the last yrh of the last row before the next stripe colour is started.

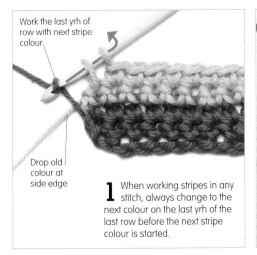

New colour will form first chain of next row

2 Drawing through the last yrh of the row completes the last stitch. The new colour is now on the hook ready to start the next stripe on the next row; this is so that the first turning chain in the next stripe is in the correct colour.

CARRYING COLOURS UP SIDE EDGE

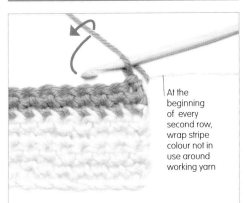

At the beginning of every second row, wrap stripe colour not in use around working yarn

If a colour is not needed for more than 2 rows, wrap it around the other colour to secure it. If it is not needed for more than 8 rows, cut it off and rejoin it later.

STRIPE COMBINATIONS

Smooth wool and fuzzy mohair stripe: The repeated double crochet stripe sequence here is two rows of a smooth wool yarn and two rows of a fuzzy mohair yarn, so each colour can simply be dropped at the side of the work and picked up when it is needed again.

Three-colour stripe: This double crochet stripe has a repeated sequence of two rows of each of three colours. Wrap the working yarn around the colours not in use on every second row to keep them snug against the edge. When changing colours, pull in the new colour firmly but not too tightly or it will pucker the edge.

Double crochet and treble crochet stripe: Each of the two stripes in this design is 2 rows tall. One stripe is worked in double crochet and the other in treble crochet. Adding in the taller trebles gives the crochet fabric a softer texture.

JACQUARD AND INTARSIA COLOURWORK

Jacquard and intarsia crochet are both worked in double crochet stitches. Jacquard is usually worked with only two colours in a row; the colour not in use is carried across the top of the row below and stitches are worked over it to enclose it. When a colour is used only in an area of the crochet rather than across the entire row, the intarsia technique is required; a different length of yarn is used for each section of colour.

COLOURWORK CHARTS

The charted crochet design will reveal which technique to use – jacquard or intarsia. If the pattern on the chart shows two colours repeated across each horizontal row of squares, then the jacquard technique is required. Motifs worked in isolation require the intarsia technique. Each square on the charts represent one double crochet.

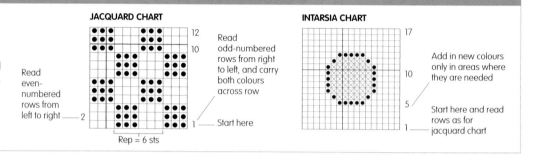

Read even-numbered rows from left to right

Read odd-numbered rows from right to left, and carry both colours across row

Start here

Rep = 6 sts

Add in new colours only in areas where they are needed

Start here and read rows as for jacquard chart

JACQUARD TECHNIQUE

1 To change to a new colour in jacquard, work up to the last yrh of the double crochet stitch before the colour change, then pass the old colour to the front of the work over the top of the new colour and use the new colour to complete the stitch.

Pass old colour to front before picking up new colour

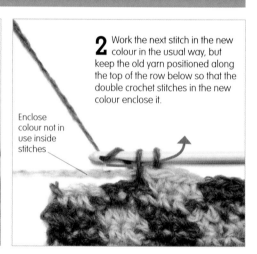

2 Work the next stitch in the new colour in the usual way, but keep the old yarn positioned along the top of the row below so that the double crochet stitches in the new colour enclose it.

Enclose colour not in use inside stitches

INTARSIA TECHNIQUE

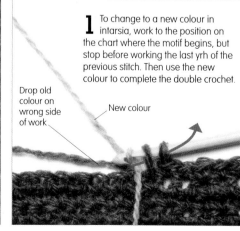

1 To change to a new colour in intarsia, work to the position on the chart where the motif begins, but stop before working the last yrh of the previous stitch. Then use the new colour to complete the double crochet.

Drop old colour on wrong side of work

New colour

2 Work all the required stitches in the new colour as shown. Then join in another ball (or length of yarn) for the next area of background colour. Use a separate yarn for each area of colour.

Pick up colours in next row to use again

Work stitches over yarn tail of new colour

SIMPLE COLOURWORK STITCH PATTERNS

Crochet colourwork stitch patterns are great fun to work. This selection of stitches, all easy-to-work, includes an array of textures, so you are sure to find one that catches your eye. Although some of the stitches have a right and wrong side, the back and front of these fabrics still look very similar. The reversibility of crochet is one of its best features. If you want to make a scarf, shawl, baby blanket, throw, or cushion cover with one of these stitches, take your time to choose the right colour combination (see Special Notes on page 131). See page 115 for abbreviations and basic stitch symbols. Any special symbols are given with the individual diagram.

SIMPLE ZIGZAG STITCH

CROCHET DIAGRAM

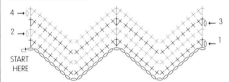

Note: When working from diagram, rep rows 2 and 3 for stitch pattern.

CROCHET INSTRUCTIONS
This pattern is worked in 3 colours (A, B, C).
Using A, make a multiple of 16 ch, plus 2 extra.
Row 1 (RS) Using A, 2 dc in 2nd ch from hook, *1 dc in each of next 7 ch, miss next ch, 1 dc in each of next 7 ch, 3 dc in next ch; rep from * to end, working 2 dc (instead of 3 dc) in last ch, turn.
Row 2 Using B, 1 ch (does NOT count as a st), 2 dc in first dc, *1 dc in each of next 7 dc, miss next 2 dc, 1 dc in each of next 7 dc, 3 dc in next dc; rep from * to end, working 2 dc (instead of 3 dc) in last dc, turn.
Row 3 Using B, rep row 2.
Rows 4 and 5 Using C, [rep row 2] twice.
Rows 6 and 7 Using A, [rep row 2] twice.
Rep rows 2–7 to form patt.

COLOURED TWEED STITCH

CROCHET DIAGRAM

CROCHET INSTRUCTIONS
This pattern is worked in 3 colours (A, B, C).
Using A, make a multiple of 2 ch.
Row 1 Using A, 1 dc in 2nd ch from hook, *1 ch, miss next ch, 1 dc in next ch; rep from * to end, turn.
Row 2 Using B, 1 ch (does NOT count as a st), 1 dc in first dc, 1 dc in next 1-ch sp, *1 ch, 1 dc in next 1-ch sp; rep from * to last dc, 1 dc in last dc, turn.
Row 3 Using C, 1 ch (does NOT count as a st), 1 dc in first dc, *1 ch, 1 dc in next 1-ch sp; rep from * to last 2 dc, 1 ch, miss next dc, 1 dc in last dc, turn.
Row 4 Using A, rep row 2.
Row 5 Using B, rep row 3.
Row 6 Using C, rep row 2.
Row 7 Using A, rep row 3.
Rep rows 2–7 to form patt.

GEM STITCH

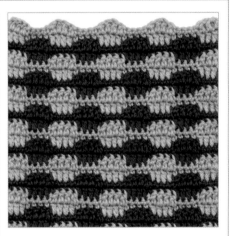

CROCHET DIAGRAM

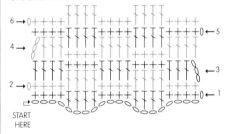

CROCHET INSTRUCTIONS
This pattern is worked in 2 colours (A, B).
Using A, make a multiple of 8 ch, plus 5 extra.
Row 1 (RS) Using A, 1 dc in 2nd ch from hook, 1 dc in each of next 3 ch, *1 tr in each of next 4 ch, 1 dc in each of next 4 ch; rep from * to end, turn.
Row 2 Using A, 1 ch (does NOT count as a st), 1 dc in each of first 4 dc, *1 tr in each of next 4 tr, 1 dc in each of next 4 dc; rep from * to end, turn.
Row 3 Using B, 3 ch (counts as first tr), miss first dc, 1 tr in each of next 3 dc, *1 dc in each of next 4 tr, 1 tr in each of next 4 dc; rep from * to end, turn.
Row 4 Using B, 3 ch (counts as first tr), miss first tr, 1 tr in each of next 3 tr, *1 dc in each of next 4 dc, 1 tr in each of next 4 tr; rep from * to end, working last tr of last rep in top of 3-ch at end, turn.
Row 5 Using A, 1 ch (does NOT count as a st), 1 dc in each of first 4 tr, *1 tr in each of next 4 dc, 1 dc in each of next 4 tr; rep from * working last dc of last rep in top of 3-ch at end, turn.

SPIKE STITCH STRIPES

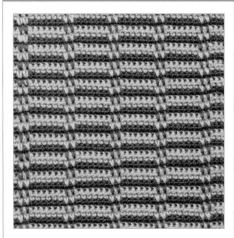

CROCHET DIAGRAM

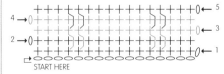

KEY

✝ spike st in st one row below next st

CROCHET INSTRUCTIONS

Note: spike st = do not work into next st, but instead insert hook front to back through top of st one row below this st, yrh and draw a loop through, lengthening the loop to the height of the row being worked (and enclosing the missed st), yrh and a draw through both loops on hook to complete an elongated dc.
This pattern is worked in 2 colours (A, B).
Using A, make a multiple of 8 ch, plus 1 extra.
Row 1 (RS) Using A, 1 dc in 2nd ch from hook, 1 dc in each of rem ch, turn.
Row 2 Using A, 1 ch (does NOT count as a st), 1 dc in each dc to end, turn.
Row 3 Using B, 1 ch (does NOT count as a st), *1 dc in each of next 3 dc, [1 spike st in top of st one row below next st] twice, 1 dc in each of next 3 dc; rep from * to end, turn.
Row 4 Using B, rep row 2.
Row 5 Using A, rep row 3.
Rep rows 2–5 to form patt.

DOUBLE ZIGZAG STITCH

CROCHET DIAGRAM

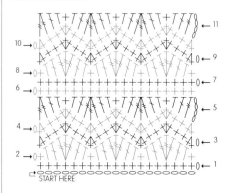

CROCHET INSTRUCTIONS

Note: cluster (also called dtr3tog) = [yrh twice and insert hook in next st, yrh and draw a loop through, (yrh and draw through first 2 loops on hook) twice] 3 times (4 loops now on hook), yrh and draw through all 4 loops on hook; **dtr2tog** = [yrh twice and insert hook in next st, yrh and draw a loop through, (yrh and draw through first 2 loops on hook) twice] twice (3 loops now on hook), yrh and draw through all 3 loops on hook.
This pattern is worked in 4 colours (A, B, C, D).
Make a multiple of 6 ch, plus 2 extra.
Work the following rows in stripes, repeating this stripe sequence – 2 rows A, 2 rows B, 2 rows C, 2 rows D.
Row 1 (RS) 1 dc in 2nd ch from hook, 1 dc in each of rem ch, turn.
Row 2 1 ch (does NOT count as a st), 1 dc in first dc, *1 htr in next dc, 1 tr in next dc, 3 dtr in next dc, 1 tr in next dc, 1 htr in next dc, 1 dc in next dc; rep from * to end, turn.
Row 3 1 ch (does NOT count as a st), dc2tog over first 2 sts, 1 dc in each of next 2 sts, *3 dc in next st, 1 dc in each of next 2 sts, dc3tog over next 3 sts, 1 dc in each of next 2 sts; rep from * to last 5 sts, 3 dc in next st, 1 dc in each of next 2 sts, dc2tog over last 2 sts, turn.
Row 4 Rep row 3.
Row 5 4 ch, miss first st, 1 dtr in next dc (counts as first dtr2tog), 1 tr in next dc, 1 htr in next dc, 1 dc in next dc, 1 htr in next dc, 1 tr in next dc, *1 cluster over next 3 sts, 1 tr in next dc, 1 htr in next dc, 1 dc in next dc, 1 htr in next dc, 1 tr in next dc; rep from *, ending with dtr2tog over last 2 sts, turn.
Row 6 1 ch (does NOT count as a st), 1 dc in first st, 1 dc in next st and each st to end (do NOT work a dc in top of 4-ch turning ch at end), turn.
Row 7 1 ch (does NOT count as a st), 1 dc in each dc to end, turn.
Rep rows 2–7 to form patt, while continuing stripe sequence.

BOBBLE STRIPE

CROCHET DIAGRAM

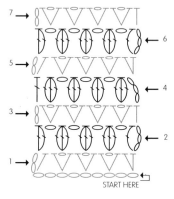

CROCHET INSTRUCTIONS

Note: bobble = [yrh and insert hook in specified st, yrh and draw a loop through, yrh and draw through first 2 loops on hook] 3 times all in same st (4 loops now on hook), yrh and draw through all 4 loops on hook to complete 3-tr bobble (see page 113).
This pattern is worked in 3 colours (A, B, C).
Using A, make a multiple of 2 ch, plus 1 extra.
Work the following rows in stripes, repeating this stripe sequence – 1 row A, 1 row B, 1 row C.
Row 1 (WS) 1 htr in 3rd ch from hook, *miss next ch, work [1 htr, 1 ch, 1 htr] all in next ch; rep from * to last 2 ch, miss next ch, 2 htr in last ch, turn.
Row 2 (RS) 3 ch (counts as first tr), 1 tr in first htr, *1 ch, 1 bobble in next 1-ch sp; rep from *, ending with 1 ch, work [yrh and insert hook in top of 2-ch at end of row, yrh and draw a loop through, yrh and draw through first 2 loops on hook] twice all in same place (3 loops now on hook), yrh and draw through all 3 loops on hook, turn.
Row 3 2 ch (counts as first htr), *work [1 htr, 1 ch, 1 htr] all in next 1-ch sp; rep from *, ending with 1 htr in top of 3-ch, turn.
Row 4 3 ch (counts as first tr), 1 bobble in next 1-ch sp, *1 ch, 1 bobble in next 1-ch sp; rep from *, ending with 1 tr in top of 2-ch at end, turn.
Row 5 2 ch (counts as first htr), 1 htr in first tr, *work [1 htr, 1 ch, 1 htr] all in next 1-ch sp; rep from *, ending with 2 htr in top of 3-ch at end, turn.
Rep rows 2–5 to form patt, while continuing stripe sequence.

TRIANGLES SPIKE STITCH

CROCHET DIAGRAM

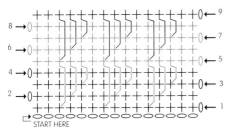

KEY

┼ spike st in st one row below next st

┼ spike st in st 2 rows below next st

┼ spike st in st 3 rows below next st

CROCHET INSTRUCTIONS

Note: spike st = do not work into next st, but instead insert hook front to back through top of st 1, 2 or 3 rows below this st, yrh and draw a loop through, lengthening the loop to the height of the row being worked (and enclosing the missed st), yrh and a draw through both loops on hook to complete an elongated dc.

This pattern is worked in 2 colours (A, B).

Using A, make a multiple of 4 ch, plus 4 extra.

Row 1 (RS) Using A, 1 dc in 2nd ch from hook, 1 dc in each of rem ch, turn.

Row 2 Using A, 1 ch (does NOT count as a st), 1 dc in each dc to end, turn.

Rows 3 and 4 Using A, [rep row 2] twice.

Row 5 (RS) Using B, 1 ch (does NOT count as a st), 1 dc in first dc, *1 dc in next dc, 1 spike st in top of dc one row below next dc, 1 spike st in top of dc 2 rows below next dc, 1 spike st in top of dc 3 rows below next dc; rep from * to last 2 dc, 1 dc in each of last 2 dc, turn.

Rows 6, 7 and 8 Using B, [rep row 2] 3 times.

Row 9 (RS) Using A, rep row 5.

Rep rows 2–9 to form patt, ending with a patt row 5 or 9.

COLOURED CLUSTER AND SHELL STITCH

CROCHET INSTRUCTIONS

This pattern is worked in 2 colours (A, B).
Work as for cluster and shell stitch on page 117 as follows:
Using A, make the foundation ch. Then work in stripe patt, repeating the following stripe sequence – 2 rows A, 2 rows B.

COLOURED CLOSE SHELLS STITCH

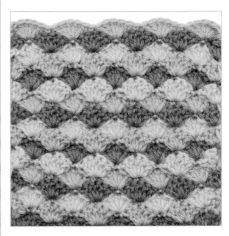

CROCHET INSTRUCTIONS

This pattern is worked in 3 colours (A, B, C).
Work as for close shells stitch on page 116 as follows:
Using A, make the foundation ch. Then work in stripe patt, repeating the following stripe sequence – 1 row A, 1 row B, 1 row C.

SPECIAL NOTES

• When following the diagrams, use colours as explained in the written instructions. The symbol tones are used to denote row change and not colour change (except for the spike stitches). See page 115 for a list of crochet abbreviations and basic stitch symbols.

• Choose yarn colours with care. Always buy only one ball of each colour first and test that the colours work well together. For a successful combination, the chosen colours should stand out well against each other, either in tone (darkness and lightness) or in hue. It is best to work several colour combinations before deciding on the final one, especially if the item you are making is a large one like a blanket. Pin the swatches up and stand back to study them – the right one will pop right out at you.

FOLLOWING A CROCHET PATTERN

Followed step by step and slowly, crochet patterns are not as difficult to work from as they appear. The guides here for a simple accessory and a garment give many tips for how to approach your first crochet patterns. This section also includes other techniques needed for working from a crochet pattern – simple increases and decreases for shaping garments, finishings such as edgings and button loops, and blocking and seams.

SIMPLE ACCESSORY PATTERNS

A beginner should choose an easy accessory pattern for a first crochet project. A striped cushion cover is given here as an example. Follow the numbered tips of the guide to familiarize yourself with the parts of a simple pattern.

1 The skill level required for the crochet is given at the beginning of most patterns. When starting out, work several easy patterns, before progressing to the intermediate level.

2 Check the size of the finished item. If it is a simple square like this cushion, you can easily adjust the size by adding or subtracting stitches and rows.

3 It is best to use the yarn specified. But if you are unable to obtain this yarn, choose a substitute yarn as explained on page 15.

8 Make a tension swatch before starting to crochet and change the hook size if necessary (see opposite page).

9 Instructions for working a piece of crocheted fabric always start with how many chains to make for the foundation chain and which yarn or hook size to use. If there is only one hook size and one yarn, these may be absent here.

10 Consult the abbreviations list with your pattern for the meanings of abbreviations (see page 115).

14 The back of a cushion cover is sometimes exactly the same as the front or it has a fabric back. In this case, the stripes are reversed on the back for a more versatile cover.

15 After all the crocheted pieces are completed, follow the Finishing (or Making Up) section of the pattern.

STRIPED CUSHION COVER

Skill level
Easy

Size of finished cushion
40.5 x 40.5cm (16 x 16in)

Materials
7 x 25g/⁷∕₈oz (110m/120yd) balls of branded Scottish Tweed 4-Ply in Thatch 00018 (**A**)
4 x 25g/⁷∕₈oz (110m/120yd) balls of branded Scottish Tweed 4-Ply in Skye 00009 (**B**)
3.5mm (US size E-4) crochet hook
Cushion pad to fit finished cover

Tension
22 sts and 24 rows to 10cm (4in) over double crochet using 3.5mm (US size E-4) hook or size necessary to achieve correct tension. To save time, take time to check tension.

Front
Using 3.5mm (US size E-4) hook and A, make 89 ch.
Row 1 1 dc in 2nd ch from hook, 1 dc in each of rem ch, turn. 88 dc.
Row 2 1 ch (does NOT count as a st), 1 dc in each dc to end, turn.
Rep row 2 throughout to form dc fabric.
Always changing to new colour with last yrh of last dc of previous row, work in stripes as follows:—
26 rows more in A, 8 rows B, [8 rows A, 8 rows B] twice, 28 rows A.
Fasten off.

Back
Work as for Front, but use B for A, and A for B.

Finishing
Darn in loose ends.
Block and press lightly on wrong side, following instructions on yarn label.
With wrong sides facing, sew three sides of back and front together. Turn right-side out, insert cushion pad, and sew remaining seam.

4 Always purchase the same total amount in metres/yards of a substitute yarn; NOT the same amount in weight.

5 If desired, select different colours to suit your décor; the colours specified are just suggestions.

6 Alter the hook size if you cannot achieve the correct tension with the specified size (see 8 left).

7 Extra items needed for your project will usually be listed under Materials or Extras.

11 Work in the specified stitch pattern, for the specified number of rows or cm/in.

12 Colours for stripes are always changed at the end of the previous row before the colour change so the first turning chain of the new stripe is in the correct colour (see page 127).

13 Fastening off completes the crochet piece.

16 See page 107 for how to darn in loose ends.

17 Make sure you look at the yarn label instructions before attempting to press any piece of crochet. The label may say that the yarn cannot be pressed or it can be pressed only with a cool iron. (See page 140 for blocking tips.)

18 See pages 140 and 141 for seaming options. Take time with seams on crochet, and when working your very first seams, get an experienced crocheter to help you.

GARMENT PATTERNS

Garment instructions usually start with the Skill Level, followed by the Sizes, Materials, and finally the instructions. Most important for achieving a successful garment – or other fitted items such as hats, mittens, gloves, and socks – is choosing the right size and making a tension swatch.

TIPS

- **Choose a skill level** that suits your crochet experience. If in doubt or if you haven't crocheted for many years, stick to an Easy or Beginner's level until you are confident you can go to the next level.

- **White is a good colour** to use for your first crocheted sweater because the stitches are so easy to see clearly. But if you do choose white yarn, be sure to wash your hands every time you start crocheting; and when you stop, put away the yarn and sweater in a bag to keep it from becoming soiled.

- **Avoid black** or other very dark yarn for a first crocheted sweater, as the stitches are very difficult to distinguish, even for an accomplished crocheter.

- **Purchase yarn balls** that have the same dye-lot number (see page 15).

- **Have a set** of hook sizes at hand if you are starting to crochet sweaters. When checking tension (see above), you will need other sizes in order to alter your hook size if necessary.

- **Always make the pieces** in the order given in the instructions, whether you are crocheting a garment, accessory or toy. On a garment, the back is usually crocheted first, followed by the front (or fronts if it is a cardigan or jacket), and lastly the sleeves. Pockets that are integrated into the fronts are crocheted before the fronts and those applied as patches are worked last.

- **It is not advisable** to attempt to alter sweater patterns. They are carefully designed for the back, front/s and sleeves to fit together precisely. For example, altering an armhole length will mean the sleeve head will not fit into it in the right way. The total length of the sleeve or sweater are sometimes adjustable, however, at the points specified in the pattern – usually right before the armhole shaping on the body and before the sleeve head shaping on the sleeve. But only adjust lengths where your instructions suggest it.

CHOOSING A GARMENT SIZE

Crochet garment sizes are usually listed as specific bust/chest sizes or in generic terms as Small, Medium, Large. (Children's sweater sizes are given in ages and chest sizes.) The best advice is not to stick strictly to choosing your preferred size by these criteria. Decide instead how you want the garment to fit you – how close-fitting or loose-fitting it should be. If you are planning to crochet a sweater, find one in your wardrobe that is comfortable and flattering and has a fabric weight and shape similar to the garment you are going to crochet. Smooth out the sweater and measure the width. Find the same, or closest, width to this on the sweater diagram of your crochet pattern – this is the size for you.

Make a photocopy of your pattern and circle or highlight all the figures that apply to your size throughout the pattern, starting with the number of balls of yarn to purchase, followed by the number of chains in the foundation chain for the sweater back, the length to the armhole, and so on. The figure for the smallest size is given first and all the figures for the larger sizes follow in parentheses. Where there is only one figure given in the instructions – be it a measurement, the number of rows, or the number of stitches – this figure applies to all sizes. Before starting your crochet, always check your tension.

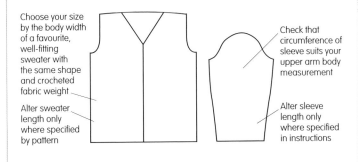

Choose your size by the body width of a favourite, well-fitting sweater with the same shape and crocheted fabric weight

Alter sweater length only where specified by pattern

Check that circumference of sleeve suits your upper arm body measurement

Alter sleeve length only where specified in instructions

MEASURING TENSION

It is essential to check your tension (stitch size) before beginning a crochet pattern. Not everyone crochets stitches with exactly the same tightness or looseness, so you may well need to use a different hook size to achieve the stitch size required by your pattern.

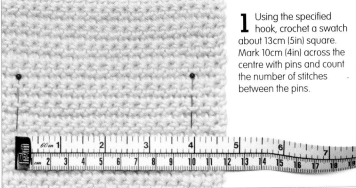

1 Using the specified hook, crochet a swatch about 13cm (5in) square. Mark 10cm (4in) across the centre with pins and count the number of stitches between the pins.

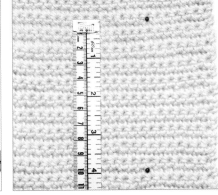

2 Count the number of rows to 10cm (4in) in the same way. If you have fewer stitches and rows than you should, try again with a larger hook size; if you have more, change to a smaller hook size. Use the hook size that best matches the correct tension. (Matching the stitch width is much more important than matching the row height.)

SHAPING
CROCHET

To move from making simple squares and rectangles, a crocheter needs to know how to increase and decrease the number of stitches in the row to make shaped pieces. The most commonly used simple shaping techniques are provided here.

DOUBLE CROCHET INCREASES

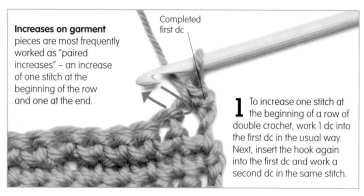

Increases on garment pieces are most frequently worked as "paired increases" – an increase of one stitch at the beginning of the row and one at the end.

Completed first dc

1 To increase one stitch at the beginning of a row of double crochet, work 1 dc into the first dc in the usual way. Next, insert the hook again into the first dc and work a second dc in the same stitch.

2 This completes the increase. Continue across the row, working 1 dc into each dc in the usual way.

2 dc worked into same stitch

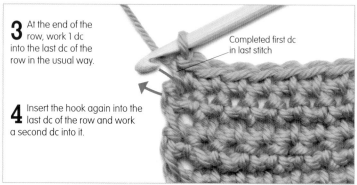

3 At the end of the row, work 1 dc into the last dc of the row in the usual way.

4 Insert the hook again into the last dc of the row and work a second dc into it.

Completed first dc in last stitch

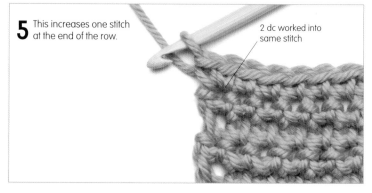

5 This increases one stitch at the end of the row.

2 dc worked into same stitch

TREBLE CROCHET INCREASES

Increases on garment pieces worked in treble crochet are worked using the same techniques as for double crochet. Again, these increases are most frequently worked as "paired increases" – one stitch is increased at each end of the row.

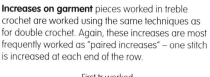

First tr worked into first tr in row below instead of missing it

1 To increase one stitch at the beginning of a row of treble crochet, first work the turning chain, then work 1 tr into the first tr in the row below. Because the first treble in the row below is usually missed, this creates an increase at the beginning of the row.

2 Continue across the row, working 1 tr into each tr in the usual way. At the end of the row, work 1 tr into the top of the turning chain in the row below in the usual way. Then work a second tr into the same turning chain.

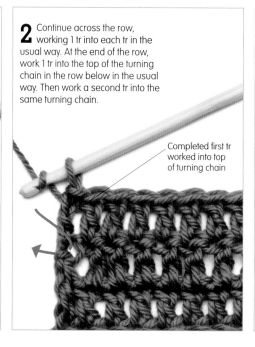

Completed first tr worked into top of turning chain

3 This completes the one stitch increase at the end of the row as shown.

2 tr worked into same chain

STEP INCREASE AT BEGINNING OF ROW

1 Increases are also frequently worked in crochet so that they form little steps at the edge. As an example, to add a 3-stitch step increase at the beginning of a row of double crochet, begin by making 4 chains as shown here. (Always make one chain more than the number of extra double crochets required.)

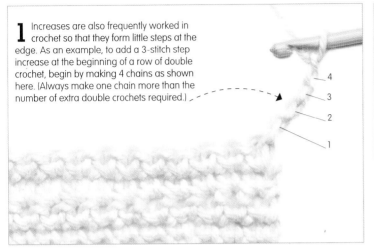

2 Work the first dc into the second chain from the hook. Then work 1 dc into each of the remaining 2 chains. This creates a 3-dc increase at the beginning of the row.

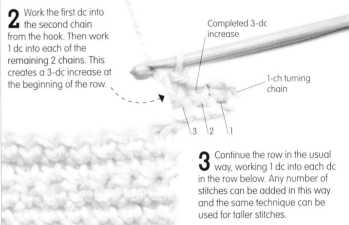

Completed 3-dc increase

1-ch turning chain

3 Continue the row in the usual way, working 1 dc into each dc in the row below. Any number of stitches can be added in this way and the same technique can be used for taller stitches.

STEP INCREASE AT END OF ROW

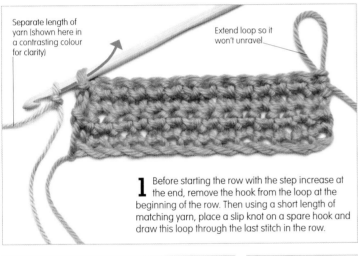

Separate length of yarn (shown here in a contrasting colour for clarity)

Extend loop so it won't unravel

1 Before starting the row with the step increase at the end, remove the hook from the loop at the beginning of the row. Then using a short length of matching yarn, place a slip knot on a spare hook and draw this loop through the last stitch in the row.

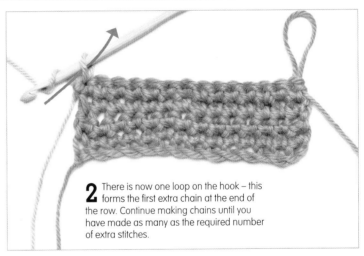

2 There is now one loop on the hook – this forms the first extra chain at the end of the row. Continue making chains until you have made as many as the required number of extra stitches.

3 So for a 3-stitch step increase, make a total of 3 chains. Then fasten off.

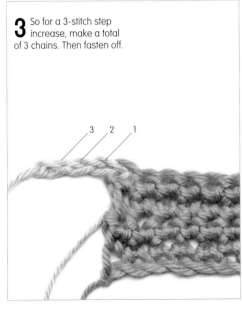

4 Return to the beginning of the row, slip the loop back onto the hook and tighten it, then work to the end of the row in the usual way until you reach the added chains.

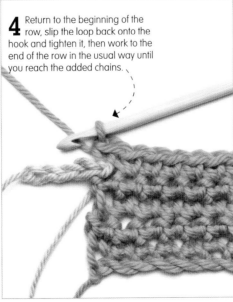

5 Work 1 dc into each of the 3 added chains. This creates a 3-dc increase. Any number of stitches can be added in this way and the same technique can be used for taller stitches.

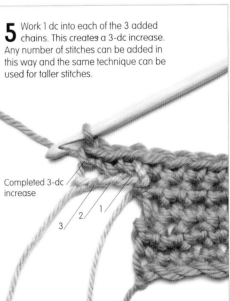

Completed 3-dc increase

DOUBLE CROCHET DECREASES (Abbreviation = *dc2tog*)

Decreases on garment pieces, like increases, are most frequently worked as "paired decreases" – a decrease of one stitch at the beginning of the row and another at the end.

1 To decrease one stitch at the beginning of a row of double crochet, work up to the last yrh of the first dc in the usual way, but do not complete the stitch – there are now 2 loops on the hook. Insert the hook through the next stitch as shown and draw a loop through.

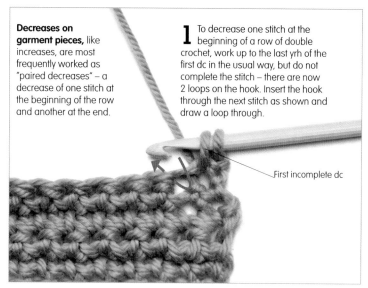

First incomplete dc

2 There are now 3 loops on the hook. Wrap the yarn around the hook and draw a loop through all 3 loops at once as shown.

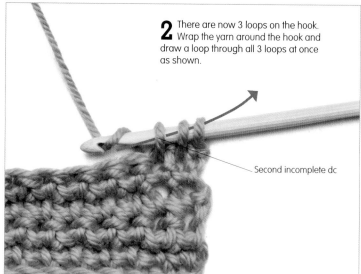

Second incomplete dc

3 This completes the decrease – where there were 2 stitches, there is now only one.

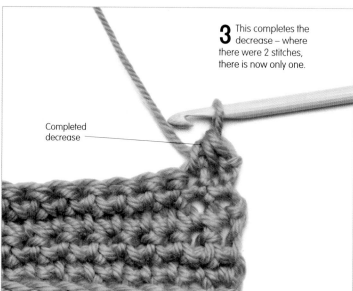

Completed decrease

4 Continue across the row, working 1 dc into each dc in the usual way up to the last 2 stitches of the row.

5 At the end of the row, insert the hook through the top of the second to last stitch and draw a loop through – there are now 2 loops on the hook.

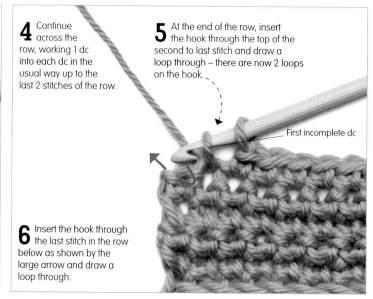

First incomplete dc

6 Insert the hook through the last stitch in the row below as shown by the large arrow and draw a loop through.

7 There are now 3 loops on the hook. Wrap the yarn around the hook and draw a loop through all 3 loops at once as shown.

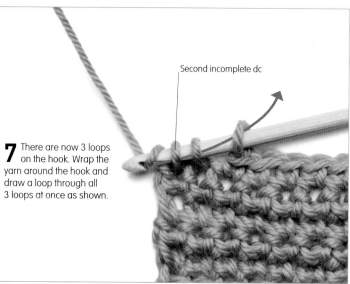

Second incomplete dc

8 This completes the decrease at the end of the row. (The same principle can be used for a "double decrease", where 2 stitches are decreased at once. For this, work 3 incomplete dc and join them together at the top with the last yrh – this is called dc3tog.)

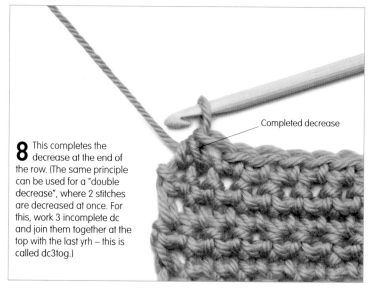

Completed decrease

TREBLE CROCHET DECREASES (Abbreviation = *tr2tog*)

1 To decrease one stitch at the beginning of a row of treble crochet, first work the turning chain. Miss the first tr and work 1 tr in each of the next 2 tr but only up to the last yrh of each stitch. Draw a loop through all 3 loops at once as shown.

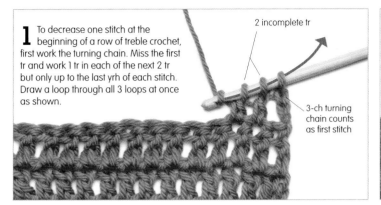

2 incomplete tr

3-ch turning chain counts as first stitch

2 This completes the decrease – where there were 2 stitches, there is now only one.

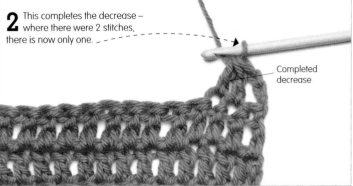

Completed decrease

3 Continue across the row in the usual way up to the last tr in the row below. Now work a tr into the last tr but only up to the last yrh. Wrap the yarn around the hook and insert the hook into the top of the turning chain in the row below as shown.

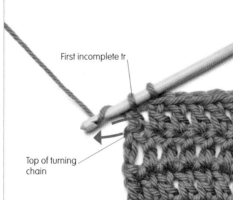

First incomplete tr

Top of turning chain

4 Work the tr in the top of the chain up to the last yrh of the stitch. There are now 3 loops on the hook. Wrap the yarn around the hook and draw a loop through all 3 loops at once as shown.

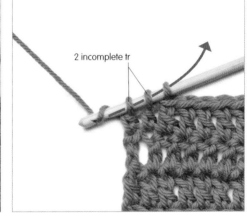

2 incomplete tr

5 This completes the decrease at the end of the row. (The same principle can be used for a "double decrease", where 2 stitches are decreased at once. For this, work 3 incomplete tr and join them together at the top with the last yrh – this is called tr3tog.)

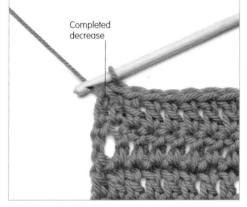

Completed decrease

STEP DECREASES

At beginning of row: Decreases, like increases, can also be worked so that they form little steps at the edge. As an example, to decrease 3 stitches at the beginning of a row of double crochet, work 1 chain and then 1 slip stitch into each of the first 4 dc. Next, work 1 chain, then work the first dc in the same place that the last slip stitch was worked. Continue along the row in the usual way.

Slip stitch to correct position

At end of row: For a 3-stitch step decrease at the end of the row, simply work up to the last 3 stitches at the end of the row and turn, leaving the last 3 stitches unworked. This technique can be used for all crochet stitches.

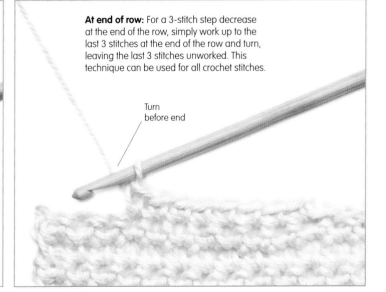

Turn before end

FINISHING
DETAILS

Finishings are often more difficult for crocheters than making the pieces. Some of the techniques most frequently used are shown here. Take your time with all finishings, and practise the methods on small swatches before adding them to your completed pieces.

DOUBLE CROCHET EDGING

Along top or bottom of a piece of crochet: Adding a simple double crochet edging is a good way to tidy up the edges of a piece of crochet. To work a double crochet edging along the top or bottom of a piece of crochet, join the yarn to the first stitch with a slip stitch, work 1 ch, 1 dc in the same place as the slip stitch, then work 1 dc in each stitch below all along the edge.

Along row-ends of a piece of crochet: A double crochet edging is worked the same way along the row-ends of a piece of crochet, but it is not as easy to achieve an even edging. To create a perfect result, experiment with how many stitches to work per row-end. If the finished edging looks flared, try working fewer stitches per row-end; and if it looks puckered, try again working more stitches per row-end.

CROCHETING EDGING DIRECTLY ONTO EDGE

Any of the edgings starting with a row of double crochet on pages 144–149 can easily be worked directly onto the crochet.

1 Using a contrasting colour for the edging, start by working the row of double crochet onto the base, then turn and work the next row of the edging (the second row of the simple shell edging on page 145 is being worked here).

Row of double crochet

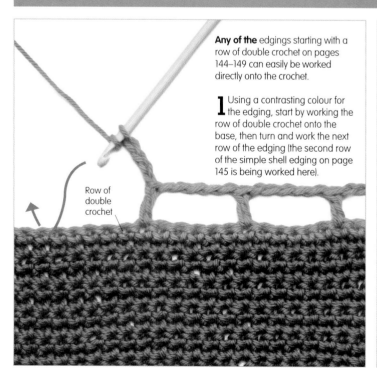

2 At the end of the second row, turn the crochet and work the remaining rows of the edging (the third and final row of the simple shell edging is being worked here).

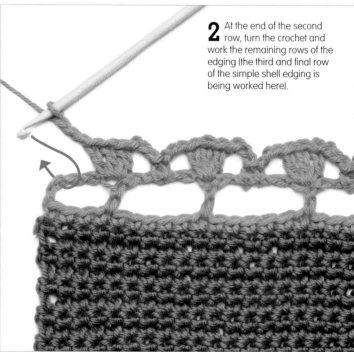

ROUND BUTTONS

Making matching crochet buttons is a great finishing detail. Experiment with different yarn and hook sizes to make round buttons of the desired size. The buttons here are made using a super-fine cotton yarn and a 2mm (US size 5 steel or B-1) hook for a button approximately 1.5cm (⅝in) in diameter.

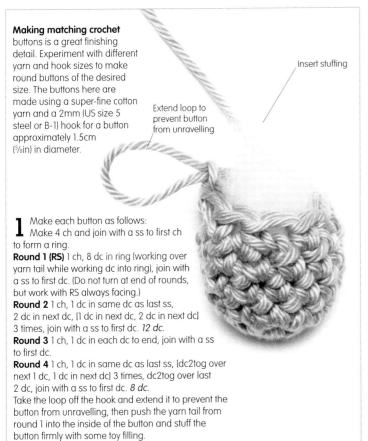

Insert stuffing

Extend loop to prevent button from unravelling

1 Make each button as follows:
Make 4 ch and join with a ss to first ch to form a ring.
Round 1 (RS) 1 ch, 8 dc in ring (working over yarn tail while working dc into ring), join with a ss to first dc. (Do not turn at end of rounds, but work with RS always facing.)
Round 2 1 ch, 1 dc in same dc as last ss, 2 dc in next dc, [1 dc in next dc, 2 dc in next dc] 3 times, join with a ss to first dc. *12 dc.*
Round 3 1 ch, 1 dc in each dc to end, join with a ss to first dc.
Round 4 1 ch, 1 dc in same dc as last ss, [dc2tog over next 1 dc, 1 dc in next dc] 3 times, dc2tog over last 2 dc, join with a ss to first dc. *8 dc.*
Take the loop off the hook and extend it to prevent the button from unravelling, then push the yarn tail from round 1 into the inside of the button and stuff the button firmly with some toy filling.

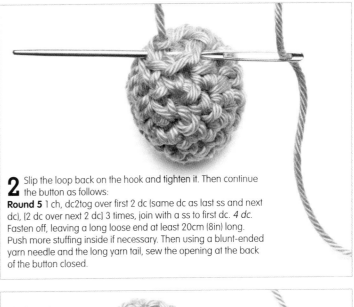

2 Slip the loop back on the hook and **tighten it**. Then continue the button as follows:
Round 5 1 ch, dc2tog over first 2 dc (same dc as last ss and next dc), [2 dc over next 2 dc] 3 times, join with a ss to first dc. *4 dc.* Fasten off, leaving a long loose end at least 20cm (8in) long. Push more stuffing inside if necessary. Then using a blunt-ended yarn needle and the long yarn tail, sew the opening at the back of the button closed.

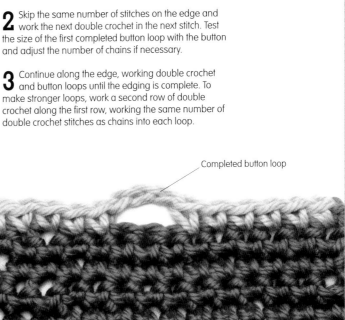

3 Do not cut off the yarn tail, but keep it for sewing on the button.

Retain long yarn tail for sewing on button

BUTTON LOOPS

Button loops are very easy to make along the edge of a cushion cover, the front of a cardigan, or for closings on baby garments.

1 Work in double crochet to the position of the button loop. Make 2, 3, or more chains, depending on the size of the button.

3-ch button loop

2 Skip the same number of stitches on the edge and work the next double crochet in the next stitch. Test the size of the first completed button loop with the button and adjust the number of chains if necessary.

3 Continue along the edge, working double crochet and button loops until the edging is complete. To make stronger loops, work a second row of double crochet along the first row, working the same number of double crochet stitches as chains into each loop.

Completed button loop

BLOCKING
AND SEAMS

Always sew the seams on a garment or accessory using a blunt-ended needle and a matching yarn (a contrasting yarn is used here just to show the seam techniques more clearly); and work them in the order given in the crochet pattern. But before sewing any seams, block your crochet pieces carefully. Press the finished seams very lightly with a cool iron on the wrong side after completion.

WET BLOCKING

If your yarn will allow it, wet blocking is the best way to even out crochet. Wet the pieces in a sink full of lukewarm water. Then squeeze out the water and roll the crochet in a towel to remove excess dampness. Smooth the crochet into shape right-side down on layers of dry towels covered with a sheet, pinning at intervals. Add as many pins as is necessary to refine the shape. Do not move the crochet until it is completely dry.

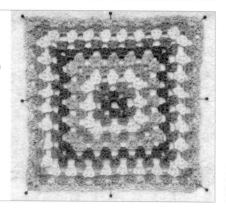

STEAM BLOCKING

For a speedier process you may prefer steam blocking (if your yarn label allows it). First, pin the crochet right-side down into the correct shape. Then steam the crochet gently using a clean damp cloth, but barely touching the cloth with the iron. Never rest the weight of an iron on your crochet or it will flatten the texture. Leave the steamed piece to dry completely before unpinning it.

BACKSTITCH SEAM

Backstitch produces durable seams and is frequently recommended in crochet patterns for garments and accessories.

1 Align the crochet pieces with right sides together and secure the yarn with two or three overcast stitches in the same place. Then inserting the needle close to the edge, work the seam taking one stitch forwards and one stitch back.

Blunt-ended yarn needle

2 On the backwards stitch, be sure to insert the needle through the same place as the end of the last stitch. At the end of the seam, secure the yarn in the same way as at the beginning of the seam.

OVERCAST STITCH SEAM

Simple overcast seam: Align the crochet pieces with right sides together and secure the yarn as for backstitch. Then inserting the needle close to the edge, make stitches through the two layers as shown.

Wrong side of crochet

Right side of crochet

Pull seam yarn tight to make seam stitches disappear

Flat overcast seam: For a flat seam along the tops of stitches, lay the pieces right-side up and edge-to-edge. Work as for the simple overcast seam, but inserting the needle through only the back loops of the stitches.

EDGE-TO-EDGE SEAM

This method creates a neat flat seam line. It can be used, as here, on treble crochet as well as on all other types of crochet fabrics.

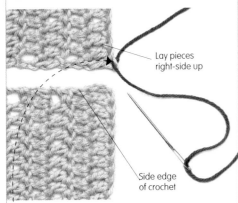

Lay pieces right-side up

Side edge of crochet

1 Align the pieces of crochet right-side up and edge-to-edge. Insert the needle through the corner of the top piece, leaving a long loose end.

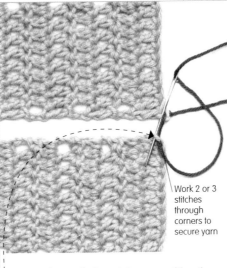

Work 2 or 3 stitches through corners to secure yarn

2 Insert the needle through the corner of the other piece, then through both pieces again in the same place at the corner to secure firmly.

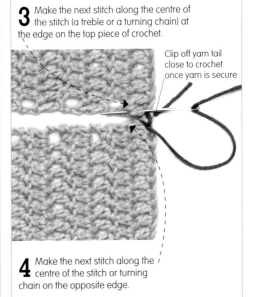

3 Make the next stitch along the centre of the stitch (a treble or a turning chain) at the edge on the top piece of crochet.

Clip off yarn tail close to crochet once yarn is secure

4 Make the next stitch along the centre of the stitch or turning chain on the opposite edge.

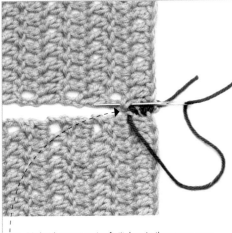

5 Make the next pair of stitches in the same way, working a stitch along one stitch or turning chain on the top piece then on the opposite piece.

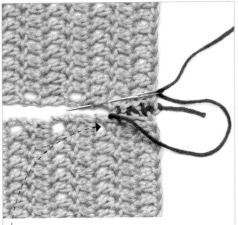

6 Continue along the seam taking a stitch in each side alternately. Take shorter stitches on each piece if the yarn used for the pieces is bulky.

When a matching yarn is used, seam disappears more readily

7 After every few stitches, pull the yarn tight so that the seam yarn disappears and is not visible on the right side of the crochet.

SLIP STITCH SEAM

1 Instead of using a yarn needle to join your seam, you can use a crochet hook to work a quicker seam. Although seams can be worked with double crochet, slip stitch seams are less bulky. Start by placing a slip knot on the hook.

Start with a slip knot on the hook

Seam yarn

2 Align the two layers of crochet with the right sides together.

3 Then with the slip knot on the hook, insert the hook through the two layers at the starting end of the seam, wrap the yarn around the hook and draw a loop through the two layers and the loop on the hook.

4 Continue in this way and fasten off at the end. When working the seam along the tops of stitches (as here), insert the hook through only the back loops of the stitches. Along row-end edges, work through the layers one stitch in from the edge.

EMBELLISHMENTS FOR CROCHET

There are many ways to add subtle or bold embellishments to your crochet. Although it may seem unimportant, choosing the right buttons when they are required comes top of the list, so always select buttons carefully and take your finished crochet along to try them out before purchasing any. Other adornments that will dress up your crochet include beads, ribbons, pompoms and fringe, edgings, and embroidery.

BEADED CROCHET

Beads can be sewn onto your finished crochet if you are only adding a few. But for an allover effect, work the beads into the fabric as you crochet. The most common beaded crochet technique uses double crochet as the background to the beads.

WORKING BEADED DOUBLE CROCHET

Beaded crochet is suitable for a range of simple spaced-out allover geometric patterns. But beware of using too many beads on the crochet or beads that are too big, as they can add so much extra weight to the fabric that they stretch it out.

1 Beaded double crochet is usually worked from a chart that shows the positions of the beads on the fabric. The chart is read as for a chart for colourwork (see page 128) and the key provided with the chart indicates which stitches are worked as plain double crochet and which have beads.

Sewing thread

Sewing needle

2 Loop the end of the yarn into a loop of sewing thread as shown, then thread the beads onto the needle and down onto the yarn.

Yarn going to ball

3 Follow the chart for the bead pattern, sliding the beads along the yarn until they are needed. The beads are always positioned on wrong-side rows. When a bead position is reached, work the next double crochet up to the last yrh – there are now 2 loops on the hook. Slide a bead up close to the crochet and wrap the yarn around the hook.

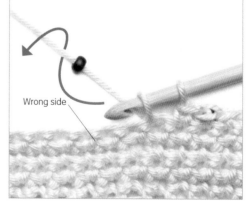

Wrong side

4 Draw a loop through both loops on the hook to complete the double crochet.

5 Complete the double crochet tightly so that the bead sits snugly against the fabric on the right side of the crochet.

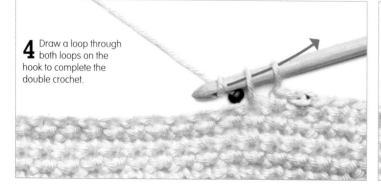

EMBROIDERY
ON CROCHET

Because double crochet creates such a firm fabric, it is easy to work embroidery onto it. Many embroidery stitches are suitable for crochet and a few of the most popular are given here. Use the same yarn for the embroidery as the yarn used for the crochet, or a slightly thicker yarn, so that the stitches will show up well. Always work the stitches with the same type of blunt-ended yarn needle that is used for seams.

BLANKET STITCH

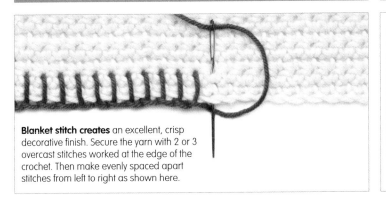

Blanket stitch creates an excellent, crisp decorative finish. Secure the yarn with 2 or 3 overcast stitches worked at the edge of the crochet. Then make evenly spaced apart stitches from left to right as shown here.

CHAIN STITCH

Chain stitch is perfect for curved motifs. Hold the yarn on the wrong side of the fabric and draw loops through with the hook. To fasten off, pull the yarn end through the last loop and then back to the wrong side over the loop. Darn in the ends on the wrong side.

CROSS STITCH

1 Work each individual cross stitch on double crochet over a single double crochet stitch. Complete each cross stitch before moving on to the next. Keep the stitches fairly loose so they don't distort the crochet.

2 Adding lines of cross stitches is an effective way to create an interesting plaid pattern on a base of plain double crochet. This is the perfect technique for dressing up a drab piece of plain double crochet.

EDGINGS
ON CROCHET

Several edging patterns are provided on pages 144–149 because they are excellent simple adornment for your crochet. Some edgings can be worked directly onto your crochet (see page 138), and others made separately and then sewn on.

ADDING EDGINGS

To sew an edging in place, use a yarn that matches the base crochet and a blunt-ended yarn needle. Secure the yarn at the right-hand end of the seam with 2 or 3 overcast stitches. Then work evenly spaced overcast stitches through both the base crochet and the edging as shown.

SIMPLE EDGING
PATTERNS

Adding a decorative crochet edging to an otherwise mundane-looking piece of crochet (or knitting) can transform it, giving it a touch of elegance. All the simple crochet edgings that follow are worked widthwise, so you start with a length of chain roughly equivalent to the length of edging you need. Suitable even for beginners, these edgings are perfect for dressing up towel ends, throws, baby blankets, necklines and cuffs. When making an edging that will encircle a blanket, be sure to add extra for turning the corners; the edging can then be gathered at each corner to allow for the turning. Use a short test swatch to calculate how much extra you will need at each corner. See page 115 for abbreviations and symbols.

CHAIN FRINGE

CROCHET DIAGRAM

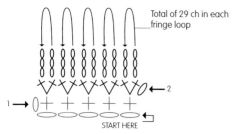

Total of 29 ch in each fringe loop

START HERE

CROCHET INSTRUCTIONS
Note: This fringe is worked onto a row of dc. The length of the fringe can be altered by changing the number of chains in each fringe loop. To start edging, make 1 ch more than required number of dc.
Row 1 (WS) 1 dc in 2nd ch from hook, 1 dc in each of rem ch, turn.
Row 2 (RS) 1 ch, 1 dc in first dc, 29 ch, 1 dc in same place as last dc, *1 dc in next dc, 29 ch, 1 dc in same place as last dc; rep from * to end. Fasten off.

STEP EDGING

CROCHET DIAGRAM

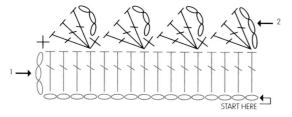

START HERE

CROCHET INSTRUCTIONS
Make a multiple of 4 ch, plus 3 extra.
Row 1 (WS) 1 tr in 4th ch from hook, 1 tr in each of rem ch, turn.
Row 2 (RS) 3 ch, 3 tr in first tr, *miss next 3 tr, work [1 dc, 3 ch, 3 tr] all in next tr; rep from * to last 3 tr, miss last 3 tr, 1 dc in top of 3-ch at end. Fasten off.

TRIPLE PICOT EDGING

CROCHET DIAGRAM

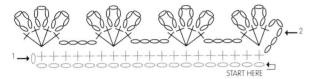

CROCHET INSTRUCTIONS

Make a multiple of 6 ch, plus 2 extra.
Row 1 (WS) 1 dc in 2nd ch from hook, 1 dc in each of rem ch, turn.
Row 2 (RS) 5 ch, work [1 dc, (5 ch, 1 dc) twice] all in first dc, *4 ch, miss next 5 dc, [1 dc, (5 ch, 1 dc) 3 times] all in next dc; rep from * to end.
Fasten off.

PICOT SCALLOP EDGING

CROCHET DIAGRAM

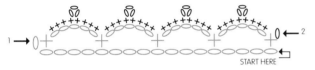

CROCHET INSTRUCTIONS

Make a multiple of 4 ch, plus 2 extra.
Row 1 (WS) 1 dc in 2nd ch from hook, *5 ch, miss next 3 ch, 1 dc in next ch; rep from * to end, turn.
Row 2 (RS) 1 ch, *work [4 dc, 3 ch, 4 dc] all in next 5-ch loop; rep from * to end.
Fasten off.

SIMPLE SHELL EDGING

CROCHET DIAGRAM

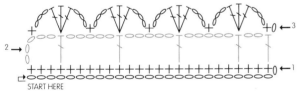

CROCHET INSTRUCTIONS

Make a multiple of 6 ch, plus 2 extra.
Row 1 (RS) 1 dc in 2nd ch from hook, 1 dc in each of rem ch, turn.
Row 2 5 ch, miss first 3 dc, 1 tr in next dc, *5 ch, miss next 5 dc, 1 tr in next dc; rep from * to last 3 dc, 2 ch, miss next 2 dc, 1 tr in last dc, turn.
Row 3 1 ch, 1 dc in first tr, 3 ch, 3 tr in next tr, *3 ch, 1 dc in next 5-ch space, 3 ch, 3 tr in next tr; rep from *, ending with 3 ch, miss first 2 ch of last 5-ch, 1 dc in next ch.
Fasten off.

GRAND EYELET EDGING

CROCHET DIAGRAM

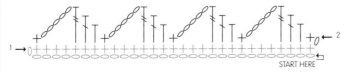

CROCHET INSTRUCTIONS

Make a multiple of 7 ch, plus 2 extra.
Row 1 (WS) 1 dc in 2nd ch from hook, 1 dc in each of rem ch, turn.
Row 2 (RS) 1 ch, 1 dc in first dc, 1 htr in next dc, 1 tr in next dc, 1 dtr in next dc, *5 ch, miss next 3 dc, 1 dc in next dc, 1 htr in next dc, 1 tr in next dc, 1 dtr in next dc; rep from * to last 4 dc, 5 ch, miss next 3 dc, 1 dc in last dc.
Fasten off.

PILLAR EDGING

CROCHET DIAGRAM

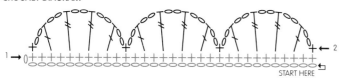

START HERE

CROCHET INSTRUCTIONS
Make a multiple of 10 ch, plus 2 extra.
Row 1 (WS) 1 dc in 2nd ch from hook, 1 dc in each of rem ch, turn.
Row 2 (RS) 1 ch, 1 dc in first dc, *2 ch, miss next dc, 1 tr in next dc, [2 ch, miss next dc, 1 dtr in next dc] twice, 2 ch, miss next dc, 1 tr in next dc, 2 ch, miss next dc, 1 dc in next dc; rep from * to end.
Fasten off.

DOUBLE LOOP EDGING

CROCHET DIAGRAM

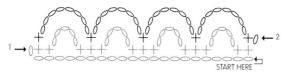

START HERE

CROCHET INSTRUCTIONS
To start edging, make a multiple of 5 ch, plus 2 extra.
Row 1 (WS) 1 dc in 2nd ch from hook, 1 dc in next ch, *5 ch, miss next 2 ch, 1 dc in each of next 3 ch; rep from * to last 4 ch, 5 ch, miss next 2 ch, 1 dc in each of last 2 ch, turn.
Row 2 (RS) 1 ch, 1 dc in first dc, *8 ch, 1 dc in centre dc of next group of 3-dc (at other side of 5-ch loop); rep from * working last dc in last dc of row 1.
Fasten off.

TWIRL FRINGE

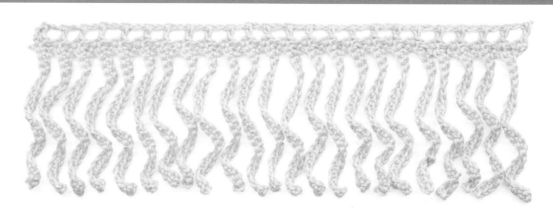

CROCHET DIAGRAM

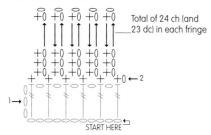

Total of 24 ch (and 23 dc) in each fringe

START HERE

CROCHET INSTRUCTIONS
Note: The fringe will twirl naturally; do not press out the twirls.
To start edging, make a multiple of 2 ch.
Row 1 (WS) 1 tr in 4th ch from hook, *1 ch, miss next ch, 1 tr in next ch; rep from * to end, turn.
Row 2 (RS) 1 ch, 1 dc in first tr, *24 ch, 1 dc in 2nd ch from hook, 1 dc in each of rem 22 ch, 1 dc in next tr; rep from * to end.
Fasten off.

CLUSTER SCALLOP EDGING

CROCHET DIAGRAM

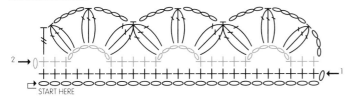

CROCHET INSTRUCTIONS

Make a multiple of 8 ch, plus 2 extra.
Row 1 (RS) 1 dc in 2nd ch from hook, 1 dc in each of rem ch, turn.
Row 2 1 ch, 1 dc in first dc, 1 dc in each of next 2 dc, *6 ch, miss next 3 dc, 1 dc in each of next 5 dc; rep from * to last 6 dc, 6 ch, miss next 3 dc, 1 dc in each of last 3 dc, turn.
Row 3 3 ch, work [yrh, insert hook in ch sp, yrh and draw a loop through, yrh and draw through first 2 loops on hook] 3 times in next 6-ch sp, 4 loops now on hook, yrh and draw through all 4 loops on hook to close 3-tr group—called 3-tr cluster –, *4 ch, 3-tr cluster in same ch sp, 4 ch, 3-tr cluster in same ch sp BUT do not close cluster (leave last 4 loops on hook), 3-tr cluster in next 6-ch sp and close this cluster and last cluster at same time by drawing a loop through all 7 loops on hook; rep from * to last 6-ch sp, [4 ch, 3-tr cluster in same ch sp] twice, 1 tr in last dc of row 2.
Fasten off.

CLUSTER AND SHELL EDGING

CROCHET DIAGRAM

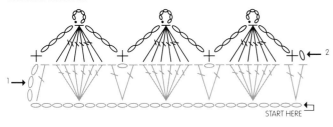

CROCHET INSTRUCTIONS

Make a multiple of 8 ch, plus 4 extra.
Row 1 (WS) 1 tr in 4th ch from hook, *miss next 3 ch, 6 tr in next ch (to make a shell), miss next 3 ch, work [1 tr, 1 ch, 1 tr] all in next ch; rep from * to last 8 ch, miss next 3 ch, 6 tr in next ch, miss next 3 ch, 2 tr in last ch, turn.
Row 2 (RS) 1 ch, miss first tr, 1 dc in next tr, *4 ch, [yrh, insert hook in next tr, yrh and draw a loop through, yrh and draw through first 2 loops on hook] 6 times (once into each of 6 tr of shell), yrh and draw through all 7 loops on hook to complete cluster, 6 ch, 1 ss in top of cluster just made, 4 ch, 1 dc in next 1-ch sp (between 2 tr); rep from * to end, working last dc of last rep in top of 3-ch at end.
Fasten off.

BOLD SCALLOP EDGING

CROCHET DIAGRAM

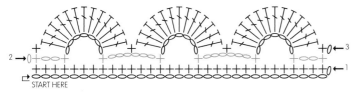

CROCHET INSTRUCTIONS

Make a multiple of 10 ch, plus 2 extra.
Row 1 (RS) 1 dc in 2nd ch from hook, 1 dc in each of rem ch, turn.
Row 2 1 ch, 1 dc in first dc, 2 ch, miss next 2 dc, 1 dc in next dc, 7 ch, miss next 3 dc, 1 dc in next dc, *6 ch, miss next 5 ch, 1 dc in next dc, 7 ch, miss next 3 dc, 1 dc in next dc; rep from * to last 3 dc, 2 ch, miss next 2 dc, 1 dc in last dc, turn.
Row 3 1 ch, 1 dc in first dc, 14 tr in 7-ch loop, *1 dc in next 6-ch sp, 14 tr in next 7-ch loop; rep from *, ending with 1 dc in last dc.
Fasten off.

LONG LOOP EDGING

CROCHET DIAGRAM

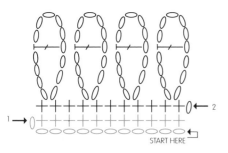

CROCHET INSTRUCTIONS
Make a multiple of 3 ch.
Row 1 (WS) 1 dc in 2nd ch from hook, 1 dc in each of rem ch, turn.
Row 2 (RS) 1 ch, 1 dc in first dc, 9 ch, 1 tr in 6th ch from hook, 4 ch, *1 dc in each of next 3 dc, 9 ch, 1 tr in 6th ch from hook, 4 ch; rep from * to last dc, 1 dc in last dc.
Fasten off.

DIAMOND EDGING

CROCHET DIAGRAM

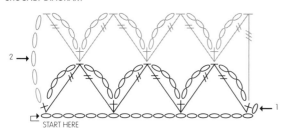

CROCHET INSTRUCTIONS
Make a multiple of 6 ch, plus 2 extra.
Row 1 (RS) 1 dc in 2nd ch from hook, *4 ch, yrh twice and insert hook in same place as last dc, [yrh and draw first 2 loops on hook] twice, yrh twice, miss next 5 ch and insert hook in next ch, [yrh and draw first 2 loops on hook] twice, yrh and draw through all 3 loops on hook – called dtr2tog –, 4 ch, 1 dc in same place as last dtr; rep from * to end, turn.
Row 2 5 ch, 1 dtr in first dtr2tog, 4 ch, 1 dc in same place as last dtr, *4 ch, dtr2tog over last dtr worked into and next dtr, 4 ch, 1 dc in same place as last dtr; rep from *, 4 ch, yrh twice and insert hook in same place as last dc, [yrh and draw first 2 loops on hook] twice, yrh 3 times and insert hook in next last dc in previous row, [yrh and draw first 2 loops on hook] 3 times, yrh and draw through all 3 loops on hook.
Fasten off.

DOUBLE SCALLOP EDGING

CROCHET DIAGRAM

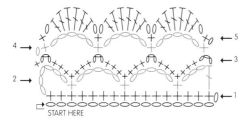

CROCHET INSTRUCTIONS
Make a multiple of 5 ch, plus 2 extra.
Row 1 (RS) 1 dc in 2nd ch from hook, 1 dc in each of rem ch, turn.
Row 2 6 ch, miss first 2 dc, 1 dc in next dc, *5 ch, miss next 4 dc, 1 dc in next dc; rep from * to last 3 dc, 3 ch, miss next 2 dc, 1 tr in last dc, turn.
Row 3 3 ch, 3 dc in first 3-ch sp, 1 dc in next dc (between loops), *work [3 dc, 3 ch, 3 dc] all in next 5-ch loop, 1 dc in next dc; rep from *, ending with [3 dc, 3 ch, 1 dc] in last 6-ch loop, turn.
Row 4 1 ch, 1 dc in first 3-ch picot, *5 ch, 1 dc in next 3-ch picot; rep from * to end, turn.
Row 5 1 ch, 1 dc in first dc, *1 ch, 6 tr in next 5-ch loop, 1 ch, 1 dc in next dc; rep from * to end.
Fasten off.

CROCHET

SIMPLE MULTIPLE-STITCH EDGING

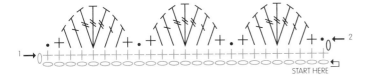

CROCHET DIAGRAM

CROCHET INSTRUCTIONS
Make a multiple of 8 ch, plus 2 extra.
Row 1 (WS) 1 dc in 2nd ch from hook, 1 dc in each of rem ch, turn.
Row 2 (RS) 1 ch, 1 ss in first dc, *1 dc in next dc, 1 htr in next dc, 1 tr in next dc, 3 dtr in next dc, 1 tr in next dc, 1 htr in next dc, 1 dc in next dc, 1 ss in next dc; rep from * to end.
Fasten off.

PETAL EDGING

CROCHET DIAGRAM

CROCHET INSTRUCTIONS
Make a multiple of 14 ch, plus 2 extra.
Row 1 (RS) 1 dc in 2nd ch from hook, 1 dc in each of rem ch, turn.
Row 2 1 ch, 1 dc in first dc, *6 ch, miss next 6 dc, work [2 tr, 2 ch, 2tr] all in next dc, 6 ch, miss next 6 dc, 1 dc in next dc; rep from * to end, turn.
Row 3 1 ch, 1 dc in first dc, *6 ch, work [2 tr, 2 ch, 2 tr] all in next 2-ch sp, 6 ch, 1 dc in next dc; rep from * to end.
Fasten off.
Note: When blocking this edging, pin out each point at each 2-ch sp to achieve correct shape.

CIRCLES EDGING

CROCHET DIAGRAM

CROCHET INSTRUCTIONS
Make a multiple of 6 ch.
Row 1 (RS) 1 dc in 9th ch from hook, *7 ch, miss next 5 ch, 1 dc in next ch; rep from * to last 3 ch, 3 ch, miss next 2 ch, 1 dc in last ch, turn.
Row 2 1 ch, 1 dc in first tr, 2 ch, 1 tr in next dc, *5 ch, 1 tr in next dc; rep from *, ending with 2 ch, 1 dc 4th ch from last dc in previous row, turn.
Row 3 1 ch, 1 dc in first dc, *3 ch, 1 tr in next tr, 3 ch, 1 dc in 7-ch loop of row 1 (catching 5-ch loop in previous row inside dc); rep from * to end working last dc of last rep in last dc of row 2.
Fasten off.

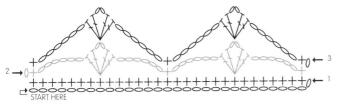
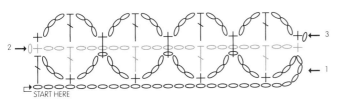

CIRCULAR CROCHET

Crochet can be worked not only back and forth in rows, but round and round in circles to form tubes or flat shapes started from the centre (called medallions). The basic techniques for crocheting in the round are very easy to learn, even for a beginner, so it is not surprising that many popular crochet accessories are made with circular crochet, including flowers and afghan motifs, as well as seamless toys, hats, mittens, containers, and bags.

CROCHETING TUBES

Tubular crochet is started on a long foundation chain joined into a ring, and the rounds of stitches are worked around this ring. The easiest of all crochet cylinders is double crochet worked in a spiral without turning chains.

STARTING A TUBE

1 Start the crochet cylinder, or tube, with the length of chain specified in your crochet pattern. Then, insert the hook through the first chain.

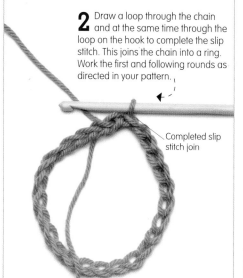

Make sure chain is not twisted

2 Draw a loop through the chain and at the same time through the loop on the hook to complete the slip stitch. This joins the chain into a ring. Work the first and following rounds as directed in your pattern.

Completed slip stitch join

DOUBLE CROCHET SPIRAL TUBE

1 Make the foundation ring and work one chain. Work the first double crochet into the same place as the slip stitch. Then work 1 dc into each of the remaining chains of the ring.

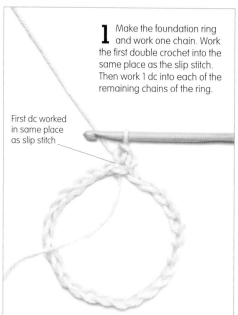

First dc worked in same place as slip stitch

2 Place a stitch marker on the last stitch of the first round to keep track of where the rounds begin and end.

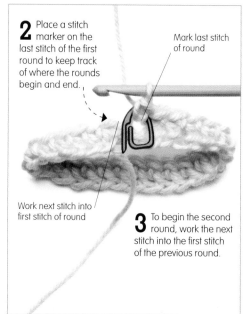

Mark last stitch of round

Work next stitch into first stitch of round

3 To begin the second round, work the next stitch into the first stitch of the previous round.

4 On the second round, work 1 dc in each dc in the round below.

Move marker up at end of each round

5 At the end of the round move the marker up onto the last stitch of this round. (As the spiral grows, the beginning of the round moves gradually to the right.)

Work with right side always facing

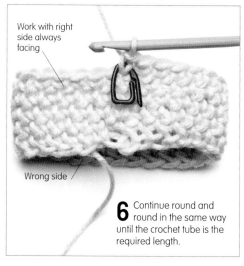

Wrong side

6 Continue round and round in the same way until the crochet tube is the required length.

TREBLE CROCHET TUBE WITHOUT TURNS

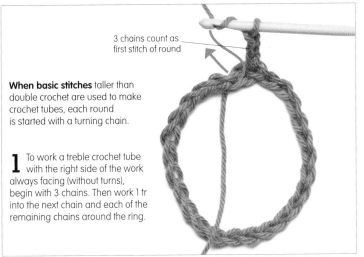

3 chains count as first stitch of round

When basic stitches taller than double crochet are used to make crochet tubes, each round is started with a turning chain.

1 To work a treble crochet tube with the right side of the work always facing (without turns), begin with 3 chains. Then work 1 tr into the next chain and each of the remaining chains around the ring.

2 At the end of the round, join the last stitch to the top of the turning chain at the beginning of the round by working a slip stitch into the third of the 3 chains.

Join with a slip stitch to top of 3 chains

3 Start the second round with 3 chains. There is no need to mark the end of the round with a stitch marker as the turning chain shows where each round begins. Continue around the tube again, working 1 tr into each tr in the previous round.

3 chains count as first stitch.

4 At the end of the second round, join the last stitch to the top of the turning chain with a slip stitch. Continue in the same way, beginning all following rounds with 3 chains.

Right side shows fronts of trebles

Wrong side shows back of trebles

TREBLE CROCHET TUBE WITH TURNS

If a treble crochet tube needs to match crochet worked in rows in other parts of an item, then the work can be turned at the end of each round.

1 Work the first round in treble crochet as for a tube without turns. Then turn the work, make 3 chains as shown and complete the round.

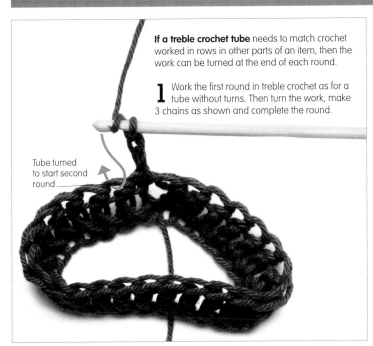

Tube turned to start second round

2 To begin the third round, turn the work and start with 3 chains.

3 Continue in this way, joining the last stitch with a slip stitch to the top of the turning chain at the end of each round, then turning the work to start the next round. The fabric looks just like treble crochet that has been worked in ordinary rows.

Second round shows backs of trebles

First round shows fronts of trebles

FLAT CIRCLES

The circular crochet techniques for making flat shapes are a little more difficult than those for making tubes. Making a simple circle is a good example for how other flat medallion shapes are started and then worked round and round from the centre. The circle is also used in conjunction with the crochet tube to make containers (see page 162) or the parts of toys (see page 159), so it is well worth practising.

CROCHETING A CIRCLE

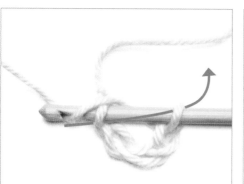

1 Follow these steps when working the simple circle below for the first time. The circle is worked from the centre outwards. Start with 4 ch. Then work a slip stitch into the first chain as shown by the large arrow.

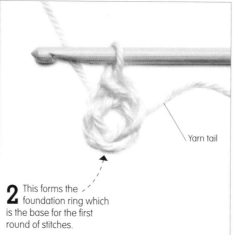

Yarn tail

2 This forms the foundation ring which is the base for the first round of stitches.

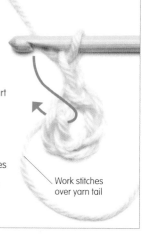

3 For a double crochet circle, start the first round with 1 chain. Then lay the yarn end around the top of the chain and start working the double crochet stitches of the first round through the centre of the ring and around the yarn tail.

Work stitches over yarn tail

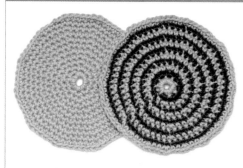

Safety pin stitch marker

Clip off yarn tail

4 When all 8 double crochet stitches of the first round are complete, mark the last stitch of the round with a stitch marker as shown. Then pull the yarn tail to close the centre hole and clip it off close to the crochet.

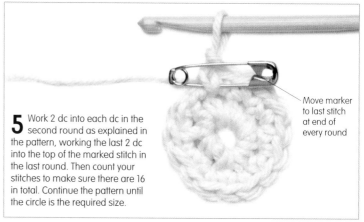

5 Work 2 dc into each dc in the second round as explained in the pattern, working the last 2 dc into the top of the marked stitch in the last round. Then count your stitches to make sure there are 16 in total. Continue the pattern until the circle is the required size.

Move marker to last stitch at end of every round

SIMPLE 11-ROUND CIRCLE MEDALLION

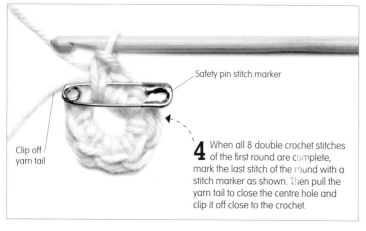

This pattern is for a classic simple crochet circle. (See page 115 for abbreviations.)

Note: Work the circle in a single colour or in two colours (A and B). For a two-colour circle, work the foundation ring and round 1 in A, then work the following rounds in B and A alternately, changing to the new colour with the last yrh of the last dc of each round and carrying the colours up the wrong side of the circle.
Make 4 ch and join with a ss in first ch to form a ring.
Round 1 (RS) 1ch, 8 dc in ring. Do not turn at end of rounds, but work with RS always facing.

Note: Mark the last stitch of round 1, and at the end of each of the following rounds, move this marker to the last stitch of the round just worked.
Round 2 2 dc in each dc. *16 dc.*
Round 3 *1 dc in next dc, 2 dc in next dc; rep from *. *24 dc.*
Round 4 1 dc in each dc.
Round 5 *1 dc in next dc, 2 dc in next dc; rep from *. *36 dc.*
Round 6 Rep round 4.
Round 7 *1 dc in each of next 2 dc, 2 dc in next dc; rep from *. *48 dc.*
Round 8 Rep round 4.

Round 9 *1 dc in each of next 3 dc, 2 dc in next dc; rep from *. *60 dc.*
Round 10 Rep round 4.
Round 11 1 dc in each of first 2 dc, 2 dc in next dc, *1 dc in each of next 4 dc, 2 dc in next dc; rep from *, ending with 1 dc in each of last 2 dc. *72 dc.*
Work 1 ss in next dc and fasten off.
To make a bigger circle, continue in this way, adding 12 extra dc in every alternate round (by working one more stitch between increases) and altering the position of the first increase on every increase round.

TIPS FOR
MEDALLIONS

The principle for starting any medallion shape and working it in rounds is the same as for the simple circle, and many simple crochet flowers are also worked using these techniques (see pages 156–157). If you find it awkward to fit all the stitches of the first round into a tiny foundation ring (see opposite page), try the simple loop ring below. Two other useful tips are the techniques for starting new colours and for joining motifs together.

MAKING A SIMPLE LOOP RING

1 Making the simple loop ring is a quick way to start working a flat shape in the round, and it allows you to make the centre hole as tight as desired, or as open as desired. Start as if you are making a slip knot (see page 99), by forming a circle of yarn and drawing the yarn through the centre of it.

2 Leave the circle of yarn open. Then to start a round of double crochet stitches, make 1 chain.

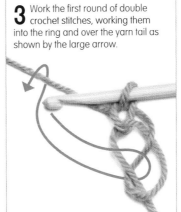

3 Work the first round of double crochet stitches, working them into the ring and over the yarn tail as shown by the large arrow.

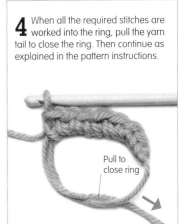

4 When all the required stitches are worked into the ring, pull the yarn tail to close the ring. Then continue as explained in the pattern instructions.

Pull to close ring

JOINING IN A NEW COLOUR

When starting a new colour at the beginning of a medallion round, you can either change to the new colour with the last yrh of the previous round or fasten off the old colour and join in a new colour with a slip stitch.

New colour   Old colour
Slip knot

1 Joining on the new colour with a slip stitch makes a firm attachment. Make a slip knot with the new colour and remove it from the hook. Then insert the hook at the specified position and draw the slip knot through.

2 Start the new round with the specified number of chains, drawing the first chain through the slip knot. Work the stitches of the round over both yarn tails (the new colour and the old colour) so that there aren't so many ends to darn in later.

Work stitches over yarn tails

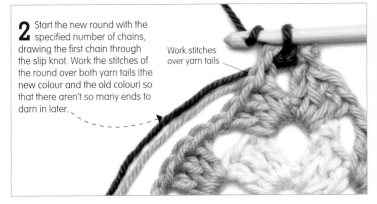

JOINING MEDALLIONS

Right sides facing upwards

Flat slip-stitch seam: Working seams with crochet stitches are the quickest way to join medallions. For a slip-stitch seam, lay the two medallions side by side. Work each slip stitch through only 1 loop (the back loop) of the top of a stitch on each medallion. (Use a hook size one size smaller than the hook used for the medallions, but work the stitches very loosely.)

Right sides together

Double-crochet seam: A double crochet seam is also quick to work, but it forms a ridge, so is best worked on the wrong side. Place the two medallions with the right sides together. Then work each double crochet through only 1 loop of the top of a stitch on each medallion (the loop closest to you on the top medallion and the loop farthest from you on the bottom medallion).

SIMPLE MEDALLION PATTERNS

Making crochet medallions is a great way to use up yarn scraps, and this was probably the reason they became so popular. You can stitch medallions together to form small items like bags or cushion covers, or to form larger items like throws and baby blankets. Joined medallions also make great scarves and shawls, especially when made in gossamer mohair. But if you are a beginner, stick to less hairy yarns when making your first medallions as it is easier to learn the technique with a smooth standard lightweight or medium-weight wool yarn.

TRADITIONAL AFGHAN SQUARE

CROCHET DIAGRAM

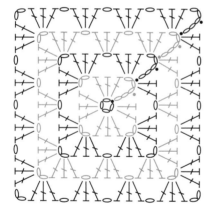

CROCHET INSTRUCTIONS

This square is worked in 4 colours (A, B, C, D), a different colour for each round.
Using A, make 4 ch and join with a ss to first ch to form a ring.
Round 1 (RS) Using A, 5 ch (counts as 1 tr and a 2-ch sp), [3 tr in ring, 2 ch (these 2-ch form a corner sp)] 3 times, 2 tr in ring, join with a ss to 3rd of 5-ch. Fasten off A.
Round 2 Using B, join with a ss to a 2-ch corner sp, 5 ch, 3 tr in same corner sp, *1 ch, [3 tr, 2 ch, 3 tr] in next 2-ch corner sp; rep from * twice more, 1 ch, 2 tr in same corner sp as 5-ch at beg of round, join with a ss to 3rd of 5-ch. Fasten off B.
Round 3 Using C, join to a 2-ch corner sp, 5 ch, 3 tr in same corner sp, *1 ch, 3 tr in next 1-ch sp, 1 ch, [3 tr, 2 ch, 3 tr] in next 2-ch corner sp; rep from * twice more, 1 ch, 3 tr in next 1-ch sp, 1 ch, 2 tr in same sp as 5-ch at beg of round, join with a ss to 3rd of 5-ch. Fasten off C.
Round 4 Using D, join to a 2-ch corner sp, 5 ch, 3 tr in same corner sp, *[1 ch, 3 tr in next 1-ch sp] twice, 1 ch, [3 tr, 2 ch, 3 tr] in next 2-ch corner sp; rep from * twice more, [1 ch, 3 tr in next 1-ch sp] twice, 1 ch, 2 tr in same sp as 5-ch at beg of round, join with a ss to 3rd of 5-ch.
Fasten off.

PLAIN SQUARE

CROCHET DIAGRAM

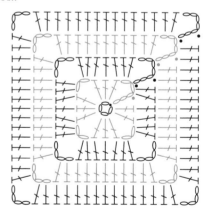

CROCHET INSTRUCTIONS

This square is worked in 3 colours (A, B, C).
Using A, make 4 ch and join with a ss to first ch to form a ring.
Round 1 (RS) 5 ch (counts as 1 tr and a 2-ch sp), [3 tr in ring, 2 ch sp) 3 times, 2 tr in ring, join with a ss to 3rd of 5-ch.
Round 2 1 ss in next ch, 7 ch (counts as 1 tr and a 4-ch sp), 2 tr in same 2-ch corner sp, *1 tr in each of next 3 tr, [2 tr, 4 ch, 2 tr] in next 2-ch corner sp; rep from * twice more, 1 tr in each of next 3 sts (working last of these tr in top of turning ch at beg of previous round), 1 tr in same sp as 7-ch at beg of round, join with a ss to 3rd of 7-ch. Fasten off A.
Round 3 Using B, join to a 4-ch corner sp, 7 ch, 1 tr in each of tr along this side of square, [2 tr, 4 ch, 2 tr] in next 4-ch corner sp; rep from * twice more, 1 tr in each of tr along this side of square (working last of these tr in top of turning ch at beg of previous round), 1 tr in same sp as 7-ch at beg of round, join with a ss to 3rd of 7-ch. Fasten off B.
Round 4 Using C, rep round 3.
Fasten off.

SPECIAL NOTES

• When following diagrams, use colours as explained in the written instructions. The symbols tones are used to distinguish the rows and do not indicate colour changes. (See page 115 for a list of crochet abbreviations and basic stitch symbols.)

• Join on new colours as explained on page 153.

• Do not turn the medallions at the end of the rounds, but work with the right side always facing.

SIMPLE HEXAGON

CROCHET DIAGRAM

CROCHET INSTRUCTIONS

Note: cluster (cl) = [yrh and insert hook in sp, yrh and draw a loop through, yrh and draw through first 2 loops on hook] 3 times all in same sp (4 loops now on hook), yrh and draw through all 4 loops on hook.

This hexagon is worked in 3 colours (A, B, C).

Using A, make 6 ch and join with a ss to first ch to form a ring.

Round 1 (RS) 3 ch, tr2tog (counts as first cl), [3 ch, 1 cl in ring] 5 times, 1 ch, join with 1 htr in top of first cl.

Round 2 3 ch, tr2tog in sp formed by 1-htr, *3 ch, [1 cl, 3 ch, 1 cl] in next 3-ch sp; rep from *4 times more, 3 ch, 1 cl in next 1-ch sp, 1 ch, join with 1 htr in top of first cl changing to B with last yrh of htr. Cut off A.

Round 3 Using B, 3 ch, tr2tog in sp formed by 1-htr, *3 ch, [1 cl, 3 ch, 1 cl] in next 3-ch sp, 3 ch, 1 cl in next 3-ch sp; rep from * 4 times more, 3 ch, [1 cl, 3 ch, 1 cl] in next 3-ch sp, 1 ch, join with 1 htr in top of first cl changing to C with last yrh of htr. Cut off B.

Round 4 Using C, 3 ch, 1 tr in sp formed by 1-htr, *3 tr in next 3-ch sp, [3 tr, 2 ch, 3 tr] in next 3-ch sp, 3 tr in next 3-ch sp; rep from * 4 times more, 3 tr in next 3-ch sp, [3 tr, 2 ch, 3 tr] in next 3-ch sp, 1 tr in next 1-ch sp, join with a ss to 3rd of 3-ch at beg of round.

Fasten off.

FLOWER HEXAGON

CROCHET DIAGRAM

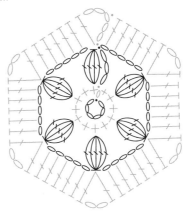

CROCHET INSTRUCTIONS

Note: bobble = [yrh and insert hook in dc, yrh and draw a loop through, yrh and draw through first 2 loops on hook] 5 times all in same dc (6 loops now on hook), yrh and draw through all 6 loops on hook.

This hexagon is worked in 2 colours (A, B).

Using A, make 6 ch and join with a ss to first ch to form a ring.

Round 1 (RS) 1 ch, 12 dc in ring, join with a ss to first dc.

Round 2 3 ch, [yrh and insert hook in same dc as last ss, yrh and draw a loop through, yrh and draw through first 2 loops on hook] 4 times all in same dc (5 loops now on hook), yrh and draw through all 5 loops on hook (counts as first bobble), *5 ch, miss next dc, 1 bobble in next dc; rep from * 4 times more, 5 ch, join with a ss to top of first bobble. Fasten off A.

Round 3 Using B, join with a ss to top of a bobble, 5 ch (counts as 1 tr and a 2-ch sp), 1 tr in same place as ss, *5 tr in next 5-ch sp, [1 tr, 2 ch, 1 tr] in top of next bobble; rep from 4 times more, 5 tr in next 5-ch sp, join with a ss to 3rd of 5-ch at beg of round.

Fasten off.

SIMPLE FLOWER PATTERNS

Crochet flowers are very seductive – even simple ones like these, which are all easy and very quick to make. You may want to try them out right away but wonder what to do with them. First, they make great individual brooches, which, in turn, are perfect gifts. Just sew a safety pin to the back and maybe a button or an artificial pearl to the flower centre. Flowers and leaves can also be used to decorate crocheted (or knitted) hats, the ends of scarves, glove cuffs, or bags. Sprinkled over a cushion cover, they will make a bold statement in a room, as well.

SHORT LOOP FLOWER

CROCHET DIAGRAM

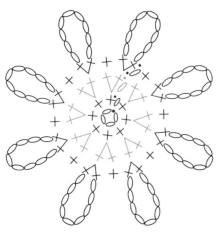

CROCHET INSTRUCTIONS

This flower is worked in 2 colours (A, B).
Using A, make 4 ch and join with a ss to first ch to form a ring.
Round 1 (RS) 1 ch (does NOT count as a st), 8 dc in ring, join with a ss to first dc of round. 16 dc. Fasten off A.
Round 2 1 ch (does NOT count as a st), 2 dc in same place as ss, *2 dc in next dc; rep from * to end, join with a ss to first dc of round. 16 dc.
Round 3 Using B, join with a ss to a dc, 1 ch, work [1 dc, 9 ch, 1 dc] all in same place as last ss, 1 dc in next dc, *work [1 dc, 9 ch, 1 dc] all in next dc, 1 dc in next dc; rep from * 6 times more, join with a ss to first dc of round. Fasten off.

LONG LOOP FLOWER

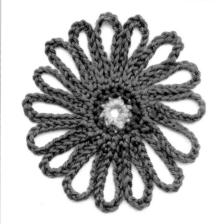

CROCHET DIAGRAM

Total of 17 ch in each loop

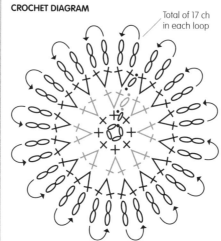

CROCHET INSTRUCTIONS

This flower is worked in 3 colours (A, B, C).
Using A, make 4 ch and join with a ss to first ch to form a ring.
Round 1 (RS) 1 ch (does NOT count as a st), 8 dc in ring, join with a ss to first dc of round. Fasten off A.
Round 2 Using B, join with a ss to a dc, 1 ch (does NOT count as a st), 2 dc in same place as last ss, *2 dc in next dc; rep from * to end, join with a ss to first dc of round. 16 dc. Fasten off B.
Round 3 Using C, join with a ss to a dc, 1 ch, work [1 dc, 17 ch, 1 dc] all in same place as last ss, *work [1 dc, 17 ch, 1 dc] all in next dc; rep from * 14 times more, join with a ss to first dc of round. Fasten off.

BUTTON FLOWER

CROCHET DIAGRAM

CROCHET INSTRUCTIONS

Note: cluster = [yrh twice and insert hook in sp, yrh and draw a loop through, (yrh and draw through first 2 loops on hook) twice] 4 times all in same sp (5 loops now on hook), yrh and draw through all 5 loops on hook.
This flower is worked in 2 colours (A, B).
Using A, make 4 ch and join with a ss to first ch to form a ring.
Round 1 (RS) 4 ch (counts as first dtr), 20 dtr in ring, join with a ss to 4th of 4-ch. Fasten off A.
Round 2 Using B, join with a ss to same place as last ss, 1 ch (does NOT count as a st), 1 dc in same place as last ss, [5 ch, miss next 2 dtr, 1 dc in next dtr] 6 times, 5 ch, join with a ss to first dc of round.
Round 3 *Work [1 ss, 4 ch, 1 cluster, 4 ch, 1 ss] all in next 5-ch loop; rep from * 6 times more, join with a ss to last dc in round 2.
Fasten off. Sew a small button to centre of flower.

SPECIAL NOTES

• When following diagrams, use colours as explained in written instructions. The symbol tones are used to distinguish the rows and do not indicate colour changes. (See page 115 for a list of crochet abbreviations and basic stitch symbols.)

• Join on new yarn colours as explained on page 153.

• Do not turn at the end of the rounds, but work with the right side of the flowers always facing.

PENTAGON FLOWER

CROCHET DIAGRAM

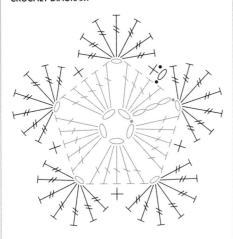

CROCHET INSTRUCTIONS
This flower is worked in 2 colours (A, B).
Using A, make 5 ch and join with a ss to first ch to form a ring.
Round 1 (RS) 3 ch (counts first tr), 4 tr in ring, [1 ch, 5 tr in ring] 4 times, 1 ch, join with a ss to top of 3-ch at beg of round. Fasten off A.
Round 2 Using B, join with a ss to a centre dtr of a 5-tr group, 1 ch, 1 dc in same place as last ss, [7 dtr in next 1-ch sp, 1 dc in centre dtr of next 5-tr group] 4 times, 7 dtr in next 1-ch sp, join with a ss to first dc of round.
Fasten off.

SQUARE PETAL FLOWER

CROCHET DIAGRAM

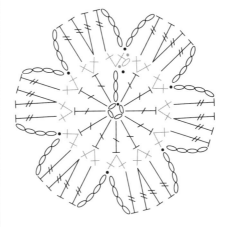

CROCHET INSTRUCTIONS
This flower is worked in 3 colours (A, B, C).
Using A, make 4 ch and join with a ss to first ch to form a ring.
Round 1 (RS) 3 ch (counts as first tr), 11 tr in ring, join with a ss to top of 3-ch at beg of round. Fasten off A.
Round 2 Using B, join with a ss same place as last ss, 1 ch (does NOT count as a st), 2 dc in same place as last ss, 2 dc in each tr to end, join with a ss to first dc of round. 24 dc. Fasten off B.
Round 2 Using C, join with a ss to a dc, *4 ch, 1 dtr in next dc, 2 dtr in next dc, 1 dtr in next dc, 4 ch, 1 ss in next dc; rep from * 5 times more working last ss in same place as first ss of round.
Fasten off.

SIMPLE LEAF

CROCHET DIAGRAM

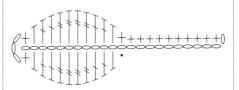

CROCHET INSTRUCTIONS
Note: The leaf is worked in one row, around both sides of the foundation chain.
To begin leaf and stem, make 23 ch.
Row 1 (RS) Working into only one loop of each foundation chain, work 1 dc in 2nd ch from hook, 1 dc in each of next 10 ch (this completes the stem), 1 htr in next ch, 1 tr in each of next 2 ch, 1 dtr in each of next 4 ch, 1 tr in each of next 2 ch, 1 htr in next ch, 1 dc in next ch (this is the last ch), 3 ch, then continue working around other side of foundation ch (working into other loop of each ch) as follows – 1 dc in first ch, 1 htr in next ch, 1 tr in each of next 2 ch, 1 dtr in each of next 4 ch, 1 tr in each of next 2 ch, 1 htr in next ch, 1 ss in next ch.
Fasten off.
Press stem flat.

CROCHETED TOYS

Although crocheted toys look difficult, they are very easy to make, and quick as well. This step-by-step guide to crocheting a toy provides tips for making the pieces, for stuffing, for stitching the parts together and for adding facial features. (Instructions for the pieces of the featured toy are given on page 399.)

MAKING
THE TOY

This striped dog has been designed to be easy to crochet and its pattern on page 399 has been specially written to be easy to follow. Because the toy has a step-by-step guide, it is an ideal first toy project. Being able to see what the pieces look like before they are stuffed will give you confidence that your crochet is turning out the shape it should. The tips in the steps apply to all toys in general.

MATERIALS FOR THE TOY

YARN
You will need two balls of a lightweight or medium-weight yarn (see page 15) in A (the main colour), and one ball in each of the remaining colours.

CROCHET HOOK
Crochet hook that is one to two sizes smaller than size recommended for the chosen yarn weight

Six-stranded cotton embroidery thread (eyebrows, nose, and mouth)

Polyester toy filling

A, B, C (three stripe colours in three different tones – pale, light, and medium)

E (muzzle, ear, and tail colour)

D (foot and hand colour)

Metal safety-eye backs

Toy safety eyes

Button eyes

Start your toy project by selecting the yarns and hook required. For the sample toy dog, you need five colours of yarn. Although small toys can often be made with a single ball of yarn, crochet takes up more yarn than knitting, so you may need two balls of the main toy colour, and small amounts for any accent colours. Your toy instructions will specify a yarn amount. Select a crochet hook size that will produce a tight double crochet fabric, one to two sizes smaller than the size recommended for the yarn weight category (see page 15).

The extras needed for the dog are the same as those for most toys – embroidery thread for the facial features, buttons for the eyes, and toy filling. Be VERY careful if you are making any toy for a small child; for these toys, it is best to embroider the eyes or select toy safety eyes that meet safety regulations.

CROCHETING THE BODY AND HEAD

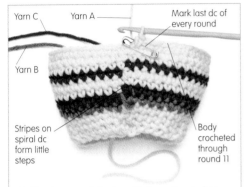

Yarn C   Yarn A   Mark last dc of every round

Yarn B

Stripes on spiral dc form little steps

Body crocheted through round 11

1 Read any special notes with the pattern before beginning the toy pieces. Then crochet the pieces in the order given; the body and head are usually first. Following the instructions carefully, work the stitches tightly and count your stitches regularly.

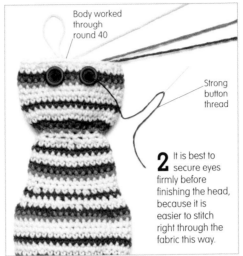

Body worked through round 40

Strong button thread

2 It is best to secure eyes firmly before finishing the head, because it is easier to stitch right through the fabric this way.

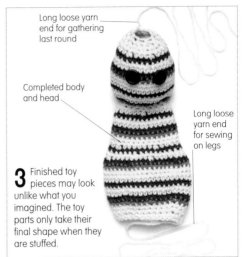

Long loose yarn end for gathering last round

Completed body and head

Long loose yarn end for sewing on legs

3 Finished toy pieces may look unlike what you imagined. The toy parts only take their final shape when they are stuffed.

CROCHETING THE LEGS AND ARMS

1 After the body and head, the legs and arms usually follow in toy instructions. As on the dog, these parts are often worked in spiral dc and started at the foot/hand end of the leg/arm. A safety pin is easiest to use as a stitch marker on a toy. (See page 000 for more about working circular crochet.)

Leg worked through round 11

2 A long loose end is often left at the top of the leg – this is used to sew the top of the leg closed. If you happen to leave a yarn end that is too short, you can join on a new length of yarn, but it is easier to use a strand already attached to the crochet.

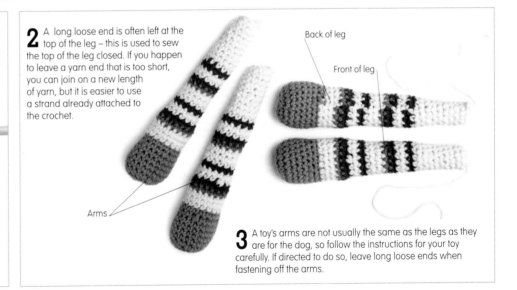

Back of leg

Front of leg

Arms

3 A toy's arms are not usually the same as the legs as they are for the dog, so follow the instructions for your toy carefully. If directed to do so, leave long loose ends when fastening off the arms.

CROCHETING OTHER BODY PARTS

1 After the main pieces of the toy are completed, there are usually other items to make, for example, ears, hairpieces, and clothes. Crochet the extra items in the order they appear in your pattern. For the dog, crochet the muzzle first.

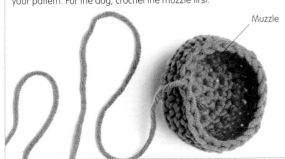

Muzzle

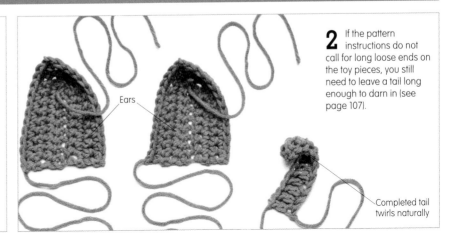

Ears

2 If the pattern instructions do not call for long loose ends on the toy pieces, you still need to leave a tail long enough to darn in (see page 107).

Completed tail twirls naturally

CROCHET

FINISHING
THE TOY

Once you have completed the pieces of a toy, take your time with the finishings. Toy pattern instructions for these are often given only in general terms, so this step-by-step guide for the sample dog gives tips useful for all toys. Stitch seams and embroider facial features very slowly and to the best of your ability. Don't hesitate to unpick stitches and try again until they look perfect – with each attempt your stitching will improve.

STUFFING AND ASSEMBLING THE TOY PIECES

1 Follow finishing instructions in the order they are given. For the dog, start by using a blunt-ended yarn needle and the long loose end at the top of the head to gather the 8 dc of the last round and close the hole. Then darn in the end invisibly to secure it.

Lace yarn through each of 8 stitches of last round to gather and close hole

2 Stuff the body and head firmly and evenly. Make sure the head is firm before starting to fill the body. Avoid lumps by spreading the stuffing out evenly and adding more where necessary. More filling than you expect will fit inside the toy.

Stuff through hole at bottom of body

3 The toy's legs and arms are usually filled next. Push the toy filling in through the top of the leg and down towards the foot. Do not stop until the leg or arm is firmly and evenly stuffed.

Poke stuffing in with end of crochet hook

Keep yarn end on arms and legs for sewing them to body

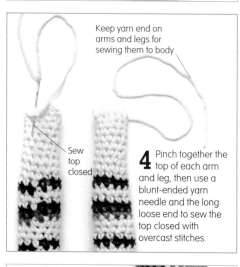

Sew top closed

4 Pinch together the top of each arm and leg, then use a blunt-ended yarn needle and the long loose end to sew the top closed with overcast stitches.

5 Pinch together the back and the front of the lower edge of the body, and pin at the centre. Using overcast stitches, sew the lower body seam between the legs, then sew the legs in place.

Position top of leg just a little inside body

Safety note: Only use pins on toys when absolutely necessary and ensure that none have been lost inside the toy.

6 Study the photo of the finished toy to position the arms. Use overcast stitches and secure the arm very firmly to the toy's body. Remember to use a blunt-ended yarn needle for all stitching on your toy.

Use arm yarn tail to sew on arm

---

7 Once the main body parts of your toy are assembled, the toy pattern will instruct you to add the smaller parts. For the dog, add the tail next. Darn in one of the yarn ends on the dog's tail and use the other to sew it to the body with overcast stitches.

Tail

8 Sew on the dog's muzzle next. To start, fill it with toy filling so that it is firm and well shaped.

Toy filling

9 Pin the muzzle to the dog's head just under the eyes, forming an oval shape covering about 10 stitches and 7 rows. Using the long loose end, sew the muzzle in place with overcast stitches.

Pull stitches tight so they disappear

ADDING FACIAL FEATURES

1 When working toy embroidery, study the photo of the toy and copy what you see. The thread must be thick enough for the features to make a statement. Use six-strand embroidery thread double if necessary. Work the dog's nose in satin stitch.

2 The best stitch for long mouths on toys is backstitch as shown here on the dog.

Position centre of dog's mouth in centre hole of muzzle

3 Once the eyes, nose, and mouth are in place, add the toy's ears. On the dog, darn in the foundation-chain yarn end on each ear first. Then using the long loose end (left when fastening off), gather the ear base to form a slightly cupped shape.

Inside of ear is wrong side of the piece

Gather bottom edge of ear with overcast stitches pulled tight

Leave yarn end to use for sewing on ears

4 Sew on the toy's ears in the position shown in the photo of the toy. The dog's ears are positioned at a slight diagonal and folded forwards after they are secure. To encourage ears into the correct shape, you can press them with steam (see page 140).

5 Leave the toy's eyebrows till last. These give your toy its unique expression. For each of the dog's eyebrows, work two stitches in the same place, on top of each other.

Try different slants for different expressions

6 Check that all the parts on your finished toy are securely sewed on and that you are satisfied with the facial features. You can always unpick and redo poor stitching until you get it just right.

CROCHET

UNUSUAL YARNS

If you want to break the monotony of working with wool yarns, why not try out some unusual materials? String, wire, rag strips, and plastic strips are great fun to crochet with, and the materials used can be recycled ones. To take you through the techniques involved, a quick-to-make item is shown with each of these "yarns". It isn't advisable to try to learn to crochet with unusual yarns, so make sure you are deft at forming double crochet stitches before attempting to work with them.

STRING
CROCHET

Tightly crocheted string forms a sturdy fabric suitable for containers. Because it is usually neither too thick nor too thin, garden twine is a good choice for a first string crochet project. It is also easy to obtain and forms a fabric that holds its shape well.

CROCHETING A ROUND STRING CONTAINER

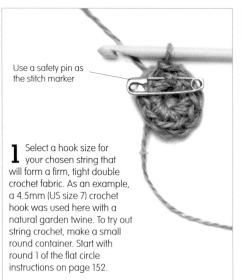

Use a safety pin as the stitch marker

1 Select a hook size for your chosen string that will form a firm, tight double crochet fabric. As an example, a 4.5mm (US size 7) crochet hook was used here with a natural garden twine. To try out string crochet, make a small round container. Start with round 1 of the flat circle instructions on page 152.

Move marker up at end of each round

2 Continuing to follow the circle pattern, work rounds 2 and 3. Work the stitches as tightly as you can. If the crochet doesn't seem tight enough, start again with a smaller hook size.

Ridge formed by working into only back loops

3 Keep working rounds of the circle pattern until the circle is the desired size for the base of the container. Then to start the sides of the container, work 1 dc into the back loop only of the top of each stitch in the next round as shown. This forms a ridge.

4 On all the remaining rounds of the container, work 1 dc in each stitch of the previous round, working through both loops of the top of the stitch below in the usual way. This will form a tube (see page 150 for tips on working spiral crochet). Continue until the container is the desired height.

5 To add some colour and interest to a natural-string container, add a trimming, such as colourful ribbon. Stitch the ribbon to the crochet using a sewing needle and matching thread.

6 When your first string container is complete, make more for a set in different sizes. For the bigger sizes, use a thicker twine and a larger hook size.

WIRE
CROCHET

As long as it is fine enough, wire is easy to crochet with even though it takes a little practice to produce even stitches. As with string crochet, it is best to stick to simple double crochet for wire – more exotic stitches are difficult to distinguish among the bendy, airy wire loops. Adding beads to wire crochet is the best way to jazz it up and turn it into simple jewellery like the easy-to-make, bendy bangle shown here.

CROCHETING A BEADED WIRE BANGLE

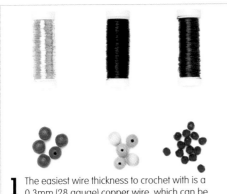

1 The easiest wire thickness to crochet with is a 0.3mm (28 gauge) copper wire, which can be obtained online from craft shops or shops that sell jewellery supplies. For this wire size, you will need a 3mm (US size D-3) crochet hook.

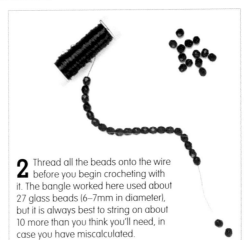

2 Thread all the beads onto the wire before you begin crocheting with it. The bangle worked here used about 27 glass beads (6–7mm in diameter), but it is always best to string on about 10 more than you think you'll need, in case you have miscalculated.

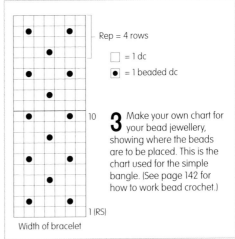

Rep = 4 rows

☐ = 1 dc

⦿ = 1 beaded dc

3 Make your own chart for your bead jewellery, showing where the beads are to be placed. This is the chart used for the simple bangle. (See page 142 for how to work bead crochet.)

Width of bracelet

4 Using the wire with the beads on it, make 8 chains to start the featured bangle. Then follow the chart to work the beaded crochet, working the stitches loosely. Whenever the position of a bead is reached (always on a wrong-side row), work up to the last yrh of the stitch, then slide the bead up close to the crochet and complete the stitch. Count the stitches frequently to make sure you still have the correct number.

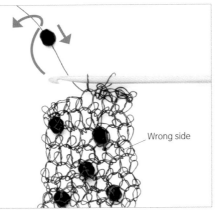

Wrong side

5 Work the bangle until it is the desired length. End with a right-side (non-bead) row so that the wrong side will be facing for the next row. Place the other end of the bangle behind the next row and work the last row through both layers of the bangle by inserting the hook through the foundation chain of the second layer as shown.

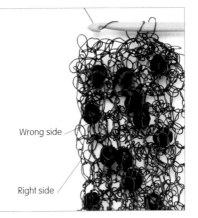

Wrong side

Right side

6 After completing the double crochet seam, cut the wire and fasten off. Darn in the wire tails along the double crochet seam, using a blunt-ended yarn needle and wrapping the wire tightly a few times around the edge of the crochet. Then cut off the remaining wire close to the bangle. Turn the bangle right-side out.

ALTERNATIVE BUTTON BANGLE

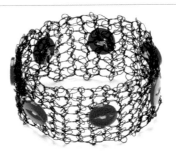

You can also make plain wire crochet bangles and decorate them once they have been completed. This bangle has been worked plain without any beads. Buttons have been sewn along the centre of the bangle with a bright contrasting silk button thread.

CROCHET

RAG-STRIP CROCHET

The biggest advantage of rag-strip crochet is its limitless colour palette – the "yarn" can be made from any cotton shirt-weight or patchwork-weight fabric. To try out the technique, work circles with rag strips and make them into a bag.

PREPARING FABRIC STRIPS

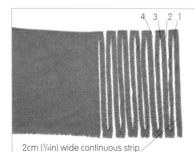

4 3 2 1

1 To make a continuous fabric strip 2cm (¾in) wide, cut or tear the fabric from selvedge to selvedge, stopping each tear/cut about 1.5cm (⅝in) from the edge.

2cm (¾in) wide continuous strip

2 As you tear the strips, wind them into balls. Rag crochet uses up a lot of fabric. To start your project, you can prepare some rag yarn in each of the colours you need and make more later as it is required.

CROCHETING TWO CIRCLES FOR A BAG

1 For a firm crochet fabric, use a 10mm (US size N-15) crochet hook and 2cm (¾in) wide patchwork-fabric-weight cotton strips. Simple double crochet is the best stitch to use for rag crochet. To begin a circle for a bag, work round 1 of the flat circle pattern on page 152 (but leave the yarn tail at the back of the work and do not attempt to work the stitches of this round over it).

A large paper clip is best stitch marker for rag-strip crochet

2 Continuing to follow the circle pattern, introduce new colours for stripes as desired. Work the circle until it is the size you want it for a bag front. Then work a second circle the same size. Using the hook, pull any yarn tails through a few stitches on the wrong side to secure them and trim off the ends.

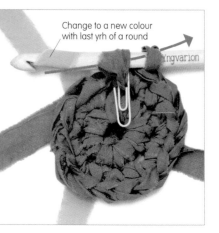

Change to a new colour with last yrh of a round

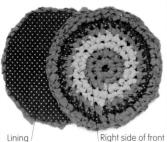

Lining | Right side of front

3 Line the two circles with a harmonizing fabric print. (The edge of the lining should reach the base of the tops of the double crochet stitches of the last row.)

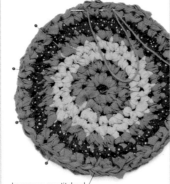

Leave an unstitched opening

4 With the wrong sides facing, pin the bag front and back together. Then using a sewing needle and matching thread or thin cotton yarn, stitch the seam just under the tops of the double crochet stitches of the last round, leaving an opening at the top.

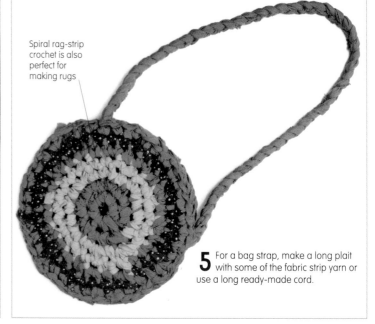

Spiral rag-strip crochet is also perfect for making rugs

5 For a bag strap, make a long plait with some of the fabric strip yarn or use a long ready-made cord.

PLASTIC-STRIP CROCHET

Recycling your colourful plastic shopping bags is a great way to help the environment. You can create plastic yarn (or plarn) in a jiffy using the quick cutting technique shown here. Then use it to experiment with plastic-strip crochet by making a simple bag.

PREPARING PLARN STRIPS

1 Use lightweight plastic bags for plarn. To cut a continuous strip from a bag, begin by laying it flat and smoothing it out. Trim off the seam at the lower edge of the bag and the handles at the top.

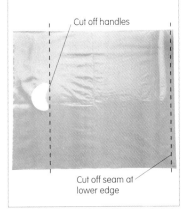

Cut off handles

Cut off seam at lower edge

2 Fold the plastic tube in half, bringing the fold at the lower edge up to 3cm (1¼in) from the top fold.

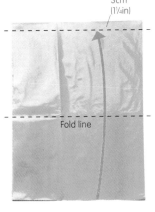

3cm (1¼in)

Fold line

3 Fold the bag twice more, bringing the lower edge up to within 3cm (1¼in) of the top with each fold.

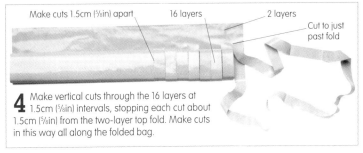

Make cuts 1.5cm (⅝in) apart | 16 layers | 2 layers | Cut to just past fold

4 Make vertical cuts through the 16 layers at 1.5cm (⅝in) intervals, stopping each cut about 1.5cm (⅝in) from the two-layer top fold. Make cuts in this way all along the folded bag.

Second cut

First cut

5 Open out the bag so that you can see the area where the strips are still joined together. To create the continuous strip, make diagonal cuts as shown and wind the strip into a ball.

CROCHETING A PLARN MAKE-UP BAG

1 Use a size 5mm (US size H-8) hook to crochet plarn prepared as above. To make a small make-up bag, work a spiral tube of double crochet (see page 150).

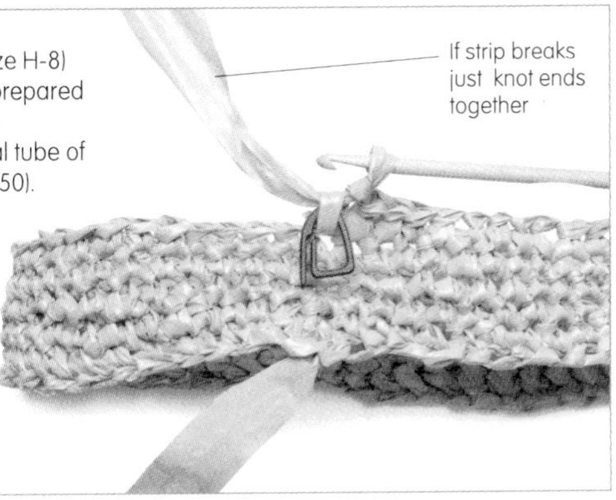

If strip breaks just knot ends together

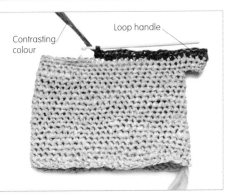

2 To add a little loop handle to the top of the bag, make extra chains before starting the next round.

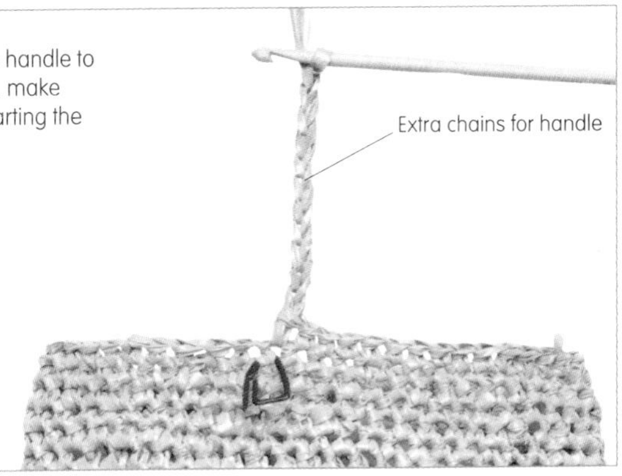

Extra chains for handle

3 On the next round, work double crochet stitches along the extra chains added for the handle. Then work more rounds until the handle is the desired width. Change to the contrasting colour of plarn for the last round and fasten off.

Contrasting colour

Loop handle

4 Join the seam along the lower edge by working a row of double crochet through both layers with contrasting plarn. Using a matching thread and a sewing needle, sew the two layers of the handle together level with the side edge of the bag to form an open loop. Line the bag with a matching fabric and add a zip.

Handle stitched together here

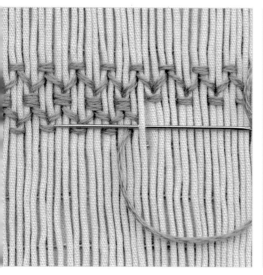 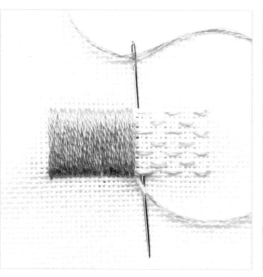 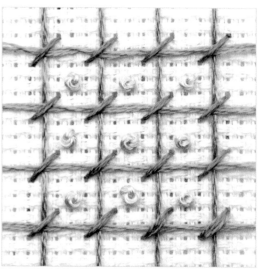

EMBROIDERY

General embroidery techniques and stitches for surface embroidery, openwork, smocking, and beadwork. Embroidery stitches can be used to add decorative stitches or embellishments to items of clothing, accessories, or home furnishing.

TOOLS AND MATERIALS

The basic tools and materials that are essential for embroidery are simple and easy to obtain, although there are a few more elaborate frames that are useful for certain advanced techniques, and some fabrics and threads that are available only through specialist suppliers. Many products can now be found via the Internet.

FABRICS

There are plenty of fabrics, particularly even-weaves, especially for embroidery, but almost any plain-weave fabric, from fine silk to cotton twill, can be used as a background. Even-weaves are linen or cotton woven in a regular square grid. Plain-weaves are ideal for freestyle embroidery.

EVEN-WEAVE FABRICS

« BINCA DOUBLE THREAD
Similar to Aida, Binca even-weave fabrics are available in many colours and textures.

« AIDA DOUBLE THREAD
Double thread even-weave fabrics are stiff and widely used for cross-stitch and other counted-stitch techniques. Aida is easy to use as the threads are clear and easy to count.

SINGLE THREAD
Single-thread cottons and linens are used mainly for drawn-thread and pulled-fabric techniques.

Thread count
Single- and double-thread even-weaves are available in a variety of sizes, which are referred to as thread counts. The more threads there are per inch, the finer the fabric.

PLAIN-WEAVE FABRICS

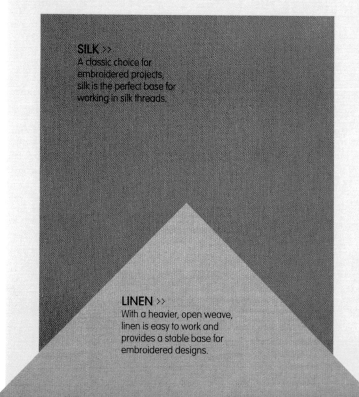

COTTON »
Easy to work and economical, cotton fabrics are a good choice for general embroidery where you do not need to count the threads in order to space the stitches evenly.

SILK »
A classic choice for embroidered projects, silk is the perfect base for working in silk threads.

LINEN »
With a heavier, open weave, linen is easy to work and provides a stable base for embroidered designs.

HOOPS
AND FRAMES

Hoops and frames are used to hold the ground fabric taut, which keeps the grain of the fabric straight and the stitches regular. Hoops consist of two thin rings; the fabric is placed between them. Frames are straight-sided. Both can be attached to floor and table stands that allow you to keep both hands free for stitching.

USING HOOPS AND FRAMES

Hoops are made of wood or plastic, and can be round or oval. The inner ring is solid, while the outer one has a screw or clamp that can be adjusted to achieve an ideal tautness. They are best used with plain-weave fabrics and fine even-weaves.

Frames, called scroll or slate frames and stretchers, are traditionally made of wood. They are used mainly for mounting even-weaves and needlepoint canvas. Scroll frames are adjustable (see below), while work in stretcher frames, whose size cannot be adjusted, should fit inside the frame.

A new type of frame of plastic tubing is particularly useful for many beading techniques, but can also be used for most types of embroidery. Called Q-Snaps, these straight-sided frames come in a variety of sizes.

‹‹ ROUND OR OVAL HOOP
Hoops are available in various sizes, from 12.5 to 36cm (5 to 14in). The outer ring is adjusted with a small tension screw or clamp mounted across a split in the ring. They are most suitable for small projects.

‹‹ SQUARE SCROLL FRAME
Scroll frames consist of two round bars that slot into squared side struts. Lengths of webbing stapled to the bars hold the work, which can be rolled up as required to expose new areas.

NEEDLES

There are several types of needle suitable for embroidery, each used for a specific purpose. All come in different thicknesses and lengths. Select one that can pass smoothly through the fabric; the eye of the needle should be large enough to take the required thread easily.

CREWEL NEEDLE ☆
Crewel needles have sharp points and an eye designed to take thicker-than-normal thread and are ideal for most surface embroidery on plain-weave fabrics.

TAPESTRY NEEDLE ☆
Blunt-ended tapestry needles should always be used on even-weaves to avoid splitting the threads of the fabric.

CHENILLE NEEDLE ☆
Chenilles are sharp-pointed and heavier, and take thicker threads for work on heavy-weight fabrics.

BEADING NEEDLE ☆
Beading needles are long and very fine, so that they can pass easily through tiny bead holes.

THREAD

Embroidery threads can be thick or thin. They are made from cotton, silk, wool, and linen as well as synthetics. Some threads are single ply, while others are spun in multiples and can be divided into single strands: the fewer the filaments, the finer the embroidered line.

COTTON THREADS

◁◁ STRANDED COTTON
This is a loosely twisted 6-strand thread that can easily be divided into single threads.

◁◁ COTTON PERLE
This is a strong, twisted thread that cannot be divided. It has a smooth sheen and keeps its shape well without kinking.

COTTON CHOICE
Cotton threads are available in a wide range of thicknesses and finishes, from lustrous to matte, and are well-suited to most embroidery techniques.

Flower thread: This is a fine, single-ply cotton thread. It has a matte finish and is good for cross-stitch.

Soft cotton: A soft, matte thread that is easy to work and suitable for half-cross stitch and long stitch. It is often used in tapestry.

Coton a broder: A pure cotton thread that is tightly twisted with a lovely lustre. It is commonly used for whitework.

SILK THREADS

◁◁ STRANDED SILK
Silk has a soft quality, and stranded threads can be divided to produce very fine threads.

◁◁ TWISTED SILK
Twisted silk has a beautiful sheen and works well on fine count canvas.

◁◁ SILK BUTTONHOLE
This is a strong thread that is similar in thickness to cotton perlé.

◁◁ RAYON SILK
This is a slightly cheaper option, but is very soft and has a rich sheen.

WOOLS

CREWEL WOOL ☆
This is a 2-ply wool yarn that is also used in tapestry work. There is another wool known as Persian wool that is loosely twisted and can be divided for embroidery.

GENERAL
EQUIPMENT

Almost all the equipment you need for embroidery can be found in a well-stocked sewing basket: large and small sharp scissors for cutting fabrics and threads, marking pens and pencils, and measuring equipment. Add a thimble if you use one, and perhaps a pincushion, and you are ready to start.

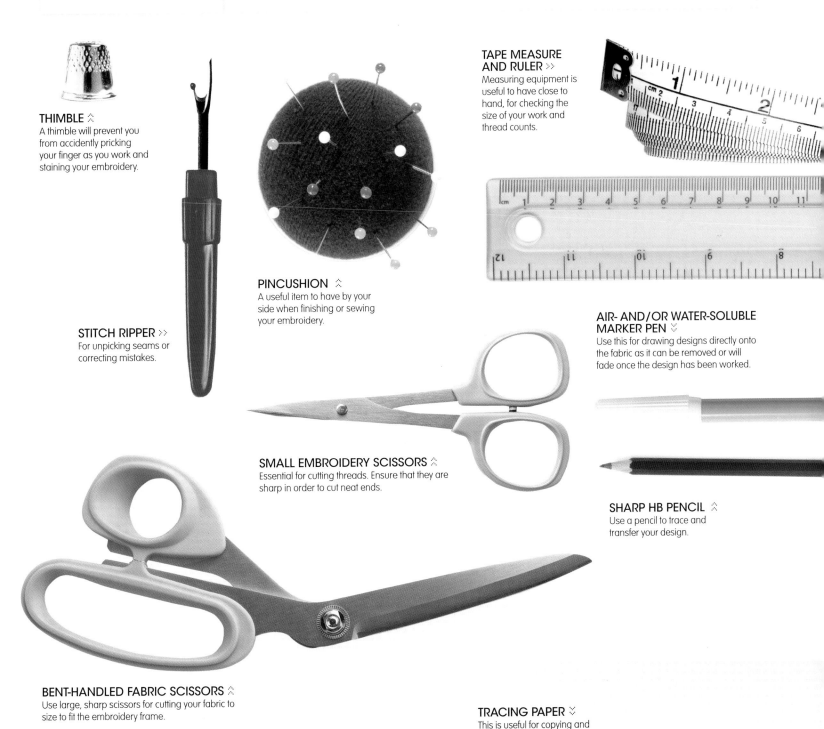

THIMBLE ⚲
A thimble will prevent you from accidently pricking your finger as you work and staining your embroidery.

STITCH RIPPER »
For unpicking seams or correcting mistakes.

PINCUSHION ⚲
A useful item to have by your side when finishing or sewing your embroidery.

SMALL EMBROIDERY SCISSORS ⚲
Essential for cutting threads. Ensure that they are sharp in order to cut neat ends.

TAPE MEASURE AND RULER »
Measuring equipment is useful to have close to hand, for checking the size of your work and thread counts.

AIR- AND/OR WATER-SOLUBLE MARKER PEN ⚲
Use this for drawing designs directly onto the fabric as it can be removed or will fade once the design has been worked.

SHARP HB PENCIL ⚲
Use a pencil to trace and transfer your design.

BENT-HANDLED FABRIC SCISSORS ⚲
Use large, sharp scissors for cutting your fabric to size to fit the embroidery frame.

TRACING PAPER ⚲
This is useful for copying and transferring designs.

DRESSMAKER'S CARBON PAPER »
This is ideal for transferring your embroidery design to the fabric ground.

EMBROIDERY

EMBROIDERY BASICS

Before you start your embroidery you need to prepare your fabric, designs, and threads. Find a suitably sized hoop or frame and mount your fabric. Once you have chosen and transferred your design, you should organize your threads, preparing skeins if required.

USING HOOPS
AND FRAMES

Before using a hoop or frame you need to prepare and mount the fabric that you will embroider onto. The inner ring of a hoop should be bound with woven cotton tape, both to protect the fabric and to help keep it taut. Make sure the fabric is larger than the hoop and, if possible, that the hoop is larger than the area to be stitched. To mount on a frame, hem or bind the edges of the fabric and attach with herringbone stitch (see page 190).

BINDING A HOOP

Secure the end of a length of cotton tape inside the inner hoop and wrap it around the ring, overlapping as you work. Secure the ends with a few stitches.

MOUNTING FABRIC IN A HOOP

1 Centre the fabric over the bound inner ring and place the outer ring on it. Hemming or binding the edges of the fabric will help to prevent it from fraying as you work.

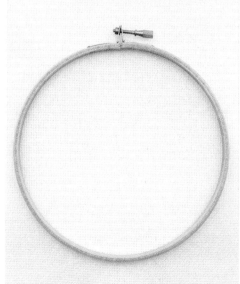

2 Press the outer ring around the inner one and tighten the tension screw slowly to hold the rings together and the fabric taut and even. Smooth any wrinkles before tightening.

TRANSFERRING EMBROIDERY DESIGNS
AND PATTERNS

Designs and patterns for embroidery are everywhere – in nature, in geometry, in our imaginations – and transferring them to fabric is not difficult. Many items such as cushion covers and table linens are available with a design already marked. Magazines and books are good sources for patterns, or you can draw your own.

DIRECT TRACING

Good for thin, light-coloured fabrics. Anchor the pattern on your work surface. Place the fabric on top, securing it with tape or drawing pins. Draw over the lines with a sharp pencil or water-soluble marker.

USING A LIGHTBOX

Another good method for transferring motifs to light-coloured plain weaves. Place the pattern on a lightbox, with the fabric on top, and draw over the lines with a sharp pencil or water-soluble marker.

DRESSMAKER'S CARBON PAPER

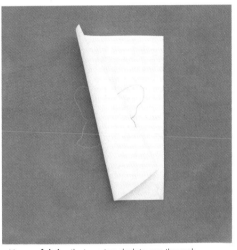

Use on fabrics that are too dark to see through. Place the fabric right-side up with the carbon paper on top. Place the design on top of the carbon paper. Draw over the lines with a sharp pencil.

TACK-AND-TEAR METHOD

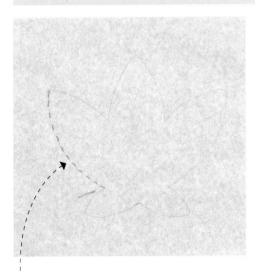

1 Good for heavier fabrics, such as wool or denim. Transfer the design to tissue paper and pin it in place on the fabric. With the knot on top, sew along the pattern lines with a small running stitch. Secure the end with a double backstitch.

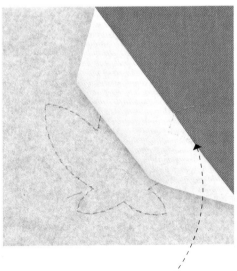

2 Pull the paper away gently without disturbing the tacking. If necessary, score the marked lines with a pin point to break the paper.

IRON-ON TRANSFERS

Follow the manufacturer's instructions to apply transfers.

PREPARING
THE THREAD

It is useful to know a few tricks of the trade before you start sewing, from learning how to unwind a skein of thread to separating strands of embroidery cotton. Most embroidery thread comes in specially wound hanks or skeins designed by the spinners to make them easier to work with, but they need special handling to keep them from becoming tangled.

LOOPED SKEINS

Do not remove looped skeins, such as stranded cotton, from their paper bands. Inside one end of the skein is a loose end of thread. Hold the other end of the skein and gently pull out the loose thread.

TWISTED SKEINS

Unwrap twisted skeins, such as cotton perle. Free the hank and cut across the threads, to give cut threads the right length for working. Slip the paper band back on and tie the threads loosely.

SEPARATING STRANDS

Stranded cotton and silk, cotton perle, and Persian wool can all be divided into strands. Cut a length and grasp the end. Gently pull the desired number of strands apart from the main thread.

THREADING
A NEEDLE

Work with a length of thread of less than 50cm (18in), unless the technique calls for a longer one. Most embroidery threads are thicker than ordinary sewing thread and, although the eyes of crewel and tapestry needles are large, they can sometimes be difficult to thread. Finer threads can be inserted using a needle threader. Use the folding method shown here for thicker types.

Fold the thread over the eye of the needle and hold the loop tight. Slide it off the end of the needle and into the eye.

STARTING
AND FINISHING

On most embroideries, knots are undesirable as they make a bump under the fabric and can sometimes show through. There are other ways to secure the beginning and end of your stitching. The method you choose will depend on the thread, fabric, and design as well as the stitches you use.

LEAVING A TAIL OF THREAD

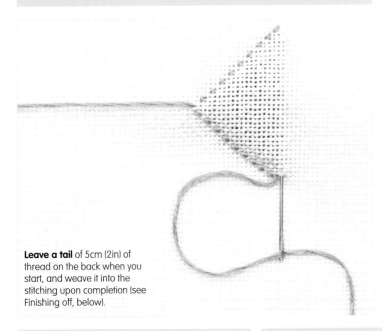

Leave a tail of 5cm (2in) of thread on the back when you start, and weave it into the stitching upon completion (see Finishing off, below).

LOST KNOT METHOD

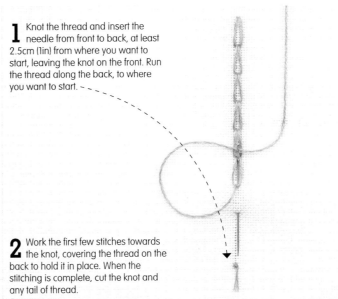

1 Knot the thread and insert the needle from front to back, at least 2.5cm (1in) from where you want to start, leaving the knot on the front. Run the thread along the back, to where you want to start.

2 Work the first few stitches towards the knot, covering the thread on the back to hold it in place. When the stitching is complete, cut the knot and any tail of thread.

BACKSTITCH METHOD

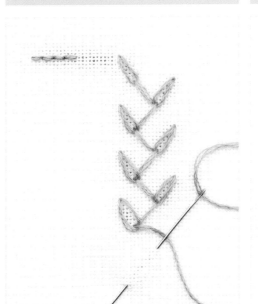

About 2.5cm (1in) from where you want to begin, take the needle from front to back, leaving a 5cm (2in) tail. Work two or three backstitches to the start. Complete the embroidery, unpick the backstitches and run in the tail on the wrong side, under the first stitches.

RUNNING-STITCH METHOD

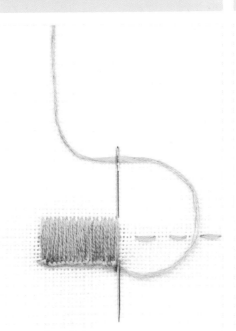

For closely worked stitches, make a short row of running stitches that will be covered by the embroidery. Leave a loose tail of thread on the back and weave it into the stitches on the reverse when completed.

FINISHING OFF

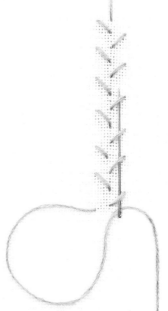

Finish a thread by weaving it under a group of stitches for at least 5–7cm (2–3in) on the back and cutting the thread. Fasten off before the thread is too short to slide under.

STITCH GALLERY

These pages provide a quick visual reference for all the stitches in this chapter. Each stitch is shown as a final sample to allow you to find the appropriate stitch quickly. The stitches are grouped according to type to show all the possibilities and alternatives at a glance.

CROSS STITCH / SURFACE EMBROIDERY

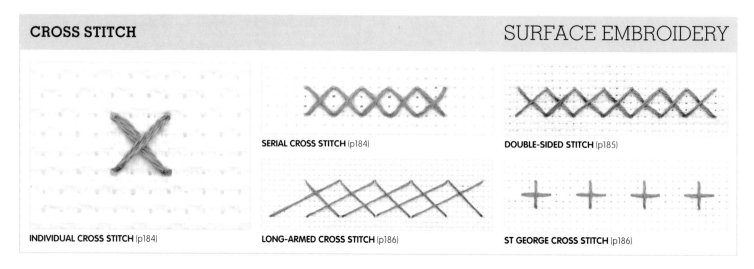

INDIVIDUAL CROSS STITCH (p184)

SERIAL CROSS STITCH (p184)

LONG-ARMED CROSS STITCH (p186)

DOUBLE-SIDED STITCH (p185)

ST GEORGE CROSS STITCH (p186)

FLAT STITCHES

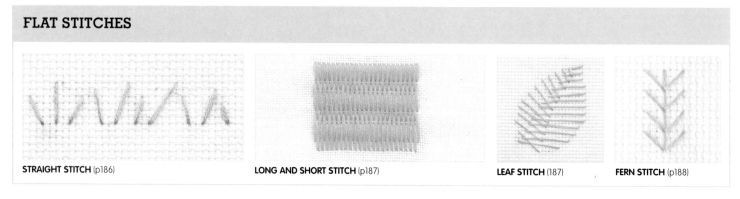

STRAIGHT STITCH (p186)

LONG AND SHORT STITCH (p187)

LEAF STITCH (187)

FERN STITCH (p188)

OUTLINE STITCHES

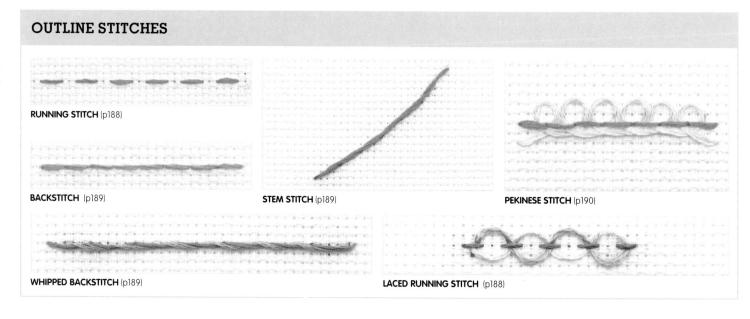

RUNNING STITCH (p188)

BACKSTITCH (p189)

WHIPPED BACKSTITCH (p189)

STEM STITCH (p189)

LACED RUNNING STITCH (p188)

PEKINESE STITCH (p190)

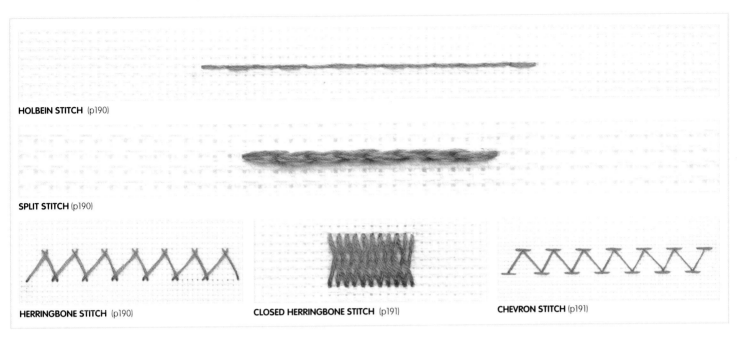

HOLBEIN STITCH (p190)

SPLIT STITCH (p190)

HERRINGBONE STITCH (p190)

CLOSED HERRINGBONE STITCH (p191)

CHEVRON STITCH (p191)

FILLING STITCH

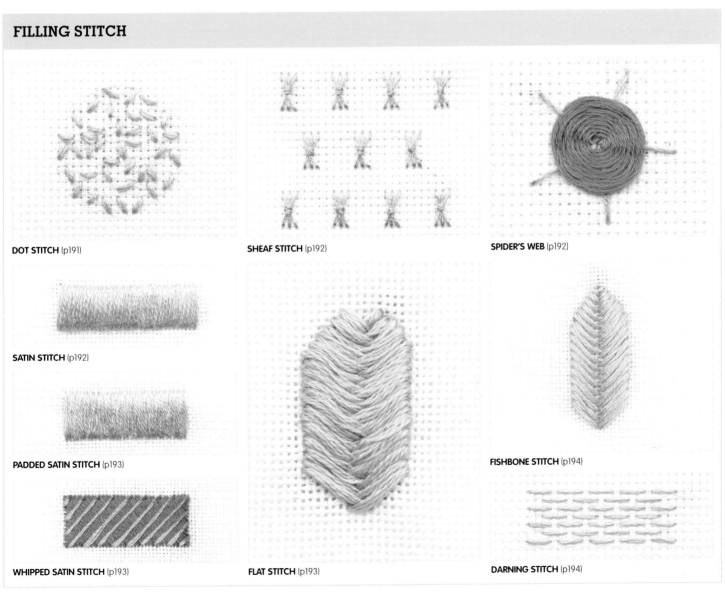

DOT STITCH (p191)

SHEAF STITCH (p192)

SPIDER'S WEB (p192)

SATIN STITCH (p192)

PADDED SATIN STITCH (p193)

FISHBONE STITCH (p194)

WHIPPED SATIN STITCH (p193)

FLAT STITCH (p193)

DARNING STITCH (p194)

EMBROIDERY

LOOPED STITCHES

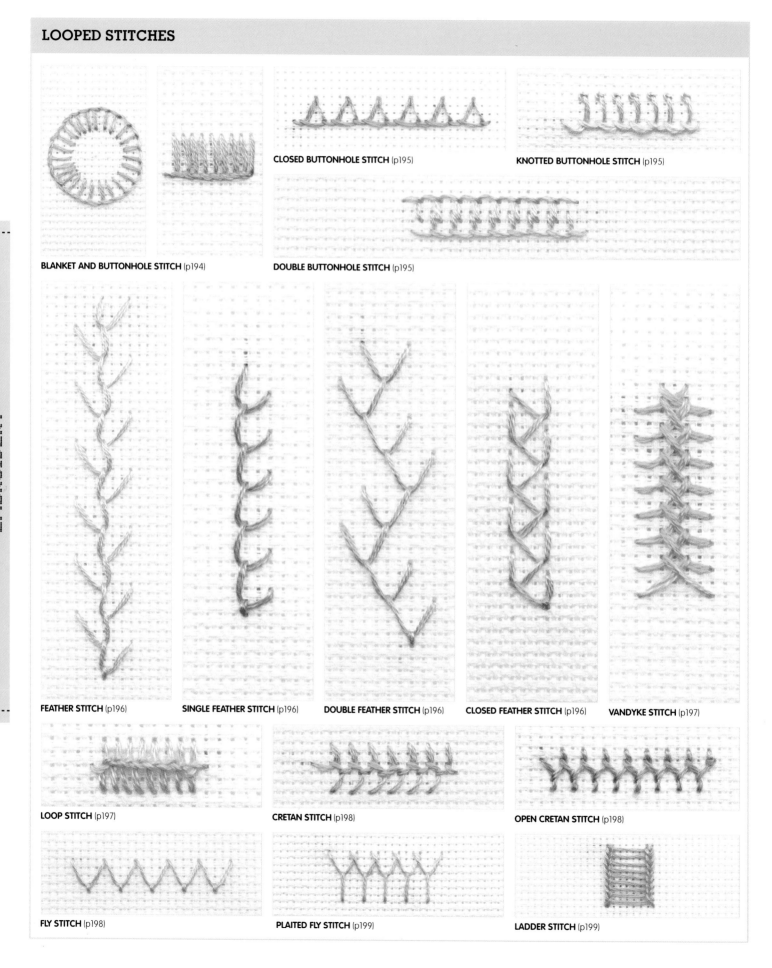

BLANKET AND BUTTONHOLE STITCH (p194)

CLOSED BUTTONHOLE STITCH (p195)

KNOTTED BUTTONHOLE STITCH (p195)

DOUBLE BUTTONHOLE STITCH (p195)

FEATHER STITCH (p196)

SINGLE FEATHER STITCH (p196)

DOUBLE FEATHER STITCH (p196)

CLOSED FEATHER STITCH (p196)

VANDYKE STITCH (p197)

LOOP STITCH (p197)

CRETAN STITCH (p198)

OPEN CRETAN STITCH (p198)

FLY STITCH (p198)

PLAITED FLY STITCH (p199)

LADDER STITCH (p199)

CHAINED STITCHES

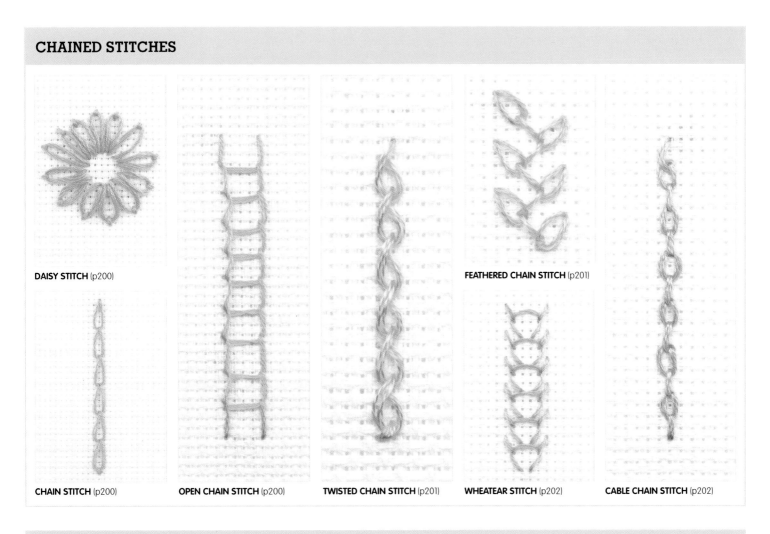

DAISY STITCH (p200)

CHAIN STITCH (p200)

OPEN CHAIN STITCH (p200)

TWISTED CHAIN STITCH (p201)

FEATHERED CHAIN STITCH (p201)

WHEATEAR STITCH (p202)

CABLE CHAIN STITCH (p202)

KNOTTED STITCHES

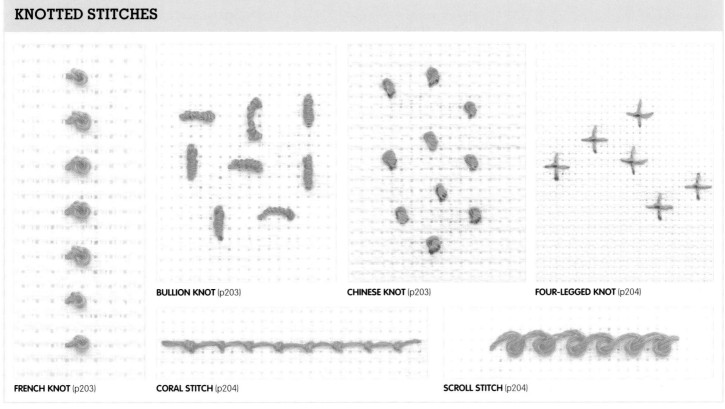

BULLION KNOT (p203)

CHINESE KNOT (p203)

FOUR-LEGGED KNOT (p204)

FRENCH KNOT (p203)

CORAL STITCH (p204)

SCROLL STITCH (p204)

COUCHING

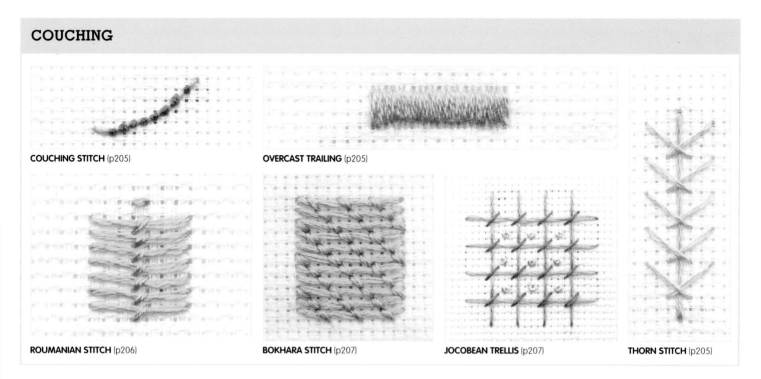

COUCHING STITCH (p205)

OVERCAST TRAILING (p205)

ROUMANIAN STITCH (p206)

BOKHARA STITCH (p207)

JOCOBEAN TRELLIS (p207)

THORN STITCH (p205)

WHITEWORK

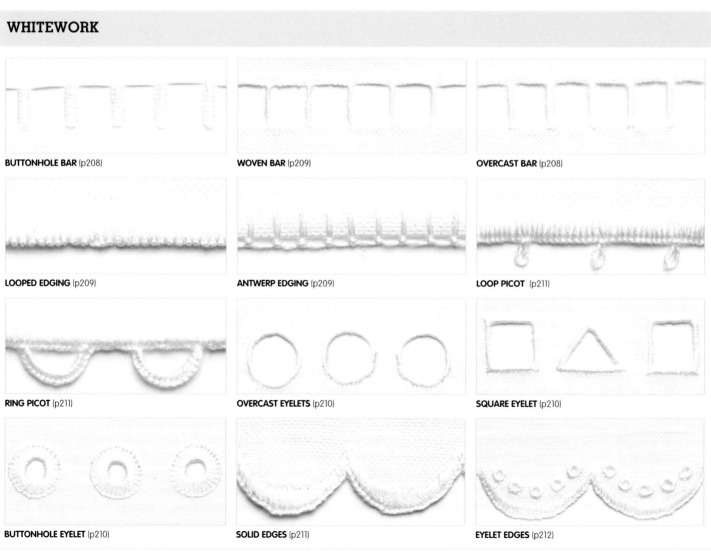

BUTTONHOLE BAR (p208)

WOVEN BAR (p209)

OVERCAST BAR (p208)

LOOPED EDGING (p209)

ANTWERP EDGING (p209)

LOOP PICOT (p211)

RING PICOT (p211)

OVERCAST EYELETS (p210)

SQUARE EYELET (p210)

BUTTONHOLE EYELET (p210)

SOLID EDGES (p211)

EYELET EDGES (p212)

PULLED THREAD WORK

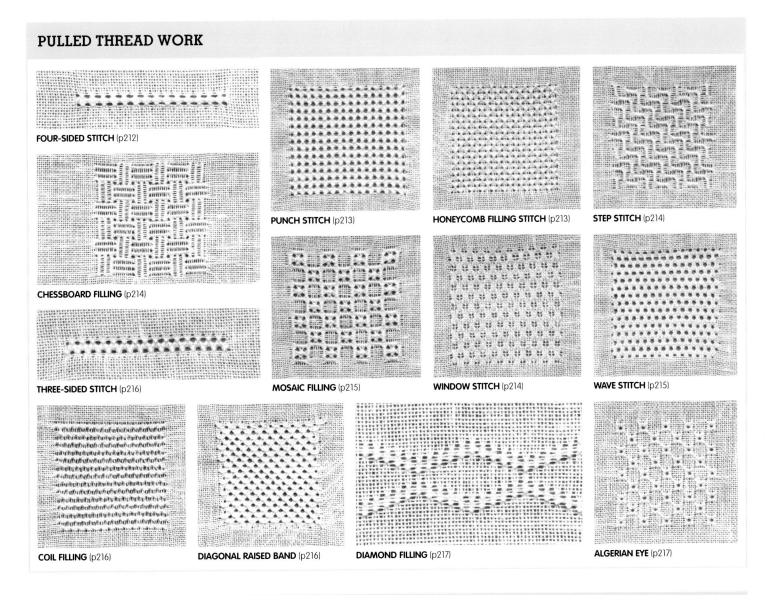

FOUR-SIDED STITCH (p212)

CHESSBOARD FILLING (p214)

THREE-SIDED STITCH (p216)

PUNCH STITCH (p213)

HONEYCOMB FILLING STITCH (p213)

STEP STITCH (p214)

MOSAIC FILLING (p215)

WINDOW STITCH (p214)

WAVE STITCH (p215)

COIL FILLING (p216)

DIAGONAL RAISED BAND (p216)

DIAMOND FILLING (p217)

ALGERIAN EYE (p217)

DRAWN THREAD WORK

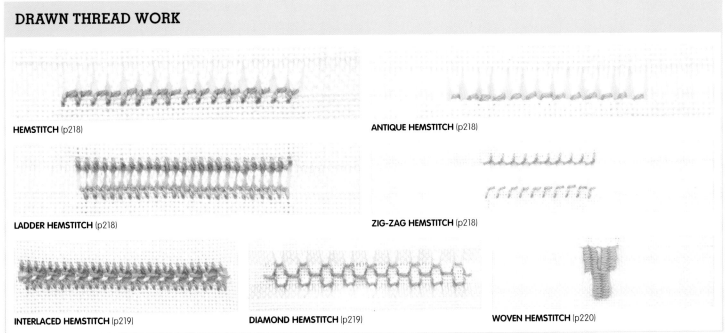

HEMSTITCH (p218)

LADDER HEMSTITCH (p218)

INTERLACED HEMSTITCH (p219)

ANTIQUE HEMSTITCH (p218)

ZIG-ZAG HEMSTITCH (p218)

DIAMOND HEMSTITCH (p219)

WOVEN HEMSTITCH (p220)

INSERTIONS

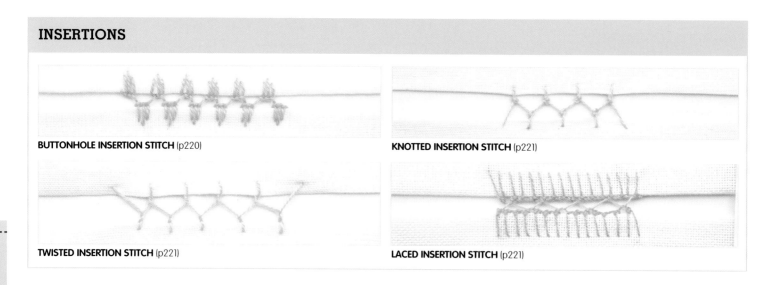

BUTTONHOLE INSERTION STITCH (p220)

KNOTTED INSERTION STITCH (p221)

TWISTED INSERTION STITCH (p221)

LACED INSERTION STITCH (p221)

SMOCKING

SMOCKING BASICS

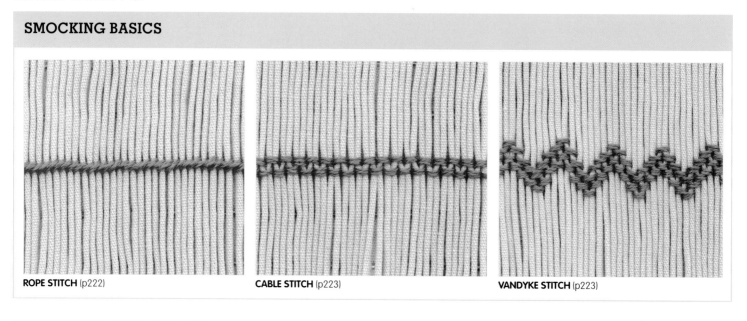

ROPE STITCH (p222)

CABLE STITCH (p223)

VANDYKE STITCH (p223)

HONEYCOMB SMOCKING

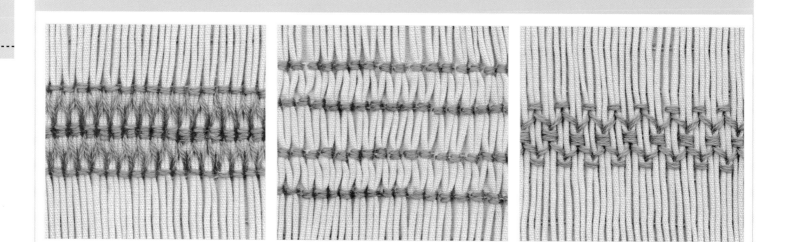

CLOSED HONEYCOMB STITCH (p223)

OPEN HONEYCOMB STITCH (p224)

HONEYCOMB CHEVRON STITCH (p224)

BEADWORK

BEADS

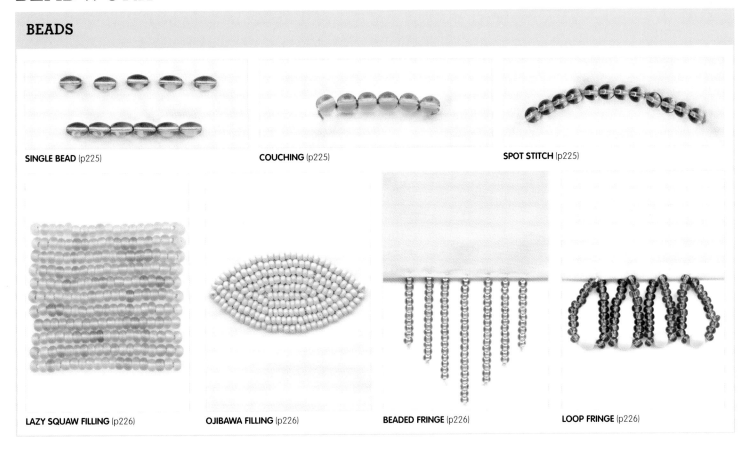

SINGLE BEAD (p225)

COUCHING (p225)

SPOT STITCH (p225)

LAZY SQUAW FILLING (p226)

OJIBAWA FILLING (p226)

BEADED FRINGE (p226)

LOOP FRINGE (p226)

SEQUINS

SINGLE SEQUIN (p227)

SEQUIN CHAIN (p227)

BEADED SEQUIN (p227)

MIRRORWORK

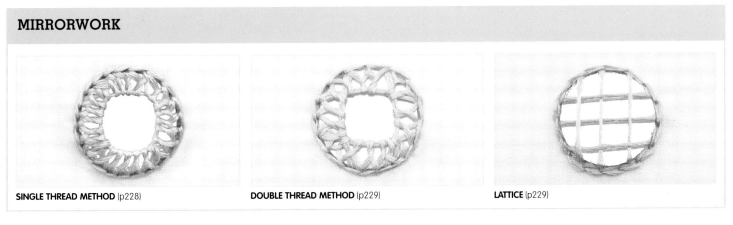

SINGLE THREAD METHOD (p228)

DOUBLE THREAD METHOD (p229)

LATTICE (p229)

EMBROIDERY

SURFACE EMBROIDERY

Decorating fabrics with embroidery is a satisfying way to make something unique, be it an article of clothing or an item for the home. Stitching the surface of cloth, whether the work is simple or complex, adds texture and interest, and can be done on virtually any fabric. Plain-weave, or common-weave, fabrics are most often used for surface embellishment, but many household textiles or accessories can be made from even-weave cloth and embroidered.

CROSS STITCH

These stitches can stand alone or be worked in rows. To work rows of stitches, complete the row of diagonal stitches from right to left, then reverse the direction to complete the cross stitches.

INDIVIDUAL CROSS STITCH

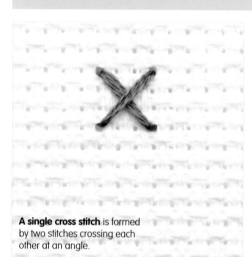

A single cross stitch is formed by two stitches crossing each other at an angle.

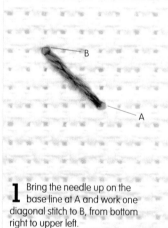

1 Bring the needle up on the base line at A and work one diagonal stitch to B, from bottom right to upper left.

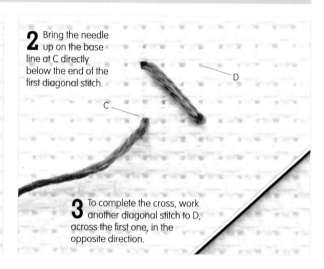

2 Bring the needle up on the base line at C directly below the end of the first diagonal stitch.

3 To complete the cross, work another diagonal stitch to D, across the first one, in the opposite direction.

SERIAL CROSS STITCH

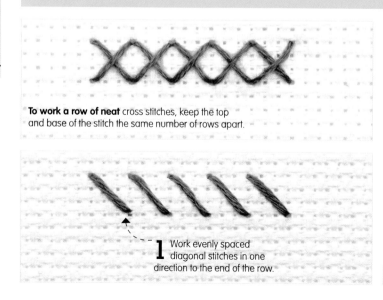

To work a row of neat cross stitches, keep the top and base of the stitch the same number of rows apart.

1 Work evenly spaced diagonal stitches in one direction to the end of the row.

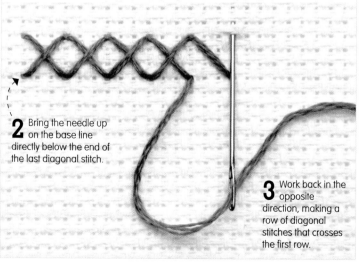

2 Bring the needle up on the base line directly below the end of the last diagonal stitch.

3 Work back in the opposite direction, making a row of diagonal stitches that crosses the first row.

DOUBLE-SIDED STITCH

1 Take a diagonal stitch in every other space, working from left to right.

This variation uses a half-diagonal stitch to complete the cross, spacing the stitches evenly and working back to complete the row.

2 At the end of the row, work a half-diagonal stitch at A on the right-hand side of the last stitch, bringing the needle up again at B on the left side of the last diagonal stitch.

3 Work another half-diagonal stitch back to the centre at A, bringing the needle out to the left of the last full diagonal stitch to complete the cross.

4 Working from right to left, work over the stitches worked in Step 1 to complete the row of crosses.

5 Return in the original direction, filling in the spaces with diagonal stitches that slant from bottom left to upper right.

6 At the end of the row take a half-diagonal stitch (as in Step 2).

7 Take another half-diagonal stitch (as in Step 3) and come up in position to finish the row.

8 Fill in the remaining single diagonals, working from right to left.

LONG-ARMED CROSS STITCH

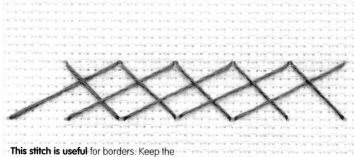

This stitch is useful for borders. Keep the proportion of twice as many vertical threads as horizontal ones as you work.

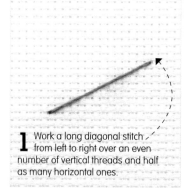

1 Work a long diagonal stitch from left to right over an even number of vertical threads and half as many horizontal ones.

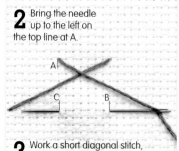

2 Bring the needle up to the left on the top line at A.

3 Work a short diagonal stitch, taking the needle down at B. Bring it up at C.

ST GEORGE CROSS STITCH

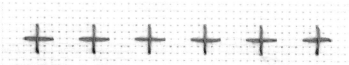

This variation is worked horizontally and vertically, combining running stitches with straight stitches.

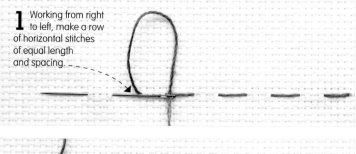

1 Working from right to left, make a row of horizontal stitches of equal length and spacing.

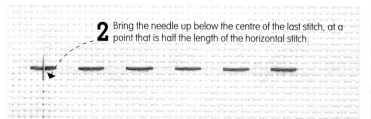

2 Bring the needle up below the centre of the last stitch, at a point that is half the length of the horizontal stitch.

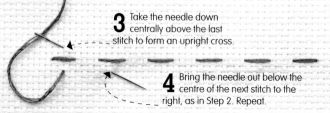

3 Take the needle down centrally above the last stitch to form an upright cross.

4 Bring the needle out below the centre of the next stitch to the right, as in Step 2. Repeat.

FLAT STITCHES

Flat stitches have an almost flat texture. There are a number of filling stitches (see pages 191–194) that are similar to the flat-stitch family but are more three-dimensional. The stitches shown here are all based on straight stitch.

STRAIGHT STITCH

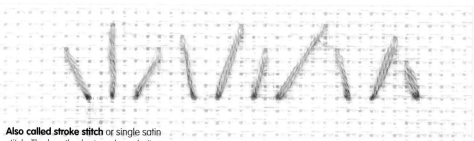

Also called stroke stitch or single satin stitch. The length, slant, and regularity can vary, but keep stitches fairly short.

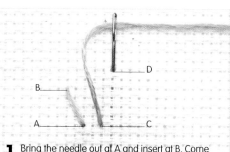

1 Bring the needle out at A and insert at B. Come out at C and insert at D. Repeat.

LONG AND SHORT STITCH

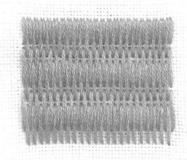

Also called shading stitch. The first row consists of alternate short and long stitches but subsequent rows are filled with stitches of the same length.

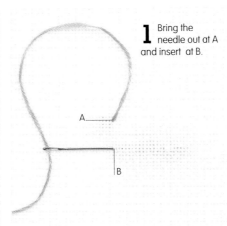

1 Bring the needle out at A and insert at B.

2 Make the next stitch longer. Bring the needle out at C and insert it next to B, at D. Repeat the short-and-long sequence along the foundation row, placing stitches as close together as possible.

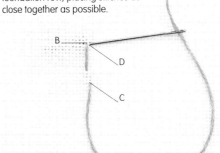

3 To work the next row, bring the needle out at E, below a short stitch, and insert it at F, almost touching the thread above.

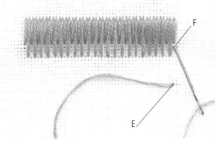

4 Repeat, coming out at G and down at H, making the stitch the same length as in Step 3. Repeat to fill the design.

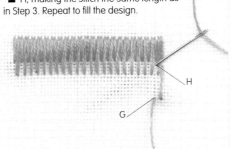

BLENDING COLOURS

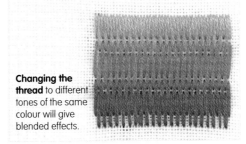

Changing the thread to different tones of the same colour will give blended effects.

LEAF STITCH

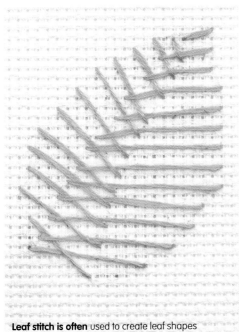

Leaf stitch is often used to create leaf shapes with a central spine and pretty veins, but it can also work well as a border stitch.

1 Draw two guidelines through the centre of the motif that meet at the top and gradually diverge. Bring the needle out at A, at the bottom of the left-hand inner line, and insert it at B, on the right-hand edge.

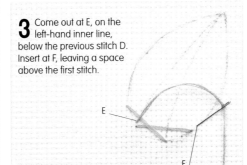

2 Come out at C, on the right-hand inner line, and insert at D, on the left-hand edge.

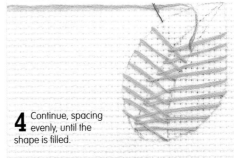

3 Come out at E, on the left-hand inner line, below the previous stitch D. Insert at F, leaving a space above the first stitch.

4 Continue, spacing evenly, until the shape is filled.

FERN STITCH

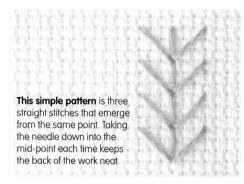

This simple pattern is three straight stitches that emerge from the same point. Taking the needle down into the mid-point each time keeps the back of the work neat.

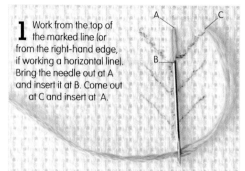

1 Work from the top of the marked line (or from the right-hand edge, if working a horizontal line). Bring the needle out at A and insert it at B. Come out at C and insert at A.

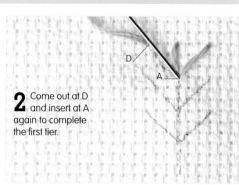

2 Come out at D and insert at A again to complete the first tier.

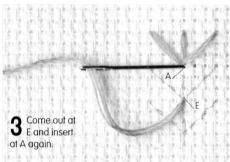

3 Come out at E and insert at A again.

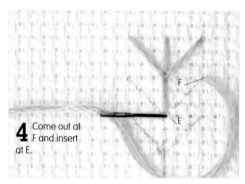

4 Come out at F and insert at E.

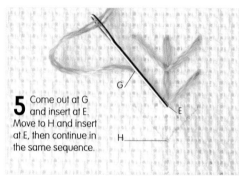

5 Come out at G and insert at E. Move to H and insert at E, then continue in the same sequence.

OUTLINE STITCHES

As the name implies, outline stitches are used to delineate the edge of a motif. They can look simple or complex, but all are straightforward to work.

RUNNING STITCH

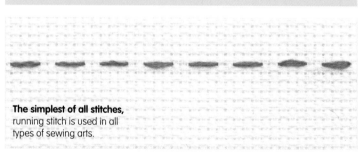

The simplest of all stitches, running stitch is used in all types of sewing arts.

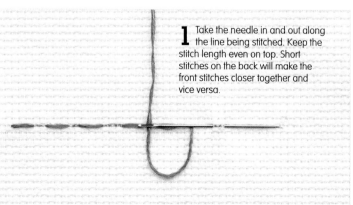

1 Take the needle in and out along the line being stitched. Keep the stitch length even on top. Short stitches on the back will make the front stitches closer together and vice versa.

LACED RUNNING STITCH

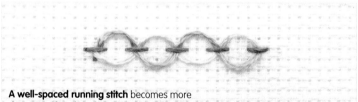

A well-spaced running stitch becomes more decorative if it is laced on top with a different colour of thread.

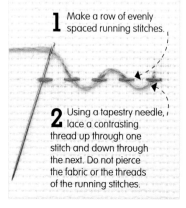

1 Make a row of evenly spaced running stitches.

2 Using a tapestry needle, lace a contrasting thread up through one stitch and down through the next. Do not pierce the fabric or the threads of the running stitches.

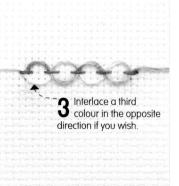

3 Interlace a third colour in the opposite direction if you wish.

STEM STITCH

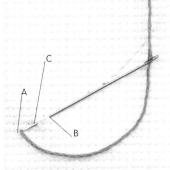

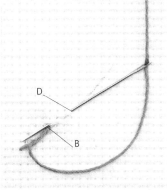

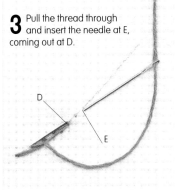

Also called South Kensington stitch and crewel stitch. This can be a single line, worked as a border or as a filling stitch. The angle of the needle determines the width of the outline.

1 Work from left to right and keep the thread below the line of stitching. Bring the needle out at A, insert it at B, and come out again at C, about halfway back towards A.

2 Insert the needle at D and come out at B. Keep an even stitch length.

3 Pull the thread through and insert the needle at E, coming out at D.

4 Repeat the sequence to continue, keeping the stitch length even.

BACKSTITCH

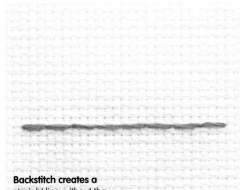

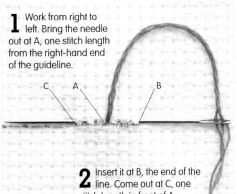

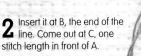

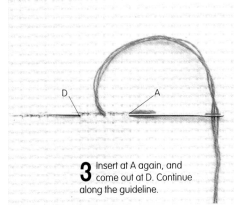

Backstitch creates a straight line without the spacing of running stitch.

1 Work from right to left. Bring the needle out at A, one stitch length from the right-hand end of the guideline.

2 Insert it at B, the end of the line. Come out at C, one stitch length in front of A.

3 Insert at A again, and come out at D. Continue along the guideline.

WHIPPED BACKSTITCH

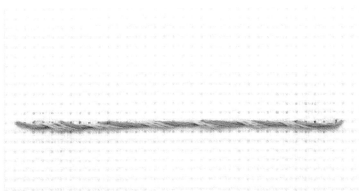

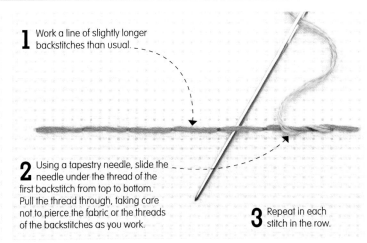

1 Work a line of slightly longer backstitches than usual.

2 Using a tapestry needle, slide the needle under the thread of the first backstitch from top to bottom. Pull the thread through, taking care not to pierce the fabric or the threads of the backstitches as you work.

3 Repeat in each stitch in the row.

Whipping an outline stitch with a matching or contrasting thread gives it extra texture.

PEKINESE STITCH

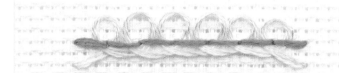

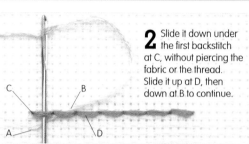

Also known as forbidden stitch, Pekinese stitch is found on ancient Chinese embroideries. It is particularly effective worked with silk or metallic threads.

1 Work a row of backstitch. Working from left to right, bring a tapestry needle with the lacing thread up at A and slide it under the second backstitch at B.

2 Slide it down under the first backstitch at C, without piercing the fabric or the thread. Slide it up at D, then down at B to continue.

HOLBEIN STITCH

Also known as double running stitch, Holbein stitch is neater when worked on even-weave fabric. It is normally worked with one thread; here, for clarity, a contrasting colour has been used for the return stitches.

1 Work a line of evenly spaced running stitch.

2 Return in the opposite direction, filling in the spaces left open with the first set of stitches.

SPLIT STITCH

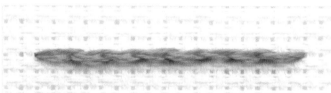

Work split stitch with a fine needle and stranded cotton or soft crewel wool for the best results.

1 Working from left to right, bring the needle up at A and down at B. Bring the needle out at C, splitting the first stitch in the middle.

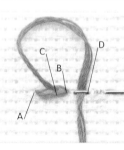

2 Insert the needle at D and repeat to continue.

HERRINGBONE STITCH

Herringbone stitch is a basic outline stitch that also works well as a border. If you are working on plain-weave fabric, mark two parallel guidelines.

1 Bring the needle out at A, on the bottom guideline.

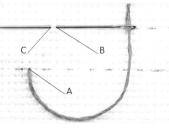

2 Take a diagonal stitch to the top guideline. Insert the needle at B and bring it out a short stitch back at C.

3 Take a diagonal stitch in the opposite direction along the bottom guideline, inserting the needle at D and coming out at E.

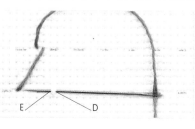

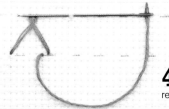

4 Repeat Step 1 to make the next stitch, then repeat Step 2 and continue.

CLOSED HERRINGBONE STITCH

Also known as double backstitch when worked on the front. This is a heavily textured stitch that can also be used as a border.

1 Work as for Herringbone stitch, opposite, but place the stitches next to each other. The tops and bottoms of the diagonal stitches should touch each other.

CHEVRON STITCH

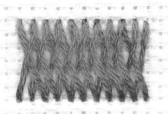

Chevron stitch is another outline stitch that also works well as a border. If you work on plain-weave fabric, mark two parallel guidelines.

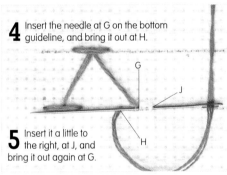

1 Bring the needle up at A on the bottom guideline and insert it at B. Come out at C.

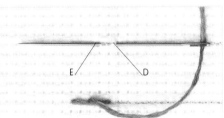

2 Insert the needle at D on the top guideline and come out a little to the left, at E. Bring the thread through to make a horizontal stitch along the top.

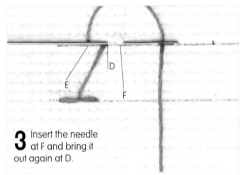

3 Insert the needle at F and bring it out again at D.

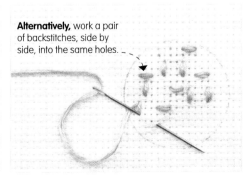

4 Insert the needle at G on the bottom guideline, and bring it out at H.

5 Insert it a little to the right, at J, and bring it out again at G.

FILLING STITCHES

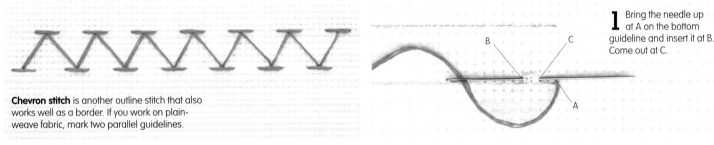

Almost any stitch can be used to fill an area of background, but some are more effective and useful than others. Filling can be worked solidly, like satin stitch, or lightly, like dot stitch, depending on the effect you want to create.

DOT STITCH

Also known as seed or seeding stitch. Dot stitch is a useful way of filling an area lightly when you want some of the background fabric to show.

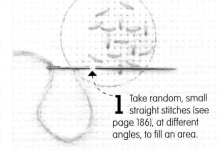

1 Take random, small straight stitches (see page 186), at different angles, to fill an area.

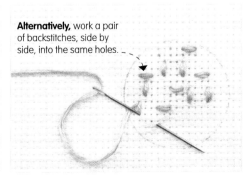

Alternatively, work a pair of backstitches, side by side, into the same holes.

SHEAF STITCH

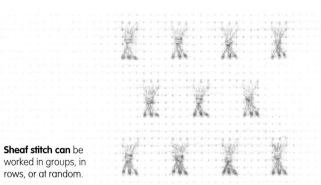

Sheaf stitch can be worked in groups, in rows, or at random.

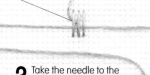

1 Take three vertical straight stitches side by side. Bring the needle out at A, behind the centre thread.

2 Slide the needle to the left, under the first stitch. Take the needle over to the right and slide it under all three stitches.

3 Take the needle to the right again and slide it under the vertical stitches. Insert at A. Do not pierce the fabric or threads.

SPIDER'S WEB

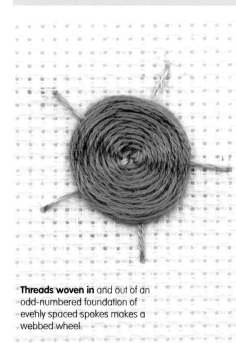

Threads woven in and out of an odd-numbered foundation of evenly spaced spokes makes a webbed wheel.

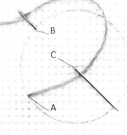

1 Mark a circular outline if using plain-weave fabric. Bring the needle out at A and insert it at B. Come out in the centre, at C.

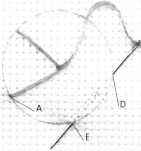

2 Catching the thread under in the centre, insert the needle at D on the other side. Come up at E, halfway between D and A.

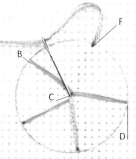

3 Take the needle back to C and insert in the centre, coming up at F, halfway between B and D. Take it back and insert at C.

4 Bring a thread to the front and use a tapestry needle to weave under and over through the spokes to fill the circle. Do not pierce the fabric or split the spoke threads.

SATIN STITCH

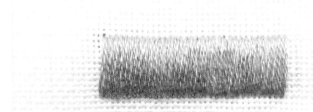

Satin stitch is a popular basic filling stitch. Use a hoop to keep your stitching smooth and even.

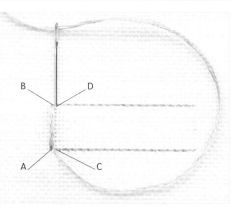

1 Bring the needle out at A and insert at B. Bring it out again at C, close to A, pulling the thread across the back smoothly. Insert at D. Continue, keeping the front and back smooth and the edges even.

PADDED SATIN STITCH

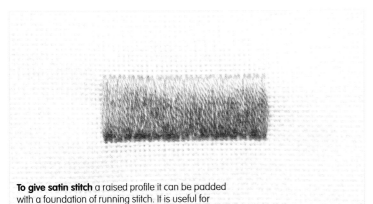

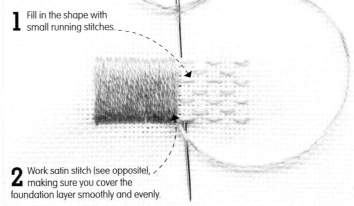

To give satin stitch a raised profile it can be padded with a foundation of running stitch. It is useful for creating elegant monograms.

1 Fill in the shape with small running stitches.

2 Work satin stitch (see opposite), making sure you cover the foundation layer smoothly and evenly.

WHIPPED SATIN STITCH

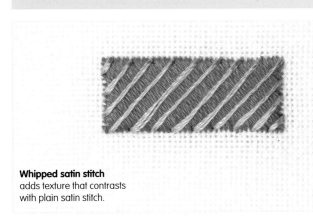

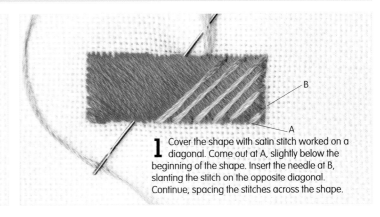

Whipped satin stitch adds texture that contrasts with plain satin stitch.

1 Cover the shape with satin stitch worked on a diagonal. Come out at A, slightly below the beginning of the shape. Insert the needle at B, slanting the stitch on the opposite diagonal. Continue, spacing the stitches across the shape.

FLAT STITCH

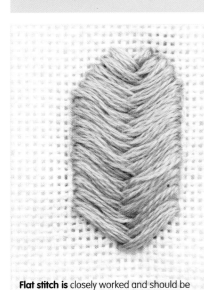

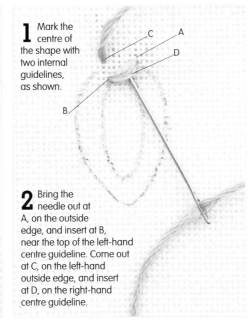

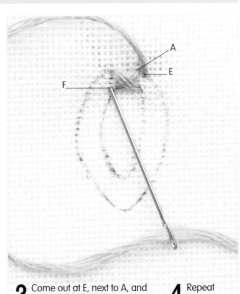

Flat stitch is closely worked and should be worked in a hoop or frame. It is ideal for making leaves and flowers.

1 Mark the centre of the shape with two internal guidelines, as shown.

2 Bring the needle out at A, on the outside edge, and insert at B, near the top of the left-hand centre guideline. Come out at C, on the left-hand outside edge, and insert at D, on the right-hand centre guideline.

3 Come out at E, next to A, and cross to F, on the left-hand centre guideline next to the stitch.

4 Repeat Steps 2–3 to continue.

FISHBONE STITCH

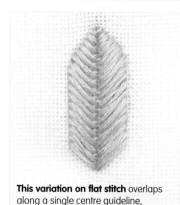

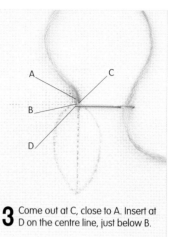

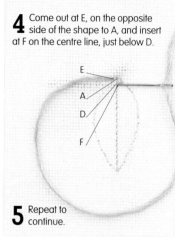

This variation on flat stitch overlaps along a single centre guideline, resulting in a more acute angle.

1 Mark a guideline along the centre of the shape.

2 Come out at A and insert needle at B to make a small stitch at the top of the guideline.

3 Come out at C, close to A. Insert at D on the centre line, just below B.

4 Come out at E, on the opposite side of the shape to A, and insert at F on the centre line, just below D.

5 Repeat to continue.

DARNING STITCH

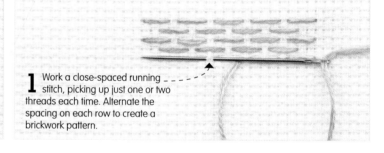

A variation on running stitch, this is worked with less spacing between stitches in regular rows. It makes a good stitch for borders and filling backgrounds.

1 Work a close-spaced running stitch, picking up just one or two threads each time. Alternate the spacing on each row to create a brickwork pattern.

LOOPED STITCHES

Looped stitches are all based on looping a thread around the needle before securing it. Many of them can be used as outline or border stitches, while others can fill in shapes or occur in isolation.

BUTTONHOLE STITCH AND BLANKET STITCH

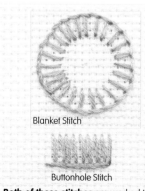

Blanket Stitch

Buttonhole Stitch

Both of these stitches are worked the same way, from left to right. They differ only in the spacing between each vertical stitch.

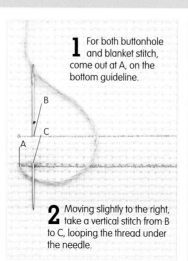

1 For both buttonhole and blanket stitch, come out at A, on the bottom guideline.

2 Moving slightly to the right, take a vertical stitch from B to C, looping the thread under the needle.

3 Repeat, keeping the stitches close together for buttonhole stitch.

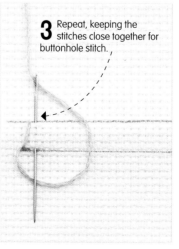

4 For blanket stitch, leave a space between each vertical stitch.

CLOSED BUTTONHOLE STITCH

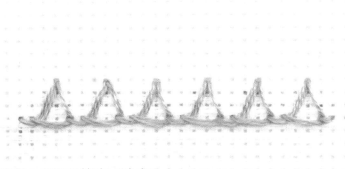

In this variation on blanket stitch, the vertical stitches are worked in pairs and slanted to form inverted V-shapes.

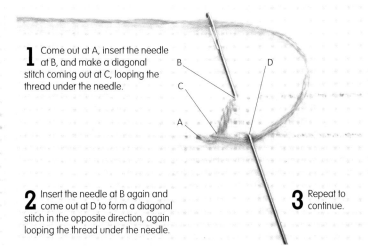

1 Come out at A, insert the needle at B, and make a diagonal stitch coming out at C, looping the thread under the needle.

2 Insert the needle at B again and come out at D to form a diagonal stitch in the opposite direction, again looping the thread under the needle.

3 Repeat to continue.

KNOTTED BUTTONHOLE STITCH

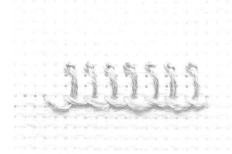

A decorative knot is formed at the top of each vertical stitch in this variation.

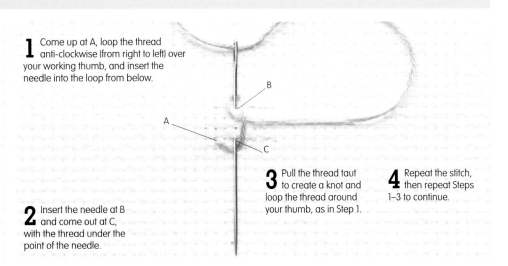

1 Come up at A, loop the thread anti-clockwise (from right to left) over your working thumb, and insert the needle into the loop from below.

2 Insert the needle at B and come out at C, with the thread under the point of the needle.

3 Pull the thread taut to create a knot and loop the thread around your thumb, as in Step 1.

4 Repeat the stitch, then repeat Steps 1–3 to continue.

DOUBLE BUTTONHOLE STITCH

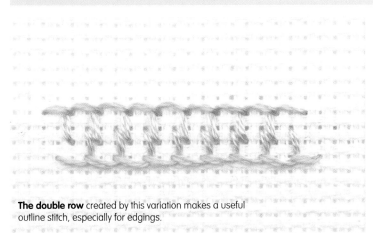

The double row created by this variation makes a useful outline stitch, especially for edgings.

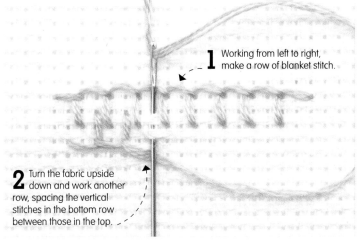

1 Working from left to right, make a row of blanket stitch.

2 Turn the fabric upside down and work another row, spacing the vertical stitches in the bottom row between those in the top.

EMBROIDERY

FEATHER STITCH

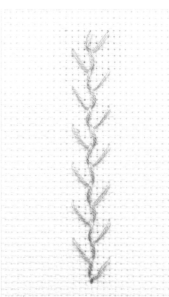

Also called briar stitch and coral stitch. Feather stitch is often used to decorate the seams on crazy quilts (see page 337) and to outline appliqué motifs, as well as making feathery patterns for embroidery.

1 Draw a guideline on the fabric – it can be straight or curved.

2 Work from top to bottom. Bring the needle up at A, at the top of the guideline, and hold the thread with your non-working thumb.

3 Insert the needle at B, level with and to the right of A. Take a slanted stitch to C, with the thread under the needle.

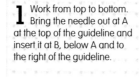

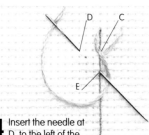

4 Insert the needle at D, to the left of the guideline and level with C, and take a slanted stitch to E, with the thread again looped under the needle. Repeat to continue.

SINGLE FEATHER STITCH

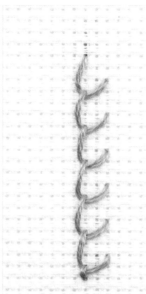

Single feather stitch is worked like feather stitch, but the loops are positioned on only one side of the guideline.

1 Work from top to bottom. Bring the needle out at A at the top of the guideline and insert it at B, below A and to the right of the guideline.

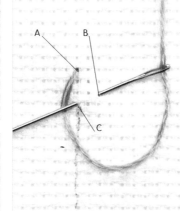

2 Take a stitch to C on the guideline, with the thread looped under the needle. Repeat to continue.

DOUBLE FEATHER STITCH

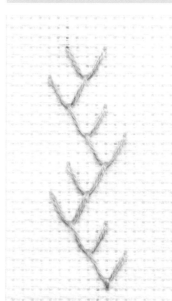

In this variation on feather stitch, extra stitches are made on each side of the line to fill a broader area. Use a hoop to stretch the fabric taut.

1 Work as for feather stitch (left), working from top to bottom and alternating from left to right – but on each side of the first stitch make two or more stitches.

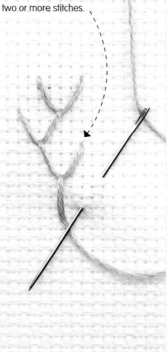

CLOSED FEATHER STITCH

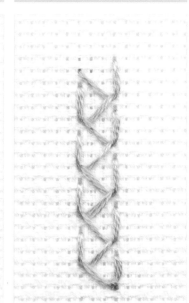

This variation on feather stitch is a useful border or outline stitch that can also be used for couching (see page 205). As with feather stitch, work from top to bottom.

1 Mark two parallel guidelines and bring the needle up at A, at the top of one line. Insert the needle at B and bring it up at C on the opposite guideline, looping the thread under the needle.

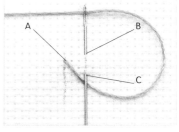

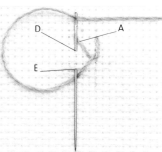

2 Insert the needle at D, below A on the first guideline, and come out at E, again looping the thread under the needle and parallel to the previous stitch. Repeat to continue.

LOOP STITCH

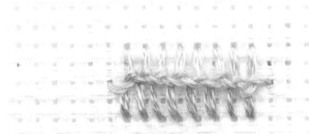

Like many looped stitches, loop stitch is usually worked in straight lines. The looping creates a raised knot in the centre of each stitch with two "legs", which gives the stitch its other name of centipede stitch.

1 Mark two parallel guidelines on the fabric and work from right to left. Bring the needle out in the centre at A, in between the marked lines. Insert it diagonally at B on the top line and come out at C, directly below B between the guidelines. Take the needle under the stitch (A–B) and over the working thread.

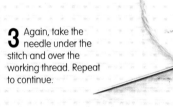

2 Pull the resulting knot gently and make another stitch from D to E.

3 Again, take the needle under the stitch and over the working thread. Repeat to continue.

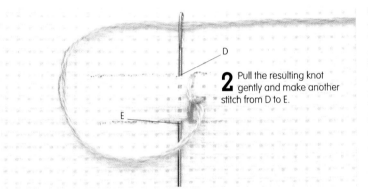

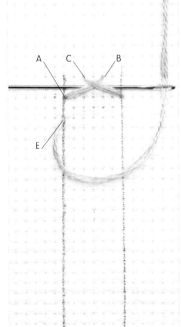

VANDYKE STITCH

1 Work from top to bottom along parallel guidelines. Bring the needle out at A, on the left-hand guideline. Insert it at B, slightly above A and mid-way between the guidelines, and bring it out at C, slightly to the left of B.

3 Gently pull the thread taut and slide the needle behind the crossed threads without piercing the fabric.

4 Insert the needle at F, below D on the right-hand line, and come out at G, below E on the left-hand side. Again, slide the needle behind the crossed threads. Repeat to continue.

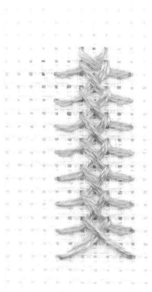

Vandyke stitch, with its braided look, can be used as a border or as a filling stitch.

2 Take a stitch across A–B, inserting the needle level with A at D on the right-hand guideline and coming out at E, below A on the left-hand guideline.

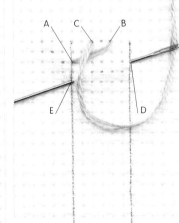

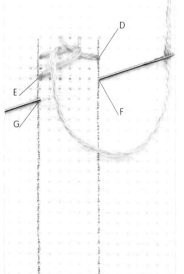

CRETAN STITCH

Cretan stitch has a braided effect and works well as a filling or border stitch.

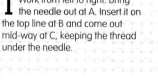

1 Work from left to right. Bring the needle out at A. Insert it on the top line at B and come out mid-way at C, keeping the thread under the needle.

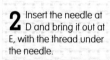
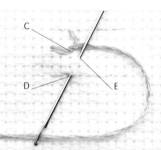

2 Insert the needle at D and bring it out at E, with the thread under the needle.

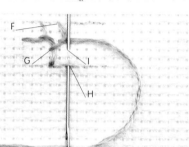

3 Repeat at F to G, then at H to I, and continue.

OPEN CRETAN STITCH

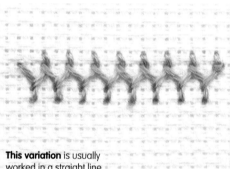

This variation is usually worked in a straight line.

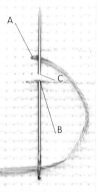

1 Bring the needle out at A. Insert it at B and take a small vertical stitch to C, with the thread behind the needle.

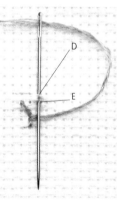

2 Insert the needle at D and take a small vertical stitch to E, with the thread behind the needle. Repeat.

FLY STITCH

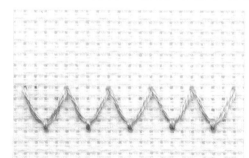

Fly stitch, also called open lazy daisy and Y stitch, can be worked in horizontal or vertical rows, or randomly, as a border or filling stitch. The length of the tying stitch can vary.

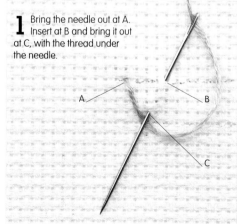

1 Bring the needle out at A. Insert at B and bring it out at C, with the thread under the needle.

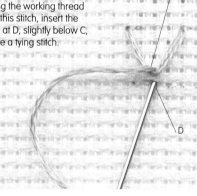

2 Pull the thread through to form a V-shaped stitch. Keeping the working thread above this stitch, insert the needle at D, slightly below C, to make a tying stitch.

PLAITED FLY STITCH

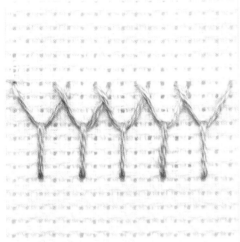

In this variation the tails are longer and the arms overlap the next stitch. It can be worked in rows or randomly.

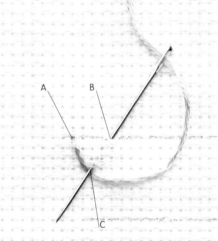

1 Bring the needle out at A. Insert at B and bring it out at C, with the thread under the needle.

2 Pull the thread to form a V-shaped stitch. With thread above stitch, insert the needle at D to make a long tying stitch.

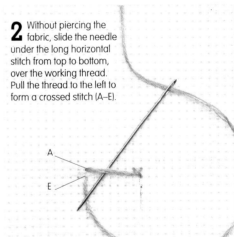

3 Bring the needle out at E, left of B, overlapping the stitches. Continue as in Step 1.

LADDER STITCH

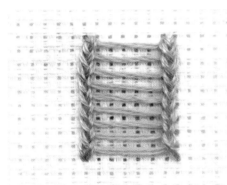

Also known as step stitch. The loops at the side of the horizontal stitches give it the look of braid.

1 Mark parallel vertical guidelines on the fabric. Work from top to bottom. Bring the needle out at A. Insert it at B and bring it out at C, keeping the thread on top of the horizontal stitch. Insert the needle at D to form a short crossed stitch (C–D). Come out at E.

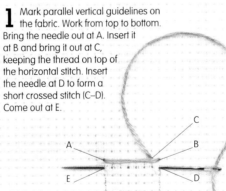

2 Without piercing the fabric, slide the needle under the long horizontal stitch from top to bottom, over the working thread. Pull the thread to the left to form a crossed stitch (A–E).

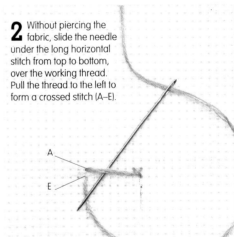

3 Slide the needle behind the crossed stitch (C–D) on the right-hand guideline.

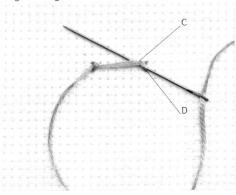

4 Insert the needle at F and come out at G, on the left.

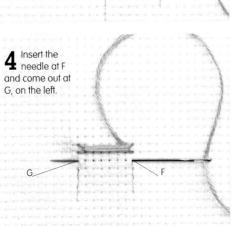

5 Slide the needle under the crossed stitch on the left-hand side (A–E), take it across the front to H, and repeat Steps 3 and 4.

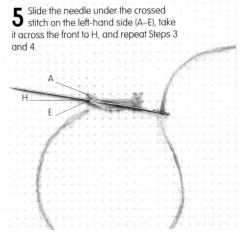

CHAINED STITCHES

The stitches in this group are useful for borders, outlining, and filling. All except daisy stitch are worked as a continuous chain.

DAISY STITCH

Also known as lazy daisy or detached chain stitch, daisy stitch is simply a single chain stitch. It is often used to make flower petals.

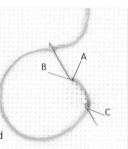

1 Bring the needle out at A and insert it at B, next to A. Bring the needle out at C with the thread under the needle.

2 Pull gently to make a loop and take a tiny stitch over the thread at C to hold it in place.

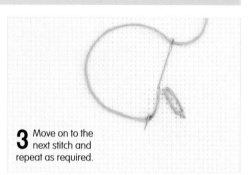

3 Move on to the next stitch and repeat as required.

CHAIN STITCH

Chain stitch is worked from top to bottom; a marked guideline makes stitching easier.

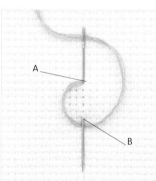

1 Bring the needle up at A at the top of the line and insert it in the same hole. Hold the thread under the needle and come out below at B. Pull gently.

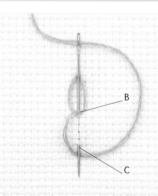

2 Re-insert the needle at B in the same hole and repeat, coming up at C with the thread under needle. Each loop will be held in place by the next.

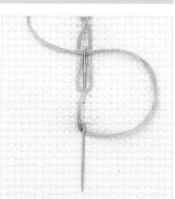

3 Tie the last loop in place by working a tiny stitch over the bottom of the loop.

OPEN CHAIN STITCH

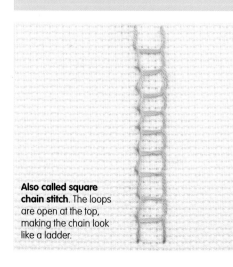

Also called square chain stitch. The loops are open at the top, making the chain look like a ladder.

1 Mark parallel guidelines. Bring the needle out at A, on the left. Insert the needle at B, on the right, and bring it out at C, below A. Keep the thread under the needle as you pull the stitch taut.

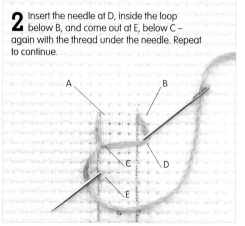

2 Insert the needle at D, inside the loop below B, and come out at E, below C – again with the thread under the needle. Repeat to continue.

TWISTED CHAIN STITCH

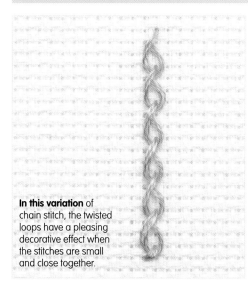

In this variation of chain stitch, the twisted loops have a pleasing decorative effect when the stitches are small and close together.

1 Come out at A, holding thread below. Insert the needle at B, slightly to the left, come out at C, below A, with thread under the needle.

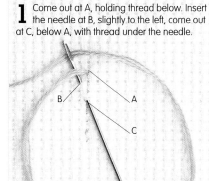

2 Again holding the thread, insert the needle at D, to the left of the line, and come out at E, with the thread under the needle. Make another twisted loop and continue.

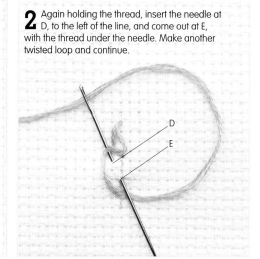

FEATHERED CHAIN STITCH

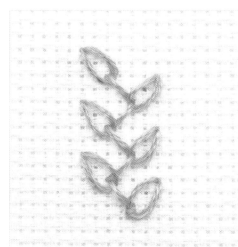

This chain stitch variation creates a zigzag line made of diagonal stitches with a chain loop at the top.

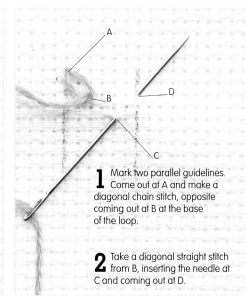

1 Mark two parallel guidelines. Come out at A and make a diagonal chain stitch, opposite coming out at B at the base of the loop.

2 Take a diagonal straight stitch from B, inserting the needle at C and coming out at D.

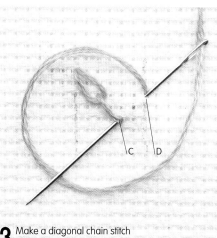

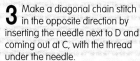

3 Make a diagonal chain stitch in the opposite direction by inserting the needle next to D and coming out at C, with the thread under the needle.

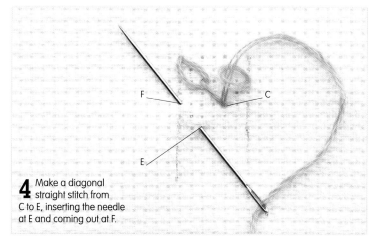

4 Make a diagonal straight stitch from C to E, inserting the needle at E and coming out at F.

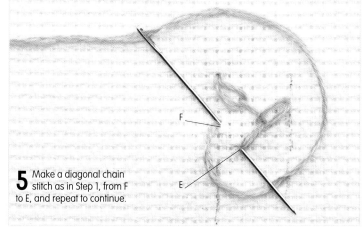

5 Make a diagonal chain stitch as in Step 1, from F to E, and repeat to continue.

WHEATEAR STITCH

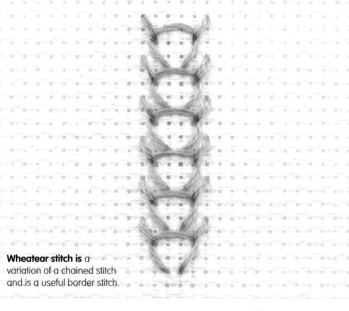

Wheatear stitch is a variation of a chained stitch and is a useful border stitch.

1 Bring the needle out at A. Take two diagonal stitches in opposite directions, from A–B and C–D, to form a V-shape with a slight gap in the middle. Come up at E, between B and D.

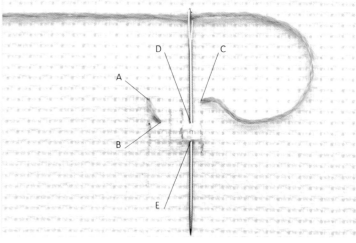

2 Slide the needle under the two diagonal stitches from right to left without piercing the fabric.

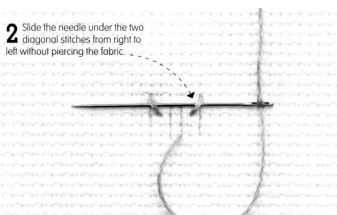

3 Insert the needle at F, beside E, to complete one stitch. Come out at G, on the left. Repeat the sequence to continue, sliding the needle under the two diagonal stitches each time.

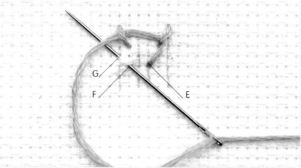

CABLE CHAIN STITCH

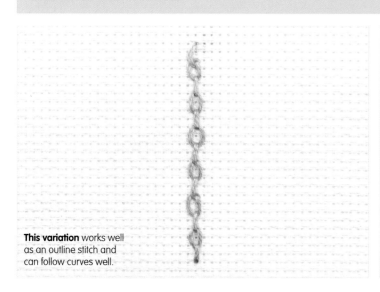

This variation works well as an outline stitch and can follow curves well.

1 Bring the needle out at A and wrap the thread over and under the needle, from right to left. Hold the thread, insert the needle at B. Come out at C, taking the thread under the needle. This forms a single chain with a straight link stitch at the top. Repeat.

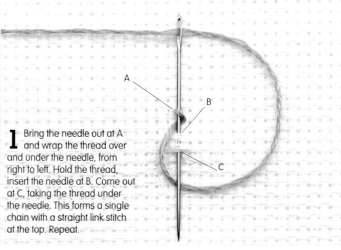

KNOTTED
STITCHES

The stitches shown here all include a decorative surface knot that gives three-dimensional texture. Single knots can be scattered across a surface or tightly grouped to make a solid filling.

FRENCH KNOT

French knots can be worked individually or in groups massed together.

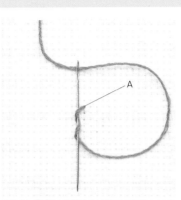

1 Come out at A, where the knot is wanted. Wrap the thread twice around the needle. For a bigger knot, make another wrap or two.

2 Pull the wraps tight against the fabric and insert the needle back next to A.

3 Hold the knot against the fabric and take the thread through to the back.

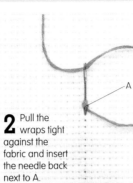

4 To work a closely spaced group, take the needle to the next position and repeat.

5 If you are making an individual knot, secure it on the back with a small backstitch.

BULLION KNOT

This long knotted stitch is best worked using a relatively thick needle with a small eye to make the coil wide enough to slide through.

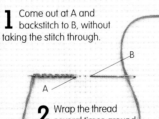

1 Come out at A and backstitch to B, without taking the stitch through.

2 Wrap the thread several times around the needle, making the wrap the same length as the stitch.

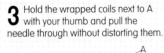

3 Hold the wrapped coils next to A with your thumb and pull the needle through without distorting them.

Press thumb here

4 Insert the needle back at B and pull the stitch tight. The coils will flip back to cover the backstitch area. Repeat.

CHINESE KNOT

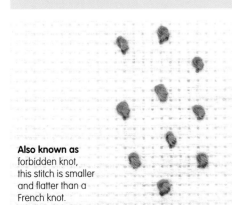

Also known as forbidden knot, this stitch is smaller and flatter than a French knot.

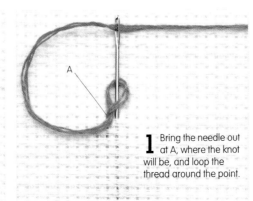

1 Bring the needle out at A, where the knot will be, and loop the thread around the point.

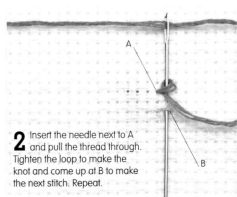

2 Insert the needle next to A and pull the thread through. Tighten the loop to make the knot and come up at B to make the next stitch. Repeat.

FOUR-LEGGED KNOT

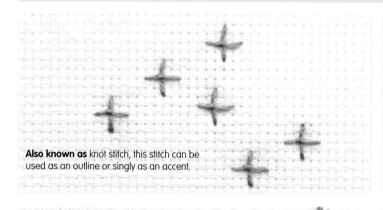

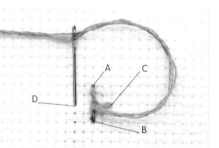

Also known as knot stitch, this stitch can be used as an outline or singly as an accent.

1 Begin as though you are making an upright cross stitch. Come out at A, insert needle at B and come out again at C, halfway up and to the right.

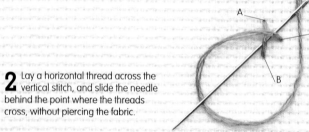

2 Lay a horizontal thread across the vertical stitch, and slide the needle behind the point where the threads cross, without piercing the fabric.

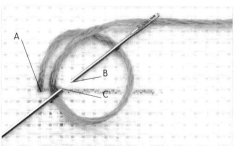

3 Pull up the knot and insert the needle at D to finish the crossed stitch.

CORAL STITCH

Coral stitch makes a knotted line; the knots can be evenly or randomly spaced.

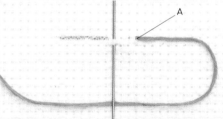

1 Mark a guideline on the fabric. Work from right to left. Bring the needle out at A.

2 Take a small stitch to where you want the first knot, looping the thread under the needle.

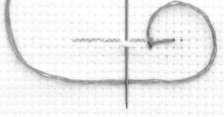

3 Pull the stitch through to form the first knot. Repeat to continue.

SCROLL STITCH

Similar to coral stitch (above), this is worked from left to right, with the thread under both ends of the needle.

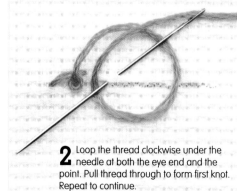

1 Come out at A, at the left end of the guideline. Take a small stitch B–C on the line where you want the first knot.

2 Loop the thread clockwise under the needle at both the eye end and the point. Pull thread through to form first knot. Repeat to continue.

COUCHING

Couching is the name given to the technique of anchoring laid threads, which are attached to the background fabric only at the ends, with small stitches along their length. The couching is often worked in contrasting colours for a decorative effect.

COUCHING STITCH

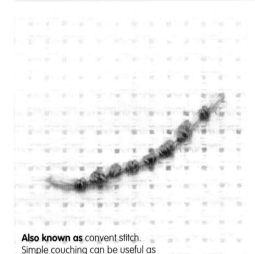

Also known as convent stitch. Simple couching can be useful as outlining or filling.

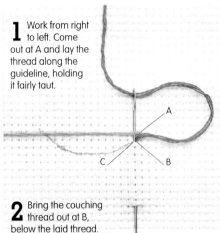

1 Work from right to left. Come out at A and lay the thread along the guideline, holding it fairly taut.

2 Bring the couching thread out at B, below the laid thread. Take a small stitch over the laid thread to C.

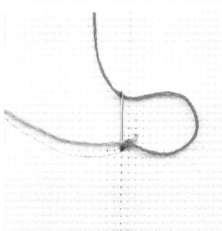

3 Repeat, taking small stitches along the laid thread to continue. Then take the end of the laid thread to the back and tie both threads off.

OVERCAST TRAILING

Also known as satin couching, this makes a raised line that looks like a cord.

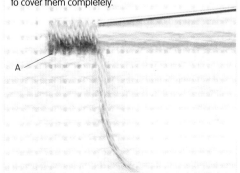

1 Bring the laid thread out at A and lay it along the guideline, holding it fairly taut. Bring the couching thread out at A and work small satin stitches (see page 192) next to each other over the laid threads to cover them completely.

THORN STITCH

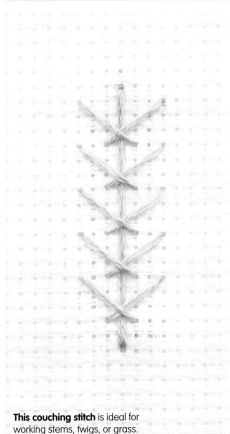

This couching stitch is ideal for working stems, twigs, or grass.

1 Come out at A, at the top. Hold the thread taut. Bring the couching thread out at B and insert at C, crossing diagonally over the laid thread.

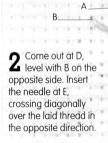

2 Come out at D, level with B on the opposite side. Insert the needle at E, crossing diagonally over the laid thread in the opposite direction.

3 Repeat along the length of the laid thread.

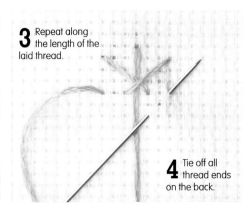

4 Tie off all thread ends on the back.

ROUMANIAN STITCH

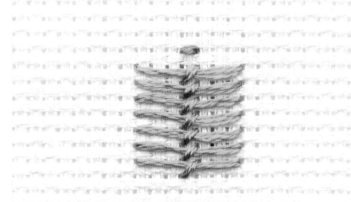

Also called oriental stitch, in this technique the same thread is used for both the laid work and the couching. Roumanian stitch is used for borders and works well to fill leaf and flower shapes.

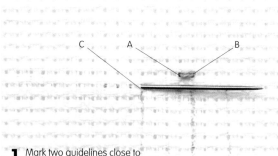

1 Mark two guidelines close to the centre of the area to be filled. Bring the needle out at A, on the left line. Take a horizontal stitch from edge to edge, inserting the needle at B and coming out at C.

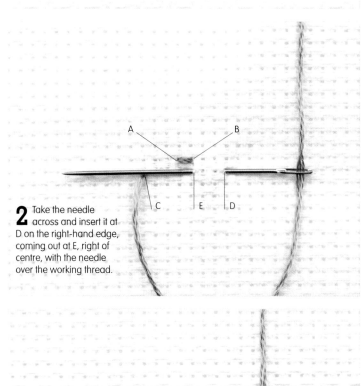

2 Take the needle across and insert it at D on the right-hand edge, coming out at E, right of centre, with the needle over the working thread.

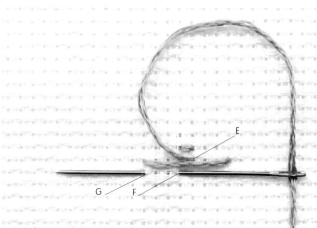

3 Take a small diagonal stitch over the horizontal one, inserting the needle at F, left of centre, and coming out at G, on the edge.

4 Make another horizontal stitch to H on the right-hand edge, coming out at I, right of centre, with the needle over the working thread.

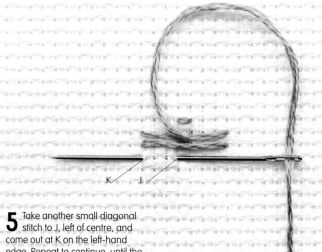

5 Take another small diagonal stitch to J, left of centre, and come out at K on the left-hand edge. Repeat to continue, until the line or shape is filled.

BOKHARA COUCHING

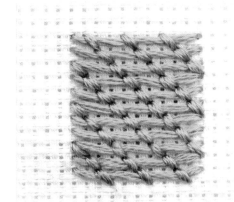

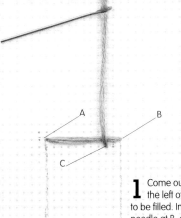

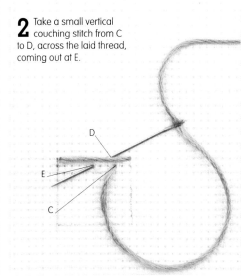

Bokhara couching is similar to Roumanian stitch, but uses more stitches in the couching. It is suitable for filling large shapes. The couching stitches are worked over the laid thread from below.

1 Come out at A, on the left of the area to be filled. Insert the needle at B, on the right, and come out at C, near the right-hand edge.

2 Take a small vertical couching stitch from C to D, across the laid thread, coming out at E.

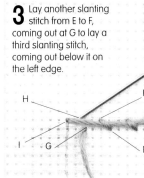

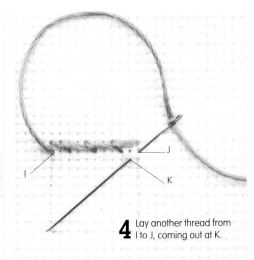

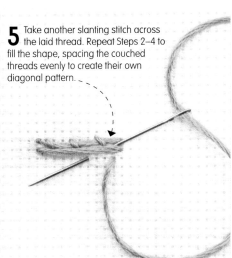

3 Lay another slanting stitch from E to F, coming out at G to lay a third slanting stitch, coming out below it on the left edge.

4 Lay another thread from I to J, coming out at K.

5 Take another slanting stitch across the laid thread. Repeat Steps 2–4 to fill the shape, spacing the couched threads evenly to create their own diagonal pattern.

JACOBEAN TRELLIS

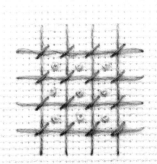

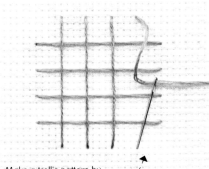

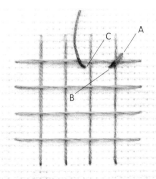

Also called trellis couching, this is an open filling stitch for large areas. The intersections can be tied down with a single stitch or a cross stitch, and the spaces filled with decorative stitches. The trellis can be horizontal and vertical, or diagonal, or a combination.

1 Make a trellis pattern by working a series of long, straight horizontal stitches, and then vertical ones.

2 Starting in one corner, tie each intersection with a diagonal stitch from A to B. Come out at C and repeat in the same direction to continue.

OPENWORK

Openwork embroidery includes cutwork and broderie anglaise or eyelet work, which are known as whitework, drawn and pulled thread work, and insertion work, also known as faggoting. Each of these techniques opens up areas of the background fabric to create lacelike effects, each very different. Most of the techniques can be worked on plain- or even-weave fabric.

WHITEWORK

Whitework includes several embroidery techniques that were used on delicate clothing and household linens that in the past were white. Whitework includes cutwork, a technique in which areas are stitched and then the background fabric is cut away. Broderie anglaise is the other main form of whitework. Delicate plain-weave fabrics, such as lawn and voile, and fine linen and cambric are suitable. Traditionally white thread is used; we have used a coloured thread to show the process clearly.

OVERCAST BAR

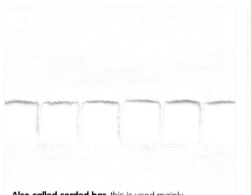

Also called corded bar, this is used mainly on delicate work that will not be subjected to wear and tear.

1 Work as for Step 1 of Buttonhole bar, below, to create two or more working threads.

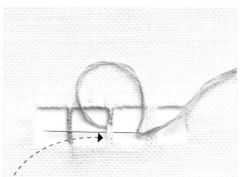

2 Working from left to right, overcast the thread sets with closely spaced stitches. Tie off or weave the overcasting threads into the fabric to secure.

BUTTONHOLE BAR

Buttonhole bars are used to connect separate pieces of fabric. You need at least three working threads to build on.

1 Even-weave fabric: withdraw vertical threads to the desired width and cut away the horizontal threads between sets of three threads (see page 217).

2 Plain-weave fabric: work three threads across the space to be filled or work running stitch across the centre of the bar.

3 Both fabrics: work buttonhole stitch (see page 194) along each bar, or set of threads.

4 A double buttonhole bar is stronger: work a close blanket stitch (see page 194) from right to left. Fill spaces between stitches with another row of blanket stitch, from left to right.

WOVEN BAR

1 Work as for Step 1 of buttonholed bar, opposite, to create an even number of at least four working threads.

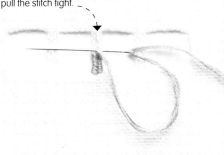

2 Come up in the centre of the bar of threads. Take needle to the left, then behind the bar and back up in the centre; pull the stitch tight. Take the needle to the right, behind the bar, and back up in the centre; pull the stitch tight.

Also called needleweaving bar, this is a strong stitch that is useful on table linens.

LOOPED EDGING

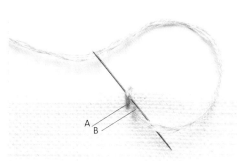

1 Press a narrow single hem. Come up at A. Slightly to the right, take a vertical stitch from back to front at B. Pull the thread through, leaving a small loop on the edge (see Step 2). Take the needle through the loop and pull gently to make a small knot on the edge.

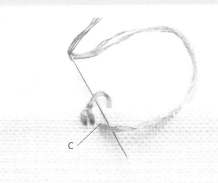

2 Come up at C and repeat to continue.

Looped edging looks similar to buttonhole stitch, but the working method is slightly different.

ANTWERP EDGING

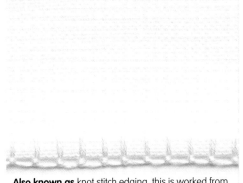

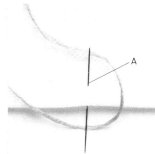

1 Insert the needle at A along a stitched hemline, which acts as a guide. Come out under edge of fabric, leaving a tail of thread on the front. Loop the thread under the needle.

2 Pull thread through, leaving a tail at the end. Slide needle behind both threads and over working thread, below where looped threads cross. Pull knot to secure it next to the folded hem.

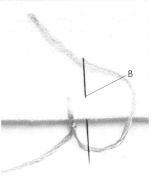

3 Insert needle at B to continue. Darn both ends into the hem to finish.

Also known as knot stitch edging, this is worked from left to right and creates a decorative lacy edging on plain-weave fabrics. Hem before beginning.

OVERCAST EYELET

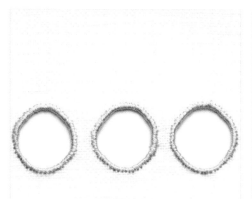

Eyelets are outlined with a variety of stitches. Overcast eyelets, which can be round or oval, are simple to work.

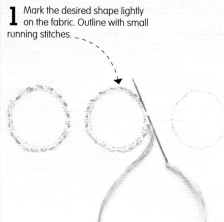

1 Mark the desired shape lightly on the fabric. Outline with small running stitches.

2 Cut the centre area, but do not remove. Fold the fabric flaps to the back and overcast along the edge of the shape.

3 Cut away any excess fabric that has not been caught in the overcasting. Do not cut into the stitching.

BUTTONHOLE EYELET

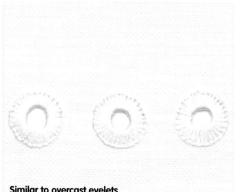

Similar to overcast eyelets, buttonhole eyelets are more substantial. They can be any shape.

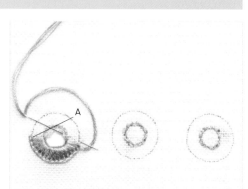

1 Draw two circles, one inside the other. Outline the inner one with small running stitches.

2 Cut across the inner circle as in Step 2 of overcast eyelets, above. Fold the cut fabric under and fingerpress it to the wrong side.

3 Come out at A on the outer circle and work buttonhole stitch around the shape, covering the running stitch and the marked outer line.

SQUARE EYELET

Eyelets with corners – squares, diamonds, or triangles – are handled slightly differently from curved ones.

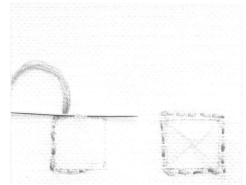

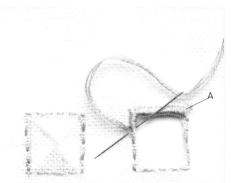

1 Draw the shape on the fabric and outline it with small running stitches. Cut diagonally across the shape into the corners and fingerpress the fabric to the wrong side.

2 Come up at A in a corner and make closely spaced overcasting stitches around the shape. Angle the stitches at the corners to make a sharp outline. To finish, weave the thread into the stitching on the wrong side and trim away excess fabric.

SOLID EDGES

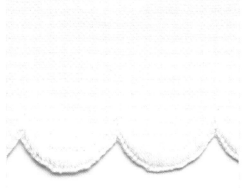

Most broderie anglaise is edged with delicate stitching rather than a hem.

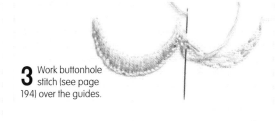

1 Mark the desired pattern on the fabric and draw in both outer and inner edges as guidelines.

2 Work a foundation between the guidelines. Use a line of running stitch inside each outline, filling with rows of running stitch, or fill with chain stitch.

3 Work buttonhole stitch (see page 194) over the guides.

4 Cut away the outer fabric carefully, without cutting into the stitching.

LOOP PICOT

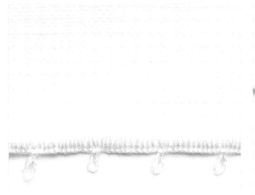

Picots are tiny loops used to decorate edgings and bar stitches. Loop picots are the easiest to work.

1 Working from right to left, buttonhole stitch (see page 194) along the folded edge. Where you want to add a loop, place a pin next to the last stitch you took, facing inwards from the edge (so that you don't catch your finger).

2 Loop thread under the pin from right to left and make a vertical stitch next to the pin on the left. Make sure the loop is the correct size, then slide needle under loop from the right, over the pin, under the other side of the loop, and over working thread. Remove pin and repeat.

RING PICOT

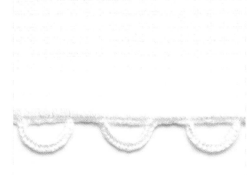

Like loop picots, ring picots are added to a buttonholed edging as decoration.

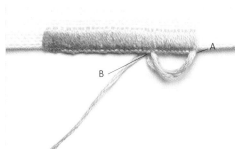

1 Working from left to right, buttonhole stitch (see page 194) along the folded edge. To add a ring picot at A, move the needle back several stitches and slide it through one stitch at B, on the edge, to create a loop.

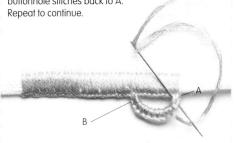

2 Take the needle through the loop and cover it with buttonhole stitches back to A. Repeat to continue.

EYELET EDGES

1 Follow Steps 1 and 2 for solid edges (see page 211), to prepare the work.

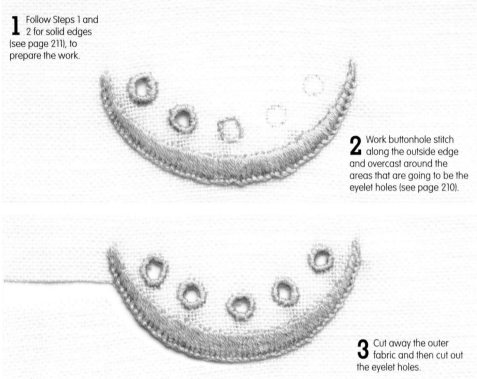

2 Work buttonhole stitch along the outside edge and overcast around the areas that are going to be the eyelet holes (see page 210).

3 Cut away the outer fabric and then cut out the eyelet holes.

When edges incorporate eyelet holes, they are worked with a combination of buttonhole stitch and overcasting.

PULLED THREAD
WORK

This is a counted-thread embroidery technique in which threads are pulled together with tight stitches to create regular open spaces in the work. Use a tapestry needle with matching thread on soft single-thread, even-weave fabric. Work loosely in a hoop.

FOUR-SIDED STITCH

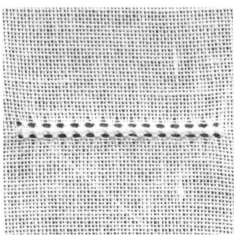

This stitch makes a lacy openwork pattern for a border or filling.

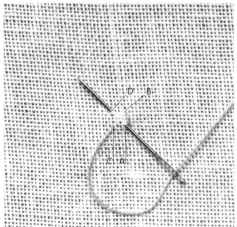

1 Come out at A. Count 4 threads up and insert needle at B. Come out at C, 4 threads down from B and 4 to the left of A. Insert needle at A again and come out at D, 4 threads up and 4 diagonally across.

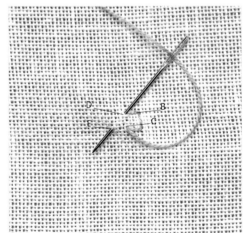

2 Insert the needle at B and come up at C. Go down at D to complete the first stitch, then come up at E, 4 down and 4 to the left of C. Repeat to make a row. To add another row, turn the work 180 degrees.

PUNCH STITCH

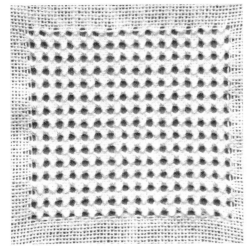

Here, **double stitches** worked in squares are pulled tight to leave open spaces at each corner. Working in rows keeps the pattern regular.

1 Come out at A. Insert needle at B, 4 threads above. Come out at A again and back in at B. Come up at C, 4 threads to the left.

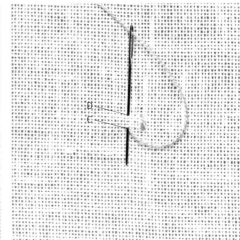

2 Work two vertical stitches from C to D.

3 Continue to make a row of evenly spaced upright stitches.

4 At the end of the row, come out at D, go down at E, 4 threads above. Work another double stitch, then come up at F. Work another row under the first.

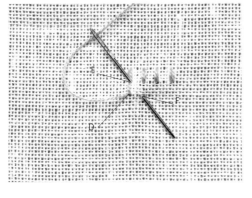

5 Come out at G. Go down at H, 4 threads to the right. Work another stitch G–H, come up at I. Continue filling in the spaces with double stitches. Pull each stitch tight.

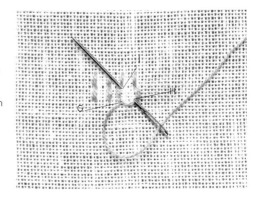

HONEYCOMB FILLING STITCH

This **light filling stitch** needs to be worked tightly.

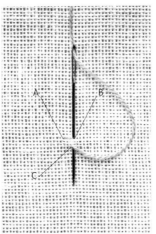

1 Come out at A. Count 3 threads to the right and insert at B. Come out at C, 3 threads below.

2 Count 3 threads to the left and insert at D. Come out 3 threads down, at E.

3 Continue back-and-forth to end of row. Turn the work 180 degrees. Repeat to create a mirror image in the next row.

STEP STITCH

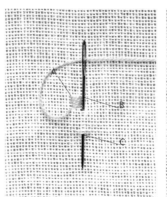

This filling stitch forms a lively zigzag pattern, consisting of horizontal and vertical blocks of straight stitches.

1 Come up at A and down at B, 4 threads to right. Work 4 horizontal stitches below, coming up at C, 8 threads below.

2 Work 5 vertical stitches over 4 threads starting at C. Come up at D and down at E. Complete a block of 5 horizontal stitches.

3 Work block of vertical stitches. Come up at F, work block of horizontal stitches. Come up at G to begin next block of vertical stitches.

CHESSBOARD FILLING

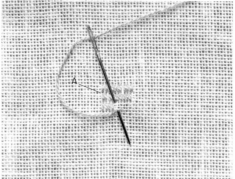

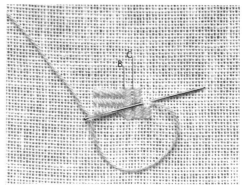

Triple rows of tightly worked alternating satin stitch (see page 192) make a solid filling with a basketweave texture.

1 Start at A, in the top left corner. Work 10 vertical straight stitches over 3 threads.

2 Reversing direction each time, repeat twice to make two more identical rows.

3 Come up at B and down at C, where previous row finished. Work 10 horizontal stitches using holes of previous block.

4 Reversing direction each time, repeat to make more identical rows.

WINDOW STITCH

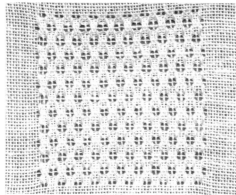

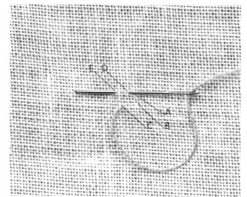

Worked in a similar way to wave stitch (opposite), window stitch uses a separate hole for each stitch, leaving a single thread in between.

1 Start at A, go down 4 threads and 2 to right at B. Come up at C, 5 threads to left. Insert 2 threads to right and 4 up at D. Come out at E, 5 threads to left.

2 Repeat the sequence to complete a row, then return from left to right, reversing the diagonal stitch each time.

MOSAIC FILLING

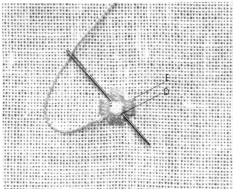

Worked in groups, this gives a dense texture that has an openwork effect if the stitches are pulled tightly.

1 Start at A, work 5 vertical straight stitches over 4 threads, finishing at B.

2 Work 5 horizontal stitches over 4 threads, from B to C.

3 Repeat from C to D to make 5 vertical stitches. Work 5 horizontal stitches, finishing at E.

4 From E, come out at D and work a four-sided stitch (see page 212) inside the open square, finishing at D.

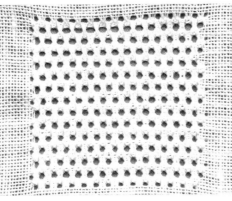

5 Work a cross stitch from D to B, and then another from C to A.

6 To work subsequent stitches in a diagonal row, for a chequerboard formation, bring needle up 8 threads down and 8 to the right. Repeat the same sequence.

WAVE STITCH

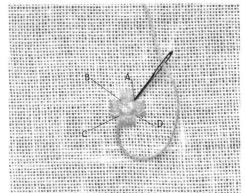

This diagonal filling stitch creates a closely worked trellis effect.

1 Come out at A, go down at B, 4 threads up and 2 to the right. Come up at C, 4 threads to the left. Insert at A and come up 4 threads to the left, at D.

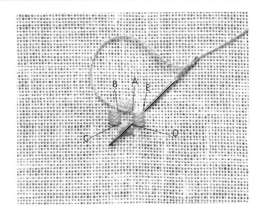

2 Insert the needle at C and come out at E. Continue in this sequence to make a row. Repeat to work subsequent rows.

3 For the new row, go down at the top of the last stitch you made, at F, and come up at G, 8 threads below. Re-insert 4 threads above and 2 to the left at H. Work from left to right, forming a mirror image of the preceding row.

EMBROIDERY

THREE-SIDED STITCH

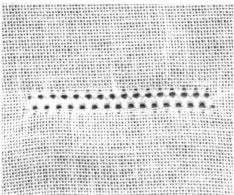

This stitch makes rows of triangles with each stitch worked twice.

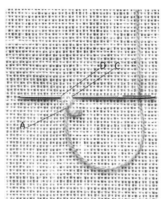

1 Come out at A and go down at B, 4 threads to right. Work another stitch A–B. Come out at A.

2 Take the needle down at C, 2 threads to the right and 4 up. Come out at A.

3 Work a second stitch A–C, coming up at D, 4 threads to the left.

4 Work 2 stitches D–C, coming up at D. Go down at A and work 2 stitches D–A. Repeat across row.

COIL FILLING

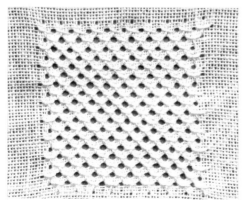

This is simple to work and creates a lacy openwork pattern.

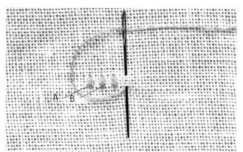

1 Come out at A and work 3 vertical satin stitches (see page 192) over 4 threads into the same hole.

2 Move to B, 4 threads to the right, and repeat. Repeat sequence to finish a row.

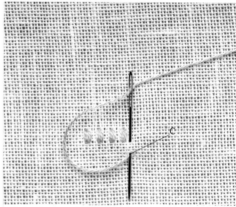

3 Begin second row at C, 4 threads down and 2 to right, repeating sequence. Make as many alternating rows as desired, pulling the thread tight.

DIAGONAL RAISED BAND

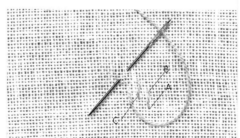

This stitch creates an open texture. It is worked in rows of upright crosses.

1 Come out at A and insert the needle at B, 6 threads above A. Come out at C, 3 threads to the left and 3 above A.

2 Continue the sequence to make a row of stepped vertical stitches.

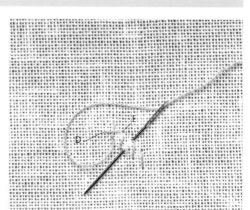

3 Begin the second row at D, 4 threads down and 2 to left, making horizontal stitches. Make as many rows as desired, pulling the thread tight.

DIAMOND FILLING

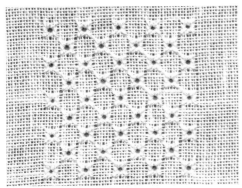

Diamond filling consists of lines of staggered straight stitches. To form a diamond shape, work a row below or above the first, in mirror image.

1 Come out at A and take a backstitch over 3 threads to right, to B. Come out at C, 3 threads below A, and repeat. Come out at D, 1 thread below previous top stitch, and repeat the sequence.

2 Repeat, making pairs of backstitches and dropping each pair 1 thread lower than previous pair.

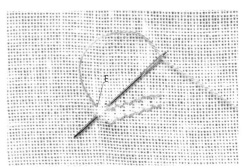

3 After working six descending pairs of stitches, come up at E, 1 thread above last upper stitch. Continue to work pairs of stitches, placing them 1 thread above preceding pair.

ALGERIAN EYE

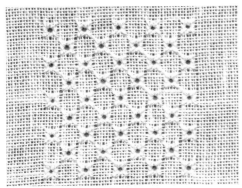

Also known as star eyelet, this can be used singly or as a chequerboard filling, with eyelets positioned so that corner stitches share holes.

1 Start at A. Go down 3 threads and 3 to right at B. Come up at C, 3 threads to left. Insert at B again. Come up 3 threads down and 3 to left at D.

2 Come up at E, 3 threads to right of D. Reinsert at B. Come up at F, 3 threads to right of E, go down at G, the centre of the next eyelet, and up at H.

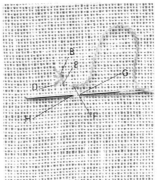

3 Repeat Steps 1–2 to make another half-eyelet. On lowest eyelet, continue around centre to make 8 stitches. Come up at I to complete the next eyelet.

DRAWN THREAD WORK

These techniques are used to decorate hems and create borders. They must be worked on even-weave fabrics from which individual threads are withdrawn, leaving a "ladder" of threads. Finish removed threads to prevent fraying.

REMOVING THREADS

1 Mark the area to be removed with pins. Cut a single horizontal thread in the centre, leaving the vertical threads in place.

2 Carefully unpick it from the centre to each end, but do not remove it completely.

3 Thread each unpicked thread in turn onto a tapestry needle and weave it in and out beside the next thread to hide it. This will secure it so that it doesn't unravel.

TURNING A HEM

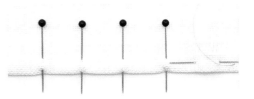

After removing the threads, turn under a double hem up to the edge of the drawn threads. Pin and then tack in place. The embroidery will hold it secure. Remove the tacking when the decorative stitching is complete.

HEMSTITCH

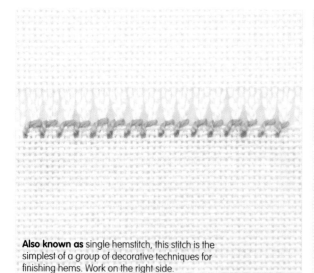

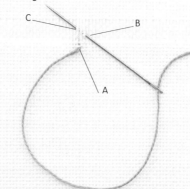

1 Remove the required number of threads, usually two or three. Tack a hem to the lower edge of the withdrawn threads.

2 Come out at A, two threads below edge, picking up top edge of hem. Slide needle under three to four threads, from B to C.

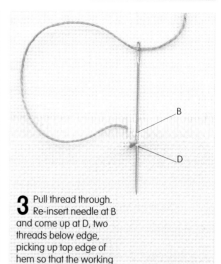

3 Pull thread through. Re-insert needle at B and come up at D, two threads below edge, picking up top edge of hem so that the working thread is looped around the vertical threads.

4 Pull loop tight. Repeat.

Also known as single hemstitch, this stitch is the simplest of a group of decorative techniques for finishing hems. Work on the right side.

ANTIQUE HEMSTITCH

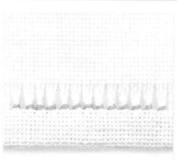

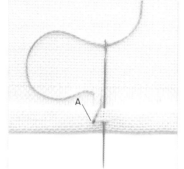

Antique hemstitch is worked like hemstitch, but from the wrong side.

Prepare the fabric. With wrong side facing, hide end of working thread and come out at A. Work as for hemstitch (above) – the right side shows only a small stitch.

LADDER HEMSTITCH

Ladder hemstitch, or ladder stitch, is worked on both sides of the row of withdrawn thread. Ladder stitch can also be worked in the same way as antique hemstitch.

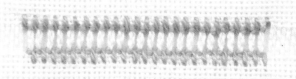

1 Prepare the fabric. Work as in Step 1 of hemstitch. At the end of the bottom row, turn the work upside down. Still with right side facing, work a row along the top. The stitching must match the groups of threads on the first row.

ZIG-ZAG HEMSTITCH

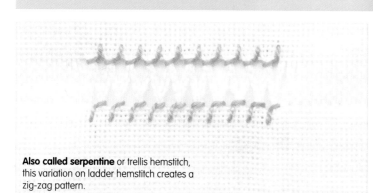

Also called serpentine or trellis hemstitch, this variation on ladder hemstitch creates a zig-zag pattern.

1 Prepare the fabric. Work hemstitch along lower edge of drawn threads. Ensure an even number of threads in each group.

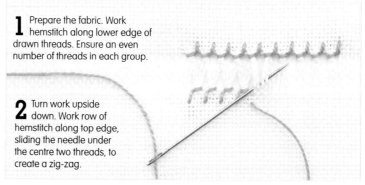

2 Turn work upside down. Work row of hemstitch along top edge, sliding the needle under the centre two threads, to create a zig-zag.

INTERLACED HEMSTITCH

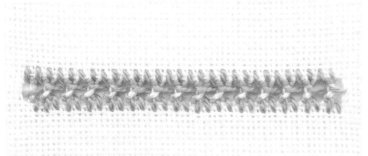

Interlaced hemstitch is a more complex variation on ladder hemstitch, but it is not difficult to work.

1 Prepare the fabric and work as for ladder hemstitch (see opposite). For the lacing thread, cut a length longer than the row of drawn threads. Secure with a couple of tiny backstitches centrally at the right-hand end of the row, at A. Slide the needle behind the second upright thread group at B and over the first group at C.

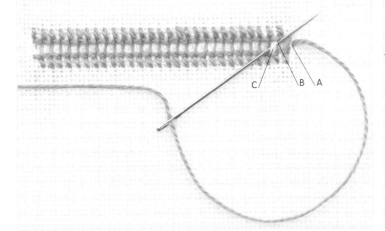

2 Turn needle and slide it behind C, to pull B across and over C. Repeat the sequence to continue to the end of the row.

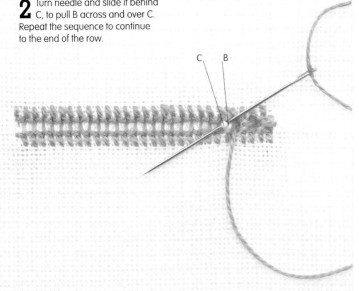

DIAMOND HEMSTITCH

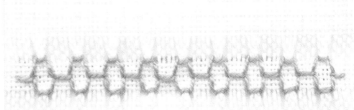

Also called diamond border, this variation is worked along two rows of withdrawn threads and over the band of remaining threads between them.

1 Prepare the fabric, but withdraw threads from two parallel rows, leaving an undisturbed row with an even number of threads in between.

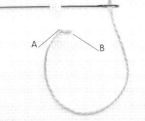

2 Come out at A, in the centre of the uncut row. Insert at B, four threads to the right. Slide needle back to A behind the thread group. Pull tightly.

3 Insert the needle at C, at the base of the top drawn-thread row. Come out at D, four threads to the left. Slide needle from C to D. Pull stitch tightly.

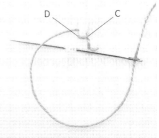

4 Repeat Step 2 to make a stitch on the uncut row.

5 Insert the needle at E, behind the next group of threads in the withdrawn row. Come out at F. Repeat Steps 2–5 to continue.

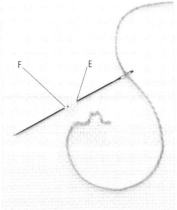

6 At the end of the row, turn the work upside down and work the second row in the same way, using the same holes as before in the centre row.

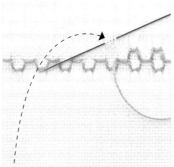

EMBROIDERY

WOVEN HEMSTITCH

Woven hemstitch, also called needleweaving, is similar to a woven bar (see page 209).

1 Prepare the fabric as in Step 1 of hemstitch (see page 218), removing four or five threads. Come out at A. Insert at B four threads to the right. Come out at A. Insert at C, four threads to the left, and come out again at A.

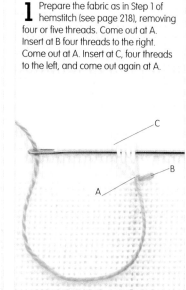

2 Repeat to halfway up the row of withdrawn threads. Come out at D, insert at E and come out at F, four threads to the left of E.

3 Bring the needle out on the right-hand edge, insert in the centre of the row, and come out again four threads to the left and work to the top of the withdrawn threads.

4 Turn the work upside down. Insert the needle on right of new row. Weave as before. To finish, slide the needle under a row of stitches on the wrong side.

INSERTIONS

Insertions, also called faggoting, are decorative stitches that hold two pieces of fabric together in an openwork seam. The technique developed from a need to join the narrow widths of fabric woven on early looms to make household textiles, and it adds a pretty effect to table and bed linens.

MOUNTING THE FABRIC

Tacking stitches

To begin, both fabrics should be hemmed along the edges to be joined. Draw parallel lines 5mm (¼in) apart on a strip of stiff paper, line up the edges of the fabric along them and tack to stabilize the surface and keep the stitches even.

BUTTONHOLE INSERTION STITCH

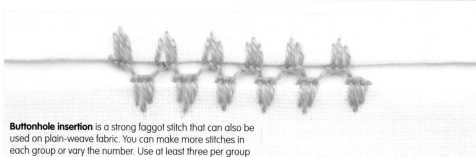

Buttonhole insertion is a strong faggot stitch that can also be used on plain-weave fabric. You can make more stitches in each group or vary the number. Use at least three per group for strength and stability.

1 Mount on paper (see left). Work a buttonhole stitch (see page 194) on one edge from A to B. Work a set of three stitches along the top edge. Insert needle at C on the lower edge, with needle over the working thread.

The middle stitch is longer

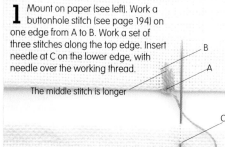

2 Work a similar set of buttonhole stitches on the bottom. Move to the top edge and repeat.

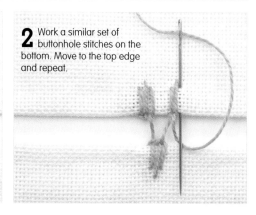

KNOTTED INSERTION STITCH

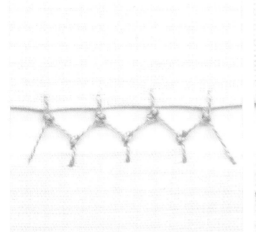

This stitch makes a textured insertion suitable for a narrow join.

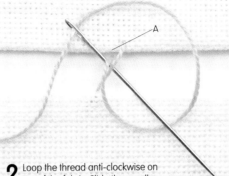

1 Mount on paper. Secure the working thread and take a diagonal stitch from the bottom edge to the top. Come out on the wrong side at A.

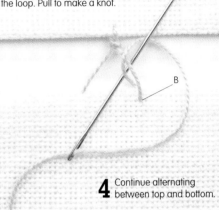

2 Loop the thread anti-clockwise on top of the fabric. Slide the needle under both threads and through the loop. Pull to make a knot at the top edge.

3 Take a diagonal stitch to the lower edge, coming out on the wrong side at B. Loop the thread clockwise. Slide the needle under both threads and through the loop. Pull to make a knot.

4 Continue alternating between top and bottom.

TWISTED INSERTION STITCH

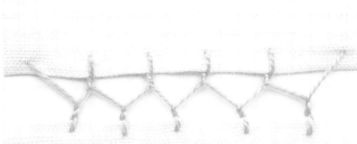

Also known as faggoting, twisted insertion stitch is a quick way of making a pretty openwork join.

1 Mount on paper. Secure the working thread on the left side of the top edge. Take a diagonal stitch to the lower edge. Bring the needle out at A, on the right side.

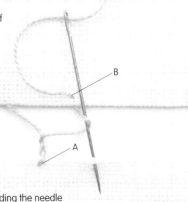

2 Take the next stitch to the top, sliding the needle through the working thread to create a twist. Come out at B on the right side. Repeat the sequence.

LACED INSERTION STITCH

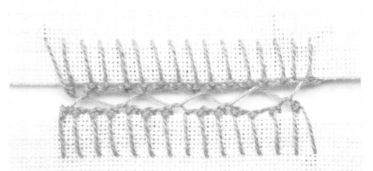

This stitch depends on the lacing thread for its strength, so choose carefully and keep the tension equal.

1 Work a row of Antwerp edging (see page 209) or knotted buttonhole edging along each edge. Mount on paper. Come out at A, through a loop on the lower edging.

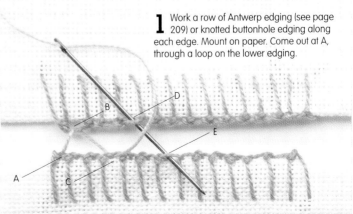

2 Take a diagonal stitch to B. Slide the needle from front to back through a loop on the edging two or three stitches along. Bring the needle from back to front at C, up to D and down to E. Repeat.

SMOCKING

Smocking has traditionally been used to decorate the gathers in the bodices of dresses, blouses, christening robes, and, of course, smocks. Because the gathers add depth and weight to the finished garment, it is recommended to use a lightweight, closely woven fabric such as cotton or silk. Stranded cotton thread is best, traditionally in a colour to match the fabric, but contrasting coloured threads can create wonderful effects.

SMOCKING BASICS

Many basic embroidery stitches can be worked over the gathers, alone or in combination. Remember that smocking takes more fabric, usually about three times the desired finished width. Fabrics with even checks, such as gingham and dotted patterns, can be used since they provide in-built guidelines. The gathering thread should be strong, but the colour doesn't matter as the thread will be removed.

MARKING THE GATHERS

1 Mark the fabric to ensure that the gathers are even. To mark by hand, measure vertical lines to delineate the spaces between folds in the gathers and then mark horizontal threads with a dot to create stitching lines.

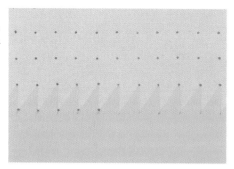

2 It is quicker, however, to use a printed transfer that has evenly spaced dots that can be ironed onto the wrong side of the fabric. Make sure there are an even number of horizontal rows.

STITCHING THE GATHERS

1 To stitch the gathers, cut a length of thread long enough to finish a row with thread left over and knot it securely.

2 Take a small stitch at each marked dot, but do not pull the thread tight. Use a new thread for each marked row.

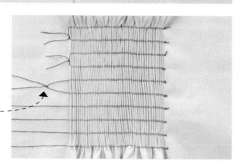

3 Pull the loose ends of the threads gently, one row at a time, until the piece measures the correct width.

4 Tie the loose ends in pairs and, working from the right side, even up the gathers.

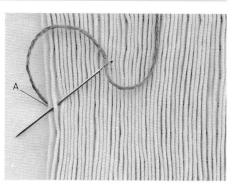

ROPE STITCH

Rope stitch is simply stem stitch (see page 189), worked along the gathers.

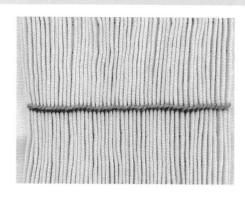

1 Bring the needle out at A, on the left-hand fold, and work stem stitch in a straight line, picking up the top of each gather. Keep the thread consistently either above or below the needle.

CABLE STITCH

Cable stitch is stronger than rope stitch and holds the gathers firmly.

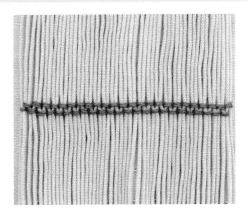

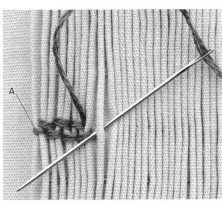

1 Bring the needle out at A as for rope stitch, opposite. Work stem stitch in a straight line, picking up the top of each gather, but alternating the position of the thread (above and then below the needle) with each stitch.

VANDYKE STITCH

Vandyke stitch is another, more decorative smocking stitch based on stem stitch.

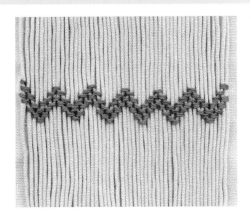

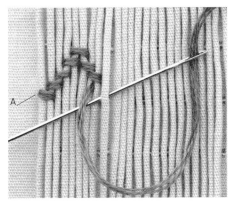

1 Bring the needle out at A as for rope stitch, opposite, and work stem stitch in a chevron pattern.

2 Keep the thread below the needle to work in an upward line and above the needle to work down.

HONEYCOMB
SMOCKING

Honeycomb stitch (see page 213) can be stitched with the working thread on either side of the fabric. The effect from the front is very different from that of the back.

CLOSED HONEYCOMB STITCH

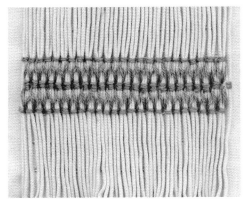

Closed honeycomb stitch is worked with the thread on the right side of the work.

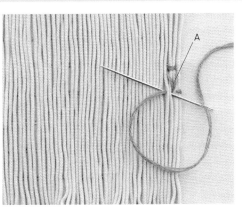

1 Come out at A, on the second fold of the second row. Backstitch through the first two folds. On the first row, backstitch through folds 2 and 3. Repeat.

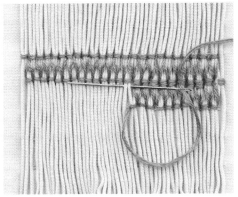

2 On the next row of stitching, work backstitches along the third row, but simply slide the needle under the backstitches on row 2.

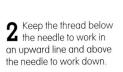

OPEN HONEYCOMB STITCH

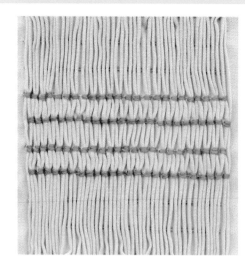

Open honeycomb stitch is worked with the thread on the wrong side of the work.

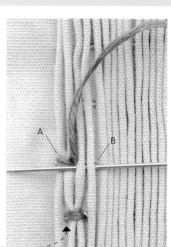

1 Bring the needle out at A and take a horizontal backstitch through the first two folds, working from left to right.

2 Bring the needle out at the second fold on row 2 and make a backstitch that pulls folds 2 and 3 together.

3 Go back to the first row, go in at B, and come out at the third fold.

4 Backstitch to pull folds 3 and 4 together. Repeat the sequence to finish the row. Work subsequent rows the same way.

HONEYCOMB CHEVRON STITCH

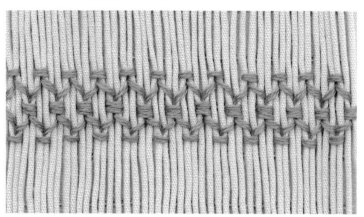

Honeycomb chevron is a stitch often found on traditional smocks. Work it from left to right, on the right side.

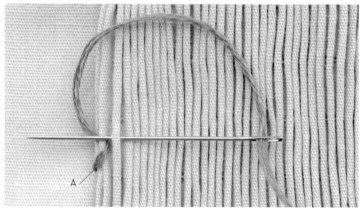

1 Bring the needle out at A on the first fold on the second row. Take it up to the first row to the right and into the second fold. Backstitch over the second and third folds and come out between them, keeping the thread below the backstitch.

2 Go down to the second row again to the right and insert the needle at B into the fourth fold. Backstitch over folds 4 and 5 and come out between them, with the thread above the backstitch.

3 Continue the sequence, alternating up and down to the end of the row.

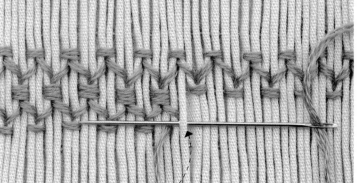

4 Work the next row in the same way, alternating the ups and downs to make a diamond pattern.

BEADWORK

Beads have been used to decorate textiles throughout history and in virtually every civilization in the world. Beadwork as an embroidery technique includes beads of an astonishing variety, sequins, and shisha mirrors, all of which are held on a fabric ground by stitching. The variety provides an excellent way to embellish everything from sachets and soft furnishings to quilts, clothing, and accessories.

BEADS

Beads can be used as accents or applied in rows in several ways. It is best to use a beading needle, which is thin enough to pass through almost any bead, and a polyester thread. Invisible nylon thread is ideal on plain-weave fabrics; alternatively, you can choose a thread that matches either the beads or the fabric.

SINGLE BEAD

Beads can be applied individually, either randomly or following a line. If the stitch is the same length as the bead, the next bead can be attached so they touch.

1 Knot the thread on the back. Bring the needle out at A and thread a bead on it.

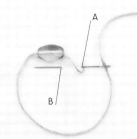

2 Take the needle back in at A and come out at B. Repeat to secure the bead with a double stitch on the back.

3 Move to the next position and repeat to apply subsequent beads.

COUCHING

Couching beads is similar to couching threads (see page 205). Cut lengths of thread that are longer than the line to be covered.

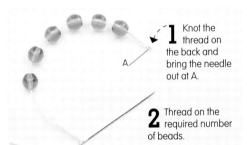

1 Knot the thread on the back and bring the needle out at A.

2 Thread on the required number of beads.

3 Position the first bead at A.

4 Bring a second needle out at B and make a couching stitch over the beaded thread.

5 Slide the next bead alongside the first and repeat. Continue until the row is filled. Take both needles to the back and finish off.

SPOT STITCH

Spot stitch is another couching technique in which several beads are grouped between each couching stitch. It is quicker to work than individual couching, but it is also less secure.

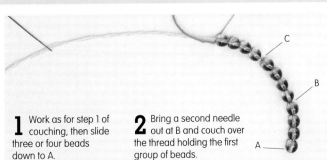

1 Work as for step 1 of couching, then slide three or four beads down to A.

2 Bring a second needle out at B and couch over the thread holding the first group of beads.

3 Slide three or four more beads down to B and couch the beaded thread at C.

4 Continue until the row or line is filled, then take both needles to the back and finish off both threads securely.

LAZY SQUAW FILLING

This is a quick method for filling an area with beads. Work in a hoop.

1 Mark guidelines on the area to be filled if necessary.

2 Cut a length of thread and knot it on the back.

3 Come out at A. Slide enough beads onto the thread to fill one row. Insert the needle at B, on the other side of the area. Come out at C, directly below B, to secure the beads. Repeat, working from side to side.

OJIBWA FILLING

This is a much more secure way of beading. Outline the area to be filled with tacking, which will be covered by the beads. Work in a hoop.

1 Knot the thread on the back. Come out at A, on the edge. Thread on one bead and apply as for a single bead (see page 225).

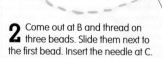

2 Come out at B and thread on three beads. Slide them next to the first bead. Insert the needle at C.

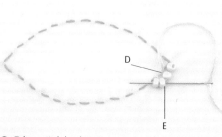

3 Take a stitch back to D, coming out between the first and second beads of group of three. Insert the needle at E, through the second and third beads in the group.

4 Add another three beads. Repeat to fill the shape from the outside in.

BEADED FRINGE

Use a strong thread that is thin enough to go through the holes in the beads.

1 Knot the end of the thread. Slide the required number of beads onto the thread.

2 Take a small backstitch in the fold of the hem. Secure the thread.

LOOP FRINGE

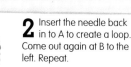

This is a quick and easy way to embellish edges.

1 Hide the knot in the hem. Bring the needle out at A. Slide the required number of beads onto the thread.

2 Insert the needle back in to A to create a loop. Come out again at B to the left. Repeat.

SEQUINS

A sequin is a small disc of metal or plastic with a hole in the centre through which it can be attached to fabric. Traditionally sequins are round, but they are available in a myriad of shapes and colours. They can be attached individually, in groups, or rows.

SINGLE SEQUIN

Single sequins can be attached on one or more sides. Sequins can be placed edge to edge or scattered across the surface.

1 To secure individual sequins with a single stitch, knot the thread on the back and bring the needle out at A.

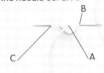

2 Slide a sequin onto it and, with the sequin flat on the background, take a backstitch at B on the right-hand edge of the sequin, coming out at C, where the next sequin will be placed.

3 Slide another sequin on the needle and pull the thread through. Repeat the backstitch and come out at the next position.

SEQUIN CHAIN

An overlapping chain of sequins can be worked to create many interesting effects.

1 Knot the thread on the back and bring the needle out at A.

2 Lay the first sequin just to the right of the thread and backstitch into the hole.

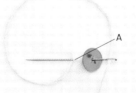

3 Come out again at A. Slide the second sequin onto the needle.

4 Backstitch into the hole of the first sequin and come out on the left-hand edge of the second sequin. Repeat to complete the chain. Secure the thread on the back.

BEADED SEQUIN

Sequins can also be anchored to the fabric by a bead.

1 Lay a sequin in position and bring the needle out through the hole.

2 Slide a bead onto the thread and insert the needle through the hole in the sequin again.

3 Pull gently to settle the bead on top of the sequin and secure the thread on the back.

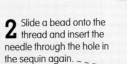

MIRRORWORK

Also called shisha work, mirrorwork is a traditional form of textile decoration from Central Asia. Shisha are small discs of mirror, glass, or tin, that are held in place by a foundation framework on which a decorative edge is stitched. On plain-weave fabrics, use a crewel needle and a single-ply thread or doubled stranded cotton with enough body to hold the disc securely and give a firm edge.

SINGLE THREAD METHOD

This traditional shisha stitch shows off the mirrored surface well.

1 Hold the disc in place. Bring the needle out at A.

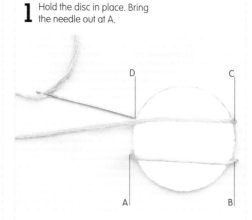

2 Insert the needle at B and come out at C. Insert at D to make two parallel stitches.

3 Bring the needle out at E and loop the thread under and over the bottom securing stitch, then under and over the top stitch.

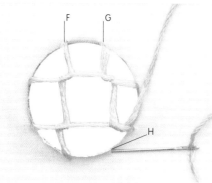

4 Insert the needle at F and come out at G.

5 Loop the working thread around the horizontal stitches as before, to make a parallel vertical stitch. Insert the needle at H.

6 Bring the needle out at I and slide the needle under the crossed threads in the bottom left corner, keeping the thread left of the needle.

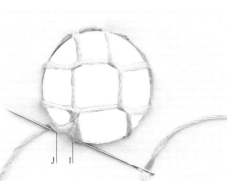

7 Insert the needle at I again and come out at J, with the needle on top of the working thread.

8 Slide the needle under the left-hand vertical thread and over the working thread.

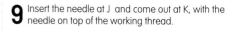
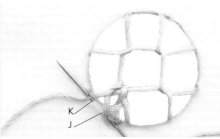

9 Insert the needle at J and come out at K, with the needle on top of the working thread.

10 Repeat the sequence of taking a small stitch through the fabric and a loop under the foundation threads to create a decorative edge.

DOUBLE THREAD METHOD

The mirror is held in place by a "frame" of four pairs of straight stitches. To keep the disc securely in place, work all the stitches as tightly against the edge of the mirror as possible, inserting the needle vertically against the edge each time.

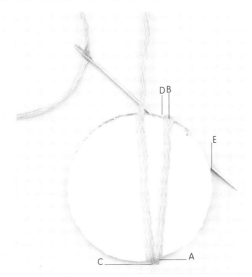

1 Hold the disc in place. Bring the needle out at A. Insert it at B and come out at C, next to A. Insert it at D, next to B, and come out at E.

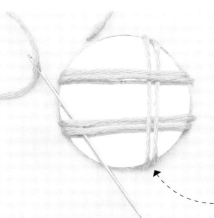

2 Repeat, making pairs of threads on all four sides. Each pair should cross on top of the previous pair; take the final pair under the first pair of threads.

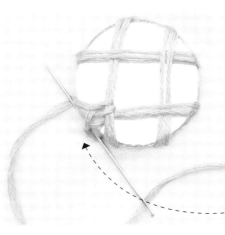

3 Working as close to the edge as possible, repeat Steps 4–7 of Single thread (see opposite). If you prefer, you can work a simple buttonhole stitch (see page 194).

LATTICE

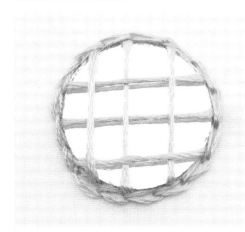

This is a simple, non-traditional mirrorwork method. Make sure that the edges of the disc are smooth so that they don't cut into the thread.

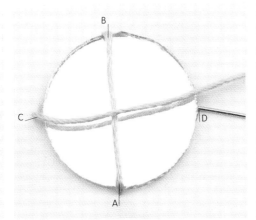

1 Work a lattice of at least three threads. Holding the disc in place, bring the needle out at A and take it across to B. Then take a stitch horizontally across the centre from C to D. Add a stitch in each direction on either side, alternating sides as you work.

2 Add lattice threads as desired, then outline the disc with chain stitch or one of its variations (see pages 200–201), worked as close as possible to the edge.

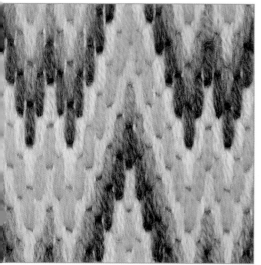  

NEEDLEPOINT

The key stitches and techniques of needlepoint, popular for making hard-wearing household and personal accessories, from spectacles cases to chair seats, as well as purely decorative items such as pictures.

TOOLS AND MATERIALS

Needlepoint requires only a few basic pieces of equipment to get started and is an easily transportable craft. With just canvas, needle, and thread you can produce many different types of design. A selection of artist's materials will aid you if you choose to design your own patterns.

TYPES OF CANVAS

Needlepoint is worked on a fabric known as canvas (hence the alternative name "canvaswork"). This has an open mesh construction: strong threads, usually of cotton, are woven with spaces in between and the stitches are worked over one or more of these threads. The number of threads per 2.5cm (1in) is called the count, gauge, or mesh. Needlepoint canvas comes in several colours – tan, white, cream, and yellow – and also in paper or plastic versions.

SINGLE, OR MONO, CANVAS ⌄

This is constructed of single threads crossing each other in a simple over-and-under weave. It comes in a wide range of gauges and is suitable for nearly all stitches. Its only drawback is that some stitches – or a tight tension – can pull it out of shape; however, a little distortion can be put right in the blocking process (see page 278).

PERFORATED PAPER ⌲

Available in several colours, this 14-count material is especially suitable for greeting cards.

INTERLOCK CANVAS >>

This is a special type of single-thread canvas in which each lengthwise, or warp, thread actually consists of two threads twisted around the crosswise, weft, threads. The result is a more stable construction – less likely to become distorted. Unlike ordinary single canvas, interlock can be used for half-cross stitch (see page 255).

DOUBLE, OR PENELOPE, CANVAS >>

In this type of canvas both warp and weft are formed of pairs of threads. This, too, is a relatively strong construction. The gauge is often expressed as the number of holes, sometimes with the thread count given afterwards. For example a 10/20 penelope canvas has 10 pairs of threads per 2.5cm (1in). Stitches are normally worked over the paired threads, treating them as one, but the threads can be separated and worked over singly to produce areas of fine stitching if desired.

RUG CANVAS >>

Available in 3-, 5-, and 7-count, this has two paired threads in each direction, which can be in an open, penelope-type weave or joined in an interlock-type weave. Some rug canvas has contrasting threads marking out 10-hole squares. This canvas is often used for wall hangings and large cushions, as well as rugs.

THREADS AND YARNS

The most popular threads for needlepoint are made of wool. There are three types of wool yarn suitable for this work: crewel, Persian, and tapestry. Other kinds of thread, such as stranded cotton and silk floss, pearl cotton, and metallic threads are also used.

WOOL

‹‹ CREWEL WOOL
This is a fine 2-ply yarn that can be used in any multiple of strands to suit the gauge of the canvas. Individual strands blend together smoothly, producing a soft texture.

TAPESTRY WOOL ⋙
This comes in a smooth, uniform 4-ply strand, which is normally used singly, on 10- to 14-count canvas.

PERSIAN WOOL
Thicker than crewel wool, this comes in a triple strand, of which the individual strands can easily be separated. You can use one or more strands in the needle.

COTTON

‹‹ PEARL COTTON
Pearl cotton is a strong, glossy thread with a twisted construction and is used singly, on fine-gauge canvas. It comes in three weights: No. 3 (the thickest), No. 5 (which comes in the greatest range of colours), and No. 8 (the finest).

‹‹ STRANDED COTTON FLOSS
This versatile thread consists of six fine strands of lustrous, mercerized cotton, which can easily be separated if desired. It is suitable for the finer gauges of canvas.

OTHER THREADS AND BEADS

BEADS ⋙
Beads add texture to a needlepoint project. They can be used for beaded tent stitch (see page 256) or simply sewn to the finished surface.

‹‹ KNITTING YARN
It is possible to use knitting yarn in a project but some soft yarns may fray and those that stretch may cause tension problems.

METALLIC THREAD ⋩
Combine metallic threads with a more conventional wool or cotton yarn in the needle to avoid them kinking.

SILK THREAD ⋩
A glossy, silk thread will add some sheen or highlights to stitches but use with care as it may snag.

EQUIPMENT

Only a few pieces of equipment are required for working needlepoint: tapestry needles, scissors, and tape to bind the canvas are the bare essentials. However, you will need some other tools and materials for finishing a project, for creating your own designs, and simply for convenience.

FOR STITCHING AND FINISHING

TAPESTRY NEEDLES
The blunt point is designed to slip through the canvas mesh and the stitches without snagging or splitting them. These needles have large eyes to accommodate the relatively thick threads and come in sizes ranging from 26 (the smallest) to 13 (the largest).

WOVEN TAPE
This is used, along with string, for attaching the canvas to a scroll frame.

MASKING TAPE
Used for binding the edges of the canvas to protect it while you work.

DRAWING PINS
These are used for attaching canvas to a stretcher frame.

SCISSORS
You will need a pair of dressmaker's scissors to cut the canvas and embroidery scissors for cutting threads.

FRAMES

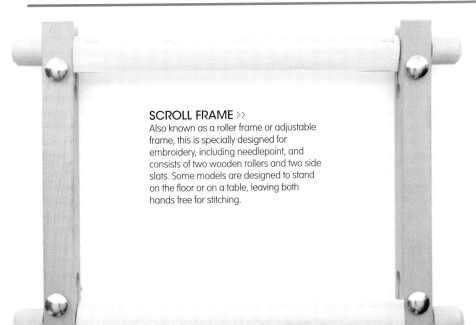

SCROLL FRAME
Also known as a roller frame or adjustable frame, this is specially designed for embroidery, including needlepoint, and consists of two wooden rollers and two side slats. Some models are designed to stand on the floor or on a table, leaving both hands free for stitching.

FRAME CHOICE
The use of a frame is optional. The main advantages of using one are that it helps to prevent the canvas from distorting and assists you in maintaining an even stitch tension. Only rectangular frames are suitable for needlepoint; canvas is too stiff for a hoop frame and would become distorted if forced into one.

An upholstered frame: This is less widely available but provides a pleasant way to work. You simply pin the canvas to the padding and move it around if necessary. A matching sandbag will hold the frame balanced on the edge of a table for two-handed stitching.

Artist's stretcher frame: This consists of two pairs of wooden (painter's) canvas stretchers, which slot into each other at the corners. They are available at art-supply shops. Make sure that the inner edges of the frame will be larger than the stitching area of the needlepoint.

NEEDLEPOINT

FOR DESIGNING

DRAWING PAPER ≫
Keep a sketch pad to hand for copying designs or sketching ideas.

ARTIST'S PAINTBRUSH ⌃
Choose a suitably-sized brush for applying paints to canvas.

ACRYLIC PAINTS (PERMANENT) ≫
These are specially made for crafts; they are easy to brush or sponge onto canvas and can be mixed to produce desired shades.

≪ PENCIL
Essential for sketching and tracing designs.

≪ FIBRE-TIP PEN
This is useful for darkening outlines on motifs before tracing or transferring.

SCISSORS ⌄
Keep a separate pair of scissors dedicated to cutting paper, to avoid blunting the blade of dressmaker's scissors used for cutting canvas or fabric.

PERMANENT FABRIC MARKER ⌄
This is useful for transferring or tracing the design outline onto the canvas.

≪ COLOURED PENCILS
Keep a selection in a wide range of colours for making charts or sketching designs.

TRACING PAPER ⌄
This is ideal for converting designs. Gridded tracing paper is ideal for translating designs to chart form.

GRAPH PAPER ⌄
This is used for tracing motifs and complete designs. Gridded tracing paper is ideal for converting designs to chart form.

COLOURED PAPER ⌄
Use coloured paper to cut out shapes when designing motifs.

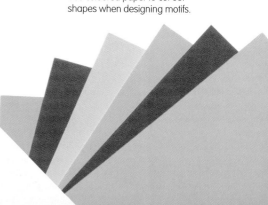

ADDITIONAL EQUIPMENT

TWEEZERS >>
These are very useful for pulling out mistakes.

NEEDLE THREADER ⌃
This is useful when working with fine threads.

TAGS >>
Use these for labelling yarns with shade numbers.

SET SQUARE >>
Useful for drawing right angles when re-shaping needlepoint.

THIMBLE >>
Although not necessary when working needlepoint, a thimble is useful for hand-sewing when making up a finished piece.

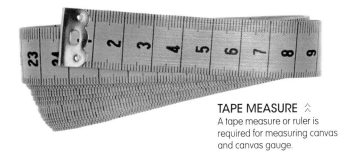

TAPE MEASURE ⌃
A tape measure or ruler is required for measuring canvas and canvas gauge.

SHARP-POINTED NEEDLES ⌃
Use crewel (embroidery) or chenille needles for making up projects.

MAGNIFIER >>
This is useful for detailed or fine work.

NEEDLEPOINT DESIGNS

Deciding what to stitch can be an exhilarating, but also sometimes bewildering, experience. There is such a wealth of commercially produced designs, as well as a wealth of needlepoint stitches tempting you to create your own designs. Here are some of the options.

READY-MADE DESIGNS

You can find many needlepoint designs ready for you to stitch – either in the form of a kit (with materials included), a printed canvas, or given in a book in chart form. These have one obvious advantage: all the design decisions have been made for you by a professional; all you need to do is the stitching and the making up of the project. The better-quality kits contain good materials. However, they usually include only enough yarn for the half-cross version of tent stitch (see page 255), so if you want to use a different form of Tent stitch, you will have to buy extra yarn.

TYPES OF READY-MADE DESIGNS

Kits: A needlepoint kit usually consists of a canvas with the design printed on it in colours approximating those of the yarns, the yarns themselves, and a tapestry needle. If the design is to be worked in half-cross stitch, this should be stated in the instructions. If so, make sure that the canvas is either double or interlock (see page 233). Otherwise, there is a risk of stitches slipping between intersecting canvas threads. Or you could work the design in a different form of tent stitch. You will need to buy more thread for those stitches (see page 243). If the kit does not state the brand of thread used, you will need to contact the manufacturer for this information.

Printed canvases: These designs consist only of a printed canvas, with a colour key designating the recommended shades of a certain brand of yarn. Their main advantage, relative to a kit, is that you can choose your own yarn (useful if that brand is not easily available) and, if you like, buy it in stages. You will need to amend the colour key, of course. If you intend to work the design in half-cross stitch, make sure the canvas is of interlock or double-thread construction.

Partially worked canvases: On some canvases a central motif has been completed – or marked with tramé (see page 256). The purchaser then works just the background (or, in the latter case, also the tent stitches over the tramé). Some traméed canvases are very complex and challenging. However, if you choose one that includes a large background of solid-coloured tent stitch, you may find the work rather boring. Consider working the background in a larger, more textured stitch, such as gobelin filling (page 261), encroaching gobelin (page 257) or long stitch (page 263). The work will be finished more quickly and you will have given it your own creative stamp.

CHARTED DESIGNS

Box chart: There are many books containing needlepoint designs in chart form, with yarn or thread colours specified. A box chart is most often used for designs worked in tent stitch; each box in the chart represents one stitch. The thread colours can be represented either by printed colours or by symbols or, sometimes (in complex designs), by both.

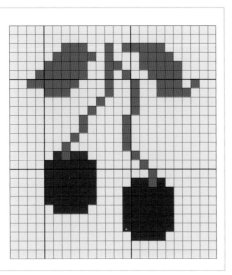

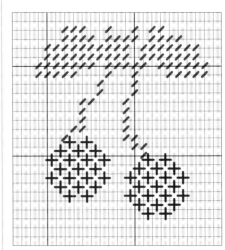

Line chart: A line chart is most often used for designs consisting of, or including, novelty stitches. The lines of the grid represent the actual canvas threads and the stitches are marked on top of them.

YOUR OWN
DESIGNS

Don't be afraid of creating your own needlepoint designs; it's not as hard as you may think. Once you start looking for ideas, you'll find them all around you – in nature, in paintings and photographs, and in the textures of needlepoint stitches themselves.

NEEDLEPOINT SAMPLERS

Begin by making a sampler of some of your favourite stitches. Work a few of each of these on spare canvas and study their shape and texture. Select a few harmonizing and/or contrasting colours of thread and work stripes of the various stitches in these colours across a narrow piece of canvas. Alternatively, work stripes concentrically around a small block of stitches (cushion stitch, for example). Keep adding stripes until the work is large enough to make the front of a cushion cover.

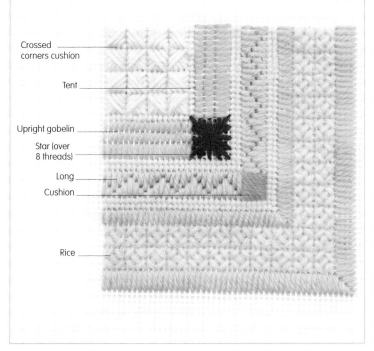

Crossed corners cushion

Tent

Upright gobelin

Star (over 8 threads)

Long

Cushion

Rice

DESIGNING WITH SHAPES

You can create both abstract and pictorial designs with cut-out shapes. For an abstract design, cut some squares, rectangles, triangles, or circles from coloured paper. Draw the area of the finished needlepoint on a sheet of paper. Move the shapes around on this area, trying different combinations until you find one that pleases you. Remember to pay attention to the spaces between the shapes; these are an important part of any design. Attach the shapes with adhesive putty and leave the design for a few hours, then come back and look at it with fresh eyes.

USING CROSS-STITCH MOTIFS

You can find hundreds of appealing cross-stitch motifs in books. Draw one on a piece of graph paper containing the same number of lines as your chosen canvas, or repeat a small one across the area of the grid.

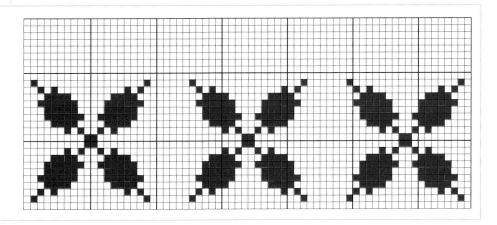

CHARTING FROM AN IMAGE

To create more realistic pictorial designs, either draw or paint the design freehand or follow these instructions to make a chart from an existing image.

1 Isolate an image from a larger source by moving strips of paper over the image until you find the best detail for your project. Enlarge the detail on a photocopier to the desired size.

2 To make a chart, place gridded tracing paper over the image and then fill in the squares on the tracing paper, using coloured pencils. Or, if you are using textured stitches, indicate these with lines.

TIPS

● **To make an** entirely original needlepoint, start with your own drawing or painting. If you lack confidence, practise! Carry a sketchbook around with you and sketch interesting shapes and textures. Make a note of colours and develop your sketches in colour when you get home. Use strips of paper (see left) to find interesting details that can be enlarged.

● **As you can** see from the stitches illustrated on pages 254–270, needlepoint stitches have their own distinctive character – some smooth and shiny, some knobbly, some with a strong vertical, horizontal or diagonal direction. You can exploit this in your design. For example, you might use encroaching gobelin (see page 257) in shades of blue to depict sky; stem stitch (see page 260) for a field of corn; or upright cross (see page 264) for a pebbly beach.

TRANSFERRING TECHNIQUES

If you are working from a chart (see page 238), the process of counting the lines/blocks of the chart and the canvas threads will transfer the design as you stitch. Otherwise you will need to trace or paint the design onto the canvas.

TRACING OUTLINES

1 Begin by going over the outlines of your design with a black fibre-tip marker. Choose a marker that is thick enough to be visible through your chosen canvas. Using the same marker, draw an outline enclosing the area to be stitched.

2 Prepare the canvas: cut it to size, adding at least 10cm (4in) to the dimensions of the area to be stitched. Using a permanent fabric marker, draw the outline of this area in the centre of the canvas, leaving a 5cm (2in) border all around. Cover the edges with masking tape.

3 Tape or weight the design onto a flat, hard surface, and position the canvas on top; tape it in place. Trace the design outlines onto the canvas using a permanent fabric marker.

4 If your design is coloured you may wish to colour in the outlines on the canvas too. Use permanent acrylic paints for this. Avoid clogging the mesh with paint and leave the canvas to dry thoroughly.

CHOOSING THE RIGHT CANVAS

In choosing canvas for a project you need to consider its type, its gauge, and its colour. For most projects an ordinary single-thread canvas will be suitable, but in some cases an interlock or double canvas will be preferable or even required. If you wish to use a certain kind of thread, this may limit the choice of gauge. The predominant colour tones of the work may influence the colour of canvas you choose.

FOR USING HALF-CROSS STITCH

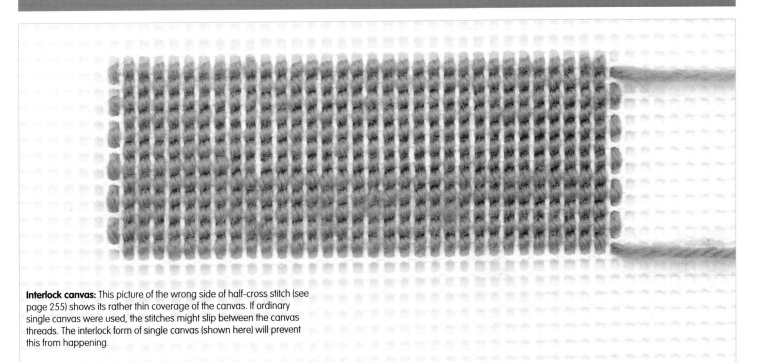

Interlock canvas: This picture of the wrong side of half-cross stitch (see page 255) shows its rather thin coverage of the canvas. If ordinary single canvas were used, the stitches might slip between the canvas threads. The interlock form of single canvas (shown here) will prevent this from happening.

Double, or penelope, canvas: Another option, when using half-cross stitch, is double-thread canvas, shown here. This, too, has a very stable weave. An even firmer fabric – suitable for chair seats and other objects that receive hard wear – can be produced by working the half-cross stitches over rows of tramé (see page 256), here worked in a contrasting shade of pink for visibility; normally a matching thread would be used. Double canvas can be used for many other stitches as well, but it is not suited to most straight stitches, including Florentine work (see pages 271–277), because the vertical pairs of canvas threads are likely to show between the individual stitches. However, the use of tramé will prevent this problem.

CHOOSING THE RIGHT GAUGE FOR THE CHOSEN THREAD

If you wish to use a single strand of thread for the stitching, this will limit your choice of gauge. The thread should fill the hole comfortably – neither too tightly, which would produce a lumpy, distorted surface, nor loosely, which would produce a thin effect. A few successful combinations are shown here.

Tapestry wool is suitable for 10-, 12-, or 14-count canvas (if tent stitch is used).

Pearl cotton (No. 5) works well on 18-count canvas.

A single strand of Persian wool will also cover the mesh of an 18-count canvas.

CHOOSING THE RIGHT GAUGE FOR THE AMOUNT OF DETAIL

Another consideration is the amount of detail you wish to include. The finer the canvas, the more detail you can include and the more easily you can represent curved lines.

These two monograms, for example, are based on the same printed source and were first charted onto graph paper having 10 and 18 squares to 2.5cm (1in). The finer grid and canvas mesh allows a more faithful representation of the curves. However, the more angular "S" has a certain appeal and might be the sort of look you are aiming for. A lot depends on the nature of the design material.

10-count canvas

18-count canvas

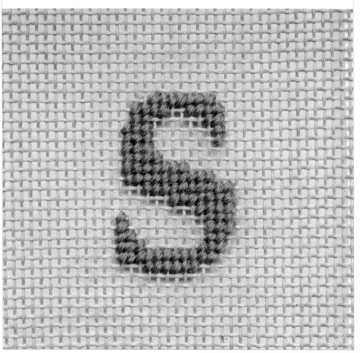

MATCHING THREAD AND CANVAS

For most projects, you'll want to choose a thread that covers the canvas well. This depends partly on the stitches you plan to use: a dense stitch such as tent (see pages 254–255) will cover better than a less-dense one, such as long stitch (see page 263), using the same thread and canvas. Before beginning a project, make some samples to ensure that your chosen materials and stitches are compatible.

This chart provides a guide to choosing suitable yarns for working tent stitch (either continental or basketweave) on various gauges of canvas. (English crewel wool is assumed; for French crewel more strands may be required.)

GAUGE OF CANVAS	TYPE AND NUMBER OF STRANDS
10-count	1 strand of tapestry wool 2 strands of Persian wool 4 strands of crewel wool
12-count	1 strand of tapestry wool 2 strands of Persian wool 3 strands of crewel wool
14-count	1 strand of tapestry wool 2 strands of Persian wool 3 strands of crewel wool
18-count	1 strand of No. 5 pearl cotton 1 strand of Persian wool 2 strands of crewel wool 6 strands of stranded floss

ESTIMATING THREAD QUANTITIES

If your design uses a large area of a single colour, buy enough yarn or thread at the outset to avoid changes in dye lots. The following amounts are based on diagonal tent stitch (see page 255) worked on single-thread canvas, using 45cm (18in) lengths and allowing about 8cm (3in) waste per thread. If you are using half-cross stitch (see page 255), divide the amounts by one half.

10-count	5.5m (6yd) to 25sq cm (4sq in)
12-count	6m (6½yd) to 25sq cm (4sq in)
14-count	7m (7½yd) to 25sq cm (4sq in)
16-count	7.5m (8yd) to 25sq cm (4sq in)
18-count	9m (10yd) to 25sq cm (4sq in)

CHOOSING THE CANVAS COLOUR

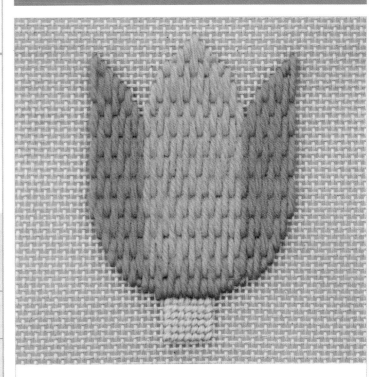

Woven canvas is available in tan, yellow, cream, and white. The choice depends partly on personal preference (threads are easiest to count on white but tan is easier on the eyes) and partly on the predominating colours of the yarns. White or cream canvas would be a good choice for a piece worked in pastel colours, whereas tan would be more suitable for darker hues.

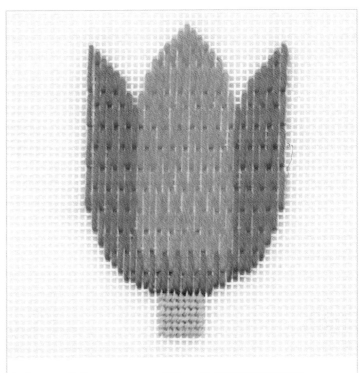

In this example, the same yarn and stitches worked on white canvas are less successful than they are in the tulip worked on tan canvas. The colour is more important for straight stitches (here Gobelin filling) than for diagonal ones, such as continental tent stitch.

GETTING STARTED

Before beginning to stitch a commercially printed canvas, all you need to do is bind the edges with masking tape, although you may wish also to mount the canvas on a frame. To follow a chart you need to cut the canvas to size first.

PREPARING
THE CANVAS

If you are following a chart or creating your own design, a few more preliminary steps are involved. Make a note of the canvas measurements and keep this handy, as you will need it for blocking the finished work (see page 278). If you have drawn or painted your own design on the canvas, you can treat it as you would a commercially printed canvas and simply begin stitching after binding the edges.

MARKING AND CUTTING THE CANVAS

1 Ascertain how many canvas threads the chart represents in both directions. Using a fabric marker, mark off an area on your canvas including the same number of threads.

2 To work out the size required, divide the number of squares/lines in the chart by the canvas gauge. For example, on 10-count canvas for a chart with 120 squares/lines, divide 120 by 10 and mark off an area 30cm (12in) square. (For accuracy use inches, as canvas is graded this way.)

3 Add a margin of at least 5cm (2in) to all edges of the marked area. For a stitched area of 30cm (12in) square, cut a piece measuring at least 40cm (15¾in) square.

4 Some charts mark the centre with a small cross or arrows along each edge. You can mark your canvas with intersecting lines, using either a fabric marker or tacking.

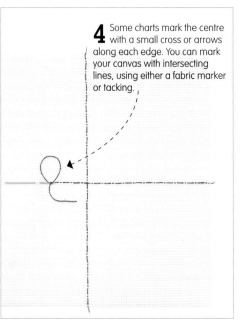

BINDING THE EDGES

Whether working on a pre-printed or blank canvas, you need to bind the edges using masking tape. Alternatively, bind them with woven tape. The bound edges are cut off when your project is complete.

1 Cut a strip of masking tape slightly longer than one edge. Lay the canvas on a flat surface and gently stick the tape on top, overlapping the edge by about half. Fold the tape to the other side and press in place. Trim the ends. Repeat on all edges.

MOUNTING CANVAS ON A FRAME

The use of a frame is optional. A small piece of work or one using stitches that are unlikely to distort the canvas, can be held in the hand. However, using a frame will help you to maintain a smooth stitching tension.

USING ARTIST'S STRETCHERS

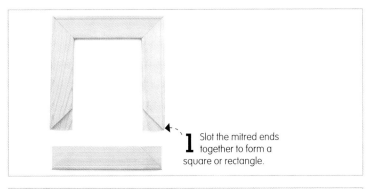

1 Slot the mitred ends together to form a square or rectangle.

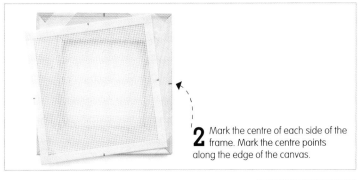

2 Mark the centre of each side of the frame. Mark the centre points along the edge of the canvas.

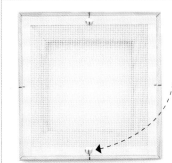

3 Align the centre of the top edge of the canvas with the centre of the top of the frame. Attach the canvas to the frame at this point with a drawing pin. Repeat at the bottom edge, pulling the canvas taut.

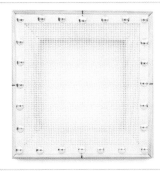

4 Repeat on adjacent sides. Working outwards from the centre and pulling the canvas taut, insert more drawing pins along all edges at 2cm (¾in) intervals.

USING A SCROLL FRAME

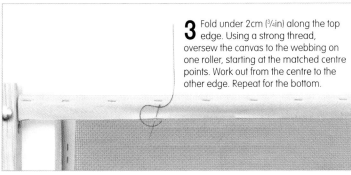

1 Remove the slats from the frame.

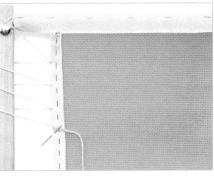

2 Bind the short canvas edges with woven tape, by hand or machine. Mark the vertical centre of the canvas, either with running stitch or with a fabric marker.

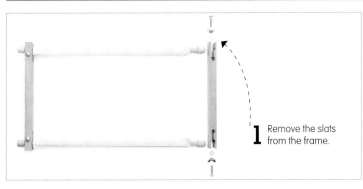

3 Fold under 2cm (¾in) along the top edge. Using a strong thread, oversew the canvas to the webbing on one roller, starting at the matched centre points. Work out from the centre to the other edge. Repeat for the bottom.

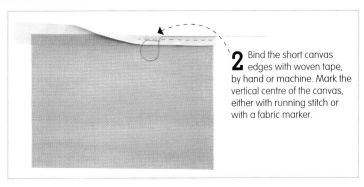

4 Insert the slats into the rollers and fasten to stretch the canvas taut. Cut a long length of string and fasten to one top corner of the frame. Working over the slats and through the canvas and binding tape, sew the canvas to the slats. Fasten off. Repeat on the opposite side.

STARTING
TO STITCH

You've got your design and your yarn and prepared your canvas. Now you just need to thread a tapestry needle and start stitching (see tips below). There are several ways of getting thick or multi-stranded threads through the eye of a needle.

TIPS

• **To sew or stab?** Whether you stitch with a horizontal (sewing) or a vertical (stabbing) movement is a matter of personal preference. With stabbing it is generally easier to avoid pulling the canvas out of shape. If you use a self-supporting frame you can work with one hand above the canvas and one below, and so will handle the work less, which helps to keep it clean.

• **Practise stitching** with a smooth, even tension; avoid pulling the stitches too tightly.

• **Wherever possible,** take the needle down – rather than up – through a hole that already contains a thread; this tends to produce a neater effect.

• **To thread stranded floss** flatten the strands between your tongue and upper teeth and then between forefinger and thumb. A needle threader may also be helpful.

• **Avoid using too long a thread.** About 45cm (18in) is the maximum recommended for crewel or tapestry wool; Persian wool may be cut longer because it is more robust.

• **Most of the stitch** descriptions and illustrations on pages 254–277 assume a right-handed stitcher. You can reverse the direction of stitching (try turning the book upside down) or use the stabbing method, or both.

THREADING THE NEEDLE: PAPER STRIP METHOD

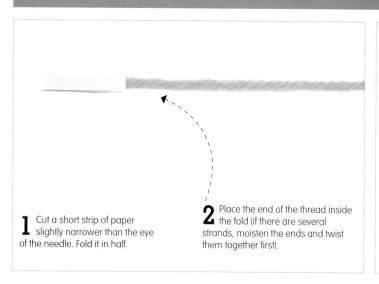

1 Cut a short strip of paper slightly narrower than the eye of the needle. Fold it in half.

2 Place the end of the thread inside the fold (if there are several strands, moisten the ends and twist them together first).

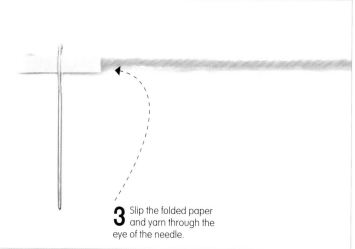

3 Slip the folded paper and yarn through the eye of the needle.

THREADING THE NEEDLE: LOOP METHOD

1 This method, too, can be used for one or more strands. Loop the strands around the needle and pinch the loops tightly together.

2 Slip the needle out of the loops, then push the eye down over them. Once the loops emerge, pull them through the eye of the needle.

STARTING AND ENDING A THREAD

In order to avoid unsightly bumps or fluffy strands of thread on your finished piece of needlepoint, you need to start and end the thread neatly, securing it on the back of the canvas to prevent your work from unravelling.

STARTING A THREAD ON EMPTY CANVAS

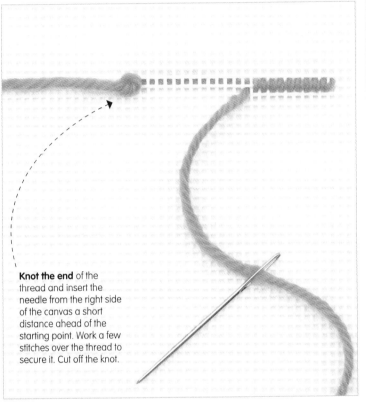

Knot the end of the thread and insert the needle from the right side of the canvas a short distance ahead of the starting point. Work a few stitches over the thread to secure it. Cut off the knot.

ENDING A THREAD

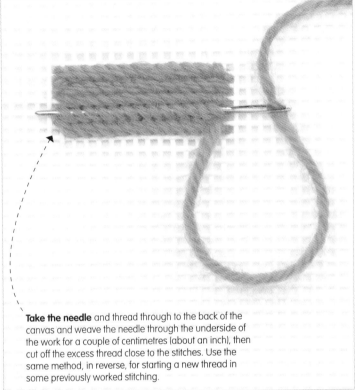

Take the needle and thread through to the back of the canvas and weave the needle through the underside of the work for a couple of centimetres (about an inch), then cut off the excess thread close to the stitches. Use the same method, in reverse, for starting a new thread in some previously worked stitching.

STARTING A THREAD ON PLASTIC CANVAS

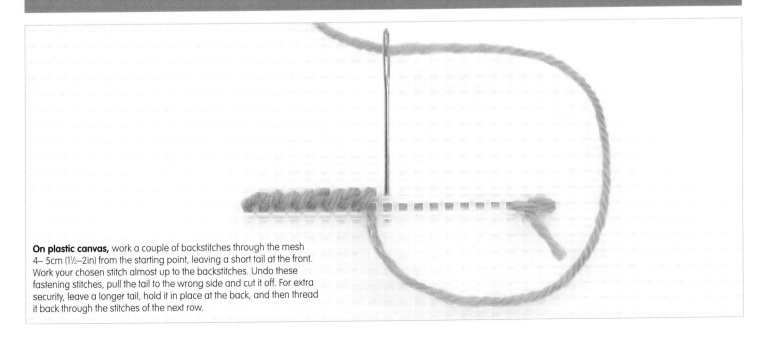

On plastic canvas, work a couple of backstitches through the mesh 4–5cm (1½–2in) from the starting point, leaving a short tail at the front. Work your chosen stitch almost up to the backstitches. Undo these fastening stitches, pull the tail to the wrong side and cut it off. For extra security, leave a longer tail, hold it in place at the back, and then thread it back through the stitches of the next row.

STITCH GALLERY

These pages provide a quick visual reference to the stitches that follow. Use this gallery to find the best stitches for your needlepoint projects. The stitches are grouped according to type to show all the possibilities and alternatives at a glance, whether you are looking for a simple textured stitch or trying something more complicated, such as a Florentine design.

DIAGONAL STITCHES

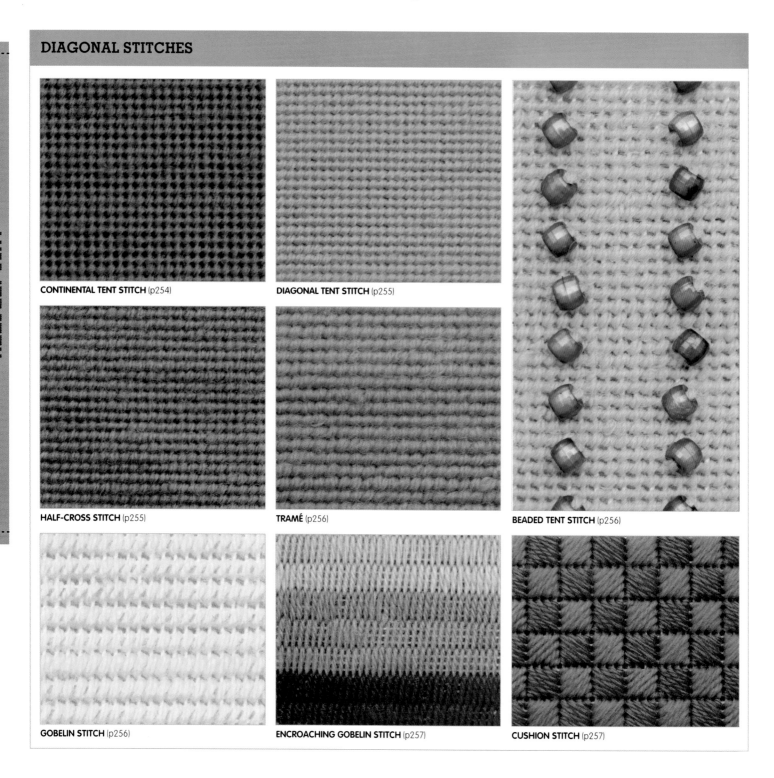

CONTINENTAL TENT STITCH (p254)

DIAGONAL TENT STITCH (p255)

HALF-CROSS STITCH (p255)

TRAMÉ (p256)

BEADED TENT STITCH (p256)

GOBELIN STITCH (p256)

ENCROACHING GOBELIN STITCH (p257)

CUSHION STITCH (p257)

CHEQUER STITCH (p258)

SCOTTISH STITCH (p258)

MOSAIC STITCH: CHEQUERBOARD EFFECT (p258)

DIAGONAL STITCH (p258)

MOORISH STITCH (p259)

BYZANTINE STITCH (p259)

JACQUARD STITCH (p259)

ORIENTAL STITCH (p260)

MILANESE STITCH (p259)

STEM STITCH (p260)

CROSSED CORNERS CUSHION STITCH (p260)

STRAIGHT STITCHES

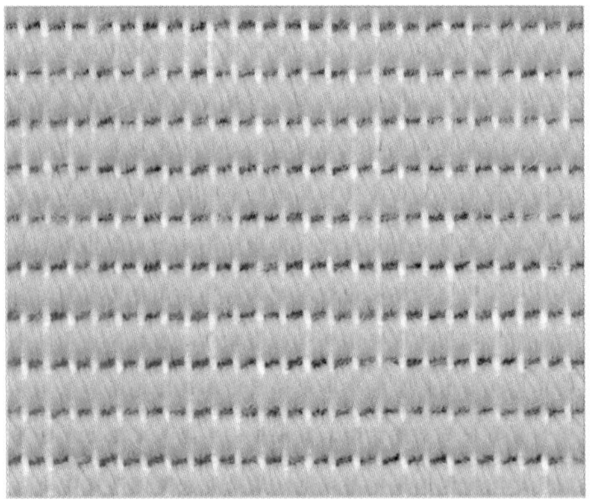

UPRIGHT GOBELIN STITCH (p261)

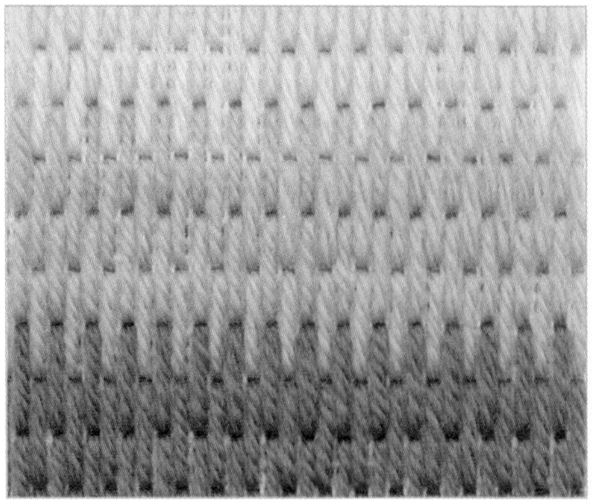

GOBELIN FILLING STITCH (p261)

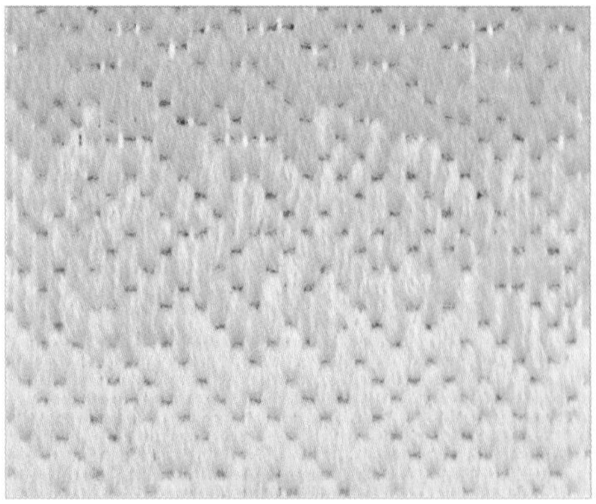

RANDOM STRAIGHT STITCH (p262)

DOUBLE TWILL STITCH (p262)

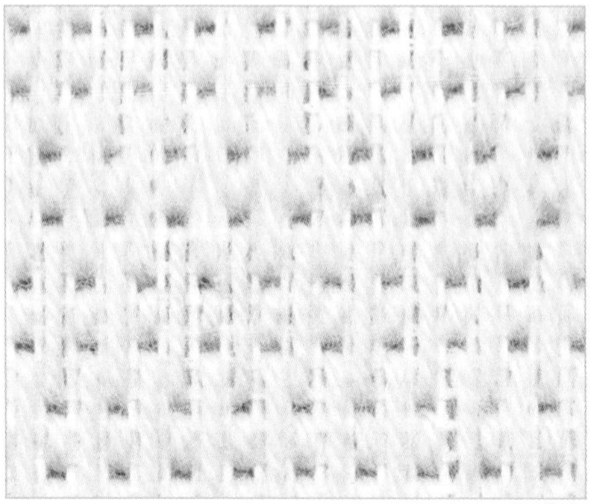

PARISIAN STITCH (p262)

TWILL STITCH (p262)

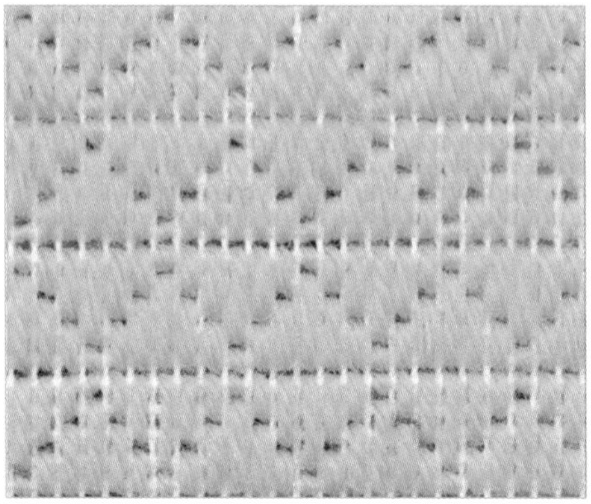

LONG STITCH (p263)

WEAVING STITCH (p263)

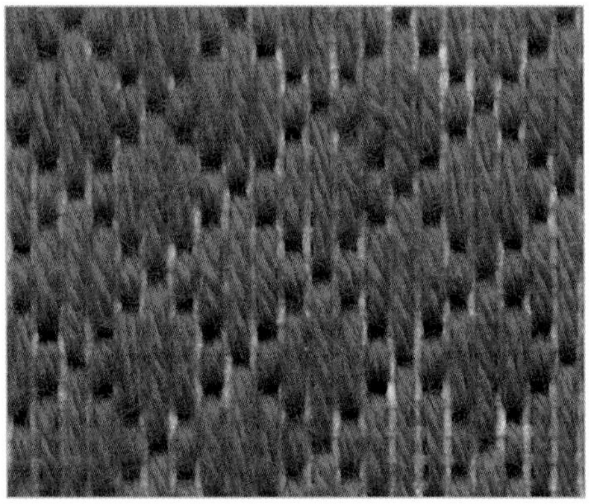

HUNGARIAN DIAMOND STITCH (p263)

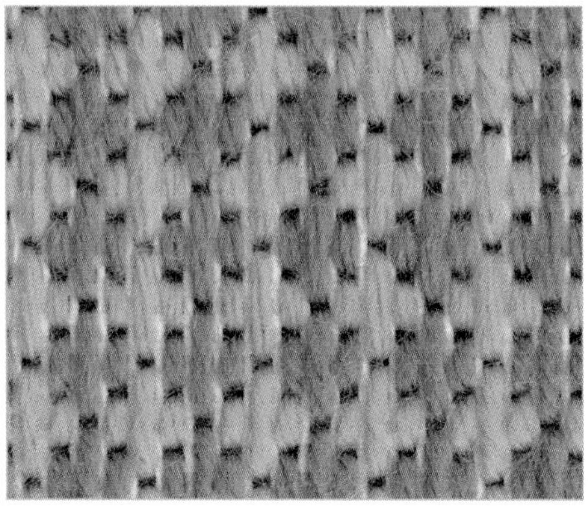

HUNGARIAN STITCH (p263)

CROSSED STITCHES

CROSS STITCH (p264)

DIAGONAL CROSS STITCH (p264)

UPRIGHT CROSS STITCH (p264)

OBLONG CROSS STITCH (p265)

LONG-ARMED CROSS STITCH (p265)

ALTERNATING CROSS STITCH (p266)

DOUBLE STRAIGHT CROSS STITCH (p266)

SMYRNA STITCH (p266)

FISHBONE STITCH (p267)

KNOTTED STITCH (p267)

RICE STITCH (p267)

NEEDLEPOINT

LOOP STITCHES

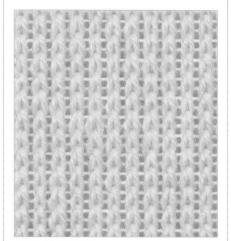

CHAIN STITCH (p268)

PILE STITCH (p268)

STAR STITCHES

STAR STITCH (p269)

FAN STITCH (p269)

DIAMOND EYELET STITCH (p270)

LEAF STITCH (p270)

FLORENTINE WORK

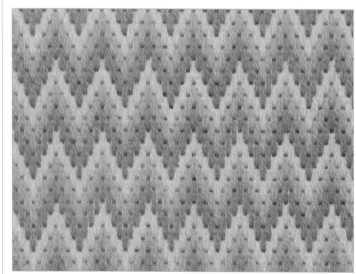

BASIC FLORENTINE STITCH (p271)

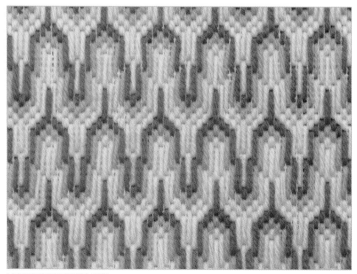

HUNGARIAN POINT (p273)

FLAME STITCH (p277)

Ws (p277)

LATTICE (p277)

POMEGRANATE (p276)

UNDULATING STRIPES (p277)

NEEDLEPOINT STITCHES

A design can be worked using a single stitch or several different stitches. Pictorial designs are often worked entirely in tent stitch (also called *petit point*), whereas the larger-scale textured stitches generally lend themselves better to abstract designs. Experiment with these stitches to discover their character.

DIAGONAL STITCHES

All of these stitches involve crossing at least one thread intersection, or mesh, producing a diagonal effect. Work with a relaxed tension or on a frame to avoid distorting the canvas. Unless otherwise stated, either single or double canvas can be used.

CONTINENTAL TENT STITCH

This stitch covers the canvas well and produces a hard-wearing fabric. However, it is apt to distort the canvas, so should be worked on a frame and/or on interlock canvas.

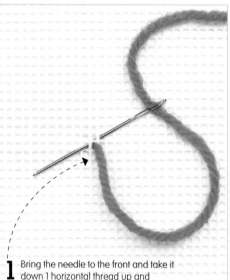

1 Bring the needle to the front and take it down 1 horizontal thread up and 1 vertical thread to the right (1 mesh). Take it under 2 vertical threads to the left and 1 horizontal thread down, bringing it out ready to form the next stitch.

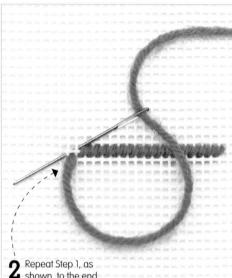

2 Repeat Step 1, as shown, to the end of the row. On finishing the last stitch, leave the needle on the wrong side of the canvas.

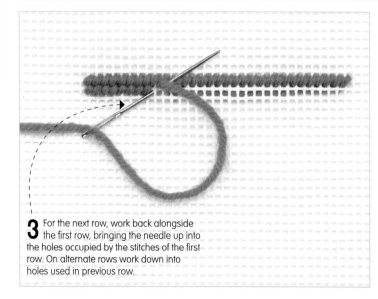

3 For the next row, work back alongside the first row, bringing the needle up into the holes occupied by the stitches of the first row. On alternate rows work down into holes used in previous row.

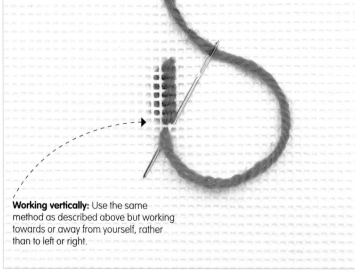
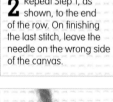

Working vertically: Use the same method as described above but working towards or away from yourself, rather than to left or right.

DIAGONAL TENT STITCH

Also called basketweave tent because of the woven effect produced on the wrong side, this stitch is recommended for larger areas of a single colour. For practice, begin at the top right-hand corner as shown here.

HALF-CROSS STITCH

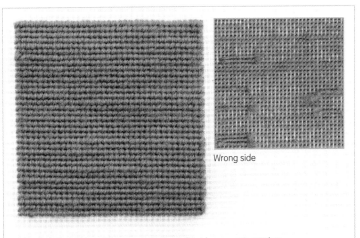

Wrong side

This stitch looks almost the same on the right side as continental or diagonal tent stitch, but on the wrong side the threads do not completely cover the canvas, and so the resulting fabric is not so strong. Use interlock, double, or plastic canvas for this stitch.

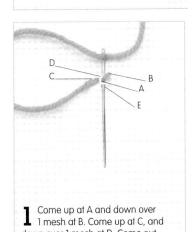

1 Come up at A and down over 1 mesh at B. Come up at C, and down over 1 mesh at D. Come out 2 horizontal threads below at E to work the third stitch.

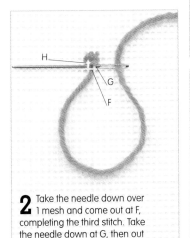

2 Take the needle down over 1 mesh and come out at F, completing the third stitch. Take the needle down at G, then out 2 vertical threads to the left at H.

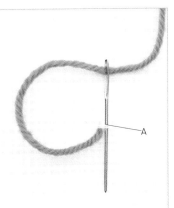

3 Continue in this way, working in diagonal rows to fill the space.

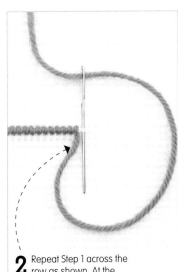

1 Bring the needle to front and take it down over 1 mesh up and to the right (A). Take it under 1 thread (or double thread) immediately below, ready to begin next stitch.

2 Repeat Step 1 across the row as shown. At the end of row, leave needle on wrong side of canvas.

DIAGONAL LINES OF TENT STITCH

Lines of tent stitch from upper right to lower left, or upper left to lower right, are essentially backstitch, taking the needle over 1 mesh and under 2 each time. If using the sewing method of stitching (see page 247), turn the work 90 degrees for one or other of these directions, depending on whether you are right- or left-handed.

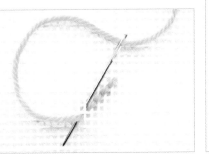

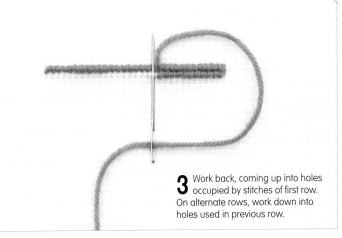

3 Work back, coming up into holes occupied by stitches of first row. On alternate rows, work down into holes used in previous row.

TRAMÉ

Tramé (or tramming) is a technique of laying long horizontal stitches to provide a foundation for other stitches, such as half-cross stitch on double canvas, or gobelin stitch on single canvas.

1 Bring the needle to the front of the canvas, between 2 paired horizontal threads. Take it down between the same pair of threads, no more than 3cm (1in) away. Repeat over following pairs of threads.

2 If additional width is needed, bring the needle up to the left of where the first tramé stitch ended, under 1 vertical canvas thread, splitting the yarn. Continue across required width.

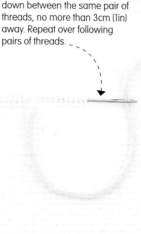

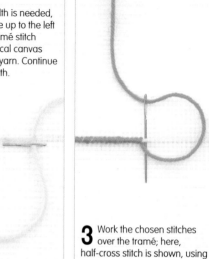

3 Work the chosen stitches over the tramé; here, half-cross stitch is shown, using a contrasting colour for clarity.

BEADED TENT STITCH

For additional texture you can add beads to tent stitch or half-cross stitch. Choose beads with holes large enough for your thread. For solid bead work choose beads the same size as the stitches.

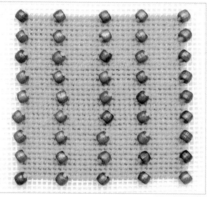

1 Bring the needle to the front. Slip a bead on the needle and slide it down the thread. Take the needle to the back to complete the stitch.

GOBELIN STITCH

Also called slanted gobelin, this easy stitch is ideal for backgrounds. The horizontal, ridged effect can be enhanced with tramé.

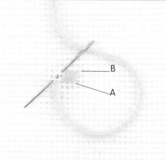

1 Bring the needle up at A and take it over 1 vertical thread to the right and 2 horizontal threads above to B. Bring it up again 2 vertical threads to the left to work the next stitch. Continue to the end of the row.

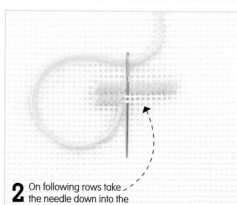

2 On following rows take the needle down into the holes occupied by the stitches of the previous row, missing the first hole in the row.

ENCROACHING GOBELIN STITCH

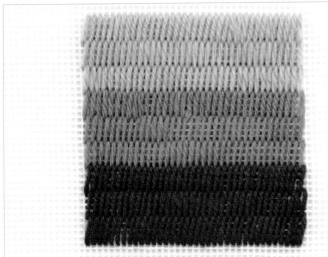

This is a smoother form of gobelin stitch. The slight overlap makes it perfect for producing a shaded effect. Encroaching gobelin stitch is useful for filling large background areas fast. Work only on single canvas.

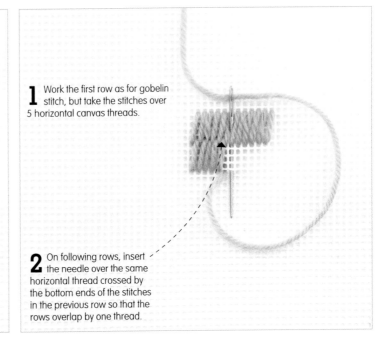

1 Work the first row as for gobelin stitch, but take the stitches over 5 horizontal canvas threads.

2 On following rows, insert the needle over the same horizontal thread crossed by the bottom ends of the stitches in the previous row so that the rows overlap by one thread.

CUSHION STITCH

Also called squares pattern or flat stitch, this is made of graduated diagonal stitches that form squares. The stitches of adjacent squares slant in opposite directions, giving the work a strong textural effect.

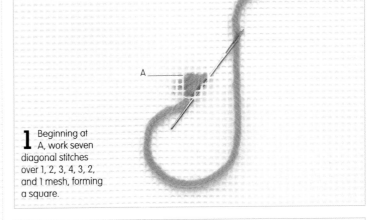

1 Beginning at A, work seven diagonal stitches over 1, 2, 3, 4, 3, 2, and 1 mesh, forming a square.

2 Work another square to the right, using a contrasting colour if desired, and with stitches slanting to the left. Here, for clarity, the first colour has been fastened off; normally you would use two needles and colours alternately.

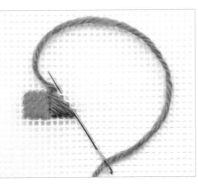

3 In following rows, continue to work squares, alternating the direction of the stitches as shown, even if working in a single colour.

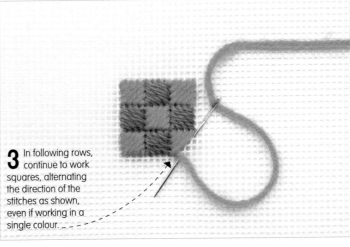

NEEDLEPOINT

CHEQUER STITCH

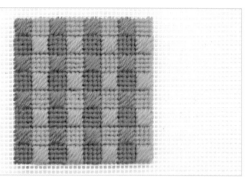

Used for covering large areas, this stitch can be worked in two (or more) colours to enhance the chequerboard effect, or in one colour to emphasize the textural contrast.

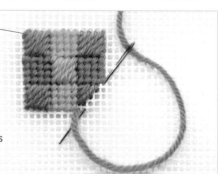

1 Starting at A, work seven graduated diagonal stitches over 1, 2, 3, 4, 3, 2, and 1 mesh, forming a square.

2 Work the next square in four rows of continental or diagonal tent stitches (see pages 254–255). Alternate these two squares to fill the area.

SCOTTISH STITCH

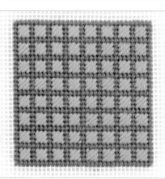

This stitch forms a lattice effect. Although it can be worked in a single colour, the effect is more pronounced if contrasting colours or different textures of yarn are used.

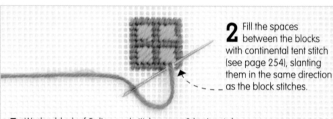

2 Fill the spaces between the blocks with continental tent stitch (see page 254), slanting them in the same direction as the block stitches.

1 Work a block of 5 diagonal stitches over 3 horizontal and 3 vertical threads. Work more blocks, slanting the stitches in the same direction, leaving 1 canvas thread free between the blocks.

MOSAIC STITCH

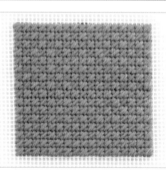

Worked in two colours, mosaic stitch forms a chequerboard pattern. It can also be worked in a single colour, producing a subtle texture.

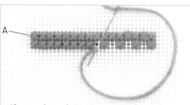

Chequerboard: Starting at A in first colour, work block of 3 stitches over 2 vertical and 2 horizontal threads. Leave 2 vertical threads. Work next block. Fill in with second colour.

Single colour: Work in rows, starting at A. Work all top short stitches and longer stitches across a row. Fill in the bottom short stitches on the next row.

DIAGONAL STITCH

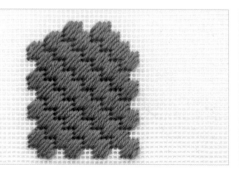

This stitch produces a strongly diagonal effect, which can be enhanced by working it in stripes of contrasting colours.

1 Work each row from top left to bottom right. Come up at A, take the needle over 2, 3, 4, and 3 mesh. Repeat sequence.

2 On subsequent rows, fit the stitches together as shown, with 4-mesh stitches next to 2-mesh stitches and vice versa.

MOORISH STITCH

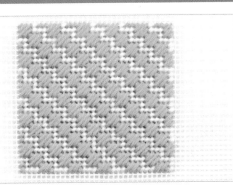

This stitch is a combination of interlinked squares, worked on the diagonal, and tent stitches. Worked in contrasting colours, the effect is a zigzag striped pattern.

1 Starting at A, work 4 diagonal stitches over 1, 2, 3, and 2 mesh. Repeat the sequence to the end.

2 For the next row, work tent stitches following the edge of the interlinked squares, using contrasting thread, if desired. Repeat two-row sequence to fill the shape.

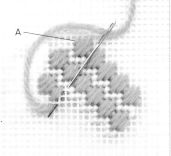

BYZANTINE STITCH

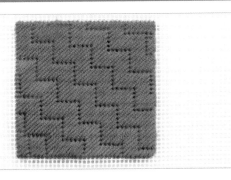

Useful for filling large areas, byzantine stitch forms a bold stepped pattern with a satiny texture.

1 Work from lower right to upper left, starting at A. Take the needle over 4 vertical and 4 horizontal threads. Work 5 more identical stitches above. Change direction, working 5 stitches horizontally to the left, then 5 vertically, and so on as required.

2 Work following rows in same way, fitting them below the preceding row.

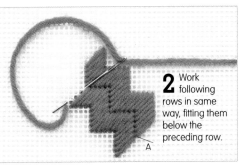

JACQUARD STITCH

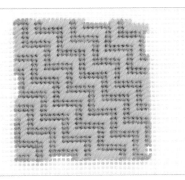

The step pattern of Jacquard stitch is accentuated by using contrasting colours or combining matt and shiny threads.

1 Work from lower right to upper left. Wider rows are worked over 2 horizontal and 2 vertical threads. Each step consists of 5 stitches.

2 Alternate rows are worked in tent stitch, either in contrasting thread, as shown, or in the same thread.

MILANESE STITCH

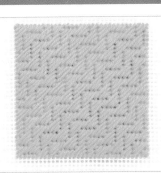

This stitch is constructed of interlocking triangles worked in backstitch. It is excellent for backgrounds.

1 Start at A. Work diagonal stitches over 1, 2, 3, and 4 mesh to form a triangle.

2 Work backwards and forwards in rows of backstitch to form the pattern: first row, work over 2, 1 and 2 mesh; next, over 2, 2, and 2; next, over 2, 3, and 2; next, over 1, 1, 4, 1, and 1. Continue to build up the pattern.

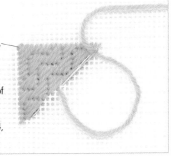

NEEDLEPOINT

ORIENTAL STITCH

This scaled-up version of Milanese stitch (see page 259) is useful for filling backgrounds. It can be worked in one colour, but its structure is easier to grasp if practised in two colours.

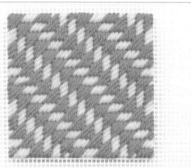
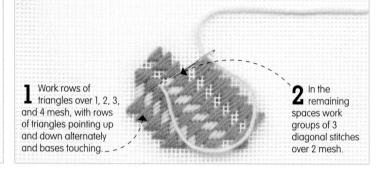

1 Work rows of triangles over 1, 2, 3, and 4 mesh, with rows of triangles pointing up and down alternately and bases touching.

2 In the remaining spaces work groups of 3 diagonal stitches over 2 mesh.

STEM STITCH

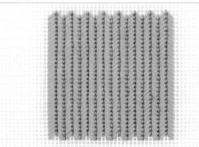

This attractive stitch is suggestive of grass or wheat. The diagonal stitches can be used on their own, but working lines of backstitch between them in a contrasting colour accentuates the vertical quality.

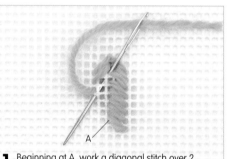

1 Beginning at A, work a diagonal stitch over 2 mesh. Continue to the top, then work down alongside these stitches, slanting the next row in the opposite direction. Work rows across the canvas.

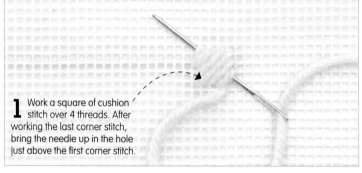

2 Using a contrasting thread, if desired, work backstitches between the rows of diagonal stitches.

CROSSED CORNERS CUSHION STITCH

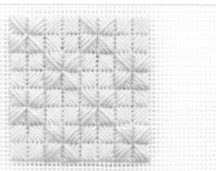

This pretty variation of cushion stitch (see page 257), is produced by covering half of a square with diagonal stitches worked at a right angle to the first ones. Many different effects can be created by varying the positions of the top stitches.

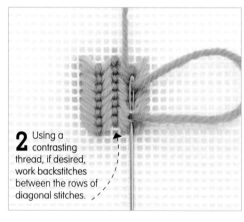

1 Work a square of cushion stitch over 4 threads. After working the last corner stitch, bring the needle up in the hole just above the first corner stitch.

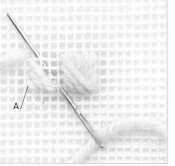

2 Work 4 diagonal stitches to cover one half of the block. Bring the needle up 5 vertical threads to the left at A. Work another cushion stitch in the same direction as the previously worked crossing stitches.

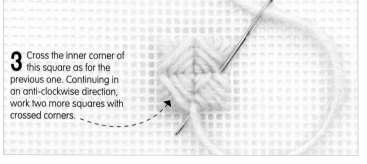

3 Cross the inner corner of this square as for the previous one. Continuing in an anti-clockwise direction, work two more squares with crossed corners.

STRAIGHT STITCHES

All of the stitches in this section are formed by working in a vertical or horizontal direction. Most of them are easy to work; in fact, many needlepoint kits are worked in a modified form of long stitch (see page 263) that covers the canvas very quickly. However, you should avoid using very long stitches for an object that will receive wear, as they are likely to snag. All the stitches in this section are best worked on single canvas.

UPRIGHT GOBELIN STITCH

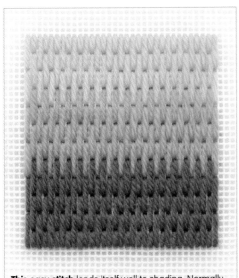

Also called straight gobelin, this simple stitch is useful for backgrounds. If worked over two horizontal threads, it produces a ridged appearance. This effect can be enhanced by working it over tramé (see page 256). For a flatter, glossier effect, work over three or four threads.

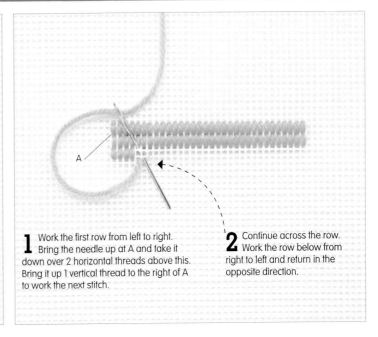

1 Work the first row from left to right. Bring the needle up at A and take it down over 2 horizontal threads above this. Bring it up 1 vertical thread to the right of A to work the next stitch.

2 Continue across the row. Work the row below from right to left and return in the opposite direction.

GOBELIN FILLING STITCH

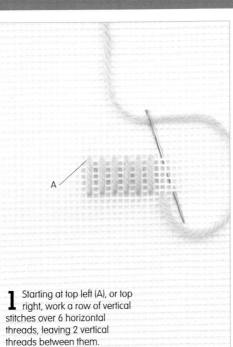

This easy stitch lends itself well to shading. Normally worked over six horizontal threads, the same basic method can be used over four threads to make a sturdier fabric.

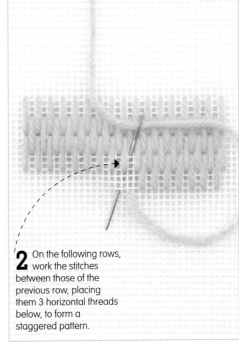

1 Starting at top left (A), or top right, work a row of vertical stitches over 6 horizontal threads, leaving 2 vertical threads between them.

2 On the following rows, work the stitches between those of the previous row, placing them 3 horizontal threads below, to form a staggered pattern.

RANDOM STRAIGHT STITCH

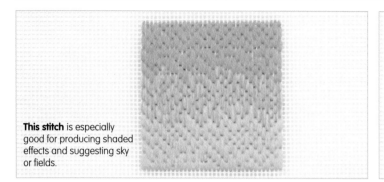

This stitch is especially good for producing shaded effects and suggesting sky or fields.

1 Work rows backwards and forwards, varying the length of stitches over 2, 3, or 4 horizontal threads. Take the needle down into the same hole as the stitch immediately above. Avoid working two adjacent stitches over the same horizontal thread.

PARISIAN STITCH

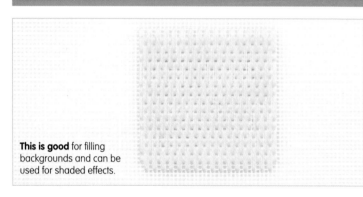

This is good for filling backgrounds and can be used for shaded effects.

1 Come out at A and take the needle down 6 horizontal threads above. Come up 4 horizontal threads down and 1 vertical thread to the right. Take it down 2 threads above. Repeat long and short stitches to end of row.

2 On next row, work long stitches below short ones.

TWILL STITCH

Quick and easy to work, this is a good choice for a smooth background. It has a strongly diagonal feel, resembling the weave of twill fabric.

1 Bring the needle up at A and take it down over 3 horizontal threads above this point. Come out 1 thread below the first stitch and 1 vertical thread to the right. Continue.

2 Work following rows also from left to right.

DOUBLE TWILL STITCH

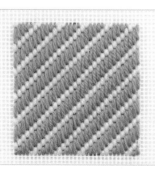

Here, the diagonal feel is accentuated by lines of short stitches alternating with longer ones. This effect can be enhanced by working the short stitches in a different colour.

1 Work from top right to lower left. Start at A. Work a vertical stitch over 4 threads. Come out 1 thread down from bottom of the first stitch and work another vertical stitch. Continue to end of row.

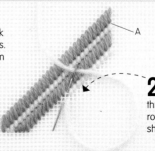

2 Work the next row over 2 threads. Alternate rows of long and short stitches.

LONG STITCH

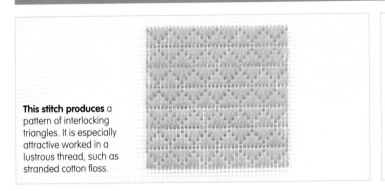

This stitch produces a pattern of interlocking triangles. It is especially attractive worked in a lustrous thread, such as stranded cotton floss.

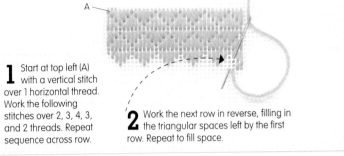

1 Start at top left (A) with a vertical stitch over 1 horizontal thread. Work the following stitches over 2, 3, 4, 3, and 2 threads. Repeat sequence across row.

2 Work the next row in reverse, filling in the triangular spaces left by the first row. Repeat to fill space.

HUNGARIAN DIAMOND STITCH

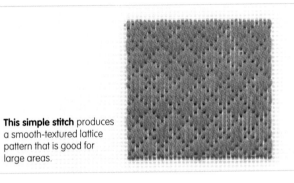

This simple stitch produces a smooth-textured lattice pattern that is good for large areas.

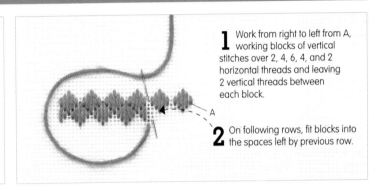

1 Work from right to left from A, working blocks of vertical stitches over 2, 4, 6, 4, and 2 horizontal threads and leaving 2 vertical threads between each block.

2 On following rows, fit blocks into the spaces left by previous row.

HUNGARIAN STITCH

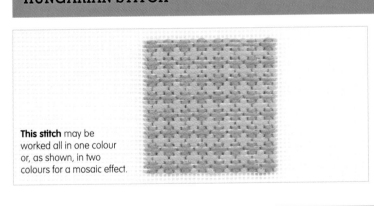

This stitch may be worked all in one colour or, as shown, in two colours for a mosaic effect.

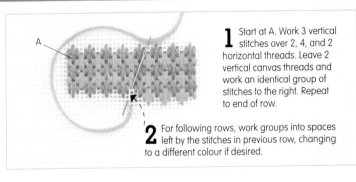

1 Start at A. Work 3 vertical stitches over 2, 4, and 2 horizontal threads. Leave 2 vertical canvas threads and work an identical group of stitches to the right. Repeat to end of row.

2 For following rows, work groups into spaces left by the stitches in previous row, changing to a different colour if desired.

WEAVING STITCH

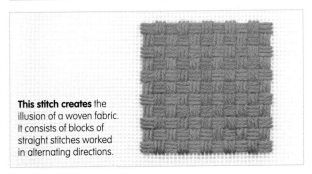

This stitch creates the illusion of a woven fabric. It consists of blocks of straight stitches worked in alternating directions.

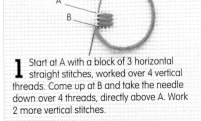

1 Start at A with a block of 3 horizontal straight stitches, worked over 4 vertical threads. Come up at B and take the needle down over 4 threads, directly above A. Work 2 more vertical stitches.

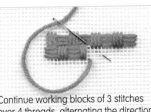

2 Continue working blocks of 3 stitches over 4 threads, alternating the direction with each block. The sides of the outer stitches in each block overlap the ends of the stitches in adjacent blocks.

CROSSED STITCHES

Stitches formed by crossing one thread over another are among the most widely used in needlepoint and create many interesting textures. Some, however, may leave areas of canvas exposed; choose a relatively thick thread to avoid this. Unless otherwise stated, work on either single or double canvas.

CROSS STITCH

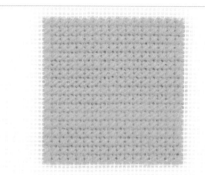

Cross stitch is one of the most widely used needlepoint stitches and creates a hard-wearing fabric. You can complete each stitch individually or work it in two stages, as shown.

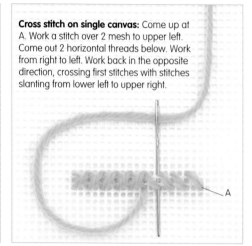

Cross stitch on single canvas: Come up at A. Work a stitch over 2 mesh to upper left. Come out 2 horizontal threads below. Work from right to left. Work back in the opposite direction, crossing first stitches with stitches slanting from lower left to upper right.

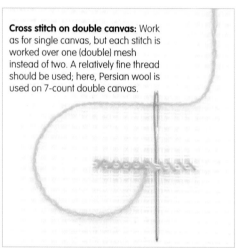

Cross stitch on double canvas: Work as for single canvas, but each stitch is worked over one (double) mesh instead of two. A relatively fine thread should be used; here, Persian wool is used on 7-count double canvas.

UPRIGHT CROSS STITCH

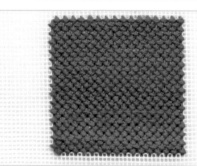

Despite its small size, this stitch is both useful and attractive, with a nubby quality that makes it ideal for depicting rough textures.

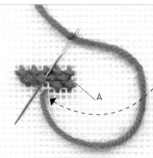

1 Start at A. Work 1 straight stitch over 2 horizontal threads. Cross this with a backstitch over 2 vertical threads. Repeat to end of row.

2 On following rows, work in alternate directions, placing stitches between those of previous row.

DIAGONAL CROSS STITCH

This is a series of upright cross stitches separated by diagonal stitches. Work on single canvas.

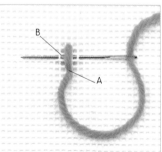

1 Work from lower right to upper left. Come out at A. Take the needle down over 4 horizontal threads above. Bring it up again at A and down over 2 mesh above and to the right. Come out 4 threads to the left at B.

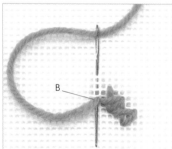

2 Work a horizontal straight stitch, coming up at B to complete first cross and first diagonal stitch. Work a vertical straight stitch over 4 threads, bringing needle out again at B.

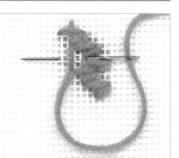

3 Continue working upright cross and diagonal stitches to complete the row. Work following rows under previous ones. Take care that all horizontal stitches lie on top of vertical ones.

OBLONG CROSS STITCH

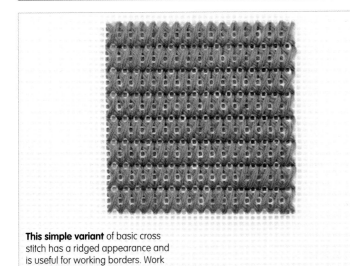

This simple variant of basic cross stitch has a ridged appearance and is useful for working borders. Work on single canvas.

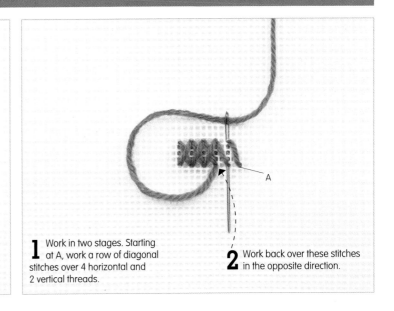

1 Work in two stages. Starting at A, work a row of diagonal stitches over 4 horizontal and 2 vertical threads.

2 Work back over these stitches in the opposite direction.

LONG-ARMED CROSS STITCH

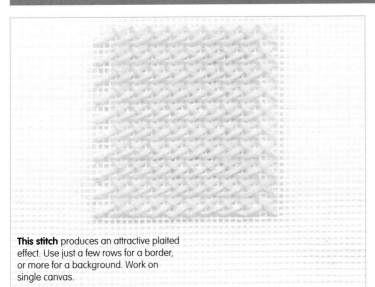

This stitch produces an attractive plaited effect. Use just a few rows for a border, or more for a background. Work on single canvas.

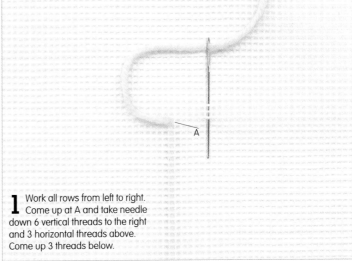

1 Work all rows from left to right. Come up at A and take needle down 6 vertical threads to the right and 3 horizontal threads above. Come up 3 threads below.

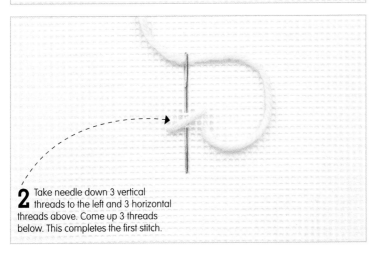

2 Take needle down 3 vertical threads to the left and 3 horizontal threads above. Come up 3 threads below. This completes the first stitch.

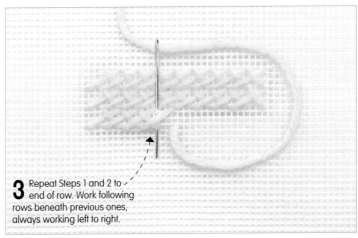

3 Repeat Steps 1 and 2 to end of row. Work following rows beneath previous ones, always working left to right.

ALTERNATING CROSS STITCH

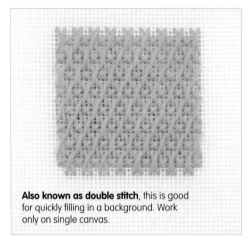

Also known as double stitch, this is good for quickly filling in a background. Work only on single canvas.

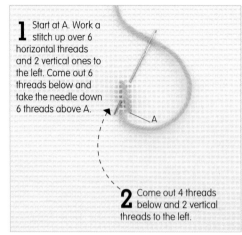

1 Start at A. Work a stitch up over 6 horizontal threads and 2 vertical ones to the left. Come out 6 threads below and take the needle down 6 threads above A.

2 Come out 4 threads below and 2 vertical threads to the left.

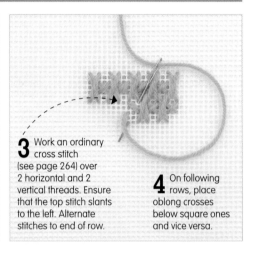

3 Work an ordinary cross stitch (see page 264) over 2 horizontal and 2 vertical threads. Ensure that the top stitch slants to the left. Alternate stitches to end of row.

4 On following rows, place oblong crosses below square ones and vice versa.

DOUBLE STRAIGHT CROSS STITCH

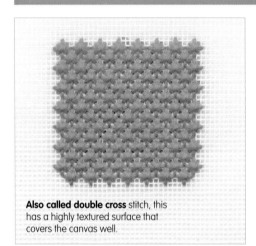

Also called double cross stitch, this has a highly textured surface that covers the canvas well.

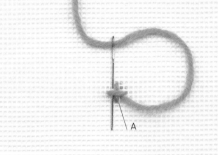

1 Start at A. Work a straight cross stitch over 4 vertical and 4 horizontal canvas threads. Come up 1 mesh below and to the right of centre and work an ordinary cross stitch (see page 264) over 4 canvas threads.

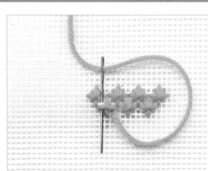

2 Work stitches from left to right, with their horizontal arms meeting as shown. On the following row, work from right to left, fitting stitches in between those of previous row.

SMYRNA STITCH

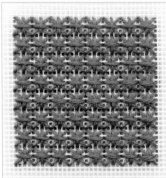

Also called leviathan stitch, this is essentially the reverse of double straight cross stitch, but it produces a square grid pattern instead of a diamond-shaped one.

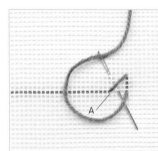

1 Start at A. Work a cross stitch over 4 vertical and 4 horizontal threads, working top stitch from lower right to upper left. Come out on the bottom line between 2 central vertical threads.

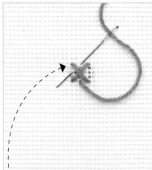

2 Work a vertical stitch over 4 threads, coming out in the centre of the left-hand side.

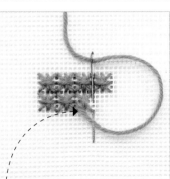

3 Complete the straight cross with a horizontal stitch, taking the needle down in the centre of the right-hand side. Come up at the lower right-hand corner, to begin the next stitch. Work additional rows from left to right under previous row.

FISHBONE STITCH

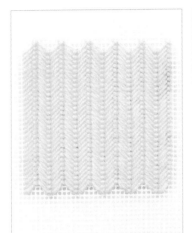

This stitch produces a striking vertical zigzag pattern. Work in vertical rows, alternately up and down. Work only on single canvas.

1 Work a diagonal stitch from lower left to upper right over 3 vertical and 3 horizontal rows, coming out 1 vertical thread to the left.

2 Cross this stitch with a stitch over 1 mesh, bringing the needle out 1 horizontal thread below starting point.

3 Repeat Step 1, coming up to the right of previously worked long stitch. Cross the long stitch with a short one, as in Step 2. Repeat Steps 1–2.

4 Work the next row upwards (to right of the first). Come up 1 thread above the end of the last crossing stitch of the completed row and down 3 threads below and to right. Cross this with a stitch over 1 mesh.

KNOTTED STITCH

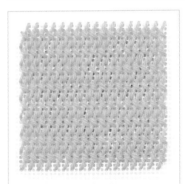

Good for backgrounds, knotted stitch fills an area quickly and easily, producing an attractive plaited effect.

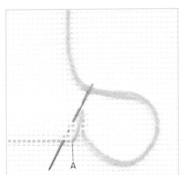

1 Start at A. Take the needle down over 6 horizontal and 2 vertical threads above and to right. Bring it up 4 threads below and cross 2 mesh up and to left. Bring it up 2 threads to left of A.

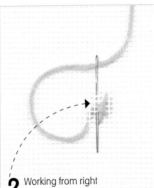

2 Working from right to left, work the next stitch in the same way as the first.

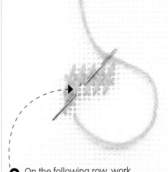

3 On the following row, work from left to right, fitting the stitches between those in the previous row and working short crossing stitches from upper left to lower right.

RICE STITCH

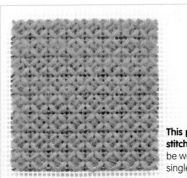

This popular stitch can also be worked in a single colour.

1 Work rows of cross stitches (see page 264), over 4 vertical and 4 horizontal threads.

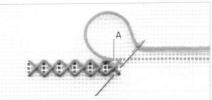

2 Using either matching or contrasting thread, and starting at A, work a diagonal stitch over 2 mesh, crossing the upper right arm of cross stitch. Come out at centre bottom.

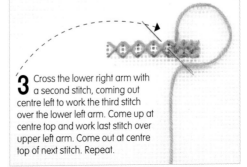

3 Cross the lower right arm with a second stitch, coming out centre left to work the third stitch over the lower left arm. Come up at centre top and work last stitch over upper left arm. Come out at centre top of next stitch. Repeat.

LOOP STITCHES

Some needlepoint stitches entail forming a loop of thread on the canvas. Here are two of the most useful. Pile stitch is worked on interlock or double canvas (including rug canvas), and preferably on a frame. These can be worked on double or single canvas.

CHAIN STITCH

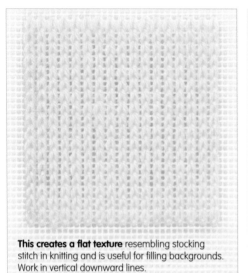

This creates a flat texture resembling stocking stitch in knitting and is useful for filling backgrounds. Work in vertical downward lines.

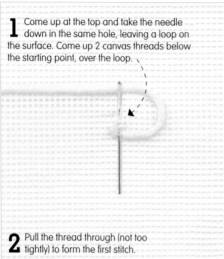

1 Come up at the top and take the needle down in the same hole, leaving a loop on the surface. Come up 2 canvas threads below the starting point, over the loop.

2 Pull the thread through (not too tightly) to form the first stitch.

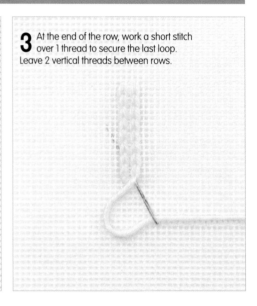

3 At the end of the row, work a short stitch over 1 thread to secure the last loop. Leave 2 vertical threads between rows.

PILE STITCH

This produces a series of loops on the canvas, which can either be left uncut as shown or cut to produce a velvet effect.

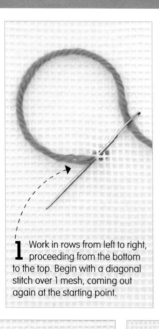

1 Work in rows from left to right, proceeding from the bottom to the top. Begin with a diagonal stitch over 1 mesh, coming out again at the starting point.

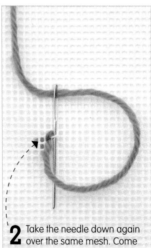

2 Take the needle down again over the same mesh. Come up 1 horizontal thread below, leaving a loop on the surface over the needle.

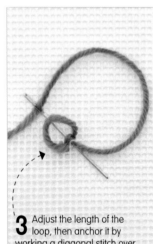

3 Adjust the length of the loop, then anchor it by working a diagonal stitch over it and over the starting stitch. Come out in the same hole to begin the next stitch.

4 To ensure loops are the same length, slip a knitting needle through them from left to right and work each one over it; slide the needle back a little to complete the stitch.

5 Work each following row over the canvas thread just above previously worked stitches. When all the stitches have been worked you can, if you wish, carefully cut through each row of loops using a small pair of scissors.

STAR STITCHES

The stitches in this section are formed of individual stitches radiating outwards from one or more points, which may be in the centre of the stitch or on one side of it. Unless otherwise stated, these stitches can be worked on either single or double canvas.

STAR STITCH

Also called Algerian eye, this simple but attractive stitch consists of eight stitches radiating from a central point. Use a relatively thick thread to cover the canvas. Work only on single canvas.

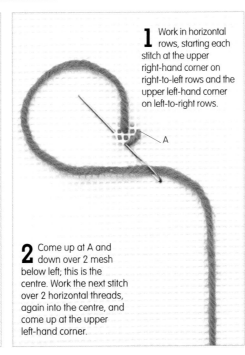

1 Work in horizontal rows, starting each stitch at the upper right-hand corner on right-to-left rows and the upper left-hand corner on left-to-right rows.

2 Come up at A and down over 2 mesh below left; this is the centre. Work the next stitch over 2 horizontal threads, again into the centre, and come up at the upper left-hand corner.

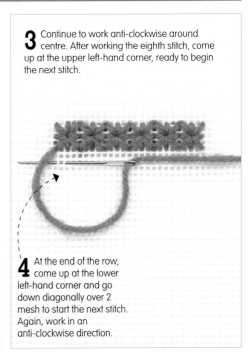

3 Continue to work anti-clockwise around centre. After working the eighth stitch, come up at the upper left-hand corner, ready to begin the next stitch.

4 At the end of the row, come up at the lower left-hand corner and go down diagonally over 2 mesh to start the next stitch. Again, work in an anti-clockwise direction.

FAN STITCH

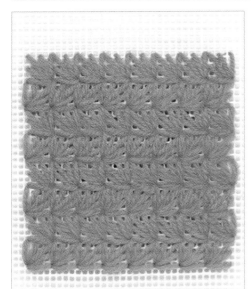

Also known as ray stitch, this is worked in alternate rows in different directions. For a denser version use nine stitches instead of five.

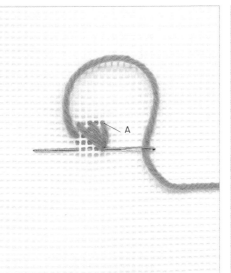

1 Start at A. Work a straight stitch over 4 horizontal threads. Work 4 more stitches radiating out from this corner point, to form a square over 4 horizontal/vertical threads. Note that there is a space (2 canvas threads) at the edge between each stitch; for a 9-stitch block, work into all the spaces.

2 Work the next fan stitch immediately to the left, coming up at the top left-hand corner of the first stitch Continue to end of row.

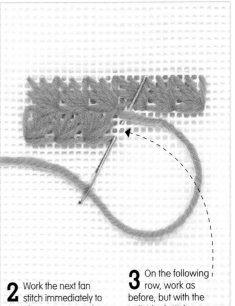

3 On the following row, work as before, but with the individual stitches pointing to the right.

DIAMOND EYELET STITCH

This decorative, large-scale stitch can be used either singly or as a background. As 16 stitches must fit into the central hole, you can widen the hole with the points of embroidery scissors or use a relatively thin thread, such as soft embroidery cotton. If you need to widen the holes to accommodate the thread, you should not use interlock (or double) canvas for this stitch.

1 Bring the needle up at A, 4 threads left of centre. Take down into centre (B). Come up 3 vertical threads to left and 1 thread above. Take down at B. Come up under 2 vertical and 2 horizontal threads.

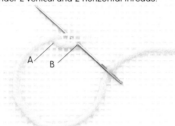

2 Continue working stitches around the centre hole to form a diamond.

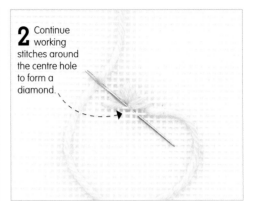

3 After working the sixteenth stitch, bring the needle up at A, where the first stitch emerged. Take it down 4 canvas threads to left; this will be the centre hole for the next stitch. Work 16 stitches.

4 Work the next row from left to right, fitting the stitches into the same holes occupied by those of the previous row. Work backstitches, if desired, between the eyelets.

LEAF STITCH

This stitch is perfect for suggesting large-scale foliage. Use a smooth thread to show its structure to best advantage.

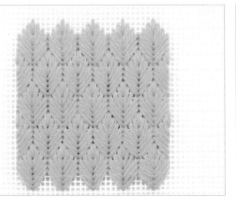

1 Work rows in alternate directions, from top to bottom. Beginning at the base of the leaf at A, work a diagonal stitch over 4 horizontal and 3 vertical threads to the left. Work 2 more identical stitches above.

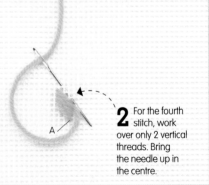

2 For the fourth stitch, work over only 2 vertical threads. Bring the needle up in the centre.

3 For the fifth stitch, take the needle over 4 horizontal and 1 vertical thread. For the top stitch, miss 2 horizontal threads and work a stitch directly above the centre line, over 3 threads.

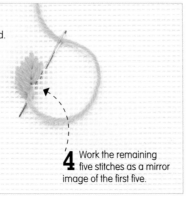

4 Work the remaining five stitches as a mirror image of the first five.

5 Begin the next stitch 6 vertical threads to the right (or left) of the base of the first one.

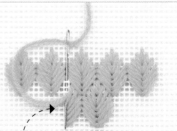

6 To begin the following row, count downwards 6 horizontal threads and 3 vertical threads to the left (or right) of the upper leaf's centre line.

FLORENTINE WORK

This distinctive style of needlepoint is named for the Italian city where it flourished in the sixteenth and seventeenth centuries. It is also called Bargello, after the palace of that name in Florence. Today, Florentine work remains very popular as it is so enjoyable to stitch.

BASIC FLORENTINE STITCH

Use single canvas for Florentine work. A smooth effect is best achieved with several strands of crewel wool, as shown in the samples that follow, although tapestry wool (shown at bottom) and Persian wool also work well.

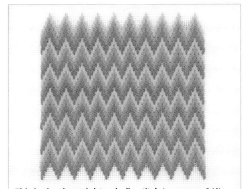

This is simply upright gobelin stitch (see page 261) worked in a stepped pattern. Each stitch is the same length, and the stitches may be worked over 3, 4, or more threads.

This sample uses the same number of stitches, worked over 4 threads, but with only a one-thread step instead of two.

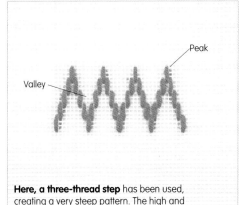

Here, a three-thread step has been used, creating a very steep pattern. The high and low points are called "peaks" and "valleys".

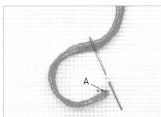

1 Come up at A and go down over 4 horizontal threads above. Come out 1 vertical thread to the right and 2 horizontal threads below.

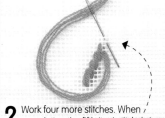

2 Work four more stitches. When completing the fifth (top) stitch, bring the needle out 2 horizontal threads below and 1 vertical thread to the right.

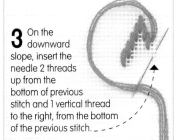

3 On the downward slope, insert the needle 2 threads up from the bottom of previous stitch and 1 vertical thread to the right, from the bottom of the previous stitch.

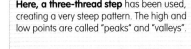

4 To begin the next upward slope, bring the needle up 2 threads above the bottom of previous stitch and 1 vertical thread to the right.

ALTERNATIVE METHOD

1 This produces longer stitches on the underside. Bring the needle out at the bottom of the "valley" at A. Take it down over 4 threads below, then bring it up 6 horizontal threads above and 1 vertical thread to right. Take it down 4 threads below and bring it up 6 threads above and 1 vertical thread to the right.

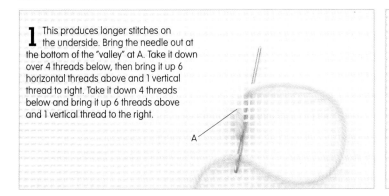

2 Continue to the top of the "peak". Begin the downward slope by bringing the needle up 2 horizontal threads beneath and 1 vertical thread to the right. Work each stitch on the downward slope, always bringing the needle up at the bottom of the stitch and taking it down at the top.

VARIATIONS ON FLORENTINE

A virtually infinite number of patterns can be created by varying the size and placement of the Florentine stitches. Here are just a few of them.

SWAGGED ZIGZAGS

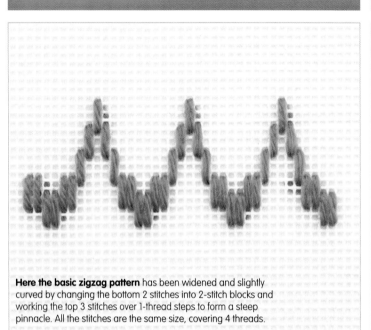

Here the basic zigzag pattern has been widened and slightly curved by changing the bottom 2 stitches into 2-stitch blocks and working the top 3 stitches over 1-thread steps to form a steep pinnacle. All the stitches are the same size, covering 4 threads.

CURVES AND PINNACLES

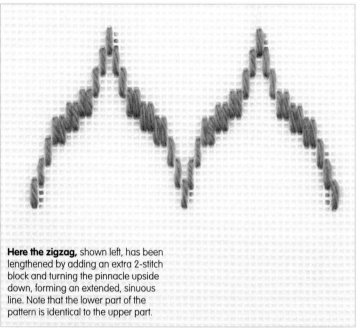

Here the zigzag, shown left, has been lengthened by adding an extra 2-stitch block and turning the pinnacle upside down, forming an extended, sinuous line. Note that the lower part of the pattern is identical to the upper part.

CURVES AND PINNACLES (WIDENED)

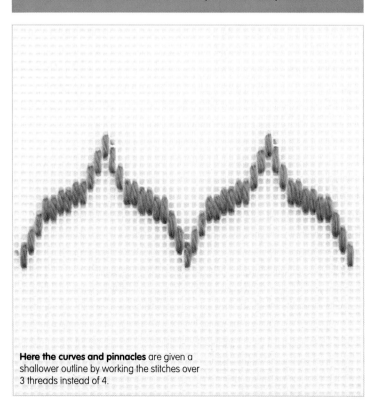

Here the curves and pinnacles are given a shallower outline by working the stitches over 3 threads instead of 4.

SCALLOPS

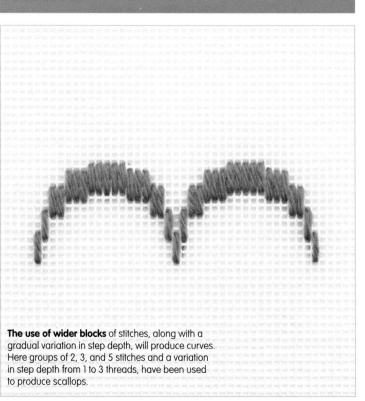

The use of wider blocks of stitches, along with a gradual variation in step depth, will produce curves. Here groups of 2, 3, and 5 stitches and a variation in step depth from 1 to 3 threads, have been used to produce scallops.

MOTIFS

Some Florentine patterns consist of motifs, rather than lines. These are produced by taking a section of a line pattern and working it as a mirror image. For example, the scallop row can be reversed to create an oval motif. Stitches within the motif can be shortened to meet in the middle.

SECONDARY MOTIFS

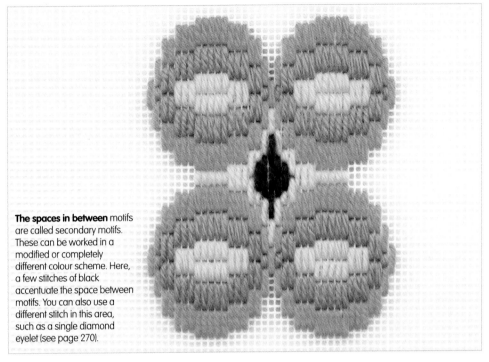

The spaces in between motifs are called secondary motifs. These can be worked in a modified or completely different colour scheme. Here, a few stitches of black accentuate the space between motifs. You can also use a different stitch in this area, such as a single diamond eyelet (see page 270).

HUNGARIAN POINT

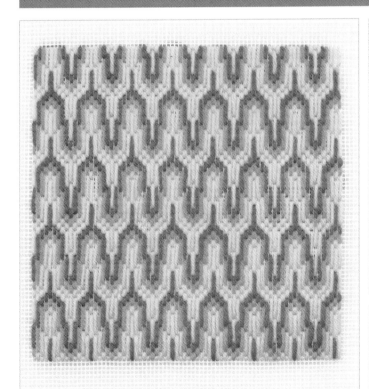

This variant of Florentine work has an ingenious pattern of long stitches combined with short ones. It is most effective worked in four closely related shades.

1 Work in rows from right to left. Establish the basic line, using the darkest colour. Come up at A and down over 6 canvas threads below. Work a stitch over 2 threads, 1 vertical thread and 1 step down to the left. Repeat. Work two long stitches, each 1 step down from the previous stitch.

2 Work a stitch over 2 threads at the bottom, as shown. Repeat this sequence in reverse on the upward slope.

3 Work the next row directly under the first one, following a sequence of 2 short, 2 long, and 2 short. On the third row, work 1 short, 2 long, and 2 short, then work a long stitch at the bottom.

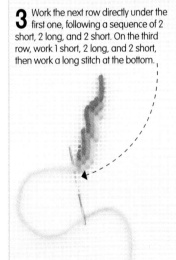

4 For the last row, work 2 long stitches, 2 short, and 2 long – the last stitch forming the lowest point of the pattern. Repeat these four rows to form the pattern.

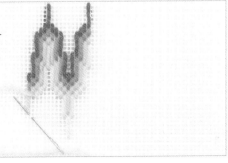

DESIGNING
A FLORENTINE PROJECT

If you'd like to try designing needlepoint but find the prospect a bit daunting, start with some Florentine designs. No drawing ability is required, and you don't have to hunt for source material. The simplest design technique is to take an existing pattern and change the colours, as shown below. You may wish first to consult a colour wheel (see page 293) to familiarize yourself with the principles of colour. Then buy some small skeins of your chosen colours and work a sample or two to see the effect.

see page 293

CHANGE THE COLOURS

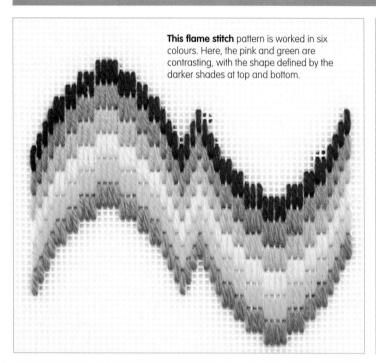

This flame stitch pattern is worked in six colours. Here, the pink and green are contrasting, with the shape defined by the darker shades at top and bottom.

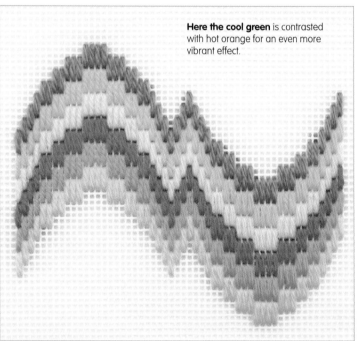

Here the cool green is contrasted with hot orange for an even more vibrant effect.

Hot colours can be combined successfully. Here pink and magenta are paired with warm yellows, with an intervening band of lilac to cool things down a little.

WORKING A FLORENTINE PROJECT

It is important, when beginning a piece of Florentine work, to get the main line of the design correct, so take a little time over this. Mark the vertical centre of your canvas; if the design is of the motif type (see page 273) you will also need to mark the horizontal centre. Then find the centre of the chart. Begin stitching at the centre and work to one side; then work out to the other side. Check the stitches carefully against the chart. Once you are sure that the pattern has been correctly established, you will find that (in most designs) the remaining rows will follow naturally.

If the design is of the motif type (see for example the Pomegranate on page 276), you should begin by working the outline of the motif; then work the filling stitches. The same is true of the lattice-type design, such as the one shown on page 277.

see page 273; see for example the Pomegranate on page 276; the one shown on page 277

STARTING FROM SCRATCH

To create your own Florentine design you will need some large-scale graph paper, a ruler, a pencil, some coloured pencils, fibre-tip pens or crayons. A small rectangular mirror will also be useful

PLANNING A ROW DESIGN

1 Begin by marking a random row of stitches across a piece of large-scale graph paper. Make sure they're all the same length and that any steps overlap the adjacent stitch by at least one grid (canvas) line.

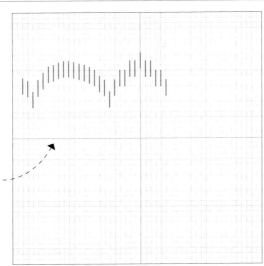

2 Choose a section of the row that could make a pleasing design. If you have a mirror, move it along the row until you see a pattern that you like reflected symmetrically in it. Draw a line along the mirror, and draw another line to each side, equidistant from the centre. This marks the repeat pattern.

3 Take another piece of graph paper large enough for your complete design, and mark the vertical centre on it. Near the top of the paper, chart the stitches of the main row, starting at the centre and working outwards. Using coloured pencils, pens, or crayons, add more rows below the main row; change the colour scheme if necessary. If you wish to design a motif-type Florentine pattern (see page 273), start with a row design, as in step 2, then run a mirror across the grid, at a 90-degree angle to the marked stitches until a pleasing motif emerges.

PLANNING A FOUR-WAY DESIGN

Also called kaleidoscope or mitred Florentine, these fascinating patterns consist of four identical quarters that meet in the centre. Again, you should start with the dominant line of the pattern. You can begin at the outer edge of the design and work inwards or vice versa.

1 Using graph paper and a mirror, create a row pattern as described above. Draw a line through the centre of the row, parallel to the stitch lines. Now place the mirror over the row at a 45-degree angle and move it along until a pleasing pattern appears. Draw a line diagonally to the centre at this point.

2 Take another piece of graph paper, large enough for one quarter of the whole design. Mark off a right angle in one corner. Mark a broken line through the grid at a 45-degree angle. Referring to the original, chart the stitches on the quarter of the design. Fill in the other colours. Apart from the dominant lines, these can be confined to one triangle.

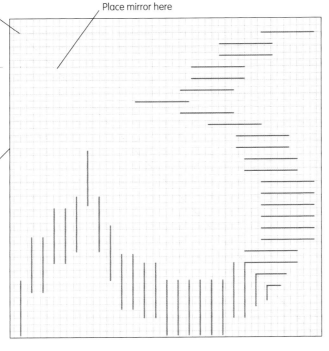

Centre hole

Place mirror here

Place mirror here

TIPS FOR ADJUSTING

• **When charting** a symmetrical section of a row, check the position of two corresponding stitches by running a pencil lightly from the bottom of one stitch to the bottom of its "opposite number" to make sure they are aligned. Also check that you have the same number of stitches in both halves of the line or motif.

• **Some trial and error** is involved in designing Florentine work – especially the four-way designs. Once you've established your dominant line and transferred it to the full-size graph paper, make a few photocopies to use, if necessary, for colour changes.

• **If you're not pleased** with the way a four-way pattern is developing along the diagonal, make a new chart, moving the dominant line inwards or outwards.

• **If the dominant line** will be interrupted at the edge of the design, you can either plan to make the needlepoint larger or smaller or choose a different-gauge canvas.

NEEDLEPOINT

FLORENTINE
DESIGNS

Here are five Florentine designs, which you can work as shown or vary as you please, changing the colours or the patterns themselves, as described on pages 272–274.

POMEGRANATE

The Pomegranate motif is a Florentine classic. When the motifs are placed together a fascinating 3-D effect is produced. You could, instead, work a single line of joined motifs on a background of shaded rows of upright gobelin stitch (see page 261). Each stitch goes over 4 canvas threads.

UNDULATING STRIPES

These undulating stripes have a restful rhythm. To accentuate the horizontal character just three colours are used, but you could add more colours for more vertical interest. Each stitch goes over 3 canvas threads.

FLAMES

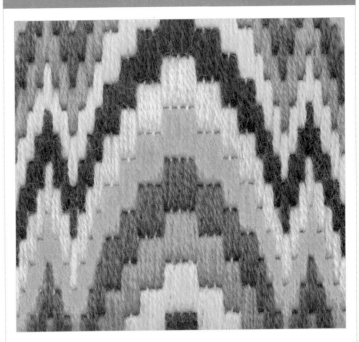

This is a typical "flame stitch" Florentine pattern, using six colours; you can use more or fewer if you prefer. Each stitch in this version goes over 6 canvas threads.

Ws

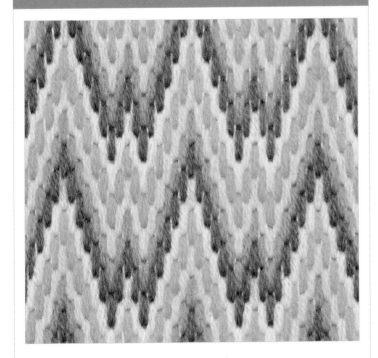

Another traditional Florentine pattern, "Ws" produces a jagged, spiky effect. Here five colours are used, and each stitch goes over 4 canvas threads.

LATTICE

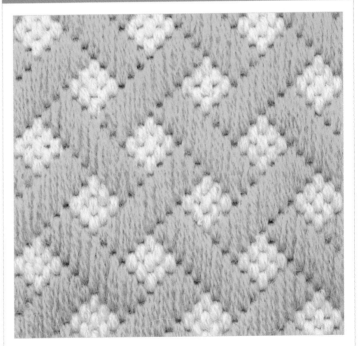

This fascinating lattice design requires a bit of study to get right, but is well worth the effort. There are 7 long (6-thread) stitches in each strip of the lattice, and each strip finishes with a 4-thread and a 2-thread stitch at each end. If you like, you could use two shades of one colour for the lattice and two colours in the central spaces.

FINAL TOUCHES

When you've worked the last stitch in your needlepoint, you now face the task of making it up into the finished article – a cushion cover or wall hanging perhaps. The first step is to get the work itself into pristine condition.

BLOCKING AND PRESSING

Blocking needlepoint gets the work back into shape if it has become distorted during stitching. Before you do this, hold the piece up to a strong light to check no stitches are missing, and pull any wisps of yarn to the wrong side with the point of a tapestry needle.

WET BLOCKING

If the corners of your work are not square, you will need to wet-block it on a blocking board. This should be a piece of plywood or softwood that will accommodate fairly large pieces of work.

1 Measure two adjacent sides of the canvas. On a sheet of blotting paper, using a permanent marking pen and a set square and ruler, draw the correct outline of the canvas. Fasten the paper to the board at the corners with masking tape or drawing pins.

2 Lay the needlepoint face down on the ironing board or on a clean turkish towel and dampen it thoroughly with a wet sponge or a spray bottle.

3 Pull on the canvas in the direction opposite the distortion, starting at diagonally opposite corners and working towards the centre.

4 Lay the wet needlepoint on the blocking board within the marked canvas outline (face down unless the work is highly textured). Secure it in place with drawing pins, stretching the canvas to fit the outline.

5 Leave the work to dry before removing it from the board. Check the corners of the needlepoint with the set square to make sure they are square.

DAMP PRESSING

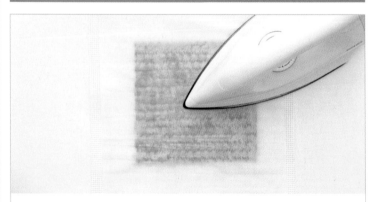

In some cases, the needlepoint will fit the marked outline perfectly and can simply be damp-pressed. Place it face down on an ironing board (or face up if it is highly textured) and lay a damp cotton cloth on top. Gently place a hot, dry iron over the whole area, repeatedly setting the iron down and lifting it up – do not use an ironing motion. Leave the needlepoint to dry naturally before handling it.

SEAMS
AND EDGES

Before joining a piece of needlepoint to a piece of fabric (as for a cushion cover), you should trim the edges to about 2–3cm (¾–1in); this will remove the selvedge, if any, and any uneven edges of canvas caused in the blocking.

STITCHING SEAMS

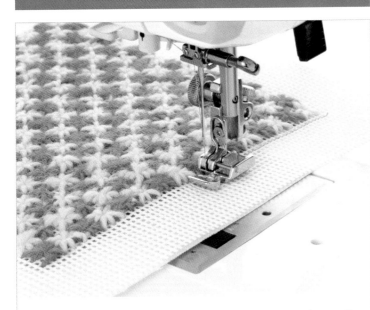

If you are joining the work to fabric, use the zip foot of the sewing machine, working on the needlepoint side and stitching as close to the needlepoint as possible. Use a heavy-duty needle (size 90 or 100) and strong thread. If you haven't got access to a sewing machine, you will need to sew the seam by hand, using backstitch. Or take the work to a company that offers a making-up service.

REDUCING BULK

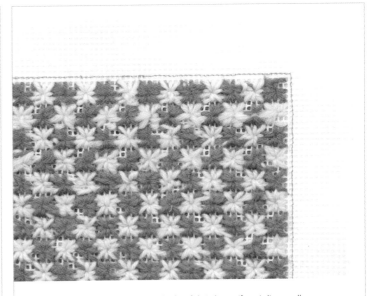

At the corners, trim the canvas (and other fabric layer, if any) diagonally across, as shown, leaving a scant 1cm (⅜in) between the stitched corner and the diagonally cut edge. Steam-press the seam open. Turn the work right side out, and gently but firmly push the corners out to a neat point.

MITRING A CORNER

A piece that will be lined – for example, a wall hanging – will need to have the canvas edges turned to the wrong side. At the corners the canvas must be neatly mitred to produce as little bulk as possible. (Here, the mitre is shown on bare canvas; in actuality, the needlepoint would extend to the fold).

1 Cut a small square out of the corner of the canvas, leaving two or three canvas threads at the inner corner. With the wrong side facing, fold the two canvas corners down to leave a diagonal fold.

2 Fold the canvas edges to the wrong side, pressing them firmly with your fingers. Bring the folded edges over to meet diagonally, forming a mitre, as shown.

3 Thread a chenille or large crewel needle with strong thread, such as button thread. Anchor this to the corner with a few backstitches, then oversew the mitred edges together firmly.

LINING A PIECE
OF NEEDLEPOINT

You can line a piece of needlepoint by sewing it to the lining fabric right sides together, turning through a gap and slipstitching the opening closed. A neater result may be achieved by hand-stitching the lining in place. Use a firmly woven fabric for the lining.

1 Cut the lining the same size as the needlepoint, including seam allowances. Mitre the corners of the needlepoint (see page 279). Steam-press the canvas seam allowances down over the wrong side. (Here only canvas and lining are shown, to illustrate the principle).

2 Press the lining seam allowances to the wrong side and mitre the corners.

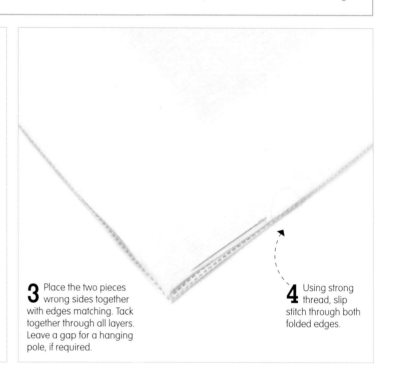

3 Place the two pieces wrong sides together with edges matching. Tack together through all layers. Leave a gap for a hanging pole, if required.

4 Using strong thread, slip stitch through both folded edges.

LACING
NEEDLEPOINT
OVER CARD

If your project is a picture, intended for framing, you will need to lace it over a piece of card. This method is also used for other embroidered pictures, but in the case of needlepoint, it is advisable to leave a small margin of bare canvas on the front, which can then be covered by the mount.

1 Cut a piece of thick card the size of the needlepoint plus 5mm (¼in) all around. Remove the tape from the canvas edges, but leave a margin of canvas, 4–5cm (1½–2in) wide. Lay the canvas face down on a clean surface and place the card on top.

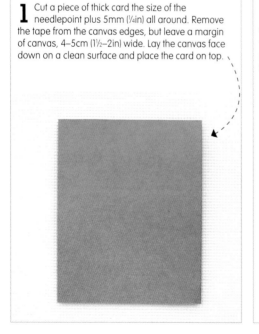

2 Fold the longer edges of canvas over the card; hold them in place temporarily with pins stuck in the card edges. Using a tapestry needle and strong thread attached to the spool, work herringbone stitches (see page 190) from one canvas edge to the other. Start at the centre and work out to each side in turn.

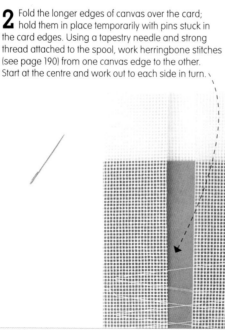

3 Repeat Step 2 to lace the two shorter sides together. Oversew the overlapping canvas edges at the corners.

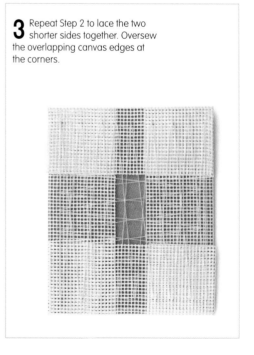

FINISHING AND JOINING
PLASTIC CANVAS

One advantage of plastic canvas is that you needn't worry about raw edges. You can finish or join plastic edges by oversewing with thread, using a tapestry needle.

FINISHING

1 Run the needle through a few stitches close to the edge on the wrong side, towards the starting point. Bring the needle to the front through the first hole, take it over the edge and bring it to the front again through the next hole. Oversew to the end.

2 When you reach a corner, work two or three stitches into the same hole to cover the plastic edge completely.

3 Fasten off by taking the needle through a few stitches on the underside. Trim the end close to the stitches.

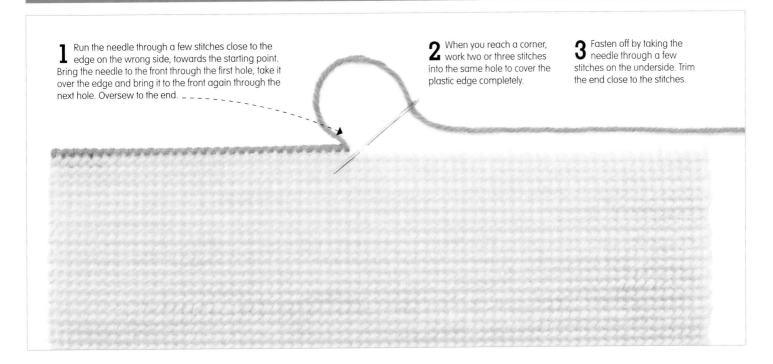

JOINING

1 Fasten the thread on the wrong side of one piece (see above). Place the two pieces together with wrong sides facing and edges aligned.

2 Oversew through the corresponding holes. Pinch the edges together as you stitch so that the stitches along the edge will lie smoothly.

PATCHWORK, APPLIQUÉ, AND QUILTING

The central skills of quiltmaking – patchwork is the piecing of fabric shapes into new patterns, appliqué is the application of fabric shapes to a background cloth, and quilting is the stitching process that secures the layers of the quilt together.

TOOLS AND MATERIALS

Making a quilt does not require a lot of equipment. If you are a beginner, you probably won't need more than needles and thread or a sewing machine, scissors, pins, ruler or measuring tape, a pencil, and a thimble. There is, however, a gigantic selection of specialized tools that have been designed to make the process easier.

GENERAL SEWING EQUIPMENT

For quiltmaking you will need a set of hand-sewing needles – both "sharps" and "betweens". Both types come in several lengths, thicknesses, and eye size. Needles are sized by number: the higher the number, the finer the needle. Pins are essential for pinning the layers of a quilt together while you work (see page 365). Always press seams as you go, with an iron or by fingerpressing.

SHARPS
"Sharps" are standard sewing needles and are usually used for processes such as tacking, hand piecing, and binding.

BETWEENS
"Betweens" are generally smaller than sharps and are most commonly used for appliqué and hand quilting.

QUILTERS' PINS
Long quilters' pins with a decorative motif such as a small yellow paper flower on top, make them easy to spot in the fabric.

GLASS QUILTERS PINS
These extra-long pins are easy to handle. Extra-short pins called appliqué pins are also available to secure pieces as you stitch.

GLASS-HEADED STRAIGHT PINS
Ordinary dressmaking pins are used to hold pieces together during hand piecing.

SAFETY PINS
If the layers of the quilt are not too thick, you can use ordinary safety pins to hold them together.

HERA
A plastic, blade-like device for fingerpressing. A little wooden iron with a flat, chisel-shaped edge can also be used.

THIMBLE
Thimbles are made from metal, leather, plastic, and even ceramic, and are designed to protect both the sewing finger and the hand underneath in quilting.

IRON
It is essential to press seams as you work, so have an iron and ironing board set up in your work area.

PIN CUSHION
Pin cushions range from traditional sawdust-filled felt shapes to magnetic pin-catchers. Magnetic types can interfere with the smooth operation of computerized sewing machines.

SEWING MACHINE

All the main manufacturers have sewing machines designed with the quiltmaker in mind, with numerous attachments available. For machine quilting, you will need to be able to drop the feed dogs. Machine needles in sizes 70–90 universals, are recommended for quiltmaking.

MACHINE FEATURES >>

Before you buy a machine, decide which features will be most useful to you and, if you're planning to quilt, make sure it's sturdy enough to be able to stitch through the quilt top, wadding, and backing fabric.

FEET

All sewing machines come with a standard presser foot as well as a selection of specialized feet for various purposes. Among the most useful for quiltmaking are:

¼-inch foot: Designed to measure a seam of exactly ¼in (5–6mm), rather than the ⅜in (10mm) presser foot that is standard in dressmaking.

Zipper foot: Useful for piping the edges of a quilt, when you need to stitch close to the piping cord.

Open-toe foot: Useful for appliqué and quilting.

Free-style quilting foot: "Floats" on a spring mechanism for free-motion quilting.

Walking foot: Guides the layers of fabric and wadding through the feed dogs at an even speed.

Twin-needle foot: Gives interesting textured effects.

THREADS

For piecing, match the thread to the fabric, such as cotton with cotton, and either match the colour to the lighter fabric, or use a neutral shade. For appliqué, match the thread colour to the piece being stitched. Speciality threads include silk, metallics, and rayon.

SEWING THREAD >>
Threads come in a dazzling choice of colours, types, and weights. Sewing thread is used for hand- and machine-sewing.

QUILTING THREAD >>
Quilting thread is heavier than sewing thread and is waxed to prevent breaks.

MEASURING TOOLS

Most of the basic measuring and marking tools that a quiltmaker needs are standard items in a home office or workshop. Some can be found in a general sewing kit or a desk drawer.

T-SQUARE >>
Useful for squaring corners and measuring.

SEAM GAUGE ⌄
Very useful for measuring and marking off seam allowances.

RULER ⌄
A metal or plastic ruler is useful for measuring and drawing straight lines.

ROTARY RULER ⌄
Useful for drafting patterns and templates, as well as for determining seam allowances.

TAPE MEASURE ⌄
An essential item for quiltmaking and patchwork, for measuring fabric widths and template sizes.

SET SQUARE >>
Useful for measuring and guiding square corners on quilt blocks and for cutting individual pattern pieces.

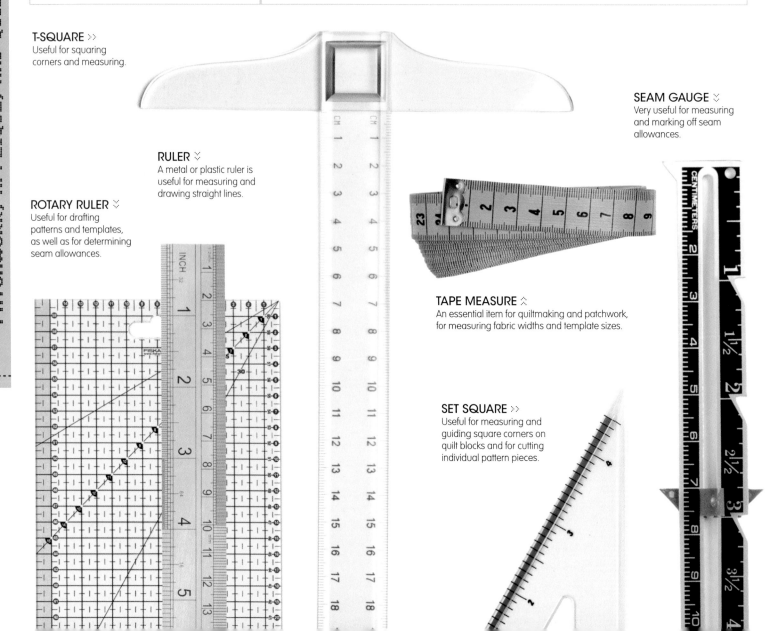

MARKING
TOOLS

Various kinds of pencils and pens are used to draw designs and mark seam allowances on both paper and fabric. Some markers, such as tailor's chalk and washaway pen, are non-permanent.

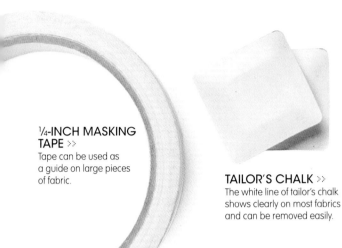

¼-INCH MASKING TAPE »
Tape can be used as a guide on large pieces of fabric.

TAILOR'S CHALK »
The white line of tailor's chalk shows clearly on most fabrics and can be removed easily.

PENCILS »
A selection of light coloured pencils will show up clearly on darker fabrics or paper when tracing or transferring patterns or designs.

BLUE WASHAWAY PEN »
A water-soluble pen can be used for transferring patterns or drawing around templates.

FINE-POINT LEAD PENCIL »
A sharp point is essential for drawing designs and templates.

TEMPLATES
AND STENCILS

Templates and stencils are more durable if they are cut from translucent template plastic, rather than card. Cut using a sharp scalpel to ensure accuracy. Freezer paper can also be used to create templates and is especially useful in some appliqué work.

FREEZER PAPER »
A good option for appliqué templates, freezer paper can be ironed onto the fabric and removed later.

READY-MADE WINDOW TEMPLATE »
Made from sturdy template plastic or metal, a window template is used to mark both the outline and the seamline without the need for two templates.

READY-MADE QUILTING STENCIL »
A quilting stencil can be used to transfer a pattern onto the fabric. Trace the stencil design with a non-permanent marker pen.

TRACING PAPER »
This is essential for tracing motifs or pattern pieces onto template plastic, or card, before cutting out.

CARD »
Stiff card can be used to make templates but will no be as long lasting as plastic.

MISCELLANEOUS ITEMS

Other useful items for quiltmaking can include graph paper, dressmaker's carbon paper, slivers of soap, flexible curves, drawing compasses, protractors, and erasers, which can all help with designing and transferring pattern pieces or motifs.

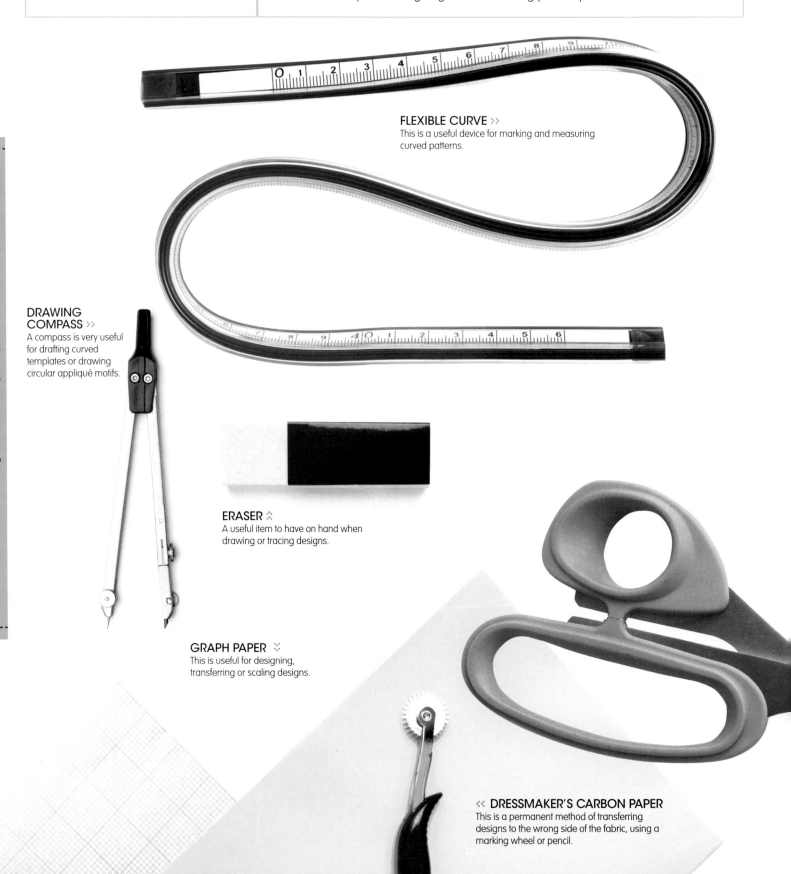

FLEXIBLE CURVE >>
This is a useful device for marking and measuring curved patterns.

DRAWING COMPASS >>
A compass is very useful for drafting curved templates or drawing circular appliqué motifs.

ERASER
A useful item to have on hand when drawing or tracing designs.

GRAPH PAPER
This is useful for designing, transferring or scaling designs.

<< **DRESSMAKER'S CARBON PAPER**
This is a permanent method of transferring designs to the wrong side of the fabric, using a marking wheel or pencil.

CUTTING EQUIPMENT

Scissors are absolutely essential in quiltmaking and you should have at least three pairs: one dedicated to cutting fabric; one for paper and wadding; and a small, sharp pair for snipping threads. A rotary cutter speeds up quiltmaking.

ROTARY CUTTER >>
Cutters come in numerous shapes and several blade sizes, as well as decorative-edge cutting blades.

SEAM RIPPER >>
Used for removing stitching that has gone awry and for "reverse sewing".

PINKING SHEARS
Useful for cutting fabric that tends to fray.

ROTARY RULER >>
With measurements broken into 3mm (⅛in) segments and angled lines for measuring 45- and 60-degree angles, rotary rulers can be square, rectangular, or triangular.

CRAFT KNIFE
This is invaluable for cutting stencils from template plastic.

SMALL SHARP SCISSORS
Use for snipping thread ends, clipping seams, and trimming and grading seam allowances. A specialized version of small scissors called appliqué scissors can be helpful in appliqué work. The blades are curved to protect layers that are not being trimmed from being damaged by sharp points, but they should not be seen as a replacement for your ordinary pair of small scissors.

FABRIC SCISSORS
These have bent handles, which allow the fabric to lie flat on the surface while you are cutting out your pieces.

SELF-HEALING MAT >>
Marked with a grid in 2.5cm (1in) increments, the surface material "heals" itself after cutting with a rotary cutter, leaving it smooth again without slits or grooves to catch the cutter next time you cut. Do not cut the top surface with a craft knife.

FABRIC
AND WADDING

The standard quilting fabric is 100 per cent cotton, which comes in a vast range of colours, patterns, and weaves and is easy to work. Wadding is used as the filling between the quilt layers. Use large frames or hoops to hold the layers in place while you quilt.

‹‹ PLAIN COTTON FABRICS
Plain fabrics are often used for the foundation of quilt designs and borders, and for the quilt backing.

‹‹ WADDING
Wadding is the soft middle layer between the quilt top and the backing. It is available in polyester, cotton, or a combination of the two. Wool and silk wadding is available for specialized work.

⌄ PRINTED FABRICS
Traditional patchwork quilts are constructed with printed fabrics, and small-scale prints work well together, especially if they share similar colour values.

CHECK FABRIC »
Checks work well combined with plains for simple patchwork or quilting designs.

MEDIUM-SCALE PRINTS »
Ideal for patchwork, medium-scale prints can be successfully combined with plain fabric and small-scale prints for texture and interest.

LARGE-SCALE PRINTS
Large-scale prints work best in large-size blocks. Individual motifs can be cut out and used in appliqué, or fussy cut for patchwork.

<< **HAND-DYED FABRIC**
The natural variations in hand-dyed fabrics look very attractive in quilted or patchwork projects.

DESIGN PRINCIPLES

Most patchwork and many appliqué quilts are based on patterns comprised of blocks – that is, squares made following the same pattern, which are then assembled to make the quilt top. This means that they can be broken down into working units that are easier to cope with than a large overall design. There are literally hundreds of existing blocks that you can make in fabrics and colours of your own choice but, once you understand the basic principles, it's fun to come up with patterns of your own.

PLANNING YOUR OWN BLOCKS

The main patchwork block categories are four-patch (see pages 311–312), nine-patch (see pages 313–314), five-patch and seven-patch (see pages 315–316). Each one lends itself to certain finished block sizes. Four-patch patterns can always be divided by even numbers, while nine-patch blocks are easiest to work with if the finished size is divisible by three. Five-patch and seven-patch patterns are more limited; they are multiples of 5 x 5 and 7 x 7 units (or patches) per block respectively.

If you want to design your own block pattern, start by deciding what size you want your finished block to be and draw it on paper, sub-dividing it into the relevant number of patches. Further sub-divide each patch into strips, triangles, smaller squares, or rectangles to create your design. When you are satisfied, transfer each element to another piece of paper and add a seam allowance to each side of each separate element.

With appliqué patterns, enlarge or reduce the pattern if necessary (see page 294) and copy it onto tracing paper. Decide which elements should be cut as separate pieces and trace them individually onto another piece of tracing paper so they can be cut out and used as patterns.

Many blocks can be super-sized by dramatically increasing the dimensions of a single block, making quilts of an ideal size for baby quilts. Combining several of these bigger blocks allows the quick creation of a full-size quilt.

USING TEMPLATES

Some elements require templates, which are copies of the pieces of the pattern. Ready-made templates are available from quilt stores and online. Find out if the seam allowances have been added. Elements to be machine pieced must include the exact seam allowances, while appliqué patterns and those for hand piecing do not need a precise allowance, but are generally cut larger than the finished shape. Many templates are cut with a "window" that shows the area of fabric you will finish up with; this also enables you to mark the seamline and the cutting line without moving the template. Alternatively, you can make your own long-lasting or limited-use templates following these instructions.

Limited-use templates using freezer paper: Trace the pattern pieces onto freezer paper and cut them out. Iron onto the wrong side of the fabric and then cut out around the shape.

Limited-use templates using tracing paper: Pin the template in place and cut out the shape, again adding the seam allowances by eye.

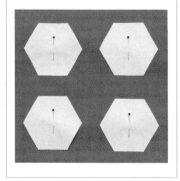

Durable templates using heavy card: Draw the shapes on paper or tracing paper. Cut them out, draw around them again on heavy card, and cut them out, or glue the shapes to card and cut out.

Durable templates using template plastic: Trace the shapes directly onto the template plastic, or cut the desired shapes from paper and glue them to template plastic. Cut them out with paper scissors.

UNDERSTANDING
COLOUR

Understanding the basic principles of colour theory is crucial to designing a successful quilt. Even a simple design gains impact from good colour choices. The three primary colours, red, yellow, and blue, can be placed side by side to create a colour wheel. When two adjacent colours are combined, they create "secondaries". Red and yellow make orange, yellow and blue make green, and blue and red make purple. Intermediate colours called tertiaries occur when a secondary is mixed with the nearest primary.

Colour wheel

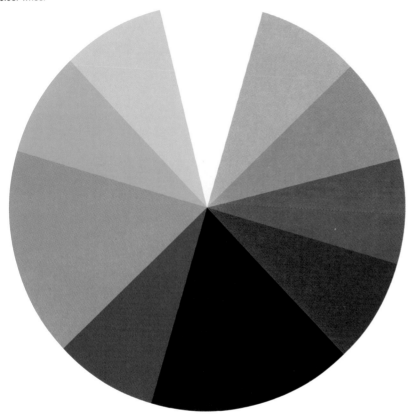

Complementary colours: Colours that lie opposite one another on the wheel, such as red and green, or yellow and violet, are called complementaries. They provide contrasts that accent design elements and make both colours stand out. Don't forget black and white, the ultimate opposites.

Colour temperature: Colour has a visual "temperature", with some colours being perceived as "warm" and others as "cool". Many people tend to think of blue and its adjacent colours as being cool, while the reds and yellows are warm, but in fact there are warm and cool versions of all the primaries; think, for example, of a warm, azure blue and a cold, icy blue. Colour temperature is an important element in whether a colour recedes or advances – that is, in whether it stands out from or blends in with the background and surrounding colours.

Colour tone: Tone, or value, is the relative lightness or darkness of a particular colour. While some fabrics are obviously dark or light in value, others take their value from the colours surrounding them. Almost all successful quilts rely on contrasting values. These are not necessarily just differences in their qualities of lightness and darkness, but in how the colours react to each other. A quilt made entirely of middle values, even if the colours themselves are quite different, will lack impact and eye appeal.

Monochromatic designs: These use different versions of the same colour. So a quilt based on greens will not stray into the red section of the colour wheel, but might have shades and tints of yellow and blue mixed in, which can then become "harmonious" combinations of colours that are next to each other on the colour wheel. These "adjacent" colours can also be combined to great effect, as long as there are differences in value between them.

FABRIC: PRINTS AND PLAINS

The scale: The size of the image – its scale – is an important factor when working with print fabrics. A large-scale pattern is generally more difficult to work with, but it can be used successfully, especially in bigger blocks. Try combining large prints with plain fabrics, especially conversation prints with themed motifs. These are useful for making quick-and-easy baby and children's quilts. Medium-scale prints can be fussy-cut (see page 298) quite effectively, and small-scale patterns are usually simple to use as they can be cut into small units that have a consistent look. There are also hand-dyed fabrics (or fabrics printed to look as if they have been hand dyed) and tone-on-tone fabrics that have tiny motifs printed on a background of the same colour that look almost like plain colours from a distance. These give more visual texture than a solid plain colour and can really help to bring a design to life.

Geometric-patterned fabrics: fabrics like stripes, checks, and tartans can make fascinating secondary patterns when they are cut and re-assembled. Widely used in country-style quilts, they need careful handling to be most effective. Stripes, in particular, can be set in different directions to create visual movement within a block, while checks and plaids can be combined with each other or with plain fabrics to great effect.

Borders and sashing: A plain colour can act as a foil to a busy print, giving the eye somewhere to rest and providing the keen quilter with a place to show off skills. Plain sashing (see page 359) can direct a viewer to the block pattern within, and while borders can be patterned and pieced, plain borders frame and contain a quilt in a special way. Balance – between prints and plains, lights and darks, warmth and coolness – is key to any successful design, and the more quilts you look at, and make, the better your judgement will become. One way to work is to choose a main print first and then coordinate the plains and other prints around it.

Creating a design wall: Working on a design wall is a good way to test how fabrics will look as it allows you to step back and view options from a distance. Hang a plain white sheet over a door to make a temporary version, or fashion a moveable one from foam board covered with white flannel over a layer of wadding. If you have room for a permanent version, mount cork or foam board on a wall in your sewing area.

GENERAL TECHNIQUES

Quiltmaking involves different stages, different techniques, and a multitude of ideas, but some aspects of making a quilt, whether it is pieced, appliquéd, or wholecloth, are the same. The skills outlined in this section will help you, whichever type of quilt you choose to make.

ALTERING THE SIZE OF A DESIGN OR PATTERN

The easiest way to alter the size of a motif is to photocopy it. To enlarge, take the size that you want the motif to be and divide it by the actual size of the template. Multiply that figure by 100. To reduce, divide the size that you want the motif to be by the actual size of the template and multiply by 100. You can also use gridded paper to alter the size of a design.

1 For non-geometric designs, trace the outline onto gridded paper. To make a pattern twice the size of the original, double the grid on another piece of paper. If you trace on 1cm (½in) squares, for example, increase the size of each square in your new grid to 2cm (1in).

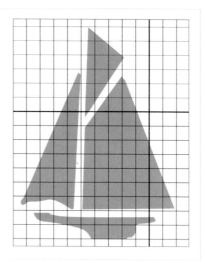

The original motif traced onto paper gridded into 1cm (½in) squares

2 Transfer the lines within each square to correspond to the original image. Trace the pattern again to smooth out any distortions.

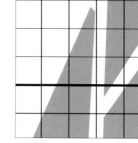

The motif enlarged onto a 2cm (1in) grid

PREPARING FABRIC

All cotton fabrics shrink a little during the first wash. Shrinkage is usually minimal, but it can distort the finished quilt. Using fabrics that have been washed with those that haven't can cause seams to pucker. Always test fabrics for colour fastness, especially dark ones. Before you start to cut, iron each piece and make sure the straight of grain is true by checking against the selvedge.

Fabric has three grains: the lengthways grain, (warp); the horizontal grain (weft); and the diagonal grain (bias). The rigid edge on each side is called the selvedge. The bias should be handled carefully as it stretches easily, which can lead to distortions.

Weft threads

Selvedge

Warp threads

TIPS

• **If you think colour may bleed,** test it by pressing a small damp piece of white fabric on the fabric to be used.

• **When prewashing fabric,** snip off a small triangle at each corner to prevent fraying. Washing small pieces of fabric in a lingerie bag will help prevent fraying.

• **Cut borders on the lengthways grain** to minimize stretching.

• **To find the lengthways grain,** pull it gently along both straight grains. The stretch will be greater along the weft, or widthways, grain.

• **Try to position bias edges** away from the edges of a block to minimize stretching and keep the size of the block accurate.

ROTARY CUTTING

Many of the most popular patterns can be rotary cut. You will need a rotary cutter, transparent plastic ruler, and a self-healing mat. When cutting a square into other shapes, such as right-angled triangles, start with a square that is larger than a simple square in the same size block, to allow for a seam allowance on bias seams.

BASIC ROTARY CUTTING

1 Fold washed and pressed fabric to fit on the mat. Place the ruler over the fabric that you intend to use. Level off the end of the fabric by cutting away from your body. Keep the hand holding the ruler steady and away from the cutter.

2 Turn the mat so as not to disturb the newly cut edge and place the ruler over the area that you want to use. Align the correct measurement on the ruler carefully along the vertical cut edge and line up the folded edge with a horizontal mark. Cut a strip of the desired width along the grain.

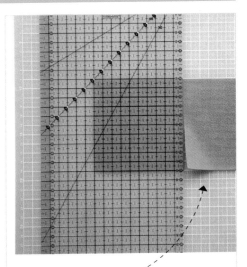

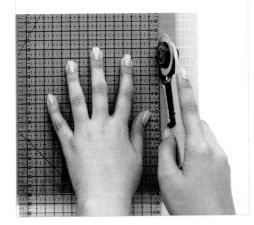

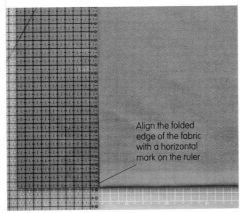

Align the folded edge of the fabric with a horizontal mark on the ruler

3 To cut strips into smaller units, position the cut strip horizontally on the mat and measure as before.

CUTTING SQUARES AND RECTANGLES

Squares and rectangles can also be cut using a square rotary ruler, which has a guideline marked across the diagonal from corner to corner. Add 2.25cm (⅞in) seam allowance for right-angle triangles and 2.75cm (1⅛in) for quarter-square triangles.

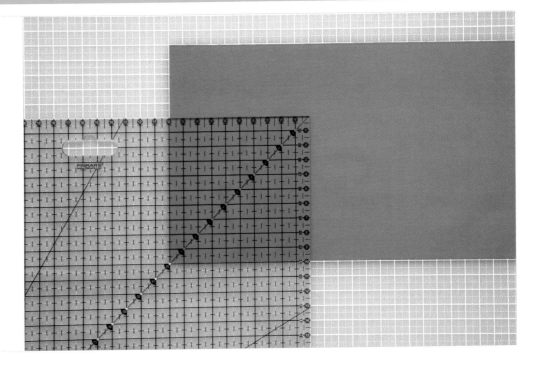

CUTTING PIECED STRIPS

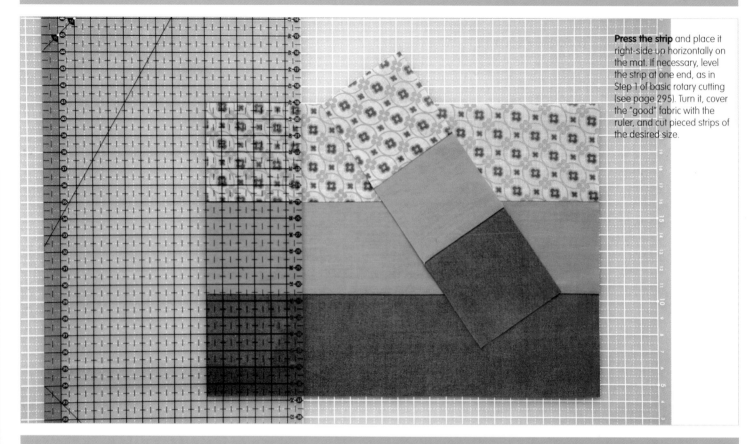

Press the strip and place it right-side up horizontally on the mat. If necessary, level the strip at one end, as in Step 1 of basic rotary cutting (see page 295). Turn it, cover the "good" fabric with the ruler, and cut pieced strips of the desired size.

CUTTING PIECED STRIPS ON THE BIAS

Trim one end of the pieced strip at a 45-degree angle, using the line marked on the ruler. Cut strips of the desired width at the same angle by measuring along the straight edge of the ruler.

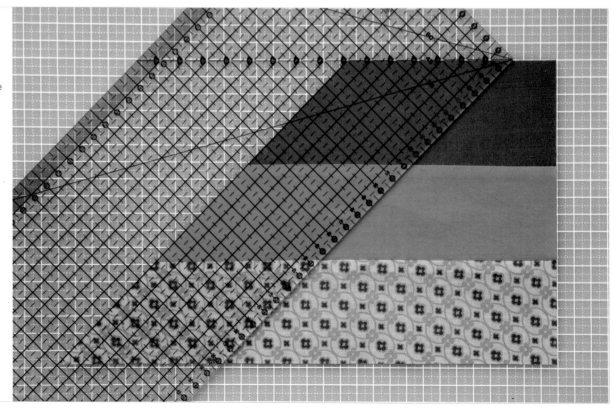

CUTTING TRUE BIAS STRIPS

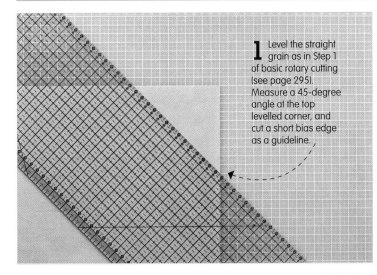

1 Level the straight grain as in Step 1 of basic rotary cutting (see page 295). Measure a 45-degree angle at the top levelled corner, and cut a short bias edge as a guideline.

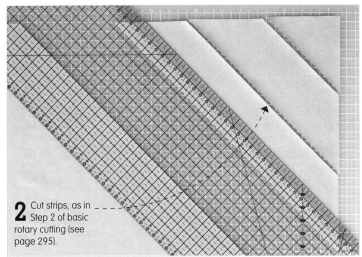

2 Cut strips, as in Step 2 of basic rotary cutting (see page 295).

CUTTING HALF-SQUARE TRIANGLES

Cut half-square triangles across the diagonal of a square, taking particular care when cutting the sides that are not on the straight of grain.

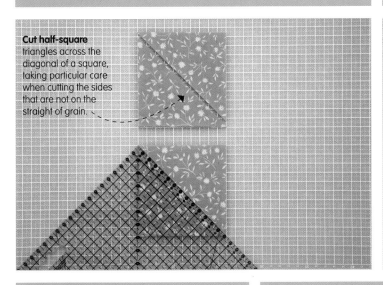

CUTTING QUARTER-SQUARE TRIANGLES

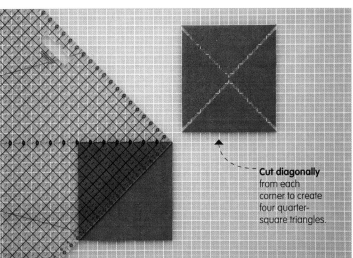

Cut diagonally from each corner to create four quarter-square triangles.

CUTTING IRREGULAR TRIANGLES

Cut a rectangle across the diagonal to create two irregular long triangles. For a matching pair, cut another rectangle starting at the opposite corner. Triangular rotary rulers are also available.

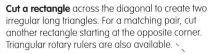
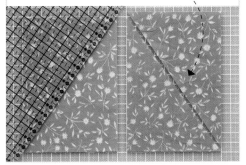

CUTTING 45 DEGREE DIAMONDS

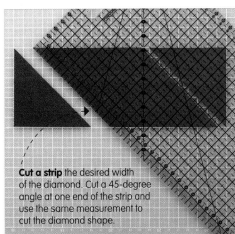

Cut a strip the desired width of the diamond. Cut a 45-degree angle at one end of the strip and use the same measurement to cut the diamond shape.

CUTTING CURVES

Gentle curves can also be rotary cut, but it is advisable to use a small blade.

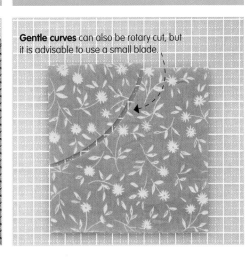

CUTTING BY
HAND

Quiltmakers generally cut with scissors if the pieces are small, or intricate, or have unusual angles or shapes. Appliqué motifs are almost always best cut by hand. You should keep at least one pair of good-quality sharp dressmaker's scissors dedicated only to cutting cloth. Paper, template plastic, wadding, and the like should not be cut with the same pair. Most quiltmakers have several pairs of scissors in different sizes.

CUTTING WITHOUT A PATTERN

1 Mark the outline of the shape to be cut on the wrong side of the fabric and add a seam.

2 Using fabric scissors, cut out the shape along the marked cutting line – or cut a short distance away if only the stitching line is marked.

CUTTING WITH A PATTERN

Patterns made from paper are familiar to dressmakers, and sometimes they provide an easy way for quiltmakers to cut a few similar shapes. Pin the pattern to the fabric and cut around it, adding the seam allowance if necessary.

FUSSY CUTTING

This is a method of isolating particular motifs in printed fabric and cutting them to show as a feature in a block of patchwork or appliqué. It can seem wasteful of fabric, but the results are usually worth it. It is easier to delineate the desired area if you cut a window template to the finished size and shape.

UNPICKING
SEAMS

Everyone makes mistakes and sometimes seams must be removed; moreover, some patterns depend on taking out seams during construction. It is vital that the ripping-out process does not stretch the fabric edges. Unpicking works best on seams that haven't been pressed. Never use scissors to unpick a seam.

METHOD 1

1 Hold the seam open and insert the point of the unpicker between the layers to break the thread.

2 Pull the seam apart gently as you work to the end of the seam.

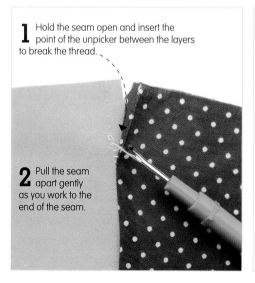

METHOD 2

1 Hold the seam taut and insert the point of the unpicker into every third or fourth stitch, breaking the thread as you work your way along the seam.

2 Hold the bottom strip flat and pull gently on the top strip to separate the layers. Do not use this method on bias seams.

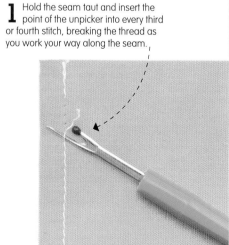

STARTING AND FINISHING

Securing the thread at the beginning and end of any stitching is, of course, essential. Traditional hand sewing begins and ends with a knot at the end of the thread, but knots can interfere with quilting and sometimes show on the quilt top. There are several knots that are useful for quiltmaking, including quilters' knots (see page 367). Backstitched loops have almost no depth to them and are a secure way of tying off.

THREADING A NEEDLE

1 Thread the end of the thread that comes off the reel through the eye of the needle, then cut the desired length. Working in the same direction as the spinning process that wraps the thread around the reel means that it is less likely to knot and tangle as you work.

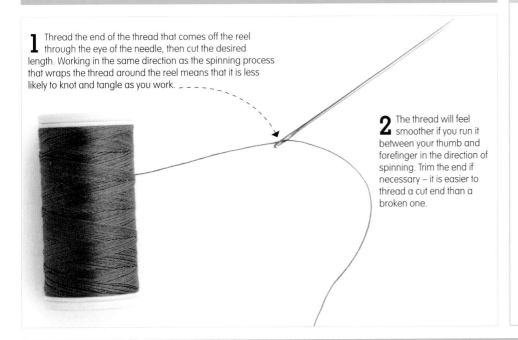

2 The thread will feel smoother if you run it between your thumb and forefinger in the direction of spinning. Trim the end if necessary – it is easier to thread a cut end than a broken one.

TIPS

● **Thread weight:** Use a thread weight appropriate to the needle size and a needle size appropriate to the weight of the fabric.

● **Thread length:** Keep the thread length to no more than 50cm (18in) long, as it is less likely to kink and fray.

● **Needle threader:** Use a needle threader if you have difficulty getting the thread through the eye.

● **Cutting direction:** Always cut away from your body when possible.

● **Knot size:** Knots make a lump wherever they occur, so make sure that they are small so that they can be hidden easily.

WRAPPED KNOT

1 For a knot that is suitable in quiltmaking, wrap the end of the thread around the shaft of the needle three times, leaving a 10mm (½in) tail. (For a bigger knot, use more wraps.)

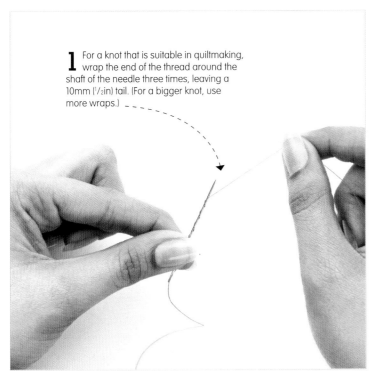

2 Anchor the wraps with your thumb and forefinger, and pull the needle through gently with your other hand. Hold the wraps until the knot is tight at the end of the thread.

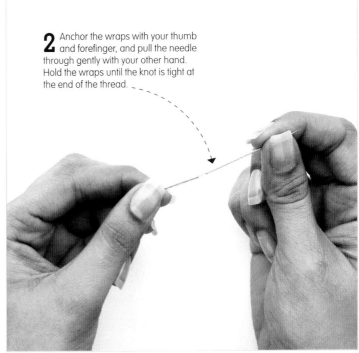

BACK-STITCHED LOOP

1 This method doesn't have the bulk of a knot but is secure. Back stitch once at the end of a line of stitching, and pull the needle through; do not pull the thread taut, but leave a small loop of thread.

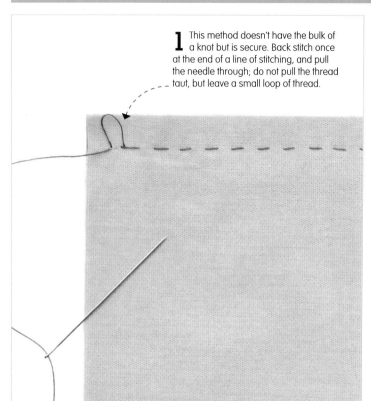

2 Take the needle through the loop and pull the thread tight.

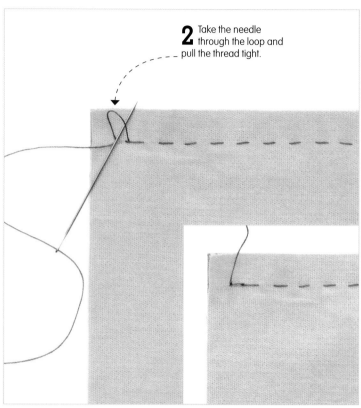

DOUBLE BACK-STITCHED LOOP

1 This method is even more secure. Back stitch once at the end of a line of stitching, leaving a small loop of thread as in Step 1 of the backstitched loop. Insert the tip of the needle through the loop and pull it through to form a second loop, creating a figure of eight.

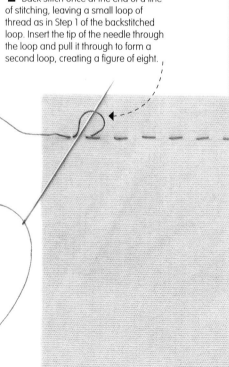

2 Insert the tip of the needle through the second loop.

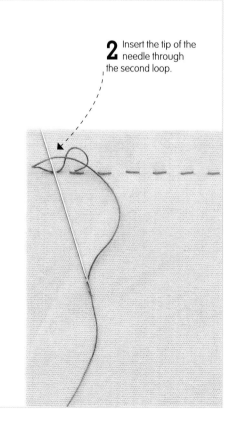

3 Pull the thread taut to form a knot.

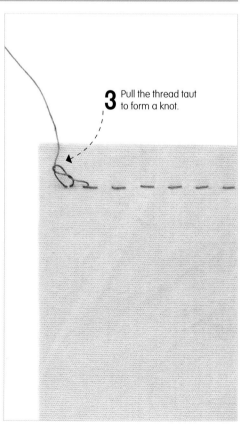

HAND STITCHES
FOR QUILTMAKING

Although most quilts today are made on a machine, there are a number of techniques that are hand sewn and it is important to choose the correct stitch for the best result.

RUNNING STITCH

This is the most common stitch for hand piecing. Take the needle in and out of the fabric several times, taking small, evenly spaced stitches. Pull the needle through gently until the thread is taut, but not tense. Repeat to the end of the seam.

STAB STITCH

This stitch is useful for sewing several layers or thick fabrics and is popular for quilting.

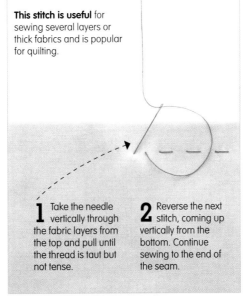

1 Take the needle vertically through the fabric layers from the top and pull until the thread is taut but not tense.

2 Reverse the next stitch, coming up vertically from the bottom. Continue sewing to the end of the seam.

BACK STITCH

Back stitch can be used in rows instead of running stitch to join units; it is also recommended as single stitches to make seams more secure. Bring the needle through all the layers to the right side, then insert it a short distance behind the entry point. Bring it up to the right side of the fabric again, the same distance in front of the point from which it first emerged. Repeat to the end of the seam.

OVERSEWING

Also known as whipstitch and overcasting, oversewing is used to join two edges with an almost invisible seam. Bring the needle through the back edge to the front, picking up a few threads from each side. Pull gently and repeat.

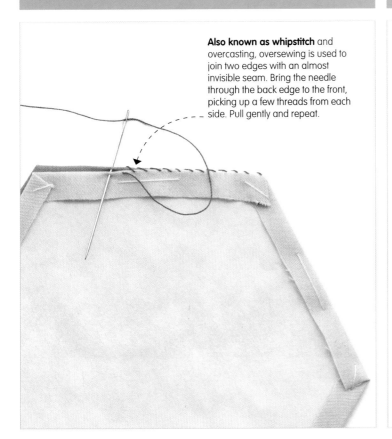

SLIP STITCH

Used mainly in appliqué, slip stitch makes an invisible line of stitching. Knot the thread and hide the knot in the folded edge of the top piece. Pull the needle through and pick up a thread or two on the back piece. Take the needle through the top piece next to this stitch and slide it along the fold in the fabric a short distance. Repeat, catching a few threads on each piece with each stitch.

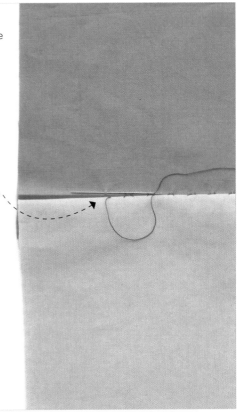

PATCHWORK

The majority of quilt tops, traditional and contemporary, are patchwork. While many of the basic techniques are the same or overlap, each method has its own issues and solutions. While making a patchwork quilt by machine is quicker, sewing by hand offers a satisfying pastime for many quiltmakers.

HAND PIECING

Mark all seamlines on the wrong side of the fabric as guides to accuracy. Take care when sewing seams on bias-cut edges (on diamond, triangle, or hexagon shapes) or around curves, as the raw edge is prone to stretching. Secure the seam with a small backstitch each time you bring the needle through and use a double backstitched loop (see page 300) at the end of a bias seam; do not sew into the seam allowance.

SEWING STRAIGHT SEAMS

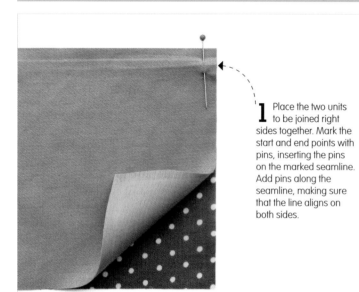

1 Place the two units to be joined right sides together. Mark the start and end points with pins, inserting the pins on the marked seamline. Add pins along the seamline, making sure that the line aligns on both sides.

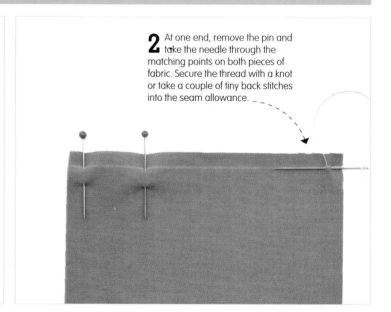

2 At one end, remove the pin and take the needle through the matching points on both pieces of fabric. Secure the thread with a knot or take a couple of tiny back stitches into the seam allowance.

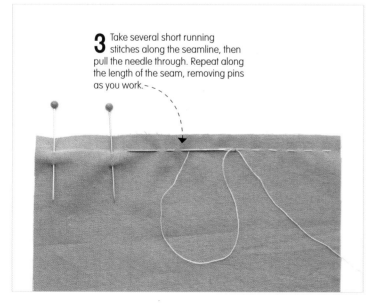

3 Take several short running stitches along the seamline, then pull the needle through. Repeat along the length of the seam, removing pins as you work.

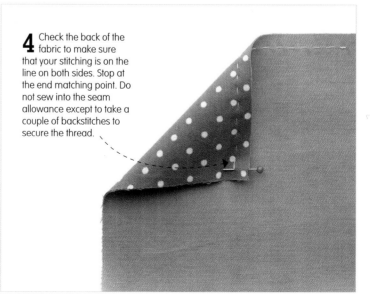

4 Check the back of the fabric to make sure that your stitching is on the line on both sides. Stop at the end matching point. Do not sew into the seam allowance except to take a couple of backstitches to secure the thread.

SEWING CURVED SEAMS

1 Mark the seamlines and any registration marks, especially the centre point, on the wrong side of each piece. If the centre isn't marked on the pattern, fold each piece in half, fingerpress it at the centre seamline, and use the crease as the centre mark.

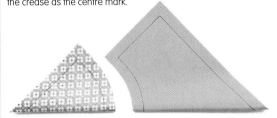

2 Place the smaller convex piece right sides together on the concave one, aligning the centre points. Pin the centre point through both pieces.

Pin the end and centre points through both pieces

Pin along the seamline, distributing the fabric evenly

3 Pin the end points of the marked seamline. Then pin along the seamline every 8mm (³⁄₈in) or so, manipulating the fabric to eliminate creases.

4 Take out the pin at one end and take the needle through the matching points. If you don't wish to use a knot, use a double backstitched loop in the seamline to secure the thread. (Do not sew into the seam allowance as you would for machine-piecing curved seams.)

5 Take several short running stitches along the seamline, then pull the needle through. Repeat along the length of the seam, removing pins as you work. The seam will be more secure if you take a small backstitch each time you bring the needle through.

6 Check the back to make sure your stitching is on the line on both sides and stop at the matching point at the end. Do not sew into the seam allowance, but use a double backstitched loop to secure the thread. Do not clip the seam allowance.

7 Press the seam towards the convex piece. If your stitching is accurate, the piece will lie flat.

SETTING-IN BY HAND

1 Diamonds and triangles sometimes meet at oblique angles. To set a piece into the resulting space needs careful pinning and sewing. Here, a square is set in the space between two diamond shapes. Cut the square to size and mark the seamlines. Match one corner of the square to the inner point on the first diamond and pin, right sides together. Then match the outer point and pin. Pin the edges together along the marked seamline.

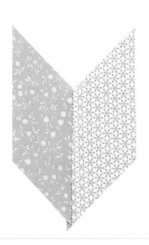

2 Sew along the marked seamline from the outer point to the inner, removing pins as you work. Take a few small backstitches into the seam at the inner corner, avoiding the seam allowance. Do not cut the thread.

3 Match the adjacent side of the square to the corresponding side of the diamond. Pin. Sew as in Step 2.

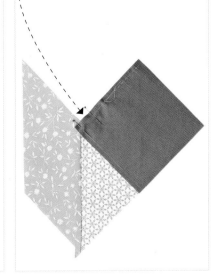

Wrong side

4 Press the seam allowances on the square towards the diamonds.

PATCHWORK, APPLIQUÉ, AND QUILTING

JOINING ROWS BY HAND

Because hand-pieced seams stop at the seam allowance, you need to match corners in a different way from machine piecing when joining rows.

1 Match the seamlines of the rows to be joined right sides together. Pin through both layers at the matching point at every corner of the row. Align the seamlines and pin at various points to make sure the seams are accurate on both sides.

2 Start sewing at one end of the row, working as for straight seams (see page 302), until you reach the first join.

3 Sew through the matching points on both layers, avoiding all the seam allowances.

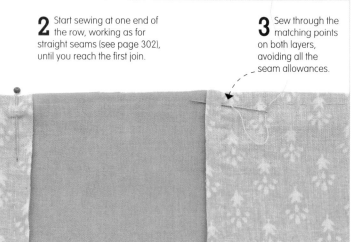

4 Take a stitch in the second pair of units, then back stitch next to the seam allowance.

5 Continue in this way to the end of the row and tie off with a back-stitched loop.

6 Press the seams on each row to opposite sides and press the just-completed seam to the other side.

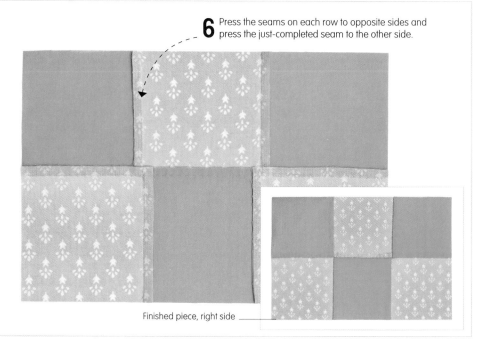

Finished piece, right side

MACHINE
PIECING

Stitching patchwork pieces by machine is a quick way of assembling a piece. As for hand piecing, always ensure that your fabrics are aligned with right sides facing and with raw edges matching. Take a 5mm (¼in) seam allowance and use a standard straight stitch.

PIECED STRIPS

1 Place two contrasting strips of fabric right sides together, raw edges aligned. Sew a straight 5mm (¼in) seam along the strip.

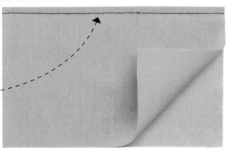

2 Press the seam towards the darker fabric.

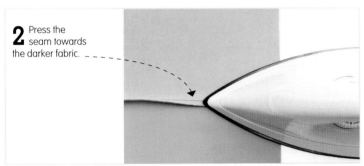

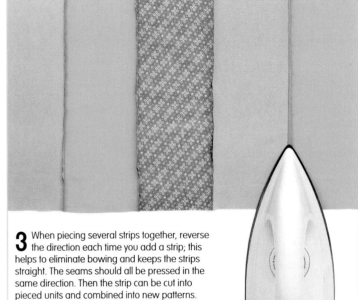

3 When piecing several strips together, reverse the direction each time you add a strip; this helps to eliminate bowing and keeps the strips straight. The seams should all be pressed in the same direction. Then the strip can be cut into pieced units and combined into new patterns.

CHAIN PIECING

1 Feed the units through the machine in sequence without lifting the presser foot or breaking the thread, so that they form a chain, leaving a short length of thread between each.

 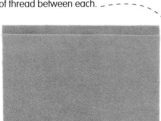  

2 Cut the units in the chain apart, using a small, sharp pair of scissors.

TRIANGLE SQUARES

1 To make a unit made of two right-angle triangles, cut two squares of contrasting fabric and place them right sides together, with the lighter colour on top.

2 Using a pencil, mark a diagonal line in one direction across the wrong side of the lighter-coloured square.

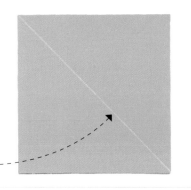

3 Machine stitch on each side of the marked line, stitching 5mm (¼in) from the line. Pivot without breaking the thread.

4 Using a rotary cutter or scissors, cut along the central pencil line. Open out the pieces of fabric and press the seams towards the darker fabric to make two identical triangle squares.

Wrong side

Right side

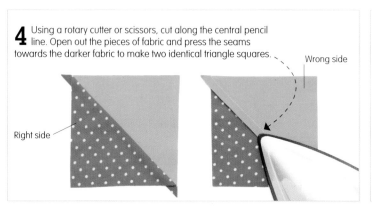

5 Trim the "dog-ear" points at each end of the seam.

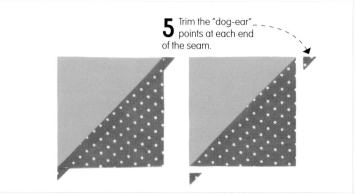

MULTIPLE TRIANGLE STRIPS

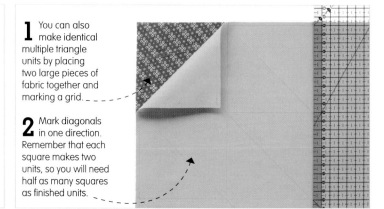

1 Multiple units of triangle squares can be made by cutting strips that are the width you want the finished squares to be plus 15mm (⅞in). Place them right sides together and mark squares on the wrong side of the lighter-coloured strip.

2 Draw a diagonal line across each square, alternating the direction of the line.

3 Place the strips right sides together with the lighter-coloured strip on top. Sew a 5mm (¼in) seam on each side of the marked diagonal lines, as described above.

4 Cut along the marked lines to separate triangles and press, as above.

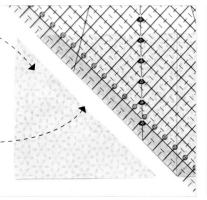

IDENTICAL MULTIPLE STRIPS

1 You can also make identical multiple triangle units by placing two large pieces of fabric together and marking a grid.

2 Mark diagonals in one direction. Remember that each square makes two units, so you will need half as many squares as finished units.

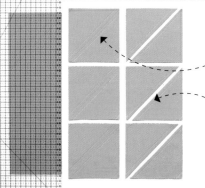

3 Machine stitch on either side of each marked diagonal line, stitching 5mm (¼in) from the lines.

4 Using a rotary cutter, cut the fabric into squares along the marked lines and then into triangles. Press.

QUARTER-SQUARE TRIANGLES

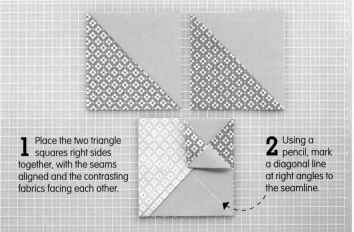

1 Place the two triangle squares right sides together, with the seams aligned and the contrasting fabrics facing each other.

2 Using a pencil, mark a diagonal line at right angles to the seamline.

3 Sew a 5mm (¼in) seam on each side of the marked line.

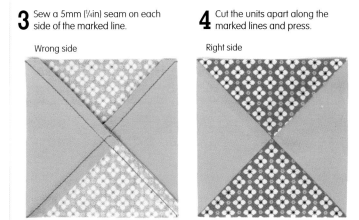

Wrong side

Right side

4 Cut the units apart along the marked lines and press.

JOINING PIECED AND PLAIN UNITS

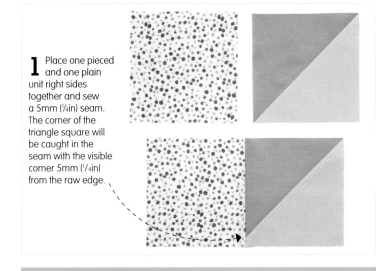

1 Place one pieced and one plain unit right sides together and sew a 5mm (¼in) seam. The corner of the triangle square will be caught in the seam with the visible corner 5mm (¼in) from the raw edge.

2 Combining two of these units takes up the seam allowance and means that the corners meet in the centre.

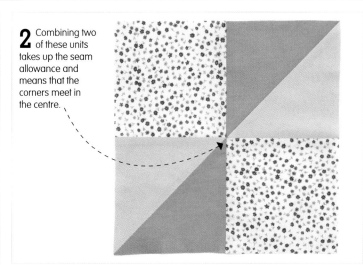

CURVED SEAMS

1 Make templates and mark the centre of the curve on each one. Cut out the fabric pieces, adding a 5mm (¼in) seam allowance.

2 Centre the templates on the wrong side of your fabric pieces, draw around them to mark the seam allowances, then mark the centre point of the curve on the fabric pieces.

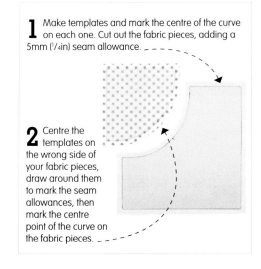

3 Pin the two fabric pieces together at the centre point on the seam allowance, then pin at each end.

4 Pin along the edge to stabilize the curve.

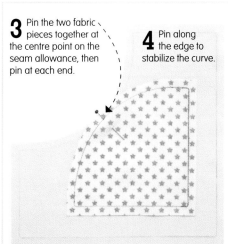

5 Stitch along the marked curve without stretching or pulling. Remove the pins as you sew.

6 Press the seam towards the larger piece. It should lie flat without being clipped.

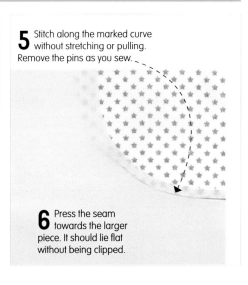

SET-IN SEAMS

1 Using a pencil or fabric marker, make a dot 5mm (¹/₄in) in from each end of the two pieces that are to be joined first. This marks the point where you start and finish stitching: do not to go to the very end of the seam.

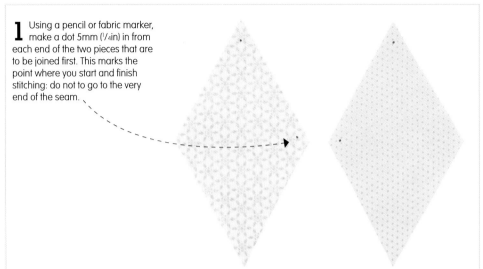

2 Place the shapes right sides together and sew from dot to dot, backstitching at each end. Do not overshoot the dots.

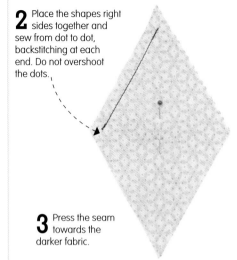

3 Press the seam towards the darker fabric.

4 On the wrong side of the piece that is to be set in, mark a dot 5mm (¹/₄in) in at the three corners of the piece.

Dot

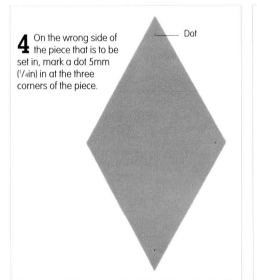

5 Match the middle marked corner of the piece that is to be set in with the corresponding dot on one of the two pieces that have already been joined. Pin the seam at each end and sew from the inside corner to the outer dot.

6 Match the outer dot on the second side of the piece that is to be set in with the outer dot on the other shape. Pin them together at the dot and sew, again stitching from the inside corner to the outer dot.

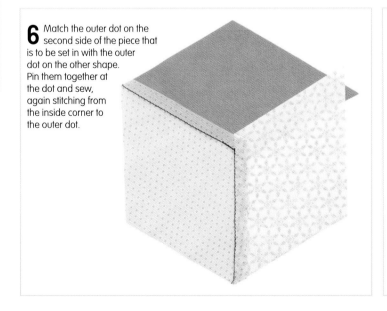

7 Press the unit flat.

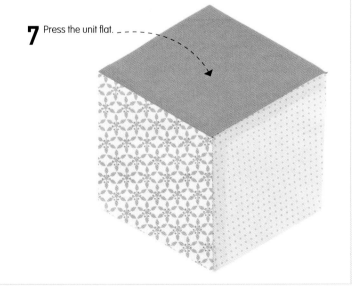

PRESSING

Pressing is essential when making accurate patchwork. When pressing, press down in one place, then lift the iron and move it before pressing down on another area. Ironing causes fabric and seams to distort. Set pieces aside to cool after each pressing and always press the seam towards the darker fabric to prevent darker colours from showing through. The temperature of the iron should be appropriate to the fabric.

PRESSING STRAIGHT SEAMS

1 Place the unit or sewn strips with right sides together on the board. Press the iron along the seam. Keep the darker fabric on top and lift the iron at regular intervals. This is called setting the seam, and helps ensure accuracy by locking the threads and smoothing the fibres. – – – – –

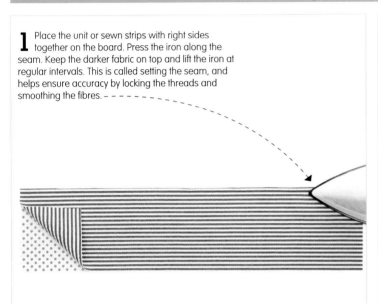

2 Open the pieces and press from one end to the other. If you keep the lighter piece nearest you and press with the tip of the iron, you can press the seam to the darker side at the same time as you open the unit. – – – – –

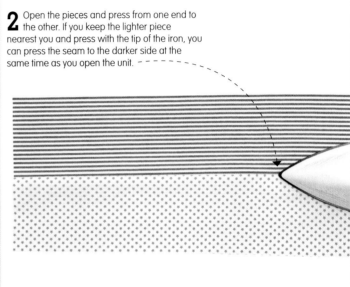

PRESSING BIAS SEAMS

Work along the straight grain to keep from pulling the seam out of shape.

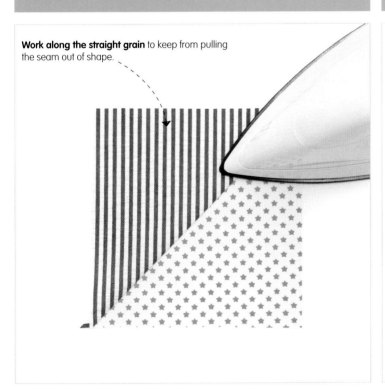

WORKING IN ROWS

Press the seams in adjoining rows in opposite directions to eliminate bulkiness at the joins.

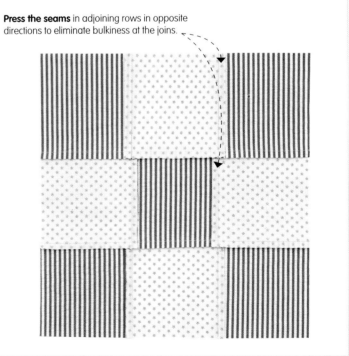

PRESSING A PIECED BLOCK

Place the block wrong side up on the ironing board. Do not press hard, but make sure the seams lie as flat as possible.

PRESSING SEAMS OPEN

Where several seams meet, you may need to press seams open to reduce bulk. After setting the seam as in Step 1 of Pressing straight seams (see page 309), open the seam and press along the length with the tip of the iron.

THUMBNAIL

Work on a hard surface. Open the unit out and press first on the wrong side, then on the right, running your thumbnail gently but firmly along the seamline so that the fabric is pressed towards the darker fabric.

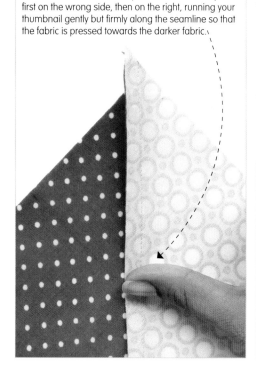

LITTLE WOODEN IRON

Place the flat, chisel-shaped edge of the tool on the seamline and run it gently along the seam.

HERA

A hera is a plastic, blade-like device. It is used in certain embroidery techniques but is also useful for fingerpressing.

FOUR-PATCH
BLOCKS

A simple four-patch block consists of four equal square units joined two by two. It relies on a strong contrast of value to be most effective. Individual units can be pieced to provide variety and secondary patterns. A double four-patch consists of sixteen units made up of four four-patch units.

STRIP-PIECED FOUR-PATCH BLOCK

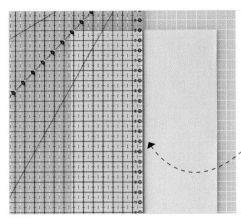

1 Using a rotary cutter, cut two contrasting strips across the width of the fabric. Here, the finished block will be 15cm (6in) square, so each unit will be 7.5cm (3in) wide, plus a 1cm (½in) seam allowance – so we cut 8.5cm (3½in) wide strips.

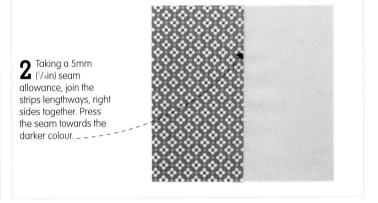

2 Taking a 5mm (¼in) seam allowance, join the strips lengthways, right sides together. Press the seam towards the darker colour.

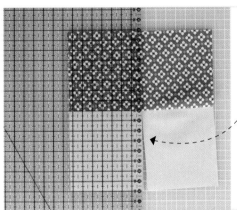

3 Cut the pieced strip across the seam into units 8.5cm (3½in) wide, the same width as the original strips.

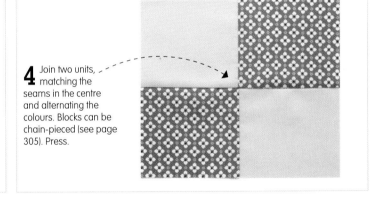

4 Join two units, matching the seams in the centre and alternating the colours. Blocks can be chain-pieced (see page 305). Press.

MAKING INDIVIDUAL BLOCKS

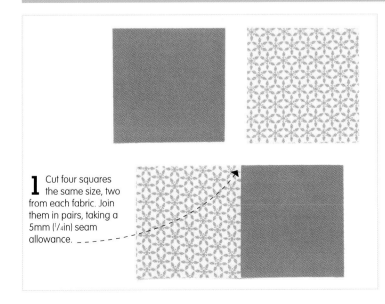

1 Cut four squares the same size, two from each fabric. Join them in pairs, taking a 5mm (¼in) seam allowance.

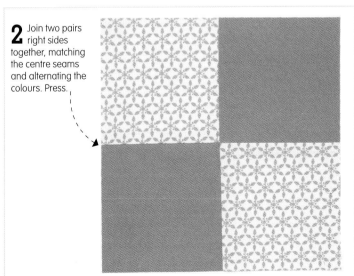

2 Join two pairs right sides together, matching the centre seams and alternating the colours. Press.

COMBINING PIECED AND PLAIN UNITS

1 Make two four-patch blocks. Cut two squares the same size as the pieced blocks from a third fabric.

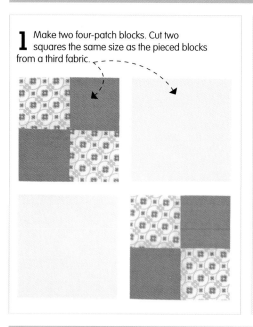

2 Join the blocks in pairs, taking a 5mm (¼in) seam allowance, and press.

3 Join the two pairs right sides together, matching the centre seams and alternating the colours. Press.

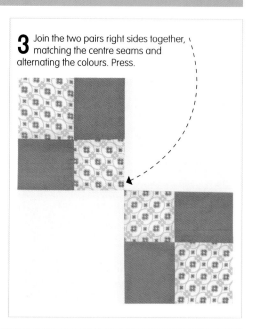

PIECED FOUR-PATCH BLOCK

1 Make four identical half-square triangle units (see page 306).

2 Join them in pairs and press.

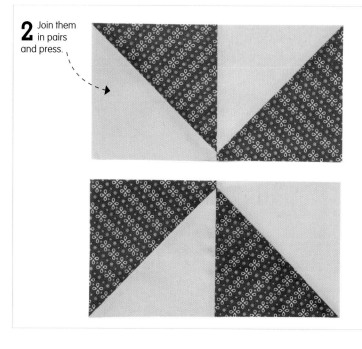

3 Join the two pairs together to complete the block. The block shown here is a traditional pattern known as Pinwheel.

NINE-PATCH
BLOCKS

Nine-patch blocks, based on three rows of three squares each, are among the most versatile and widely used patchwork patterns. Each unit in the grid can either be a plain colour or pieced, resulting in a huge variety of patterns. In Double Nine-patch, small nine-patch units are combined in a larger nine-patch grid. As with four-patch blocks, units can be subdivided to form complex patterns.

INDIVIDUAL NINE-PATCH BLOCKS

1 Cut nine squares the same size, five from fabric A and four from fabric B.

Cut 5 from fabric A

Cut 4 from fabric B

2 Arrange them in a grid, A–B–A, B–A–B, A–B–A. Join them in three rows of three, matching the seams and taking a 5mm (1/4in) seam allowance.

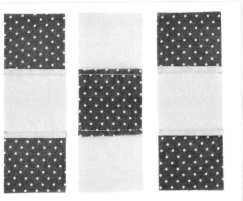

3 Join the three rows to complete the block.

STRIP-PIECED NINE-PATCH BLOCK

1 Using a rotary cutter, cut strips across the width of the fabric from two contrasting fabrics. Here, the finished block will be 15cm (6in) square, so each strip will be 5cm (2in) deep plus a 10mm (1/2in) seam allowance. Arrange the strips to alternate fabrics, A–B–A and B–A–B, and join them taking a 5mm (1/4in) seam. Press towards the darker fabric.

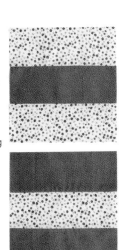

2 Cut both pieced strips across the seams into units 5cm + 1cm (2in + 1/2in) wide. Note that the cut strips are the same width as the original strips.

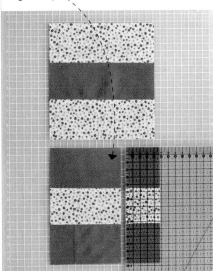

3 Arrange the cut strips in rows of three, alternating the A and B fabrics, and join them, matching the seams. Blocks can be chain-pieced (see page 305). Press.

PIECED NINE-PATCH BLOCK: JACOB'S LADDER

1 Make five Four-patch blocks using fabrics A and B (see page 311).

Make 5

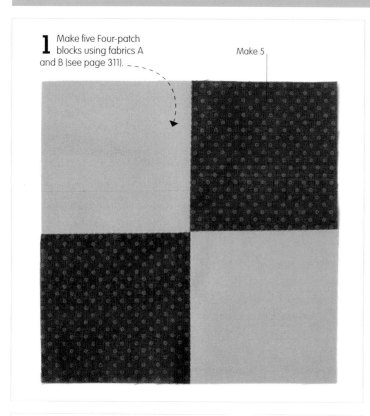

2 Make four triangle squares the same size, using fabrics A and C (see page 306).

Make 4

3 Arrange the units in rows, as shown, and join them, taking a 5mm (¹/₄in) seam allowance. Press the seams in opposite directions in each row.

4 Join the three rows, matching the seams and taking a 5mm (¹/₄in) seam allowance. Press.

FIVE- AND SEVEN-PATCH BLOCKS

Five-patch consists of a grid of five units in each direction, or 25 units in total. Seven-patch blocks have seven units each way, for a total of 49. Because these numbers don't divide easily, the size of the finished block should be carefully considered when planning a quilt to make cutting easier. They lend themselves to larger finished blocks – 35, 37.5, 50, or 52.5cm (14, 15, 20 or 21in) – so you need fewer to make a quilt.

FIVE-PATCH: LADY OF THE LAKE

1 Divide the size of the finished block by five to determine the size of each unit. Add a 10mm (½in) seam allowance.

2 Cut three squares from fabric A and three from fabric B. Make 19 triangle squares the same size from fabrics A and B (see page 306).

Cut 3 from fabric A

Cut 3 from fabric B

Make 19 from fabrics A and B

3 Following the layout carefully, combine the units into five rows of five units each, taking 5mm (¼in) seam allowances. Make sure the triangle squares face in the correct direction.

4 Join the five rows together, matching the seams and taking 5mm (¼in) seam allowances. Press.

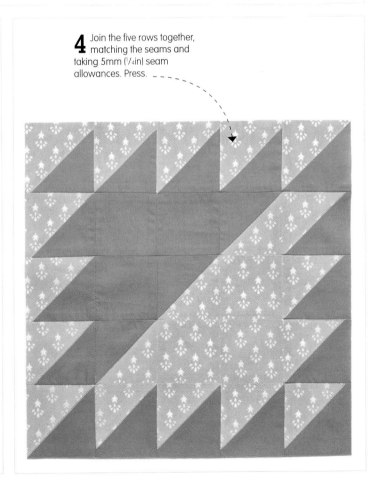

SEVEN-PATCH: BEAR'S PAW

1 Divide the size of the finished block by seven to determine the size of each unit. Add a 10mm (1/2in) seam allowance to this measurement and cut one centre square from fabric A. Cut four squares the same size from fabric B for the corner squares. The arms of the centre cross are one unit wide and three units long. Add the seam allowance and cut four strips from fabric B. The large squares are two units by two. Add the seam allowance and cut four large squares from fabric C.

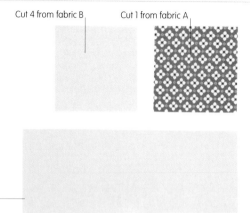

Cut 4 from fabric B   Cut 1 from fabric A

Cut 4 from fabric B

Cut 4 from fabric C

2 Make 16 triangle squares from fabrics A and B (see page 306). Join them in pairs, taking a 5mm (1/4in) seam allowance.

Make 16 from fabrics A and B

3 Following the layout carefully, add a corner square to four pairs of triangle squares, taking a 5mm (1/4in) seam allowance. Note that two of the strips face in the opposite direction to the other two.

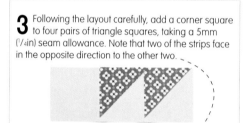

4 Join one of the remaining pairs of triangle squares to one side of each large fabric C square, taking a 5mm (1/4in) seam allowance. Note that two of the strips face in one direction and two the opposite way.

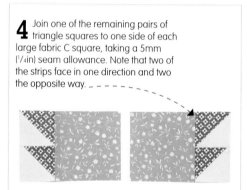

5 Following the layout and matching seams carefully, join one strip from Step 3 to one side of each unit made in Step 4. Note that two sets will face in one direction and two will face the opposite way.

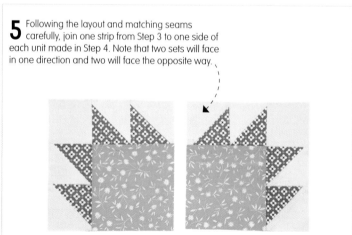

7 Join one short side of the two remaining centre strips to opposite sides of the centre square.

6 Join one large unit to each long side of two centre strips.

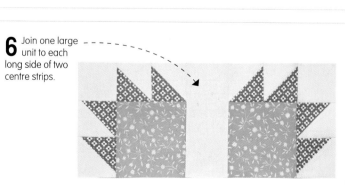

8 Join the three rows to finish the block.

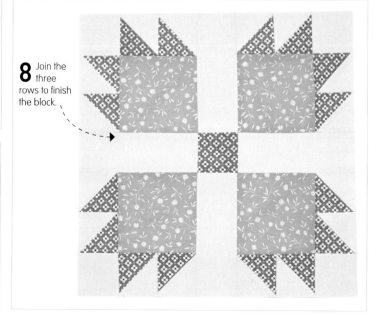

STRIP PIECING

Strip piecing is a good way to build blocks quickly. In principle, several long strips are joined and then cut apart before being stitched together again in a different sequence. It is the method by which many blocks are made, including log cabin (see pages 319–321) and seminole patchwork (see pages 321–323).

STRIP-PIECED BLOCKS: RAIL FENCE

1 From three contrasting fabrics, cut three strips of equal width. Join them lengthways taking a 5mm (¼in) seam allowance. To prevent the pieced strip from bowing, sew to the end of strips 1 and 2, then reverse the direction to add strip 3. Press the seams to one side away from the centre.

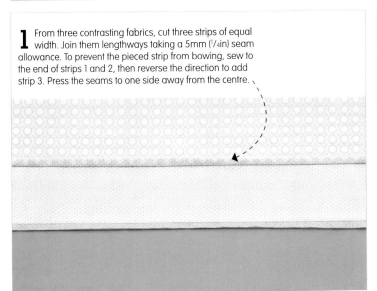

2 Using a rotary cutter, cut across the seams to make squares the same size as the width of the pieced strip set.

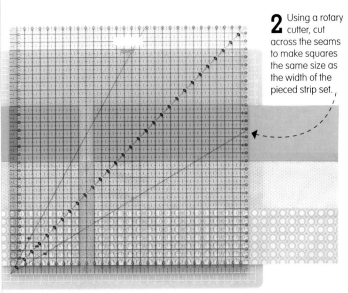

3 Following the layout, arrange the squares in rows.

4 Join the squares to make three horizontal rows, taking a 5mm (¼in) seam allowance. Press, alternating the direction in each row.

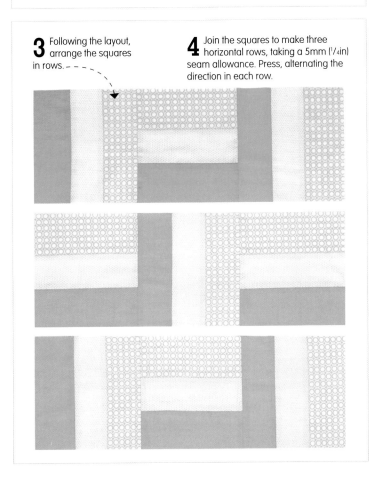

5 Join the rows, matching the seams and taking a 5mm (¼in) seam allowance.

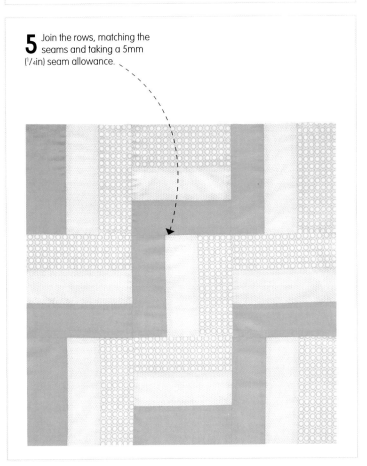

STRING
PIECING

String piecing is similar to strip piecing, but the lengths of fabric are referred to as "strings" and are not necessarily straight strips. This is a good way of using up leftover pieces of uneven widths. String-pieced blocks can be combined to make larger units.

METHOD 1

1 Select a number of "strings" of fabric with plenty of contrast in colour and pattern. Join them lengthways, taking a 5mm (¼in) seam allowance. Alternate the angle in each piece and the direction of stitching to keep the finished piece even.

2 Press the seams to one side. Trim the piece to the desired size and shape.

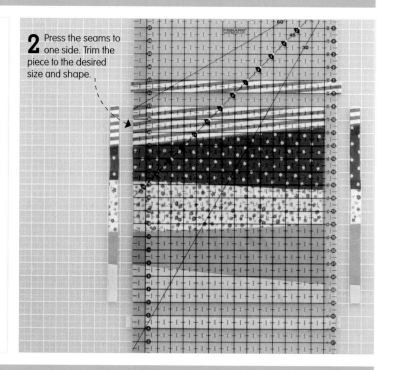

METHOD 2

1 Cut a muslin or paper foundation block, plus seam allowances. Place the first string right-side up in the centre of the foundation and lay the second piece right-side down on top. Make sure both pieces are longer than the widest point on the foundation.

2 Machine stitch along one edge of the strips through all layers. Flip the pieces open and press.

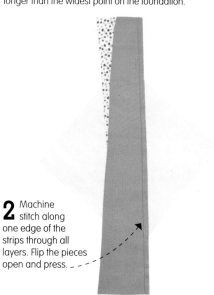

3 Turn the foundation and add a new string, right-side down, to the opposite edge of the first piece. Flip it open and press.

4 Continue to add strings, flip, press, and stitch, until the foundation is covered. Trim the edges level with the foundation. Leave a 5mm (¼in) allowance if the foundation is to be removed. Carefully tear away paper foundations. Press.

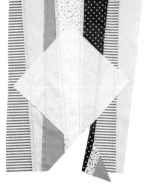

Finished piece

LOG
CABIN

Log Cabin is perhaps the most versatile block of all. Blocks can be made individually or chain-pieced. Log Cabin lends itself to scrap quilting if the values have a strong contrast, and is stunning in simple two-colour versions. The crucial centre piece can be virtually any shape, and the order of piecing can vary. Blocks can be set (see page 357) in many ways to create secondary patterns. Always use a 5mm (1/4in) seam allowance.

METHOD 1: INDIVIDUAL BLOCKS

1 Cut a centre square of the desired size, plus seam allowances. Cut a second square the same size from fabric A and join them right sides together along one edge. Press open.

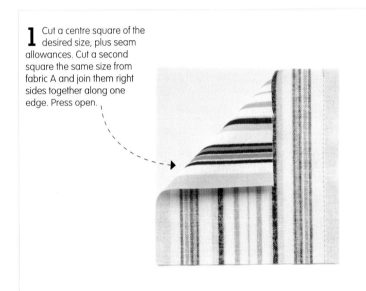

2 Cut strip 3 from fabric A the width of the centre square and the same length as the pressed unit and join it right sides together along the long side. Start at the corner of the second square and finish at the bottom of the centre square. Press open.

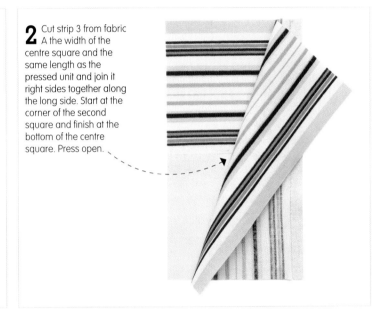

3 Now add two strips from fabric B in the same way, working in a clockwise direction to help the centre stay square.

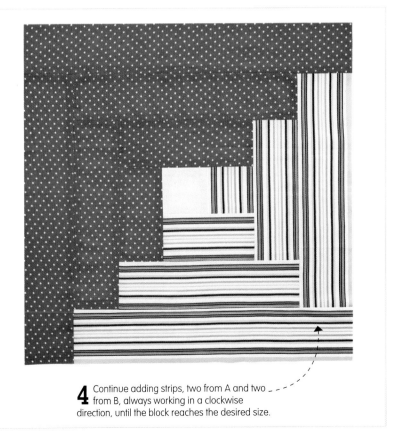

4 Continue adding strips, two from A and two from B, always working in a clockwise direction, until the block reaches the desired size.

METHOD 2: CHAIN PIECING

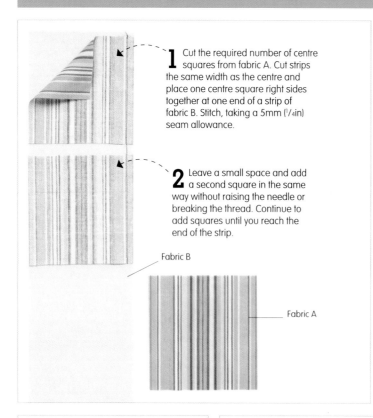

1 Cut the required number of centre squares from fabric A. Cut strips the same width as the centre and place one centre square right sides together at one end of a strip of fabric B. Stitch, taking a 5mm (¼in) seam allowance.

2 Leave a small space and add a second square in the same way without raising the needle or breaking the thread. Continue to add squares until you reach the end of the strip.

Fabric B

Fabric A

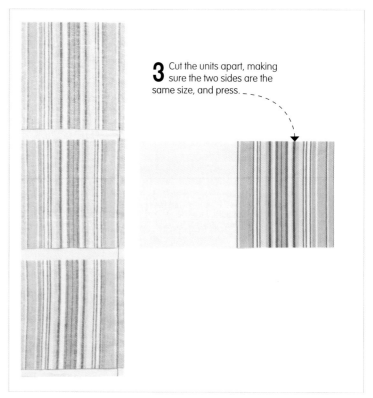

3 Cut the units apart, making sure the two sides are the same size, and press.

4 Place the pieced units on a second light-coloured strip right sides together with the centre square at the bottom. Stitch and press, then trim, making sure the unit is square.

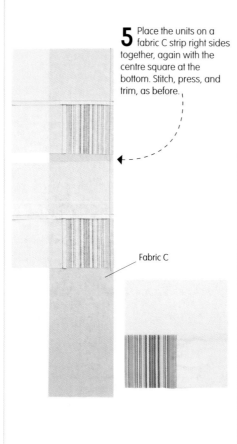

5 Place the units on a fabric C strip right sides together, again with the centre square at the bottom. Stitch, press, and trim, as before.

Fabric C

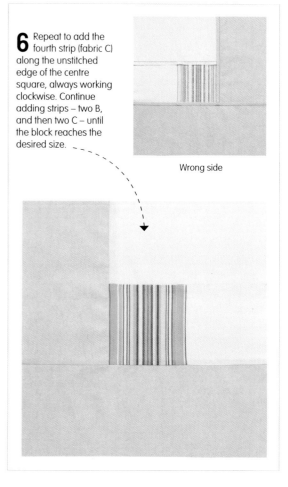

6 Repeat to add the fourth strip (fabric C) along the unstitched edge of the centre square, always working clockwise. Continue adding strips – two B, and then two C – until the block reaches the desired size.

Wrong side

METHOD 3: COURTHOUSE STEPS

1 Cut a centre square.

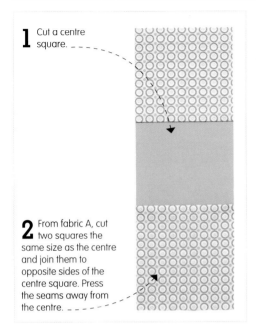

2 From fabric A, cut two squares the same size as the centre and join them to opposite sides of the centre square. Press the seams away from the centre.

2 Cut strips the same width as the centre square from fabric B, and add one strip to each long side of the pieced unit. Trim to the same length as the three-piece unit. Press away from the centre.

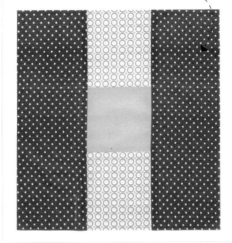

3 Continue adding strips – first two strips of fabric A, then two of fabric B – to opposite sides of the block until it reaches the desired size. Press each strip away from the centre.

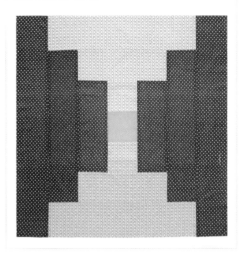

SEMINOLE PATCHWORK

Used by the Seminole tribe of Native Americans in Florida, this type of strip-pieced patchwork is useful for borders or blocks. The method often involves cutting pieced strips at an angle and re-joining them.

METHOD 1: STRAIGHT BAND

1 Cut strips from three contrasting fabrics. The width ratio here is 2:1:3, which gives an even offset.

2 Join them right sides together, with the narrow strip in the centre, taking a 5mm (¼in) seam allowance. Press towards the darker colour.

3 Using a rotary cutter and ruler, cut across the seams to the desired width.

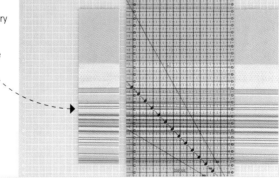

4 Alternating the top and bottom of each adjacent strip, sew them back together, taking a 5mm (¼in) seam allowance. Press the seams in the same direction.

  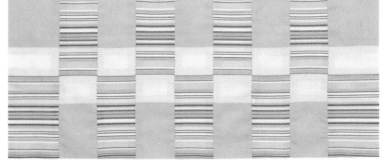

METHOD 2: ANGLED BAND

1 Cut strips from three contrasting fabrics; the widths can vary.

2 Join them right sides together, with wider strips on the outside. Press the seams in the same direction.

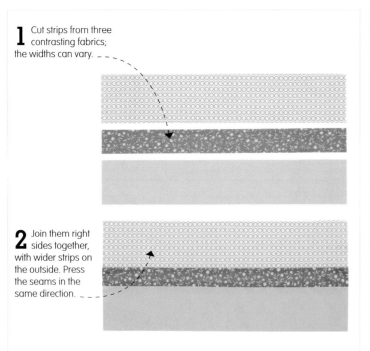

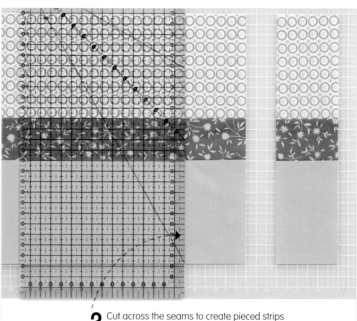

3 Cut across the seams to create pieced strips the desired width.

4 Sew the strips back together, taking a 5mm (¼in) seam allowance and offsetting the centre squares each time. Press the seams in the same direction.

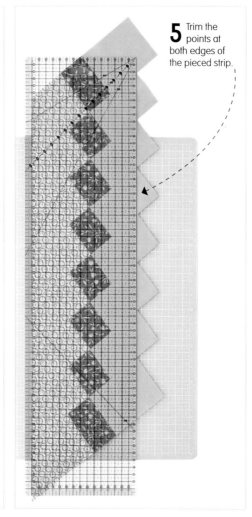

5 Trim the points at both edges of the pieced strip.

6 Square up both ends.

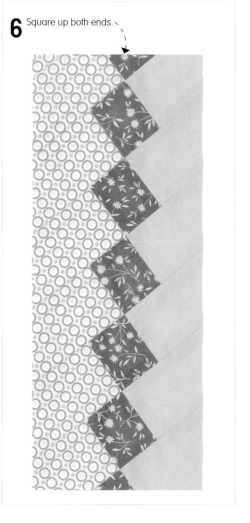

METHOD 3: CHEVRON BAND

1 Cut strips the same width from three contrasting fabrics. Join them right sides together. Press the seams in the same direction. Make a second identical pieced strip.

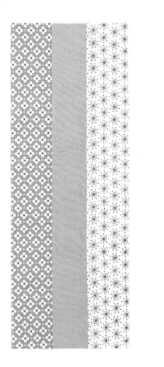

2 Cut across the seams at an angle in one direction on the first pieced strip.

3 Repeat on the second strip, using the same angle but reversing the direction of the cut.

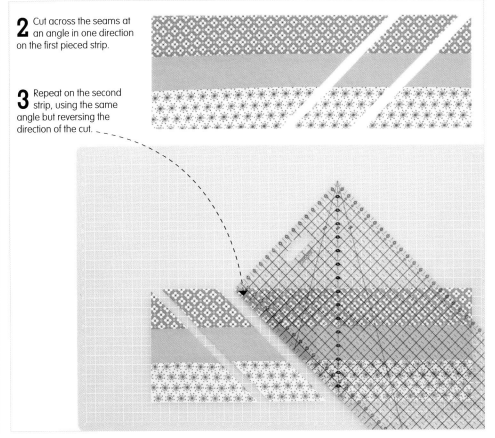

4 Match the seams of a cut strip from strip 1 to the seams of a cut strip from strip 2 and join, taking a 5mm (¼in) seam allowance. Repeat to join in pairs.

5 Join the pairs to create a chevron band. Press the seams in the same direction. Trim the points at both edges.

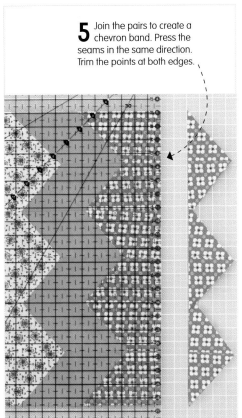

6 The central fabric creates a chevron pattern.

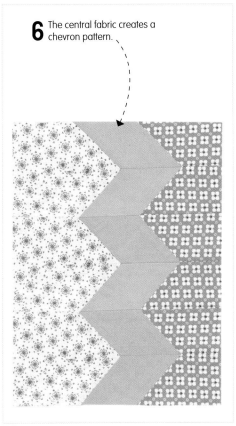

STAR BLOCKS

Star designs make up the largest group of patchwork patterns, ranging from simple four-patch examples to highly elaborate ones with multiple points. They combine many techniques and the following patterns are the starting point for numerous variations.

SINGLE STAR: DOUBLE FOUR-PATCH

1 Divide the size of the finished block by four. Add seam allowances. Cut four squares each of fabric A and fabric B. Make eight triangle squares from fabrics A and B (see page 306).

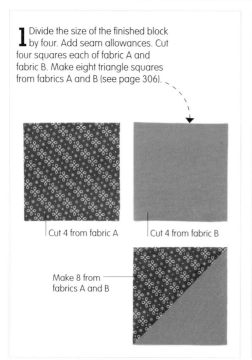

Cut 4 from fabric A

Cut 4 from fabric B

Make 8 from fabrics A and B

2 Following the layout, join the squares and triangle squares in rows of four units each, taking a 5mm (¹/₄in) seam allowance.

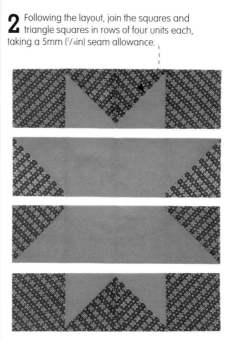

3 Join the rows, matching the seams and taking a 5mm (¹/₄in) seam allowance.

FRIENDSHIP STAR: NINE-PATCH

1 Divide the size of the finished block by three. Add seam allowances. Cut four squares from fabric A and one square from fabric B. Make four triangle squares from fabrics A and B (see page 306).

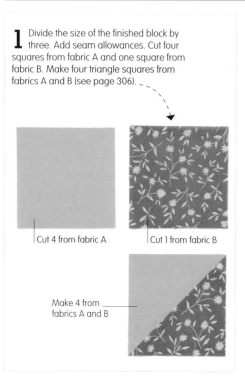

Cut 4 from fabric A

Cut 1 from fabric B

Make 4 from fabrics A and B

2 Following the layout, join the squares and triangle squares in rows of three units each, taking a 5mm (¹/₄in) seam allowance.

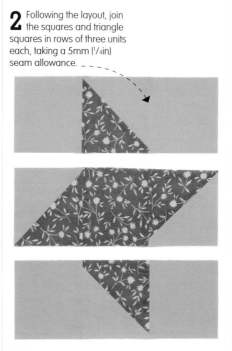

3 Join the rows, matching the seams and taking a 5mm (¹/₄in) seam allowance.

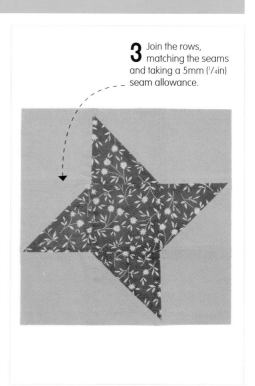

OHIO STAR: NINE-PATCH WITH QUARTER-SQUARE TRIANGLES

1 Divide the size of the finished block by three. Add seam allowances. Cut four squares from fabric A and one square from fabric B. Make four quarter-square units from fabrics A and B (see page 307).

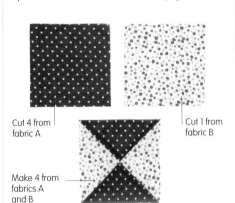

Cut 4 from fabric A

Cut 1 from fabric B

Make 4 from fabrics A and B

2 Following the layout, join the squares and quarter-square units in rows of three, taking a 5mm (¼in) seam allowance.

3 Join the rows, matching the seams and taking a 5mm (¼in) seam allowance.

HEXAGON STAR: 60-DEGREE ANGLES

1 Copy the template to the desired size and cut a pattern. Cut three star points each from fabrics A and B, and six setting diamonds (see page 297) from fabric C, adding a seam allowance all around when you cut out each piece.

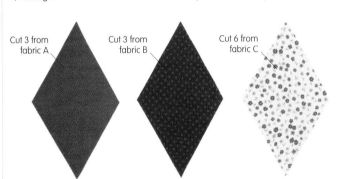

Cut 3 from fabric A

Cut 3 from fabric B

Cut 6 from fabric C

2 Join the three star points in sets, alternating the fabrics.

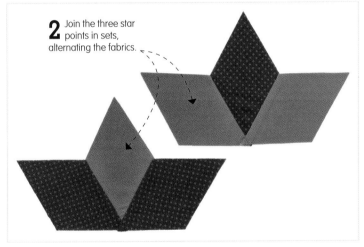

3 Join the units to make the star.

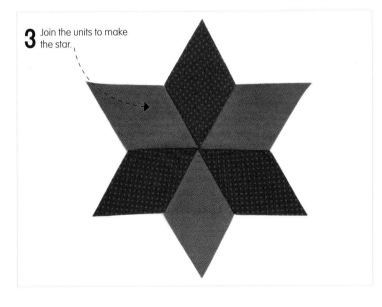

4 Set in the diamond units (see page 303).

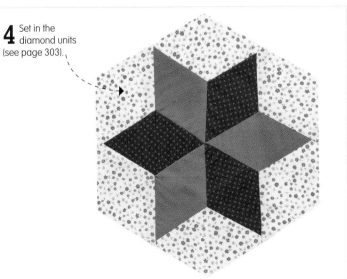

EIGHT-POINT STAR: 45-DEGREE ANGLES

1 Make templates to the desired size for the star points, corner squares, and setting triangles. Cut four star points (see page 297) each from fabrics A and B, and four corner squares (see page 295) and four setting triangles (see page 297) from fabric C.

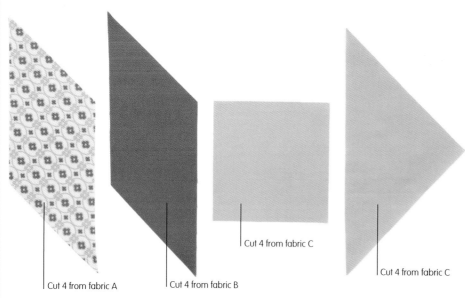

Cut 4 from fabric A

Cut 4 from fabric B

Cut 4 from fabric C

Cut 4 from fabric C

2 Join the star points in four identical pairs, alternating the fabrics.

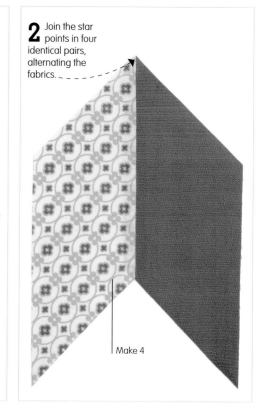

Make 4

3 Join two pairs together to make half the star, then join the two halves to complete the star.

4 Set in the triangle units, then set in the corner squares (see pages 303 and 308).

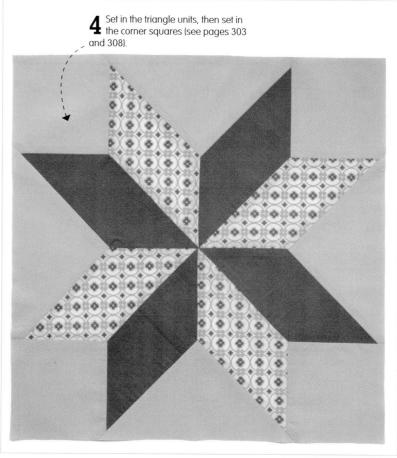

PICTORIAL BLOCKS

Most pictorial quilt blocks are appliquéd, but there are a number of representational blocks, traditional and modern, that are pieced. Many of them, such as flowers and leaves, derive from nature, and most look best if they are spaced out on a quilt, not set together edge to edge. Sashing (see page 359) can be used to separate blocks to show them off, or they can be alternated with plain spacer blocks.

MAPLE LEAF: NINE-PATCH

1 Divide the size of the finished block by three. Add seam allowances. Cut two squares that size from fabric A and three from fabric B. From fabric B cut a strip 4cm (1½in) wide and long enough to fit across the diagonal of one square for the "stem". Make four triangle squares (see page 306) from fabrics A and B.

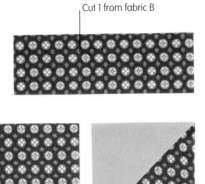

Cut 1 from fabric B

Cut 2 from fabric A

Cut 3 from fabric B

Make 4 from fabrics A and B

2 Apply the stem strip diagonally across one of the fabric A squares. Turn under the raw edges on the long edges and one short edge. Trim the other corner level with the corner of the square.

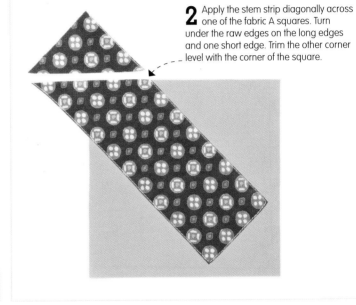

3 Following the layout, join the units in three rows of three.

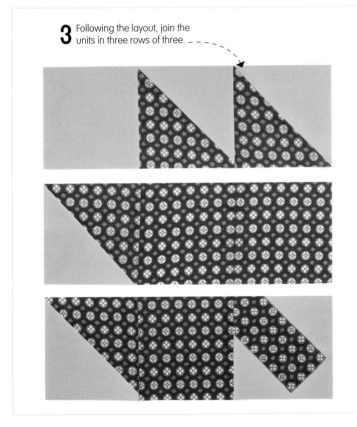

4 Join the rows, making sure you catch the raw edge of the "stem" strip in the seams.

LILY: EIGHT-POINT STAR

1 Cut six "petal" points (see page 297) from fabric A, two petal points from fabric B, and four corner squares and eight right-angled triangles (see page 297) from fabric C. From fabric D, cut a strip 2.5cm (1in) wide and long enough to fit across the diagonal of one square for the "stem".

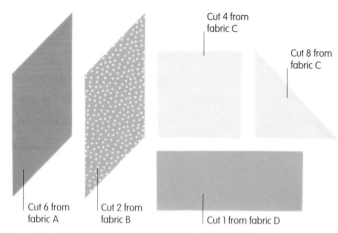

Cut 4 from fabric C

Cut 8 from fabric C

Cut 6 from fabric A

Cut 2 from fabric B

Cut 1 from fabric D

2 Apply the strip diagonally across one of the fabric C squares. Turn the raw edges under on the long edges and level both short ends even with the corners of the square (see Maple leaf, page 327).

3 Matching the colours, join the "petals" in pairs.

4 Add a right-angled triangle to both long sides of each pair of "petals".

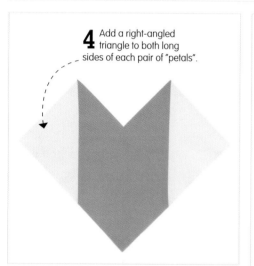

5 Set in the corner squares to make four units. Make sure you catch the raw edges of the "stem" square in the seams.

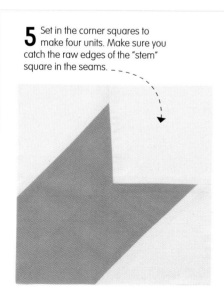

6 Join the units in pairs, then join the pairs, manipulating the seams in the centre to help them lie flat.

CAKE STAND BASKET: FIVE-PATCH

1 Divide the size of the finished block by five. Add seam allowances. Cut eight squares this size from fabric A. Make eight triangle squares (see page 306) from fabrics A and B.

Cut 8 from fabric A

Make 8 from fabrics A and B

2 The finished centre triangle square is three times the size of the outside squares. Cut one triangle from fabric A and one from fabric B to this size and join them on the diagonal.

3 Join three small triangle squares.

4 Join one small triangle square to two small plain squares. Following the layout, add the strips to opposite sides of the large triangle square.

5 Following the layout, join the remaining small squares into two strips and add one strip to opposite sides of the large unit. Match all seams carefully.

SHIP: DOUBLE FOUR-PATCH

1 Divide the size of the finished block by four. Add seam allowances. Cut four squares this size from fabric A and two from fabric B. Divide this by three and add 10mm (¹/₂in) to determine the size of the strips that make up the "sea". Cut four strips in each of three colours to that measurement times the width of the square units. Make two triangle squares from fabrics A and B and four from fabrics A and C (see page 306).

2 Join the sea strips to make four units the same size as the plain squares. You can make the "sea" from three long strips if you prefer. They should be the width determined in Step 1. The length of each strip is the same as the finished measurement of the block plus seam allowances.

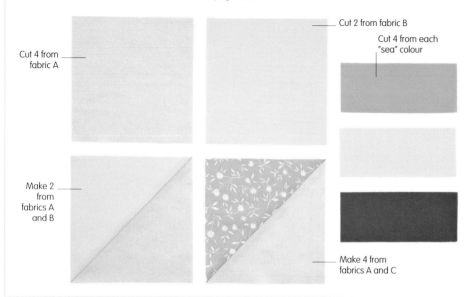

Cut 4 from fabric A

Cut 2 from fabric B

Cut 4 from each "sea" colour

Make 2 from fabrics A and B

Make 4 from fabrics A and C

Make 4

3 Following the layout, join the units in four rows.

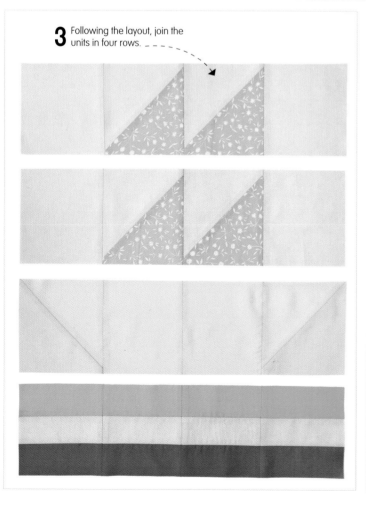

4 Join the rows to complete the block.

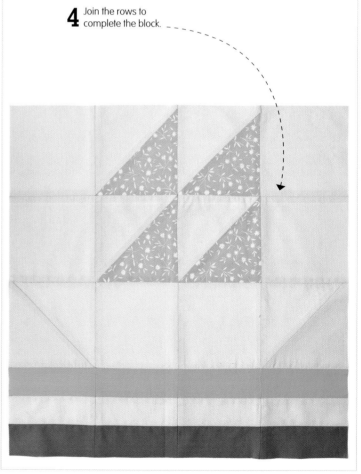

HOUSE

1 Fabric A: cut five 6.5 x 9cm (2¹/₂ x 3¹/₂in) rectangles and four 4 x 21.5cm (1¹/₂ x 8¹/₂in) strips. Fabric B: cut one 6.5 x 21.5cm (2¹/₂ x 8¹/₂in) strip and one 4cm (1¹/₂in) square. Fabric C: cut two rectangles 9 x 11.5cm (3¹/₂ x 4¹/₂in) and one 6.5 x 14cm (2¹/₂ x 5¹/₂in), one strip 21.5 x 4cm (8¹/₂ x 1¹/₂in), and one 9 x 4cm (3¹/₂ x 4in).

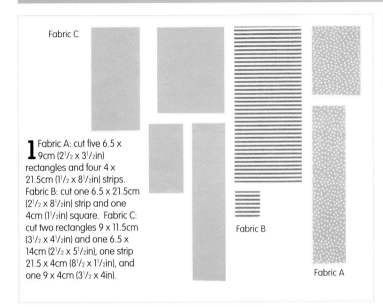

Fabric C

Fabric B

Fabric A

2 Cut one 6.5 x 11.5cm (2¹/₂ x 4¹/₂in) rectangle from fabric B and one from fabric C. Cut them in half diagonally and make two triangle rectangles (see page 306). Join one to each end of the 4 x 21.5cm (2¹/₂ x 8¹/₂in) fabric B strip to make the "roof".

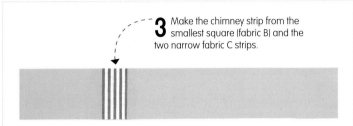

3 Make the chimney strip from the smallest square (fabric B) and the two narrow fabric C strips.

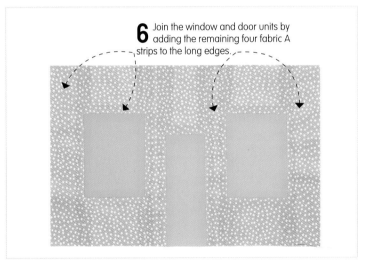

4 Make two window units by adding a 6.5 x 9cm (2¹/₂ x 3¹/₂in) fabric A rectangle to the short ends of each 9 x 11.5cm (3¹/₂ x 4¹/₂in) fabric C rectangle.

Make 2

Make 1

5 Make the door unit by joining the remaining fabric A rectangle to the 6.5 x 14cm (2¹/₂ x 5¹/₂in) fabric C rectangle.

6 Join the window and door units by adding the remaining four fabric A strips to the long edges.

7 Join the chimney and roof elements together.

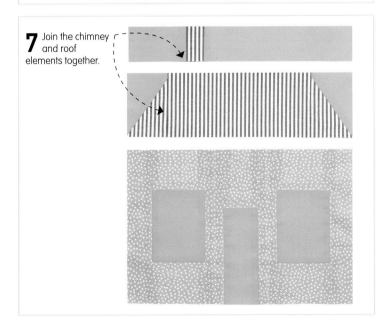

8 Join the roof and house to complete the block.

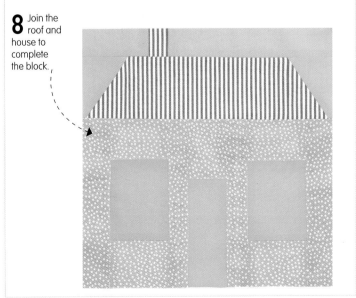

CURVES

Patchwork patterns based on curves are less common than those with straight seams, which are easy to cut and stitch. But although curves can be fiddly, they give more options and, with careful preparation at every stage from template making to cutting and pinning, they are straightforward to sew. Many people find curves easier to work by hand, but it is not difficult to machine stitch them (see page 307).

DRUNKARD'S PATH

1 Make two sets of templates from card or plastic – set 1 for the cutting lines, and set 2 with the seam allowances trimmed off the curved edges for the stitching line. Place the registration marks precisely on both sets.

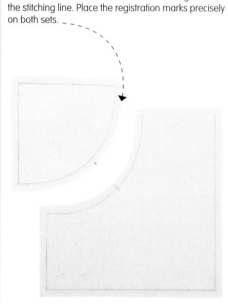

2 Transfer the larger outlines to the wrong side of the chosen fabrics. Make sure the registration marks are transferred accurately.

3 Cut out the shapes. If you are using scissors, cut around the curve, not into it. If you prefer to cut with rotary equipment, use the smallest size blade and a perfectly smooth cutting mat for best results.

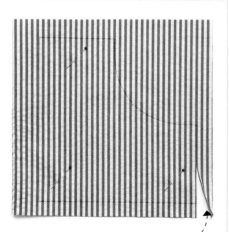

4 Separate the cut-out shapes and, using the set 2 templates, transfer the seamlines and registrations marks to the wrong side of each fabric piece.

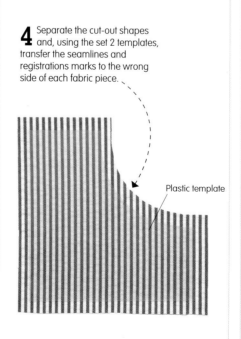

Plastic template

5 Pin one of each shape and fabric right sides together, with the convex piece on top of the concave one. Match and pin the centre marks first, then pin the corners.

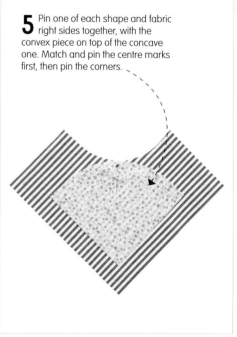

6 Place pins in between, every 8mm (³/₈in) or so, matching the seamlines on both pieces as necessary and using your fingers and thumbs to manipulate the fabric to eliminate uneven distribution.

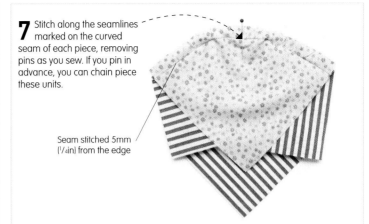

7 Stitch along the seamlines marked on the curved seam of each piece, removing pins as you sew. If you pin in advance, you can chain piece these units.

Seam stitched 5mm (¹/₄in) from the edge

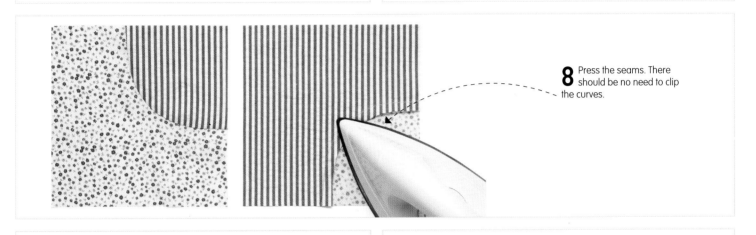

8 Press the seams. There should be no need to clip the curves.

9 Following the layout and alternating colours, combine the units in four rows of four. Press the seams in opposite directions on alternate rows.

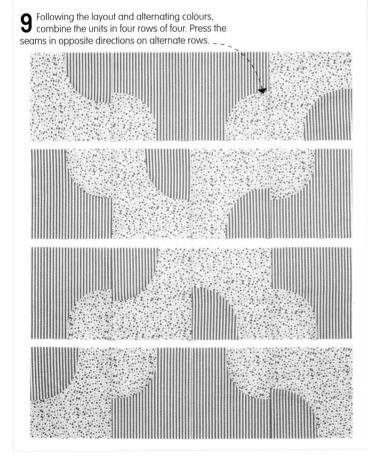

10 Join the rows, matching the seams carefully. Press.

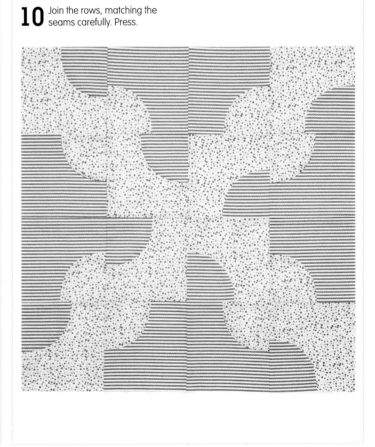

FANS

1 Transfer the outlines to card or template plastic and cut out the shapes. Make two sets of templates – set 1 for the cutting lines, and set 2 with the seam allowances trimmed off the curved edges for the stitching line.

2 For a six-blade fan, cut three blades each from fabrics A and B. Cut a small corner piece from fabric C and a background from fabric D.

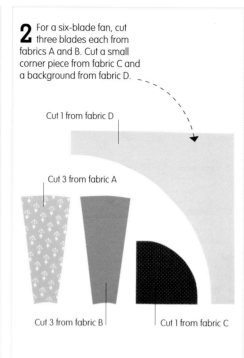

Cut 1 from fabric D

Cut 3 from fabric A

Cut 3 from fabric B

Cut 1 from fabric C

3 Join the fan blade pieces, alternating the colours and taking a 5mm (¹/₄in) seam allowance. Press the blades in the same direction.

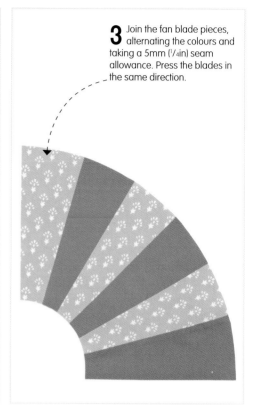

4 Mark the seam allowances on the top and bottom edges of the fan unit.

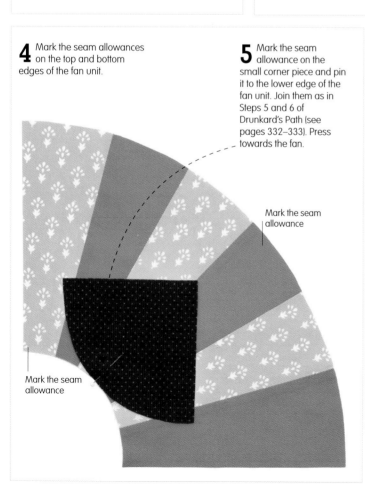

Mark the seam allowance

Mark the seam allowance

5 Mark the seam allowance on the small corner piece and pin it to the lower edge of the fan unit. Join them as in Steps 5 and 6 of Drunkard's Path (see pages 332–333). Press towards the fan.

6 Mark the seam allowance on the background piece and pin the background piece to the upper edge of the fan unit. Join them as before. Press towards the background.

ENGLISH PAPER PIECING

This is a traditional method for making a quilt of mosaic shapes. The fabric pieces – hexagons, honeycombs, diamonds, and triangles, all of which have at least two bias edges – are tacked to pre-cut paper templates the size of the finished element. The technique is usually done by hand. The backing papers can be cut from virtually any heavy paper but freezer paper can be ironed on quickly and is easy to remove.

BASIC PAPER-PIECING TECHNIQUE

1 Unless you are using pre-cut paper shapes, make a template. Draw around it to make the necessary number of shapes. Using paper scissors, carefully cut out the backing papers.

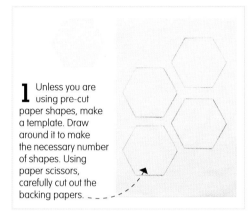

2 Pin a plain-paper shape or iron a freezer-paper shape (paper side up) to the wrong side of the fabric. Leave enough space for seam allowances.

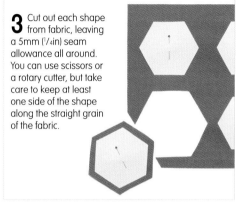

3 Cut out each shape from fabric, leaving a 5mm (¼in) seam allowance all around. You can use scissors or a rotary cutter, but take care to keep at least one side of the shape along the straight grain of the fabric.

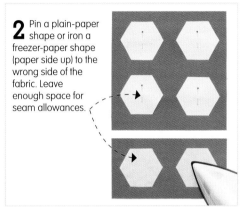

4 Turn the seam allowance to the wrong side over the edge of the paper shape. Tack along each side in turn, folding each corner neatly and stitching through the fold to hold it securely.

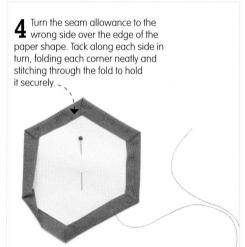

5 To join patches into units, place two shapes right sides together. Make a back-stitched loop (see page 300), and oversew to the corner. Do not sew through the backing papers.

6 Oversew along the same edge to the opposite corner, again taking small stitches. When you reach the corner, backstitch in the opposite direction for 5mm (¼in).

7 Continue adding shapes until complete.

8 If you wish to re-use papers, you can remove them once all the shapes adjoining a particular piece have been added.

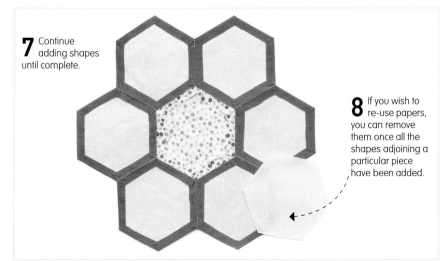

9 Remove the tacking stitches.

SETTING IN HEXAGONS

1 To set in a third hexagon, oversew one side of the seam, starting at the centre point.

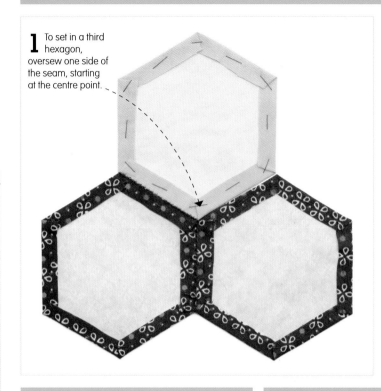

2 Align the second sides to be joined at their outer points, folding back the pieces as necessary, and stitch as before.

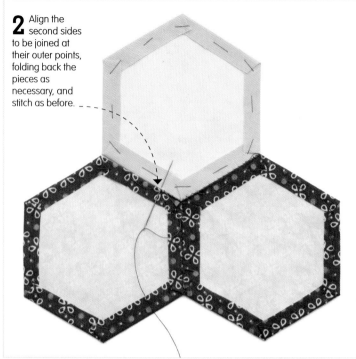

NEAT FOLDS

1 To make a neat fold at the sharp points when tacking diamonds and triangles, start sewing in the middle of one side. When you reach the point, fingerpress the extended seam allowance.

2 Fold over the allowance from the next side neatly. Take a stitch through the fold and continue. Do not trim off the fabric extensions.

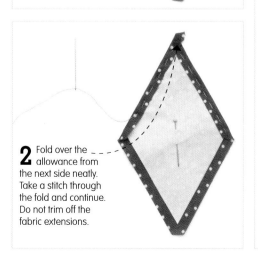

NEAT JOINS

To make a neat join when you sew pieces together, fold the extension to the side so that you don't stitch through it. Where several come together, the unstitched extensions will form a spiral around their meeting point and lie flat.

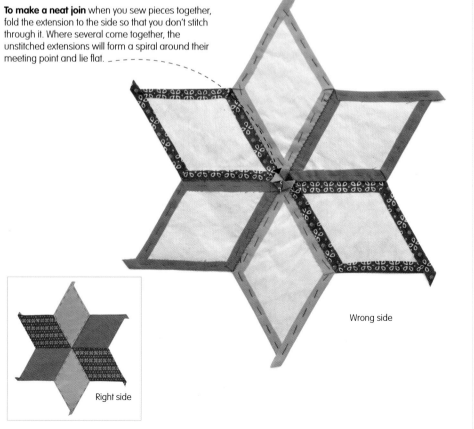

Right side

Wrong side

WORKING ON A
FOUNDATION

Several patchwork techniques are worked on a foundation, also known as stitch-and-flip. Crazy patchwork uses random shapes and is a great way to use up scraps. It is best made on a lightweight foundation fabric, such as calico. Reverse-pieced foundation piecing ensures accuracy and is a quick way to make blocks. You can make patterns for each segment, or cut the shapes with generous seam allowances.

FOUNDATION PIECING: TOP PIECED

1 Cut a foundation of lightweight calico the size you want the finished block to be plus a 2.5cm (1in) seam allowance all around.

2 Gather a selection of straight-sided pieces of various shapes and colours. Starting in the centre, place two pieces right sides together and sew along one side. Take a 5mm (¹/₄in) seam allowance, whether you are working by hand or machine.

3 Press or fingerpress the pieces open.

4 Add piece 3 along one edge of the combined shape made in Step 1. Open and press. If necessary, trim the seam allowance level before you add the next piece. Snip off thread ends if machining.

5 Continue clockwise around the centre piece until the foundation is completely filled. Keep the arrangement random and avoid parallel lines. Run the seams in different directions and vary the angles. Press each piece open as you work.

6 Trim the edges level with the edges of the foundation fabric. Embellish the finished piece if you wish.

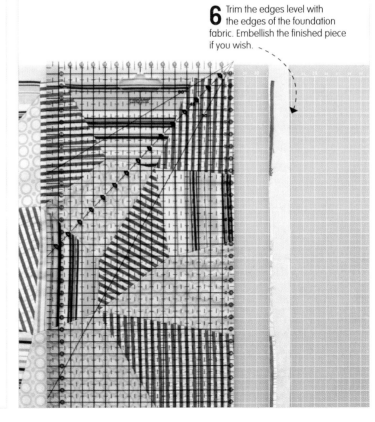

FOUNDATION PIECING: REVERSE PIECED

1 Cut the chosen foundation (you can use paper, calico, wadding, or non-woven interfacing) to size, with a generous amount added all around.

2 Trace or transfer the design to the foundation. Number the piecing order clearly on the foundation. You will be sewing from the back of the foundation, so the block will be the reverse of the foundation itself.

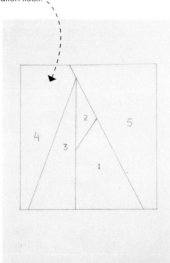

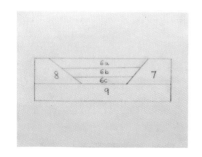

3 Cut out piece 1 and pin it right side up on the reverse side of the foundation. Make sure that it extends beyond the stitching lines; you can check this by holding it up to the light.

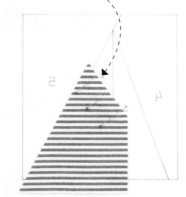

5 Turn the foundation right side up and re-pin carefully to avoid catching any pins in the feed dogs of your sewing machine.

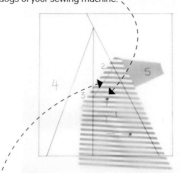

6 Stitch the seam, joining pieces 1 and 2. If your foundation is paper, use a short stitch to make it easier to remove. If necessary, trim the seam allowance to 5mm (¼in).

4 Cut out piece 2 and place it right sides together on piece 1, along the seam to be sewn. Pin through all layers.

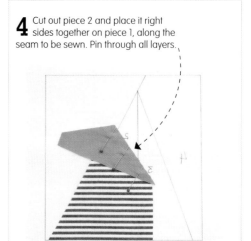

7 Turn the foundation fabric right side up, remove the pins, open the pieces and press.

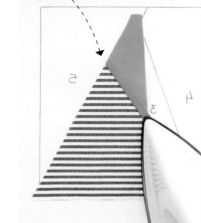

8 Cut piece 3 as before and align it next to piece 2. Pin it on top, then turn the foundation over and stitch as in Steps 3–7.

9 When the top section is complete, make the bottom section the same way.

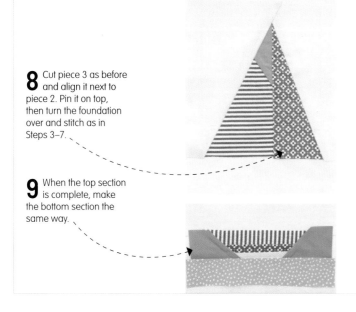

10 Join the sections. Then trim the foundation level with the edges of the patchwork design. If the foundation is removable, carefully tear it away.

FOLDED PATCHWORK

There are a number of specialized patchwork techniques that involve manipulating fabric by folding it in specific ways before joining pieces together. They can all be used to make quilts, but because they are, by definition, made from more than one layer, they are also good for making household items, such as placemats.

CATHEDRAL WINDOW

1 Decide the size of the finished square (10cm/4in) and multiply the measurement by two (20cm/8in). Add 10mm (½in) seam allowance and cut four squares this size from the background, fabric A.

2 Fold each square diagonally one way and press, then fold along the other diagonal and press firmly to mark the exact centre. Open out. Turn the seam allowance to the wrong side on all sides of all squares. Press firmly.

3 Fold each corner of each square to the centre and press the folds firmly. Make sure that the new corners are sharply defined.

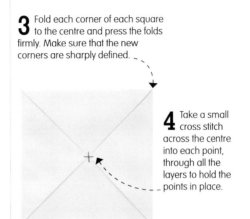

4 Take a small cross stitch across the centre into each point, through all the layers to hold the points in place.

5 Fold each corner to the centre again and press firmly. Take a small cross stitch as before through all the layers to hold the points in place. The square is now half the size of that cut in Step 1.

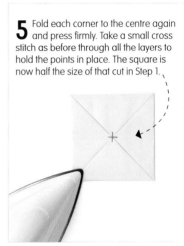

6 With folded edges together, join the four squares in pairs, oversewing with tiny stitches along the edge. Then join the two pairs to make a square. If you are making a large piece, you can also work in rows that are joined before the windows are added.

7 Cut four contrasting window squares from fabric B. (Each window square should just fit inside a quarter segment of the background square; to work out the size, measure the distance from the centre of one folded square to the outside corner.)

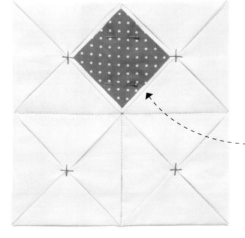

8 Place the first window square over a seam, on the diagonal. Pin in place. If necessary, trim the edges slightly to make it fit.

9 Roll one folded edge in the background square over the raw edge of the first window square.

10 Matching the thread to the background fabric, sew the rolled, slightly curved overlap in place with tiny stitches, catching in the raw edge completely. Do not stitch through the background fabric. Repeat to catch in the other three edges of the window.

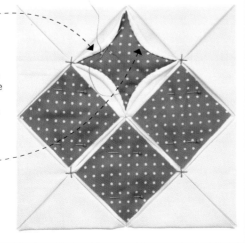

11 Repeat Steps 7 to 9 to fill the other spaces in the square. If you work in rows, add windows after you join rows together.

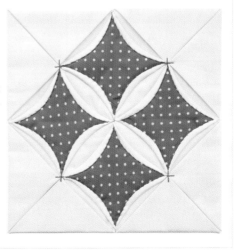

SECRET GARDEN

1 Make a folded square as for Steps 1 to 3 of Cathedral Window (see page 339). Fold and press the corners, as in Step 4, but do not stitch in place. Cut a window square the size of the finished square.

2 Open the pressed corners and place the window square on point within the lines. If necessary, trim the raw edges to fit and anchor with small tacking stitches.

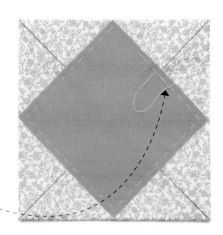

3 Fold the four corners of the background square in to the centre. Press. Anchor each corner in the centre with a small cross, stitching through all layers.

4 Pin 5mm (¼in) in from each corner through all layers to stabilize the square.

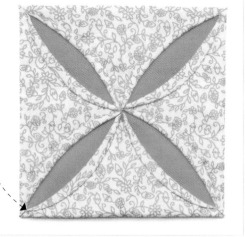

5 Turn under one edge of the background square to form a curving "petal" shape. Sew in place, working outwards from the centre and using thread to match the background fabric.

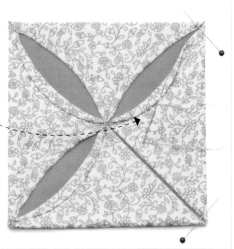

6 Repeat on all eight folded edges of the background square, removing the pins and securing each corner with a double tacking stitch.

FOLDED STAR

1 Cut a foundation from calico the finished size plus 5cm (2in) on all sides. Our star has four rounds, or layers, each one in a contrasting fabric. For round 1, the central star, cut four 10cm (4in) squares. For rounds 2, 3 and 4, cut eight 10cm (4in) squares.

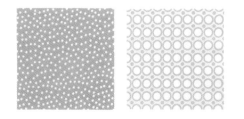

3 For a square foundation, fold the foundation fabric in half horizontally and vertically and press to create guidelines. Fold in half again along the diagonals and press. For a circle, fold the foundation in quarters and press.

4 Place the four folded squares (the right-angled triangles), along the pressed guidelines, so the points meet in the centre, with folded edges on top. Pin or tack in place along the raw edges. Secure each point with a small hidden stitch.

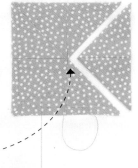

2 With wrong sides together, press each square in half. Fold the top corner of the resulting rectangle to the centre of the raw edges and press, then repeat to make a right-angled triangle with the raw edges along the long side.

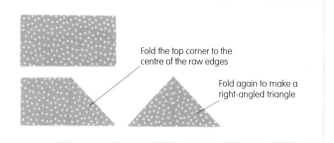

Fold the top corner to the centre of the raw edges

Fold again to make a right-angled triangle

5 Add the next round by placing four triangles in fabric B, made as in Step 2, with the points 10mm (¹/₂in) from the centre, with the raw bottom edges aligned with the four sides of the square. Secure as in Step 4.

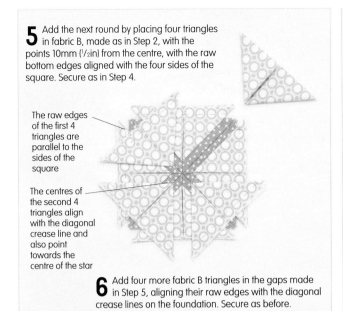

The raw edges of the first 4 triangles are parallel to the sides of the square

The centres of the second 4 triangles align with the diagonal crease line and also point towards the centre of the star

6 Add four more fabric B triangles in the gaps made in Step 5, aligning their raw edges with the diagonal crease lines on the foundation. Secure as before. Measure 10mm (¹/₂in) from the points and mark.

7 Add subsequent rounds in the same way. Trim the edges to match the foundation shape. Remove the tacking and trim and finish the edges as desired.

GATHERED
PATCHWORK

Yo-yos, also called Suffolk puffs, are fabric circles that have been gathered to make two layers. They are widely used as decorations in appliqué and can be further embellished (see page 373). Joined edge to edge, they can be made into tablecloths, cushion covers, or openwork bedcovers. Yo-yo projects are a great way to use up small scraps of fabric.

YO-YOS

1 Cut circles of fabric twice the desired finished size. You can use almost anything circular as a template, from cotton reels to bottles or cups.

2 Knot a length of strong thread, doubled if necessary, and secure it close to the edge on the wrong side of the circle. Turn the raw edge 5mm (¹/₄in) to the wrong side and take small gathering stitches through both layers all around the edge, to make a single hem.

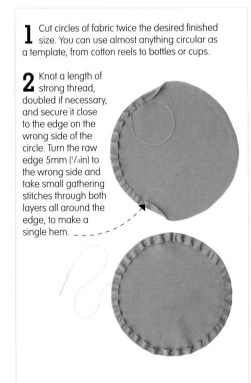

3 Finish next to where you started. Do not remove the needle or cut the thread, but pull the thread gently to gather the circle into a smaller one, with pleats around the centre. The raw edge will disappear inside the circle. Secure the thread with a couple of tacks or backstitches, then knot it. Cut the thread.

4 Flatten the circle by gently fingerpressing the edges. The gathered side is normally the front, but sometimes the back is used instead.

5 To join yo-yos, place them gathered sides facing and oversew the flattened edges for a short distance, taking small, tight stitches. Join yo-yos together until you have a row that is the desired length; join rows together in the same way.

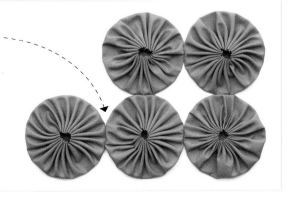

PATCHWORK
BLOCK GALLERY

There are literally hundreds of traditional patchwork patterns and we have space to show only a few – but once you've mastered the basic construction techniques shown in the preceding pages, you will be able to look at a block pattern and work out both the constituent elements and how to piece it together.

FOUR-PATCH BLOCKS

The simplest four-patch blocks are made up of just four squares (patches), but those four squares can also be created by piecing together two half-square triangles, or four quarter-square triangles, or various combinations thereof.

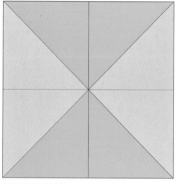
YANKEE PUZZLE

CHEVRON, OR STREAK OF LIGHTNING

BROKEN PINWHEEL

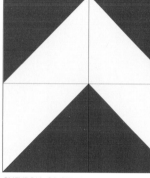
FLYFOOT

NINE-PATCH BLOCKS

Nine-patch blocks are made of nine units in three rows of three. By adding a third colour to a simple nine-patch of two colours, you can create myriad variations.

PICTORIAL BLOCKS

Patchwork pictorial blocks tend to be highly stylized, with the individual elements of the design being made up of square and triangle units in varying combinations.

RED CROSS – THREE-COLOUR NINE-PATCH

THREE-COLOUR DOUBLE NINE-PATCH

GRAPE BASKET

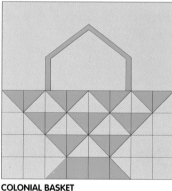
COLONIAL BASKET

ROCKY ROAD TO CALIFORNIA

BUILDING BLOCKS

BASKET OF SCRAPS

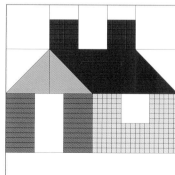
HOUSE WITH FENCE

FIVE- AND SEVEN-PATCH BLOCKS

Five-patch blocks consist of a grid of five units in each direction, or 25 units in total, while seven-patch blocks have no fewer than 49 units (seven in each direction). With so many elements, each one of which can be sub-divided in several ways, there is almost infinite scope for creating different patterns.

STAR AND CROSS PATCH

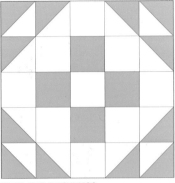

DUCK AND DUCKLINGS

HENS AND CHICKENS

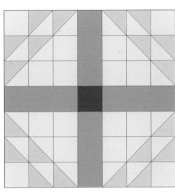

DOVE IN A WINDOW

STRIP-PIECED BLOCKS

Strip-pieced patterns can be put together in random colour and fabric combinations or in repeating patterns. If two fabrics are pieced A–B–A and B–A–B, the resulting squares can be alternated to create a Basketweave block. Use more fabrics for a more complex effect. Seminole bands can be angled or set square and are wonderful for creating pieced border strips.

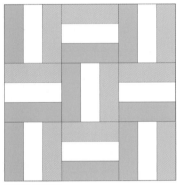

BASKETWEAVE

STRING-PIECED DIVIDED SQUARE

DOUBLE CHEVRON SEMINOLE

LOG CABIN BLOCKS

There are many variations in Log Cabin blocks and settings. Strips of light and dark fabrics can be alternated, placed on adjacent or opposite sides, made of varying widths, or pieced from a combination of smaller squares and rectangles. The centre square can be pieced, turned "on point", or made from a rectangle, triangle, or diamond.

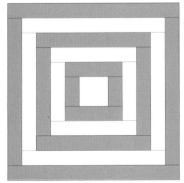

CABIN IN THE COTTON

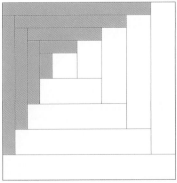

THICK AND THIN

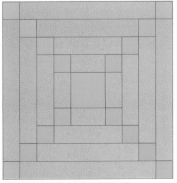

CHIMNEYS AND CORNERSTONES

PINEAPPLE

STAR BLOCKS

There are probably more kinds of star blocks than any other patchwork motif; the construction ranges from simple four-patch stars to extremely complex designs created by cutting 60-degree diamonds in half lengthways or crossways. The basic eight-point star alone, with its 45-degree angles, is the starting point for numerous variations, including the intricate lone star.

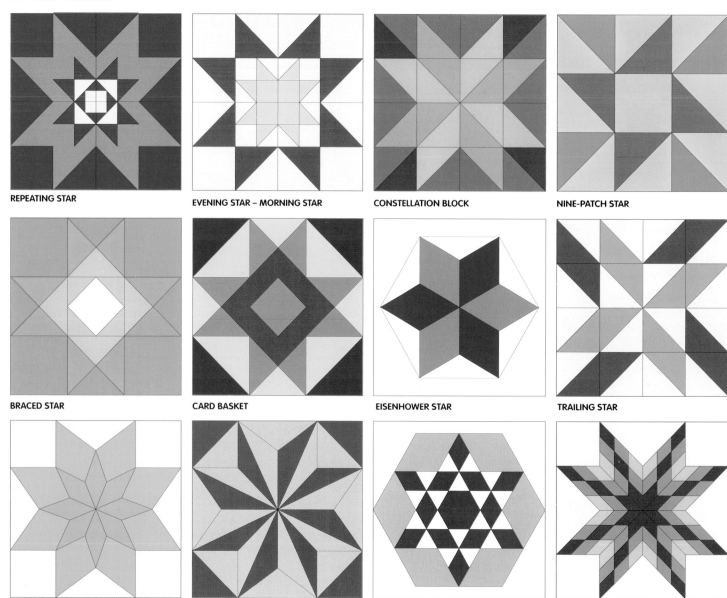

REPEATING STAR

EVENING STAR – MORNING STAR

CONSTELLATION BLOCK

NINE-PATCH STAR

BRACED STAR

CARD BASKET

EISENHOWER STAR

TRAILING STAR

TENNESSEE STAR

SILVER AND GOLD

OZARK DIAMONDS

LONE STAR

TIPS

• **When marking,** make sure the marker has a sharp point. If you mark with dashes, not a continuous line, the fabric is less apt to shift or stretch.

• **Remember the rule:** measure twice, cut once. And bear in mind that measurements from one brand of ruler or mat are not always exactly the same as another brand. For accuracy, try to use the same ruler and mat, as well as the same machine foot, throughout the piecing process.

• **If you make a sample block to begin,** you can measure your finished blocks against it to ensure accuracy.

• **Whenever possible,** sew a bias edge to a straight edge to minimize stretching.

• **If you need to trim a block to make it smaller,** trim back an equal amount from all sides to keep the design of the block accurate.

CURVED BLOCKS

Probably the most popular of all traditional curved blocks is the drunkard's path (see page 332) – a double four-patch. When the orientation or colour values of the four units is altered, a number of complex curving patterns result. Changing the size and shape of the curves also alters the block considerably.

FALLING TIMBERS

WONDER OF THE WORLD

CHAIN LINKS

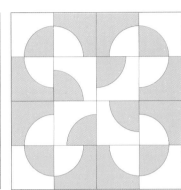

DRUNKARD'S PUZZLE

ROBBING PETER TO PAY PAUL

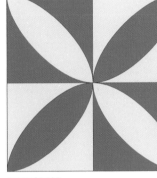

ORANGE PEEL

MOSAIC BLOCKS

Though many of these can be machined, but most are made by piecing together geometric shapes using the "English" paper-piecing method (see page 335). The most familiar block is grandmother's flower garden.

GRANDMOTHER'S FLOWER GARDEN

FLOWER BASKET

FAN BLOCKS

Fans are based on quarter-circles and can be arranged in a number of different ways. However they are arranged, a curving pattern results. Fan variations such as Dresden plate patterns are full circles and are often appliquéd to a background. The segments can be curved or pointed, or a combination of the two. The centre can be open to allow the background to show through or applied separately for contrast.

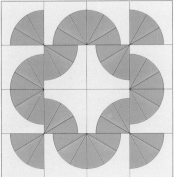

MOHAWK TRAIL

DRESDEN PLATE

TUMBLING BLOCKS

1000 PYRAMIDS

APPLIQUÉ

Appliqué is a decorative technique in which shapes are cut from one fabric and applied to a background fabric. It has been used in quiltmaking for centuries and is found on many other items, from clothing to cushions. Hand appliqué is the traditional method but working by machine can be effective.

TIPS FOR APPLIQUÉ

- **Blanket stitch** (below) is the most popular decorative stitch for hand appliqué, but many basic embroidery stitches can be used as decoration, including cross stitch (see page 184), herringbone (see page 190), chain stitch (see page 200), and feather stitch (see page 196).

- **Make sure that** decorative stitches sit tight against the turned-under edge and are in proportion with the size of the applied pieces.

- **In most appliqué** techniques, a seam allowance has to be added to the shapes. The secret is to make an allowance that is wide enough to keep fraying at bay and narrow enough to be undetectable once it has been stitched.

- **Most seam allowances** for appliqué can be cut by eye, following the outline of the shape. Remember that you can trim away any excess as you work, but you can't add it once it has been removed. The ideal seam allowance is around 3mm ($\frac{1}{8}$in).

- **If you need** only one piece of a particular shape, draw it on tracing paper and cut it out. Pin the tracing paper shape to the fabric and cut it out, in the same way as a dressmaking pattern.

- **Appliqué designs** usually have a right and a wrong side. When transferring a design, make sure that the right side of the fabric will be the right way around when the shape is cut out and applied.

- **Some methods call** for the outline of a design to be marked on the background fabric. In this case, make sure that the outline will be covered or can be removed when the stitching is completed. Draw the design lightly on the right side of the fabric or tack around the outlines.

- **When tacking,** make sure that any knots are on the wrong side of the background fabric, as this will make it easier to remove the thread later.

- **If the fabric is light** or you have access to a lightbox, you may be able to trace from an original pattern directly onto fabric.

- **When working machine appliqué,** work a practice row or two using the same fabrics as the design to make sure your settings are correct.

STITCHES FOR APPLIQUÉ

Appliquéd shapes can be attached to the background in two ways, either hidden (using blind stitch) or calling attention to themselves as part of the design. Machine appliqué is almost always worked with decorative stitches such as zigzag or satin stitch, or with one of the many stitches programmed into modern sewing machines.

BLIND STITCH OR SLIP STITCH

Bring the needle up on the right side of the background fabric, next to the turned-under edge of the shape being applied. Insert it a few threads into the folded edge. Go back through the background fabric and continue taking tiny stitches 3mm ($\frac{1}{8}$in) apart around the entire shape.

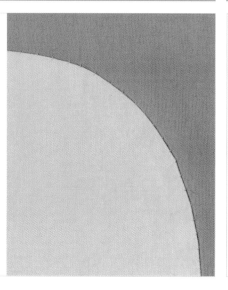

BLANKET STITCH

Bring the needle up on the right side of the background fabric, next to the turned-under edge of the shape being applied. Take a stitch into the shape 3–5mm ($\frac{1}{8}$–$\frac{1}{4}$in) to the right and perpendicular to the edge. Bring the needle out at the edge and loop the thread under the point. Pull tight and repeat.

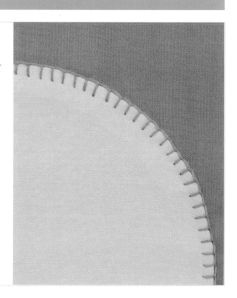

DEALING WITH
PEAKS AND VALLEYS

Both "peaks" (shapes that come to a sharp point) and "valleys" (sharp points between two sides of a shape) can be pointed or curved, and both can be difficult to work neatly. The points of peaks should, of course, be pointed, and you risk creating a lump under the point where you turn the edges under. The seam allowance in valleys needs to be clipped to make the edge neat.

PEAKS

1 Trim the tip of the point a few threads shy of the seam allowance.

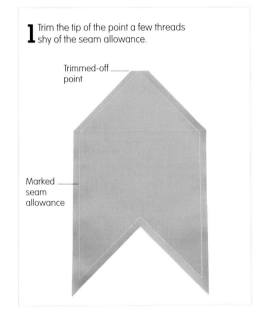

Trimmed-off point

Marked seam allowance

2 Fold the sides of the point along the seam allowance. Ensure that the raw edge at the point is hidden. Press the edges.

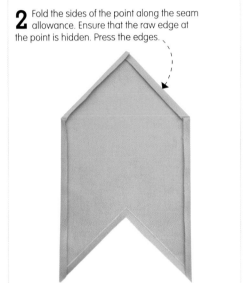

VALLEYS

At the bottom of the valley, clip to within a few threads of the marked seam allowance. Fold the edges to the wrong side. When applying the piece, take several tiny stitches in the valley to secure the cut threads.

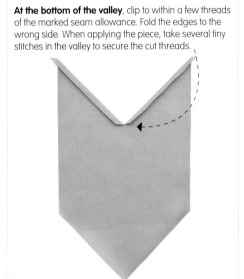

DEALING WITH
CURVES

Curves can be difficult to keep smooth. The raw edge of an outward (convex) curve is slightly longer than the folded-under edge and can cause bunching under the fold unless the seam allowance is clipped. Inward (concave) curves will sometimes stretch smoothly, but shallow curves may need to be clipped before being stitched.

CONVEX CURVES

1 Cut tiny V-shaped notches into the seam allowance to remove excess fabric.

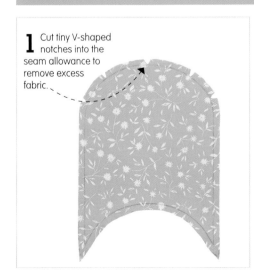

2 When it is turned under, the curved edge will lie flat.

CONCAVE CURVES

Clip straight cuts into the seam allowance as you work, one section at a time. The clips will form notches that will spread open and allow the edge to lie flat.

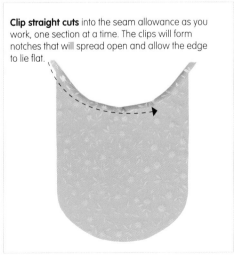

NEEDLE-TURNED APPLIQUÉ
AND BIAS STEMS

Needle-turned or turned-edge appliqué is the traditional method for applying shapes to a background. This motif also incorporates narrow bias strips that must be applied first.

1 Wash and press the background fabric.

2 Make templates for the appliqué shapes. Transfer the shapes to the right side of the appliqué fabric and cut them out, adding a scant 5mm (¹⁄₄in) seam allowance all around.

3 Cut the bias stems three times the finished width. Here they are 15mm (³⁄₄in) wide and cut on the true bias. With wrong sides together, fold each strip in half and machine stitch a seam 5mm (¹⁄₄in) from the folded edge. Do not press. Trim the raw edge close to the seam.

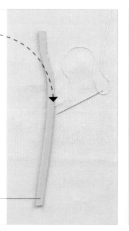

4 Lay the stitched strip folded edge down and press flat, pressing the seam open. This makes a strip with the seam running down the centre of the back.

Seam

5 Lay the stems in position on the background fabric and pin in place. Blind stitch along first one edge, then the other, with the seam hidden under the stitched strip.

The raw edges will be covered by other pieces

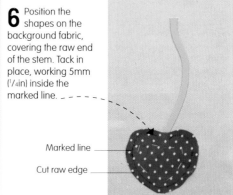

6 Position the shapes on the background fabric, covering the raw end of the stem. Tack in place, working 5mm (¹⁄₄in) inside the marked line.

Marked line

Cut raw edge

7 With the needle point, turn under a small section of the seam allowance until the raw edge touches the tacked line. Blind stitch in place.

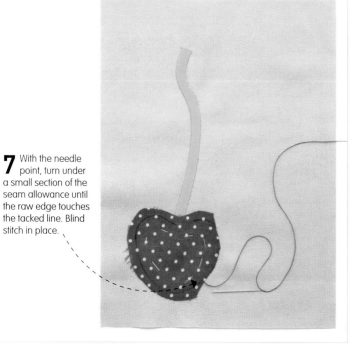

8 Repeat, taking small stitches along the edge until the piece is stitched. Fasten off on the back. Add any remaining pieces. Remove the tacking and press the piece from the wrong side.

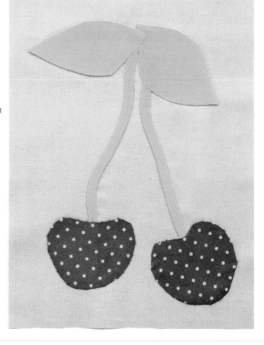

FREEZER PAPER
APPLIQUÉ

Freezer paper is a stiff, white paper coated on one side with a film that can be ironed on fabric and easily removed without leaving a residue. The paper side is ideal for drawing on patterns. It can be found in quilt shops, at supermarkets, and online. Seam allowances can be pressed over the edge to the wrong side to give a hard crease that makes it easy to sew shapes in place accurately.

1 Trace the templates in reverse on the paper side of the freezer paper and cut out. Iron the paper pieces to the wrong side of the fabric.

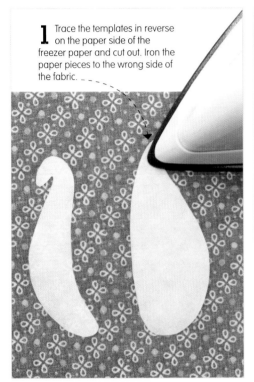

2 Cut out the fabric shapes, leaving a 5mm (¼in) seam allowance all around. Clip or notch any corners and difficult curves up to the paper. Press the seam allowance to the wrong side, using the edge of the freezer paper as a guide.

3 Remove the paper shapes by peeling them off gently. Make sure that the raw edges lie flat on the wrong side.

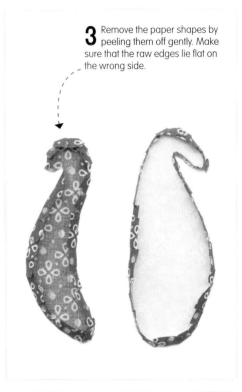

4 Decide on the order in which to work, making sure that any underlapping pieces are covered. Pin or tack the first piece in place, then blind stitch it to the background.

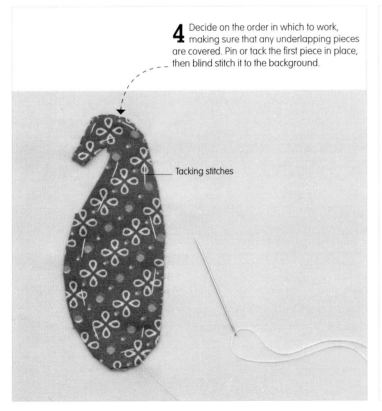

Tacking stitches

5 Add the remaining pieces in order, one at a time. If you pin the pieces in place, remove the pins as you work. If you tack them in place, remove all the tacking stitches when the work is complete.

RAW-EDGE APPLIQUÉ

Non-woven fabrics, such as felt and felted wool, that won't fray can be used effectively in decorative appliqué, but remember that they cannot be laundered. No seam allowances are needed.

1 Trace your entire pattern onto the background fabric. Then trace the pattern pieces separately on tracing paper. Cut out each paper pattern and pin to the fabrics.

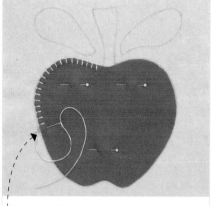

2 Cut out the appliqué pieces (without a seam allowance). Pin the first piece to the background and stitch in place, using a decorative stitch (see page 346).

3 Add pieces in order. Remove all the pins and press from the wrong side.

BRODERIE PERSE

Persian embroidery, or broderie perse, is a technique in which motifs are cut from one printed fabric and applied to a different background. Several motifs, not necessarily from the same fabric, can be layered and re-arranged to create a new design.

1 Cut out the motif with a generous 5mm (¼in) seam allowance. Clip any curves inside the seam allowance. If there are areas that are too small to cut away, leave the background fabric in place.

Clipped curve

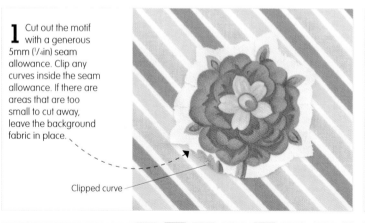

2 Pin the motif in position on the background and tack it 10mm (½in) inside the outline. For narrow areas such as stems, tack along the centre. Trim outside seam allowances to reduce bulk wherever possible.

3 Using the needle tip, turn the seam allowance under and blind stitch the motif to the background, using thread to match the motif, or use a decorative stitch and contrasting thread as shown.

4 This appliqué technique allows you to make a small piece of expensive printed fabric go a long way, as individual motifs can be applied over a larger and less costly background fabric.

HAWAIIAN APPLIQUÉ

Hawaiian appliqué originated in Hawaii when women native to the islands were taught to sew by early missionaries. The patterns are usually square and cut as eight-sided motifs from a single piece of folded fabric. The designs are traditionally based on flora indigenous to the Pacific outpost, but six-sided snowflake motifs can also be used. Finished pieces are usually echo quilted (see page 369).

1 Cut a piece of paper to the size of the finished block. Fold the paper in half twice, then along the diagonal once to make a triangle. Draw on the triangle or cut freestyle through all the layers, with the main part of the design on the folded edge.

2 Cut out one triangular section and transfer it to card to use as a template in Step 3.

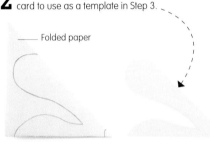

Folded paper

3 Cut a square of freezer paper the same size as the original paper pattern. Fold it in half twice, paper side out, then fold it once along the diagonal to make a triangle. This matches the template. Transfer the template outline to the paper, making sure that the fold of the paper matches the fold on the template.

4 Staple the layers together inside the design lines. Cut out along the marked line.

5 Remove the staples carefully and open out the paper pattern.

6 Cut a square of the appliqué fabric and one of the background fabric, both 5cm (2in) larger than the pattern square. Fold both in half twice to find the centre and position them, wrong side of the appliqué fabric to right side of the background.

7 Centre the freezer paper pattern on the right side of the appliqué fabric, sticky side down, and iron it in position (see page 349).

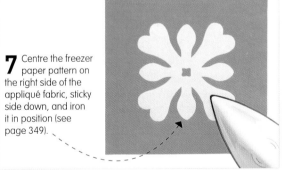

8 Tack the layers together 5mm (¼in) from the inside edge of the paper pattern.

9 Work a small section at a time by cutting away the appliqué (top) fabric along the edge of the pattern, leaving a 5mm (¼in) seam allowance outside the pattern. Turn the seam allowance under so that it's level with the edge of the pattern and blind stitch the fabric to the background.

10 Continue cutting and stitching until the entire pattern has been applied to the background (see page 347 for dealing with curves). Remove the tacking and peel the pattern away.

REVERSE HAND APPLIQUÉ

This technique uses two or more layers of fabric, cutting away the top layers to reveal the fabric beneath. The raw edges are turned under to finish the shape. Floral, pictorial, and geometric designs work well.

1 Choose two or three fabrics and tack them together, right-sides up, around the outside edge.

2 Trace the motif onto the non-shiny side of freezer paper and cut it out. Iron it to the centre of the fabric sandwich.

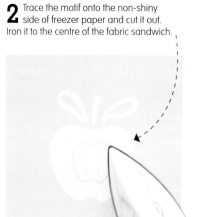

3 Using a removable marker, draw around the freezer-paper shape on the top fabric. Remove the template. Tack around the outline 10mm (½in) from the outside edge.

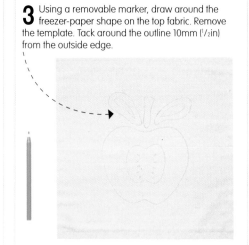

4 Using small sharp scissors, begin cutting away the shape 5mm (¼in) inside the marked line, being careful to cut only the top layer of fabric. Cut one section at a time, clipping or cutting small notches into any curves.

5 Turn under the seam allowance along the marked line. Using thread to match the top fabric, slip stitch the edge in place.

6 Mark the areas to be cut out from the second layer. Tack as in Step 3. Cut away the second layer, which will be smaller than the top layer. Always cut inside the marked line.

7 Using thread to match the second layer of fabric, slip stitch as in Step 5.

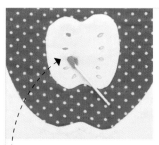

8 To add small areas of different colours under the second layer, cut a piece of fabric slightly larger than the area to be filled. Insert it into the cut-out area, using a toothpick or the tip of your needle. Turn under the edge on the second fabric and slip stitch. Remove all tacking stitches.

Finished piece

MACHINE APPLIQUÉ
GENERAL TECHNIQUES

Machine appliqué is quick and will stand many washes, especially if you use a tightly woven fabric and finish the edges with zigzag or satin stitch. Before you begin, it's a good idea to practise on scraps of your material. Try out different stitch widths and lengths to see what works best.

OUTER CORNERS

To work outer corners, stop with the needle outside the shape on the right-hand side. Lift the foot, turn the work, and continue.

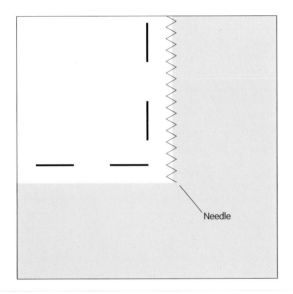

Needle

INNER CORNERS

To work inner corners, stop with the needle inside the shape on the left-hand side. Lift the foot, turn the work, and continue.

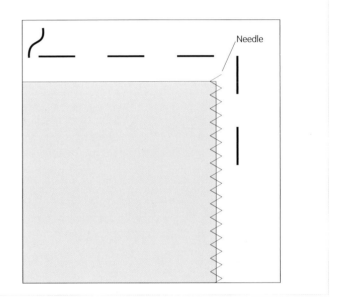

Needle

CONVEX CURVES

For convex (outer) curves, stop with the needle just outside the shape. Lift the foot, turn the work, and continue.

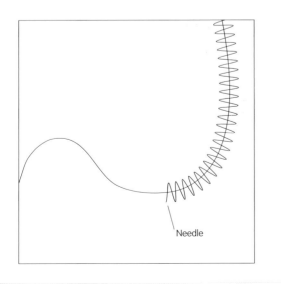

Needle

CONCAVE CURVES

For concave (inner) curves, stop with the needle inside the shape. When working any kind of curve, you may need to stop frequently to turn the work slightly, then take a few stitches, then stop, and turn again.

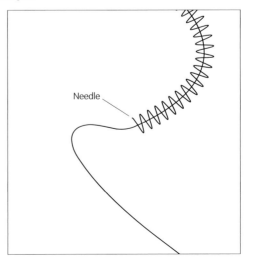

Needle

STITCH AND CUT
APPLIQUÉ

In this quick machine method, the motif is marked on the appliqué fabric and then sewn along the marked line before being cut out along the stitching line. The edges can then be finished by machine or by hand.

1 Make templates for the shapes. Draw around each shape on the right side of the fabric and add a 10mm (½in) seam allowance all around. Cut out the fabric shapes.

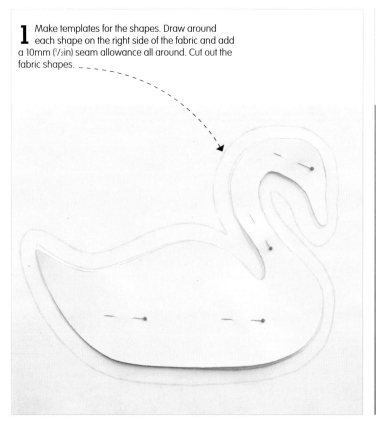

2 Pin the shapes to the background fabric, making sure that the pins will not get caught in the machine foot, and use straight stitch to sew along the marked line. (Here, we've used a contrasting colour of thread for clarity.)

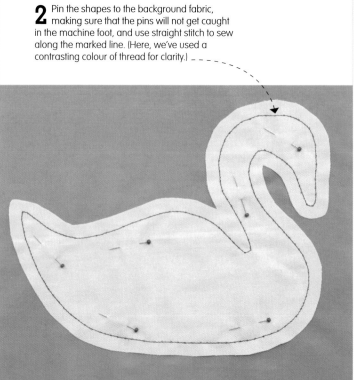

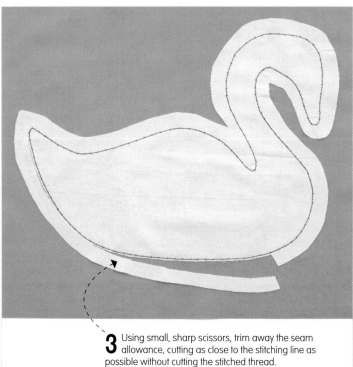

3 Using small, sharp scissors, trim away the seam allowance, cutting as close to the stitching line as possible without cutting the stitched thread.

4 Zigzag or satin stitch along the trimmed edge to finish the raw edge and hide the straight stitching.

FUSED
APPLIQUÉ

Fusible bonding web is a non-woven fabric impregnated with glue that is activated by heat. One side is anchored to paper on which shapes can be drawn. When ironed to the wrong side of a shape and then to the background fabric, it forms a firm bond that is almost impossible to remove. It is most suitable for machine appliqué, because it creates a stiffness that is difficult to sew by hand.

1 Transfer the shapes, in reverse, to the paper side of the web and cut them out roughly. If you group pieces that are to be cut from the same fabric close together, you can cut the whole group in one go, rather than cutting each individual shape separately.

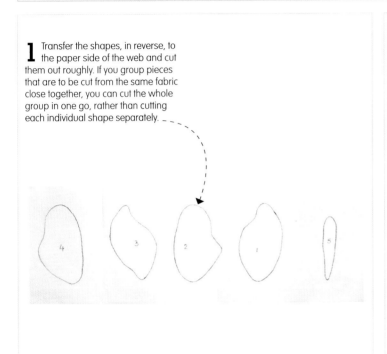

2 Following the manufacturer's instructions, place the rough, non-paper side on the wrong side of the fabric and press in place.

3 Cut out the shapes, cutting carefully along the drawn line, and peel off the backing papers. Position the shapes on the background fabric and iron in place.

4 Finish by stitching around the edges of each appliquéd piece with machine zigzag or satin stitch.

STAINED-GLASS APPLIQUÉ

Stained glass appliqué gets its name from the bias strips that separate the elements in the design, which resemble leading in church windows. You can make bias strips yourself (see page 378) or purchase bias strips with fusible bonding web on the back, which can be ironed in place to secure the strip while you stitch it in place. If your design features straight lines, you can use strips cut on the straight grain.

1 Transfer the pattern onto the background fabric. If the design is complicated, number the shapes on the background.

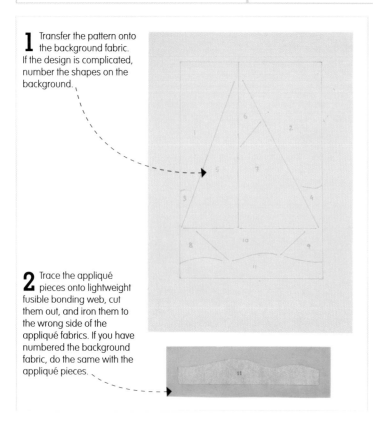

2 Trace the appliqué pieces onto lightweight fusible bonding web, cut them out, and iron them to the wrong side of the appliqué fabrics. If you have numbered the background fabric, do the same with the appliqué pieces.

3 Cut out the appliqué shapes without adding any seam allowances. Iron them in place on the background.

4 Butt each piece up tightly against its neighbour, so that it will be easier to catch the raw edges under the bias strips.

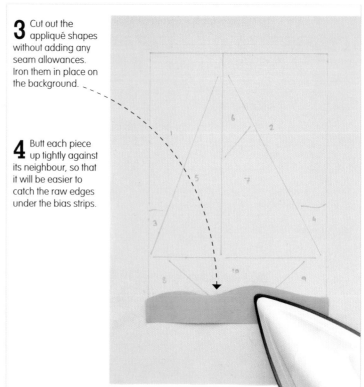

5 Plan the order in which you apply the bias strips so that you can cover any raw ends with another strip. Iron on the strips and stitch them in place, using a machine blindstitch.

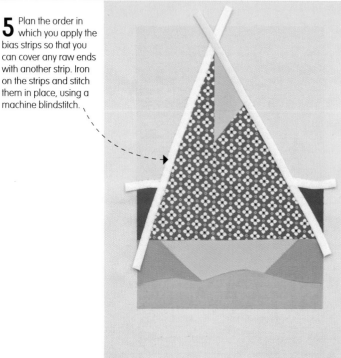

6 The bias strips cover the raw edges of the pieces over which they are placed.

SETTING

The way quilt blocks are arranged in a finished top is called the set, or setting. The following section can give only an outline of the virtually infinite possibilities for putting blocks together. The way to work out the best setting for a quilt is to lay the blocks out and view them from a distance.

QUILT LAYOUTS

Many quilt blocks, even fairly simple ones, can create interesting secondary patterns when they are joined, and rotating or reversing blocks makes a quilt look entirely different.

STRAIGHT SETS

The simplest sets are rows of repeating blocks stitched together edge to edge, referred to as "straight set".

ALTERNATING PIECED AND PLAIN

Alternating a pieced block with a plain one means fewer blocks to put together and allows large, open areas for quilting in the plain squares.

ON POINT: SOLID SET

Blocks can be set "on point" (turned on the diagonal), with setting triangles around the edges.

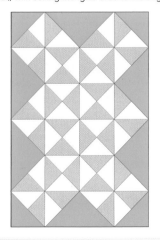

ON POINT: ALTERNATING PIECED AND PLAIN BLOCKS

This setting needs triangles added to each corner and along each side to fill the edges.

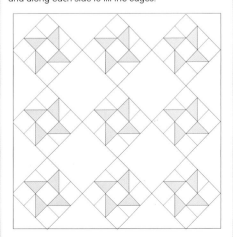

ROTATING BLOCKS

This setting creates new patterns once several blocks are set, particularly with asymmetrical patterns.

LOG CABIN

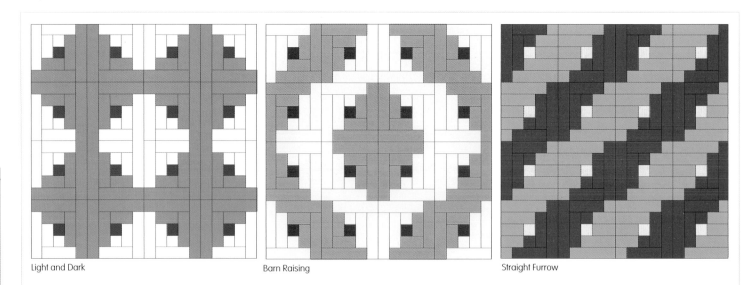

Light and Dark

Barn Raising

Straight Furrow

There are so many possible sets for Log Cabin designs that each version has its own name. These examples all have the same number of identical blocks. In each case, the way each row is turned determines the final effect.

FRAME SETTINGS

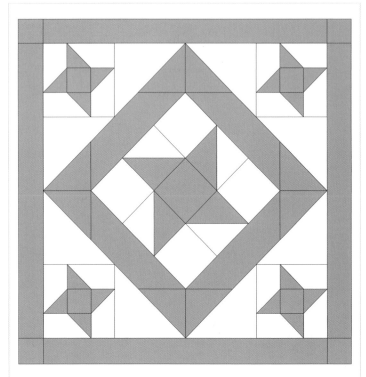

Also known as medallion settings, these have a central block, sometimes an elaborate appliqué, surrounded by several borders of various widths, some pieced, some plain. The centre can be set square or on point as here.

STRIPPY SET

When blocks are arranged vertically, a strippy set results. The first strippy quilts were usually simple strips of fabric joined to make the width of a quilt, but beautiful strippy quilts can be made from pieced blocks.

SASHING

Sashing is comprised of strips of fabric placed between blocks to frame them. Sampler quilts and star blocks are usually sashed to give each block the chance to shine. The space created by the sashing is flexible: try out various widths and colours before you cut the strips. Squares, plain or pieced, can be placed at the corners of each block within sashing strips to delineate the pattern further or continue a chained effect.

Each block in this piece is framed by straight-set simple sashing.

Straight-set simple continuous sashing

Adding a square in each corner between the blocks can create additional pattern. The corner squares can also be pieced; simple pinwheel, four-patch, and nine-patch designs work well.

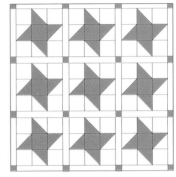

Straight set with corner square sashing

Blocks can be assembled in vertical or horizontal rows with sashing in only one direction.

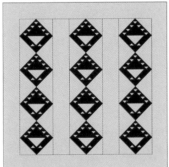

Vertical set with sashing

Blocks set on point can be sashed and assembled in strips with side triangles added to make a chevron sash.

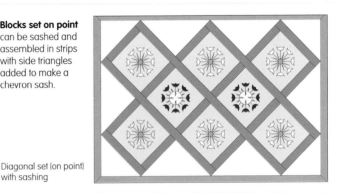

Diagonal set (on point) with sashing

SIMPLE CONTINUOUS SASHING

1 Cut strips to the desired width plus 10mm (1/2in) seam allowance and the same length as the measurement of one side of the blocks. With right sides together, taking a 5mm (1/4in) seam allowance, alternate strips and blocks to make a vertical row. Press seam allowances towards the sashing.

2 Cut strips to the desired width plus 10mm (1/2in) seam allowance and the same length as the joined row of blocks.

3 With right sides together, taking a 5mm (1/4in) seam allowance, sew a strip along the top and bottom of the row of blocks. Press seam allowance towards the sashing.

4 Continue alternating rows of sashing strips and blocks until the quilt top is the required size.

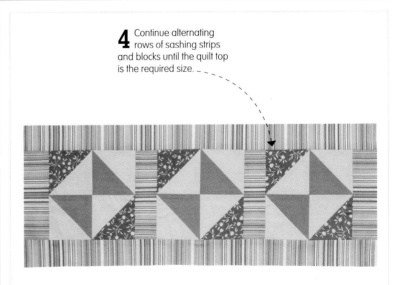

SASHING WITH CORNER SQUARES

1 Repeat Step 1 of simple continuous sashing (see page 359) to make rows of blocks.

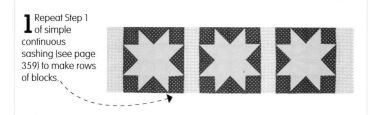

2 Cut strips the same length as the width of the block, and squares the same width as the strips. With right sides together, taking a 5mm (¹⁄₄in) seam allowance, alternate squares and strips to make a long strip.

3 With right sides together, taking a 5mm (¹⁄₄in) seam allowance, machine stitch one long strip along the top and bottom edges of the first row of blocks. Ensure that the corners of the blocks and the corner squares match up. Continue alternating rows of sashing strips and blocks until the quilt is the required size.

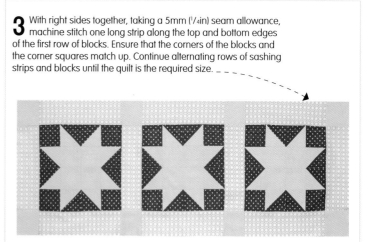

BORDERS

The outside edges of most quilts are finished with strips called the border, which frame the piece and protect the edges. They can be single or multiple, wide or narrow, pieced or plain. To help choose a size, try dividing the block measurement in half or three-quarters. If possible, strips should be cut along the lengthways grain, selvedges removed, in one long piece. Never cut borders on the bias.

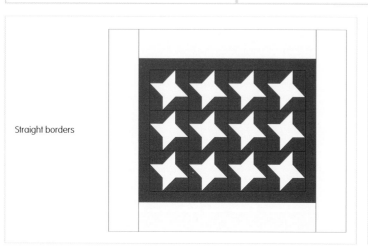

Straight borders

Mitred borders

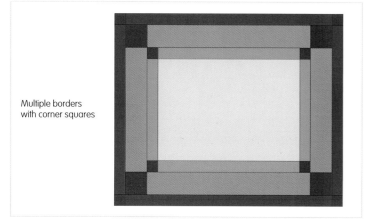

Multiple borders with corner squares

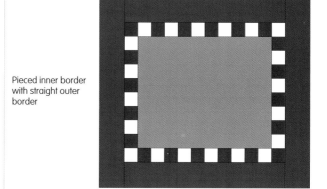

Pieced inner border with straight outer border

JOINING STRIPS TO MAKE A BORDER

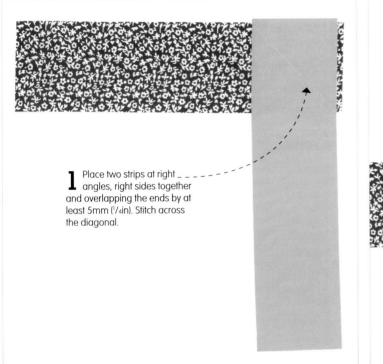

1 Place two strips at right angles, right sides together and overlapping the ends by at least 5mm (1/4in). Stitch across the diagonal.

2 Trim the seam to 5mm (1/4in) and trim the sides level. Press seam to one side.

STRAIGHT BORDERS

1 Cut or piece two border strips the same length as the sides of the quilt, plus 10mm (1/2in) seam allowances. Mark the centre of the strips and the sides of the quilt, and pin right sides together. Join, taking a 5mm (1/4in) seam allowance. Press seams towards border strips.

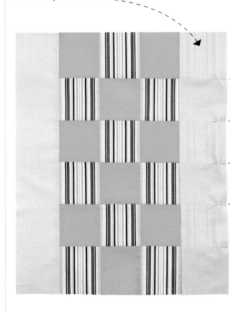

2 Measure the top and bottom of the quilt plus borders and cut two strips to that length. Mark the centre of the strips and top and bottom of the quilt, as in Step 1, and pin right sides together. Join, taking a 5mm (1/4in) seam allowance. Press seams towards the border strips. Repeat Steps 1 and 2 to add additional borders.

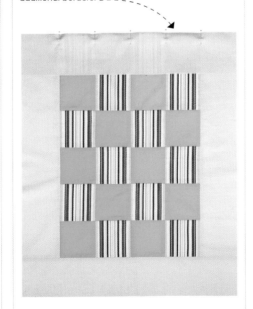

3 The quilt top is now completed and ready to be quilted (see pages 364–373).

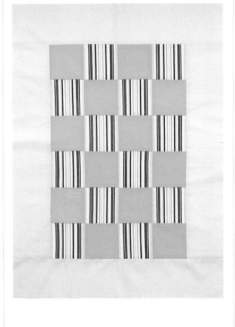

CORNER SQUARES ON A STRAIGHT BORDER

1 Follow Step 1 of straight borders (see page 361) to add the two side borders. Press seams towards the borders.

2 Cut two strips the same length as the top and bottom of the quilt without the side borders, plus a 10mm (½in) seam allowance.

3 Cut four corner squares the same size as the width of the border strips. Add a square to each end of the strips. Press the seams towards the centre.

4 Add the pieced strips to the top and bottom of the quilt. Press the seams towards the border strips.

5 The quilt top is now completed and ready to be quilted (see pages 364–373).

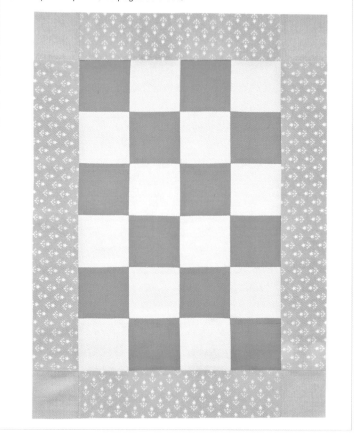

MITRED BORDERS

1 Cut border strips to the desired width, plus 10mm (¹/₂in) seam allowance, and 10cm (4in) longer than the sides of the quilt.

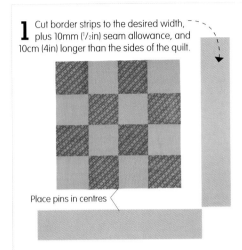

Place pins in centres

2 Place a pin as a marker in the centre of the strips and the top and bottom of the quilt. Pin them right sides together. Place a pin as a marker 5mm (¹/₄in) from each corner.

3 Join the border strips to all sides of the quilt, taking a 5mm (¹/₄in) seam allowance. Do not stitch into adjoining border strips. Press the seams towards the borders.

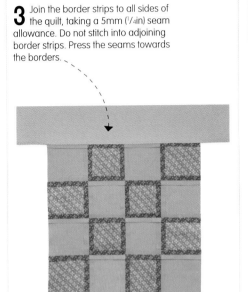

4 Place the quilt right side up on a flat surface and fold under each end of each strip to the wrong side, at a 45-degree angle. Pin the folds in place from the right side and make sure the angle is correct. Remove the pins and press the folds.

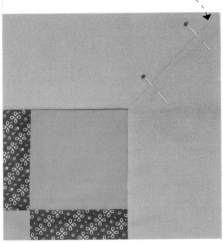

5 Working from the wrong side, re-pin the mitre along the pressed fold. Tack if desired. Stitch from the quilt edge to the outside corner. Trim the seam allowance and press it open. Repeat to mitre all corners.

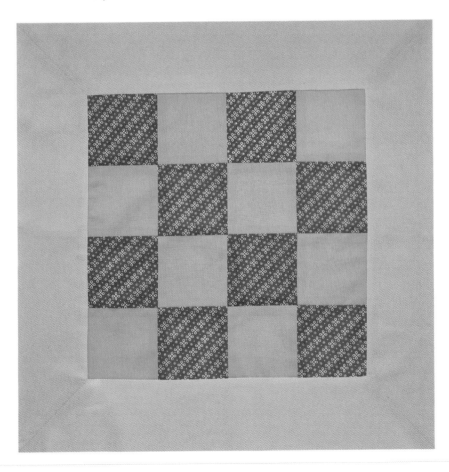

MULTIPLE MITRED BORDERS

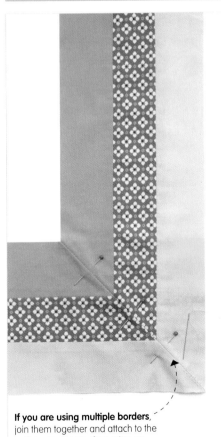

If you are using multiple borders, join them together and attach to the quilt top in one go, then mitre as above, making sure you match the seams for each border in the mitre.

QUILTING

Quilting holds the layers of a quilt together, gives a quilt its texture, and should add to the overall beauty of the piece. Quilting motifs range from geometric grids and simple heart shapes to elaborate scrolls. Some appliqué motifs look best if they are outlined or echoed by quilting.

TRANSFERRING DESIGNS

Once the quilt top is finished, you need to transfer the quilting pattern onto it. Use equipment that can be removed, such as water- or air-soluble pens or light pencil marks, to mark the pattern. Tailor's chalk applied lightly can usually be removed. Slivers of soap can make effective and washable marks on dark fabrics. Dressmaker's carbon paper is indelible and not recommended.

MASKING TAPE

1 After the quilt has been layered with wadding and backing, apply 5mm (¼in) masking tape in lines as a guide. This method only works for quilting designs in straight lines.

2 Stitch along the edge of the tape by hand or machine, then remove the tape as soon as possible. When the rows are complete, repeat in the other direction.

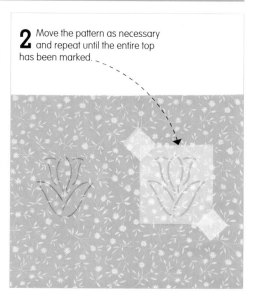

TRACING

If your project is small and light in colour, you can trace the pattern directly on the fabric. Place the quilt top over the pattern on a lightbox or a glass-top table with a table lamp underneath. Alternatively, tape it to a clean window. Trace the design lightly onto the fabric.

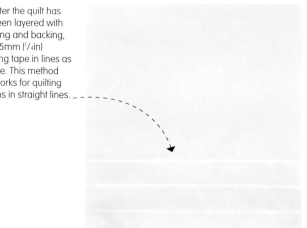

TEMPLATES OR STENCILS

1 Mark the design on the finished top before you layer it. Place the pattern on the quilt top and secure it with masking tape or weights. Draw around a template or in the channels of a stencil with a very sharp pencil. Keep the line as light as possible.

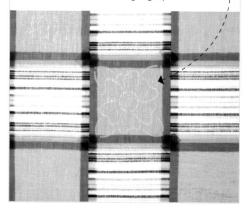

2 Move the pattern as necessary and repeat until the entire top has been marked.

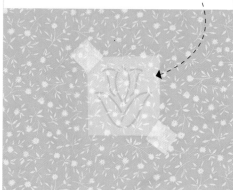

TRACE AND TACK

1 Use on fabrics that are hard to mark. Transfer the pattern to the quilt top before you layer it. Transfer the design to tissue paper and pin in place. With the knot on top, sew along the pattern lines with a small running stitch. Secure with a double backstitch.

2 Pull the paper away gently without disturbing the tacking. If necessary, score the marked lines with a pin to break the paper.

ASSEMBLING THE QUILT LAYERS

Once you have marked the quilting pattern on the quilt top, it is time to assemble the quilt "sandwich", which is the layers of top, wadding, and backing that make up the quilt. If the wadding has been folded, open it out flat and leave it for several hours to relax the wrinkles.

1 Trim the wadding and backing 7.5–10cm (3–4in) larger all around than the finished top. Lay the backing wrong side up on the work surface and smooth it flat. Secure it to the surface with masking tape.

Backing fabric (wrong side)

Wadding

2 Centre the wadding on the backing, and smooth it out.

3 Position the quilt top right side up, centring it on the wadding. Use a ruler to check that the top is squared up. Using large quilter's straight pins, temporarily pin along each squared edge as you work.

Backing fabric (wrong side)

Wadding

Quilt top (right side)

4 Working from the centre out diagonally, horizontally, and vertically, tack or safety pin the layers together. Remove the pins along the edge as you reach them. Keep smoothing the layers. Take tacking stitches 5cm (2in) long – first vertically and horizontally, then diagonally. If pinning, follow the same pattern and insert the pins at 7.5–10cm (3–4in) intervals.

BAGGING OUT

Sometimes you may want to finish the edges of the quilt before you quilt it. The technique works well on smaller projects, such as baby quilts. Cut the wadding and backing slightly larger than the quilt top.

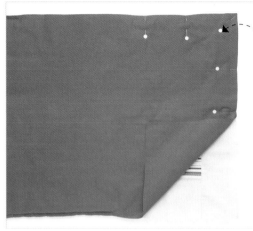

1 Centre the quilt top right-side up on the wadding. Centre the backing on the quilt top, right-side down. Pin or tack the layers together around the edge.

2 Start machine stitching at the bottom edge, several centimetres (about an inch) from the corner, taking a 5mm (¼in) seam. Secure with backstitching.

3 At the corners, stop 5mm (¼in) from the edge with the needle down. Raise the presser foot. Pivot the fabric, lower the presser foot and continue sewing. On the fourth side leave an opening of 12–25cm (5–10in). Secure with backstitching.

4 Clip the corners to reduce bulk. If necessary, trim and grade the seams, then turn right-side out through the opening.

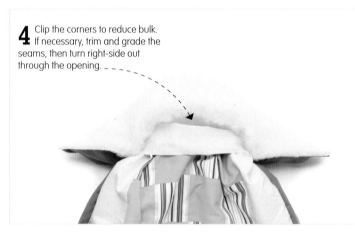

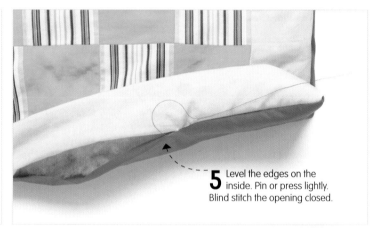

5 Level the edges on the inside. Pin or press lightly. Blind stitch the opening closed.

MAKING A BIGGER BACKING

Most bed quilts are wider than most fabrics, so it is often necessary to piece the backing. There are several ways to do this, but you should avoid having a seam down the vertical centre of the quilt.

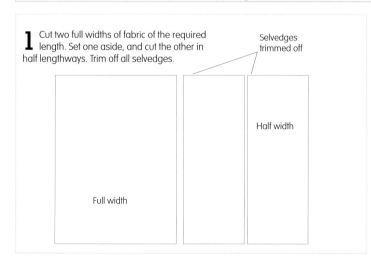

1 Cut two full widths of fabric of the required length. Set one aside, and cut the other in half lengthways. Trim off all selvedges.

Selvedges trimmed off

Half width

Full width

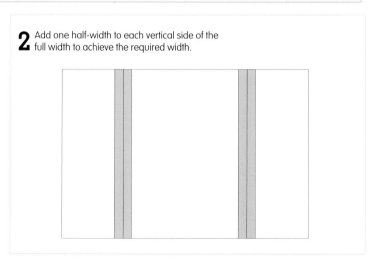

2 Add one half-width to each vertical side of the full width to achieve the required width.

HAND QUILTING
BASICS

Quilting by hand gives a soft look. Straight, even stitches are worked, ideally with the needle at an angle of 90 degrees, and the same stitch length on front and back. Because of the thickness of the quilt layers, the stitches are executed using a technique known as "rocking" the needle, which uses both hands. Use quilting threads and needles, and wear a thimble on your middle finger and a protective guard underneath.

KNOTTING TO BEGIN

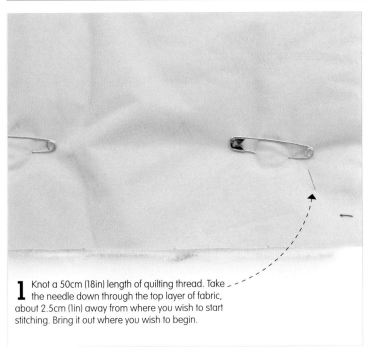

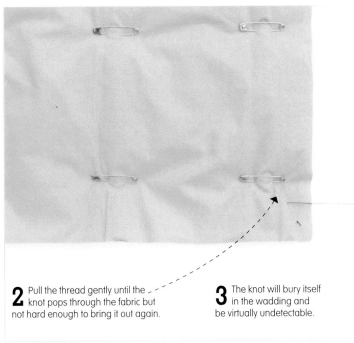

1 Knot a 50cm (18in) length of quilting thread. Take the needle down through the top layer of fabric, about 2.5cm (1in) away from where you wish to start stitching. Bring it out where you wish to begin.

2 Pull the thread gently until the knot pops through the fabric but not hard enough to bring it out again.

3 The knot will bury itself in the wadding and be virtually undetectable.

FINISHING OFF

1 To secure the thread at the end, take a small back stitch through the top layer and pull the thread through to the top. Make a French knot (see page 203), close to the end of the stitching. Secure the wraps with your finger and pull the knot tight.

2 Insert the needle point into the top layer only, next to where the thread emerges and in the opposite direction to the stitching. Slide the needle within the wadding and bring it out about 2cm (³/₄in) from the end of the stitching. Gently pull the French knot through into the wadding.

3 Carefully cut the thread close to the surface and let the tail sink into the wadding.

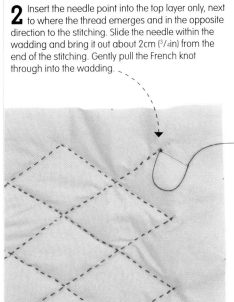

QUILTING OR ROCKING STITCH

1 Bury the knot as in knotting to begin (see page 367). Place one hand under the quilt where the needle should emerge.

2 With the needle between thumb and forefinger of your needle hand, push the needle with your thimbled finger straight down until you feel the point with your underneath hand. Stop pushing.

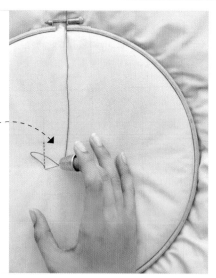

3 With your underneath finger, push up gently against the side of the needle and the quilt. At the same time, push down with your top thumb and make a bump in the layers while you push the needle to the top.

4 Stop when the length of the needle protruding on the top is the same length as the next stitch.

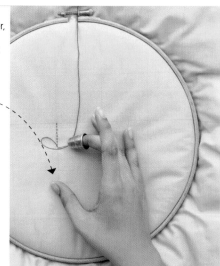

5 Use the thimbled finger to bring the eye of the needle upright again, while at the same time pushing in front of it with your thumb. When the needle is upright and the point breaks through the fabric, push down as in Step 1.

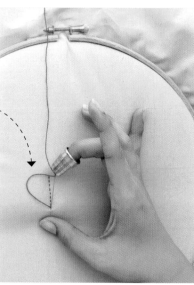

6 Continue this motion until the needle has as many stitches as it will hold. Pull the thread through. Repeat.

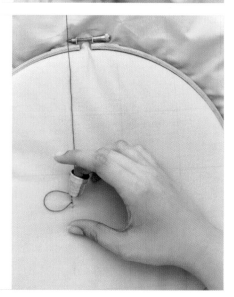

STAB STITCH

1 Stab stitch is an alternative way to work on thick quilts. Use a thimble on each middle finger. Bury the knot as in knotting to begin (see page 367). Push the upright needle straight down through all layers. Pull the needle and thread through to the back.

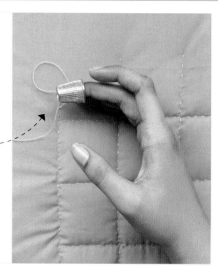

2 Push the upright needle back up through all layers, working a stitch length away from the previous stitch. Pull the needle and thread through to the top. Repeat.

MACHINE
QUILTING BASICS

Beautifully machined quilts are in no way second best to those worked by hand. Because the stitches are continuous, the finished product is usually flatter than a hand-quilted one. An even-feed, or "walking", foot, which feeds the layers through at the same speed top and bottom, is useful. Start and finish either by setting the stitch length to 0 and taking a few stitches before re-setting, or leave a tail of thread to tie off.

PREPARING A QUILT FOR MACHINING

1 To work on a small area at a time, roll up both sides of the quilt towards the centre, leaving 30cm (12in) open in between. Hold the edges with clips.

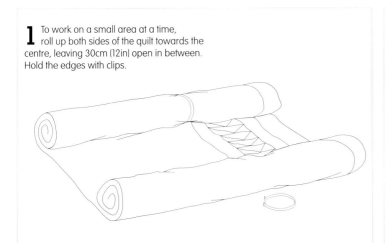

2 Fold or roll up the open ends of the piece and secure them using clips, leaving space to work on. Repeat the rolling and/or folding process as you work.

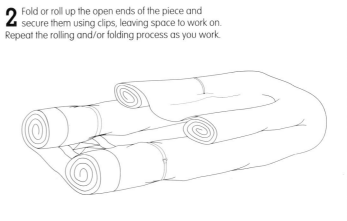

CONCENTRIC
QUILTING

Concentric quilting lines can be worked by hand or machine. Outline quilting emphasizes a pieced or appliquéd design and requires minimal marking. Straight lines can be marked with 5mm (¼in) masking tape; curves can be drawn lightly. Echo quilting is similar, but consists of a series of evenly spaced concentric quilted lines. It is most often used in Hawaiian appliqué (see page 351.

OUTLINE QUILTING

Follow the seamlines or outlines of the motif, working 5mm (¼in) away inside or outside, or on both sides of, the lines.

ECHO QUILTING

Make a row of outline quilting (see left). Then add evenly spaced rows to fill the background around the motif.

SEEDING

Also known as stippling, this hand-quilting method uses small, straight stitches to fill the background.

1 Bury the knot (see page 367). Bring the needle and thread out near the motif. Take to the back and come up a short distance away from the first stitch.

2 Take another stitch straight down and pull the thread through and come up a short distance away. Work outwards from the motif. Keep the stitches small on the front and back and position them randomly to look like seeds.

QUILTING IN THE DITCH

Here, the stitching follows the piecing lines on the quilt top and is hidden in the seams.

Secure the thread. Stitch along each row of piecing in turn. Stop and start as little as possible.

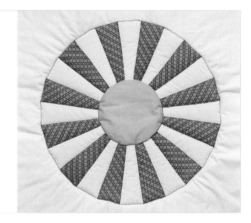

QUILT AS YOU GO

If you work patchwork directly onto layers of wadding and backing fabric, you will end up with a finished piece that needs no further quilting. The technique works best when piecing strips or assembling a medallion quilt with a border. Borders can be pieced and added as strips.

1 Cut backing and wadding to size of finished piece plus 2.5cm (1in) all around. Tack together along all edges.

2 Cut a central medallion and the strips for the first border. Position the medallion face up in the centre of the backing and apply the first strip, right sides together, sewing through all layers. Add side strips first, fingerpress open, then apply top and bottom strips. Fingerpress the first round open.

3 Add strips in your chosen order. Trim backing and wadding to correct size and add binding (see page 379).

CORDED QUILTING
AND TRAPUNTO

Corded quilting, or Italian quilting, and trapunto, or stuffed quilting, are techniques that can be used separately, but they work well together. Both involve stitching a design through a top and a thin backing layer, usually of butter muslin. The motif is then filled from the back with lengths of quilting, knitting wool or soft cord, or with stuffing material. The outline is traditionally worked by hand.

1 Cut a background fabric and transfer the design to the right side, using a water-soluble pen. Cut a piece of butter muslin or similar fabric the same size. Tack them together around the edges.

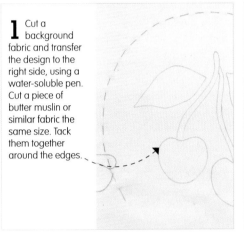

2 Outline the motif(s) with a small running stitch. Here we have used a contrasting colour thread for clarity. Where lines meet, keep stitches separate so they don't cross over.

3 When stitching is complete, remove the marking.

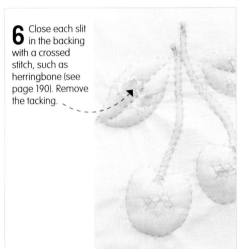

4 Thread a tapestry needle with quilting or knitting wool or cord. From the back, slip the needle through the first channel, leaving a short tail at each end.

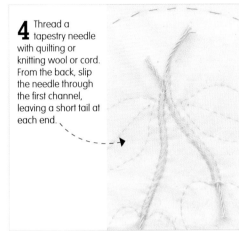

5 Make small slits in the centre of each element through the backing layer only and stuff small pieces of wadding between the top and the muslin.

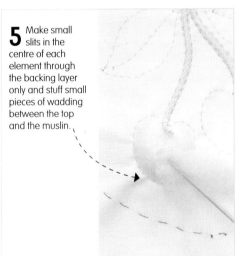

6 Close each slit in the backing with a crossed stitch, such as herringbone (see page 190). Remove the tacking.

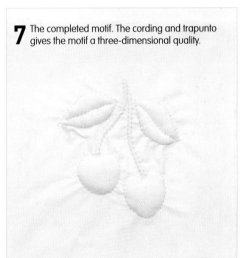

7 The completed motif. The cording and trapunto gives the motif a three-dimensional quality.

GRID
PATTERNS

Traditional gridded quilting patterns can be square or diamond shaped. Mark the grid by drawing the centre line in each direction, or use 5mm (¼in) masking tape. If you set a quilting guide on your walking foot, you can use it to measure the distance between rows as you work.

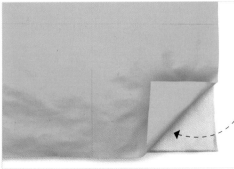

1 Take a few short stitches. Set the quilting guide to the correct distance on one side and stitch the first marked row from edge to edge. Turn the work and use the quilting guide to measure each vertical row in turn.

2 Repeat to work the horizontal rows.

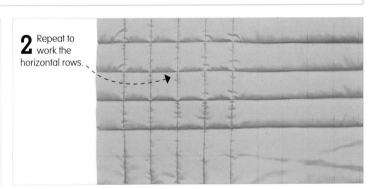

FREESTYLE QUILTING

Freestyle, or free-motion, quilting gives machine quilters a great deal of freedom to create their own designs. Mastering the technique requires practice, but the effort can be well rewarded with unique work. You need a darning foot or a free-motion foot and to know how to lower the feed dogs. If your machine has the option to stop work with the needle always down, use it.

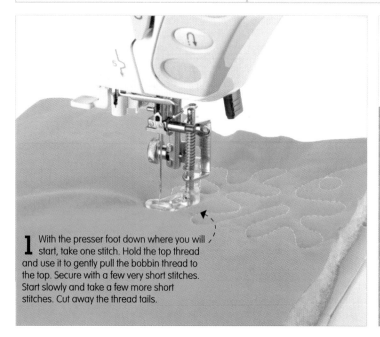

1 With the presser foot down where you will start, take one stitch. Hold the top thread and use it to gently pull the bobbin thread to the top. Secure with a few very short stitches. Start slowly and take a few more short stitches. Cut away the thread tails.

2 Guide the fabric with your hands, moving the work in any direction. Position your hands in an open circle around the machine foot and press the layers gently. Keep a moderate speed and make the stitches the same length. Tie off with a few short stitches, as in Step 1.

TYING

Tying involves tying lengths of thread, lightweight wool, or ribbon through the layers of a quilt to hold them together. Cotton perle and stranded cotton both work well. You will need a sharp-pointed needle with an eye that is large enough to hold the thread but small enough to avoid making holes in the quilt. Space the ties according to the type of wadding, the block pattern, and the size of the quilt. Cotton and wool wadding shift easily and should be tied more closely than polyester. A general guide is 10–15cm (4–6in) apart.

1 Working from the centre out, take a stitch through all the layers and pull the needle and thread through, leaving a 10cm (4in) tail on the top.

2 Take a second stitch in the same place.

3 Tie the ends of thread in a reef knot. Cut the thread from the reel and trim the ends to the same length. Repeat, double-stitching and knotting over the entire quilt.

EMBELLISHING
QUILTS

From surface embroidery and beading to adding buttons, bows, and found objects, the ways to embellish a quilt are endless. You can use sequins, charms, or shisha mirrors, or add machine embroidery. Many embellishing techniques, including beading, adding sequins, and surface embroidery, can be found in the Embroidery chapter, pages 166–229.

BUTTONS

Novelty buttons make charming embellishments on theme quilts or folk-art versions. Buttons can also become "flowers" at the end of stems in a basket or accents in any number of places. Stitch buttons to the quilt top and knot them if you don't want to stitch through the backing. Otherwise, tie a knot at the back.

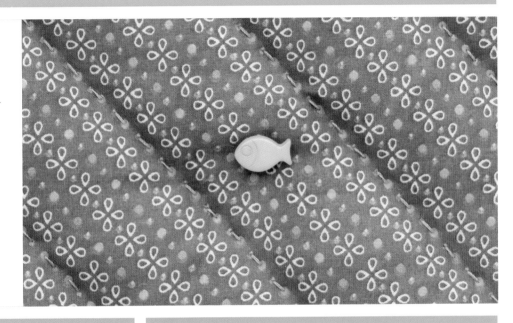

CHARMS

Simply tie charms in position on the quilt top, depending on the type and size. Charms are usually used to add a personal touch to a quilt – wedding motifs for a bride's quilt, for example. They are best reserved for decorative pieces such as wall hangings and should not be used on quilts for children and babies, since they can become detached.

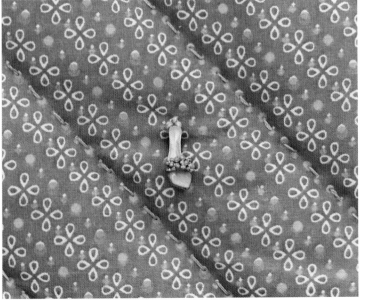

BOWS

Tie ribbon bows to the desired size and stitch them in place on the quilt top. They can be single or double bows. Make sure the knot is secure before stitching.

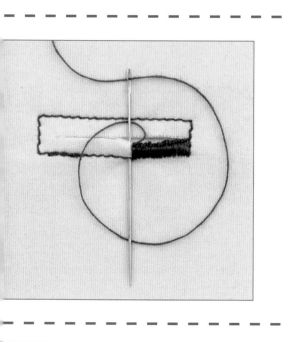  

FINISHING

The general and decorative techniques you need to finish your
item of needlecraft, such as hemming, binding, and adding fastenings
and decorative edgings.

GENERAL FINISHING TECHNIQUES

Finishing the edges of a quilt or an embroidery is the final stage in their creation. Quilts must always be bound in some way and some needlepoint benefits from binding, while embroidered work can be hemmed or bound depending on its proposed use and personal preference.

HEMMING
NEEDLEWORK

A variety of hems can be used to finish the edges of needlecrafted pieces. Hems can be turned to the back or the front; they can be straight or mitred at the corners. The choice depends mainly on the desired look, but also on the fabric and the use to which the piece will be put. Hems along drawn-thread borders (see page 217) can be caught into the stitching as the embroidery is being worked.

DOUBLE-TURNED HEM

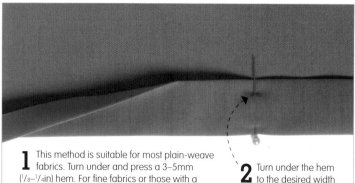

1 This method is suitable for most plain-weave fabrics. Turn under and press a 3–5mm (¹/₈–¹/₄in) hem. For fine fabrics or those with a tendency to fray, tack and machine in place.

2 Turn under the hem to the desired width and pin in place.

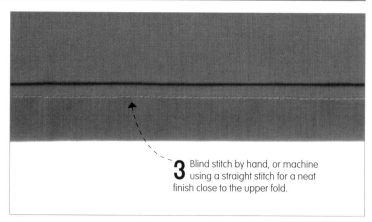

3 Blind stitch by hand, or machine using a straight stitch for a neat finish close to the upper fold.

SINGLE-TURNED HEM

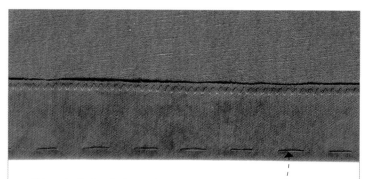

1 This method is best for heavy plain weaves. Finish the raw edge with a zigzag or overlocking stitch, or bind it with bias binding (see page 378). Turn the hem to the wrong side, press lightly and tack in place.

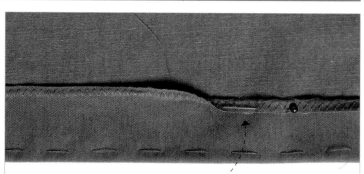

2 Either slip stitch in place by hand or blind stitch the hem in place by machine. Remove tacking.

FACED HEM

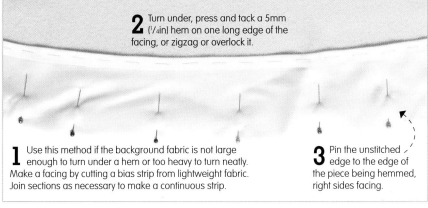

2 Turn under, press and tack a 5mm (¹⁄₄in) hem on one long edge of the facing, or zigzag or overlock it.

1 Use this method if the background fabric is not large enough to turn under a hem or too heavy to turn neatly. Make a facing by cutting a bias strip from lightweight fabric. Join sections as necessary to make a continuous strip.

3 Pin the unstitched edge to the edge of the piece being hemmed, right sides facing.

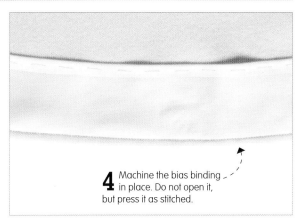

4 Machine the bias binding in place. Do not open it, but press it as stitched.

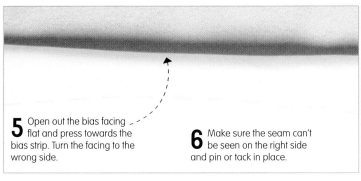

5 Open out the bias facing flat and press towards the bias strip. Turn the facing to the wrong side.

6 Make sure the seam can't be seen on the right side and pin or tack in place.

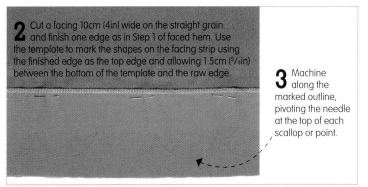

7 Blind stitch along the hemmed top edge of the bias strip. Remove tacking.

DECORATIVE FACINGS

The same technique for making a faced hem can be used to make decorative hems, such as scallops or points, for finishing a hanging or embellishing an edge on a cushion or piece of patchwork.

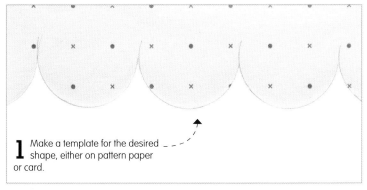

1 Make a template for the desired shape, either on pattern paper or card.

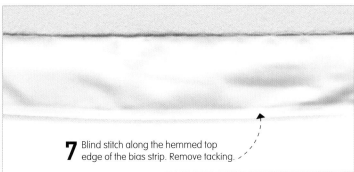

2 Cut a facing 10cm (4in) wide on the straight grain and finish one edge as in Step 1 of faced hem. Use the template to mark the shapes on the facing strip using the finished edge as the top edge and allowing 1.5cm (⁵⁄₈in) between the bottom of the template and the raw edge.

3 Machine along the marked outline, pivoting the needle at the top of each scallop or point.

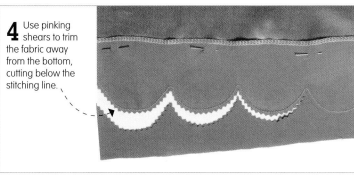

4 Use pinking shears to trim the fabric away from the bottom, cutting below the stitching line.

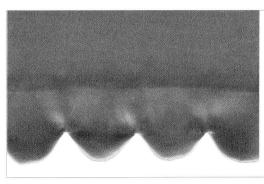

5 Turn through to the right side and press. Blind stitch the finished edge of the facing to secure it.

BINDINGS

Bias binding is available in various colours and widths, or you can make your own. Bindings should be applied as a continuous strip. If possible, cut straight binding strips along the lengthways grain of the fabric or join pieces before applying (see page 361). Bias binding has more stretch than straight binding, making it suitable for binding work with curved edges.

MAKING A STRAIGHT BINDING STRIP

1 Measure the edges of the piece being bound and decide on the width of the finished binding. Cut strips twice this width plus 10mm (½in), allowing extra length for mitring corners and joining pieces.

2 Ensure your edges are square and cut along the straight grain of the fabric. Add about 40cm (16in) to the length for full quilts, 30cm (12in) for baby quilts, wall hangings, and large embroideries, and 20cm (8in) for small works.

MAKING A BIAS STRIP

1 Buy at least 1.5m (1³/₄yd) of fabric so you can cut very long strips. Cut off selvedges and smooth the fabric flat. Straighten the right-hand edge of the fabric, then fold this edge back so that it aligns with the top edge and forms an exact 45-degree angle. Cut along this bias fold.

2 Using a metal ruler and a sharp piece of tailor's chalk, mark lines on the fabric parallel to the bias edge and 4cm (1½in) apart. Cut out the strips along the chalked lines. Cut as many strips as you need for your project plus a little extra.

3 Join strips together to make a continuous strip. Pin the strips together at a 90-degree angle with right sides facing and sew a 5mm (¼in) seam on the bias. The seam should run from edge to edge of each strip, with a triangle of fabric left at either end of the seam.

4 Press the seam open and trim off the seam allowances. You can also make bias binding with these prepared strips. To do this, press under the edges or run the strip through a bias binding maker.

MAKING A CONTINUOUS BIAS STRIP

1 Cut a square of binding fabric with 90-degree corners. Mark two opposite sides as A and B and draw a diagonal line. Cut along the marked line.

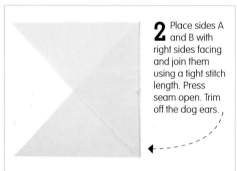

2 Place sides A and B with right sides facing and join them using a tight stitch length. Press seam open. Trim off the dog ears.

3 Mark lines parallel to the bias edges the desired width of the strip.

4 Bring the remaining two straight-grain edges together and offset the marked lines by aligning one tip of the fabric to the first marked line on the other side. Pin carefully to match the marked lines and sew together, right sides facing, to make a tube.

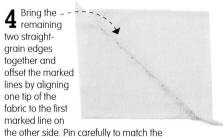

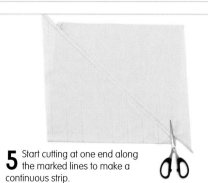

5 Start cutting at one end along the marked lines to make a continuous strip.

CALCULATING METERAGE

- **Multiply the length** of two sides and divide by the width of the binding strip to calculate the length of a binding strip. For example, for a 5cm (2in) binding, from a 90cm (36in) square, 90 x 90cm = 8100cm (36 x 36in = 1296in). Divide by 5cm (2in) to get 1620cm (648in). You can make 16.2m (18yd) of binding, which should be sufficient for a king-size quilt. Always work in either the metric or imperial system.

BINDING EMBROIDERY
OR NEEDLEPOINT

Needlepoint and embroidered pictures and some single-layer appliqué work can be finished effectively by binding the edges using a single binding. Single binding can also be used to bind a quilt, but it is not as durable as double binding.

SINGLE BINDING

1 Cut a binding strip to the desired width and press a 5mm (¹/₄in) seam allowance along one long edge. Align the top of the binding strip with one corner of the piece and pin along the unpressed edge with right sides facing. Stitch the strip in place. Repeat on the opposite side.

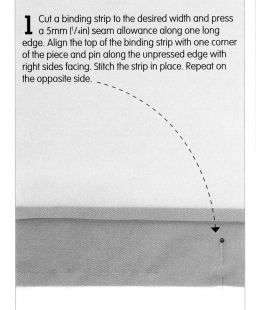

2 Turn the strips to the wrong side, pin or tack in place and blind stitch along the folded edge, making sure the stitches don't show on the front.

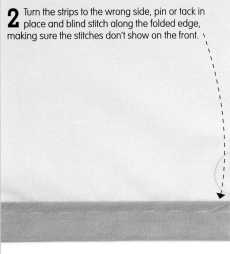

3 Measure the remaining sides and cut two strips to that length, plus 10mm (¹/₂in) seam allowances. Turn under a 5mm (¹/₄in) allowance at each end of each strip, and aligning the top and bottom, pin one strip to each of the remaining sides along the unpressed edge.

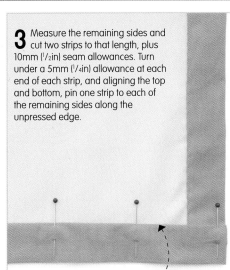

4 Stitch in place, then turn to the wrong side and repeat to blind stitch in place along the fold. Blind stitch the ends of these strips to finish.

BINDING A QUILT:
DOUBLE BINDING

Double binding is stronger than single binding and is recommended for binding bed quilts. Quilted wall hangings and other small, layered items that won't get routine wear and tear can be single-bound.

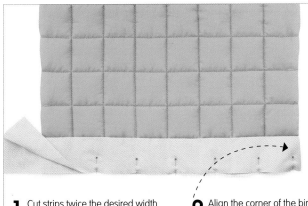

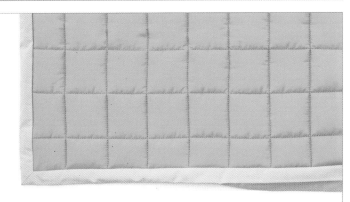

1 Cut strips twice the desired width plus 10mm (¹/₂in) seam allowances. Fold in half lengthways, wrong sides together, and press. Mark each corner of the quilt top 5mm (¹/₄in) from each side edge.

2 Align the corner of the binding strip to one corner of the right side of the quilt and pin with the doubled raw edges along the quilt edge. Repeat on the opposite side. The raw ends will be covered by the final strips.

3 Start and finish stitching from the marked seam allowance along the raw edges. Turn the folded edge of the binding to the back and slipstitch in place. Repeat on the opposite side.

4 Turn under a 5mm (¹/₄in) allowance at each end of the two final strips and apply them in the same way.

CORDING AND PIPING

Cushion covers, home accessories, or bags made up in various needlework techniques often require a contrasting decorative edging of cording or piping. Cording is the easiest to apply; however, with piping your choice of colour is endless.

SEWING ON CORDING

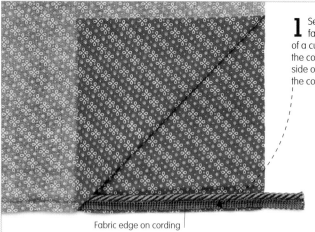

Fabric edge on cording

1 Sew cording in between two layers of fabric, for example, along the seamline of a cushion cover. Align the fabric edge of the cording with the raw edge of the right side of the front piece. Tack in place along the cording.

2 Lay the back piece over the cording, with the right sides of the fabric pieces together, and machine stitch along the cording using a zip foot.

3 Remove the tacking and turn the fabric pieces right-side out. Press the fabric away from the cord so that the cord sits neatly along the seamline.

COVERING AND INSERTING PIPING CORD

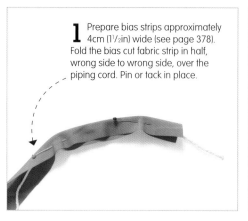

1 Prepare bias strips approximately 4cm (1½in) wide (see page 378). Fold the bias cut fabric strip in half, wrong side to wrong side, over the piping cord. Pin or tack in place.

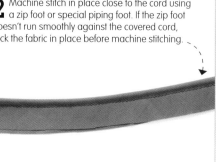

2 Machine stitch in place close to the cord using a zip foot or special piping foot. If the zip foot doesn't run smoothly against the covered cord, tack the fabric in place before machine stitching.

3 Trim the seam allowance on the piping cover so that it is the desired seam allowance width – it can be less than this width, but not more.

4 Align the seam on the piping cover with the seamline on the right side of the front of the fabric. Pin or tack in place with the piping facing inwards.

5 If you are sewing the piping around a corner, bend it carefully to form a 90-degree angle and continue tacking.

6 Place the back fabric piece over the front piece with the right sides together. Using a zip foot, machine stitch the layers together, stitching on top of the piping cord seam.

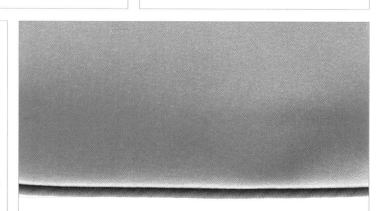

7 Turn the piece right-side out and carefully press the fabric away from the piping.

FASTENINGS

Although fastenings have a practical use – securing closings on cushion covers, bags, garments, and home accessories – many of them also serve as decorative finishing details. Techniques for adding very simple fastenings are provided here, including easy-to-work button loops, hand-stitched buttonholes, ties, snap fasteners, and zips. There are also helpful tips for sewing on buttons.

MAKING SIMPLE BUTTON LOOPS

1 Work simple button loops directly onto the seamline at the edge of fabric so that the securing stitches are worked through four layers of fabric – the front fabric layer, the two seam allowance layers, and the back fabric layer.

2 Thread the needle with one strand of thick, strong buttonhole thread. Run it between the layers of fabric and out at the right of the loop position. Make three small stitches through the layers in the same place, close to the edge.

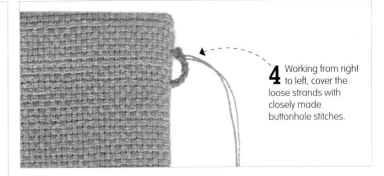

4 Working from right to left, cover the loose strands with closely made buttonhole stitches.

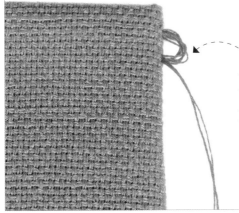

3 Insert the needle through the fabric to the left, leaving a gap the same width as the button's diameter. Create four loose strands of thread back and forth over this gap, making one stitch through the edge at each end of each loop.

5 Once the strands are completely covered, secure the end in the same way as in Step 2.

HAND-STITCHED BUTTONHOLES

Practise on scrap fabric to improve your skills before stitching directly onto your needlework. Always work buttonholes through two layers of fabric that have an interfacing in between them.

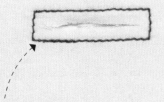

1 Mark the desired finished length of the buttonhole on the right side of the piece, then machine stitch a rectangle 5mm (¼in) wide and as long as the required finished buttonhole length. Carefully cut a slit along the exact centre of this rectangle.

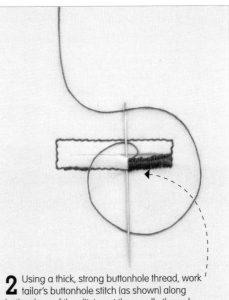

2 Using a thick, strong buttonhole thread, work tailor's buttonhole stitch (as shown) along both edges of the slit. Insert the needle through the fabric just outside the machine stitches, so that the stitches are 3mm (⅛in) long.

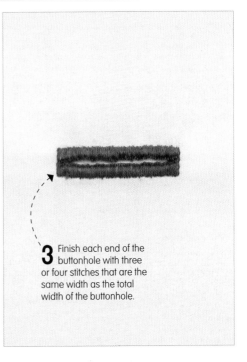

3 Finish each end of the buttonhole with three or four stitches that are the same width as the total width of the buttonhole.

ROULEAU BUTTON LOOPS

1 Cut a bias strip 4cm (1¹/₂in) wide from a lightweight cotton fabric (see page 378). A strip 10cm (4in) long (excluding the pointed ends), is long enough for a loop for buttons up to 2.5cm (1in) in diameter. Fold the strip in half lengthways with right sides together and pin.

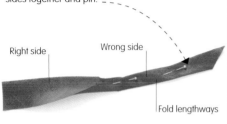

Right side   Wrong side

Fold lengthways

2 Machine stitch lengthways along the folded strip, 5mm (¹/₄in) from the fold, leaving long thread ends. Then machine stitch along the seam allowance, 3mm (¹/₈in) from the first line of stitching.

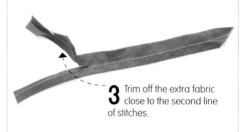

3 Trim off the extra fabric close to the second line of stitches.

4 Thread the two long loose ends of thread at one end of the rouleau strip onto a blunt-ended needle and pass the needle through to pull the rouleau right-side out. Alternatively use a loop turner.

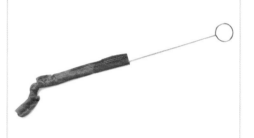

5 Press the rouleau strip flat, aligning the seamline along one edge. With the seamline along the inside of the button loop, fold the rouleau as shown. Ensure the folded loop is long enough to accommodate the button, with a sufficient seam allowance at the ends.

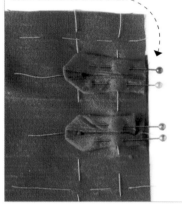

6 Machine stitch the folded rouleau loop face down to the right side of the garment or accessory, with raw edges aligned.

7 Machine stitch the first line inside the seam allowance just outside the seamline. Stitch the second line 4mm (³/₁₆in) from the first.

8 Sew on the facing, catching the button loop in the seam. Turn right-side out and press.

SEWING ON BUTTONS

1 Thread your needle with a doubled strand of thread. Secure the thread to the fabric where the button is to be positioned. Pass the needle up through one hole of the button, down through the other hole to the back. Do not pull the thread taut yet – first insert a cocktail stick (or match stick) under the button and between the button's holes. Then pull the thread taut.

2 Continue working back and forth through the holes of the button and through the fabric, until at least five stitches have been worked.

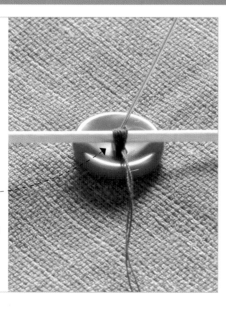

3 Remove the cocktail stick. Wrap the working thread several times around the thread under the button to form a shank. Secure the thread end with three small stitches at the back.

SEWING ON PLASTIC SNAPS

Although snaps or press studs are not visible, align them carefully when sewing them on. Use a doubled thread and work three or more stitches through each hole around the edge of the press stud pieces.

SEWING ON TIES

You can sew ties on a finished item with decorative stitching. Fold under the ends of the ties and tack them in place on the wrong side. Machine stitch a square with a cross at the centre over the end. Remove the tacking.

SEWING ON HOOKS AND EYES

Work a ring of straight stitches through the loops provided. Work the stitches only through the back layer of fabric and the seam allowances underneath. Ensure that the hook and the eye remain aligned by tacking the necks in position before stitching.

SEWING ON A ZIP

1 The easiest method for sewing on a zip is centring it on an opening in a seamline. To begin, machine stitch the seamline, leaving a gap in the stitches that is the length of the zip.

———— Gap in seamline

2 Tack the opening closed, working the tacking stitches along the seamline.

———— Tacking stitches

3 Open out the seam and press the seam allowance open on the wrong side. Open the zip and place it face down on top of the wrong side of the seam.

4 Centring the zip teeth carefully on top of the seam, tack one side of the zip tape in place 3mm ($^1/_8$in) from the teeth.

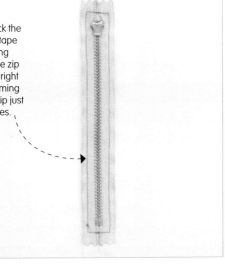

5 Close the zip and tack the other side of the zip tape in place. Using a matching thread, machine stitch the zip in place, stitching on the right side of the fabric and forming a rectangle around the zip just outside the tacking stitches.

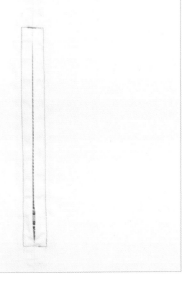

6 Remove the tacking around the zip tape and along the opening. Press.

EMBELLISHMENTS

Finishing instructions sometimes involve the addition of simple handmade or ready-made embellishments. For other types of needlework, you can finish your project by adding trimmings of various sorts. Here are some helpful tips for successfully applying these finishing touches.

HANDMADE YARN EMBELLISHMENTS

Yarn embellishments for knitting or crochet are easy to make, but be sure to take your time so that they look absolutely perfect. Fringe is often used to edge throws and scarves; tassels are ideal for the corners of a cushion cover or the top of a hat. Instructions for making fringe and tassels are given here, but you could also apply pompoms – handmade or ready-made – on almost any accessory.

MAKING FRINGE

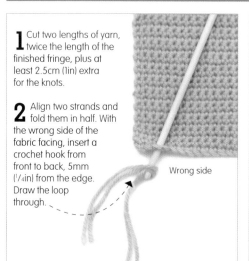

1 Cut two lengths of yarn, twice the length of the finished fringe, plus at least 2.5cm (1in) extra for the knots.

2 Align two strands and fold them in half. With the wrong side of the fabric facing, insert a crochet hook from front to back, 5mm (¼in) from the edge. Draw the loop through.

Wrong side

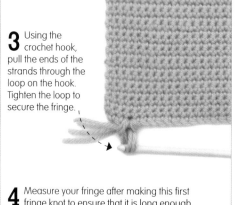

3 Using the crochet hook, pull the ends of the strands through the loop on the hook. Tighten the loop to secure the fringe.

4 Measure your fringe after making this first fringe knot to ensure that it is long enough, and adjust the length of the strands if necessary.

Right side

5 Add fringe knots along the edge of the fabric, spacing them evenly apart. For a plumper fringe, use more than two strands at a time. If you have trouble pulling the fringe through the fabric, experiment using a smaller or larger hook size.

6 After completing the fringe, trim it slightly to straighten the ends if necessary.

MAKING A TASSEL

1 Cut a piece of cardboard 8cm (3¼in) wide and twice as long as the desired length for the finished tassel. Fold the cardboard in half widthways with the fold at the top.

2 Wrap yarn round and round the cardboard lengthways to form a plump tassel.

3 Using a blunt-ended needle, pass a length of yarn under the yarn strands at the top and tie tightly.

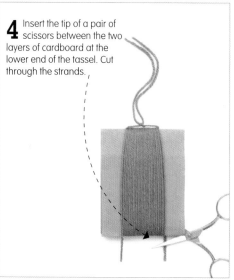

4 Insert the tip of a pair of scissors between the two layers of cardboard at the lower end of the tassel. Cut through the strands.

5 Wrap one of the long strands at the top several times around the tassel, about 2cm (³⁄₄in) from the top. Thread this strand onto a blunt-ended needle and pass it through the centre of the tassel and out at the top next to the other strand.

6 Use the long strands to attach the tassel to your knitting or crochet.

APPLYING
DECORATIVE EDGINGS

A pretty decorative edging can bring a piece of needlework to life and add a professional touch. Sometimes trim is applied only along one of its sides. These trims usually overhang the edge, adding a lacy or frilly outline. Depending on the fabric and personal preference, the trim can be attached to the front or the back of the piece by hand or machine.

APPLYING SINGLE-EDGE TRIM TO THE FRONT

1 Measure the edge to be trimmed and allow an extra 10–15cm (4–6in) for the trimming to take account of any mitred corners or overlaps at joins. Hem the piece first (see page 376).

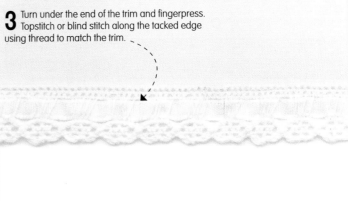

2 Pin the trim along the edge, starting in the middle of one side (or the bottom edge if there is a direction) as close to the edge of the trim as possible. Tack in place, removing pins as you work.

3 Turn under the end of the trim and fingerpress. Topstitch or blind stitch along the tacked edge using thread to match the trim.

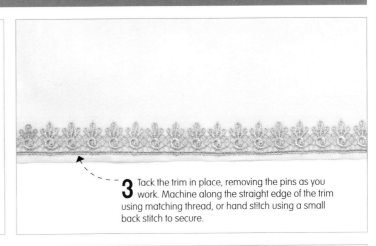

APPLYING SINGLE-EDGE TRIM TO THE BACK

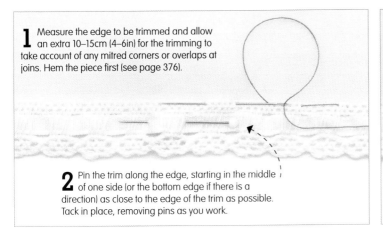

1 Turn under and tack a narrow hem (see page 376). Position the straight, top edge of the trim along the folded edge on the right side of the piece, with the decorative edge facing inwards.

2 Pin the trim along the edge, starting in the middle of one side.

3 Tack the trim in place, removing the pins as you work. Machine along the straight edge of the trim using matching thread, or hand stitch using a small back stitch to secure.

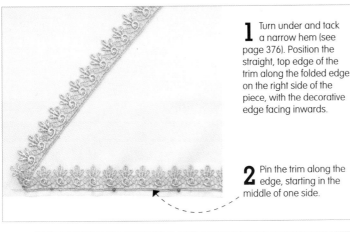

4 Turn the stitched edge to the wrong side and press.

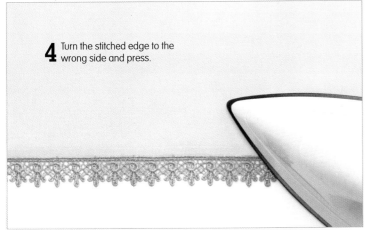

5 Machine topstitch along the fold on the right side or hand whipstitch along the top fold on the wrong side. Use thread to match the fabric.

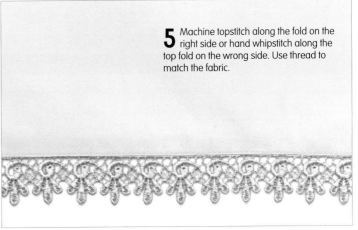

APPLYING FLAT TRIMS

Some lace and most braids are flat and have two edges that make them more suitable as decoration inside the outer edges of the piece. Like single-edge trim, flat trim can be sewn by hand or machine, but it is almost always applied to the right side of the piece before it is backed, lined, or hemmed.

1 Measure the edge to be trimmed and add an extra 10–15cm (4–6in) to the trimming.

2 Starting in the middle of one side, or at the bottom if the piece is directional, pin the trim parallel to the edge. Be sure to leave room on the edge of the fabric to turn a hem or a seam.

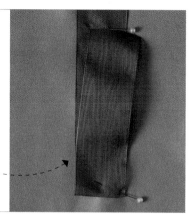

3 At each corner make a mitre. Fold the trim back on itself and pin the point. Mark a 45-degree angle to the opposite, inside edge on the trim and machine across from the inside to the outside point.

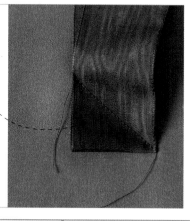

4 Trim the excess from the corner, lay the trim along the next side and continue pinning. Repeat to mitre all corners and at the end, turn the raw end under overlapping the starting point and pin in place.

5 Stitch the edges of the trim to the fabric using thread to match the trim. Hem the piece as desired.

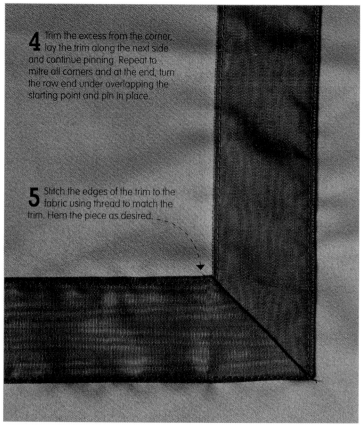

INSERTING TRIM IN A SEAM

If a piece is to be lined or backed, trims, in addition to piping (see page 380), can be inserted between the top and the other layer, such as in the seam joining the front and back of a cushion or placemat.

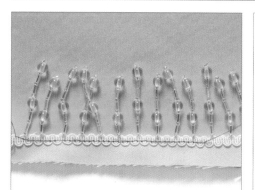

1 Measure the edge to be trimmed and add an extra 10–15cm (4–6in) to the trimming. Starting in the centre of the bottom edge on the right side of the top, align the top edge of the trim on the seamline with the decorative edge pointing away from the raw edge. Pin and tack, then machine in place.

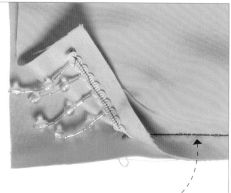

2 With the trim inside and pointing inwards, position the back and top right sides facing. Machine along the same seamline.

3 Turn through to the right side and press on both sides. Topstitch the edge if desired.

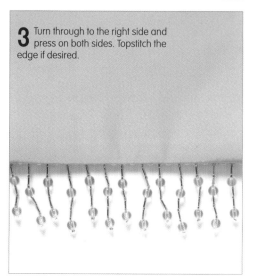

CARE OF NEEDLEWORK

As you have invested so much time and effort in your needlework, take care when cleaning and storing it. Start by referring to the care instructions on the labels supplied with the textile components of your needlework, which might include wadding and fabrics for patchwork, embroidery threads and ground fabrics, needlepoint canvases, yarns, and so on.

CARE OF KNITS AND CROCHET

Keep a thorough record of all projects, to include the pattern, the tension swatch, a small winding of the yarn/s, and most importantly a yarn label for each of the yarns used. Care instructions for any special ready-made trimming, ribbons, zips, or press studs should also be included.

Preparing for washing

Remove any special buttons or trims that can be damaged by water or dry-cleaning. To retain the shape of openings, tack them closed using a fine cotton yarn that can be easily pulled out when dry. Measure the piece in all directions and record these dimensions so you can mould it into the correct shape when it is still damp.

Washing

Refer to your yarn label for washing instructions. Yarns labelled "superwash" or "machine washable", can be washed in a washing machine on a gentle cycle and at a cool temperature. The majority of yarn labels, however, recommend hand washing.

Wash your knits and crochet with great care, avoiding friction (rubbing), agitation (swirling the water), and hot water, which can cause felting in wool yarns and damage other fibres.

Dissolve a mild detergent in a large sink full of lukewarm water. Submerge a single item and gently press up and down on it. Soak for a few minutes, then rinse to remove the soapy water.

Squeeze out the water very gently, pressing the item against the sink. Do not wring. Supporting the damp item, move it onto a large towel. Roll in the towel to remove more moisture.

Drying

Dry washed knitwear and crochet flat on a fresh towel, turning over occasionally to speed up the process and avoid damage by mildew.

Large items, such as throws, can be dried on the floor; cover the floor first with a large plastic sheet, then lay towels on top of this before positioning the throw.

Mould damp knitting or crochet into its correct size and shape before leaving to dry, and never leave in direct sunlight or near a heating source. Once completely dry, you can block and steam the piece if necessary, see pages 69 and 140.

Storing and moth control

Check regularly for telltale holes. If storing all summer, place an anti-moth product in the drawer or closet with your wool knits and crochet and renew it as directed.

Before repairing a hole in a moth-infested item, place it in the freezer overnight to kill any eggs. Knits or crochet too large for the freezer, such as throws and afghans, can be placed all day in the sun to achieve the same result.

CLEANING QUILTS

Modern quilts in everyday use will probably be made from washable fabrics such as cotton and filled with polyester or cotton wadding. Give a good shake when you change the bed and an airing outdoors, weather permitting. Dry-cleaning is not recommended for quilts.

Machine washing

If a quilt needs to be laundered, make sure there is no damage to the fabrics. Small items such as baby quilts can be laundered in the washing machine, as can bed quilts. Use a gentle cycle, a mild detergent, and lukewarm water.

Hand washing

Large quilts can be soaked in the bath. Run the water lukewarm, fold the quilt until it fits into the bath and leave to soak. Use a gentle washing solution if necessary, but bear in mind that it will need to be rinsed out completely. If the water looks murky, drain and refill the bath. Once the water remains clear, drain the bath and leave the quilt to continue to release water for several hours. Use a clean sheet to lift the quilt out.

Drying

Dry washed quilts flat. Spread a white sheet on the floor, lay the quilt flat on top, and cover it with another white sheet. When the top side feels dry, turn the "sandwich" upside down.

Vacuuming

Fragile quilts can be vacuumed with extreme caution. Set the vacuum on low and use an upholstery brush to work lightly over the surface, which should be protected by a clean nylon screen or a piece of fine netting.

Storing quilts

Store flat: a bed is an ideal place. Fold quilts as few times as possible and store them on a cupboard shelf or in a blanket box. Refold them occasionally if they will be stored for a long time. An alternative is to hang them as a wall display.

CLEANING EMBROIDERY AND NEEDLEPOINT

Any work done on canvas should be cleaned dry if possible. If you wish to wash it, make sure the threads are colorfast before you start. Wet a cotton bud and press it against a thread. If the colour bleeds on to the cotton bud, do not wash it.

Washing

Many plain-weave and even-weave fabrics can be carefully washed if they pass the colour-bleed test. Hand-embroidered items should be washed by hand. Use barely warm water, a mild washing solution, if any, and agitate or squeeze gently. Rinse thoroughly and squeeze out the water. Do not wring. Block (see page 278) while wet to maintain the shape.

Vacuuming

Needlework items can also be vacuumed as described, above. Use a hand vacuum and if the piece is particularly dusty, cover the nozzle with a piece of fine butter muslin held in place with an elastic band.

TOY PATTERNS

KNITTED MONKEY FROM PAGES 82–85

Yarns, needles, and extras
Refer to page 82 for yarns, needles, and extras required for making the toy.

Body and head
The body and head are worked in one piece, starting at the lower end of the body.
Using a stripe colour (B, C, D, or E), cast on 20 sts, leaving a long loose end for back seam.
Row 1 (RS) [Kfb, K1] 10 times. 30 sts.
Row 2 P.
Row 3 K1, [M1, K3] 9 times, M1, K2. 40 sts.
Row 4 P.
Row 5 K2, [M1, K4] 9 times, M1, K2. 50 sts.
Cont in st st in random stripes for 13 rows more, ending with RS facing for next row.
Cont in st st in random stripes (of B, C, D, and E) throughout as foll:
Next row (RS) K6, [K2tog, K10] 3 times, K2tog, K6. 46 sts.
P 1 row.
Next row K1, [K2tog, K4] 7 times, K2tog, K1. 38 sts.
P 1 row.
Next row K3, [K2tog, K8] 3 times, K2tog, K3. 34 sts.
P 1 row.
Next row K4, [K2tog, K3] 6 times. 28 sts.
Work 9 rows without shaping, ending with RS facing for next row.
Shape shoulders
Next row (RS) K6, K2tog, K12, K2tog, K6. 26 sts.
P 1 row.
Next row K5, sl 1-K2tog-psso, K10, sl 1-K2tog-psso, K5. 22 sts.
P 1 row.
Next row K4, sl 1-K2tog-psso, K8, sl 1-K2tog-psso, K4. 18 sts.
P 1 row.
Head
Next row (RS) K2, [Kfb, K1] 8 times. 26 sts.
P 1 row.
Next row K2, [M1, K3] 8 times. 34 sts.
P 1 row.
Next row K4, [M1, K5] 6 times. 40 sts.
Work 17 rows without shaping, ending with RS facing for next row.
Next row K2 [K2tog, K3] 7 times, K2tog, K1. 32 sts.
P 1 row.
Next row K1, [K2tog, K2] 7 times, K2tog, K1. 24 sts.
P 1 row.
Next row [K2tog, K1] 8 times. 16 sts.
P 1 row.
Next row [K2tog] 8 times. 8 sts.
Next row [P2tog] 4 times. 4 sts.
Cut off yarn, leaving a long loose end. Thread end onto a blunt-ended yarn needle and pass needle through 4 remaining sts as they are dropped from needle. Pull yarn to gather stitches and secure with a few stitches.

Legs (make 2)
Each leg is started at the foot end.
Using A (foot and hand colour), cast on 6 sts using the single cast-on method (see page 22) and leaving a long loose end.
Row 1 (RS) [Kfb] 5 times, K1. 11 sts.
Row 2 P.
Row 3 K1, [M1, K1] 10 times. 21 sts.
Beg with a P row, work 9 rows in st st, ending with RS facing for next row.
Row 13 (RS) K2, [K2tog, K3] 3 times, K2tog, K2. 17 sts.
Row 14 P.
Cut off A.
Cont in st st in random stripes (of B, C, D, and E) throughout as follows:
Work 10 rows without shaping, ending with RS facing for next row.

Next row (RS) K4, K2tog, K6, K2tog, K3. 15 sts.
Work 15 rows without shaping.
Next row (RS) K3, [K2tog, K2] twice, K2tog, K2. 12 sts.**
Work 11 rows without shaping.
Cast off knitwise.

Arms (make 2)
Each arm is started at the foot end.
Work as for leg to **.
Work 7 row without shaping.
Cast off 2 sts at beg of next 4 rows.
Cast off rem 4 sts, leaving a long loose end for sewing arm to body.

Muzzle
Using a stripe colour (B, C, D, or E), cast on 6 sts, using single cast-on method (see page 22) and leaving a long loose end.
Row 1 (RS) [Kfb] 5 times, K1. 11 sts.
Row 2 P.
Row 3 K1, [M1, K1] 10 times. 21 sts.
Row 4 P.
Cut off first stripe colour and change to a second stripe colour for remainder of muzzle.
Row 5 K1, [M1, K2] 10 times. 31 sts.
Beg with a P row, work 5 rows in st st.
Cast off knitwise, leaving a long loose end for sewing muzzle to body.

Ears (make 2)
Using F (ear and tail colour), cast on 3 sts.
Row 1 (WS) [Kfb] twice, K1. 5 sts.
Note: Work the remaining increases as yarn-overs, ensuring that each yarn-over is crossed when it is knit in the following row to close the hole by knitting it through the back of the loop.
Row 2 (RS) [K1, yfwd] 4 times, K1. 9 sts.
Row 3 K to end, knitting each yfwd through back loop.
Row 4 [K2, yfwd] 4 times, K1. 13 sts.
Row 5 Rep row 3.
Row 6 K.
K 2 rows.
Cast off loosely knitwise, leaving a long loose end for gathering ear into cupped shape and sewing to head.

Tail
Using F (ear and tail colour), cast on 3 sts, leaving a long loose end for sewing tail to body.
Work in garter stitch (K every row) until tail is a little longer than leg (or desired length).
Next row Sl 1-K2tog-psso, then fasten off.
Tail will swirl naturally – do not press out this swirl.

Finishing
Finish as explained on pages 84 and 85.

CROCHETED DOG FROM PAGES 158–161

Yarns, needles and extras
Refer to page 158 for yarns, needles, and extras required for making the toy.

Special stripe notes
• When changing to a new colour, introduce the new colour by using it for the last yrh at the end of the previous round.
• Do not cut off A and C when they are not in use, but drop them inside piece until they are needed again. Begin and end B in the rows it is needed.
• When introducing colours and cutting off colours, work over the yarn ends for 4 or 5 stitches to secure them, then clip off inside the toy part.

Body and head
The body and head are worked in one piece in spiral dc, starting at the lower end of the body.
Using A, make 28 ch and join with a ss to first ch to form a ring, leaving a long loose end for sewing on legs later.
Round 1 (RS) 1 ch (does NOT count as a st), 1 dc in same place as ss, 1 dc in each of rem ch. 28 dc. (Do not turn at end of rounds, but work in a spiral with RS always facing.)
Note: Mark last st of round 1 with a safety pin and move this marker onto last st at end of every round (see page 150 for working spiral dc).

Begin stripe sequence
Begin the stripe sequence of [3 rounds A, 1 round B, 1 round C, 2 rounds A, 1 round C], which is repeated throughout, **and at the same time** continue shaping body as follows:
Round 2 [2 dc in next dc, 1 dc in each of next 6 dc] 4 times. 32 dc.
Round 3 1 dc in each dc to end of round.
Round 4 [1 dc in each of next 3 dc, 2 dc in next dc] 8 times. 40 dc.
Round 5 Rep round 3.
Round 6 [1 dc in each of next 9 dc, 2 dc in next dc] 4 times. 44 dc.
Rounds 7–12 [Rep round 3] 6 times.
Round 13 [1 dc in each of next 9 dc, dc2tog] 4 times. 40 dc.
Round 14 1 dc in each of next 4 dc, [dc2tog, 1 dc in each of next 8 dc] 3 times, dc2tog, 1 dc in each of next 4 dc. 36 dc.
Round 15 [1 dc in each of next 7 dc, dc2tog] 4 times. 32 dc.
Round 16 Rep round 3.
Round 17 1 dc in each of next 3 dc, [dc2tog, 1 dc in each of next 6 dc] 3 times, dc2tog, 1 dc in each of next 3 dc. 28 dc.
Rounds 18–24 [Rep round 3] 7 times.

Shape neck and head
Round 25 [1 dc in each of next 5 dc, dc2tog] 4 times. 24 dc.
Round 26 [1 dc in next dc, dc2tog] 8 times. 16 dc.
Round 27 Rep round 3.
Round 28 [1 dc in next dc, 2 dc in next dc] 8 times. 24 dc.
Round 29 1 dc in each of next 3 dc, 2 dc in next dc] 6 times. 30 dc.
Round 30 1 dc in each of next 4 dc, 2 dc in next dc] 6 times. 36 dc.
Rounds 31–39 [Rep round 3] 9 times, marking centre of rounds 37 and 38 with a coloured thread when they are reached (for position of eyes).
Round 40 [1 dc in each of next 4 dc, dc2tog] 6 times. 30 dc.
Using a strong button thread, sew on eyes now (or attach safety eyes), positioning them over rounds 37 and 38 in the centre of the rounds and about 12mm/½in apart. Then complete head as follows:
Round 41 Rep round 3.
Cut off C and cont with A only.
Round 42 [1 dc in each of next 3 dc, dc2tog] 6 times. 24 dc.
Round 43 Rep round 3.
Round 44 [1 dc in next dc, dc2tog] 8 times. 16 dc.
Round 45 [Dc2tog] 8 times. 8 dc.
Fasten off, leaving a long loose end.

Legs (make 2)
Each leg is started at the foot end.
Using D (foot and hand colour), make a loop ring by forming a circle with

the yarn and drawing a loop through it with the hook (see page 153), then begin as follows:
Round 1 (RS) 1 ch (does NOT count as a st), 8 dc in loop ring. (Do not turn at end of rounds, but work with RS always facing.)
Pull yarn end to close loop ring.
Note: Mark last st of round 1 with a safety pin and move this marker onto last st at end of every round (see page 150 for working spiral dc).
Round 2 [2 dc in next dc] 8 times. 16 dc.**
Round 3 [1 dc in each of next 3 dc, 2 dc in next dc] 4 times. 20 dc.
Before proceeding, pull yarn end at beg of foot again and darn it in securely on WS.
Round 4 1 dc in each to end of round.
Rounds 5–7 [Rep round 4] 3 times.
Round 8 [1 dc in each of next 3 dc, dc2tog] 4 times. 16 dc.
Round 9 Rep round 4.
This completes the foot.

Begin stripe sequence
Begin repeated stripe sequence as for body **and at the same time** cont leg as follows:
Rounds 10–14 [Rep round 4] 5 times.
Round 15 [1 dc in each of next 2 dc, dc2tog] 4 times. 12 dc.
Rounds 16–25 [Rep round 4] 10 times.
Cut off D and cont with A only.
Rounds 26–28 [Rep round 4] 3 times.
Round 29 [Dc2tog, 1 dc in each of next 4 dc] twice. 10 dc.
Rounds 30–34 [Rep round 4] 5 times.
Work 1 ss in next dc and fasten off, leaving a long loose end.

Arms (make 2)
Make 2 arms in exactly same way as legs.

Muzzle
Using E throughout, work as for leg to **.
Round 3 [1 dc in next dc, 2 dc in next dc] 8 times. 24 dc.
Before proceeding, pull yarn end at beg of muzzle again and darn it in securely on WS.
Round 4 1 dc in each to end of round.
Rounds 5–7 [Rep round 4] 3 times.
Work 1 ss in next dc and fasten off, leaving a long loose end for sewing muzzle to head.

Ears (make 2)
Using E, make 10 ch.
Row 1 (WS) Working into only one loop of each foundation chain, work 1 dc in 2nd ch from hook, 1 dc in each of next 7 ch, 2 dc in last dc, then continue working around other side of foundation ch (working into other loop of each ch) as follows – 1 dc in first ch (same ch last 2-dc group was worked but on other side of this ch), 1 dc in each of rem 8 ch on this side of ch, turn. 19 dc.
Row 2 (RS) 1 ch (does NOT count as a st), 1 dc in each of first 9 dc, 3 dc in next dc, 1 dc in each of rem 9 dc, turn. 21 dc.
Row 3 1 ch (does NOT count as a st), 1 dc in each of first 10 dc, 3 dc in next dc, 1 dc in each of rem 10 dc, turn. 23 dc.
Row 4 1 ch (does NOT count as a st), 1 dc in each of first 11 dc, work [1 dc, 2 ch, 1 dc] all in next dc, 1 dc in each of rem 11 dc.
Fasten off, leaving a long loose end for sewing on ear.

Tail
Using E, make 14 ch.
Row 1 1 tr in 4th ch from hook, 1 tr in each of rem ch.
Fasten off. (Tail will twirl naturally – do not press out this twirl.)

Finishing
Finish as explained on pages 160 and 161.

Glossary

APPLIQUÉ
From the French verb appliquer, meaning "to apply", a decorative technique in which shapes are cut from one fabric and applied to another, either by heat bonding with fusible bonding web or by stitching them in place.

BAGGING OUT
In quilting, a technique that involves placing the quilt top and backing right sides together, on top of the wadding, and then stitching around the edges before turning the quilt through to the right side – thereby obviating the need for a separate binding.

BIAS
The diagonal grain of a woven fabric, at 45 degrees to the straight grain.

BINDING
A narrow strip of fabric used to cover the raw edges of a quilt top or piece of embroidery to provide a neat finish and prevent it from fraying. For straight edges, the binding can be cut on the straight grain; bias-cut binding has more stretch, and should always be used for curved edges.

BLOCK
In patchwork and appliqué, a single design unit. Patchwork blocks traditionally fall into one of four main categories: four-patch (2 rows of two patches), nine-patch (3 rows of three patches), five-patch (5 rows of five patches), and seven-patch (7 rows of seven patches).

BLOCKING
In knitting, crochet, and needlepoint, manipulating a finished piece into the correct shape by wetting and pinning it out, or pinning it out and steam pressing it.

BRODERIE ANGLAISE
A type of openwork embroidery in which the design consists mainly of small holes edged with buttonhole stitch; also known as eyelet lace. Broderie anglaise is traditionally worked in white thread on white fabric.

CASTING OFF
In knitting, removing all the stitches from the needle in order to complete a piece of knitted fabric and stop it unravelling.

CASTING ON
In knitting, making new stitches on the needle.

CHAIN LOOP, CHAIN SPACE
In crochet, a length of chain stitches worked between basic stitches to create a space in the fabric.

CHAIN PIECING
In patchwork, a method of piecing together units by feeding them through the sewing machine in sequence without lifting the presser foot or breaking the thread so that they form a chain with a short length of thread between each one.

CIRCULAR KNITTING
Also known as knitting in the round, rows of knitting are worked as rounds on a circular needle or with a set of four or five double-pointed needles to form a tube or a medallion.

COUCHING
An embroidery technique in which a thread is laid over the surface of the fabric and attached by means of tiny "tying" stitches worked vertically or diagonally across it.

COUNT
The number of threads or holes per 2.5cm (1in) in each direction of an even-weave fabric or needlepoint canvas; the more threads, the finer the fabric.

CUTWORK
A type of openwork embroidery in which areas of the fabric are stitched and the background fabric is then cut away to form lacy patterns. Like broderie anglaise, it is traditionally worked in white thread on white fabric.

DECREASE
In knitting and crochet, removing a stitch or stitches in order to reduce the number of working stitches and shape the fabric.

DRAWN THREAD WORK

An openwork embroidery technique that involves pulling individual threads from an even-weave fabric, leaving a "ladder" of threads in one direction, or an area that can be worked by stitching over groups of threads in a regular pattern.

ENGLISH PAPER PIECING

In patchwork, a traditional method for making a quilt of mosaic shapes by tacking the fabric pieces (all of which have at least two bias edges) to pre-cut paper templates the size of the finished element.

EVEN-WEAVE FABRIC

A fabric that has the same number of threads running from left to right as from top to bottom. It is used for counted-thread techniques such as cross stitch and needlepoint. Examples of even-weave fabrics include even-weave linen, Aida cloth, Binca, and Hardanger.

FAIR ISLE KNITTING

A type of colourwork knitting in which no more than two colours are used in a row (although there may be more than two colours in the pattern as a whole). The colour not in use is either stranded or woven in across the back of the work.

FILET CROCHET

A form of openwork crochet created by working a combination of squares or rectangles of open mesh and solid blocks.

FLORENTINE WORK

A style of needlepoint that developed in Florence, Italy, in the sixteenth and seventeenth centuries and is characterized by stepped stitches that create curved or zigzag patterns; also known as Bargello.

FOUNDATION CHAIN

In crochet, a length of chain stitches that forms the base of the piece of crochet.

FOUNDATION PIECING

A patchwork technique in which fabric pieces, or patches, are stitched to a lightweight foundation fabric such as calico.

FUSSY CUTTING

In patchwork and appliqué, isolating an individual motif on a printed fabric and cutting it out to use as a feature in a block.

INCREASE

In knitting and crochet, adding a stitch or stitches to increase the number of working stitches and shape the fabric.

INSERTIONS

Decorative embroidery stitches worked over an open space between two pieces of fabric to join them together; also known as "faggoting".

INTARSIA

A term used in both knitting and crochet to refer to a technique in which a colour appears only in a section of a row and is not needed across the whole row. Unlike Fair Isle knitting and jacquard crochet, more than two colours may be used in a row. In both crochet and knitting, a separate ball or length of yarn is used for each area of colour and carried vertically up to the next row when it is needed again.

JACQUARD CROCHET

A type of colourwork crochet worked in double crochet stitch, with no more than two colours in each row, in which the colour not in use is carried across the top of the row below and covered with the stitches of the other colour so that it is hidden from view. This results in a thicker-than-normal fabric, so it is best worked in a fine yarn.

LACE KNITTING

A series of techniques used to create holes, or eyelets, resulting in a knitted fabric that has an airy, lacelike texture.

MEDALLION

In knitting and crochet, a flat shape worked from the centre outwards. In quilting, a style in which a large central motif is surrounded by several borders.

MIRRORWORK

Also called shisha work, a traditional form of textile decoration from Central Asia and India that involves stitching around or over small discs of mirror, glass, or tin to hold them in place on the fabric.

MITRE

To finish a corner by stitching adjacent sides of fabric together at a 45-degree angle.

OPENWORK CROCHET

A lacelike effect created by working chain spaces and/or loops between the basic stitches.

OPENWORK EMBROIDERY

An overall term for a number of embroidery techniques that open up areas of the background fabric to create lacelike effects. See also broderie anglaise, cutwork, drawn thread work, insertions, pulled thread work, whitework.

PATCH

A small piece of fabric used in making a patchwork design. Patches may be whole squares, or sub-divided into half-square triangle units, quarter-square triangle units, curved units, or combinations thereof.

PATCHWORK

The technique of stitching together small pieces of fabric to make a larger one.

PLAIN-WEAVE FABRIC

A tightly woven fabric in which the warp and weft form a simple criss-cross pattern. The number of threads in each direction are not necessarily equal. Examples of plain-weave fabrics include cotton, linen, and silk.

PULLED THREAD WORK

An openwork embroidery technique in which threads on an even-weave fabric are pulled together with tight stitches to create regular spaces.

QUILTING

The process of stitching the three layers of a quilt (top, wadding, and backing) together. In addition to serving a practical purpose in holding the three layers together, the quilting stitch pattern often forms an integral part of the quilt design. It is normally marked out on the quilt top in advance and may consist of a geometric grid of squares or diamond shapes, concentric lines that echo shapes within the design, or intricate shapes such as hearts, feathers, and swags.

RIGHT SIDE

The front of a piece of fabric, the side that will normally be in view when the piece is made up.

ROUND

A row of knitting or crochet worked in a circle, with the last stitch of the row being joined to the first to complete the foundation circle.

SASHING

Strips of fabric interspersed between blocks when making a quilt top.

SEAM

The join formed when two pieces of fabric are sewn together.

SELVEDGE

The rigid edge woven into each side of a length of fabric to prevent the fabric from fraying or unravelling. It occurs when the weft thread turns at the edge of the warp threads to start the next row.

SET OR SETTING

The way the blocks that make up a quilt top are arranged. Blocks may be straight set (stitched together edge to edge, with each block oriented the same way), or set "on point" (turned on the diagonal so that they appear as diamonds rather than squares); pieced and appliqué blocks may be alternated with plain "spacer" blocks; or blocks may be rotated to create secondary patterns.

SETTING IN

In patchwork, sewing one shape or patch into an acute angle formed when two other shapes have been joined together.

SMOCKING

A form of embroidery that involves gathering fabric into tight folds and then working decorative stitches over the gathers. Traditionally used to decorate the gathers in the bodices of dresses, blouses, christening robes, and smocks.

STRAIGHT GRAIN

The threads of a woven fabric running parallel to, or at 90 degrees to, either the lengthways (warp) or crossways (weft) direction of the weave.

STRANDING IN

Fair Isle knitting, the technique of carrying a yarn across the wrong side of the work to a new position.

STRING PIECING

In patchwork, similar to strip piecing, but the strips can be of uneven width.

STRIP PIECING

A patchwork technique in which long strips of fabric are sewn together and then cut apart before being reassembled in a different sequence. The method is used to create many popular blocks, including log cabin and seminole patchwork.

SURFACE EMBROIDERY

The general term for decorative surface stitchery usually worked on plain-weave fabric. Most techniques on even-weave fabric are open work.

TENSION

In knitting and crochet, the number of stitches and rows over a given area, usually 10cm (4in) square. Also, the relative tightness used by the needlecrafter, in needlepoint and pulled-thread work, as well as in knitting and crochet.

TRAMÉ, TRAMMING

In needlepoint, the technique of laying long horizontal stitches to provide a foundation for other stitches.

TURNING CHAIN

In crochet, a length of chain stitches worked at the start of a row in order to bring the hook up to the necessary height to work the first stitch of that row.

WARP

The vertical threads of a woven fabric, also known as the lengthways grain.

WEFT

The horizontal threads of a woven fabric, also known as the crossways grain.

WHITEWORK

A generic term for the embroidery techniques of cutwork and broderie anglaise, which are traditionally worked in white thread on delicate white plain-weave fabrics such as lawn, fine linen, cambric, and voile.

WRONG SIDE

The reverse of a piece of fabric, the side that will normally be hidden from view when the piece is made up.

Index

USEFUL WEBSITES

A world of needlecraft websites are available to both inspire you and help you stock up. These websites offer some helpful starting points.

KNITTING AND CROCHET

UK online yarn and equipment suppliers
Angel Yarns www.angelyarns.com
The Black Sheep www.blacksheepwools.co.uk
Dragon Yarns www.dragonyarns.co.uk
Lana Pura www.lanapura.com
Modern Knitting www.modernknitting.co.uk
Purplelinda Crafts www.purplelindacrafts.co.uk
Whichcrafts? www.whichcrafts.co.uk
The Toft Alpaca Shop www.thetoftalpacashop.co.uk

Australia and New Zealand online yarn and equipment suppliers
Knit World www.knitting.co.nz
Morris and Sons www.morrisandsons.com.au
The Wool Shack www.thewoolshack.com

Local yarn shop listings
Knitmap www.knitmap.com

Online yarn index
Yarndex www.yarndex.com

Free knitting and crochet patterns
Crochet Me www.crochetme.com
Free Crochet.com www.free-crochet.com
Free Knit Patterns.com www.free-knitpatterns.com
Free Vintage Crochet www.freevintagecrochet.com
Free Vintage Knitting www.freevintageknitting.com
Knit on the Net www.knitonthenet.com
Ravelry www.ravelry.com

EMBROIDERY AND NEEDLEPOINT

UK online materials and equipment suppliers
Barnyarns www.barnyarns.co.uk
Burford Needlecraft www.needlework.co.uk
The Craftlight Company www.craftlights.co.uk
House of Smocking www.smocking.co.uk
Tandem Cottage Needlework Ltd. www.threadsite.co.uk
Willow Fabrics www.willowfabrics.com

Australia and New Zealand online materials and equipment suppliers
The Embroiderer www.theembroiderer.co.nz
The Thread Studio www.thethreadstudio.com
Needlecraft Mailbox www.needlecraft.com.au

Needlepoint and Embroidery kit designers
Beth Russell www.bethrussellneedlepoint.com
Ehrman Tapestry www.ehrmantapestry.com
Elizabeth Bradley Ltd. www.elizabethbradley.com

PATCHWORK, QUILTING, AND APPLIQUÉ

UK online materials and equipment suppliers
The Cotton Patch www.cottonpatch.co.uk
Inhouse Quilting www.inhousequilting.com
Pelenna Patchworks www.pelennapatchworks.co.uk
The Quilt Room www.quiltroom.co.uk

Australia and New Zealand online materials and equipment suppliers
Fabric Patch www.fabricpatch.com.au
Kiwi Quilts www.kiwiquilts.co.nz
Oz Quilts www.ozquilts.com.au

CLUBS, ASSOCIATIONS, AND CLASSES
Embroiderer's Guild www.embroiderersguild.com
Irish Patchwork Society www.irishpatchwork.ie
The Knitting and Crochet Guild of Great Britain www.knitting-and-crochet-guild.org.uk
Quilter's Guild of the British Isles www.quiltersguild.org.uk
Stitch'n Bitch www.stitchnbitch.org
UK Hand Knitting Association www.ukhandknitting.com

SHOWS AND EVENTS
UK
Creative Exhibitions www.twistedthread.com
Grosvenor Exhibitions www.grosvenorshows.co.uk
UK Hand Knitting Association www.ukhandknitting.com
Knit Happenings www.knithappenings.com

Australia and New Zealand
Australasian Quilt Convention www.aqc.com.au
Textile Art Festivale www.textileart.com.au

ABOUT THE AUTHORS

Maggi Gordon, author of the patchwork, quilting, appliqué, and embroidery chapters, is a freelance editor and author specializing in craft, home, and lifestyle. She lives in Wisconsin, USA, and is the author of 14 needlecraft books, including *The Ultimate Quilting Book* (1999), *The Ultimate Sewing Book* (2002), and *The Complete Book of Quilting* (2005).

Sally Harding, author of the knitting and crochet chapters, is a needlecraft technician, author, designer, and editor. Born in the United States, she now lives in London. She was the Technical Knitting Editor for Vogue Knitting from 1982, and has for many years

edited needlework books by acclaimed textile designer Kaffe Fassett. Her books include *Crochet Style* (1987), *Fast Knits Fat Needles* (2005), and *Quick Crochet Huge Hooks* (2005).

Ellie Vance, author of the needlepoint chapter, is a writer and freelance editor specializing in needlecrafts. She has designed and made original embroidery, needlepoint, and patchwork projects for various books and magazines. Born in the United States, she now makes her home in England.

ACKNOWLEDGMENTS

Authors' acknowledgments
Maggi Gordon: Thanks to everyone at Dorling Kindersley who contributed to this book, especially Mary-Clare Jerram, who commissioned me, and Danielle Di Michiel, the most patient of editors, and to Heather, who was my original point of contact. And as always to David, whose support has been unwavering.

Sally Harding: I would like to thank the whole DK team in London and Delhi for their hard work making samples, shooting steps, and laying out all those pages. Thanks also to Maggi Gordon for suggesting that I take part in the project and to Mary-Clare Jerram for commissioning me. Biggest thanks to Katie Hardwicke, my editor, for being such a joy to work with and to Danielle Di Michiel at DK for giving me so much support throughout.

Ellie Vance: I would like to express my thanks to Katie Hardwicke, for her sensitive editing and fine attention to detail, and to the team at Dorling Kindersley for all their hard work, especially to Danielle Di Michiel, for her outstanding efficiency and unfailing good humour.

Dorling Kindersley would like to thank:
Tia Sarkar for editorial assistance; Jenny Latham for proofreading; Hilary Bird for indexing; Coral Mula for the crochet diagrams; Lana Pura, Willow Fabrics, House of Smocking and The Contented Cat for materials, equipment, and resources; Usha International for sewing machines.

Creative technicians: Arijit Ganguly, Archana Singh, Amini Hazarika, Bani Ahuja, Chanda Arora, Christelle Weinsberg, Eleanor Van Zandt, Evelin Kasikov, Geeta Sikand, Indira Sikand, Kusum Sharma, Medha Kshirsagar, Meenal Gupta, Nandita Talukder, Nalini Barua, Neerja Rawat, Resham Bhattacharjee, Rose Sharp Jones, Suchismita Banerjee. Special thanks to Bishnu Sahoo, Vijay Kumar, Rajesh Gulati, Tarun Sharma, Sanjay Sharma.